BUSINESS

ITS NATURE AND ENVIRONMENT
AN INTRODUCTION
STEADE·LOWRY·GLOS

TENTH EDITION

Richard D. Steade
Professor of Management
College of Business
Colorado State University
Fort Collins, Colorado

James R. Lowry
Head, Department of Marketing
Ball State University
Muncie, Indiana

Raymond E. Glos
Dean Emeritus
School of Business Administration
Miami University
Oxford, Ohio

Published by

G74   **SOUTH-WESTERN PUBLISHING CO.**

CINCINNATI   WEST CHICAGO, ILL.   DALLAS   PELHAM MANOR, N.Y.   PALO ALTO, CALIF.

Contents

PREFACE   xi

PART I · OVERVIEW OF AMERICAN BUSINESS

Chapter 1   The American Business Enterprise System   2

Elements of Our Business Enterprise System   **4**
Economic Theories of Capitalism   **14**
Other Economic Systems   **16**

Chapter 2   Business in a Changing Environment   22

The Social Environment of Business: Basic American Values   **24**
Social Values and Models of Business Responsibility   **26**
The Physical Environment of Business   **30**
Business Legitimacy and Corporate Accountability   **35**

Chapter 3   Forms of Business Ownership   40

            Proprietorships **42**
            Partnerships **44**
            Corporations **48**
            Other Unincorporated Forms of Business Ownership **56**
            Other Incorporated Forms of Business Ownership **58**

PART II • MANAGEMENT AND ORGANIZATION OF HUMAN RESOURCES

Chapter 4   Organizing for Management   66

            The Meaning of Organization **68**
            The Organizing Process: Dividing and Coordinating **68**
            Departmentation of Operating Tasks **70**
            Establishment of Authority Relationships **74**
            Division of Managerial Work **76**
            The Process of Delegation **79**
            Organization Structure **80**
            Developing Effective Organizations **85**

Chapter 5   The Manager's Job   88

            Managerial Levels, Skills, and Tools **90**
            Process of Decision Making **93**
            Managerial Functions **94**
            Managerial Leadership **101**
            Motivation **104**
            Communication **106**
            Management by Objectives **108**
            Organizational Complexity and Contingency Management **109**

Chapter 6   Staffing the Organization   114

            Changes in the Staffing Function **116**
            Basic Steps in Staffing **117**
            Discrimination in Employment **128**

Chapter 7   Compensation for Human Resources   138

            Base Pay   *140*
            Wage Incentives   *147*
            Fringe Benefits   *151*

Chapter 8   Labor-Management Relations   160

            The Emergence and Growth of Organized Labor   *162*
            Labor Goals and Bargaining   *165*
            Bargaining Tactics and Tools   *169*
            Labor Legislation   *173*
            Current Labor Issues and Trends   *178*

PART III · PRODUCTION AND PRODUCTIVITY

Chapter 9   American Productivity   188

            Why Productivity Is Important   *190*
            The Measures of Productivity   *191*
            Our Declining Productivity   *193*
            Steps to Improve Our Productivity   *198*

Chapter 10   Production and Manufacturing Systems   210

            Basic Factors in Manufacturing Systems   *212*
            Mass Production and the Assembly Line   *216*
            The On-Going Production Function   *216*
            Toward the Automated Factory   *221*

Chapter 11   Materials Management   230

            The Evolution of Materials Management   *232*
            Nature and Functions of Purchasing   *234*
            Distribution Management   *241*

PART IV · MARKETING

Chapter 12   Marketing Management   260

                        Marketing and Its Importance **262**
                        Marketing as a Productive System **264**
                        Marketing Organization Structure **264**
                        Marketing Functions **267**
                        Marketing Mix **267**
                        Uncontrollable Factors in the Marketing Environment **272**
                        Consumer Behavior **277**
                        Marketing Research **280**

Chapter 13   Products and Their Distribution   286

                        Types of Goods **288**
                        Product Policies **290**
                        Distribution Policies **295**
                        Wholesaling **299**
                        Retailing **302**

Chapter 14   Personal Selling and Advertising   312

                        Personal Selling **314**
                        Advertising **320**

Chapter 15   Prices and Pricing Policies   342

                        Pricing Objectives **344**
                        Approaches in Determining Prices **344**
                        Pricing Policies **352**
                        Price Legislation **359**
                        Pricing Theories **360**
                        Price Indexes and Trends **362**

Chapter 16   International Business   368

                        Why Nations Trade **370**
                        Conducting World Trade **375**
                        Promoting World Trade **381**
                        Protectionism and Economic Integration **385**
                        International Payments and Balance of Trade **390**
                        Multinational Corporations **391**

PART V · ACCOUNTING AND FINANCE

Chapter 17   Accounting and Financial Statements   400

    Types of Accountants   403
    Basic Steps in Accounting Procedures   404
    Financial Statements   407
    Interpretation of Financial Statements   417
    Audits   422
    Budgets   423
    Standardization and Regulation   425

Chapter 18   Long- and Short-Term Financing   432

    Long-Term Financing   434
    Short-Term Financing   449

Chapter 19   Security and Commodity Exchanges   462

    Organized Security Exchanges   464
    Over-the-Counter Markets   477
    Development of a National Market System   478
    Option Markets   479
    Commodity Exchanges   480

Chapter 20   Money and Banking   488

    Basic Aspects of Money   490
    Our Banking System   492
    The Federal Reserve System   498
    International Monetary Operations   503
    Electronic Funds Transfer Systems   506

Chapter 21   Risk Management and Insurance   510

    Business Risks   513
    The Insurance Business   516
    Health Insurance   518
    Property and Liability Insurance   520
    Life Insurance   529

PART VI • INFORMATION MANAGEMENT AND CONTROLS

Chapter 22   Business Information and the Computer   540

Scope of Data Processing   *543*
Analog and Digital Computers   *544*
Components of a Computer System   *545*
Computer Hardware   *549*
Computer Software   *555*
Applications of Electronic Data Processing   *557*
Social Impact of the Computer   *562*
Management Information Systems   *564*

Chapter 23   Laws and Ethics for Business   572

Distinctions Between Torts and Crimes   *574*
Our Legal and Court Systems   *575*
Nature and Scope of Business Law   *577*
Business Ethics   *584*

Chapter 24   Regulation of Business   592

Competitive Businesses and Approved Monopolies   *595*
Regulation of Competitive Businesses   *595*
Regulation of Approved Monopolies   *604*
Principles of Taxation   *606*
Variation in State and Local Taxes   *608*
Federal Taxes   *613*

PART VII • BUSINESS AND YOU

Chapter 25   Business Career Opportunities   624

Factors to Consider in Career Planning   *626*
Aids to Occupational Selection   *629*
Areas of Employment Opportunities   *632*
Planning a Job Campaign   *639*

Chapter 26   Small Business and Franchising   652

Importance of Small Business   *654*
Factors Necessary for New-Business Success   *654*
Distinctions Between Small and Large Businesses   *657*
The Five P's of Entrepreneurship   *665*
Choice of Business Ownership Form   *666*
Small Business Administration Services   *667*
Franchising   *670*

COMPREHENSIVE CASE • PAWS, INC.—THE TALE OF GARFIELD   687

Starting a New Comic Strip   *689*
Creating GARFIELD   *689*
The Advantages of a Licensing Program   *690*
Building the Foundation of a Licensing Program   *691*
Developing Licensing Programs for GARFIELD Products   *692*
Keeping GARFIELD Purring   *695*

GLOSSARY   699

INDEX   713

Preface

The number "10" has taken on a new meaning in recent times. It is now seen as a measure of perfection on a scale of 10 — a point that few people or objects can hope to reach. In a sense, the same can be said for the 10th edition of a textbook. Few books survive to reach this point, much less still enjoy wide acceptance.

So, we are pleased to bring you this 10th edition of a long-standing book that often has been called the standard against which other introduction to business texts are compared. Although this book has been widely imitated over the years, its popularity continues to hold. We feel this is because the text carefully balances enduring topics with the coverage of new topics that will remain current throughout the entire edition. For example, some current business topics in this edition include R&D limited partnerships, intuitive decision making, the middle-management bulge, job burnout and mid-life career crises, equity and comparable worth in wage and salary administration, give-backs and labor-management concessionary bargaining, robotics, research focus groups, personal computers, computer security, government regulation and deregulation, and electronic funds transfer systems, to name a few.

As for the organization of the material in this textbook, the seven parts have been carefully developed so that they reflect the close relationships between allied business activities. The three major functional areas of business — production, marketing, and finance — are significant parts of this text. Part I presents an overview of American business by examining our business system and its changing environment. Part II looks at the management and organization of human resources. Part III discusses the critical areas of production and productivity. Part IV introduces the concepts of marketing to students. Part V reviews the principles of accounting and finance. Part VI covers the important topics of managerial information and controls with a discussion of the roles of computers, laws, ethics, and regulations in business. Part VII focuses on your career opportunities as either an employee in a large corporation or a proprietor of your own business.

The number of chapters in this edition has been reduced to 26 from the 27 in the last edition, and the content of many chapters has been extensively revised. Because of their significance in business today, chapters on American productivity, money and banking, and small business and franchising (formerly an appendix) have been added. The former chapter on multinational business has been broadened in scope, moved to the Marketing part, and renamed "International Business." The chapter on business law now includes business ethics. As in the 9th edition, this edition concludes with a comprehensive case that permits a student to apply many of the principles which are discussed in the text.

Each chapter is introduced with a statement of learning objectives. These can be used by students as a guide for study and as a check on their understanding of the material covered. Also, at the opening of each chapter is a thought-provoking excerpt that describes an actual business situation related to the chapter content. At the end of each chapter, there are five questions that tie the material in the excerpt to the chapter's topics. Each chapter concludes with a summary that identifies the most important points that have been covered. Thus, the format follows the sequence of telling you what you are to learn, providing the learning experience, and telling you what you have learned.

For many students, the language of business is difficult to remember and confusing to understand. In order to resolve these difficulties, at the end of each chapter is a list of important business terms that are used and defined within that chapter. These terms are readily identified by being printed in boldface type. Another feature is a comprehensive glossary that eliminates the need for a chapter-by-chapter search for the definition of a business term and provides a handy reference for students.

Also, in this edition you will note the abundant use of lively graphics and relevant illustrations that depict more clearly the role of business in our society.

Although the changes seem substantial, this revision has been made with one thought in mind—to improve our introductory business text. With the use of this text, an introduction to business course should be able to accomplish the following objectives:

1. For nonbusiness majors it is a very worthwhile general education course.
2. For business majors it gives an overview of all business activities, thus providing a valuable perspective for subsequent specialized business courses.
3. It is an excellent vocabulary builder for students.
4. Students gain an appreciation and understanding of our capitalistic business enterprise system.
5. It generates an awareness of the social responsiveness of business.
6. It gives students an insight into and practice in decision making.
7. For many, it provides an opportunity to evaluate and possibly choose a lifetime career.

The *Student Supplement* that accompanies the text has been revised and strengthened. It continues to serve three important purposes. First, for each chapter there is a series of review questions whose answers are in the back of the Supplement. Second, two short incidents for each chapter provoke discussion and often involve decision making. Third, in each chapter is a timely article that complements the text material. These three features make the Supplement a programmed learning aid, a case book, and a readings collection. Other supplementary publications are the *Instructor's Manual,* the printed objective tests, the key to the printed objective tests, and the transparencies prepared by Mr. Joel J. Lerner of Sullivan County Community College.

We would like to thank the many instructors who used the 9th edition and shared with us their thoughtful comments and suggestions for changes. We would also like to express our appreciation to a large number of businesses and business publications, who have graciously given us permission to use their various types of materials for illustrative purposes.

R.D.S.
J.R.L.
R.E.G.

I. Overview of American Business

Chapter 1. The American Business Enterprise System
2. Business in a Changing Environment
3. Forms of Business Ownership

Photo courtesy of Haworth, Inc., Holland, MI.

Profits and Free Market in Communist Bulgaria?

Bulgaria, smallest of the East-bloc nations, has stolen a head start on its East European allies and adopted a far-reaching economic reform in which the market is to replace the classic form of communist plan almost entirely.

Amid East-bloc concern over impoverished Poland, Bulgaria's step was announced quietly a few days ago. It could prove the most notable development in the area in many years.

The report delivered by Grisha Filipov, who is chairman of the Council of Ministers and acknowledged to be second only to President Todor Zhikov in the Communist Party leadership, was published at the weekend.

The general tenor of the Filipov report was that the market is to replace the plan. "Market forces will decide relations between enterprise and enterprise and between enterprise and the center," he said.

The whole present process is being reversed, with responsibility from below — from enterprises, their work forces, agro-industrial complexes, and local government. Only overall guidance will be exercised at the top chairman level. As chairman Filipov outlined them, the main features are:

- A speeding up of the switch-over from extensive to intensive production and productivity, with establishment of direct market links. This means abandoning the emphasis on mere production figures (the old bugbear of communist planning) and replacing it with efficiency and quality criteria.
- Market forces alone are to determine production and meet the needs of society.
- The role of central government and planning will be confined to ensuring economic "balance" and guiding the "general proportions" of the economy. Specific decisions and action are left to individual enterprises.
- Every economic unit will have to operate on the basis of cost-effectiveness in its use of labor and materials and be strictly self-supporting.
- Incentives for management and workers alike will depend on competitiveness, the quality of the final product, and its profitable marketing "inside and outside the country."

The new economic mechanism makes no direct reference to workers' councils as such. But it stresses the role of the "work team" in enterprise production and other planning.

Under the Bulgarian reform the state is the "owner of social property." The workers are its "keep."

SOURCE: Adapted from Eric Bourne, "Profits? Free Market? Can This Be Communist Bulgaria?" *The Christian Science Monitor* (January 20, 1982), pp. 1, 14. Used by permission of Eric Bourne.

The American Business Enterprise System

1

Objectives:

- Identify the three main elements that form our business enterprise system.
- Explain why business is a key social institution in the United States.
- Distinguish between industrial and commercial businesses.
- Identify and explain three basic freedoms in our capitalistic economic system.
- Explain the importance of capital and risk to capitalism.
- Explain three ways in which profit is crucial to our capitalist economic system.
- Explain the gainful relationship represented in the circular flow of economic activity.
- Distinguish between the classical (supply-side) and Keynesian (demand-management) economic theories of capitalism.
- Distinguish between the use of monetary policy and fiscal policy as economic policy tools.
- Distinguish among capitalist, socialist, and communist economic systems.

Over two hundred years ago Thomas Jefferson noted that agriculture, manufacturing, commerce, and navigation were the four "pillars of our prosperity." To this we can add that individual enterprise, or initiative, is the foundation on which these pillars stand. In fact, it was largely enterprising individuals and organizations seeking private gain who spurred the founding of our colonies before the break with England.

So, our capitalistic business enterprise system has been a key force in the growth of our nation since its founding. Business is the activating element—the engine of growth and productivity—in this system. **Business** is defined as all the commercial and industrial activities that provide goods and services to maintain and improve our quality of life. The purpose of this book is to explain how business combines human, material, technological, and financial resources for profit. This profit is achieved by anticipating and satisfying the needs and wants of people in our society and throughout the world.

ELEMENTS OF OUR BUSINESS ENTERPRISE SYSTEM

In our complex society today, someone must accept the challenge and risk to bring human resources, materials, and capital together before a single gallon of milk can be marketed or a single automobile produced. That job rests with the businessperson. The owner of a lumber mill has to process various types of lumber as efficiently as possible in the amounts and varieties needed. A trucker has to move goods quickly from places where they are not needed to where they are needed. The person who runs a retail store must make a variety of goods available at a price the consumer is willing to pay. These are only a few examples of the almost limitless business activities in our daily lives.

However, our business enterprise system is comprised of more than business firms and activities. It results from the combination of three major elements: business as a key social institution, constitutional democracy, and the American capitalistic economy. Figure 1-1 shows the relationship of these three elements. Each of these elements will be discussed in this chapter so that we can begin to understand the factors that help shape our enterprise system into a dynamic social and economic force.

Business: A Key Social Institution

Business is a major institution in our society because its values and consequences are accepted as an important and basic part of our lives. Business is also a social institution as it is comprised of human groups working toward goals that agree with the overall goals of society.

Structure of Business

Figure 1-2 shows that the institution of business is formed by industries and business firms. An industry is a distinct group of productive firms concerned with a particular business such as automobile manufacturing or providing entertainment. A business firm is a commercial or industrial enterprise owned and organized to buy, sell, manufacture, or provide products or services to society for a profit. This is a broad definition and includes all sizes and types of business firms.

Sizes and Types of Business Firms

American business is carried on by firms of various sizes. The definitions of small business are changed from time to time by the Small Business Administration (SBA)

Figure 1-1   Elements of Our Business Enterprise System

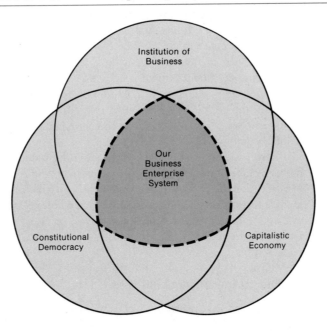

Figure 1-2   The Institution of Business

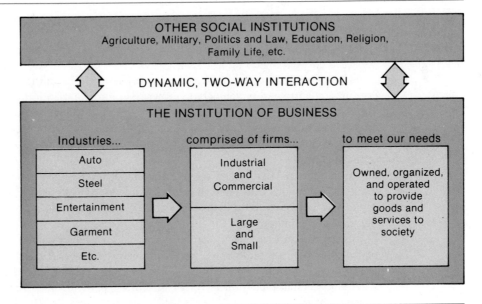

because the character of American business changes constantly. Currently retail and service businesses are considered small if their annual sales do not exceed $2 million to $7.5 million, depending on the industry. Wholesale firms with annual sales of $9.5 million or less are classified as small businesses. Construction firms are considered to be small if their annual sales do not exceed $7.5 million, averaged over a three-year period. In manufacturing, a firm with up to 250 employees is classified as a small business. (If employment is between 250 and 1,500, a size standard for the particular industry is used.) Table 1-1 shows some data for the 20 largest industrial corporations in the United States for 1981. Note the wide variations among these firms in assets, employees, and especially in the net income as a percentage of sales and stockholders' equity.

Two basic types of business firms are industrial and commercial. Industrial businesses include firms that are engaged in producing things by extraction from the earth, by fabrication in a factory, or by construction on a building site. Commercial businesses include firms engaged in marketing, such as wholesalers and retailers; in finance, such as banks and investment companies; and in services, such as advertising, repair services, laundries, hotels, and theaters.

Institutional Framework of Business

Although the institution of business exerts great influence over our way of life, it exists within a framework of other social institutions such as agriculture, the military, politics and law, education, religion, and family life. As Figure 1-2 shows, business and other social institutions have a dynamic, many-sided relationship in our complex society as each affects the other.

Constitutional Democracy

Capitalism is an economic, not a political, system. Capitalism works best, however, in a country with a democratic rather than a totalitarian form of government. Totalitarianism is a political system that uses state power to impose an official ideology on its citizens. Nonconformity to this ideology is treated as resistance or opposition to the government. The political party in a totalitarian system thus becomes the means of social control.

Constitutional democracy, on the other hand, is a political system that provides for periodic elections with a free choice of candidates. Key elements of a constitutional democracy include decision by majority vote, constitutional safeguards for basic civil liberties, and limitations on the use of power.

Many countries enjoy the fruits of capitalism even though capitalism is not part of their political philosophy. Singapore, with its remarkable capitalist economy, is run by a government which calls itself socialist. France and Japan, the best all-around capitalist performers of the seventies, both practice forms of business-government enterprise.

Table 1-1   The 20 Largest Industrial Corporations Ranked by Sales

Rank '81	'80	Company	Sales ($000)	Assets ($000)	Employees Number	Net Income as % of Sales %	Net Income as % of Stockholders' Equity %
1	1	Exxon (New York)	108,107,688	62,931,055	180,000	5.1	19.5
2	2	Mobil (New York)	64,488,000	34,776,000	206,400	3.8	16.6
3	3	General Motors (Detroit)	62,698,500	38,991,200	741,000	0.5	1.9
4	4	Texaco (Harrison, N.Y.)	57,628,000	27,489,000	66,728	4.0	16.8
5	5	Standard Oil of California (San Francisco)	44,224,000	23,680,000	43,281	5.4	18.7
6	6	Ford Motor (Dearborn, Mich.)	38,247,100	23,021,400	404,788	—	—
7	9	Standard Oil (Indiana) (Chicago)	29,947,000	22,916,000	58,665	6.4	18.0
8	8	International Business Machines (Armonk, N. Y.)	29,070,000	29,586,000	354,936	11.4	18.2
9	7	Gulf Oil (Pittsburgh)	28,252,000	20,429,000	58,500	4.4	12.3
10	11	Atlantic Richfield (Los Angeles)	27,797,436	19,732,539	54,200	6.0	19.3
11	10	General Electric (Fairfield, Conn.)	27,240,000	20,942,000	404,000	6.1	18.1
12	15	E. I. du Pont de Nemours (Wilmington, Del.)	22,810,000	23,829,000	177,235	6.1	13.4
13	12	Shell Oil (Houston)	21,629,000	20,118,000	37,273	7.9	18.4
14	13	International Telephone & Telegraph (New York)	17,306,189	15,052,377	324,000	3.9	11.1
15	16	Phillips Petroleum (Bartlesville, Okla.)	15,966,000	11,264,000	34,500	5.5	16.0
16	17	Tenneco (Houston)	15,462,000	16,808,000	103,200	5.3	16.1
17	18	Sun (Radnor, Pa.)	15,012,000	11,822,000	45,062	7.2	21.5
18	20	Occidental Petroleum (Los Angeles)	14,707,543	8,074,543	47,804	4.9	25.2
19	19	U. S. Steel (Pittsburgh)	13,940,500	13,316,100	141,623	7.7	17.2
20	21	United Technologies (Hartford)	13,667,758	7,555,103	190,000	3.3	14.2

SOURCE: "The *Fortune* Directory of the 500 Largest U. S. Industrial Corporations," FORTUNE (May 3, 1982), pp. 260–261, © 1982 Time Inc. All rights reserved.

Constitutional Support for Business

The Constitution of the United States, drawn up in Philadelphia in 1787, was a victory for businesspersons and lawyers such as Alexander Hamilton, James Madison, and Robert and Gouverneur Morris. They wanted to establish the financial credit of the United States and provide a stable and supportive environment for the ownership of private property and for trade and manufacturing.

Various Constitutional provisions helped set the stage for American business growth. Federal tariffs provided revenue and the means to protect our infant industries. The federal issuance of money allowed the starting of a strong central banking system and the governmental backing of public debt. Both of these provisions served to reinvite foreign investment in America.

Other Constitutional provisions were written to restrain tariffs and taxes on interstate trade, state issuance of currency, and any federal taxation on bases other than population. Uniform bankruptcy laws were established, and the rights of authors and inventors to copyrights and patents were recognized. Perhaps the most basic and necessary clause is Amendment V which states, in part, that the federal government shall not deprive any person of life, liberty, or property without due process of law.

Business and Government Relationship

American business has never operated independently of our government. Rather, it continues to benefit from a balanced relationship with our government. Beyond providing our national defense, the federal government has helped finance the nation's infrastructure—roads, ports, and facilities—that make commerce possible.

Business enjoys the enforcement of contracts and the protection of property rights by our stable and vigorous government. And, to a large degree, government shapes industrial development through its research and development programs. For example, our present competitive advantage in aircraft is based on government initiative. The federal government accounted for 92 percent of all aircraft sales in the 1950s, and a whole generation of commercial aircraft was spun off from these defense-related prototypes.

So, we have partly a free-enterprise economy and partly a government-controlled one. The problem is to have both the private and the government sectors doing what each does best. Generally, we can recognize that saving, investment, and risk-taking are encouraged when the power of the government is not forced on the system, as is often the case in totalitarian countries.

American Capitalism

Economics is a social science that studies the creation, distribution, and consumption of a nation's goods and services. It includes many areas such as the study of the behavior of prices, levels of employment, and national income. An economic system, or economy, deals with the structure and processes of a society's economic activity.

American **capitalism** is an economic system in which individuals competitively produce goods and services for society with comparative freedom from outside controls. These goods and services are usually sold for money. And the main motivating force for this system is private profit.

Capitalism in its purest form is called *laissez-faire,* a French term meaning noninterference by government in the decisions and actions of businesspersons and firms. Early American business enjoyed a relatively high degree of laissez-faire capitalism. In recent times, however, the increase in government constraints on business has led our economy to be called modified capitalism. Despite the impact of governmental policies and practices on our capitalistic system, we still have the basic freedoms and strengths of capitalism working for us.

Basic Freedoms of Capitalism

The three basic freedoms of capitalism are private property, private enterprise, and freedom of choice.

Private Property. The freedom of private property is necessary to capitalism. Individuals and businesses must have the right to purchase, own, and sell property including land, buildings, machinery, and equipment. Businesspersons must also have the right to sell the goods they produce and to keep the after-tax profits from these sales.

Private Enterprise. Where there is freedom of private enterprise, most businesses are owned by individuals rather than by federal, state, or local governments. This is true regardless of the size of the business. General Motors, Exxon, and General Electric, as well as small hardware stores and hair styling shops, are all private enterprises. In no sense are they public or government ventures like the United States Postal Service or the Tennessee Valley Authority.

Even though a corporation must secure a state charter to conduct its business, it is still a private enterprise. In granting a charter the state does not enter into partnership with the corporation, does not supply any of the capital, and does not agree to share in any of the gains or losses. The state ordinarily cannot require the firm applying for a charter to show any proof that the firm's services are needed or refuse a charter without this proof.

Freedom of Choice. An outstanding feature of capitalism, especially in a country with a democratic form of government, is freedom of choice in economic actions. In our country businesspersons are free to choose their type of business. They can combine the factors of production — land, labor, capital, and management — to generate profits as they see fit, so long as they conform to the laws of society. Businesspersons may also choose their customers with almost complete freedom. Workers are free to choose the jobs that they wish, in the trades they prefer, and with the companies that offer them the best deal for their efforts. Consumers are free to buy the goods and services they wish.

Freedom of contract is an offshoot of freedom of choice. This means that persons or firms are free to use their judgment about entering into contracts that call for legally providing services or goods to others.

Key Factors of Capitalism: Capital, Risk, Profit

The U.S. economy is unrivaled in the world for its output of goods and services. With only 5.1 percent of the world's population, the U.S. accounts for over 21 percent of the world's output. By itself, the output of California exceeds that of Africa. Pennsylvania about equals Australia in economic power, and the Nebraska economy ranks close to Ireland's in size. This performance is the result of the self-confidence and resourcefulness of Americans in our capitalistic enterprise system. To understand our capitalistic system, we must understand three factors that are basic to its operation: capital, risk, and profit.

Capital. The word "capital" can best be understood in terms of its two forms: capital goods and capital funds. Examples of capital goods are tools, equipment, buildings, fixtures, patents, and land. Capital funds refer to money that a firm uses, mainly to buy capital goods. These funds may be obtained from the investments of individual owners or by borrowing from financial institutions or individual lenders.

The owners of capital are known as capitalists. They provide resources to a business either as owners or as lenders (creditors). The term capitalist often evokes an image of a cigar-chomping fat cat. Actually, capitalists may be "ordinary" people who run clothing shops, insurance agencies, or drive around in pickup trucks with their construction equipment in the back.

Figure 1-3

SOURCE: From *The Wall Street Journal,* February 12, 1982, p. 24. Permission—Cartoon Features Syndicate.

Risk. The element of risk is always present in private enterprise. The essence of capitalism is risk-taking, and the most striking characteristic of business operators is faith—faith in their ability to compete and faith in the virtues of a system that emphasizes individual effort and rewards, with a minimum of government interference.

Profit. The capitalist is not so much one who takes but one who gives. Capitalists invest money, resources, and irreplaceable energy in the hope of future rewards for society and themselves. A capitalist's reward comes in the form of monetary profit, along with nonmonetary gains such as prestige or growth. Society's reward comes in the form of effective economic activity. It is through profits in the private sector of our economy that funds become available for programs of social improvement in other sectors of the economy.

If the key factors discussed in this chapter are the primary building blocks of capitalism, then profit is the mortar that holds these blocks together. Our business system could not operate effectively in its existing form without the profit incentive. Yet on no other topic are businesspersons and students less convincing than in their efforts to explain this vital aspect of business in our society. Part of this problem comes from confusing the definitions of "profit" and "profitability" with the way profits are used to benefit our nation.

For practical business purposes, **profit** is defined as the earnings that remain in a firm after the costs of its operations are covered. This bottom-line figure (on a firm's income statement) serves two important purposes. First, it provides a basic measure of effectiveness—that is, how well the firm is doing relative to similar firms. Second, the bottom-line figure tells the owner whether or not the risks and effort required to run the business are worth it and are profitable. An enterprise that earns less on the money invested in it than the going rate of interest for the use of capital is not a profitable business. In fact, it is virtually operating at a deficit.

All profits—high or low—don't go into the owner's pocket. As Figure 1-4 shows, profits are the lifeblood of our economic system in three basic ways. Profits provide savings to cover bad times, reinvestment to provide for growth, and a reward for risk-taking.

In sum, profit is the legitimate reward for the investment, effort, and risk-taking of those persons who provide the goods and services the public needs.

Roles and Gainful Relationships in Capitalism

The critics of capitalism often claim that this system benefits a few people at the expense of the working masses—that for one group to gain, the others must lose. Figure 1-5 rejects this claim. It shows that each person in our society potentially plays a gainful role in this economic activity as she or he fulfills one or more of the four essential roles in capitalism: entrepreneurs, managers, workers, and consumers.

Entrepreneurs. The **entrepreneur** is the prime risk-taker in a capitalistic system. Entrepreneurs put their ideas and money on the line by entering some areas of business. In effect, they are betting that they can operate efficiently enough to earn a profit despite competition, government controls, and other risks.

Managers. Persons charged with the responsibility of operating businesses effectively and efficiently are called managers. The managerial group of a firm is called the

Figure 1-4   Three Basic Functions of Profit

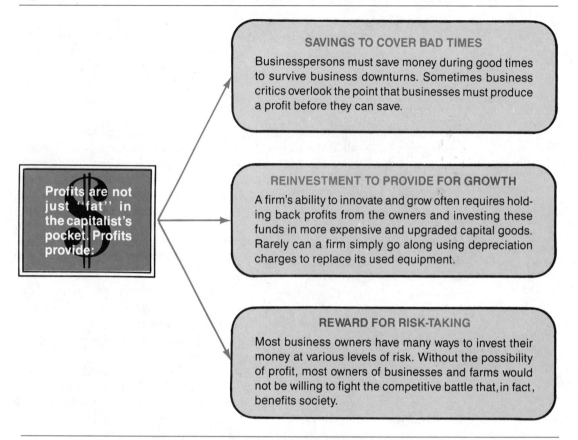

SAVINGS TO COVER BAD TIMES

Businesspersons must save money during good times to survive business downturns. Sometimes business critics overlook the point that businesses must produce a profit before they can save.

REINVESTMENT TO PROVIDE FOR GROWTH

A firm's ability to innovate and grow often requires holding back profits from the owners and investing these funds in more expensive and upgraded capital goods. Rarely can a firm simply go along using depreciation charges to replace its used equipment.

REWARD FOR RISK-TAKING

Most business owners have many ways to invest their money at various levels of risk. Without the possibility of profit, most owners of businesses and farms would not be willing to fight the competitive battle that, in fact, benefits society.

Profits are not just "fat" in the capitalist's pocket. Profits provide:

management. Sometimes the owners of a firm, especially a small one, are also its managers. In most large companies, however, managers are salaried persons who may or may not be stockholders of the companies they run. Their incentives to do a good job come from the expectation of higher salaries, profit-sharing bonuses, and the chance to move to better jobs within or between companies.

Managers occupy formal positions of responsibility as stewards of a firm's or society's resources. They must behave according to the expectations of society to justify their positions of trust. This demand on the part of society gives the business manager great challenge and opportunity for satisfaction.

Workers. Our capitalistic system relies heavily on millions of skilled, semiskilled, and unskilled workers who provide the physical and mental effort necessary to produce our many goods and services. Workers have no formal authority over other employees. When a person is given formal authority to make decisions that guide the actions of other workers, that person becomes part of management. This does not mean that workers have no control over their work lives. They are free to change jobs and better their situations. Their right to form unions that protect their interests and status is guaranteed by law.

Consumers. As Figure 1-5 notes, the role of the consumer in a capitalistic economy has two sides. On the one hand, everyone is a consumer. Each of us needs at least the basic necessities of life. Consumer demand, or the desire for goods and services backed up by purchasing power, determines the success of our nation's business activity. On the other hand, this purchasing power usually comes through the consumer being paid for doing something (producing, in the broad sense of the word). The consumer may be paid in the form of wages, rents, profit, interest, or other types of income. Thus, the consumer is also a producer.

A Gainful Relationship for All? The United States contains about 5 percent of the world's people, yet we consume about 40 percent of the world's goods. Obviously millions of persons in our society are gainfully involved in this flow of economic activity. But some persons in our society do not have the skills necessary to take part in this gainful exchange in order to provide for their families' minimum needs. Some face an existence of rigid, unyielding poverty. Depending on who they are and what their long-run work prospects are, the capitalistic system may appear to be one of racism and exploitation to these people.

Figure 1-5   The Circular Flow of Economic Activity

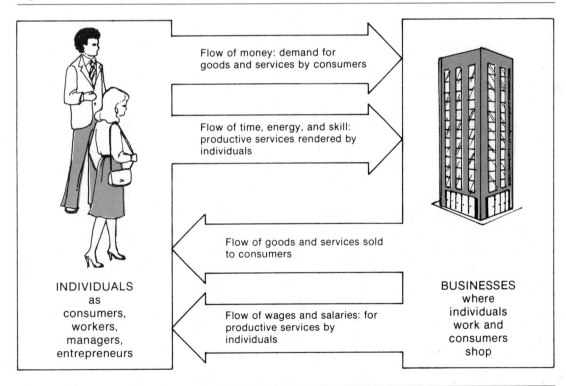

Flow of money: demand for goods and services by consumers

Flow of time, energy, and skill: productive services rendered by individuals

Flow of goods and services sold to consumers

INDIVIDUALS as consumers, workers, managers, entrepreneurs

Flow of wages and salaries: for productive services by individuals

BUSINESSES where individuals work and consumers shop

ECONOMIC THEORIES OF CAPITALISM _____

As the president of the Soviet Union reviewed the annual May Day parade, he is said to have asked an aide who the well-dressed civilians were who marched alongside the soldiers. When told they were economists, the president demanded to know why economists were in the ranks of the military. "You'd be surprised at the damage they can do," the aide responded!

As we have seen, the nature and scope of American capitalism are reasonably clear in theory. In reality, however, the theory does not always work well. Theories are the weapons of economists. Over the years, economists have developed various theories to explain how our capitalistic system should best be operated. These theories have ranged from macroeconomics (the "big picture" of capitalism as an organic whole) to microeconomics (the narrower explanation of decisions made by individual entrepreneurs about prices and profits). The two basic theories of capitalism that have influenced the economic policies of our federal government will be discussed here. These are the classical theory and the Keynesian theory.

Classical Theory

The classical theory of capitalism dates back several hundred years to Adam Smith's time. Classical theory made its earlier contributions in microeconomics, dealing with the rational allocation of scarce resources at the level of business firms. At the "macro" level this theory made the following assumptions:

1. Normally there is a high or full employment of labor.
2. All income from the production of goods and services will be spent immediately.
3. The production of goods creates an equivalent amount of demand. Therefore, total supply and demand will always be equal.

These assumptions led to the conclusion that the forces of supply and demand are adequate to keep the economy moving ahead steadily with a high level of employment. In this approach governments are expected to do little more than keep the budget in balance and let the economic fluctuations work themselves out.

Say's Law and Supply-Side Economics

The current version of classical thinking is called **supply-side economics**. In relatively few years, the great interest in supply-side economics has been sparked by the failure of Keynesian policies of demand management (discussed on page 15) to lift the economy from chronic inflation, lagging productivity, and sluggish real growth.

Supply-side economics rests on Say's Law of Markets (or Say's Law), the famous notion of the classical 18th-century French economist Jean-Baptiste Say. This law holds that people produce in order to consume; that is, supply creates its own demand. Contrary to Keynesian demand-oriented economics, Say's Law emphasizes production over consumption — or supply over demand. The idea underlying Say's Law is that workers' or businesspersons' buying power consists of their supplying power. Supply or production provides the funds to back up demand for the goods that are produced. In short, people can't buy things without income, and that income comes from producing goods and services.[1]

Supply-Side Economic Policy Tools

If supply is the only enduring source of real demand, what economic policy tools can be used to encourage saving, investment, and production over spending and consumption? We have two major economic policy tools—fiscal policy and monetary policy. **Fiscal policy** consists of the taxing and spending policies of the federal government. **Monetary policy** is concerned with our nation's supply of money and credit, as controlled by the Federal Reserve System (see Chapter 20).

Supply-siders and Keynesians both use monetary and fiscal policies, but in different ways, to accomplish our basic economic objectives of full employment and stable prices. To encourage production and capital formation, supply-siders argue for monetary policies that lower the tax rate on wages, interest, dividends, and corporate income. In addition, they rely on monetary policy to provide a stable, even supply of money and credit consistent with the full utilization of resources at stable prices.

Keynesian Theory

Keynesian theory is also known as income-expenditure analysis, national income theory, or neo-Keynesian theory. It was set forth in 1936 by a famous English economist, John Maynard Keynes, in his book *General Theory of Employment, Interest, and Money.* This major work launched macroeconomics as an independent field of economic theory.

Keynes emphasized demand and consumption rather than supply and production. A key point in Keynes' general theory states that a modern capitalistic system is naturally unstable because of a built-in lag in total demand. Once full employment is reached, people have a greater tendency to save than to invest or spend their earnings. Therefore, if the rates of consumption and investment are not great enough to insure relatively full employment, the government must spend more to raise the level of employment and demand.

Demand-Management Economics

Currently, Keynesian economics is called **demand management,** or the attempt to increase output by increasing demand for it. Economic policy since World War II has been dominated by demand-management policies. Since underutilized resources could be put to work if more demand were forthcoming, Keynesians argue that it is up to the government to design policies aimed at increasing demand.[2]

---

1. The various ideas in this section are from Robert E. Keleher, "Historical Origins of Supply-Side Economics," *Economic Review of the FRB of Atlanta* (January, 1982), pp. 12–17.

2. Much of the material on demand management is from Aris Protopapadakis, "Supply-Side Economics: What Chance for Success?" *Business Review of the FRB of Philadelphia* (May/June, 1981), pp. 11-20.

For example, the Employment Act of 1946, a federal law sometimes called the Full Employment Act, gave the federal government responsibility for taking necessary steps to maintain national economic health. It also established a federal Council of Economic Advisers (CEA) to "develop and recommend to the President national economic policies to foster and promote free competitive enterprise, to avoid economic fluctuations. . . and to maintain maximum employment, production, and purchasing power." The CEA prepares an Annual Economic Review for the President, who in turn presents an Economic Report to Congress.

More recently, the Full Employment and Balanced Growth Act of 1978, called the Humphrey-Hawkins bill, gave added emphasis to the Full Employment Act of 1946. The Full Employment and Balanced Growth Act provided for:

1. A target of 4 percent unemployment to be achieved by 1983.
2. The President to set targets each year for employment, unemployment, production, and real income.
3. The President to propose programs to achieve these goals.

Furthermore, the Act prescribed the following sequence of means for achieving these goals:

1. Regular private-sector jobs.
2. Private-sector jobs with federal assistance.
3. Conventional public-sector jobs.
4. A last-resort government employment reservoir.

In effect, the Humphrey-Hawkins bill converts into firm commitments the annual forecasts that the President of the United States makes in the Economic Report. For the past few years, however, the chance to achieve the above goals has seemed remote indeed.

Demand Management Economic Policy Tools

Theoretically, demand management calls for offsetting fiscal and monetary policies at different stages of the business cycle. A recession would call for easing the money supply, higher government spending, and tax cuts. A boom would call for tight money, cuts in government spending, and tax increases. Since the 1960s, however, the government has failed to bring these steps together at the right time.

Which of the two theories (supply-side economics and demand-management economics), with its related policy tools, is correct? This question is of great importance to the successful operation of our capitalistic enterprise system. Chances are that each may be correct under certain conditions, time constraints, and economic cycles, depending on the adjustments that are needed. Clearly these economic theories of capitalism are not just textbook exercises; they have real-world implications.

OTHER ECONOMIC SYSTEMS

Regardless of a nation's political and economic directions, it will face the basic economic issues that have remained the same over the years. These issues are:

1. What consumer and capital goods will be produced from the limited supply of available resources?
2. How will these goods be produced — by whom and with what resources?
3. How are the goods distributed among individuals?
4. How do nations bring about economic growth?

The decisions on these issues will vary depending on the economic system of a nation, both in theory and practice. It is important to note how our system differs from the other main systems — socialism and communism — in order to understand the reasons for the success of our dynamic business enterprise system.

The Socialist Economic System: In Theory and Practice

Socialism refers to an economy in which the government is heavily involved in economic decisions. Theoretically in a socialist economy the government owns and controls important economic resources, such as factories, mines, banks, stores, transportation systems, and farms, for the benefit of society as a whole. A basic level of social welfare is provided, taxes are high, and incomes are equalized through this taxation.

In practice, socialist economies vary widely in the degree of government control and in achieving their goals. For example, the socialist economy of Sweden, where democratic political processes still exist, has many capitalistic elements. The means of production are mostly privately owned, individuals can save and invest, and the market determines prices. Although a state planning commission publishes guidelines, adherence to them is not compulsory. But even Sweden's socialist economy sacrifices profit and efficiency to government-set employment levels and bureaucratic goals. It has suffered recently from high worker alienation and absenteeism, high inflation, jammed warehouses, and many unprofitable businesses.

The Communist Economic System: In Theory and Practice

In theory, **communism** describes a socialist economy which is ruled by a single political party and is based on the economic and political doctrines of Karl Marx. The goal of Marxism is to equalize the human condition within a classless society. Labor's output is distributed equally in the community, and the government is used only to achieve and maintain this equality.

The Union of Soviet Socialist Republics (U.S.S.R.) is the leading communist nation. But, in practice, the Marxist ideal does not exist in the Soviet Union. A more correct term for the Russian economy might be *state capitalism*, with all the factors of production owned and controlled by the government. The Soviet economy is called a *command economy* as opposed to our market economy. Economic planners establish the nation's basic economic objectives, both military and civilian. This total program is translated into national production objectives and imposed on the industries and plants throughout the nation. The citizens' well-being may be sacrificed to industrial growth, and a misallocation of resources often occurs.

Furthermore, there is a thinly disguised privileged class of people in the Soviet Union that mocks the Marxist theory of economic equality. For example, on major Moscow boulevards the middle lane is for the use of the sleek limousines of high Soviet officials. The privileged class enjoys resorts, yachts, and automobiles provided by the government while many of the 262 million citizens have little hope for improvement in their stark living standards. A problem here is that military aggression is the classic way of distracting attention from economic problems.

Are there any capitalistic incentives in the Soviet Union? Do Russian bears have hair? In 1981, 34 million households in Russia were farming independently in their spare time on small plots of land. Although these plots constitute a mere 17.5 million acres—only 3 percent of the total arable land in the Soviet Union—they provide 24 percent of the total farm output, according to the Soviet Ministry of Agriculture.[3] Also, a huge private underground production and distribution system thrives in the Soviet Union.

Central planning may work reasonably well when it is dealing with a simple economy that needs desperately to survive and grow. The more complex the economy, the further central planning is likely to go wrong. No longer do developing nations look only to the Soviet Union's command economy model. They are starting to realize the powerful and dynamic force of capitalistic incentives.

Figure 1-6 summarizes some of the basic differences among capitalism, socialism, and communism in five important dimensions: ownership of means of production, degree of central control, extent of managerial decision making, occupational choice, and incentives.

As Figure 1-6 suggests, because of various basic characteristics the three main economic systems respond differently to problems of resource allocation, productive balance, and distribution of goods and services. Regardless of the economic system, however, production and trade will prosper under good management (or whatever name may be used for managers) and falter under bad.

Our profit-oriented enterprise system has played a giant role in productively combining our resources to build and defend our nation and allow us to achieve great abundance and prosperity. It has achieved an almost miraculous balance in the production of consumer and capital goods in a complex economic system that involves thousands of interdependent processes and activities.

---

3. David Brand, "Russia's Private Farms Show State-Run Ones How to Raise Output," *The Wall Street Journal* (March 3, 1981), p. 1. Reprinted by permission of *The Wall Street Journal,* © Dow Jones & Company, Inc. (1981). All Rights Reserved.

Figure 1-6   **Comparisons of Representative Economic Systems**

Characteristic	Capitalism	Socialism	Communism
1. Ownership of means of production	Private ownership of business and industry with right to freedom of economic choice sanctioned by the Constitution and protected by law.	Public ownership of basic industries, distribution channels, and commerce.	Public (state) ownership of virtually all industrial and agricultural productive capacity.
2. Degree of central control	Relatively few product and pricing goals established by consumers and managers in the competitive marketplace.	Major goals of economy set by government; personal freedom exists to vary occupation and consumption within this broad governmental framework.	Central determination of prices, investments, and all major resource values and proportions in production, distribution, and consumption.
3. Extent of managerial decision making	Private managerial initiative supported by governmental actions to promote private enterprise.	Managers of major firms must obey the central control plans, thus precluding major independent business decisions.	Managers selected through state political party; highly bureaucratized, with managerial decisions imposed through state administrative hierarchy.
4. Occupational choice	Individual freedom to choose and bargain for jobs, employers, fields of business, and locations.	Individuals may own small businesses and land and choose occupations within the state-controlled economy.	State government owns all business and is the only employer. Individual's work prescribed by state.
5. Incentives	Monetary and social in the form of profit, prestige, and self-control.	"To each according to one's need, from each according to one's ability."	Nationalistic appeals, peer pressure, public recognition, threats of punitive action, and work standards.

SUMMARY   Our capitalistic business enterprise system is the means through which the United States has achieved great economic progress in its relatively short history. This system results basically from the combination and interaction of the social institution of business, constitutional democracy, and capitalism.

The social institution of business is the activating element in our enterprise system. Business is a key institution because its values and consequences are accepted as an important and basic part of our lives. It is social in nature as it is comprised of human groups working toward goals that agree with those of society. But business does not stand alone. It exists within a framework of other social institutions in a dynamic, interactive relationship.

Capitalism and business work best in a balanced relationship with a strong, stable government. In our society, constitutional democracy encourages business by providing safeguards for basic civil liberties, limitations on the use of power by government and other groups, and enforcement of contracts and property rights.

Regardless of the growing impact of governmental policies and practices on our economy, our capitalistic system still offers great freedom of opportunity. It is based on mutually gainful relationships between individuals. And it includes factors that provide the foundation for productive, innovative business activity in our society.

Three key factors of capitalism are capital, risk, and profit. Capital takes two forms: capital goods and capital funds. The essence of capitalism is risk-taking, as risk is always present in private enterprise. The reward for those persons who invest their capital and energy and who face risk to provide goods and services to society comes from profit. But profits are more than a reward for risk-taking. They are reinvested so firms can innovate and grow, and profits also are used to provide savings to cover the ups and downs of business.

The basic underpinnings of our enterprise system are in place, but there are various economic theories with widely differing ideas as to how our system should operate. Two basic models are the classical theory of capitalism and the Keynesian or income-expenditure theory. Today's classical thinking is called supply-side economics, and Keynesian theory is also called demand-management economics. The key policy tools of these two basic models are monetary policy and fiscal policy.

Regardless of a nation's political and economic leanings, its managers will face the same economic problems of how best to use its limited resources in the production and distribution of goods and services. The decisions on these questions will vary depending on the ideological framework of a nation. And there is a great difference between capitalism and various forms of socialism and communism.

Our profit-oriented capitalistic system has served our nation well during its short history. The form of our enterprise system undoubtedly will change over time as the needs of society change. But it should continue to live up to these changing expectations and remain a vital contributor to our quality of life.

BACK TO THE CHAPTER OPENER	1. What is the main difference between a market economy and a command economy?
	2. What is the usual role of a central government in communist nations? In capitalist nations?
	3. What distinguishes a socialist economy from a communist economy?
	4. Which theory of American capitalism currently emphasizes incentives to produce rather than to consume?
	5. Will Bulgaria's new economic plan be capitalist or communist?

BUSINESS TERMS

business	3-4	fiscal policy	15
American capitalism	9	monetary policy	15
profit	11	demand management	15
entrepreneur	11	socialism	17
supply-side economics	14	communism	17

QUESTIONS FOR DISCUSSION AND ANALYSIS

1. Would a profit-making racketeering activity be considered part of the institution of business?
2. Would the manufacturer of ultra-light aircraft with 25 employees be considered a small business? How about a manufacturer of yachts with 300 employees?
3. Would a firm that mines asbestos and manufactures fire-resistant insulation be an industrial or a commercial business? Explain.

4. Are an economic system and a business enterprise system essentially the same thing? Explain.
5. Do you think most automobile manufacturers and highway builders would like to have government out of their business lives?
6. Why is private property vital to capitalism?
7. Do you feel that most capitalists exploit the working classes in order to prosper? Explain.
8. Discuss how entrepreneurial and managerial roles differ and whether a person can be successful in both roles.
9. Would most corporate businesses favor supply-side over demand-management economics? Why?
10. Why would the Soviet Ministry of Agriculture allow individuals to farm small, rented plots on state-owned land in their spare time and to market the produce and livestock as capitalists might do?

PROJECTS, PROBLEMS, AND SHORT CASES

1. Two pressing problems in the United States are: our deteriorating infrastructure (system of physical facilities) and our 10 million unemployed Americans. We are all aware of the pothole explosion in our cities. In addition, more than 8,000 miles of our interstate highway system need rebuilding. Over 200,000 bridges, as well as water, sewage, and mass transportation systems, need fixing. And the list goes on.

   Prepare a five-minute oral report that covers the following three points:

   a. Should unemployed workers be trained to rebuild our nation's deteriorating physical facilities?

   b. If so, should this be handled through private-sector jobs, jobs with federal assistance, public-sector jobs, or some other means?

   c. If the government were involved, where would the revenue come from to cover its share?

2. A controversial, but growing, kind of profit-making business is the ambulatory surgical facility (ASF), where doctors perform simple operations that do not require an overnight stay. The bills for the operations include neither the room-and-bed charges of a conventional hospital nor the overhead cost of maintaining expensive hospital equipment for serious treatments. Most ASFs start making money after two years and yield an annual return of 15 percent to 20 percent on the investment in the facility. Thus, the ASF seems to be an innovative, profit-oriented answer to reducing the cost and humanizing the conditions of minor surgery.

   Discuss whether you see any problems with the profit-making ASF from the viewpoint of other groups or institutions in our society.

3. Assume you are part of the leadership group of a less-developed country (LDC) that has just emerged from a colonial era of dependence on industrialized, capitalist nations. You have been asked to make a recommendation on whether the country should opt for a Marxist system (not necessarily with Soviet ties) or a capitalist economic system.

   Prepare a two-page report giving your decision and the reasons for it.

Environmental Zeal and Economic Deals

Two years ago, some Oregon lawmakers, aflame with environmental zeal, tried to ban disposable diapers. They argued that forcing every baby bottom into good old recyclable cloth would eliminate countless tons of malodorous trash. No go, said the mothers of Oregon, threatening to dump a mountain of soiled diapers at the capitol. End of idea.

Perhaps only in Oregon would people lock horns over diaper pollution. Environmentalism hasn't been just another cause in the state; it is bred in the bone. Over the past 14 years Oregon has mounted a passionate drive to maintain its beauty, passing groundbreaking laws since copied elsewhere . . .

But if Oregon environmentalism is still strong, it isn't as strong as it was only a short time ago, for the passion it once aroused is not competing with a growing sense of economic alarm. There is a full-fledged bust in the forest products industry, and energy problems loom. Unemployment is over 10% and rising; are the jobless to eat scenery? Dirt-cheap federal hydropower can't fill the Northwest's needs anymore, and a regional nuclear construction program in Washington State has generated nothing by megabuck cost overruns. Where is the affordable electricity to come from?

In tackling these dilemmas, Oregon is trying to have its cake and eat it too. A new coal-fired power plant opened recently, but last fall voters in effect banned any more nuclear plants, and the state is banking heavily on conservation and alternative energy sources . . .

On the economic front, the sickly condition of the forest industry has spurred efforts to lure new businesses to a state that once didn't seem to want them. Some big hi-tech firms have settled in, but development officials confess that the state's anti-growth reputation isn't helping recruitment any. "We have an image problem," says one . . . but now jobs are desperately needed, and antipathy toward new industry is waning. This is apparent even in Eugene, Oregon's second-largest city, one of the most livable anywhere, and, as one resident puts it, "a last refuge for the terminally hip." . . . In this town full of beards, backpacks, and bicycles, an environmental-loving counterculture has struck deep roots . . .

Over at city hall, however, the welcome mat is out for rotten capitalist outfits who would like to settle in. The town has prepared new industrial sites and representatives have been sniffing around firms in California's Silicon Valley . . .

It's too early to tell whether Eugene's effort, as well as the state as a whole, will bear sufficient fruit. But it is clear that economic conditions have forced Oregon to pause in its once continuous drive toward an ever-cleaner, more livable environment. Bill Young, the environmental quality chief, doubts that some of the pioneering legislation passed years ago could pass today. And Liz Frenkel, the Sierra Club's lobbyist, adds: "Environmentally, 10 years ago this state was a knight on a white charger. Now we're riding a gray mule."

SOURCE: Adapted from William E. Blundell, "Oregon's Environmental Zeal Is Yielding to Economic Needs," *The Wall Street Journal* (October 13, 1981), p. 1. Reprinted by permission of *The Wall Street Journal,* © Dow Jones & Company, Inc. (1981). All Rights Reserved.

2 Business in a Changing Environment

Objectives:

- Identify and explain three representative models of American values.
- Distinguish between the manager as a trustee of profit and a trustee of power.
- Explain the relationship of social pluralism to the use of power by business.
- Define enlightened self-interest.
- Explain the self-interest concept of Adam Smith.
- Define social costs.
- Distinguish among the four basic stages in efforts to control air pollution.
- Explain the importance of cost-benefit relationships to cost-effective decisions to control air pollution.
- Explain how the concepts of business legitimacy, corporate accountability, and environmental scanning are related.
- Explain the function of the corporate social audit.

Some 80 years ago Mark Twain, in London at the time, wired a New York newspaper, "The reports of my death are greatly exaggerated." Today we see our capitalistic system, and especially the institution of business, in a Twain-like situation. Business — the vigorous engine of growth and productivity in our society — is being attacked from various directions.

As with our friend Mr. Twain, the reports of the downfall of our enterprise system seem greatly exaggerated. But the trend in the criticism of business is clear and offers little comfort to business and its managers. Ten years ago, over half of the American public expressed confidence in our business leaders. Today a clear-cut majority holds business and its managers in low esteem. A public opinion poll commissioned by *Business Week* and conducted by Lou Harris & Associates concluded that the American public does not believe the business community is pulling its weight in restoring the economy to health. Says pollster Lou Harris, "Business is perceived as falling down on the job badly. . . the more basic the responsibility, the worse the performance is perceived.[1]

The gap between the expectations of the business community and those of the American public is hard for some corporate managers to accept. Corporate managers might reason like this: "America benefits from our corporation. We meet a large payroll that allows thousands of employees to earn a living for themselves and their families. We produce a good product that is needed by many customers. We buy goods from dozens of other companies. And we pay out many thousands of dollars in dividends to our stockholders and in taxes to state and federal governments. We'll let these accomplishments speak for themselves against any criticism of business."

The public generally accepts these points but sees them as part of the *social rent* of business—the dues that business pays in return for being allowed to operate as a steward or trustee of society's scarce resources. So, it is clear that business is deeply involved in this nation's societal problems, and businesspersons cannot avoid the pressures to respond to ever-changing societal demands.

In order for business to meet responsibilities that go beyond its economic obligations, business managers must understand the environment in which they operate. In Chapter 1 we noted the importance of the economic and political environment of business. In this chapter we will cover aspects of the social and physical environment of business, especially the importance of basic American value patterns as they relate to societal expectations and business behavior. We will develop models of business responsibility that reflect these various American values. Finally, we will recognize the continuing challenge that business faces in demonstrating its legitimacy and credibility.

THE SOCIAL ENVIRONMENT OF BUSINESS: BASIC AMERICAN VALUES

Society's expectations about the obligations of business reflect our nation's values, or cultural standards of behavior. These act as guides to businesses in setting and pursuing goals. Values are also important building blocks of thought and action at the individual level. These enduring standards of right action tell us how to act, what to want, how to judge morally, and how to compare ourselves with others. Some basic American values include the following:

1. Individual rights and the freedom to compete.
2. Property rights as a guarantee of individual rights.

---

1. "Business Week/Harris Poll—The Recession Sours Voters on Business," quoted from the May 31, 1982 issue of *Business Week* by special permission.

3. Equality of opportunity.
4. Limited government.
5. Technological growth and specialization as a basis for human progress.

Thus, values are more than theoretical concepts. They are real and practical. And our nation's diverse values, along with other theories, goals, and beliefs, form our societal ideology. This ideology is the institutional "glue" of our society. It provides the overall sociopolitical framework that gives direction to our nation's efforts. It also provides the basis for the acceptability or legitimacy of our institutions (see pages 35-36).

American values change as societal circumstances change. However, three important American value patterns that have developed over time are seen in the models that we call Traditional Man, Economic Man, and Social Man.[2]

Traditional Man

The values of **Traditional Man** came to America with its first settlers. These values were rooted in the "Natural Laws" of John Locke, the Puritan ethic of John Calvin, and the self-interest concept of Adam Smith.

John Locke was an educational and political philosopher of 17th-century England. He was concerned about the growing power of the ruling royal family and sought to protect individuals from the arbitrary acts of monarchs. Locke held that individuals did not surrender all their rights to monarchs, but only the rights needed to preserve law and security. The remaining "Natural Rights," or "Natural Laws," relating to the integrity of the person and property were retained by individuals. Locke's "Natural Laws" included the right of individuals to strive for their own fulfillment, property rights, the rejection of the divine right of monarchs, and desire for limited government.

The **Puritan ethic (Protestant ethic or work ethic)** of theologian John Calvin also emphasized individual effort, hard work, self-discipline, reinvestment rather than consumption of earnings, and obedience to God's will. And Adam Smith combined the Puritan ethic with self-interest. The values of Traditional Man made possible the great effort needed to establish our nation in its first century.

Economic Man

Economic Man arrived during our industrial revolution in the late 1800s. Over the past 100 years Economic Man has been concerned mainly with producing goods and services. A person whc fits this model is rational and calculating and considers advantages and disadvantages in terms of one's own self-interest. She or he believes

---

2. The representative models of Economic Man and Social Man, and much of their descriptions, are from David P. Eastburn, "Economic Man vs. Social Man, and Other Talks" (Federal Reserve Bank of Philadelphia, 1977), pp. 1–7, 27–32.

that self-interest has served this nation well, that self-interest in a market economy is expressed largely in monetary terms, and that the Puritan ethic of hard work and self-discipline is still a major path to the good life.

More recently, however, Economic Man has been seen by some as straying from the Puritan ethic toward the **consumption ethic**, which views consumption and material comfort as the most important goals in life. A person in this image wants economic growth, and this growth is made possible by a high level of innovation and modern technology. If this growth results in the misuse of our resources and environment, it is simply the price of progress.

Social Man

Social Man sees a far different route to the good life from that of Economic Man. This model stresses people instead of things and human rather than monetary values. Social Man thinks that property rights should be replaced by a person's right to survival and enjoyment as a member of the American community or corporation. Further, Social Man believes that large firms may view partnerships with government as an alternative to vigorous competition among individual companies. As a result, community needs replace competition as the basis for the use of scarce resources. Along this line, Social Man also sees the state as a planner of goals and priorities, thus enlarging the role of government. Some key values of Social Man, as well as those of Traditional Man and Economic Man, are summarized in Figure 2-1.

SOCIAL VALUES AND MODELS OF BUSINESS RESPONSIBILITY

The basic values implied by our capitalistic enterprise system, along with one's personal values, are necessarily involved in any discussion of business or corporate responsibility. Persons and groups who believe mainly in the values of Economic Man see today's world differently from those who believe mainly in the values of Social Man. Each accepts a different model of the business manager's responsibility to society. Economic Man sees the business manager's basic role as a *trustee of profit*, while Social Man sees the manager as a *trustee of power*. Today's managers probably see their role more in terms of enlightened self-interest.

The Manager as a Trustee of Profit

In January, 1925, President Calvin Coolidge made a speech to the Society of American Newspaper Editors in which he made the famous remark, "The business of America is business." By and large that statement was regarded as an acceptable definition of what the United States was all about at that time. It was consistent with the economic philosophy of the 18th and 19th centuries. The nation was best served, it was thought, when each businessperson and company aimed for self-interest, or

Figure 2-1   Summary of Three Value Models

Value Model	Key Values or Characteristics
Traditional Man: Rooted in the Puritan ethic of John Calvin, the "Natural Laws" of John Locke, the self-interest of Adam Smith, and the need for hard work to survive in the new world.	1. Individual effort. 2. Survival of the fittest. 3. Sacredness of work as obedience to God's will. 4. Reinvestment of earnings and delayed gratification in the consumption of material goods. 5. Discipline, honesty, sobriety, and obedience to authority. 6. Right to own property. 7. Open-market competition and pursuit of self-interest. 8. Limited government interference. 9. Rejection of the divine right of monarchs.
Economic Man: Rooted in the rational, calculating use of resources and mass production to generate the highest possible income. More recently, rooted in the consumption ethic with its cravings for greater material comfort.	1. Production of goods and services. 2. Limitless growth and ever-greater material comfort. 3. Value-free technology. 4. Relatively free pursuit of self-interest. 5. Money rewards to the efficient entrepreneur. 6. Individual hard work and self-discipline. 7. Opportunity costs as a key concept in life. 8. More concern about inflation than about unemployment.
Social Man: Rooted in the stress on people and human values rather than on things and monetary values as the route to the good life.	1. Efficient distribution instead of unlimited production. 2. Stress on quality and price-value relationships. 3. Equality of result rather than equality of opportunity. 4. Cooperative involvement, often with government, to solve social problems. 5. Worker participation in managerial decision processes. 6. More concern about unemployment than about inflation.

maximum gain, in the competitive business scene. Consider, for example, this passage from Adam Smith's *The Wealth of Nations*, published in 1776:

> It is not from the benevolence of the butcher, the brewer, or the baker that we expect our dinner, but from their regard for their own interest. We address ourselves not to their humanity, but to their self-love, and never talk to them of our own necessities but of their own advantages.[3]

---

3. Adam Smith, *The Wealth of Nations* (London: George Routledge & Sons), p. 11.

In many companies and individuals this traditional acceptance of responsibility to the owner or stockholders of a company has carried over into the present. This approach argues that business cannot do everything for everyone. So, it should pursue what it does best — its economic goal of striving to earn profits over the long run. There are other institutions, such as government, religion, and the family, that should handle programs of social improvement and general well-being. If the manager, as a trustee of profit, seeks also to support social programs from business profits, this is seen as a weakening of the entrepreneurial spirit needed to maintain corporate performance.

The Manager as a Trustee of Power

Those who view the manager as a *trustee of power* hold that the manager is responsible not only to the stockholders, but also for decisions that include the well-being of society as a whole. Underpinning this demand for social involvement is the feeling that corporate managers must accept the responsibility that goes with their position of leadership and power in our pluralistic nation.

Although business is a major social institution in our society, we have noted that it exists within the framework provided by other institutions such as government, religion, politics and law, the military, agriculture, family life, and education. And within these institutions one finds diverse groups such as professional associations, trade associations, farm organizations, and fraternal and service groups that also have their own leadership and power. In other words, ours is a pluralistic society comprised of numerous institutions, associations, and groups that possess some power and leadership and use these to keep one another in balance. For example, business, government, and labor each uses its leadership and power to keep one another from growing too powerful.

Within this framework the modern business corporation is seen by many as being a semipublic, as well as an economic, unit. The manager as a trustee of power is expected to achieve a skillful balance in the firm's responsibilities not only to stockholders, but also to employees, customers, suppliers, the community, and the public at large.

Managers and Enlightened Self-Interest

To this point our discussion of some value patterns of society and the resulting expectations as to what is responsible business behavior has been arranged in basic models that are relatively clear. These include the values of Traditional, Economic, and Social Man and the expectations that business managers behave as either trustees of profit or trustees of power. The conflict between these general categories of values and expectations underlies many of our nation's problems today.

Unfortunately the business manager finds that the nature of this "gap" is not as clear as these general models suggest. First, each person is a mixture of Economic Man and Social Man, as each wants to make a living and to get along with others in society. Also, this mix of values varies *from* person to person and *within* individuals over time.

Those who are 90 percent Economic Man see our world differently from those who are 90 percent Social Man. There is little conflict within these persons. The conflict of competing values comes when a person—business manager, government official, or any citizen—approaches a 50-50 split in her or his values.

The same holds true for other levels in society. As the values, goals, and attitudes of groups, associations, and institutions change, so do their expectations as to how business should respond to issues in its changing environment.

So, today's business decisions are likely to be based on some mixture of self-interest and public interest in what is called **enlightened self-interest (ESI).** With this approach, decision makers act as trustees of both power and profit. They try to balance the social, political, economic, and natural forces in the environment in a way that lets the firm succeed in the long run.

ESI and Adam Smith

As we have noted, Adam Smith set forth a rationale for the free market. He proposed to allow the market to function as the chief allocator of investment, rewarding the diligent and astute and penalizing the tradition-bound and inefficient.

But Adam Smith was more than an economist; in fact, there were no economists in his day. Rather, he was a political and moral philosopher, concerned with the mainsprings of human behavior and of social responsibility.[4] The concepts of sympathy and intelligence had special meanings in Smith's work. As one scholar explains it:

> Sympathy was not a sentimental concept for Smith; rather, it invested the idea of one's larger interests with the new dimension, for unless self-interest is intelligent it degenerates into pandering to the passions. To be intelligent means to know others and what they would like and aspire to become themselves. To pursue one's interests can lead to mutual advantage if the enterprising spirit can identify and meet a real need that exists beyond one's self.[5]

Smith was confident that the intelligent pursuit of one's true interests would lead to an advantage for all. To him, people's ambitions needed to be directed toward power and respect that could be gained through economic success. Thus, Adam Smith's thinking seems to relate well to the concept of enlightened self-interest.

ESI and the Horns of a Dilemma

Perhaps the key point in this chapter is that every business decision of any importance in our society is based on a mix of economic and social considerations. This means that business decision makers often find themselves on the horns of a dilemma. The problem they face is that no major decision, regardless of the care that goes into making it, will satisfy all parties concerned with the decision.

An example of the pressures business decision makers face is found in the area of corporate philanthropy (or corporate giving). In fact, enlightened self-interest has also

---

4. Much of this section is from James T. Laney, "The Other Adam Smith," *Economic Review of the FRB of Atlanta* (October, 1981), pp. 26-29.
5. *Ibid.,* p. 27.

been called "critical philanthropy" and "unavoidable altruism." At first, corporate philanthropy was closely bound to the giver's self-interest. It emerged in the late 19th century, when the railroads sponsored YMCA hostels where their employees bunked down. Today the pressure is on corporations to give to a mind-boggling variety of charities and organizations. This is especially true in the face of recent cutbacks in federal spending.

In deciding whom to help, most corporate givers combine social and economic considerations that reflect at least some self-interest. For instance, according to *Fortune*:

> Xerox lends money to provide housing for the poor in Stamford, Connecticut, the company's headquarters town. The money earns no interest for Xerox, but it earns the company a reputation as a good neighbor. Similarly, Atlantic Richfield helps support native artisans in Alaska partly because the company is the largest oil producer on the North Slope and wants the goodwill of the local population.[6]

Without a doubt, one mark of a professional manager today is that person's ability to evaluate correctly the various dimensions of business decisions.

THE PHYSICAL ENVIRONMENT OF BUSINESS

So far we have been dealing with the expected economic and social performance of business. But what about its performance in dealing with the challenges and problems in its physical environment?

In most nations, including the United States, economic growth is king. Along with this growth and our high standard of living have come problems in the use of land, air, and water. In the United States, as in many other parts of the world, environmental pollution is the outcome of a national commitment to achieve growth as cheaply as possible. America has paid for part of its growth by mortgaging its physical environment. Industry, along with government and the public, has regarded air and water as free goods—a kind of national public sewage system for the discharge of industrial wastes. Although the costs of labor and materials are routinely included in the pricing of products, the pollution of water and air has not been recognized as a production cost. Thus, society has been left with the **social costs of pollution**—the harmful consequences of the productive processes that fall outside the market's regular pricing mechanisms and for which the industrial operators are not held accountable. When industrial firms and their customers pay for their share of the social costs of pollution created by the production of the needed product, this is called the **internalization of social costs.**

Obviously Economic Man has neglected the environment in our period of great growth. And business is clearly implicated in our nation's environmental issues since business is the activating element—the transforming mechanism—in our enterprise system. Business is the institution that combines our raw and semiprocessed resources

---

6. Lee Smith, "The Unsentimental Corporate Giver," FORTUNE (September 21, 1981), p. 121. © 1981 Time Inc.

and creates goods from them. It organizes and channels a high proportion of the activity of our society. Thus, it is difficult for business to escape the expectations that it also exercise its leadership and expertise to solve pollution and other ecological problems.

There are many problems in the physical environment of business. These include problems of air pollution, water pollution, noise pollution, land pollution in the forms of solid waste and litter, disposal of toxic chemical wastes and nuclear wastes, and the like. Some of these problems are the fault of business, especially as the result of our industrial processes. However, business also is on the receiving end of these problems as it tries to interpret and live up to changing governmental regulations and societal expectations. In this section, the topic of air pollution will be used as an example of the challenges faced by business in making its peace with its physical environment.

Air Pollution: Its Nature and Sources

Air pollution is defined as significant contaminants in the atmosphere or outdoor air (ambient air) that have adverse effects on a person's health, safety, comfort, or use of property, or on plant or animal life. The main types of air pollution emissions are carbon monoxide, sulfur oxides, particulates, hydrocarbons, and nitrogen oxides. These pollutants come mainly from transportation, stationary fuel combustion, industrial processes, and solid waste disposal.

Stages of Air Pollution Control

Since the early 1960s, there have been four basic stages in the strategies and legislation to control air pollution. These stages correspond roughly with the: Clean Air Act of 1963 and its 1967 Amendments, Clean Air Act Amendments of 1970, Clean Air Act Amendments of 1977, and present stance of the federal administration.

Clean Air Act of 1963 and Its 1967 Amendments

This stage was a broad effort to reverse the steady deterioration of air quality in the United States. In general, this was a period of authorizing funds for pollution research and of developing state regulatory agencies. The Act provided three federal dollars for every local dollar to develop and support regional interstate air pollution control programs. The Department of Health, Education, and Welfare (HEW) designated air quality regions and adopted air quality standards for these regions.

Clean Air Act Amendments of 1970

This comprehensive amendment, known also as the "Muskie bill" because of the efforts of its sponsor, Senator Edmund Muskie, was a major change from earlier efforts. The 1970 Act granted the newly-formed U. S. Environmental Protection Agency (EPA) the first real statutory power at the federal level to contain air pollution. The administration of the EPA was directed to set ambient levels for 10 major pollutants within 120 days after this bill became a law. Each state was to translate the federal standards into emission standards for local industry and develop strategies for their enforcement. The Act required full enforcement of the standards by June, 1975. It also required auto companies to reduce carbon monoxide and hydrocarbons in their cars' emissions by 90 percent, and nitrous oxides by 90 percent in the 1976 model year.

Clean Air Act Amendments of 1977

The 1977 Amendments directed the states to prepare new pollution control plans that would ensure compliance with all standards by December 31, 1980 (1987 for ozone and carbon monoxide). A key aspect of this third stage of air pollution control is the **Prevention of Significant Deterioration (PSD) rules.** These regulations, added to the Act in 1977, impose stricter air pollution limits than required under the national ambient air quality standards.

The PSD rules provide for three new classes of areas. Class I includes such areas as national parks, forests, and wilderness. Class I status allows little additional pollution. More pollution is allowed in Class II areas, which include most of the country's "clean" areas. Class III areas, which allow the greatest pollution increases, have not yet been designated.

In addition, the 1977 Amendment committed the EPA to rewrite the *New Source Performance Standards (NSPS)* for power plants fired by fossil fuels. The new performance standards for sulfur dioxide emissions forced the use of flue gas cleaning devices (scrubbers) in coal-fired power plants.

Air Pollution Control at the Present

This fourth stage of air pollution control is now under way. The main thrust of this stage is to ease, rather than strengthen, antipollution standards under the Clean Air Act. This change is a response to the claim by businesses and other groups that the existing law inhibits production and causes unemployment in some of the nation's largest industries.

Rather than offer detailed legislation on reforming the Clean Air Act, the White House has made public its broad guidelines or "principles" for reform and is leaving it up to Congress to fill in the details. Among the federal administration's main goals are:

1. Turn more responsibility for clean air over to the states.
2. Allow industry to expand in areas where the air is already clean as long as national standards are not violated.
3. Continue to protect air quality in Class I "pristine" areas.
4. Roll back auto-emission standards for current models to 1977 levels.
5. Extend the deadline for meeting clean-air standards for cities with tough pollution problems until 1990.
6. Set uniform pollution standards for all coal-burning utilities.

Opposing any substantial change are environmentalists and the lawmakers who drafted the original Act. They argue that the law needs only to be fine-tuned to bolster its protection of the environment.

The Complex Issues of Pollution Control

The Clean Air Amendments of 1970 and 1977 were relatively blunt instruments. Congress was specifying a set of air quality standards with the full realization that both air quality and its relationship to human health are not subject to any precise scientific legal definition. But this was tolerated because of a general recognition that cleaner air was a public good. The air in a lot of places was plainly dirty; and people, including businesspeople, wanted to clean it up. Billions of dollars already have been spent to this end.

Now various groups of business leaders, such as the Business Roundtable and the National Environmental Development Association (NEDA), feel that the blunt instrument needs refining. Business in general is seeking to change only those provisions in the law that represent obstacles to needed production and industrial growth but produce little or no improvement in air quality. This position by business requires that managers understand cost-benefit relationships and the importance of careful responses to environmental issues in general.

Cost-Benefit Relationships

Figure 2-2 shows estimated pollution control expenditures from 1979 to 1988 for air, water, and solid waste. These estimates support the viewpoint that businesses are not evading pollution control expenditures. Over 70 percent of the money spent for pollution control in the decade 1979-1988 will come from businesses.

But big business is not willing simply to throw money at various pollution control problems. It argues that carefully evaluated cost-benefit relationships should weigh more heavily in our nation's desire for a high-quality environment. This issue of cost-benefit relationships includes at least two basic questions:

1. Are the most effective and economic means being used to control pollution?
2. What is the cost of the improvements at various levels of quality and rates of accomplishment?

These questions must be answered in order to determine if a decision is cost-effective. For example, much of the $338 billion for air pollution control from 1979-1988 will be spent on desulfurization of fuels, installation of power plant flue gas scrubbers, and control of auto emissions. The effect of these projects on human health is largely immeasurable. Another way to use this money would be to ask, "What is the best way we can use $338 billion to improve health with measurable results?"

Business recognizes the need for improvement. But it seeks to achieve this improvement in ways and rates that do not threaten our economic growth, jobs, and ability to make products at a price consumers can afford. Thus, business leaders are asking the following basic question about pollution control measures: Are the most effective and economic ways being used to control pollution and to achieve a high-quality environment in the United States? Questions like this underlie the current changes noted in stage four of air pollution control.

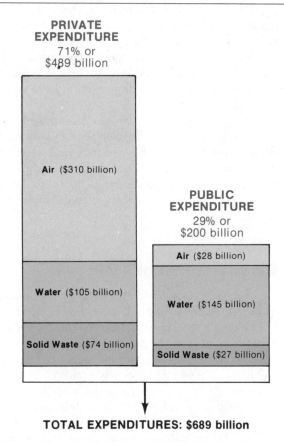

PRIVATE EXPENDITURE
71% or
$489 billion

Air ($310 billion)

Water ($105 billion)

Solid Waste ($74 billion)

PUBLIC EXPENDITURE
29% or
$200 billion

Air ($28 billion)

Water ($145 billion)

Solid Waste ($27 billion)

TOTAL EXPENDITURES: $689 billion

SOURCE: Council on Environmental Quality, "Environmental Quality," 11th Annual Report (Washington, DC: U. S. Government Printing Office), p. 397.

Managerial Responses to Environmental Issues

We have been using air pollution issues as an example of the physical environment in which businesses must operate. We have seen that the air pollution regulations are constantly changing, sometimes politically inspired, and often not measurable as to their effectiveness. When we multiply this situation by all the various types of pollution control, the picture is one of complexity and uncertainty. Critics argue that many companies have used this complexity as an excuse for inaction rather than as a situation that demands sincere responses. As with most environmental issues, there is some truth to this view. Past accidents have tarnished industry's image, cost companies millions of dollars in fines, and landed some executives in court.

Now, faced with heightened public awareness of environmental problems, most large industrial companies, such as chemical companies, are concluding that effective environmental management is as much a part of the company's profit picture as its other operations. As a result of this changing viewpoint, many companies now have organized programs and environmental staffs to deal with environmental crises. The responsibilities of these staffs are to comply with federal and local regulations, keep up with new regulations and technological developments, and generally take active measures to avert future crises.

BUSINESS LEGITIMACY AND CORPORATE ACCOUNTABILITY

In Chapter 1 we discussed business as a key social institution in our society. Earlier in this chapter we noted that business managers are seen as trustees of both power and profit. As such, they face the challenge of responding to the pressures of the total environment in a way that lets their firms succeed over the long run. To gain a better perspective of what we should expect from business, the concepts of business legitimacy and corporate accountability should be understood.

Concept of Business Legitimacy

The right or authority of business to act as a trustee of society's resources is based on the recognition and confidence of the American people that business is fulfilling the role for which it was created. This is what is meant by **business legitimacy**. In other words, business is seen as legitimate to the degree that its purposes are in harmony with those of the society of which it is a part.

But business legitimacy is not an automatic right. Instead, corporate businesses must carefully establish their good reputation or credibility over the years. Credibility is gained through the ongoing processes of identifying those considerations that seem important to the public and of meeting reasonable expectations.

Concept of Corporate Accountability

Legitimacy gives business a base of authority for its actions. The power and authority possessed by corporations — the most visible arm of the institution of business — depends on how valuable they are to those they serve. But legitimacy also means that managers are accountable for their actions. Thus, the concept of **corporate accountability** holds that corporate managers are responsible for their performance, i.e., how they handle the resources under their control.

Monitoring Corporate Performance

With corporate accountability comes the inevitable efforts to monitor corporate social performance along with its financial performance. One such effort, the

corporate social audit, is a systematic attempt to measure and evaluate a corporation's impact on society. This audit may be conducted by internal or external auditors and may focus on a few or many of a company's activities. Further, the company's social performance may be reported in financial or nonfinancial terms. To push this concern for social performance, the U. S. Chamber of Commerce has developed a **social performance index**, a voluntary measure and guide to help firms see where they can be more socially active. Some firms and trade groups already have their own social indexes. For example, Arco has "The Social Critique"; Pennsylvania Bank and Trust Company, "The Social Scorecard"; American Council of Life Insurance, "The Social Reporting Program"; and the Bank of America, "Voluntary Disclosure Program."

Other methods to report the social performance of a corporation include:

1. Written descriptions of corporate social performance efforts, included in the footnotes of financial statements.
2. Extension of financial statements to include the costs of specific corporate social performance efforts.
3. Special reports covering corporate efforts in specific areas such as pollution or occupational health.
4. Attempts to measure the costs and benefits of programs in terms of dollars spent.
5. Addition of an active public affairs committee to help the board of directors understand issues of corporate social performance.

The process of establishing effective social auditing procedures is still in its infancy, and enlightened self-interest undoubtedly will continue to play a part in the types of social programs a corporation decides to support. But as areas of social involvement are established either by choice or by public pressure, companies will be expected to monitor and report carefully their social performance on a formal basis.

Environmental Scanning

The need for a manager to know what's going on in the company's environment is most often discussed in topics like management planning and strategy. This probing of the environment sometimes is called **environmental scanning**, defined as the process that seeks "information about events and relationships in a company's outside environment, the knowledge of which would assist top management in its task of charting the company's future course of action."[7]

This sensitivity to the environment also is crucial to corporate legitimacy and accountability. It is becoming increasingly important that managers correctly perceive and respond to the current rules and standards of society. If the actions of corporations are not seen as actions that meet social needs, then business will lose the legitimacy which is the basis for its stewardship role in our society. Business must be willing to pinpoint and respond effectively to the societal expectations in its ever-changing evironment.

---

7. Francis Joseph Aguilar, *Scanning the Business Environment* (New York: Macmillan, 1967), p. 1.

SUMMARY   Business functions as the trustee of society's resources. To continue in this role, business—especially corporate business—must live up to society's expectations. This means that business managers must understand the environment in which they operate. This environment includes social and physical dimensions. In the social environment, society's expectations about the obligations of business reflect, in part, our nation's values. Three basic value patterns are those of Traditional Man, Economic Man, and Social Man. Economic Man sees the business manager's basic role as a trustee of profit, while Social Man sees the manager as a trustee of power. Managers probably see themselves as practicing enlightened self-interest, recognizing that important business decisions include both economic and social considerations.

As the activating element in our enterprise system, business contributes to our environmental problems. However, business also is on the receiving end of these problems as it tries to interpret and live up to changing regulations and expectations. Businesses expect to spend money to clean up our environment. But business leaders argue that environmental improvement should be balanced with our need for economic growth and jobs. To accomplish this, greater emphasis should be given to cost-benefit relationships in deciding how the money will be spent.

Business is seen as legitimate to the extent that it meets the needs of society, and society holds managers accountable for how they handle the resources under their control. There are growing efforts to monitor corporate social performance along with financial performance. To achieve effective corporate social performance, managers must correctly perceive and respond to the current needs of society. This environmental sensitivity can be strengthened by a formal process of environmental scanning.

BACK TO THE CHAPTER OPENER

1. How would you characterize the values of the Oregonians?
2. Do Oregonians see business as a trustee of profit or a trustee of power? How, would you guess, do businesspersons in Oregon see themselves?
3. Have cost-benefit relationships been considered in formulating Oregon's environmental standards?
4. Has large, corporate business enjoyed a stable, predictable, growth-oriented environment in Oregon?
5. Is the viewpoint in Oregon changing concerning the legitimacy of some industries?

BUSINESS TERMS

Traditional Man	25	internalization of social costs	30
Puritan ethic (Protestant ethic or work ethic)	25	Prevention of Significant Deterioration (PSD) rules	32
Economic Man	25	business legitimacy	35
consumption ethic	26	corporate accountability	35
Social Man	26	corporate social audit	36
enlightened self-interest (ESI)	29	social performance index	36
social costs of pollution	30	environmental scanning	36

1. Discuss which of the models of value patterns — Traditional Man, Economic Man, or Social Man — is most evident in our society today.
2. "Businesspersons are involved in a near-sighted, single-purpose pursuit of the almighty dollar." Do you agree with this statement? Explain.
3. Should a manager, as a trustee of power, be responsible for the well-being of employees beyond providing them with a paycheck? Discuss.
4. What do the concepts of sympathy and intelligence have to do with Adam Smith's concept of self-interest?
5. Discuss whether good managers should make decisions that satisfy all parties concerned with the decision.
6. Is enlightened self-interest a desirable basis for managerial decision making in the long run? Explain.
7. Many persons feel that it is the fault of business that social costs have not been internalized in our market-pricing process. Explain why you agree or disagree with this statement.
8. At present, the White House wants to turn more responsibility for clean air over to the states. Discuss how this action might affect the use of cost-benefit analysis in the decision to control air pollution, especially from auto emissions.
9. "Business generally has been dragging its feet in its efforts to clean up our environment." Do you agree? Explain.
10. Are the concepts of business legitimacy and credibility basically the same thing? Explain.

1. Sometimes corporate giving comes out of stockholders' pockets and sometimes — as in the case of corporate United Way fund drives — it comes out of the employees' pockets. Some employees gladly support this activity as something that is morally right and personally satisfying. Others may feel that it is an activity in which company management resorts to coercion and intimidation to achieve 100 percent participation and a certain level of contributions.

   For a term project, interview a salaried employee from each of the following four organizations: a manufacturing company; a financial institution such as a bank or a savings and loan; a government office (local, state, or federal); and a large retail chain store. Determine the following:

   a. The process by which their United Way or United Appeal contributions are collected.
   b. How important this fund drive seems to be to the employee's immediate manager.
   c. Why the employee is either for or against the activity.

   Prepare a short oral report presenting your findings to the class.

2. Does television have an antibusiness bias? It certainly seems that businesspersons on television programs often are presented as crooks, wheeler-dealers without morals, foolish, pompous, greedy, jerks, clowns, buffoons, and the like. Seldom does TV seem to portray business as socially useful or as a legitimate, economically productive activity.

   Over a month's time, watch a wider variety of TV programs, especially prime-time episodes, than you ordinarily would. Keep track of the following:

a. Whether the businesspersons portrayed were big- or small-business operators.

b. Whether the businesspersons were shown in a positive, neutral, or negative light.

c. Whether the functions they performed were illegal, foolish, only in their self-interest, or some other type.

d. Whether other professionals, such as lawyers or physicians, were portrayed as socially useful.

Prepare a written report of your findings, and share your conclusions with your class in an oral report. (This would be a good team project.)

3. Belinda Bergman is a partner in a chain of eight movie houses. This theater chain has been asked to show a nine-minute documentary film called "Two Wheels, One Life." The movie is about motorcycle-car crashes. It shows the smashed faces and maimed bodies of motorcycle riders who are crash victims. Accidents are recreated to show how the injuries occur. The film's message is that more careful motorcycle riding and the appreciation of motorcycles' capabilities by car drivers could prevent thousands of serious accidents each year. The film was produced by a group called the Institute for Motorcycle Safety and was financed by the insurance industry. The movie theaters are not charged a rental fee for the film.

Bergman's theater chain usually doesn't show short features along with its regular features. But after viewing the film, she and her partner decided that the merits far outweighed whatever negative reactions there might be. "I may lose some popcorn and candy sales, but the people who see the film will be better off," she commented.

Discuss the following:

a. Is Bergman being a socially responsible businessperson by showing these graphic lessons on motorcycle-car safety?

b. Will such documentaries help the credibility of theater chains and the film industry?

c. Which groups may resent her decision to show the film?

More Heat on Directors

A well-made board of directors is a collection of experts from diverse areas of society that proves its value most when it helps corporate management substitute foresight for hindsight. By this test, questions can be raised about what the board of Gulf Oil Corp. was doing while the company's top management maneuvered it into the current messy situation with Cities Service Co. For that matter, where was the board of Continental Illinois Bank when that institution was forging its risky link to the troubled Penn Square Bank and, later, when the resulting fiasco came to light? Or the board of Chase Manhattan Bank while that bank's management followed a growth-at-any-price philosophy that stuck it with big losses from loans to Drysdale Securities Corp. and Penn Square Bank? To ask these questions, of course, is not to pass judgment—not yet. But crisis turns a fierce spotlight on a company's board of directors, and no company can ignore that these are crisis-prone times. At the very least, prudent directors should remind themselves of some recent history.

When Penn Central RR collapsed more than a decade ago, many of its directors were surprised and dismayed to find themselves sued by stockholders who alleged that the directors had failed to meet their responsibilities. Subsequently, under prodding from the Securities & Exchange Commission, the New York Stock Exchange, and litigious stockholders, more directors began pulling up their socks and taking a broader view of their obligations and liabilities. Corporate boards began adding more outside directors, forming director audit committees to monitor corporate affairs, and enlarging director involvement in corporate policies.

But memories are short, and the Gulf, Continental Illinois, and Chase examples suggest that directors of many corporations have again slid back into the clubby atmosphere that tempts them to rubber-stamp management decisions with few questions. At the least, directors should keep in mind that if serious company troubles break into the open, shareholders and the public will want to know, and have a right to know, what the board of directors was doing, or not doing, to serve the best interests of the corporation and its owners.

SOURCE: Editorial, "More Heat on Directors," reprinted from the August 23, 1982 issue of *Business Week* by special permission, © 1982 by McGraw-Hill, Inc., New York, NY 10020. All rights reserved.

3 *Forms of Business Ownership*

Objectives:

- Define the proprietorship and its advantages and disadvantages.
- Define the partnership and distinguish among the following types of partners: general, limited, secret, silent, and dormant.
- Explain how an R&D limited partnership works.
- Explain the advantages and disadvantages of partnerships.
- Identify three elements in the definition of a corporation that make it unique.
- Identify three basic elements in the structure of a corporation.
- Describe four ways to classify corporations.
- Explain the advantages and disadvantages of corporations.
- Distinguish among joint ventures, business trusts, and unincorporated associations.
- Distinguish among cooperatives, credit unions, and mutual companies.

Nestled in the great midsection of our country is a bustling organization. It includes a medical clinic, a radio station, and a solar-heated school for children. It grosses well over $1 million a year from its book publishing, construction, and farm products businesses. What form of business ownership do you think this organization has? A corporation? A partnership? A proprietorship? Actually it's "none of the above." It is a commune called The Farm near Summertown, Tennessee. In fact, it's a true *collective*, requiring its over-1,000 members to donate all their assets to the organization's activities.

In Chapter 1 we saw that the right to own private businesses is an important characteristic of capitalism. Even a commune can be a profit-making organization in our enterprise system (although the profits may not be distributed to the members). In this chapter, however, we will focus on the three main legal forms of private ownership: the proprietorship, the partnership, and the corporation. Then we will touch on other unincorporated and incorporated forms of business ownership.

PROPRIETORSHIPS

A **proprietorship** is a business owned by one person and operated for one's own profit. This person, also called a proprietor, is classified as self-employed. The term "proprietorship" is interchangeable with sole proprietorship, individual enterprise, sole ownership, and individual proprietorship.

Have you ever asked a person what she or he does, who responded by saying, "I'm self-employed"? Usually this response is said in a way that goes beyond the question. It says, "I'm independent, have my self-respect, make money as a direct outcome of my efforts, and I do it my way!" Increasingly, people want to "be their own bosses," and the real action in our economy has shifted to smaller companies. At the beginning of the 1970s, self-employed individuals often were looked at as oddities who couldn't hack corporate life. Now they are seen more as folk heroes and heroines. There are many attractions to being a proprietor, but starting your own business also can be an economic and emotional mine field. More will be said about this in Chapter 26. At this point, we'll take a look at some characteristics, advantages, and disadvantages of the proprietorship form of business ownership.

Characteristics of a Proprietorship

Although there are some large proprietorships, typically the proprietorship is the ownership form for small businesses such as a restaurant, a TV shop, a bakery, or a bike shop. The capital needed for the business usually is provided by the owner from personal funds along with borrowed funds. The owner may hire someone to manage the business, but more often the owner is also the manager. As such, the owner-manager may find it necessary to make decisions personally rather than delegate them to others. Sometimes, however, this is a mistake, as it may reflect the owner's ego more than his or her expertise.

Sometimes a proprietorship can be identified by the name used, such as Phoebe Simon — Photographer, or Paul Snow — Cement Contractor. More commonly, however, the firm's name does not indicate the type of ownership — e.g., the University Women's Shop or even the King Paint Company. In these cases the owner must usually clear the firm's name at the county courthouse. Franchise holders operating as proprietors often use the name of the parent company, such as "Kentucky Fried Chicken."

Table 3-1 shows that in the United States more than 9 million individuals operate their own businesses on a full- or part-time basis. These do not include over 3 million persons engaged primarily in farming. Note that the largest number of

Table 3-1   **Proprietorship Income Tax Returns (Number, Receipts, Net Profits, and Average Receipts by Industries[1])**

Industry	Number of Returns	Business Receipts	Net Profit (Loss)	Average Business Receipts
		(Millions of Dollars)		
ALL INDUSTRIES[2]	9,067,383	$389,239	$55,533	$42,927
Mining	97,488	6,084	90	62,408
Construction	1,097,417	50,943	7,948	46,420
Manufacturing	235,526	12,929	1,512	54,894
Transportation, communication, electric, gas, and sanitary services	415,472	18,070	1,957	43,493
Wholesale and retail trade	2,454,720	195,655	11,174	79,706
Finance, insurance, and real estate	1,057,726	21,157	7,072	20,002
Services	3,654,001	83,290	25,531	22,794
Nature of business not allocable	55,033	1,112	248	20,206

[1]Agriculture, forestry, and fishing omitted.
[2]Due to rounding, items may not add to totals.

SOURCE: Internal Revenue Service, *Statistics of Income 1979: Sole Proprietorship Income Tax Returns* (Washington, DC: U. S. Government Printing Office, 1982), pp. 10–15.

proprietors is engaged in "services." The second largest category of proprietors deals in "wholesale and retail trade." Business receipts, on the average, are $43,000 a year, but the annual net profit of all proprietors averages only $6,124. Although Table 3-1 does not show it, retailers account for 84 percent of those engaged in "wholesale and retail trade." Similar tables for partnerships (Table 3-2) and corporations (Table 3-3) are shown later in this chapter. A comparison of the three tables shows that, of the totals for all three forms of ownership, the proprietorships account for 70 percent in number, less than 7 percent in volume of business, and 14 percent in net profit.

Advantages of a Proprietorship

Why is the proprietorship the most common form of business ownership? Aside from the urge many people have to go into business for themselves, some with the hope of high profits and others because they may enjoy being the "boss," proprietorships have the following advantages:

1. *Ease and low cost of organization.* As long as the proposed business activity is legal, anyone can organize a business without going through "red tape" and without cost.
2. *Ownership of all profits.* There is no need to share the rewards of a successful operation.

3. *Freedom and promptness of action.* The proprietor can make decisions and take action without delay.
4. *Personal incentive and satisfaction.* The proprietor has a strong urge to make the business successful. When it is, this person derives intense personal pride.
5. *Credit standing.* Because the proprietor's nonbusiness assets are available to business creditors, the credit standing of the business may well be excellent.
6. *Secrecy.* If confidential information is a key to the success of the business, it is unlikely that its owner will leak this information.
7. *Ease of dissolution.* If all debts of the business are paid, it is as easy to dissolve the proprietorship as it was to form it.

Disadvantages of a Proprietorship

While the advantages of a proprietorship are many, so are its disadvantages. Not everyone is cut out to be a business proprietor. Before deciding that the proprietorship is the best business form to take, the following possible disadvantages should be considered:

1. *Unlimited liability.* All assets owned by the proprietor, both business and personal, are subject to claims of business creditors.
2. *Limitation on size.* The size of a proprietorship is limited to the amount of money one person can raise from his or her own resources and by borrowing.
3. *Difficulties of management.* The proprietor may not be competent to manage such diverse responsibilities as purchasing, merchandising, financing, hiring, advertising, and many other necessary functions.
4. *Lack of opportunity for employees.* A good employee of the business may quit because there is no opportunity to obtain an ownership interest in it.
5. *Lack of continuity.* If the owner cannot continue to run the business for any reason — most commonly death or poor health — the proprietorship will be dissolved.

If there is one distinguishing feature among entrepreneurs who run proprietorships, it is their capacity and willingness to work hard. As one person describes it:

What is the key motivator? Curiously it is not making money. Money is the way the score is kept, not the game. It is not love either. Entrepreneurs tend to be egocentric and driven people. They are hard to love and hard to live with. What they really ask from the world is respect. Rodney Dangerfield says it all.[1]

PARTNERSHIPS

The Uniform Partnership Act defines a **partnership** as "an association of two or more persons to carry on as co-owners of a business for profit." Such a relationship is based on an agreement, written or oral, that is both voluntary and legal.[2] In a **general partnership,** all partners have unlimited liability. In the **limited partnership,** which is

---

1. Thomas P. Murphy, "Bucking the System," *Forbes* (July 19, 1982), p. 121.
2. Only two states have not adopted the Uniform Partnership Act: Georgia and Louisiana.

discussed in more detail later, one or more partners can have limited liability as long as at least one partner has unlimited liability.

Characteristics of a Partnership

The typical partnership is larger than the typical proprietorship. Yet most partnerships are relatively small businesses. Even though the average annual business receipts for a partnership amount to approximately $178,000, the average annual net profits total only $10,822. And these net profits must be shared with at least one other person! Table 3-2 shows that the largest number of partnerships is in "finance, insurance, and real estate," which accounts for close to one-half of all business partnerships.

Some of the partnerships can be identified by the firm name; others cannot. Firm names such as "Gilbert & Gomez" and "McGinnis & Daughter" usually denote a partnership. But the Masonville Food Market might or might not be owned and operated as a partnership. If a fictitious partnership name is used, such as "Read and Wright," some states require that the names of all partners be filed in the county office.

Of the three common types of business ownership, partnerships are the least used. There are over seven times as many proprietorships and about twice as many corporations.

Table 3-2   **Partnership Income Tax Returns (Number, Receipts, Net Profits, and Average Receipts by Industries[1])**

Industry	Number of Returns	Business Receipts	Net Profit (Loss) (Millions of Dollars)	Average Business Receipts
ALL INDUSTRIES[2]	1,306,399	$232,191	$14,145	$177,734
Mining	37,712	9,721	(2,508)	257,769
Construction	77,098	19,733	2,127	255,947
Manufacturing	32,015	13,108	485	409,433
Transportation, communication, electric, gas, and sanitary services	21,182	5,409	368	255,358
Wholesale and retail trade	211,548	58,229	2,858	275,252
Finance, insurance, and real estate	674,795	76,258	(521)	113,009
Services	252,621	49,728	11,339	196,848
Nature of business not allocable	238	5	(3)	21,008

[1]Agriculture, forestry, and fishing omitted.
[2]Due to rounding, items may not add to totals.

SOURCE: Internal Revenue Service, *Statistics of Income 1979: Partnership Income Tax Returns* (Washington, DC: U. S. Government Printing Office, 1982), pp. 19–23.

Kinds of Partners

The individuals who comprise a partnership are known as partners, or copartners. They may be classified in several different ways. A **general partner** assumes unlimited liability and is usually active in managing the business. Most partners are general partners. A **limited or special partner** assumes limited liability, risking only his or her investment in the business. Limited partners may not be active in management, and their names are not used in the name of the business. A **secret partner** is active in management although the general public does not know of this person's partnership status. As opposed to a secret partner, a **silent partner** is known to the general public but is inactive in management. A **dormant or sleeping partner** is neither known to the general public nor active in management.

Individuals who are not partners but who claim they are or allow others to think of them as partners are called nominal partners. Such individuals may assume some of the responsibilities of general partners. In a firm such as a law partnership, those who assume a major role in management because of age, money invested, or large share of profits are known as senior partners. Junior partners usually are those who are young, have only a small investment in the firm, and are not expected to make major decisions.

The Partnership Contract

It is most desirable, although usually not necessary, that the agreement between partners be written and signed. Such a contract, known as articles of partnership or articles of copartnership, may prevent misunderstanding and ill will among the partners in the future. A written agreement is especially important if profits and losses are *not* to be divided equally because it must be proved that the partners are not of equal standing. The common provisions of a partnership contract cover the following:

1. Date of contract and length of life of the agreement.
2. Nature of business, location, and name of firm.
3. Names of partners and their respective investments.
4. Distribution of profits and losses.
5. Duties of each partner and hours of personal service.
6. Provision for salaries of partners.
7. Provision for paying interest on capital and drawing account balances.
8. Limitation on withdrawal of funds from the business.
9. Provision for an accounting system and a fiscal year.
10. Method to be followed in the case of withdrawal of a partner.

The Limited Partnership

When people invest in a Broadway show, they usually purchase a limited partnership interest in the venture and split the profits 50-50 with the producer. This is a risky business, and even having star performers doesn't guarantee success. The musical show *Rex*, with music by Richard Rodgers and with Nicol Williamson as the lead, played only six weeks on Broadway. The investors lost all their investment of $700,000. But if a show is a hit, the rewards can be enormous. *Fiddler on the Roof* has yielded a profit of over 1,400 percent to its investors since 1964! This level of risk is a key reason why the limited partnership is used. Also, a limited partnership cannot be formed unless permitted by state legislation. But most states have passed the Uniform Limited Partnership Act, so this restriction is not usually a problem.

Another type of limited partnership that surfaced in California's Silicon Valley about 10 years ago is the **R&D limited partnership**. It is used specifically to finance research and development projects of American companies. This approach allows wealthy investors to invest money directly in the work of inventors and inventive companies that have the new ideas but don't have the money to develop them. For example, John Z. DeLorean's sleek, stainless steel motor car may not make an enduring impact on the auto industry. But he used this approach to raise funds for research on his innovative product!

The R&D limited partnership can be complicated. But here's the way *INC.* magazine explains it:

> Simply speaking, investors put tax-sheltered money into a project. If the project is marketed profitably, the partners are bought out by the inventor; if not, they lose their investment.
>
> For a rudimentary illustration, let's say a modern-day Thomas Edison wants to improve the light bulb, but his company doesn't have enough capital to pay for the necessary R&D. So Edison turns to a limited partnership. He enlists 10 well-heeled acquaintances. Each of them gives him $100, which they deduct on their tax returns. In exchange for the $1,000, Edison gives them ownership of the technology he is about to create. He makes arrangements to buy it back later if it's a smashing success, expecting to have to pay $400 to each partner to make it worth the risk that the new bulb may not work.
>
> All shake hands, and the partners leave Edison to his labors. In a year or so, Edison's brilliant idea becomes a marketed product. He sets the price at $1 and starts to sell bulbs on behalf of the owners. As a means of payment for buying back his technology for himself, Edison pays the partners 10¢ for each bulb sold. Eventually each owner gets his appointed reward and the partnership turns back everything to Edison.[3]

The R&D limited partnership will never replace other traditional forms of business ownership and venture financing, but it is one way to boost American ingenuity and technology.

Advantages of a Partnership

Because partnerships are also unincorporated, they share some of the same advantages as proprietorships. Partnerships are easy to organize (although written articles of partnership are strongly recommended). They are not singled out for regulation by government, and they are not subject to any special taxes. Other advantages are:

---

3. Robert Mamis and Susan E. Currier, "R&D Partnerships Come of Age." Reprinted with permission, *INC.* magazine, March 1982. Copyright © INC. Publishing Company, 38 Commercial Wharf, Boston, MA 02110.

1. *Larger amount of capital.* The financial resources of two or more persons can be tapped.
2. *Credit standing.* The business and nonbusiness wealth of two or more persons is available to pay business debts.
3. *Combined judgment and managerial skills.* The old adage that two heads are better than one may well apply.
4. *Retention of valuable employees.* Admission to a partnership is an excellent method of rewarding employees the firm wishes to keep.
5. *Personal interest in the business.* Partners are vitally interested in the success of the business.
6. *Definite legal status.* Many court decisions have established clear-cut answers about partnerships.

Disadvantages of a Partnership

Since partnerships are in comparatively small use, it is clear that they have some serious disadvantages. Some of these are:

1. *Unlimited liability of the partners.* Each general partner is liable for the debts of the partnership.
2. *Lack of continuity.* The withdrawal of a partner for any reason results in the dissolution of the partnership.
3. *Managerial difficulties.* Divided control can cause difficulties when two or more owners cannot agree.
4. *Frozen investment.* It is easy to invest funds in a partnership but very difficult to withdraw them.

CORPORATIONS

Corporations employ millions of workers and are owned by millions of investors. Their activities and actions have a profound effect on the lives of practically every person in the United States, as only large businesses can mass-produce and mass-market the goods and services we need and want. And, big business usually means corporate business. No other type of business ownership offers the same chance for a business firm to grow over the course of many decades.

Despite the importance of large corporations to our economy, they often exist in a love-hate relationship with other groups in society. For example, corporate critics have claimed that giant corporations fix prices, crush smaller competitors, and ignore the welfare of their own stockholders.[4]

According to Table 3-3, there are two to three million corporations in the United States. Many of these corporations are as small as the typical proprietorship or partnership. Relatively few large corporations have a great impact on our society, and this

---

4. See, for example, Ralph Nader, Mark Green, and Joel Seligman, *Taming the Giant Corporation* (New York: W. W. Norton, 1976).

Table 3-3 **Corporation Income Tax Returns (Number, Receipts, Net Profits, and Average Receipts by Industries[1])**

Industry	Number of Returns	Business Receipts (Millions of Dollars)	Net Profit (Loss) (Millions of Dollars)	Average Business Receipts
ALL INDUSTRIES[2]	2,556,794	$5,136,705	$321,650	$2,009,041
Mining	23,919	127,454	44,890	5,328,567
Construction	249,887	246,890	8,904	987,967
Manufacturing	236,564	2,072,665	139,687	8,761,540
Transportation, communication, electric, gas, and sanitary services	103,770	432,328	21,908	4,166,214
Wholesale and retail trade	772,598	1,713,929	48,189	2,218,397
Finance, insurance, and real estate	471,222	255,128	43,208	541,418
Services	603,445	235,010	12,109	389,448
Nature of business not allocable	11,900	2,079	154	174,706

[1]Agriculture, forestry, and fishing omitted.
[2]Due to rounding, items may not add to totals.

SOURCE: Internal Revenue Service, *Statistics of Income 1979: Corporation Income Tax Returns* (Washington, DC: U.S. Government Printing Office, 1982, pp. 76–78.

impact is not the same in all areas of business. Table 3-3 also shows that the corporate form of ownership is used most often by companies engaged in "wholesale and retail trade." But even though the industrial classification of "manufacturing" ranks a poor fifth in use, it accounts for the largest total of business receipts and earns almost 50 percent of net profits for all industries. Giant firms such as General Motors, General Electric, Exxon, and IBM account for this difference between numbers and dollars.

Nature of the Corporation

What is it that sets the corporation apart from the other forms of business ownership and makes it so important to our society? The answer is found in the definition of a corporation. Chief Justice John Marshall, in *Dartmouth College* v. *Woodward*, wrote probably the most famous definition of a corporation:

A **corporation** is an artificial being, invisible, intangible, and existing only in contemplation of law. Being the mere creature of law, it possesses only those properties which the charter of its creation confers upon it, either expressly or as incidental to its very existence. These are such as are supposed best calculated to effect the object for which it was created. Among the most important are immortality, and, if the expression may be allowed, individuality; properties, by which a perpetual succession of many persons are considered as the same, and may act as a single individual.

This definition emphasizes the fact that the corporation is a **legal entity**, which means that the law has created an artificial being endowed with the rights, duties, and powers of a person. The definition also includes the concept of many people united into one body that does not change its identity with changes in ownership. Finally, the definition suggests that a corporation may have perpetual life.

Formation of a Corporation

To form a corporation is easy enough although it is best to consult a lawyer. The federal government charters national banks, federal credit unions and savings and loan associations, a few government corporations, and some scientific and educational organizations. However, all industrial and commercial corporations are formed under state laws. Their status as legal entities stems from a **charter**, which is a document issued by a state authorizing and recording the formation of a corporation. The procedure is to file an application form with the Secretary of State together with the incorporation fee. All states specify a minimum amount of capital, which can be as low as $500. Many states specify a minimum of three stockholders, but in some states even just one person may incorporate. States also impose an annual levy, or franchise tax, on corporations to whom they have granted charters.

The application form must also state a name for the corporation. The only restriction is that the name chosen cannot be the same, or so nearly the same as to cause confusion, as that of another corporation doing business in the state. Some states specify that the last word of the name be Corporation, Company, Incorporated, or Limited. In the United States the abbreviations Corp., Co., or Inc. are commonly used. Corporations chartered in Canada and England usually end the firm name with the abbreviation Ltd. Still other endings and abbreviations are used for corporations organized in other countries.

The person or persons forming a corporation may select any of the 50 states in which to incorporate. Small firms usually choose the state in which they do most of their business. Sometimes the amount of the franchise tax has a bearing on the state selected. In other instances the incorporation fee or possible charter restrictions may be the determining factors in selecting the state of incorporation.

Corporate Structure

Figure 3-1 shows the basic structure of a corporation. The owners are called stockholders, or shareholders. The stockholders elect a **board of directors** who represent the stockholders and have final authority for all corporate actions. There may be thousands of stockholders. The board of directors usually has between 9 and 17 members, although this number may vary. The board is the critical link between owners and operating officers of the corporation. Therefore, we will touch on some basic aspects of boards, annual corporate meetings, and voting practices at these meetings.

Figure 3-1   Chart of Corporate Structure

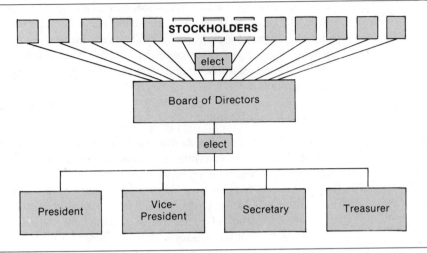

Board of Directors

A board member may be an officer of the corporation, such as its president. This person is called an *inside* board member. Other board members come from outside the corporation, such as banks, other corporations, and representatives of major stockholder groups. They are called *outside* board members.

All boards meet at least annually, but many meet monthly. An important function of these meetings is to approve or modify recommendations from the corporate officers it has appointed. Of these, the most important of the corporate officers is the chief executive officer (CEO), who is either the chairperson of the board or the company's president.

Changing Responsibilities of Board Members. There was a time when appointments of outside members to boards often was done more for prestige than for active involvement in corporate decisions. The outside board members dined lavishly, nodded their approval to decisions when told to, and pocketed their honorarium for serving on the board. This is no longer the case, as corporate directors are getting more deeply involved in their companies.

Directors also face new sources of potential liability. A corporation's annual report to the Securities and Exchange Commission (SEC) is called the 10-K report. In the past, only top officers signed the 10-K report. Now, the SEC requires a majority of the board of directors to sign it. This requirement really says that the directors have to take a meaningful hand in the operation of the company and that they may be held accountable if things go wrong. One outcome of this new rule is that good outside board members are becoming harder to get. Many of them feel that the money and prestige from board membership aren't worth the trouble. Furthermore, almost everyone who accepts this job now insists on special liability insurance.

Women as Board Members. The number of women board members throughout this country is still small. Of the 16,000 seats available on the boards of the top 1,300 companies listed by *Fortune* magazine, only 336, or 2.1 percent, are now held by women. In 1969, however, only 46 women served on the top 1,300 boards.[5] Companies no longer are looking for "token" women directors who, in the past, were often agreeable silent relatives to company owners. Now companies seek women who, because of their expertise and success, can contribute a unique perspective to the board's business.

Corporate Annual Meetings

The SEC requires private corporations to hold at least one annual stockholders' meeting. How these meetings are conducted often shows the company's attitude toward its stockholders—especially the small stockholders—as to whether they are seen as resources or a nuisance. The range of corporate management's attitudes toward the small stockholder is broad, varying from active interest to bare tolerance.

Some companies rotate the annual meeting from one large city to another, giving shareholders at least an occasional chance to attend. Others meet in remote locations to discourage the attendance of small shareholders. Starting in 1982, General Motors decided to discourage hecklers by holding two separate meetings. A bare-bones meeting in the morning fulfills legal requirements and transacts corporate business. In the afternoon, another meeting 15 miles away permits stockholders—both the serious ones and gadflies—to fire questions at management. But neither the CEO nor the board of directors of GM will attend the afternoon meeting.

The need to interact with stockholders goes beyond the annual meeting. It includes such tasks as sending quarterly and annual reports, answering letters, and mailing dividend checks. Many companies see the stockholders as business partners and customers and feel that it's worth the extra effort to do these jobs right.

Voting Practices at Corporate Meetings

In small corporations the few owners attend the annual meeting and elect themselves as board members. Then the board members select officers from among themselves. In large corporations only a small percentage of the stockholders accept the invitation to attend the annual meeting. The majority simply sign a written authorization, called a **proxy**, that gives someone else (usually a board member) the right to cast their votes. This system usually results in perpetuating the existing board members since the proxy holder frequently controls over 50 percent of the votes.

Occasionally a group of dissatisfied stockholders may attempt to solicit proxies for a rival slate of board members. Because they must do this at their own expense, proxy battles are relatively rare when the corporation has thousands of stockholders. **Cumulative voting** offers an easier way for a minority group of stockholders to secure

---

5. Marilyn Hoffman, "Women in the Boardroom," *The Christian Science Monitor* (June 10, 1982), p. 15. Reprinted by permission from *The Christian Science Monitor* © 1982 The Christian Science Publishing Society. All rights reserved.

representation on the board. For example, if there are 17 directors to be elected, a stockholder owning 100 shares could cast 1,700 votes for one director rather than 100 votes for each of 17 directors. Cumulative voting is required by law in approximately half of the states. In other states it is permitted if the corporation wishes to include such a provision in its bylaws.

In addition to voting on members of the board, stockholders vote on the following matters:

1. Selection of the outside auditors of the firm.
2. Amendments to the charter such as permission to issue more shares of stock.
3. Broad policies covering retirement plans for officers and employees, stock options for key personnel, waiving of preemptive rights to subscribe to new stock issues, and on any appropriate resolution a stockholder wishes to propose at the annual meeting.

Separation of Ownership and Management

An important feature of corporations, particularly the giants, is the distinction between ownership and management. Managers as a rule do not own many shares as a percentage of total shares outstanding. The effect of divorcing ownership from management is that managers do not consider stockholders as their "bosses" to whom they should be solely responsible. The managers' decisions take stockholders into consideration, but on a comparable basis with the rank-and-file company employees, the firm's customers, the government, and the general public.

Classifications of Corporations

Corporations may be classified in many ways. Four basic classifications are by ownership, purpose, place of incorporation, and availability of stock for purchase.

By Ownership

When classified according to ownership, a corporation is *private* if it is owned, chartered, and operated by individuals. It is *governmental* if it is organized by the federal government, a state, a city, or some other political subdivision. Governmental corporations are sometimes referred to as public corporations. But unless this meaning is made clear, public corporations may be confused with private corporations owned by the general public. Examples of governmental corporations are incorporated cities and state universities.

By Purpose

When classified according to the purpose for which it is organized, a corporation may take several forms. A *profit* corporation is privately owned and operated to make profits. Since it issues stock certificates which represent shares of ownership, it is also a *stock* corporation. A *nonprofit* corporation is somewhat of a misnomer in that its receipts may exceed its expenses but the profit is not distributed to its owners. Any excess income of the nonprofit corporation is used to further the purposes for which it was organized. If the nonprofit organization does not issue stock, it is also called a *nonstock* corporation. In general, governmental corporations, schools, churches, and hospitals are nonstock corporations.

Private, profit-making corporations are classified by *Moody's Manuals* as Industrial, Public Utilities, Banks & Finance, and Transportation. A further breakdown into such categories as aviation, chemical, and many others is found in each manual. The Office of Statistical Standards of the Bureau of the Budget is responsible for the Standard Industry Classification of Corporations. This classification was used in Tables 3-1, 3-2, and 3-3.

Many independently owned businesses that appear to be proprietorships actually are Subchapter S corporations. A **Subchapter S corporation** is one that is limited to 35 stockholders and elects to be taxed the same as proprietorships or partnerships in order to avoid corporate income taxes. This is possible under Subchapter S of the Internal Revenue Code.

If Trapper John, M. D., had to do it all over again, he probably would do it as Trapper John, M.D., P.C. The "P.C." wouldn't be some advanced degree. It's the abbreviation for *professional corporation*. A professional corporation makes possible big tax savings in the form of fringe benefits and retirement plans that ultimately can more than double a professional's assets and retirement income. Since the early 1970s, many of our physicians, lawyers, accountants, architects, surveyors, and other "professionals" have been turning their businesses into corporations. To qualify as a professional corporation, a professional must organize under state laws that recognize professionals of certain kinds. For example, Florida licenses undertakers, and California licenses marriage counselors as professionals. The licensing practices vary widely among states.

By Place of Incorporation

When classified according to place of incorporation, the business is a **domestic corporation** in the state in which it is incorporated. In every other state in which it may do business, it is considered to be a **foreign corporation**. When it has been organized in another country but is doing business within the United States, it is known in the United States as an **alien corporation**. Some states are concerned about the growing number of alien corporations. In 1979, for instance, the attorney general of Oklahoma ruled that alien corporations cannot own property in that state.

By Availability of Stock for Purchase

When classified according to the availability of its stock for purchase, the business is a *close* corporation if its stock is not available to outsiders. Family businesses that were incorporated after operating as proprietorships or partnerships typically are close corporations. If the stock is available for purchase by anyone having sufficient funds, it is an *open* corporation. Most large corporations are open corporations. Within recent years many close corporations have "gone public" because they needed funds for expansion. As previously mentioned, this has given rise to the use of the term "public corporation" for what is really an open corporation.

Advantages of a Corporation

Today's business scene would not be dominated by the corporation unless it had some outstanding advantages. The principal advantages are:

1. *Limited liability of stockholders.* Investors in corporations enjoy limited liability, which means that they risk only the amount they paid for their shares of stock. Creditors cannot look beyond corporate assets for the payment of debts owed to them.
2. *Larger size.* By issuing many shares, corporations can attract millions of dollars from thousands of stockholders.
3. *Transfer of ownership.* In almost all instances stockholders can sell their shares to anyone willing to buy them. In the case of death, the shares of deceased stockholders can be transferred to their heirs.
4. *Length of life.* Corporate charters can be perpetual so that a business can live forever. Several corporations in the United States can boast that they have been in existence for 100 or more years.
5. *Efficiency of management.* The stockholders delegate authority to a board of directors who, in turn, hire the company's managers. If the managers are unsatisfactory, they can be fired. Efficiency may also result in that specialists, such as purchasing agents, can be employed.
6. *Ease of expansion.* If the corporation wishes to expand, it can sell more stock provided that current or new investors are willing to buy additional shares. Furthermore, large corporations find it much easier to borrow funds because the amounts they need are substantial enough to interest the appropriate financial agencies to market these securities.
7. *Legal entity.* A corporation can sue and be sued in its own name, make contracts, and hold title to land and buildings. By contrast, a proprietorship or partnership must use individual names even though the business has a firm name.

Disadvantages of a Corporation

The corporate form of business ownership has its disadvantages as well as its advantages. Some of its more important disadvantages are:

1. *Taxation.* In addition to paying annual franchise taxes, a corporation may pay annual levies to other states in which it does business. Also, most corporate income is taxed by states and by the federal government. Furthermore, certain types of corporations — such as public utilities, railroads, and insurance companies — may be subjected to special taxes.
2. *Organization expenses.* Incorporation fees vary with the number of shares of stock authorized, but a charge of more than a thousand dollars would be common. Stock certificates and record books must be purchased, and lawyers' fees are incurred.
3. *Governmental restrictions and reports.* Corporations cannot do business within a state without proper registration. Also, states and the federal government require reports that can be costly and burdensome to prepare.
4. *Lack of personal interest.* All persons who work for a corporation are its employees. Unless these employees are also principal stockholders, they do not have the intense interest in the success of the business that exists on the part of proprietors and partners.

5. *Lack of secrecy.* Corporations must make annual reports to their stockholders. When these reports number in the hundreds or thousands, financial details become available to competitors, as well as to the general public.

6. *Relative lack of credit.* Size for size, corporations do not enjoy the credit standing of proprietorships and partnerships because of the limited liability of their stockholders.

7. *Charter restrictions.* At the time of securing a charter, a corporation states its intended business. It may not be able to diversify its activities later, unless it files an amendment.

Figure 3-2 gives a comparative overview of the three major types of business ownership.

OTHER UNINCORPORATED FORMS OF BUSINESS OWNERSHIP

In addition to proprietorships and partnerships, there are some other unincorporated forms of business ownership that are not widely used but fill specific needs. These include joint ventures and syndicates, business trusts, and unincorporated associations.

Joint Ventures and Syndicates

When two or more persons join together for the purpose of a single undertaking, they form a **joint venture**, or "joint adventure." Usually the undertaking is of short duration. During this relatively short life, each participant has unlimited liability; nevertheless, the management is frequently delegated to one individual. A *syndicate* is similar to a joint venture, but its purpose is always financial. Members of a syndicate can sell their interest to others, and the syndicate need not be dissolved when its purpose is completed. The most common type of syndicate in use today is the *underwriting syndicate.* This is an association of investment banking companies formed to sell a large issue of corporate bonds or shares of stock. The firm forming the syndicate is responsible for managing it, and each member firm's liability is limited to an agreed-upon portion of the total issue.

Business Trusts

Investors who form a **business trust** transfer cash or other property, under a trust agreement, to a small number of trustees who manage the firm. Business trusts are also known as common-law trusts or Massachusetts trusts. The trustees issue certificates of beneficial interest called *trust certificates,* or *trust shares,* to those who organized the trust. These shares are the basis for the distribution of profits.

If the trust agreement gives the investors any control over the firm's management, such as the right to elect trustees, courts have held that each investor has unlimited liability. Since one of the reasons for using the business trust is to secure the advantage

Figure 3-2   Comparison of Proprietorship, General Partnership, and Corporation

Characteristic	Proprietorship	General Partnership	Corporation
1. Ease and cost of formation	No legal procedures and no required costs.	Can be simple but a lawyer should draw up articles of partnership.	Incorporation fee required, and legal assistance needed.
2. Ownership of profits	Undivided.	Divided among two or more partners.	Belong to the corporation, but may be distributed to stockholders.
3. Personal incentive of owners	Extremely high since success need not be shared.	Very high, but success must be shared.	High only if managers are also owners.
4. Credit standing	Depends on personal assets of owners.	Usually better than the proprietorship as personal wealth of two or more is available.	Size for size, the lowest standing as only assets of the firm are available to creditors.
5. Liability of owners	Entire fortune available to satisfy business debts.	Entire fortunes of all owners available to satisfy business debts.	Individual owners not liable for business debts.
6. Size	Limited to wealth and borrowing ability of one person.	Limited to wealth and borrowing ability of two or more persons.	Unlimited as long as investors will buy its bonds and stocks.
7. Taxation	No special taxes as a proprietorship.	No special taxes as a partnership.	Taxed by states and by the federal government.
8. Opportunity for employees	No opportunity for an employee to become a part owner.	Opportunity for employees to be admitted to partnership.	Opportunity for employees to advance on merit.
9. Managerial efficiency	Frequently inferior as owner is responsible for all activities.	Better than the proprietorship as two or more owners bring diverse talents.	Frequently high, particularly if size allows for hiring specialists.
10. Freedom and promptness of action	Immediate action by one person within a legal framework.	Slightly slower than the proprietorship if partners consult one another.	Much slower on all matters that must be referred to the board of directors.
11. Ease of dissolution	Decision made at will by one person.	Frequently difficult as the value of partners' interests must be determined.	Requires action by board of directors and legal steps with the state.
12. Continuity	Based on good health or life of owner.	Limited to the life or good health of any and all partners.	Can be perpetual.

of limited liability without incorporating, the investors usually give up any right to elect the trustees or to have any voice in management. The holders of trust certificates do have the right to sell them to a buyer of their choice, and the death of an owner does not affect the continuation of the trust.

Unincorporated Associations

Any number of persons or companies can form an unincorporated association by drawing up and signing an agreement for the purpose of rendering a service to its members. The purpose of this form of business ownership is always nonprofit. National fraternal organizations, trade associations, security exchanges, bank clearinghouses, and retail credit associations are frequently unincorporated associations. Usually a fee to join the association is charged, and its operating expenses are divided among its members based on their use of the association's services. The members elect a board of directors who employ personnel to run the organization.

OTHER INCORPORATED FORMS OF BUSINESS OWNERSHIP

Some incorporated forms of business ownership, in addition to the regular corporation, are widely used in specific areas of business. These include cooperatives, credit unions, mutual companies, and savings and loan associations. Savings and loan associations are discussed in Chapter 20.

Cooperatives

A **cooperative or co-op** is a nonprofit business owned by its stockholders or members, each of whom casts a single vote in electing the board of directors. The cooperative is incorporated under state law. It seeks to provide goods or services that private industry either neglects or provides at what co-op members regard as an unreasonably high price. Refunds from any overpayments made are returned to members, usually on the basis of how much they have used co-op goods or services as customers. Generally co-ops differ from corporations in the following respects:

1. Each cooperative unit is owned by the user-members of the group.
2. Each member has only one vote regardless of the number of shares of stock owned.
3. There is a limitation on the amount of stock that each member may own.
4. The capital for the enterprise is subscribed only by the members.
5. Interest is paid on the investment of each member-stockholder.
6. Dividends are paid on a patronage basis, in proportion to the amount of goods that each member has bought or sold through the co-op. These are referred to as *patronage dividends*.

Various Kinds of Cooperatives

The co-op movement largely grew out of the co-ops started by militant farm organizations in the 1800s. Co-ops still are used extensively in agriculture. Nationwide, co-ops market roughly a fourth of all U.S. farm produce and provide farmers with a fifth of their supplies, such as feed, seed, and fertilizer.

Farm products marketed through cooperatives include fruits, dairy products, potatoes, wool, grains, and livestock. Such well-known brands as Sunkist oranges and Sun Maid raisins are the property of *producer* cooperative associations engaged in marketing these products grown by their members. There are about 5,000 producer cooperative associations in the United States with total annual sales of about $60 billion. In addition, there are approximately 3,000 farmer-owned *buying* or *supply* cooperatives whose purchases of seeds, gasoline, machinery, etc., run about $8 billion annually.

Consumer co-ops are user-owned retail outlets of goods and services. These range from rural electric companies and credit unions to retail clothing and food stores. Although they have long been a dominant factor in Denmark and Sweden, their influence in the United States has been relatively minor. However, in some regions consumer co-ops are widespread. This is true in the Pacific Northwest, whose large Scandinavian population has roots in Wisconsin and Minnesota. But co-ops — some very large — can be found in most parts of the United States.

Advantages and Disadvantages of Cooperatives

Cooperatives have most of the advantages of corporations. They also have some advantages and disadvantages of their own, as summarized in Figure 3-3.

Probably the greatest single obstacle to the growth of co-ops, especially consumer co-ops, has been the lack of access to capital from outside the business. Many businesses have looked upon co-ops as being "socialist" concerns in a free enterprise economy. Likewise, banks seldom lend to co-ops because most bankers are suspicious of nonprofit enterprises. However, in 1978, Congress passed the National

Figure 3-3   Advantages and Disadvantages of Cooperatives

Advantages	Disadvantages
1. Tax advantages are gained because patronage dividends are considered a refund of overpayments rather than a distribution of profits (tax rates are about one-third those of competitors).	1. Ownership by user-members limits size and ease of expansion. Also, fortunes of co-ops and people who own them are closely tied.
2. Internal funds are generated because many co-ops pay dividends in form of stock certificates that can't be redeemed in cash for 10 years or more.	2. Opposition arises from small-business groups because they see co-ops as a competitive threat.
3. Producer and consumer co-ops (but not supply co-ops) are exempt from antitrust prosecution. Some co-ops now own manufacturing facilities.	3. Bitter competition and tight profits prevail in principal businesses, including farm supply, oil refining, and grain merchandising.
4. Federal government provides financial help and technical know-how.	4. Co-ops need access to economies of scale through size and market power to stay competitive.
5. Co-ops have powerful political support in Washington, DC.	5. Co-op managers frequently lack training in business techniques.
6. Members of agricultural co-ops often are intensely loyal.	6. Bankers are fearful of co-ops as risky ventures.

Consumer Cooperative Bank Act. This Act created a quasi-government institution—the National Consumer Cooperative Bank—which was empowered to provide $1.5 billion in loans over the following five years and to offer technical assistance to co-op managers. Thus, a boost to co-ops in the United States was provided.

Credit Unions

A **credit union** is a cooperative type of financial institution in which a group of people save money and loan it to one another. For example, the group may be the employees of a firm, members of a church, or residents of a community. A credit union is an incorporated entity chartered by either the state or the federal government.

Each member of a credit union may purchase at least one share or pay a membership fee of 25 cents. The members elect a board of directors from among themselves, and the board serves without pay. The board elects officers who likewise are not paid, except that some larger credit unions may employ an office manager and the necessary clerical help. By using funds available from shares sold to members or from savings deposits made by members, loans are made to other members.

There are approximately 20,000 credit unions with 32,000,000 members in the United States. Total assets owned are in excess of $46 billion. Most credit unions are relatively small with memberships ranging from 100 to 1,000. This type of incorporated business ownership is currently operating in 70 countries. However, approximately one-half of all credit unions are located in the United States.

Mutual Companies

Like the customary corporation, a **mutual company** receives a charter from a state. But its owners are users of the service rendered rather than its "stockholders."

Mutual companies have two primary uses: as life insurance companies and as savings banks. The purchaser of a policy from a mutual life insurance company or the person who deposits money in a mutual savings bank is automatically a member. These owners theoretically elect a board of directors to manage the business. Actually, since it is unusual to solicit proxies from policyholders or depositors, the owners rarely bother to vote. Thus, boards of directors tend to be self-perpetuating.

Mutual companies have most of the advantages of corporations, including limited liability. They also enjoy special federal income tax treatment. For example, dividends on life insurance policies are considered a partial refund of premiums paid by the policyholder. Mutual savings banks can insure their accounts with an agency of the federal government and can borrow funds from the federal home loan bank system.

Only about 8 percent of all life insurance companies are organized as mutuals. However, the mutual life insurance companies based in this country own three-fifths of the assets of all life insurance companies and have written nearly one-half of all life insurance outstanding. For legal reasons most mutual savings banks are located in the Middle Atlantic and New England states. Despite this restriction, their total assets amount to $135 billion. These figures seem to indicate that, despite the lack of pressure from stockholders for dividends, mutual companies have been aggressive and efficiently managed.

SUMMARY   The three most widely used forms of business ownership are proprietorships, partnerships, and corporations. Of these, proprietorships are the most common, as about 9 million women and men operate their own full- and part-time businesses. About two-thirds of these are in two classifications of business: services, and wholesale and retail trade. A proprietorship is easy to organize, but its owner risks personal wealth if the business is unsuccessful. Furthermore, the average business receipts and net profit of proprietorships are low.

Partnerships are widely used in finance, real estate, and insurance. Generally they are much less popular than proprietorships or corporations. Partnerships have a better chance to succeed if partners prepare written partnership agreements. Unlimited liability is a big disadvantage of partnerships. This can be avoided by some individuals if they become limited partners in a limited partnership. R&D limited partnerships are a relatively recent way to finance research and development projects of American companies.

The giants of commerce and industry are corporations. These legal entities have the rights, duties, and powers of a person, along with perpetual life. Stockholders risk only their investment in a corporatin and rely on an elected board of directors to oversee the operations of their company. Despite its disadvantages, the corporate form of ownership has made possible the mass production and mass merchandising that underpin our high standard of living.

There are various other types of unincorporated and incorporated business ownership. Most other unincorporated forms, such as joint ventures and business trusts, are used for narrow, specific business purposes. Of the incorporated forms, cooperatives exist mainly for the buying and selling of agricultural products, equipment, and supplies. There also are consumer co-ops. Credit unions make loans to member-shareholders. Mutual companies are used for insurance and savings deposits, mainly in eastern states.

BACK
TO THE
CHAPTER
OPENER

1. What form of business ownership uses boards of directors?
2. To whom are boards of directors responsible?
3. What is an outside director?
4. What is the basic role of the board of directors?
5. What is the effect of enlarged board involvement on getting competent outside directors?

BUSINESS
TERMS

proprietorship	42	board of directors	50
partnership	44	proxy	52
general partnership	44	cumulative voting	52
limited partnership	44	Subchapter S corporation	54
general partner	46	domestic corporation	54
limited or special partner	46	foreign corporation	54
secret partner	46	alien corporation	54
silent partner	46	joint venture	56
dormant or sleeping partner	46	business trust	56
R & D limited partnership	47	cooperative or co-op	58
corporation	49	consumer co-ops	59
legal entity	50	credit union	60
charter	50	mutual company	60

1. Hobart McNulty, a contractor specializing in solar heating and hot water systems, decided to call his firm "McNulty and Sun." What kind of business ownership do you think he had?

2. Why might you be more inclined to buy from a bicycle shop operated as a proprietorship than from a large retail corporation that sells bikes?

3. Discuss why so few mining and manufacturing businesses are proprietorships or partnerships.

4. Shelley McCune is an accounting supervisor with a large public utility company. She also is a co-owner of a fast-food partnership located near the utility company and is active in its management. However, she is careful not to disclose her involvement in the fast-food business. What type of partner is she?

5. You are invited to invest $10,000 in a tax-sheltered R&D limited partnership with 20 other people. You have the money to do this, and the technology to be developed has promise. But you will have to wait at least five years to recover the payoff from your investment in this partnership even if the venture is successful. Why might you invest your money this way rather than in some other venture that was more of a sure thing?

6. Is there anything in the personal background of most high-level women executives today that might make them especially useful as directors of corporations? Discuss.

7. Why might a corporation decide to sell stock rather evenly in various parts of the country, even though it might be able to sell its entire public stock offering in its own geographical area?

8. Do you think medical doctors, dentists, lawyers, and other "professionals" should be able to set up professional corporations that make big tax savings possible? Discuss.

9. You are a bank loan officer, and two businesspersons come to you seeking a loan. The two businesses are similar in nature and size (both fairly small). However, one is a corporation and the other is a proprietorship. Discuss which of the two businesses you would be more likely to grant a loan.

10. As nonprofit corporations, how can producer and consumer co-ops be successful in the face of stiff competition without the profit-seeking motive?

1. Some small-business operators may begin or back into proprietorships without really considering other forms of ownership. Also, businesses and tax laws tend to change over time, but the form of ownership may not be reconsidered in the face of such changes.

   For a project, talk with the owners and/or managers of seven independently owned businesses in a shopping mall. Find out the following:

   a. Is the business a proprietorship, a partnership, or a corporation?
   b. If it is a corporation, is it a Subchapter S corporation?
   c. Why is the owner/manager satisfied (or not satisfied) with the current form of ownership?

   Summarize your findings in a short written report and share them with your class.

2. Rena Lowenberger is part of a growing number of people wanting to make a living as an independent craftsperson. Her specialty is stained-glass window hangings and lamps. In the past, her crafts have been handled on consignment by gift shops and other retail outlets. The stores paid her for the merchandise only if and when it was sold, deducting a commission of 15 to 30 percent, depending on the volume of her

work that the store handled. She feels that, in order to succeed, she must find some way to have an active voice in the sale of her work and a permanent place to display it. But she sees herself primarily as an artist, not a store owner/manager. Furthermore, she feels that other craftspersons must be in the same situation.

Lowenberger has asked your advice on whether some kind of retail store — perhaps a cooperative — could be set up to handle the goods of a group of independent craftspersons. How would you advise her on this problem?

3. To look at Dom Girardi, one wouldn't suspect that he is the head of a successful commercial fishing operation. At 35, he is small and wiry, and his hair is starting to fleck with gray. But his deep tan and agile movements suggest that his life is spent in active, outdoor work. At age 16, Girardi started shipping out during summers as a galley helper on commercial fishing boats. He rapidly rose through the ranks as a fisherman, first mate, and then skipper of a large fishing boat by age 25.

Girardi had a reputation for finding fish. He was also known to be a good employer. When Girardi was 27, some wealthy investors in the community became his limited partners and backed him in purchasing his own large, modern fishing vessel. As time went on, the partnership group backed Girardi in purchasing another fishing boat, which was managed by his cousin, Guido. Girardi prospered, but he also began to think of security. Since Girardi was the general partner, his liability in the business was unlimited; and there were plenty of risks in the business — poor catches, loss of boats to hurricanes, fires and other disasters, seizure of fishing boats in the fishing waters of other nations, and competition with Japanese fishing fleets. Girardi began to think that he should start a corporation so that he wouldn't be wiped out in the face of heavy damages. Discuss the pros and cons of Girardi's proposed plan to incorporate.

II. Management and Organization of Human Resources

Chapter 4. Organizing for Management
5. The Manager's Job
6. Staffing the Organization
7. Compensation for Human Resources
8. Labor-Management Relations

Reprinted through the courtesy of New York
Life Insurance Company.

To Decentralize or Not to Decentralize

There were two articles in the previous issue of BUSINESS WEEK (Feb. 16) that illustrate basic differences in management, matched by striking differences in performance. The first examined the unhappy case of Sears, Roebuck & Co., once the most effective retailer in the world and now a high-cost operator trying to shift capital out of its traditional business. The second told the story of Schlumberger Ltd., the giant oil service company that has done so well in providing electronic assessment of wells that it is now moving into the manufacture of semiconductors.

The top management of Sears downgraded the store managers by taking more and more of the key decisions away from them. It tried to solve problems by adding more executives, and the result was a top-heavy structure that put decision-making farther and farther away from the stores—and the ultimate customers. Territorial management teams overlapped with national merchandising groups that handled buying, market development, promotion, and pricing. And while the levels of management multiplied, the quality of the work force in the stores deteriorated.

Schlumberger says that its biggest asset is the field engineers who run the individual jobs. They have a high degree of independence and full responsibility for doing what needs to be done. They are well-paid, carefully recruited, and trained. In effect, each engineer runs his own business with a truck and sophisticated equipment worth about $1 million and a crew of two. He is expected to know what he is doing, and he is paid accordingly— a base salary plus a cut of each logging fee that he earns for the company.

In the end, it's not a question of centralization or decentralization. The question is whether a company is organized so that it focuses externally on the customer or internally on its own reports and financials.

Organizing for Management

Objectives:

- Understand the meaning of organization and why firms organize.
- Identify the elements of the organizing process.
- Distinguish between organizational differentiation and integration.
- Discuss the advantages and disadvantages of the five main bases of departmentation.
- Distinguish among line authority, staff authority, and functional authority.
- Relate span of management to levels of management in the organization.
- Distinguish between managerial decentralization and physical decentralization.
- Identify the three parts in the act of delegation.
- Distinguish between line and line-and-staff organization structures and discuss the role and structure of the matrix organization.
- Recognize the importance of the informal group to the firm.

In James Jones's novel *From Here to Eternity* the American soldiers, under surprise attack by Japanese planes at Pearl Harbor, rushed to the arsenal for weapons. There they found the arsenal door barred by a comrade-in-arms loudly proclaiming that he couldn't pass out live ammunition without a written request signed by a commissioned officer!

This misled guardian of the gates overlooked the reason for which the Army is organized, and to him the means had become the ends. The Army at Pearl Harbor is not the only organization in our society that lost sight of the job at hand. We find this situation happening today in industrial, commercial, and educational circles as well.

Nevertheless, we should not ignore both the reason why we organize and the basic fact that our society could not grow and prosper without effective organizations.

THE MEANING OF ORGANIZATION

The term "organization" is used in many ways. Some use it to mean the total pattern of behavior in a society or culture. Others use it when referring to large enterprises such as a business corporation, church, or government agency. In this chapter we define **organization** as a group of people occupying a formal structure of positions to achieve a particular purpose. Specifically, we will be concerned with the organization that is engaged in business.

Thus, an organization has three basic parts: a purpose, a structure, and a process. The purpose refers to *why* a job needs to be done; the structure refers to *what* are the means by which the job will be done; the process is *how* the job will be done. A large organization relies on many highly trained specialists in determining its structure and process. By carefully combining their individual specialties, the organization both achieves its purpose and gives its members a chance for self-fulfillment in the type of work they want to do.

THE ORGANIZING PROCESS: DIVIDING AND COORDINATING

Management uses the **organizing process** to divide and coordinate the tasks of people in the organization. The organizing process should not be haphazard but should follow a careful plan. It should cover the division of work and the assignment of authority and responsibility necessary to achieve the organization's goals. Specifically, the organizing process includes the following elements:

1. Departmentation, or the rational grouping, of operating tasks.
2. Establishment of authority relationships among those who will be performing the tasks.
3. Division of managerial work, or decentralization.
4. Process of delegation, which is needed to accomplish the first three steps.
5. Determination of the organization structure as the final step.

The basic elements of the organizing process are diagrammed in Figure 4-1 to show their relationships. These elements will be discussed in detail because each is important to a well-run organization. The organizing process is an on-going challenge to management since changing goals, jobs, and authority relationships require new ways of dividing and coordinating the tasks to be done.

Dividing the Organization

Today's large, complex organizations are based on a high degree of task speciali-zation. Most skilled workers and managers perform small parts of large tasks. Thus, the

Figure 4-1   The Organizing Process: An Overview

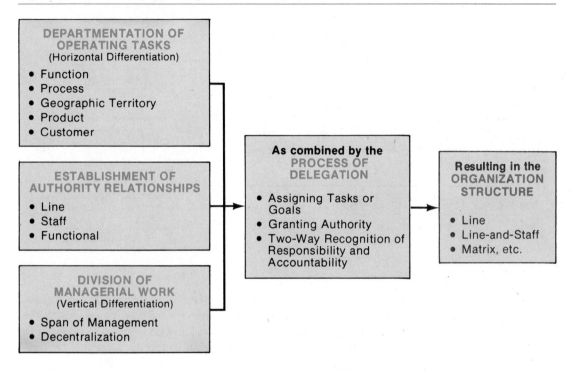

operating and managerial work of a business organization must be divided, or differentiated, to determine which departments and persons are responsible for the many specialized activities.

Differentiation is done both horizontally and vertically. **Horizontal differentiation** refers to dividing operating tasks, and **vertical differentiation** refers to the levels of managerial decision making in an organization. In Figure 4-2, for example, the top-level functions of the 3-W Company are horizontally differentiated into the tasks of finance, production, and marketing. The levels of managerial decision making in marketing are vertically differentiated among the president, the director (or vice-president) of marketing, and the different managers (or whatever titles might be used) of the several regions. Figure 4-2 also illustrates the different ways by which the operating tasks of the 3-W Company are departmentized. The discussion of departmentation later in this chapter will be referring to this illustration.

Coordinating the Organization

Most organization designers spend their time on how to divide the organizational tasks. Yet the central problem in structuring an organization today is one of coordi-

Figure 4-2   Organization of the 3-W Company

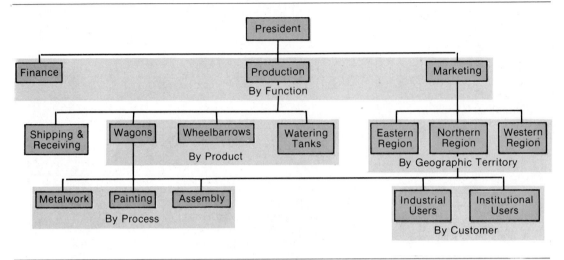

nation or integration—how to make the parts come together to accomplish organizational goals. In fact, most **organization charts** are drawn to emphasize the vertical hierarchy and superior-subordinate relationships (see Figure 4-3). Only a few of these charts indicate the horizontal relationships and integrative activities between groups or individuals at the same levels in the organization.

One reason for this apparent gap in organizational thinking is that most firms of any size and complexity rely greatly on informal, voluntary processes in place of formal processes to achieve coordination. Formal integrative processes might include the use of managerial directives, committees, administrative directives such as policies and procedures, staff people to help pull things together, and special structures such as matrix organizations with task teams and project management (see pages 82–84).

Often, however, effective integration and boundary spanning comes from the voluntary efforts of individuals or groups rather than from hierarchical and administrative procedures. This voluntary, integrative effort on their part usually reflects professional competency and commitment to goals instead of their formal positions in the organization. Integration clearly is becoming more important in organization design. Because of the growing differentiation in complex organizations, greater emphasis must be placed on innovative ways to achieve effective integration in the future.

DEPARTMENTATION OF OPERATING TASKS

In recent times, Sears, Roebuck & Co. has been restructuring itself in order to move into a new era of prestige and prosperity. Previously Sears was organized in only two basic divisions: merchandising, and everything else loosely grouped under its Allstate unit. Now there are three operating divisions: retailing, Allstate Insurance,

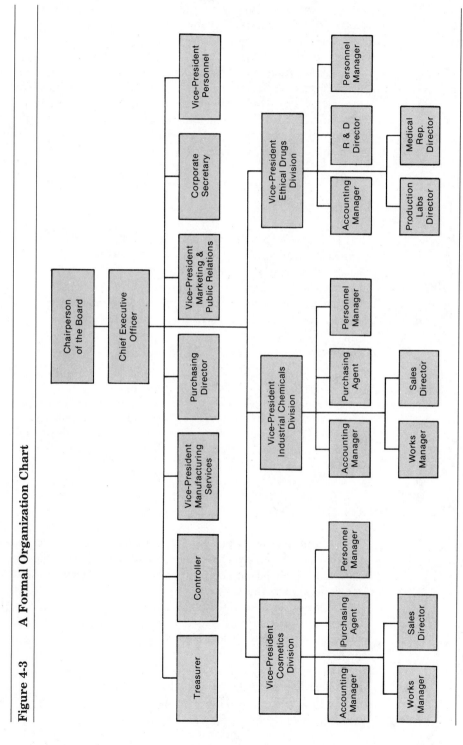

Figure 4-3   A Formal Organization Chart

and the new Seraco Group of real estate and financial service companies. Sears recognized that, as its goals changed, its structure should also be reevaluated. This change into three operating divisions illustrates Sears' departmentation of tasks to meet its goals.

Departmentation deals with horizontal differentiation. It is one element of the organizing process that rationally groups the work necessary to achieve the goals of the organization on a basis that encourages cooperation and communication. Departmentation takes place at all levels in the organization. In most cases the activities are grouped, or departmentized, on the basis of functions, processes or equipment, geographic territories, products, and customers.

Departmentation by Function

The activities of business enterprises typically are grouped by major functions such as production, finance, and marketing, as Figure 4-2 on page 70 shows. However, a manufacturing firm that sells its entire output to one customer might not have a marketing or sales department. And a research firm might not have a manufacturing department. The major functional departments of any organization should, as in the case of Sears, reflect its basic character and activities.

Advantages	Disadvantages
1. Logical, simple, and time-proven method.	1. May emphasize departmental goals and deemphasize enterprise goals.
2. Efficient use of specialized talent.	2. May sometimes be difficult to coordinate and control with other departments.
3. Clear managerial responsibility for a specific task.	3. Does not provide good training ground for top-level, all-around managers.

Departmentation by Process or Equipment

Departmentation by process or equipment groups activities together by the specialized process, equipment, or techniques that are used. The grouping of work around metalworking equipment and painting processes in Figure 4-2 is an example of this type of departmentation.

Businesses in the United States have been working with computers and robots for some time in such single-function areas as automated check-processing and computer-controlled robot welders. Now some companies are moving to integrated office and factory systems, with a huge growth coming in the use of robotics and electronic work stations. Dramatic changes will occur in factories and many service operations in the next 10 years as the computer fundamentally changes the relationship between workers and their tasks. Thus, this basis of departmentation will become increasingly important.

Advantages	Disadvantages
1. Economic use of specialized equipment, processes, and operators.	1. Often requires heavy financial investment.
2. Ability to integrate computer-controlled systems and processes.	2. Threatened by technological change and obsolescence.

Departmentation by Geographic Territory

In departmentation by geographic territory, all the activities performed in a particular region or territory are brought under a specific manager. Geographical divisions are common, for example, in the regional offices of chain-store operations. Or, as shown in Figure 4-2, the work of salespersons is often divided by regions.

Advantages	Disadvantages
1. Flexibility in serving the needs of local markets.	1. Duplication in local and centralized service activities such as personnel, purchasing, and finance.
2. Opportunities for general managerial experience.	2. Problem of controlling and coordinating distant activities through a central office.
3. Economies in transportation and distribution by using local manufacturing and warehousing.	

Departmentation by Product

All activities directly associated with a product, such as manufacturing, sales, service, and engineering, may be grouped together in product departmentation. The wagon, wheelbarrow, and watering tank divisions in Figure 4-2 are examples of product departmentation. On a smaller scale, a food market may be divided into groups for meats, groceries, and produce.

Advantages	Disadvantages
1. Divides company into small, flexible administrative units.	1. Possible conflict between competing product divisions.
2. Emphasizes consistency of profits with division-level profit responsibilities.	2. Empire building by product managers to the possible detriment of organizational goals.
3. Encourages product growth and diversification.	3. Need for general managerial abilities.
4. Provides training ground for general managers.	4. May show favoritism to certain products.

Departmentation by Customer

Customer departmentation is useful for grouping the activities of firms that cater to different types of customers. Large customers, with their purchasing departments and technical requirements, may have to be treated differently from smaller customers or, perhaps, military customers. Figure 4-2 shows that a hardware company may set up separate divisions to serve industrial users and institutional users (such as schools or hospitals).

Advantage	Disadvantages
1. Use of highly qualified salespersons and specialized skills to satisfy the special and varied needs of specific customer groups.	1. Difficulty of coordination with other departments.
	2. Pressure from managers of customer departments for special treatment.
	3. Possible underemployment of specialized personnel and facilities in business downturns.

The simplified organizational chart for the 3-W Company on page 70 shows that various departmental groupings may exist together in the various levels of a business firm. Each basis of departmentation has its advantages and disadvantages. Therefore, management must balance the strong and weak points of each grouping and set up departments that allow for effective coordination and communication in moving toward the firm's goals.

ESTABLISHMENT OF AUTHORITY RELATIONSHIPS

An organization chart of a company shows how the work load is divided and assigned to specific individuals or departments. An equally important element in the organizing process that rarely appears on organization charts describes authority-responsibility relationships between the persons doing these jobs. Managers must have an understanding of who is supposed to do what before a managerial team can run smoothly. These relationships are usually established on the bases of line authority, staff authority, and functional authority. The tasks and formal authority relationships for each position are set forth in the organization manual or management guide.

Line Authority Relationships

Managers functioning in a **line authority** relationship to other persons or departments directly supervise subordinates in the **chain of command or hierarchy of authority.** The chain of command in Figure 4-4 shows the formal authority relationships that run in a direct line from the top to the bottom of the organization.

Figure 4-4   A Chain of Command

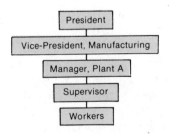

Line managers are in the chain of command because they are responsible for an activity that directly contributes to the earnings of the company. They usually are concerned with the accomplishment of quantitative objectives, cost control, and the on-going decisions that allow them to accomplish the tasks for which they are responsible.

Staff Authority Relationships

Unlike line authority, which is based on superior-subordinate relationships, **staff authority** is based on expertise in specialized activities. Staff authority includes the authority to advise, plan, gather information, and provide guidance to line managers. Figure 4-5 shows the formal relationships among persons who have staff authority.

Figure 4-5   A Staff Authority Relationship

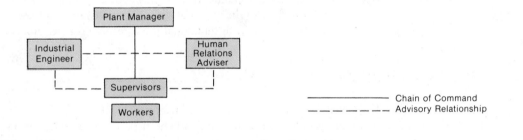

It is becoming obvious that, since World War II, staff positions in the United States have far outstripped line jobs in number and influence. Since the 1950s, bright young MBAs and other executives seeking the "fast track" to promotion have avoided line jobs. Many top managers and directors have staff backgrounds and have taken care of their staff people in pay and promotions.

In Japan, on the other hand, the brightest people are wanted in line jobs. Although these people may be rotated between line and staff jobs far more extensively than in the United States, it is felt that the key line posts in engineering, manufacturing, and marketing require the best talent available. The success of Japanese business is leading some American organization thinkers to wonder if it's really in our national interest for line jobs not to be regarded as "thinking jobs" performed by people who are the core of the business.

Functional Authority Relationships

Individuals with **functional authority** have the right to issue policies and procedures for their specialized functions throughout the organization and to expect compliance. Staff persons prepare recommendations for the line manager. Persons with functional authority issue directives in their names instead of submitting them through the line manager. A production manager may, for example, have the authority to specify maintenance schedules for machines in any part of the company. Likewise, a personnel manager may have the right to establish policies and procedures used throughout a company in hiring employees.

A Caution

The distinctions between types of authority relationships are not as neat and clean as they appear at first glance. Most managerial positions are not solely line, staff, or functional in nature. For instance, a personnel manager will be in a line relationship to the employees in the personnel department; in a staff relationship to the executive officers when serving on the advisory executive committee; and in a functional relationship to the total organization.

Therefore, every management job contains each of these three authority relationships to some degree. Understanding the changing authority of managers in their various relationships with others in the organization is a far more important issue than attempting to impose the line, staff, or functional job category on a person.

DIVISION OF MANAGERIAL WORK

We have seen how departmentation in an organization covers the horizontal division of operating tasks. Let us now turn to the third element of the organizing process — the vertical division of managerial tasks. The division of managerial work is accomplished through two organizational concepts: the span of management and the decentralization of managerial authority.

Span of Management

Both the horizontal and vertical divisions of activities in an organization are costly not only in terms of managerial and staff personnel, but also in terms of communication and coordination. Nevertheless, the underlying concept of **span of management** — the number of subordinates that a manager can effectively supervise — requires managerial work to be differentiated. Another name for span of management is *span of executive control*.

Levels of Management

As Figure 4-6 shows, the span of management is clearly related to the number of levels in an organization. The narrower the span, the more levels that are needed. As a result, more executives are needed to manage the various levels. Generally the proper number of subordinates an executive can handle will depend on the complexity of the

Figure 4-6   Span of Management

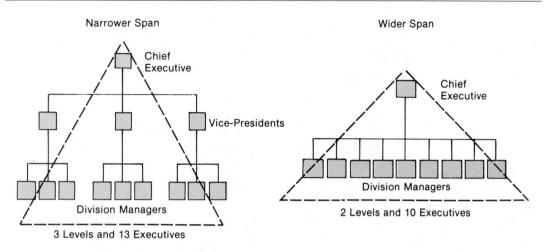

activity, the skill and experience of both the manager and the employees concerned with that activity, and other related factors.

Today's thinking about the "proper" levels and spans of management is changing as companies seek to cut overhead. In 1980, for instance, the Ford Motor Company had 11 layers of management between the factory worker and the chairman, while Toyota Motor Company had 6. By 1982, Ford had eliminated 25 percent of its North American salaried personnel. Likewise, GM has announced the layoffs of over 13,000 white-collar workers.

As with Ford and GM, many companies now are moving toward flattening their bureaucracies by eliminating whole layers of management. The managers who remain will probably have to do more for themselves and supervise more people.

Group and Sector Executives

Some companies grow internally, and some grow by acquiring other companies. When a company reaches a certain size and complexity, it often operates several distinct kinds of businesses such as automobiles, locomotives, appliances, and diesel engines. It then begins to look at *group structure with group management* as a way to keep the corporate officers' span of control within bounds.

The group executive is a manager whose position on the organization chart is between the CEO and the managers of the operating divisions. The General Electric Company went one step beyond group management with a new layer of senior management called sector executives. In doing this, General Electric combined six previous groups and six new groups into five sectors: Consumer Products and Services Sector, Power Systems Sector, Technical Systems and Materials Sector, Industrial Products and Components Sector, and International Sector. The basic movement of a company to group and sector management is illustrated in Figure 4-7. Although group structure

Figure 4-7   Group and Sector Executives

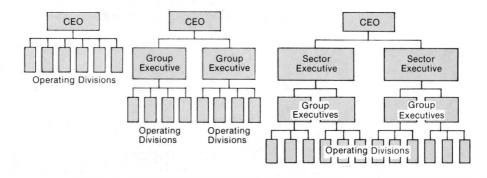

is quite common, few companies have grown to the point where sector structure is needed.

There are at least three reasons why companies use group structure to deal with problems of growth and diversification. Group structure provides:

1. BETTER COMMUNICATION. The group executive facilitates the flow of information and decisions up and down between corporate headquarters and other companies or divisions within the corporation.
2. ECONOMIES OF SCALE. Groups can be formed so that similarities or common needs among divisions can be combined for greater profit. Groups may provide equipment or sales coverage that no one division could afford on its own.
3. EXECUTIVE TRAINING. Group executives have true profit responsibility. They make important strategic decisions and often serve on top-level corporate policy-making committees.

Decentralization of Managerial Authority

In 1983, Levi Strauss & Co. started to streamline its domestic operations, which amounts to about two-thirds of the apparel company's total sales. Pressed by a recession in the clothing industry, the company expected to cut corporate expenses by about 20 percent, or $10 million, in a year's time. Levi's biggest step was to eliminate a layer of group executives tucked between the company's five domestic operating units and the head of U.S. operations.

Do you remember what happens to the span of management when the number of organizational levels is reduced? If you remember that the span of management becomes wider, you're right! But another key relationship also comes into play here. A wider span of management usually means the decentralization of managerial authority. **Decentralization** is the delegation of authority for making managerial decisions to subordinates at lower levels in the organization.

Usually a manager faced with a wide span of management will either want or be forced to share managerial decision making with others. Also, the trend toward lean corporate staffs may require a decentralized style of management. However, the degree of decentralization is not measured by the quantity of decisions that are passed down the managerial hierarchy. Rather, it is measured by both the importance and the scope of the decisions being made down the line and their impact on the entire organization.

Decentralization and Physical Dispersion

The position is sometimes taken that a firm is decentralized when its management is physically dispersed. Physical dispersion, or physical decentralization, occurs when central managers are geographically separated from division or branch managers. This viewpoint is not entirely correct, as authority to make managerial decisions may be delegated by a manager to a subordinate sitting at the next desk. Likewise, **centralized management** occurs when a central manager is heavily involved in the decisions that are made by other managers down the line. Although decentralized management usually goes hand in hand with physical dispersion, one is not necessary to the other. Care should be taken, therefore, to distinguish between the two concepts.

Factors in Decentralization

There are no simple formulas to indicate how much decision-making authority should be decentralized. The following factors are often considered when making this decision:

1. Are the persons at the lower levels capable of making sound decisions?
2. Which person down the line has the necessary facts to make a given type of decision?
3. Will changing conditions in the field require that speedy, flexible decisions be made at the local level?
4. How important is the decision in terms of dollars, its impact on other decisions in the organization, and the morale of the managers down the line?

THE PROCESS OF DELEGATION

The concepts discussed to this point — departmentation, authority relationships, and decentralization — can be worked out on paper, but they cannot be put to use in an organization without the fourth element of the organizing process — delegation. Delegation is the heart of the organizing process. Managers delegate to tie together the task responsibilities and the authority needed to carry out the tasks.

Basically, **delegation** is the key managerial technique by which a manager:

1. Assigns tasks or goals to subordinates.
2. Grants the authority necessary to carry out these assignments.
3. Helps the subordinates recognize their responsibilities to perform the assigned work and accept their accountability for this expected performance.

Ultimately, however, a boss cannot "delegate away" the responsibility for organizational performance. As the famous plaque on President Harry S Truman's desk once read, "The buck stops here" (at the top). Thus, delegation is a two-way process in which the boss and the subordinates ideally develop a working relationship that encourages agreement as to what needs to be done and how.

ORGANIZATION STRUCTURE

Organization structure is the formal pattern of relationships among the parts of an organization. Determining this structure is the final element of the organizing process. The formal structure of an organization does not simply "happen." It is the outcome of many management decisions made throughout the organizing process to balance the organization's tasks, authority relationships, and human capabilities.

Organizational Premises

The formally structured organization is based on two premises:

1. The rational person is motivated by economic incentives.
2. The organization is controlled by formal managerial authority.

Such an organization is sometimes called the closed-system organization. It does not take into account the possible influence of forces outside the organization, such as environmental and human factors, on the inner workings of the formal system. Instead, those who hold this viewpoint see management as a unifying force that achieves coordination within the organization by using formal authority relationships.

The premises of the closed-system organization are being challenged today by those who see the organization as an open system, or behavioral system. This view sees the open-system organization as a flexible social system that exists in a dynamic give-and-take relationship with its environment. In the open-system organization, managers adapt to inputs from the environment in the form of information, resources, and materials by changing the organization's formal structure and processes. Most large organizations are not solely "open" or "closed," but reflect elements of both systems.

Forms of Organization Structure

Only two forms of formal organization structure are commonly used today: line and line-and-staff. The matrix organization is a hybrid form of organization straddling both the closed-system and the open-system types. And there is always the informal organization that exists whenever groups of people work together.

Line Organization

A **line organization** is sometimes called a *scalar* or *military* organization as it is based on clear and simple relationships in a direct chain of command. Figure 4-8 shows a simplified line organization. Each person reports to an immediate supervisor, and responsibility for task performance is clearly defined. Because of its simplicity, however, the line organization rarely is suited to the needs of today's business organizations.

Figure 4-8   A Line Organization

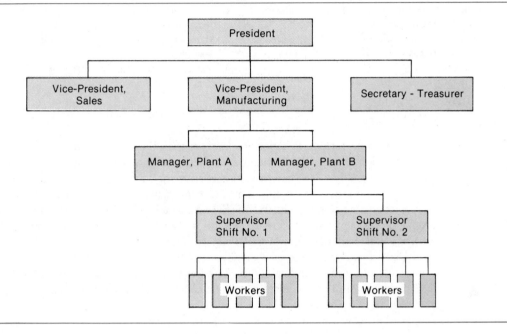

Advantages

1. It is simple and easy to understand.
2. Decisions can be made quickly.
3. Responsibility and accountability are clearly pinpointed.
4. Employees are free from criticism if they follow directions.

Disadvantages

1. The top manager may become bogged down in operating decisions to the exclusion of the necessary managerial work.
2. Managers lack staff help and must be able to handle any aspect of the job.
3. Coordination of the different "lines" is hard to achieve.

Line-and-Staff Organization

The **line-and-staff organization** releases line managers from having to master every aspect of their jobs as they can get help from others outside the chain of command. The *specialized staff* is used where specialized skills are needed. The *general staff* helps the manager with a wide variety of problems rather than dealing only with a certain specialty. The many advantages of this form of organization have made it the most popular type of organization structure.

The formal organization chart in Figure 4-3 on page 71 is a line-and-staff organization. Note the accounting, purchasing, and personnel help available to the vice-presidents of the Cosmetics and Industrial Chemicals Divisions and also the accounting, R & D, and personnel help for the vice-president of the Ethical Drugs Division.

Advantages	Disadvantages

1. Specialists can be used without losing the advantages of the line organization.
2. Authority and responsibility remain clearly placed.
3. Line managers have more time for their primary assignments.

1. The advice of staff persons may be seen by others as demands or orders.
2. Managers may refer too much of their managerial work to staff members.
3. Managers may blame problems on wrong advice from the staff.

Matrix Organization

Many modern organization theorists are critical of strict adherence to traditional organization theory. While traditional theory remains important, they feel that it should be modified by other viewpoints such as the behavioral, systems, and decision-making approaches to organization and management. For example, the **matrix or project organization** is an interesting hybrid example of modern thinking that involves temporary, fluid work teams within the framework of the pyramidal formal organization. The matrix organizational concept came from the needs of the Department of Defense and the National Aeronautics and Space Administration (NASA). New management and organization techniques were needed that could be applied across departmental lines to accomplish specific complex undertakings such as developing a missile system.

Many government agencies and private firms have adapted the matrix concept to their own needs. General Motors now uses "project centers" for every major new effort, as well as for parts and engineering problems common to all divisions such as frames, electrical systems, brakes, emission controls, and restraint systems. GM's project centers draw people and ideas from the five car divisions plus 25 other divisions and staffs. As GM sees it, the project center eliminates overlaps in work between divisions and has speeded many new technologies into production. It also encourages innovation and freedom from conventional organizational thinking.

Hewlett-Packard is basically a team-style organization. For example, it uses "small business teams" within product divisions to develop new products and coordinate joint engineering efforts. Lockheed Corporation uses an Advanced Development Projects (ADP) Section called the "Skunk Works" to develop secret projects for the Air Force.

Project Management. Large specialized companies today may have a number of complex on-going projects, each of which is in a different stage of completion and has its own problems and identity. With many projects in the mill, the traditional functional managers, such as the manager of Systems Engineering in Figure 4-9, may find it hard to keep up with the changing needs of the various projects. As numerous functional specialists contribute to a project and then leave it, the continuity of the project is not easily maintained. Therefore, most projects are run by a project manager who is responsible for guiding and controlling all aspects of a project during its life cycle. Certainly the job of the project manager requires both technical and administrative skills.

As contrasted to the traditional organization structures and relationships discussed earlier, the characteristics of a matrix organization are:

Figure 4-9 Matrix Organization with Project Management

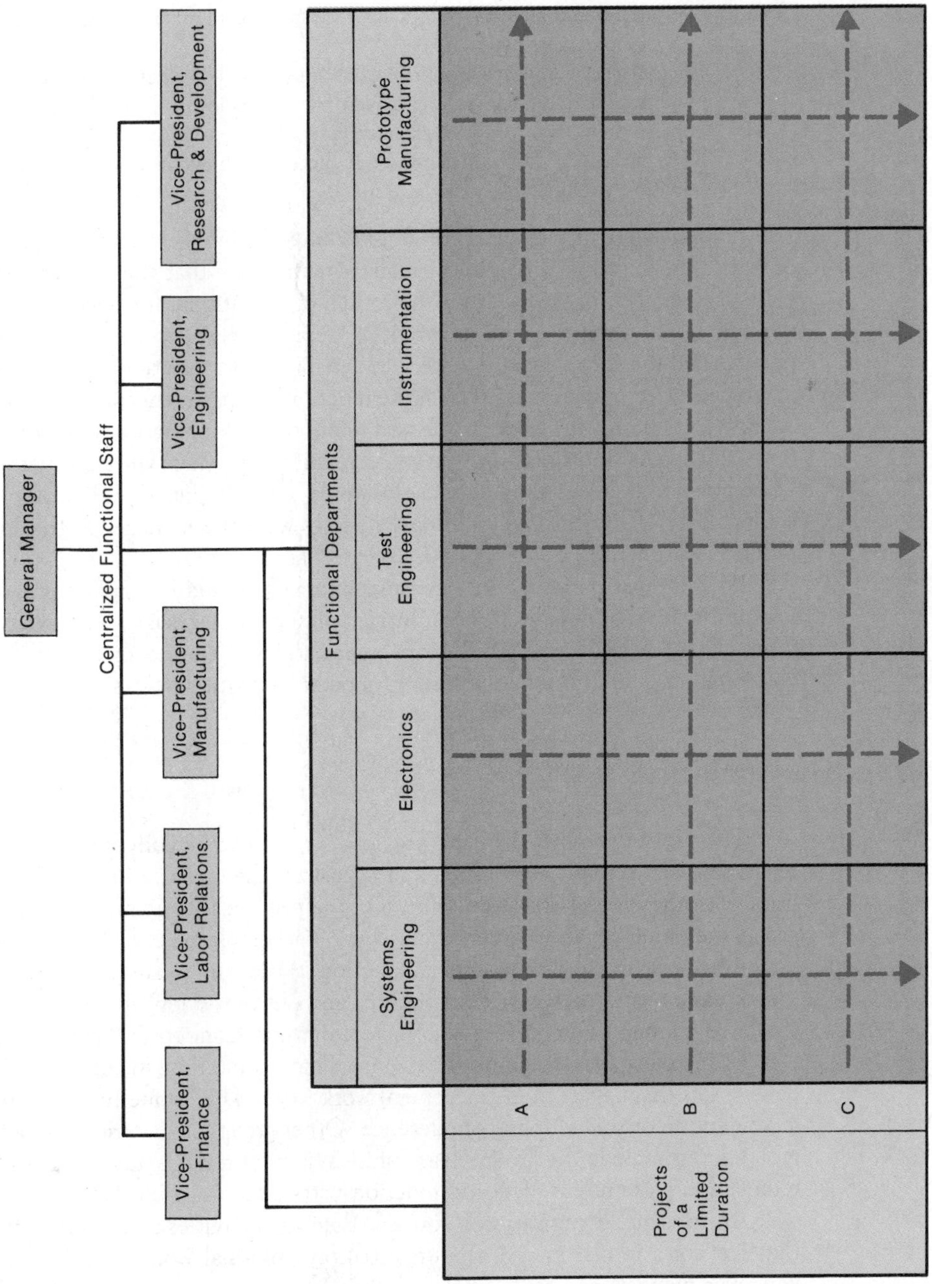

1. The project manager's authority is a combination of technical expertise, charisma, political effectiveness, and formal power. This person does not merely occupy a formal position in the chain of command. The project manager must rely heavily on persuasion and personal acceptance and must build alliances with peers, functional associations, and superiors.

2. The project manager's authority goes outside the organization lines to relationships with suppliers, subcontractors, government agencies, and the like. It emphasizes an open-system organization that must be responsive to forces in its environment.

3. The project is finite in duration. If successful, however, it may be the start of a division in the formal organization.

Relationships in a Mixed-Form Organization. Figure 4-9 shows a simple example of matrix organization with project management. Note that the project organization exists in a matrix, or grid, within the formal organizational framework that provides the functional expertise and centralized service activities needed to support the projects and the company as a whole. In the matrix organization the various projects draw specialized help as needed from the functional departments on a temporary basis. The project effort reflects work-oriented relationships. It is more concerned with the flow of work in horizontal and diagonal relationships than with the vertical chain of command. A diagonal relationship would exist in Figure 4-9 if, for example, the manager of Project C should deal directly with the manager of the Instrumentation Department.

Project organization is an expensive effort. It should be applied only to highly important jobs that require the coordination of numerous specialties. There are various forms of matrix, project, and task-team organizations. This brief discussion should give you some insights into just one form of modern organization.

Informal Organization

The projects discussed in the previous section are actually work groups or task teams that are formally established and appear on the organization chart. There are, however, other groups that form but do not appear on the organization chart. Work groups are formed by the workers themselves to accomplish a task. Informal groups are established on the job without official sanction. Social groups are established for purely social reasons, and they may exist both in and out of the job situation. An example would be a group of employees who have a bowling team on Friday evenings.

In any type of small group, the members have something in common which they believe sets them apart from the general work force. This "something" often is called a group norm or shared frame of reference. Other group characteristics in addition to group norms include the group's leadership, system of rewards and punishment, communication patterns, loyalty, and function within the organization.

An **informal organization** is formed, then, by activities and human interactions that are not a formal part of the organization. Informal work groups are inevitable wherever numbers of people work together and group acceptance and involvement may be highly prized by the group members. Informal groups may be both good or bad (functional or dysfunctional) to the formal organization. The wise manager carefully observes and analyzes the nature and activities of informal groups in order to develop effective working relationships with them.

DEVELOPING EFFECTIVE ORGANIZATIONS

It is a narrow view to judge the effectiveness of a business organization by a single standard such as profit maximization, high productivity, efficient service, or good employee morale. Modern theorists insist that a broad view must be taken. They define *organizational effectiveness* as the capacity of an organization to survive, adapt, maintain itself, and grow in the face of changing conditions. An effective business organization thinks and acts along the following criteria:

1. It has the managerial ability to solve problems and to react with flexibility to changes in the social, political, and economic environment. The current emphasis on environment places an increasing burden on management's ability and willingness to assume an active role in this vital area.
2. It has a sense of identity; it knows what its goals are and what must be done to achieve them; this knowledge is widely shared by all members of the organization.
3. It is realistic in its planning in that it can judge correctly the impact of relevant changes in markets and technology on the company's future.
4. It provides for integration or fusing of personal goals and enterprise objectives.

The traditional organizational concepts explored in this chapter will remain necessary and important as foundations of organizational thinking. However, as our society becomes more complex, dynamic, and interdependent, the organizing process will require greater managerial knowledge and skill in dealing with both the formal and the informal aspects of organization.

SUMMARY An organization is the means by which people with specialized skills combine their efforts and get things done. Organizing is the process managers use to set up an organization. This process includes the horizontal grouping of tasks to be performed, the establishment of authority relationships, the vertical dividing of the managerial work, and the determination of the overall organization structure.

Delegation is the key managerial technique used to activate the organization once it is planned. It involves assigning tasks or goals to subordinates, granting authority necessary to carry out these tasks, and creating a two-way recognition of the work to be performed.

There are various forms of formal organization today, and to a degree these represent differing viewpoints that people hold about the nature of organizations. Some see organizations as closed systems; that is, "closed" to the environment. Others see organizations as open systems that are responsive to the forces in the external environment. Most large organizations reflect elements of both systems.

The line-and-staff organization is the most popular form of formal organization structure today. But other forms, such as the matrix, or project, organization, represent interesting and useful deviations from traditional forms.

In addition to understanding the formal organization structure, the thinking manager today carefully notes informal organizations that exist outside the formal organization. Work groups, informal groups, and social groups will form wherever numbers of people work together. Such groups may be highly important to the long-run effectiveness of the formal organization.

BACK TO THE CHAPTER OPENER

1. Define centralization and decentralization.
2. Where do centralization and decentralization fit into the organizing process?
3. What are the key parts of an organization plan?
4. How has Sears recently changed its goals and organization structure?
5. Would you expect Schlumberger to have a wide or narrow span of management?

BUSINESS TERMS

organization	68	functional authority	75
organizing process	68	span of management	76
horizontal differentiation	69	decentralization	78
vertical differentiation	69	centralized management	79
organization charts	70	delegation	79
departmentation	72	organization structure	80
line authority	74	line organization	80
chain of command or hierarchy of authority	74	line-and-staff organization	81
staff authority	75	matrix or project organization	82
		informal organization	84

QUESTIONS FOR DISCUSSION AND ANALYSIS

1. What is the starting point in setting up a business organization?
2. Discuss if it is good for an organization to rely on informal voluntary efforts to coordinate or integrate the various activities in the organization.
3. What basis of departmentation would you use for a maker/seller of ultralight aircraft?
4. Where should you look to determine the authority relationships in an organization?
5. Is there any difference between "line authority" and a "line job"? Explain.
6. Since a "line job" places a person in the chain of command, are line jobs better than staff jobs? Explain.
7. If you are a chef in a restaurant, in what authority relationship do you exist to the person who is in charge of the commissary that provides the various foods and supplies to the chef?
8. How do we know when a manager's span of management is too broad?
9. Do you think a good project manager in a technical activity would be hard to find? Explain.
10. If the informal organization doesn't appear on the organization chart, how can it be a real part of the organization?

1. Over the years the Allied Resources Corporation had grown and expanded in what seemed to be a random pattern. Its ten divisions ranged from vegetable canning to oil exploration. Despite this diversity, it was run on a highly centralized basis by Fred "Bo" Didley, its president and founder, until his retirement in 1983. During his active working years, Didley felt he knew every aspect of the business, and he welcomed the chance to take part in the daily operating decisions.

   Profits were up at the time of Didley's retirement, but return on investment was less than in 1965. Some facilities were obsolescent and generated little or no profit. The lines of command were confused, and nobody knew exactly whom to go to for help when problems arose. It was almost impossible to pin down the profitability of any one division.

   Didley's successor is a 20-year veteran with the company. Discuss what steps you would expect this person to take to reorganize the company.

2. Interview a business manager and prepare a report on the following:

   a. Whether she or he occupies a position with line, staff, or functional authority, or perhaps a position involving all of these.

   b. On what basis this manager's division, unit, or department is departmentized.

   c. Whether the company has a current organization chart and organization manual.

   Note particularly the ways in which this manager's responses may differ from the discussion in the text. Share your findings with your class in a verbal report.

3. Life in the big-network broadcasting industry can be exciting, demanding, and volatile. This has been especially true for NBC, as parent RCA has been trying to yank NBC up from its third-place rank against ABC and CBS in the networks' rating race. RCA appointed two CEOs—Fred Silverman and Grant Tinker—within four years in an attempt to boost morale and ratings. These two executives differ widely in their management style and particularly in their willingness to delegate managerial decision-making authority to subordinates.

   Read about Silverman (August 12, 1980 edition of *The Wall Street Journal,* p. 31) and Tinker (February 12, 1982 issue of *Business Week,* p. 73). Then prepare a short report contrasting the way in which these two executives divide managerial work.

Managers in Atari Land

Peter Sprague, the venture capitalist who guided National Semiconductor from the brink of bankruptcy to the Fortune 500, tells a story about the time he tried to put together a deal for a young Silicon Valley entrepreneur only to have the man reject it when he discovered he would make merely $3 million the first year. "This guy had about eight dollars to his name," Sprague says, "but he had a potentially marketable product and a dream. That's the psychology of Silicon Valley. People don't want to wait for success; they want it now. They want to go straight from the Toyota to the Lear jet. It's a different world."

This thirty-mile strip of industry between San Jose and Palo Alto has become the most visible repository of the quintessential American dream—that all a man needs is one good idea and it can make him rich beyond his wildest dreams. And the dream comes true with startling regularity.

Some of the area's garage-shop-to-public-corporation wonders grow faster in a single decade than the great eastern companies did in a century. When Apple Computer went public in December, 1980, not only did its founders—Stephen Wozniak, twenty-nine, Steven Jobs, twenty-six, and Mike Markkula, thirty-nine—become seriously rich (to the tune of more than $100 million apiece) but nearly forty other Apple employees also became paper millionaires. In its first public year Apple had profits of $39.4 million on sales of $334.8 million.

Year after year new companies spring up alongside highways 280, 101, and 17, nearly all of them founded and run by young men who have never been within 3,000 miles of the Harvard Business School. Oddly enough, they stand a 95 percent chance of surviving, according to a twenty-year study run by the University of Santa Clara.

"The driving force behind growth in the Valley is innovation," says Henry M. Kaiser, a venture capitalist. "Business conditions change so rapidly that there simply is not time for traditional methods. By the time you appoint a committee, do a study, and get your flip charts together, someone else has already brought a better product to market. This is not a game for professional managers, at least not in the early stages."

SOURCE: Jerry Bowles, "Silicon Valley Days: Being a True-Life Account of the Adventures of the Micro Kids in Atari Land," *World,* No. 2 (1982), p. 24.

5

The Manager's Job

Objectives:

- Describe the three managerial levels.
- Explain the three basic managerial skills.
- Identify the steps in the decision-making process.
- Discuss the seven basic managerial functions.
- Identify the three basic leadership styles.
- Distinguish between the needs hierarchy theory and the behavior modification theory of motivation.
- Relate three types of feedback to organizational communication.
- Distinguish between communication and information.
- Identify three basic steps in the MBO technique.
- Explain how contingency management relates to managing complex organizations.

When the Chinese plan a building, they consider the *feng shui*—a blend of the winds, water, and landscape—and the precise placement of the structure. Then they build according to what the natural elements dictate. To disregard the feng shui, Chinese believe, is to invite disaster.

American business has its own version of the feng shui—it's called dynamic management! Management is a system of thought and a function. As a system of thought, it supports the intelligent use of human effort and other responses to a changing environment. It also is a function through which managers determine and achieve their organizational and personal objectives.

The job of the management group in any organization is to make cooperative, specialized efforts function properly. Rather than deal with winds, water, and landscape, management combines and converts people, machines, money, and materials into a useful, goal-oriented enterprise. A manager cannot simply adapt after the fact to changing forces in the environment, as this type of reactive management invites disaster. At all levels a manager must be a dynamic, proactive, innovating force in the business enterprise.

MANAGERIAL LEVELS, SKILLS, AND TOOLS

A manager performs a great variety of commonplace activities during a normal day's work. Managers make and receive telephone calls; go on trips; attend meetings; speak and listen to individuals and groups; and monitor the movement of people, materials, and machines.

After observing several managers at work, one may arrive at two conflicting conclusions. One conclusion is that the various managerial jobs differ so widely in content and scope that no generalization about managerial activities is possible. The other conclusion is that there is not much difference between the work of managers and nonmanagers.

However, the manager may view the work differently. When a person guides subordinates, decides how to achieve a particular goal, or checks to see that events proceed according to plans, that person acts as a manager. Although various managers may have similar objectives in mind, they face different demands at different levels. These challenges may require different skills and the use of different tools (techniques, concepts, and principles).

Levels of Management

Usually there are three managerial levels in large businesses. As Figure 5-1 indicates, these levels are: institutional management, administrative management, and operating management. The arrows in Figure 5-1 show the basic orientation of each managerial level.

Institutional management or top management is comprised of the board of directors, president, and group executives. The function of this level is to set corporate objectives and policies and to establish the relationship of the firm to other institutions in its environment.

Administrative management or middle management is comprised of managers of divisions or services. As the arrow in Figure 5-1 indicates, the orientation of this level is coordinative and unifying. Administrative management coordinates the work of the various departments at the operating level. It also provides a link between the production processes and the sale of goods that are produced, thus standing between the technical management and the firm's customers.

Operating management or technical management is comprised of department managers and persons of professional technical competence. This level is oriented

Figure 5-1   **Levels of Management**

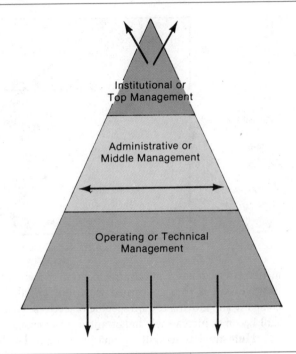

downward to basic operations such as producing the goods and moving them out the door. The technical expert often seeks recognition from peers and colleagues rather than from the managers at the administrative level.

Basic Types of Managerial Skills

The effectiveness of managers in directing others and achieving results through these efforts rests on three basic managerial skills: technical skill, human relations skill, and administrative skill. Each of these skills is used in all three managerial levels. But, as Figure 5-2 indicates, these skills have differing degrees of importance at different levels of management.

Administrative skill, sometimes called conceptual skill, involves the ability to see the company as a whole. This skill recognizes how the various departments or divisions of a company are interrelated and how the company fits into society. A manager with administrative skill sees how various parts of the company work interdependently and are affected by outside changes in the social and economic environment. For example, when a major change is made in marketing policy, the change may have an impact on the other departments such as production, finance, research, and personnel. In turn, the change in marketing policy may result from — or even create — changes in govern-

Figure 5-2   Managerial Skills at Different Levels

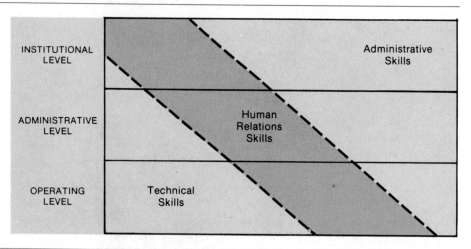

mental policy, labor relations, the location of plants, and consumer behavior. Administrative skill is thus concerned with unifying all the activities and interests of a company and moving toward specific objectives. Figure 5-2 shows that administrative skill becomes increasingly important in top management positions.

Human relations skill is primarily concerned with working with people. This skill enables a manager to work effectively as a group member and to build teamwork among the subordinates. It is based on an understanding of the differences and similarities among people. Human relations skill depends on an understanding of what subordinates mean by their words and actions and on the manager's ability to communicate clearly with them. This skill must be practiced continuously since it involves sensitivity not only in decision making and problem solving, but also in daily contact with others.

Technical skill involves functions dealing with the actual production and distribution of the company's products or services. It also includes many types of activities that utilize knowledge in research and development, market research, and accounting. In business organizations many of the technical tasks are performed by highly trained experts. Therefore, the manager may not practice a certain technical skill all the time, but must be competent to direct the technical activities. This requires an understanding of the processes, techniques, and methods used in a particular activity.

Basic Frameworks for Managerial Tools

As mentioned earlier, the tools of a manager are managerial techniques, concepts, and principles. Thus, a manager can be seen as a social mechanic who must know which tools are available and how to use them. At any given time, the manager has a great number of tools available for her or his use. Are there any frameworks that will help the manager organize these tools for use? Fortunately there are. Just as a mechanic may use a tool chest with drawers and sections to separate pliers, socket sets, etc., there are two basic frameworks a manager can use to "section off" managerial tools. These frameworks are: the process of decision making and the group of managerial functions which comprise managerial work.

PROCESS OF DECISION MAKING

Probably the foremost responsibility of management is decision making, which is used in all levels and functions of management. The types of decisions will vary by management levels. Decisions at the technical management level often are of a short-run engineering or computational nature. Decisions at the administrative level often involve short- and long-run questions of coordination and compromise. At the institutional level, decisions may involve long-run conceptual or judgmental questions that relate the organization to its environment and establish its objectives and policies.

Decisions at the institutional level often are strategic ones. Strategic decisions are major decisions regarding utilization of resources that may have a long-run impact on the accomplishment of goals. Strategic considerations include such factors as:

1. The firm's human, capital, and material resources.
2. The nature and importance of the work in process.
3. Future trends based partly on changing technical, commercial, and financial conditions.
4. The order in which each step of the decision-making plan is to be undertaken.
5. The timing of each step.
6. The communication and coordination needed so that each step is understood, accepted, and carried out.

An example of a strategic decision was that made by Cummins Engine Company in 1981 to launch the largest capital spending plan in its history. Cummins plunged into a five-year, $1.3 billion capital-spending effort to revamp its entire product line and to produce more fuel-efficient engines for light- and medium-duty trucks. To finance this program, Cummins had to raise $550 million in outside funds.

Steps in Decision Making

At all management levels, effective decision making and the willingness to face risk are essential to the well-being of the company and to our economy. The steps in the decision-making process are:

1. Recognition of the problem.
2. Definition and analysis of the problem into its essential parts.
3. Establishment of two or more alternative solutions which are comparatively evaluated.
4. Selection of the solution believed to be the most favorable.
5. Adoption and implementation of the solution by issuing the necessary orders and securing the needed acceptance of the plan from those who will be carrying it out.

These steps may be taken in a few moments on some routine decisions or may require extensive analysis by many specialists on important technical, administrative, and competitive questions.

Beyond Rational Decision Making

As our society and technology advance, business problems will become even larger and more complex. Managers will have to break away from past solutions and instead develop new solutions to these problems. This search for new solutions will require expert application of the steps in the decision-making process. The search also will require an appreciation of newer views of decision making such as intuitive decision making and consensus management.

Intuitive Decision Making

Recent studies of the brain suggest that its left side is the source of logical, sequential, rational, and verbal processes while its right side is the source of intuitive, imaginative, artistic, and creative processes. Despite the attention given to rational decision making in the management literature, top managers often use the right side—their intuitions—in making decisions. Intuition is not simply impulsiveness. Intuition welcomes data but refuses to be limited to data. Intuition often is based on much study and thought. We need to know more about the effective use of intuition as part of our decision-making process.

Consensus Management

Another view of decision making is the Japanese concept of **consensus management,** a management style keyed to group decision making and implementation. In this approach, the top manager allows the subordinate managers a voice in almost every major decision. The goal of consensus management is twofold: to encourage the manager's commitment to implementing a decision and to invite creative ideas by helping people understand what happens at different levels of the organization.

MANAGERIAL FUNCTIONS

Managerial work typically is broken down into the following seven managerial functions: planning, organizing, staffing, directing, controlling, representing, and innovating. The two-way arrows between these functions in Figure 5-3 show that these functions interact with each other. Figure 5-3 also shows that decision making and communication are the coordinative processes that tie these functions together. Managers must be skilled in these coordinative processes and functions if they are to accomplish their goals through the efforts of other people.

Figure 5-3   Management Functions and Coordinative Processes

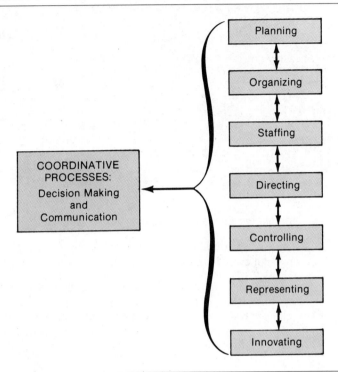

Planning

The process of establishing and clarifying objectives, determining the policies and procedures necessary to meet the objectives, and preparing a plan of action is called **planning**.

An objective is *what* one wants to accomplish. One way for a manager to identify areas in which a company should establish objectives is to consider the relationships and resources that are necessary to its survival and success. This will lead to objectives concerning the type and quality of goods produced and the desired relationship of the company to its customers, suppliers, employees, stockholders, and the surrounding community.

A policy is a broad guideline that says something about *how* objectives will be attained. Figure 5-4 gives some examples of basic objectives and related policies.

A predetermined course of action is a plan. Both objectives and policies are types of plans, as they prescribe broad future courses of action. But broad statements of what the company is trying to achieve are not enough. A plan of action must be prepared detailing the course of action and stating the specific resources required. The plan of action reflects the company's strategy.

Figure 5-4   Objectives and Related Policies

Broad Objective	Related Policy
• An efficient, customer-oriented company.	• Orders filled and shipped within three days of receipt.
• A willingness to innovate.	• A formal system for reviewing and rewarding employee suggestions.
• Participation in civic improvement.	• Time off without loss of pay to executives involved in desirable community programs.
• Opportunity for qualified workers to advance.	• All job openings posted; a yearly performance review conducted by each department head.

Information Needed for Planning

At least three kinds of information are needed for planning, especially for top-level policy and strategic issues. These types of information are:

1. Environmental information, which describes the social, political, and economic aspects of the climate in which a business operates or may operate in the future. Examples of environmental information are population trends, price-level movements, transportation costs, labor force supply, and foreign trade forecasts.
2. Competitive information, which explains the performance, programs, and plans of competitors. It includes data on present and future profitability, return on investment, share of the market, and sales trends of competitors.
3. Internal information, which indicates the company's own strengths and weaknesses. It should stress the elements that give a company an edge over its competitors. A company's strengths and weaknesses are seen in cost variations relative to changes in sales volume, delivery performance, community standing, reputation in the industry, and labor relations.

Strategic Planning for Growth

Strategic planning means fashioning goals that build on a company's strengths and steering clear of its weaknesses. Probably no company is better known for its strategic planning skill than General Electric. In the early 1970s, GE developed strategic planning as the route to corporate growth and profits. This planning technique treated GE's many ventures and product lines as business units in an investment portfolio, sorting out the winners and losers through systematic analysis.

Then, in 1981, GE launched a radical new strategy that emphasizes a new era of technical development, rather than the financial performance of the 1970s, and puts a greater emphasis on market share as the road to long-run profitability. With the new emphasis on technological competitiveness and market-share leadership, GE's effort to implement its new goals and strategies is sure to be one of the real-life corporate dramas of the 1980s. It clearly reflects the importance of the planning function of management.

Organizing

Once objectives and policies are established, the manager must determine the activities necessary to achieve the objectives and provide for the coordination of authority relationships among the persons who will be performing these activities. If a firm is running smoothly, it may seem to an outsider that the whole process is relatively simple. Goods are shipped on time because they have been made and stored in advance of receiving an order and because the proper packaging and transportation facilities are available when needed. Actually this smooth flow could not have been accomplished without an efficient organization operating under competent managerial supervision. The specific elements of the organizing function of management were covered in the previous chapter.

Staffing

In the **staffing** function the manager attempts to recruit, hire, train, and develop the right person for each job. This is an ongoing managerial activity since people quit, are promoted, are transferred, are discharged, or retire. In the case of a growing company, new positions are created that must be filled. Staffing is not solely the responsibility of the human resources department. Effective staffing requires that managers observe their subordinates' performance, noting strengths and seeking to remove weaknesses by careful counseling and training programs. Because the staffing function covers a multitude of activities that are increasingly being constrained by legislation, the next chapter will deal with this subject more extensively.

Directing

When one thinks of management in general, one may think almost instinctively of the three basic elements of the directing function: leadership, motivation, and communication. This is quite understandable since **directing** involves the ability to guide and motivate subordinates to achieve the objectives of the enterprise while at the same time building an enduring relationship between the subordinates and the enterprise. A relationship of this sort is based on the recognition that subordinates have goals that must be satisfied to some degree if they are to contribute effectively to the activity over time. The three elements of directing—leadership, motivation, and communication—are discussed later in the chapter.

Controlling

The managerial function that measures current performance against expected results and takes the necessary action to reach the goals is called **controlling**. Specifically, the control process consists of four steps:

1. Deciding what should be accomplished or what will constitute good performance.
2. Measuring current actual performance in quantitative terms if possible.
3. Comparing current performance with standards of expected performance.
4. Taking corrective action, if needed, so as to achieve or exceed the desired results in the future.

Controlling at Different Managerial Levels

At all levels of management there must be control, all the way from knowing how much money the firm is making or losing to knowing the number of parts of a particular size that are on hand. A proper organizational plan assigns differing amounts of control responsibility to individuals at various levels of management. For example, top management should not be concerned with the problem of whether 100 or 200 one-horsepower motors should be kept on hand; but it should be concerned with the total dollars tied up in inventory.

Control Efforts and Economic Climate

When the economic climate is strong, managers sometimes become careless about the control function and the steps in the control process. Too many people are hired; costly inventories and receivables are allowed to become flabby; and managers' egos may dictate which programs are added or dropped.

Recently, however, corporate liquidity has been at its lowest point in 25 years, and managerial control has once again become a prime function. Operating expenses have been cut to reflect declines in sales. Inventories and receivables have been carefully pruned. Executives and workers have been asked to accept reduced paychecks. Suppliers have been pressed for discounts. The intensity of these recent control efforts will not be easily forgotten. In the future, the control function of management will be more uniformly practiced regardless of the economic climate.

Representing

Civic affairs, politics, governmental dealings, and other "outside" obligations have come to consume a huge chunk of executive time at the top level of American businesses. Some CEOs resent participation in these activities, which they feel take up the time they should be giving to the internal affairs of their companies. But most top-level managers increasingly recognize the importance of the representing function that brings them into contact with the world outside the company. Participation in representing activities gives them an opportunity to explain the ways of business to the public, helps them to manage crises, and allows them to develop anticipative management.

Explaining the Ways of Business

Some corporate leaders, such as those at Mobil Oil, have indicated in newspaper ads lately that they're unhappy about the negative coverage of business in the media. Yet corporations need to recognize that much of today's antibusiness attitude comes from people with little exposure to the business side of public issues and questions. America's corporate executives need to be more venturesome in explaining the ways of the business enterprise system to the public in language the public can understand.

Crisis Management

Managers who have resisted their representing function may not be effective in the face of crises. When a crisis comes along — like the Three Mile Island scare — they simply may not know how to talk with the media and how best to promote an understanding of their problems. Mishandling a crisis can be ruinous.

Anticipative Management

A major part of the future top-level manager's job will be anticipative management, which means correctly evaluating and adapting to a rapidly changing environment. Anticipative management requires an understanding of how change may affect the organization. To develop this understanding, managers must become involved with groups outside the company such as government agencies, interest groups, and educational institutions.

Most companies see the representing function as a two-way street. They see it as a chance to share ideas and to learn from others, along with providing public exposure to future top-level managers. Sometimes, however, companies prefer to leave the representing function to public relations specialists, paid lobbyists, or trade associations.

Innovating

The story goes that Henry Ford once hired an efficiency expert to evaluate his company. After a few weeks, the expert made his report. It was highly favorable except for one thing. "It's that man down the hall," said the expert. "Every time I go by his office he's just sitting there with his feet on the desk. He's wasting your money." "That man," replied Mr. Ford, "once had an idea that saved us millions of dollars. At that time, I believe his feet were planted right where they are now!"

Alert managers realize that their companies cannot stand still. Remaining ahead of competition requires corporate leadership dedicated to the principle that innovation and risk-taking are the lifeblood of the company. Smart companies know that money alone does not produce innovation; people do. Most successful programs begin with an individual and succeed in a management climate that encourages creative thinking, risk-taking, and initiative. Thus, the innovating function is based on two elements: the company's innovative climate and the individual innovator.

The Innovative Climate

An individual must be liberated to innovate successfully. In an innovative climate individuals are encouraged to contribute creative ideas, communicate freely, and criticize products and goals. Also, they expect their ideas to receive consideration and recognition. Many attempts to innovate end in failure. However, the alternative to taking the risks of innovation is a worsening of the company's market position and its eventual decline.

The Individual Innovator

The job of an innovator doesn't end with the idea for a new product. The true innovator is capable of nurturing a new product from its early stages through a period of growth and profit. Of course, not all new-product managers are innovators. Yet they must be entrepreneurial risk takers and should be able to identify innovators and inspire creativity in these individuals.

Significance of Managerial Functions at Different Levels of Management

This overview of managerial functions has some hidden difficulties when one attempts to apply them to a specific managerial job. First, one cannot tell which functions are most important and how much time must be allocated to each function. All functions are important parts of a manager's job, but the significance attached to each one may vary at different times such as in different stages of a product life cycle. Furthermore, the significance of each function varies at different management levels in the same organization, as Figure 5-5 suggests.

Identifying managerial functions helps, however, to distinguish managerial work from nonmanagerial efforts. These functions show the complexity of managerial tasks

Figure 5-5   Significance of Managerial Functions at Different Managerial Levels

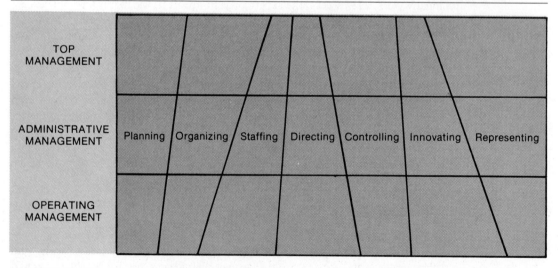

Part II • Management and Organization of Human Resources

Figure 5-6   Continuum of Leadership Behavior

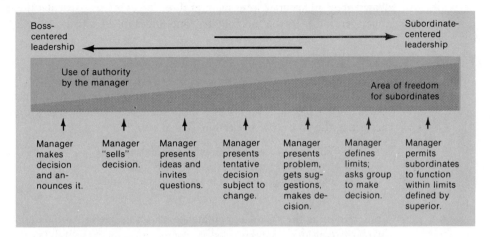

and help the manager recognize the important role of decision making. They show that the manager's work is concerned with ideas and people, rather than with impersonal operations and things.

MANAGERIAL LEADERSHIP

In performing their jobs, managers may rely basically on the authority that is officially or traditionally attached to the positions they occupy. Beyond this formal authority, however, managers must also exert leadership to motivate subordinates to contribute willingly to organizational goals. **Leadership** is defined as the ability to persuade or influence others in a dynamic, two-way process between the leader and followers. In this process the leader influences the group members and is responsive to their desires.

The skillful leader realizes that various leadership styles may affect the performance of the organization or group with which he or she is dealing in different ways. The three basic leadership styles are autocratic, democratic, and laissez-faire. The autocratic (boss-centered) leader makes decisions without consulting others; the democratic (subordinate-centered) leader invites participation of subordinates in the decisions that affect them; and the laissez-faire leader leaves many of the decisions to the subordinates by giving them a "free rein" over their activities.

In Figure 5-6, Tannenbaum and Schmidt suggest seven representative points of leadership behavior in a continuum moving from boss-centered to subordinate-centered leadership. None of these styles is always the most effective. Rather, the effectiveness of leaders will depend upon their ability to select and use a leadership style based upon an accurate assessment of three forces at any particular time: forces in the manager, forces in the subordinates, and forces in the situation.

Forces in the Manager

All managers view leadership problems in their own ways, depending on their particular background, knowledge, and experience. Four factors within the manager influence the pattern of leadership. These are:

1. The confidence placed in one's subordinates.
2. One's own preference for a leadership style.
3. One's feeling of security in an uncertain situation.
4. One's value system.

In determining the degree of confidence placed in one's subordinates, the manager is likely to consider their knowledge, competence, and adaptability. Also, there are managers who seem more comfortable and natural when they can direct their subordinates' activities. Others operate more comfortably in a team role.

Perhaps one's value system is the major force within a manager that moves him or her toward either a boss-centered or a subordinate-centered leadership pattern. How strongly does a manager feel that subordinates should have a share in making the decisions of the department? Douglas McGregor outlined two opposing managerial assumptions regarding the attitude and behavior of workers.[1] He called these Theory X and Theory Y. The basic assumptions of each of these theories are shown in Figure 5-7. A manager who accepts the assumptions of Theory X will tend to be a work-centered, authoritarian leader. Another whose values closely follow Theory Y assumptions will tend to emphasize a participative, group-centered leadership style.

Forces in the Subordinates

If a manager gets "yes" answers to most or all of certain questions, he or she will tend to stress a subordinate-centered leadership style. These questions are:

1. Do the members of my department have a high desire for independence?
2. Are they ready to assume responsibility?
3. Can they tolerate uncertainty?
4. Are they deeply interested in the problem to be solved?
5. Do they understand and accept the company's objectives?
6. Do they have the knowledge and experience to deal with the problem?
7. Do they expect to share in the decision making?

"No" answers to these questions move the manager toward a more boss-centered pattern of leadership.

1. Douglas McGregor, *The Human Side of Enterprise* (New York: McGraw-Hill Book Company, Inc., 1960).

Figure 5-7   Opposing Theories of Worker Attitude and Behavior

Theory X	Theory Y
1. Work is distasteful. It is an onerous chore to be performed in order to survive.	1. Work is as normal as play.
2. The average person has an inherent dislike of work and will avoid it if possible.	2. External control and the threat of punishment are not the only means for directing effort toward company objectives. People will exercise self-direction and self-control in working toward objectives to which they are committed.
3. Most people must be coerced, controlled, directed, or threatened with punishment to get them to put forth adequate effort toward the achievement of company objectives.	3. Commitment to objectives depends upon the rewards associated with their achievement.
4. The average person prefers to be directed, wishes to avoid responsibility, has relatively little ambition, and wants security above all.	4. The average person learns under proper conditions not only to accept but also to seek responsibility.
	5. The capacity to exercise a relatively high degree of imagination, ingenuity, and creativity in the solution of organizational problems is widely, not narrowly, distributed in the population.
	6. Under the conditions of modern industrial life, the intellectual potentialities of the average human being are only partially utilized.

Figure 5-8   "The Leader Recognizes Forces in the Subordinates"

THE WALL STREET JOURNAL

"Caruthers, this memo shows unusual insight into the human condition."

SOURCE: From *The Wall Street Journal,* May 2, 1979, p. 22. Permission—Cartoon Features Syndicate.

Forces in the Situation

A manager's pattern of leadership depends greatly on the situation. Situational factors include the type of organization, the effectiveness of subordinates, the nature of the problem to be solved, and time pressures. Furthermore, each company has its own view of how a "good manager" operates. This view becomes ingrained in the folklore of an organization and pushes managers to behave in line with tradition.

Leadership skills do not come automatically when a person is made a manager. Effective managerial leadership is earned by the active understanding of the factors that influence individuals and groups to act the way they do, the dynamics of organizational life, and the needs, goals, and prejudices of the individual as a manager.

MOTIVATION

Current management thinking about motivation has been strongly influenced by the findings of behavioral scientists. But neither managers nor scientists feel that they have the key to the complex problem of work motivation. Much of the practice and study of motivation today centers around two theories: the needs hierarchy theory and the behavior modification theory.

Needs Hierarchy Theory

Have you ever received better grades on a paper or project than a person you think is smarter or more talented than you? It could be that the other person was not as highly motivated as you. **Motivation,** or the willingness to behave or act in a certain way, depends on the strength of a person's motives, as well as abilities. Motives — or the needs, wants, and drives within a person — are the forces that move a person to action. All of us have many motives, conscious and subconscious, and our behavior at a given point is usually determined by the strongest of our needs.

In this traditional view of motivation, the effective manager creates organizational conditions that will allow a person to satisfy his or her needs and, in the process, be willing to perform at the desired level. But how much of a psychoanalyst can a manager be? How can the manager determine a person's strongest needs at a certain point? Most managers cannot be psychoanalysts. But, as a starting point, they can be aware of A. H. Maslow's **hierarchy of needs,** a theory which proposes that basic human needs can be arranged in an ascending order.[2] The hierarchy of needs is shown in Figure 5-9.

Before Maslow's theory was developed, puzzling facts were noted. For example, it was generally assumed that people work to satisfy material needs. Money was thus assumed to be the great incentive. However, when attitude surveys were taken and working people were asked what was most important to them in their jobs, good wages

---

2. Abraham H. Maslow, *Motivation and Personality* (New York: Harper & Brothers, 1954).

Figure 5-9   **Hierarchy of Needs**

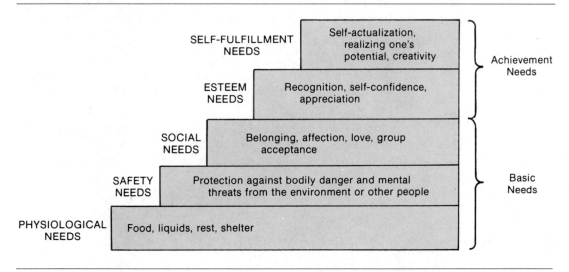

frequently took third or fourth place behind "challenging work," "chance for advancement," and even in some cases "a good boss."

Maslow's theory explains the seeming contradiction. He suggested that people emphasize the first level of these needs until it is relatively well satisfied. When the first level of needs is almost satisfied, the second level becomes dominant, and so on through the series. Once a certain level of needs is relatively satisfied, it ceases to operate as a primary motivator and is replaced by higher-order needs.

Behavior Modification Theory

Behavior modification techniques have been studied and used in both non-business and business applications. These techniques are usually identified with Harvard psychologist B. F. Skinner. His theory, known as **behavior modification or positive reinforcement,** holds that behavior is controlled by its immediate consequences. Individuals tend to repeat those behaviors which result in favorable consequences for them and avoid repeating those behaviors which result in unpleasant consequences. So, to modify an employee's behavior, proper control of a worker's environment is required. This involves the designing of methods to let individuals know how well they are meeting specific goals and the rewarding of improvements by praise, recognition, or some other positive consequence. Thus, the main tool of behavior modification is the *consequence of behavior* — how and when a desired behavior is reinforced.

Skinner's ideas were first applied to education, clinical psychology, and behavior management in public institutions such as mental hospitals. When Skinnerian techniques are used in formal business organizations as a contingency management technique, it is called **organizational behavior modification** (OB Mod.).[3] The basic steps for implementing organizational behavior modification are:

1. Specify the desired level of performance, preferably in quantitative terms.
2. Provide immediate feedback informing employees of their level of performance in relation to the standard.
3. Provide positive reinforcement in cases where feedback indicates that performance meets the standard, and encouragement where it does not. (This is in line with Skinner's belief that punishment for poor performance produces negative results in the long run.)

Major companies that have adopted all or parts of an OB Mod. program include Emery Air Freight, 3M Company, Frito-Lay, Addressograph-Multigraph, B. F. Goodrich, Weyerhaeuser, Ford Motor Co., AT&T, General Electric, and over a hundred more.

Needs Satisfaction v. Behavior Modification

The two main theories of motivation discussed above are far apart. Traditional non-Skinnerian "needs" theorists tend to concentrate on the subconscious causes of behavior to see *why* a person behaves in a given way. Skinnerian thinkers avoid psychoanalyzing the intrapersonal needs of the worker. Instead, they analyze the work situation itself, focusing on *what* causes a worker to behave as he or she does. Each approach has useful applications, especially when combined with other management techniques. As one person puts it:

> Motivation is not simply a force or condition that resides inside individuals. In addition to the personal side (personality and physical and emotional state), motivation is affected by the nature of a person's tasks or job requirements, the technology or physical support provided for the job, the actions of immediate supervisors and interactions with others in management, and the policies, rules, and structure of the organization.[4]

COMMUNICATION

Behavioral scientists have systematically studied many aspects of the process of communication. They have found, for example, that the typical manager spends about 70 percent of the working day in writing, reading, speaking, and listening. Moreover, the greater portion of the manager's time is usually spent in face-to-face, oral communication. Unfortunately not all managers are effective communicators.

---

3. Contingency management is discussed on pages 109–111.
4. Curtis W. Cook, "Guidelines for Managing Motivation," *Business Horizons* (April, 1980), p. 68.

Managers may feel that, if others hear or read what they say, communication has occurred. But hearing is not enough. The message must be interpreted, evaluated, and responded to. As one expert explains it, "Communication . . . occurs when people are led to experience shared perceptions and assumptions about what is real, what is relevant, and what is important in a particular situation."[5] Many aspects of communication could be discussed here. But two aspects that are especially important to managers if real communication is to occur are: the importance of feedback to performance and the difference between communication and information.

Importance of Feedback to Organizational Performance

Feedback can be defined as knowledge of results. Just as an atmospheric vacuum will not support life, a feedback vacuum will not support high-quality job performance. Three basic types of feedback are needed: informational feedback, corrective feedback, and reinforcing feedback.[6]

Informational Feedback

As we have noted, control is a major function of sound management. This includes monitoring results based on a flow of information to managers *up* the line. But this flow should be two-way — managers also must provide information *down* to those who do the work. A properly completed *feedback loop* of key control information allows an individual to make decisions on objective facts rather than on hunches or intuition.

Corrective Feedback

In contrast to informational feedback, corrective feedback is evaluative and judgmental. Busy managers often fight fires by pointing out mistakes, but nothing more. An effective manager, like an effective coach, not only points out mistakes, but also gets the individual headed in the right direction with corrective feedback.

Reinforcing Feedback

As we noted in the discussion of organizational behavior modification, positive consequences or reinforcements are one key to desired performance. In other words, reinforcing feedback is a prime means of achieving growth in job performance. People may find many things personally rewarding, so a manager must "fine-tune" reinforcing feedback to suit the individual.

---

5. Reed Sanderlin, "Ideational Item: Information Is Not Communication," *Business Horizons* (March/April, 1982), p. 40.
6. These three types of feedback are summarized from Robert Kreitner, "People Are Systems Too: Filling the Feedback Vacuum," *Business Horizons,* Vol. 20, No. 6 (December, 1977), pp. 56–57.

Difference Between Communication and Information

In his book *Future Shock*, published some fifteen years ago, Alvin Toffler commented upon the increased rate at which information of all types had begun to bombard us and accurately predicted that this rate could increase. Information may be defined as any type of data, perceptions, or ideas that can be arranged in a systematic, organized manner.[7] Examples of information include letters, reports, memoranda, computer printouts, and financial analyses.

These forms of information all contribute to a mass of paperwork that may reach overload proportions. People find themselves unable to handle either the volume of information or the intensity of it. An information crisis occurs when a person doesn't know how to interpret the masses of information in ways that make it relevant to action and decision making. Thus, employee performance can be directly affected by the ways that managers select, process, and transmit information as well as by the amounts transmitted. The following five points may help managers to clarify the difference between information and communication with employees:

1. More or better information directed at employees does not ensure communication.
2. Too much information, in whatever form it is transmitted, may actually prevent effective communication with employees.
3. Employees vary considerably in their abilities and willingness to process information.
4. Information is valuable only to the extent that it permits communication involving decision making and constructive action.
5. Employees need to be trained how to use the information they receive from inside and outside the organization.[8]

Thus, a starting point for managers is to realize that more information is not necessarily better communication.

MANAGEMENT BY OBJECTIVES

Perhaps no management approach is more clearly related to the management functions already discussed in this chapter than the currently popular area of **management by objectives** (MBO). Broadly, MBO is more than a technique or method. As George Odiorne, a leading MBO management thinker, puts it, "... the system of management by objectives goes beyond being a set of rules, a series of procedures, or even a set method of managing ... it is a particular way of thinking about management."[9] This way of thinking about management includes both a concept and a process.

---

7. Adapted from Sanderlin, *loc. cit.*
8. *Ibid.*, pp. 41–42.
9. George S. Odiorne, *Management by Objectives: A System of Managerial Leadership* (Belmont, CA: Fearon-Pitman Publishers, 1965), p. 54.

MBO: The Concept

An MBO system allows superiors and subordinates to establish jointly what they should accomplish. There are two key points here: participation and results. Participation in setting objectives increases the subordinates' understanding of organizational processes and what is expected of them. MBO focuses on results and not on the work itself. The MBO concept rests on the belief that organizational performance is greatly influenced by both the degree to which individuals or groups are motivated to use their abilities and the degree to which their accomplishments are recognized.

MBO: The Process

MBO clearly is a management planning and control technique because the mutually-set objectives become the standards of control. However, MBO doesn't leave planning and control to chance. As the cycle of MBO in Figure 5-10 illustrates, planning and control are practiced in a formal and precise manner. And managers are still experimenting with other ways to use the MBO process.

Even though the MBO cycle seems complex, Odiorne boils it down to three basic elements:

1. Identify common goals.
2. Define each individual's major area of responsibility in terms of expected results.
3. Use these measures as guides for operating the unit and assessing the contribution of each of its members. [10]

The MBO process is a learning process for both bosses and subordinates. Because it involves participation and feedback, it helps to provide the motivating factors of growth, development, achievement, and recognition.

ORGANIZATIONAL COMPLEXITY AND CONTINGENCY MANAGEMENT

The basic management functions, concepts, and tools discussed in this chapter form an important management base. Yet they do not, by themselves, provide a workable approach to organization and management. Instead, they are a relatively small part of the rapidly growing body of managerial knowledge needed to deal with complex organizations in modern societies.

One major area of management thinking that hopes to provide a workable framework for dealing with organizational complexities is called **contingency management.** It focuses on the relationship of the organization to its environment, rather than

---

10. *Ibid.*, pp. 55–56.

Figure 5-10   The Cycle of Management by Objectives

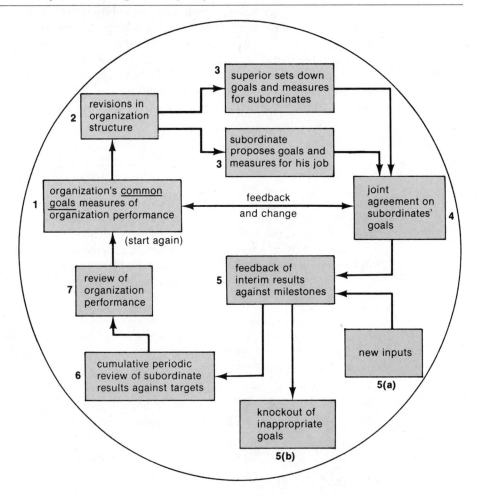

SOURCE: George S. Odiorne, *Management by Objectives: A System of Managerial Leadership* (Belmont, CA: Fearon-Pitman Publishers, 1965), p. 78. Reproduced by permission.

assuming that there is "one best way" to manage. Contingency management is concerned with the appropriate management techniques that recognize the factors, forces, and variables—i.e., the *contingencies*—in the organization and environment. Organizational contingencies include such factors as corporate philosophies, managerial personalities, and the nature and structure of work. Furthermore, the social, political, economic, and technological elements in the environment set the climate for the company. Although still in its early stages, contingency management offers the possibility of a framework for pulling together different management theories and clarifying the role of management in complex organizations.

SUMMARY   The job of management in any organization is to make cooperative, specialized efforts function properly—to combine and convert people, machines, money, and materials into a useful goal-oriented enterprise. There are many dimensions to the manager's job, and managerial work can be discussed from such standpoints as managerial levels (institutional, administrative, and technical), managerial skills (administrative, human relations, and technical), the process of decision making, and the traditional management functions (planning, organizing, staffing, directing, controlling, representing, and innovating).

These various dimensions of a manager's job are interrelated, and together they form an important management base. Nevertheless, they are a relatively small part of our growing managerial knowledge. For example, more recent managerial thinking includes such important concepts as organizational behavior modification, management by objectives, and contingency management.

Also, managerial work is people work. Effective managers must go beyond the basic dimensions of their job and recognize the importance of leadership, motivation, and communication in getting things done through other people.

Managers face a challenge that is both exciting and never-ending. They cannot simply adapt after the fact to changing forces in the environment. They must be a dynamic, innovating force at all levels of the organization.

BACK
TO THE
CHAPTER
OPENER

1. Is innovation a basic function of management?
2. What are other functions of managers?
3. Which managerial skill is more important to top managers in a new company with sophisticated technology?
4. How, would you guess, do professional managers differ from the innovative managers in the article?
5. What are three forces the innovative manager/leader might need to be aware of in choosing a leadership style?

BUSINESS
TERMS

institutional management or top management	90	directing	97
administrative management or middle management	90	controlling	97
		leadership	101
operating management or technical management	90	motivation	104
		hierarchy of needs	104
administrative skill	91	behavior modification or positive reinforcement	105
human relations skill	92	organizational behavior modification	106
technical skill	92		
consensus management	94	feedback	107
planning	95	management by objectives	108
strategic planning	96	contingency management	109
staffing	97		

1. Which managerial skill would be more important to an engineering manager at the administrative level of an organization?

2. What makes a managerial decision strategic in nature?

3. What is the difference between intuition and impulsiveness in making decisions?

4. Coordination seems just as important as the seven basic managerial functions. Why isn't coordination a basic function of management?

5. What is the difference between an objective and a plan?

6. The planning and controlling functions of management often are discussed together. Why?

7. "Our company doesn't have a PR (Public Relations) department. We expect each manager to represent our company effectively to the public." Do you think this is a good approach? Explain.

8. It seems that the ability to innovate requires specialized, technical skill. How then can managers who lack this skill be expected to innovate?

9. What type of communications feedback would be more basic to OB Mod? To MBO?

10. How does a manager know when information is effectively communicated?

1. The FunTime Company is a successful, medium-size producer of games, dolls, and novelty items. But even its president, Jerry McManus, was surprised at the company's current performance—the best in its 10-year history. He even consented to discuss its business strategy with a business reporter from a national newspaper.

   When asked by the reporter about his strategic planning, he responded, "That's easy! We just let the big boys do the skull work. We're a relatively small company, and we're willing to sit back and be number two." The reporter noted the importance of innovation in this competitive industry and wondered how FunTime could remain competitive by following the bigger companies. McManus answered that FunTime let others develop and test new products. It then watched the results to see if the item was worth copying.

   "Of course, we add our own little frills and goodies to the basic idea, and we sometimes lose out on the big initial profits of a new item," he explained. "But we also suffer far less flops than the front-row innovators, and it sure makes our planning and forecasting a lot easier."

   Prepare a two-page report evaluating McManus as a planner and innovator.

2. Elsie Kellinger was the founder of a string of donut shops in the eastern United States. An energetic, aggressive person, Kellinger rarely was seen in her headquarters office. Rather, she spent almost all her time traveling through the company's regions and pulling what she called "sneak attacks on the troops." She felt this first-hand exposure to the performance of the donut shops provided her with ammunition for her control efforts, and she didn't hesitate to take steps to ensure that performance measured up to the expected standards. In a visit to five outlets in the Atlanta area, she found four shops with old and depleted stocks of donuts, indifferent clerks, and littered parking lots. Shortly after that visit, she remarked, "The Atlanta area has made great progress under new management. That's one of the advantages of surprise visits."

   Discuss the pros and cons of Kellinger's managerial approach.

3. Analyze the style and attributes of a manager who you feel is also an outstanding leader. Include the following points in your observations:

    a. What leadership style does this person usually use?

    b. Is this person especially effective as a motivator? A communicator? Both?

    c. At what level in the organization does this person work, and which managerial functions appear to be the most important to the job?

    d. Is he or she effective in all situations, or perhaps more effective in certain kinds of situations or relationships?

    e. How does this individual recognize and reward good work?

    Discuss your findings in an oral class report.

On the Road Again

CHICAGO. They called it "Black Friday" when the first 150 people were fired without warning from the manufacturing firm I worked for. The ax didn't hit me right away, but I knew it soon would. We had been taken over by another firm, and a management purge was under way. I was a rising department head, but a sympathetic boss tipped me off: Brace yourself; you could be on their list. So I cut my travel and stayed close to the office in a kind of death watch.

The whole idea seemed impossible. As a young man, I had learned to value "the work ethic." You give of your talents, energy and loyalty. In return, you get tenure, financial security, job satisfaction. That philosophy guided me through 17 years of steady advancement.

Then came what I thought would be the keystone of my career: A responsible position with a major producer of transportation equipment. What's more, they had recruited me, a heady experience. For four years, I had worked to turn around a troubled department. It was the most satisfying work I'd ever done, and the rewards followed — recognition, salary, bonuses, everything to feed the ego.

The Ax Falls. With that background, I thought that I could handle it when the dreaded phone call finally came a month after Black Friday. Thanks to the advance warning from my boss, I'd had time to prepare severance demands, which the new management agreed to. But the magnitude of the termination finally hit me when I turned in my company ID. At 43, with one child in college and another college bound, I was out in the cold...

My severance package included the services of an outplacement specialist. I hadn't hunted a job in 17 years. We put together a professional résumé — and then the specialist began digging into my state of mind, uncovering emotions that surprised me...

On top of all that, we found out in the mock, taped employment interviews that I was a poor job applicant. Here I was, a polished professional at making business presentations, but I was doing a lousy job of selling myself. The counseling taught me how to sharpen the positive points and restore dwindling self-confidence...

Fading Chances. Some employers considered me overqualified. Two potential jobs vanished when economic pressures forced the firms to trim staff...

With anxiety growing, I shifted my sights and decided to try the defense industry, which I had left years earlier. I contacted a big company, and, at last, luck was with me.

The job I landed was comparable to the one I held long ago. But after 3½ months of looking, I was happy to be working again. Now, I feel like I am starting over, trying to earn the new company's confidence and rebuild my own self-esteem. The need to assume more challenge gnaws at me. I want to recapture that feeling that I'm in control of my destiny once again, and I want to regain that faith in the old work ethic.

SOURCE: "'You're Fired!' Memories of a Dark Day," from a copyrighted article in *U.S. News & World Report*, April 5, 1982.

6

Staffing the Organization

Objectives:

- Distinguish between the traditional personnel approach and the human resources approach to staffing.
- Describe the basic steps in the staffing function.
- Distinguish among an executive search firm, a private employment agency, and an employment or job counselor firm.
- Identify the steps in the employment process.
- Discuss training and development at the three levels of an executive career model.
- Distinguish between involuntary termination and dehiring.
- Describe the key federal legislation on equal employment opportunity and affirmative action.
- Discuss the occupational and wage status of women in the work force.
- Discuss the status of black managers in the work force.
- Explain the importance of the Age Discrimination in Employment Act in the 1980s.

The early 1980s have not exactly been vintage years for our nation and for business. In fact, many people would see this period as one of disruption and change. Some of the prime suspects in this period include restrictive government regulations, lack of capital formation, reduced R&D expenditures, and lagging productivity. Of these, human productivity is one area where management can do something. The success of organizations of all types — whether in periods of black ink or of red ink — depends on the skills and abilities of the people who comprise them. The key to an organization's survival is how effectively it builds on the talents of its people while minimizing their weaknesses.

The staffing function of management is the heart of this challenging and important effort. And human resources executives are moving higher up in the corporate ladder as firms continue their search for better workers and managers; strive to comply with federal rules in the areas of pensions, equal opportunity, and health and safety; and provide worker satisfaction in an era of high expectations.

CHANGES IN THE STAFFING FUNCTION

Activities connected with the staffing function include the recruitment, selection, hiring, training and development, job termination, and retirement of employees. In carrying out these activities, management should have a general concern for the needs of people in the organization. It is important to note that, within the past ten years, the scope and orientation of this function has changed greatly.

The Staffing Function: Then

There was a time when a paycheck was the necessary and sufficient condition to tie a person to a job, regardless of its content. In the generally smaller companies of the past, this basic need for the paycheck led the worker to accept even a barely tolerable working relationship with the boss. Owner/managers often handled the basic personnel matters involved in staffing the company. They hired, paid, and sometimes fired their employees. Employees, in turn, did their jobs as long as they were physically able. When their ability to work ceased, so did their jobs and paychecks.

By 1900, companies used a number of specialists to help in such matters as employment, wage rate-setting, safety, health, and training. These groups of specialists were the forerunners of the formal personnel department that surfaced in some larger companies around 1915.

Enter: Human Resources Management

Today many corporate personnel departments have been replaced by human resources departments, or divisions. In some instances the personnel department has become a unit within the human resources activity. This change is more than a play on words. It represents a difference in attitude and approach on the part of workers and bosses to the relationships involved in attracting, developing, and keeping a competent and productive work force.

Today's blue-collar and white-collar workers want more from their jobs than just a paycheck. They want satisfying jobs with salaries that are fair in relation to their co-workers' salaries. And they want a fair chance for promotion based on objective measurement of their performances rather than on the subjective whims of their bosses or on the basis of their sex, skin color, or age.

From the manager's viewpoint the **human resources approach** formally recognizes that all persons in an organization, regardless of their level or job, are potential sources of innovation and talent. This differs markedly from the traditional viewpoint that workers are basically lazy and unwilling to perform above the minimum level necessary to keep their jobs.

Matters that concern human resources are expected to take up to half of top management's time by the mid-1980s. Decisions about human resources are increasingly being made by an executive who reports directly to the president or the CEO. Moreover, human resources directors or managers now command salaries that match those of managers in marketing, production, and finance.

The many functions of the human resources department, or personnel department, fall naturally into the following divisions: employment, training and development, employee services, safety and health, human resources planning, wages and salary administration, and labor relations. These divisions are shown in Figure 6-1.

Figure 6-1   Organization Chart of the Human Resources Department

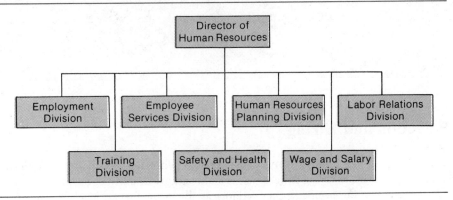

Figure 6-2 lists some representative functions performed in five human resources divisions. (Wages and salaries are discussed in Chapter 7; labor relations, in Chapter 8.) The scope and degree of these functions will vary from firm to firm. A small company may have only one person to perform a few basic functions. A large company may have an extensive human resources division that performs even more functions than those noted in Figure 6-2.

BASIC STEPS IN STAFFING

Regardless of the size or nature of an organization, the following basic steps in staffing must be handled: selection and hiring, training and development, job termination, and retirement. Each of these four steps is discussed in this section. In addition to these steps, the human resources manager often is responsible for some employee services, as well as employee safety and health.

Figure 6-2   Representative Human Resources Functions

Division	Functions
• Employment	• Job analysis, description, and specification; developing sources of workers; administration of steps in the employment process; induction and orientation to the job; follow-ups and personal job evaluations; transfers, promotions, and involuntary terminations; retirements; legal aspects of selection decisions; lie detection and psychological testing
• Training and development	• Company, or "vestibule," schools; sponsoring of new workers; apprenticeship systems; job rotation; retraining and upgrading skills; employee skills inventories; career pathing; performance rating systems; assessment centers
• Employee services	• Eating facilities; recreational opportunities; insurance and hospitalization plans; employee counseling; legal advice; credit unions; "cafeteria" approaches to benefits and compensation; suggestion systems
• Safety and health	• Installation of safety devices in buildings and on machines; dissemination of safety information; conformance to requirements of workers' compensation acts; periodic physical exams; programs to reduce industrial fatigue
• Human resources planning	• Records and reports; statistical analysis of personnel records; publication of manuals for the guidance of other departments; development of systems and procedures, including computerized information retrieval systems for human resources; audits and evaluations; research in employee motivation and productivity

Selection and Hiring

Today many companies are in either an official or an unofficial hiring freeze, and this hiring pattern may remain with us for a while. So, selection and hiring now focus on specific, specialized jobs at all but the highest levels. Companies want a precise fit in skills and expectations between themselves and the people they hire. This precise fit requires care in pinpointing the nature and requirements of the positions to be filled.

Analyzing the Jobs

The first step in selecting and hiring for a group of jobs involves **job analysis,** which means collecting and organizing information about jobs. The purpose of job analysis is to pinpoint the requirements of each position that needs to be filled. These requirements include the following:

1. Location of the job.
2. Tasks, duties, and responsibilities of the job.
3. Mental and physical level of work to be performed.
4. Equipment, tools, and machines to be used.
5. Working conditions and hazards.
6. Compensation and the opportunities for promotion.
7. Extent of job training required.

All this information about a job is written up in a **job description,** as shown in Figure 6-3.

Sometimes a job specification is also prepared. The **job specification** lists the personal qualifications and special skills, aptitudes, or professional background needed of the person filling the job.

Figure 6-3   **Job Description**

JOB TITLE: HUMAN RESOURCES CLERK

Department: Human Resources   **Date:** March 26, 198-

Employees in Department: 12

Employees on this Job: 3

General Description of the Job

Works under the supervision of the Human Resources Manager; assists in clerical routine of induction which involves interviewing new workers; performs a variety of clerical and stenographic work.

Specific Duties of the Job

1. Interviews new workers after they have been given induction information such as hours, working conditions, services, etc., to verify personnel information and prepare records; checks information on application, statement of availability, draft, citizenship, and the like; obtains necessary information for income tax withholding, and determines classification; prepares forms for hospitalization, group insurance, and bond deductions; assigns clock number, makes up time card and badge card.

2. Calls previous employer to get reference information while applicant is being interviewed; may check references by mail after employee is hired, and occasionally records information from Dun & Bradstreet on personnel card.

3. Telephones employee's department or home after extended absence to determine when employee is expected to return, if at all; follows same procedure at end of leave of absence.

4. Handles stenographic work of the Human Resources Manager.

5. Does miscellaneous clerical work; assigns clock numbers and makes up time cards for employees transferred between departments; keeps record of equipment loaned to employees, such as micrometers, goggles, etc.; maintains current address file of employees in service; performs other clerical duties as assigned.

6. May substitute for Receptionist for short periods; give induction information to new employees in absence of Human Resources Induction Clerk; escort new workers to departments; administer tests.

Recruiting Employees

There are many sources from which to recruit new employees. The source to be used depends on the level of education and degree of skill needed for the jobs to be filled. Other factors to consider in recruiting are the nature of the organization's business and the population of the area in which it is located. Common sources of nonmanagement employees include referrals by current employees, walk-in applicants, private employment agencies, trade and technical schools, classified ads, and union hiring halls.

In recruiting executive-level employees, the two greatest sources are a company's own employees and referrals to people known personally by the company's own employees. Other sources include consultants or executive search agencies, placement services of professional societies and alumni groups, career centers at conventions, advertisements in newspapers and technical journals, and private employment agencies.

It is important to one's job-hunting success and checkbook to know the differences among three types of agencies: executive search firms, private employment agencies, and employment or job counselor firms.

Executive Search Firms. An **executive search firm or "headhunter"** is an organization hired by the employer to seek out someone for a specific position. Headhunters get paid by the employer in all cases, usually on an annual retainer. The fees often run from 30 to 33 percent of the executive's first-year salary and expected bonus. These stiff fees are encouraging some companies to bypass executive recruiters and search for executives on their own.

Private Employment Agencies. A **private employment agency** interviews and classifies job candidates, usually for a fee, and sends the best prospects to employers who have job openings. The agency usually is paid by the employer and sometimes by the job-seeker. In either case, usually the fee is paid only when the job is filled. Hoping to collect a fee, some agencies send job-seekers out on interviews for jobs even though the job-seekers may not be ideally suited for the job openings.

Employment or Job Counselor Firms. Especially noteworthy for the job-seeker is the **employment or job counselor firms.** These firms may be large or small. Sometimes they don't make it clear that they are *not* employment agencies. Actually, they are "packagers" of talent. They offer help in preparing résumés, conduct seminars on job-search techniques, and mail lists of large companies that are available in school and public libraries. Most important, they ask the job-seeker to pay anywhere from $500 to several thousand dollars in advance for this service, with no guarantee of being placed in a job.

The Employment Process

With a job description, a job specification, and a group of applicants for the job, the human resources department can begin a series of steps in the employment process, as shown in Figure 6-4. The combination of steps usually progresses from the less expensive to the more expensive steps. These include:

Figure 6-4   **The Employment Process**

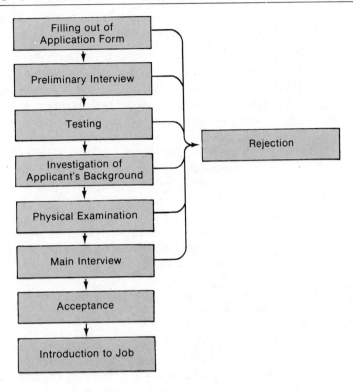

1. Completed application form.
2. Preliminary interview.
3. Tests.
4. Investigation of applicant's background.
5. Physical examination.
6. The main interview.

The first few steps in the employment process are relatively inexpensive to the company, and each may indicate basic reasons why the applicant is unsuited for the job. The applicant usually is hired or rejected in the main interview. In some companies the interviewer must follow a form with a fixed series of questions. Other companies allow their interviewers a free hand in conducting discussions with job applicants. In either case, interviewers should know what types of questions they can and cannot legally ask during the interview.

The responsibility of the employment division for the new employee does not end when the person accepts the job and is officially hired. At this point most new employees are concerned about their fit with the company and their new job, and they are eager to get off to a good start. So, the effective employment process includes a program of job induction and job orientation.

Induction to the Job. The details of **job induction,** which involves properly introducing a new employee to the job and to fellow employees, vary with different firms. Many companies have found that a careful and friendly job induction effort encourages the best abilities and frame of mind of the new employee right from the start.

Job Orientation. New employees need to be oriented to certain policies, rules, and other matters concerning the company and their jobs in order to fit into the big picture. **Job orientation** may include the daily work routine, safety rules, company pay practices, employees' organizations, recreational facilities, the availability and location of medical services, and the business of the company. This information often is provided in a handbook that the new employee is given and asked to read. Unfortunately not all handbooks are easy to read, and some provide little information to the new employee. Many orientation programs supplement the handbook with discussions, films, and company tours.

Proper selection and hiring should include an effective induction and orientation program that is carefully tailored to strengthen the security and sense of belonging of each new employee. The long-term relationship between the company and its human resources is too important to overlook these vital steps in the employment process.

Training and Development

All employees require some degree of training to develop into effective, valued human resources. Training and development are related concepts. Training refers to the many various programs that may be offered to employees—both managers and workers—to help them develop their capabilities and to progress in their work. Development is the progress the person actually makes and may include conceptual or intellectual growth along with practical performance. Often the term "training" means vocational skill training in the short run, and managerial development is viewed as a long-run process. We will emphasize managerial training and development.

The bird is the fastest moving creature. Speeds higher than 185 mph have been attributed to peregrine falcons. Humans, of course, move less quickly. But there is one group which is known for its remarkable mobility—the American business executive. This mobility occurs both within and between companies, and most companies hope not to lose their up-and-coming executives after extensive training and development.

Two related trends in managerial succession planning are evident for the 1980s. These are: a concern for succession into general management and an emphasis on experience and performance in management succession. A survey of human resources managers from 329 American corporations revealed that 41 percent of these companies are deeply concerned about management succession. Furthermore, 50 percent of them felt that general line management positions would be most critical.[1]

---

1. Allan D. R. Stern, "Retaining Good Managers Without Golden Handcuffs," *Business Horizons* (November/December, 1981), pp. 76–77.

The second trend—an emphasis on performance and experience in management succession—favors the insider with a proven track record of results obtained over the years of employment. Thus, most companies prefer to "grow their own" executives rather than to hire from outside the company. This practice provides managerial resources with known abilities and attitudes. It also helps to maintain the morale of the junior executives in the company. As we noted in Chapter 5, there are three management levels: technical or operating, administrative or middle, and top or institutional. An in-house career plan leading to a top-level managerial position might resemble the model in Figure 6-5.

Figure 6-5   Executive Career Model

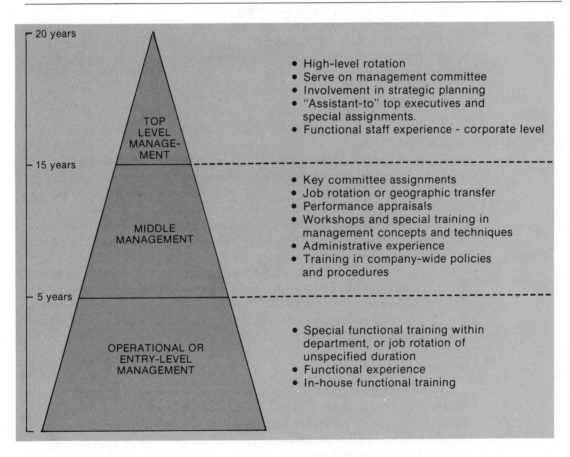

Training for Operating Managers

Front-line supervisors and management trainees at the operating level are concerned with building the skills needed to carry out their programs and duties within the budget and getting the product out the door. On-the-job training by the managers is often the best type of training at this level, especially when accompanied by a clear effort to demonstrate and practice the techniques. Another procedure is job rotation, which is designed to familiarize junior executives with the details of the many positions that may be available and to reveal any special interests and abilities they may possess.

If a company, large or small, sees a shortage of executives developing at higher levels, it may take steps to protect itself by identifying and isolating its "superstars" early and placing them on a *fast-track.* These promising persons will receive intensified training and increased responsibilities along with pay and benefit packages to hold them with the company. IBM, for example, routinely places some of its fastest-track young managers in 18-month to 3-year assistant jobs with factory managers, top company scientists, or higher-up executives.

Fast-trackers may also be provided with a *mentor* — a trusted advisor, sounding board, and coach. Ordinarily, mentors are not provided but must be sought out. Smart young executives — fast-trackers or not — will seek out mentors as an important aspect of their development.

Training for Middle Managers

Until recently, a transfer to the personnel department was seen as a trip to a corporate Siberia. Fast-rising executives wanted to be in departments like finance or marketing, which had a clear impact on corporate profits. But in the 1980s, U. S. companies are expected to face some human resources "hot-spots." As a result some young, fast-track managers are being shifted into personnel work to help the companies deal with human resources problems.

Perhaps the toughest human resources problem on the horizon is the crowding on the promotion ladder in the middle-management ranks. A large number of young workers from the post-war baby boom entered corporations in the mid-1960s and early 1970s. This baby-boom generation will be reaching its 30s and 40s during a time of reduced business growth. This push into middle-management compounds the problem that most companies are like pyramids. The higher a person goes, the fewer slots there are. Therefore, many companies face two problems at the middle-management level. First, who should be trained and developed for higher-level slots? Second, how can the company stimulate the large group of middle managers who will not be able to move up or don't want to move up?

Who Should Move Up? Not everyone at the middle management level is suited to become a top-level manager. Therefore, a key developmental activity at this level is performance appraisal to determine which managers should be groomed for upward progress in the organization. In a smaller company, performance appraisal often is handled subjectively on a person-to-person basis over the course of time. In larger companies, however, many people from various divisions may appear qualified for top-level responsibilities. Since present job performance does not necessarily measure potential for a new job, an assessment center may be used to judge the potential for future performance.

The first industrial assessment center was pioneered by AT&T in 1956. It is estimated that over 1,000 companies now have used this method of employee evaluation. In this approach groups of managers are rated in a 3- to 5-day program by teams of upper-level managers, human resources specialists, and psychologists. These ratings are derived from the results of extensive interviews, performance in situational decision-making exercises, analysis of personality tests, and peer evaluations by others being assessed. The judgments are pooled by the assessors at an evaluation meeting, and they agree on the overall evaluation. Usually only large companies can afford the time and effort required for an assessment center.

Managers moving into the middle-management level need broader management theory and techniques than the specific techniques they have been using at the operating level. Possible means to develop the appreciation of broader managerial concepts are university "case courses," conference programs and workshops, and geographical transfers.

Who Will Not Move Up? Many managers may welcome a career plateau as a relief from competition and pressure. At this point, they may work harder to maintain their job situation rather than move upward. So, human resources managers must try to stimulate both those who don't want promotions and those who do but won't get them. To do this, companies are trying flexible programs such as horizontal job moves, assignments to special-project teams, and tasks that permit more independence on the job.

Training for Top-Level Managers

According to a *Wall Street Journal*/Gallup survey, "chief executive officers of the 1,300 largest U. S. corporations typically work 60 to 70 hours a week, travel 6 to 10 days a month, and often give up their weekends for business meetings. On their way to the top, many have relocated six or more times."[2] Furthermore, according to the same survey, "two-thirds of these chief executives say they already have a clear idea who their successors will be . . . but the smaller the company, the less certain the chief executive is likely to be about a successor."[3]

Not everyone at the top-level management becomes a CEO. In fact, no universal definition of "top-level executive" exists. However, one or more of the following criteria have been suggested for a person to be considered a top-level executive. Such a person receives an annual salary of $100,000 or more, reports directly to the CEO

2. Frank Allen, "Chief Executives Typically Work 60-Hour Weeks, Put Careers First," *The Wall Street Journal,* August 19, 1980, p. 31. Reprinted by permission of *The Wall Street Journal,* © Dow Jones & Company, Inc. (1980). All Rights Reserved.

3. Frank Allen, "Many Bosses Already Have Decided Who Successors Will Be and Why," *The Wall Street Journal,* November 18, 1980, p. 33. Reprinted by permission of *The Wall Street Journal,* © Dow Jones & Company, Inc. (1980). All Rights Reserved.

or the chairperson, carries the title of executive vice-president or higher, or is a group executive in a conglomerate.[4] Training and development at this level varies greatly by company size and degree of product diversification. A small company usually will rely on a one-to-one training of the top officer's successor. This can be done by an "assistant-to" position and by special assignments.

Large companies often find that senior managers know much about their own divisions or groups but not enough about the rest of the company. Training and development for such managers is in the form of a "broadening" program. This can be achieved by service on the corporate-level management committee, participation in strategic planning units, lateral transfer through the rotation of jobs with other executives included in the broadening program, and appointment to group- or sector-executive slots.

One consistent theme holds among companies of various sizes. Personal character apparently matters most to heads of companies when they evaluate their possible successors. "More than half the chiefs of large- and medium-size companies specifically mention such traits as honesty, intelligence, good judgment, and self-reliance, as do 43 percent of chiefs of small companies."[5]

Job Termination

As the story goes, when Henry Ford wanted to fire someone, he did it quickly and absolutely. The terminated person would return from a vacation to find the office furniture stacked in the hall and a note on the door informing this person that he was fired! Today, however, firing a subordinate is probably one of the most unpleasant tasks that a superior must face. From an organizational point of view, the pattern of firing managers differs from that of terminating lower-echelon employees. Managers may be dehired while lower-level employees are subject to some form of involuntary termination.

Dehiring

The process of getting an employee to quit voluntarily so that it is unnecessary to fire that person is called **dehiring**. Other terms used in place of dehiring are *selecting-out* and *outplacing*. When a firm wants to help a dehired executive get a job elsewhere, it may retain an outplacement counselor to help the executive with her or his self-appraisal, résumé, job-search strategy, and interviewing techniques. On the other hand, if the firm wants to keep an executive but cannot correct his or her failings, it may turn to mid-career counseling. Such counseling should help the executive under-

---

4. Judson Gooding, "Firing at the Top," *Across the Board* (October, 1981), p. 17.
5. *Ibid.*

stand what the problem is, how his or her behavior affects the other people on the job, and how to correct the problem.

One of the reasons that may lead to dehiring is **job burnout,** a syndrome in which victims suffer a specific set of job-related symptoms. Such symptoms may be a negative attitude toward themselves and their jobs, chronic fatigue, low energy, and irritability. Job burnout differs from mid-life crises, which are often related to personal difficulties such as divorce, money problems, or aging. Job burnout can occur early in careers and may lead to apathy or "retiring on the job." More often it affects employees who deal extensively with other people on the job.

Involuntary Termination

The involuntary termination of an employee's services may take either of two forms: a discharge or a layoff. A **discharge** is a permanent separation from a company and may be a blot on the person's work record. While a **layoff** may be either permanent or temporary, it usually does not reflect on the employee's character or competence. In bad economic times, some companies resort to a type of partial layoff called **nonvoluntary rotation.** Such rotation is only a short-term solution which allows employees to work shorter weeks to keep fellow employees on the job at least part-time. Rotated employees do get to keep their fringe benefits, which they otherwise would lose.

Retirement

In 1950 almost 27 percent of women and men age 65 or older stayed in the labor force. Now, fewer than 12.5 percent of them remain in the labor force once they reach the age of 65. Prior to the 1978 amendments to the Age Discrimination Act, about half the employers in the United States had policies requiring employees to step down at 65. The mandatory retirement age now is 70.

As a general rule, the desire to retire decreases the higher up a person climbs on occupational and career ladders. Auto workers and miners, for example, work long and hard years. Many of them welcome the chance to retire even before age 60. On the management side of the coin, the senior executive who at age 65 is in good physical and mental shape may be at the peak of possible contributions to the organization.

Human resources management faces increasing challenges in matching the attitudes toward retirement with the human resources needs of the company. More and more companies are taking at least two basic steps. The first step is offering pre-retirement planning programs (PREPPs) to encourage employees to think about the problems and benefits of retirement before they actually stop working. The second is to develop career continuation, or career extension, programs for senior executives. Such programs provide for the senior executive to leave the executive suite at age 65, but to continue working for the company in some other professional capacity, sometimes with reduced hours.

DISCRIMINATION IN EMPLOYMENT

Major federal laws and regulations to end discrimination in hiring and in training and development have been on the books for some time. But human resources management, in general, still has a long way to go in recognizing the rights and abilities of certain groups which have suffered employment discrimination in our society. The two main areas that human resources managers must deal with are equal employment opportunity and affirmative-action programs for such groups as women, minorities, the elderly, and the disabled.

The Civil Rights Act and the EEOC

The key federal legislation on equal employment opportunity is Title VII of the Civil Rights Act of 1964. This Act forbids discrimination by employers, labor unions, or employment agencies based on an individual's race, color, religion, sex, or national origin. It applies to hiring or firing; wages; fringe benefits; classifying, referring, assigning, or promoting; assigning use of facilities; training, retraining, or apprenticeships; or any other terms, conditions, or privileges of employment.

Title VII also created the five-member Equal Employment Opportunity Commission (EEOC) to administer Title VII. Prior to 1972 the EEOC was limited to informal conciliation efforts to eliminate alleged discriminatory employment practices. The Equal Employment Opportunity Act of 1972 amended Title VII of the Civil Rights Act of 1964 to permit the Commission to sue in a U. S. District Court on its behalf or for other claimants when it believes discrimination has taken place.

Affirmative-Action Programs

To ensure that the equal employment opportunity clause is observed by employers who have contracts with the federal government, Executive Order No. 11246 was issued in 1965 and later amended by Executive Order No. 11375. While these executive orders required "affirmative action" by employers with federal government contracts, they did not specify what this really meant. The new standards for affirmative action were set forth in 1972 under Revised Order No. 4. This Order requires that, within 120 days from start of a contract, each prime government contractor and subcontractor with 50 or more employees and a contract of $50,000 or more must develop a written affirmative-action compliance program for each of its establishments.

The Office of Federal Contract Compliance (OFCC) considers an **affirmative-action program** acceptable when it includes:

1. An analysis of areas within which the contractor is deficient in the utilization of minority groups and women.
2. Goals and timetables to which the contractor's effort must be directed in achieving prompt and full utilization of minorities and women in areas where deficiencies exist.

These goals are not rigid, but they require the employer's good-faith effort in living up to them. Human resources management must accept the challenge and opportunity to achieve balance in the staffing function. This includes eliminating discrimination against women and minorities or on the basis of age, religion, or disabilities.

Discrimination Against Women

Sometimes charts and tables seem cold and impersonal, but they provide a way of presenting useful comparative data without making the reader wade through a lot of words. For example, Table 6-1 shows that by mid-1982 about 48 million women were in the work force, forming about 43 percent of the country's entire work force. Table 6-1 also shows that the participation rate for women was 52.4 percent, and this rate is expected to reach about 65 percent by 1990. Despite this remarkable increase of women in the work force, the twin problems of working women — under-employment and underpay — still remain.

Table 6-1   **Employment Status of the Population 16 Years and over by Sex, Race, and Hispanic Origin: Second Quarter, 1982 (Numbers in Thousands)**

EMPLOYMENT STATUS	BLACK		HISPANIC ORIGIN[3]		WHITE		TOTAL	
	Men	Women	Men	Women	Men	Women	Men	Women
Civilian labor force[1]	5,769	5,441	3,577	2,398	55,339	40,872	62,594	47,505
Participation rate[2]	68.9	52.9	80.4	49.2	77.8	52.3	76.9	52.4
Employed	4,561	4,485	3,123	2,065	50,710	37,598	56,684	43,148
Unemployed	1,118	956	454	332	4,630	3,273	5,910	4,357
Unemployment rate	19.4	17.6	12.7	13.9	8.4	8.0	9.4	9.2

[1]All persons classified as employed or unemployed.
[2]The civilian labor force as a percent of the civilian noninstitutional population.
[3]Includes all persons who identify themselves as of Mexican, Puerto Rican (living on the mainland), Cuban, Central or South American, or other Hispanic origin or descent. Persons of Hispanic origin may be of any race; hence, they are included among the numbers for whites, blacks, and other races.

SOURCE: U.S. Department of Labor, Bureau of Labor Statistics, *Employment in Perspective: Minority Workers* (Second Quarter, 1982).

Occupational Discrimination

The jobs held by women today are generally in the same fields as 25 years ago. But, as Table 6-2 shows, from 1976 to 1982 women have made some inroads in two occupational groups: (1) managers and administrators, and (2) operatives. In fact, in 1950 only 13.8 percent of the managers and administrators were women. However, in 1982 the ax was swinging once again against women. As noted in *The Wall Street Journal:*

> Because of the widespread white-collar cutbacks, women business managers are getting axed in record numbers. In August (1982), 175,000 female managers and administrators were out of work in the U. S., the most ever. Their 4.9 percent jobless rate . . . exceeded the 3.6 percent unemployment rate for all managers. Women seem more likely than men to fall victim to cutbacks because they lack seniority or they hold managerial positions in vulnerable support functions, such as personnel, marketing, finance, and public relations.[6]

Table 6-2   **Median Usual Weekly Earnings of Year-Round Full-Time Workers: First Quarter, 1982**

OCCUPATION	NUMBER OF WORKERS (In Thousands)		WOMEN AS PERCENT OF WORKERS IN OCCUPATIONAL GROUP		MEDIAN WEEKLY EARNINGS		WOMEN'S EARNINGS AS PERCENT OF MEN'S
	Men	Women	1976	1982	Men	Women	
Professional and technical workers	7,346	5,712	42.0	43.7	465	330	71.0
Managers and administrators	5,728	2,175	20.8	27.5	502	301	60.0
Sales workers	2,346	1,215	42.9	34.1	362	195	53.9
Clerical workers	3,044	10,665	78.7	77.8	342	232	67.8
Craft workers	9,163	657	4.8	6.7	377	278	73.4
Operatives	5,316	3,487	31.3*	38.7*	304	198	65.1
Transport	2,498	133			321	239	74.5
Nonfarm laborers	2,617	324	9.3	11.0	249	223	89.6
Service workers	3,382	3,583	57.8	51.4	245	175	71.4
Farm workers	591	59	16.2	9.0	189	n.a.	—

*Includes transport.

SOURCE: U. S. Department of Labor, *News: Earnings of Workers and Their Families* (May 24, 1982), and *U. S. Working Women: A Databook* (Bulletin, 1977).

---

6. Joann S. Lublin, "White-Collar Cutbacks Are Falling More Heavily on Women Than Men," *The Wall Street Journal,* November 9, 1982, p. 9. Reprinted by permission of *The Wall Street Journal,* © Dow Jones & Company, Inc. (1982). All Rights Reserved.

Some companies are trying to expand the job opportunities for women through the use of assessment centers, formal career paths, and job posting that publicizes upper-level job opportunities that are open to any qualified person. Basically, however, the increase of women in the work force is doing little more than increasing the size of the traditional women's occupations.

Wage Discrimination

Generally the more education women have, the more likely they are to be in the work force. And the more education they bring to their jobs, the higher their earnings. Nevertheless, as Table 6-2 shows, in certain occupations the great majority of women have not yet attained parity with working men in earned income. Median annual earnings of women in full-time jobs in 1982 were about 65 to 70 percent of those of men. Despite this imbalance in earnings, women make substantial contributions to their family's economic well-being. And the family with more than one wage earner has become an important feature of American life.

Sexual Harassment

Until recently, sexual harassment in the workplace has been a serious, but generally ignored, problem for women. Since the first farm girls went to work in the cotton mills of New England at the start of the Industrial Revolution, experience has led women employees to suppose that verbal and even physical abuse came with the job. Now, the issue of sexual harassment is gaining increased awareness as the number of women in the work force increases — especially as women enter jobs traditionally held by men. Although women themselves may be accused of sexual harassment, most cases involve sexual harassment by men.

Sexual harassment can be defined as deliberate or repeated unsolicited verbal comments, gestures, or physical contact of a sexual nature which are unwelcome.[7] This covers a wide range of behavior, but most forms of sexual harassment tend to fall into two categories. One type consists of comments, gestures, and other actions that treat women as sex objects rather than employees. The second type demands sexual favors which, when refused, result in firing, demotions, denials of pay raises or promotions, and the like.

The EEOC takes the position that such harassment constitutes sex discrimination under Title VII of the Civil Rights Act, which guarantees women employees a working environment free of discriminatory intimidation. The EEOC's guidelines of 1979 apply to governments and any private business employing more than 15 people.

---

7. Office of Personnel Management, *Spotlight: OPM Issues Policy on Sexual Harassment* (November/December, 1979), p. 1.

These guidelines make clear that employers have an "affirmative duty" to prevent and eliminate such abuses. As a result, many corporations, colleges, government agencies, and other institutions are issuing formal policies denouncing sexual harassment. Some human resources managers also are making employees more sensitive to the problem through training and strengthened grievance procedures. In all, employers now are expected to view and handle sexual harassment as intolerable misconduct in the workplace.

Discrimination Against Minorities

In late 1982, America recorded its highest unemployment rate—about 10 percent—in 41 years. Not since June of 1941, when the United States was still suffering from the Great Depression, had the nation experienced an unemployment rate this high. We noted earlier that tables provide data without using a lot of words. But tables also mask many important points such as the unevenness of unemployment rates and the scarcity of management jobs for minorities.

Unevenness of Unemployment Rates

The nation's unemployment rate of around 10 percent doesn't tell the whole story. Minorities, persons under 20 years old, and blue-collar workers have been hit the hardest. As Table 6-3 shows, the rate for black persons between 16 and 21 years old

Table 6-3	Unemployment by Sex, Age, and Race, 1980 and 1982 (July)		
Employment Status		**Unemployment Rates**	
		1980	**1982**
All workers 20 years old and over		7.1	9.8
Men		5.9	8.8
Women		6.4	8.4
Men and women over 20 years			
White		6.3	8.7
Black		14.3	18.5
Hispanic		10.1	13.9
Both sexes between 16 and 21 years old			
White		17.8	24.1
Black		35.7	40.2
Hispanic		n.a.	n.a.

SOURCE: U. S. Department of Labor, *Monthly Labor Review* (September, 1982), p. 56, and *News: Youth Employment Situation* (August 31, 1982).

was over 40 percent in 1982, which is almost double the rate for white persons of the same age group. This is what economists call the "two-for-one rule" — generally there will be two blacks for every white on the unemployment rolls. This rule, which has remained remarkably constant over the past 20 years, also holds true for the overall rates, as shown in Table 6-1 on page 129. Unemployment rates for Hispanics fall between those of whites and blacks, but there is a great variation among the several Hispanic groups.

Ratios and tables tend to erase the fact that numbers represent real people — white, black, Hispanics, and others. To these people, unemployment is a deep personal tragedy. Furthermore, the traditional safety nets for the unemployed have been reduced by the severe cuts in recent federal budgets. The Equal Pay Act of 1963 established a federal policy of equal pay for equal work. We have noted that Title VII of the 1964 Civil Rights Act outlawed various types of discrimination and created the EEOC to enforce these provisions. These antidiscrimination efforts, along with affirmative-action programs, should have increased the relative employment of minorities since 1964. Unfortunately this has not happened in terms of a long-term trend.

Scarcity of Blacks in Management Jobs

Almost 20 years after the phrase "affirmative action" entered our vocabulary, blacks remain all but absent from executive suites. The country's 11 percent black population, plus Hispanics of black racial origin, are only beginning to enter middle management in significant numbers, with an occasional vice-president at the higher levels. That vice-president, moreover, is likely to hold a visible post in public relations, which is hardly the most promising route to the top.

Some corporate officials will argue that executive development takes time — 15 to 25 years — for anyone, white or black, to rise to the top. But many black male executives see themselves in much the same situation as do women. They feel that white corporate executives are comfortable dealing with one another and have not really tried to bring minorities or women into their circle.

Blacks entering the corporate world may face difficult adjustments and uneven progress. Discrimination in minority employment and promotions continues to exist, sometimes in obvious ways and sometimes in subtle forms that reflect the social contacts and politicking that are part of the corporate culture.

Discrimination Against Older Employees

Age discrimination has long been a fact of corporate life, with Wall Street's emphasis on youthful, dynamic management. Some companies see two advantages to firing or forcing early retirement on highly paid older executives. It cuts salary and pension costs and makes room at the top for young achievers trapped in the middle-management ranks.

Older executives, however, are starting to fight back. Age bias is becoming a major corporate issue. The Age Discrimination in Employment Act (ADEA) of 1967, as amended in 1978, protects persons 40 to 70 years of age from discrimination in hiring, discharge, compensation, leaves, promotions, and other areas of employment. The 1978 amendment is favorable to employees because it assures trials by jury. Under the ADEA, a six-month deadline is allowed for filing a claim of age discrimination. In states with their own antibias agencies, this deadline is extended to 300 days.

In 1979 the EEOC assumed jurisdiction of the ADEA from the Department of Labor. The demographic trends in the United States suggest that the EEOC should have plenty to do because, by 1985, 36 percent of the labor force will be more than 40 years of age. In the 1990s, the ADEA will be the source of a high percentage of litigation on age discrimination, perhaps eclipsing Title VII, which covers race and sex discrimination.

Discrimination Against the Disabled

While the jobless rate for the nation as a whole stands near 10 percent, about half of the 15 million disabled citizens fit to work cannot find jobs. A growing number of them are no longer content to live outside the mainstream of workaday life. They want to be judged on what they can do, not on what they cannot do.

Three federal programs cover the employment of disabled people: Section 503 of the Vocational Rehabilitation Act of 1973, Section 504 of the same act, and the Vietnam Era Veterans Readjustment Assistance Act. These programs are enforced by the Office of Federal Contract Compliance Programs (OFCCP) under the jurisdiction of the Department of Labor.

Section 503 calls for affirmative action, which means that every employer doing business with the federal government under a contract for more than $2,500 must take affirmative action to hire disabled people. This affirmative action also covers job assignments, promotions, training, transfers, working conditions, and terminations. Section 504 calls for nondiscrimination, which means that every institution in the United States that gets federal financial assistance must take steps to assure that disabled people are not discriminated against in employment. Under the Vietnam Era Veterans Readjustment Assistance Act, every employer with a federal government contract of $10,000 or more must take affirmative action to hire disabled veterans of all wars, including the Vietnam Era.

Not every disabled person is eligible for these programs. A person must be capable of performing a particular job, with reasonable accommodation to the handicapping condition if it is needed. But employers covered by the three programs mentioned above no longer may screen out people simply because of their disabilities. The emphasis has shifted to their abilities, not their disabilities.

Only through specific programs of affirmative action can most large employers live up to today's standards regarding equal employment opportunities. The implementation of an effective affirmative-action program to remove discriminatory employment barriers rests on competent supervision, responsive human resources management, and sound training.

SUMMARY   Increasingly, corporations are realizing that their employees are more than simply workers. Rather, they are valuable human resources who hold the key to an organization's survival and success. An effective staffing function is at the heart of the effort to hire, train, and keep productive, motivated human assets who have equal access to employment opportunities.

In most companies the staffing function includes selection and hiring, training and development, job termination, and retirement of human resources. The tools and procedures for each of these activities vary with the type of organization and the staffing level within the organization. In addition, the human resources manager often is responsible for a variety of employee services and the provisions for employee safety and health.

Human resources managers must also deal with problems of discrimination as an integral part of the staffing function. The Civil Rights Act of 1964, as amended, is a federal mandate to end discrimination in employment on the basis of race, color, religion, sex, or national origin. At this time, however, most minorities and women continue to face the problems of unemployment, underemployment, and underpay. Also, backed by Title VII of the Civil Rights Act, women are starting to fight long-established aspects of sexual harassment as an intolerable condition in the workplace.

There are also federal laws against discrimination on the basis of age and disability. Age bias is becoming a major corporate staffing issue, as is disability bias for companies doing business with the federal government.

Since World War I, personnel and human resources managers have provided an increasingly wide group of services to their organizations in efforts to hire and train productive human resources. Today, human resources managers must strive to do this while also responding to the social, political, and legal forces in their organization's environment.

BACK TO THE CHAPTER OPENER

1. At which level on the executive career model was the writer of this article? What are the other two levels?
2. When the writer was recruited for a specific job by the manufacturer of transportation equipment, what kind of firm probably was used by the prospective employer to handle this?
3. Was the writer fired or dehired?
4. What is the usual role of an outplacement counselor?
5. The writer found he did poorly in job interviews. What are some other steps in the employment process?

BUSINESS TERMS

human resources approach	117	job induction	122
job analysis	118	job orientation	122
job description	119	dehiring	126
job specification	119	job burnout	127
executive search firm or		discharge	127
"headhunter"	120	layoff	127
private employment agency	120	nonvoluntary rotation	127
employment or job counselor		affirmative-action program	128
firms	120	sexual harassment	131

QUESTIONS FOR DISCUSSION AND ANALYSIS

1. What is the difference between a job analysis and a job description?
2. Why should college students be especially careful about dealing with private employment agencies or job counseling firms?
3. How does job induction differ from job orientation?
4. Having a mentor as an adviser and sounding board can be very helpful to a junior executive. Discuss how having a mentor might also work to one's disadvantage.
5. What problems do you see in the "fast-track" approach to training and developing managers from the standpoints of the company and of employees aiming toward management jobs?
6. When might it not be to the advantage of a 55-year-old executive, who is outplaced, to accept the company's offer to provide an outplacement counselor's help for, say, six months?
7. What effect may the Civil Rights Act have on the preparation of job specifications?
8. Is the percentage of women in the country's entire work force the same as the participation rate for women?
9. What myths or erroneous attitudes have contributed to the lack of upgrading in women's occupations?
10. What effect may the Age Discrimination in Employment Act (ADEA) have on employee handbooks and the appeals that companies use to recruit employees?

PROJECTS, PROBLEMS, AND SHORT CASES

1. For persons born between 1945 and 1964, the 1980s may be a decade of scarce promotions, frustrated expectations, and job hopping. Millions of baby-boomers crowded on the first rungs of management will be forced to stay put. Popular thinking holds that the crowding on the promotion ladder is a menace faced only by middle-aged managers. But with the baby-boom generation reaching its 30s and 40s during a time of widespread unemployment and record numbers of business-school graduates, a career plateau can come to anybody at an early age. The impact on some younger executives will be more stress and dissatisfaction. Others will revise their expectations fairly gracefully and fairly early.

   Prepare an oral report on how you think the younger executive should deal with the problem of career planning.

2. Human resources managers must be sensitive to discrimination in all aspects of the staffing function. This is true not only with regard to discrimination on the basis of sex, age, race, and disability but also with regard to other types of discrimination (obesity, smoking habits, etc.) that are likely to become especially troublesome in the future.

   Discuss the topic of discrimination with the human resources manager of a large business organization and prepare a two-page report on the following issues:

   a. Which types of discrimination that person feels will be more troublesome in the 1980s.

   b. Whether or not the company has changed its employees' handbook or orientation program recently, or taken other formal steps to confront the types of discrimination that may be on the rise in the 1980s.

3. Steve Weiss is now the purchasing director of a company for which he has worked 18 years. As the assistant purchasing director for the past 8 years, he was conscientious in his job and was a well-liked member of the company team because of his pleasant, cooperative manner.

After the resignation of the purchasing director, Weiss was promoted to that position. While Weiss had been a good assistant, it now appears that his former boss had never really developed Weiss's initiative, critical self-evaluation, and managerial skills such as the ability to plan and understand current material requirements systems. Weiss is still 15 years from retirement. His boss feels that the company has an obligation to Weiss as a loyal employee whose professional and managerial training and development have never really been stressed. Yet Weiss cannot be allowed to hinder the ability of the purchasing department to respond to the growing needs of the company.

Discuss the following:

a. Whose fault is this situation?

b. What can be done with a loyal employee who is no longer able to cope with the greater demands of the job?

How to Bargain for a Bigger Paycheck

(Interview with Sherry Chastain, Expert on Salary Negotiation)

Q. Ms. Chastain, are there secrets for successfully negotiating the salary on a new job or for asking for a raise in one's present job?

A. Yes. Most people don't realize that they can bargain on pay. They think they have to accept whatever the employer offers. You may not be accustomed to negotiating with employers, but they're always negotiating with you — for the lowest sum they can get away with.

The truth is that most salaries are negotiable, from a few dollars to many thousands. If you don't speak up in your own self-interest, an employer may decide you're not much of a bargain at any price.

Q. Why aren't people more aggressive in dickering about pay?

A. For several reasons: First, many employees think that if they work hard, they'll be justly rewarded without having to speak up. That ignores the fact that the employer's task is to keep profits up and costs down — and your pay is part of the costs...

Q. Are they afraid they might be demoted or fired?

A. Perhaps. But that's not likely to happen to the person who works hard, does a good job and negotiates in a tactful and professional way. If you have what the organization wants, it will bargain with you.

Q. Do people often put too low a price on their skills?

A. Yes. Some think they'll stand a better chance of getting a good job or getting a raise in a tight job market if they mark down their value. That's a fundamental mistake. Low aspirations actually can disqualify you from jobs. If you don't think you're worth much, neither will the employer.

Q. How does a person know what he or she is worth on the job market?

A. By talking with friends and associates, reading trade and professional journals and seeking out salary surveys that are available in libraries and on college campuses.

Employers have to maintain a competitive salary range, but remember that some companies put more value on certain skills than others.

Q. What's the best way to use this information in negotiating a starting salary?

A. The best strategy is not to discuss pay at all during the interview process. Wait until you have a firm job offer, or feel certain that you do. That's the time to raise the money issue. If the employer brings up the question of pay early in the interview, you might say, "Before we get into salary, tell me about your company's goals and how my role would fit into your plans."

The reason behind this is simple: Until the employer has decided to hire you, you aren't worth anything to that person. By delaying the money issue and stressing your accomplishments, you can make yourself worth more in the employer's eyes than you were in the beginning....

Q. We've been talking mostly about salary on a new job. When is a good time to ask for a raise in one's present job?

A. If you have taken on added responsibilities — say a fellow worker has left and you've assumed much of his or her workload — that's a reason to ask for an immediate pay boost. If you have scored some sort of spectacular success that's widely commended, that also should call for a raise. And, of course, if you get another job offer, you certainly should bring up the pay question....

SOURCE: "How to Bargain for a Bigger Paycheck," from a copyrighted interview in *U.S. News & World Report,* March 23, 1981.

Compensation for Human Resources

Objectives:

- Identify the three distinctive aspects of most wage systems.
- Distinguish between the internal phase and the external phase of compensation equity.
- Discuss the Fair Labor Standards Act and explain the arguments for and against minimum wages.
- Discuss the Equal Pay Act and the issue of "comparable worth."
- Distinguish among the piece-rate plan, the commission plan, and the bonus plan.
- Distinguish among gains-sharing plans, profit-sharing plans, and ESOPs.
- Distinguish among incentive stock options (ISOs), performance shares, and Stock Appreciation Rights (SARs).
- Explain pension portability and vesting rights.
- Identify the three sources of financial security on which most people depend during their retirement years.
- Discuss five types of unemployment benefits.

In ancient Rome different things circulated as money. When the emperors were firmly established, they issued coins of gold and silver and these were used throughout the Empire. In the early days of the Empire, however, Caesar paid his legionnaires in cakes of salt; and the Roman emperors did this again in the later days of the Empire when they began to run out of metal. This custom may be the origin of the saying that a person is — or is not — "worth his salt."

Our word **salary,** meaning a regularly paid compensation of a fixed amount, also finds its roots in this use of salt, as it comes from the Latin word "salarium" or "salt money." Over the long span of history, money has assumed many other shapes and forms. Different societies at different times have been willing to exchange goods or services for seashells, whale's teeth, boar's tusks, stones, feathers, bricks, coconuts, cocoa beans, iron rings, beaver pelts, blankets, bronze axes, and stone wheels. Any number of different materials, including paper IOUs, may serve as money. Money is anything that people will accept in exchange for goods or services in the belief that they may, in turn, exchange it at any time for other goods and services.

For most people the satisfaction of human needs is the force that moves them to work for money to satisfy their needs and desires. In a capitalistic enterprise system these efforts are broadly known as production, and for employees the combined reward and stimulus is employee compensation, or wages. The term "wages" is synonymous with "salaries" and is used more widely than "employee compensation." "Wages" is used in this chapter as an all-inclusive term to cover not only the pay received by employees in stores, factories, offices, banks, mines, and farms, but also the salaries of executives and managers and the commissions paid to salespeople.

The determination of compensation policies in any organization is a top management task, but the overall responsibility for the many aspects of employee compensation usually rests with compensation management. The purpose of compensation management is to provide adequate and equitable compensation to all employees. Compensation managers face a distinct challenge in handling such important matters in the maintenance of a productive employee group. No employee—minority or majority, executive or operator, man or woman—is willing to tolerate poorly administered compensation plans for long. These must be carefully planned, clearly communicated, and consistently monitored and carried out.

A well-designed compensation system is based on many factors. In this chapter we will cover three distinctive aspects of most wage systems: the base pay, the incentives, and the fringe benefits. These three aspects do not explain the entire wage picture, but they provide a foundation for understanding many parts of it.

BASE PAY

The base pay comes from setting rates of pay for various levels of jobs in an organization. Figure 7-1 shows that there are a great many determinants that may influence the pay differences within a firm. It indicates that a sound pay program reflects both external and internal considerations, as well as factors regarding the individual employees in the firm. We discussed the job factors (job analysis and job description) in the previous chapter. In this section we will focus on three key considerations in setting pay rates. These are: external competitiveness of the firm, compensation equity, and federal legislation.

Figure 7-1   Pay Difference Determinants

I. EXTERNAL TO THE ENTITY
  A. Market Factors
    1. Supply and demand
      a. Learning time
      b. Experience and education
      c. Transferability of skills between industries
      d. Geographic transferability of skills
      e. Employee's perception of the job's desirability
      f. School(s) attended
    2. Union—impact of other entities' settlements
    3. Industry patterns or values
    4. Economic conditions
    5. Historical relationship of jobs
    6. Geographical pay differences
  B. Government Regulations and Laws
II. INTERNAL TO THE ENTITY
  A. Entity Factors
    1. Definition of entity
    2. Union relationship
    3. Ability to pay
    4. Size
    5. Capital or labor intensive
    6. Other peculiarities of industry
    7. Philosophies of the entity
      a. Mix of pay and benefits—total compensation relationship
      b. Relationship to market
      c. Historical job relationships
      d. Compensation policies, practices, and procedures
      e. Part time/full time
      f. Entity's organizational approach
  B. Job Factors
    1. Skill
      a. Mental requirement
      b. Analytical ability
      c. Complexity of duties
      d. Personal qualifications needed
      e. Ability to make decisions
      f. Managerial techniques
      g. Character of supervision given
      h. Preparation for the job
      i. Essential education, training, and/or knowledge
      j. Capacity for getting along with others
      k. Capacity for self-expression
      l. Ability to do detailed work
      m. Ability to do routine work
      n. Manual dexterity or motor skill
      o. Creative ability
      p. Judgment
      q. Initiative
      r. Resourcefulness
      s. Versatility/flexibility
      t. Previous experience
      u. Training time
      v. Social skill
    2. Effort
      a. Physical requirement, effort, or demand
      b. Mental effort
      c. Physical or mental fatigue
      d. Attention to details
      e. Pressure of work
      f. Attention span required
      g. Volume of work
    3. Responsibility (for)
      a. Commitments, property, cash, or records
      b. Decision making
      c. Supervision of others
      d. Work of others
      e. Financial results
      f. Contact with public, customers, and personnel
      g. Dependability and accuracy
      h. Quality
      i. Effect of errors
      j. Material
      k. Equipment
      l. Confidential data
      m. Goodwill and public relations
      n. Work methods
      o. Determining company policy
      p. Contact with others
    4. Working conditions
      a. Job conditions
      b. Tangible surroundings
      c. Personal hazard
  C. Other Factors
    1. Desirability of job—employee's perception
    2. Title
    3. Status
    4. Perquisites
    5. Security of pay
    6. Amount of risk involved
    7. Value added by the employee's work
    8. Group productivity and incentives
    9. Job evaluation system used
    10. Hours of work
    11. Monotony
    12. Out-of-town travel
III. INDIVIDUAL EMPLOYEE
  A. Seniority
  B. Experience
  C. Performance
    1. Productivity
    2. Individual incentives
  D. Potential/Promotability
  E. Personal Preferences

SOURCE: The American Society for Personnel Administration and the American Compensation Association, *Elements of Sound Base Pay Administration* (1981), p. 22.

External Competitiveness of the Firm

An employer's goal is to pay what is necessary to attract, retain, and motivate qualified employees. An employer who wants a high-quality work force may have to pay an above-the-market average. Other employers may set pay policies of matching the market or paying less than the market.

How competitive a firm's pay policies are in the marketplace can be judged by looking at the supply and demand of human resources who have the required skills and by noting employee turnover and morale. As jobs become more complex and require higher-level skills, they become harder to fill and command higher wages. This is especially true in high-level executive positions with their high salaries and extra benefits. Among industries, a higher degree of skill is required of workers in contract construction such as carpenters, structural steel workers, plumbers, electrical workers, and painters as compared to that required of retail workers. The average hourly and weekly earnings in selected industries pictured in Figure 7-2 reflect the variations in pay among these workers. So, compensation programs must consider the job market for various skills—whether the market be local, regional, national, or industrywide.[1]

Compensation Equity

The concept of **compensation equity** is closely related to the concepts of fairness and consistency in the eyes of employees. This concept has both an internal and an external aspect.

Internal Equity

When employees within an organization compare their pay and their jobs, they typically focus on four elements of job content: skill, effort, responsibility, and working conditions. Difficulties may arise when two employees are paid the same rates even when they perform far differently. Likewise, differences in length of service, when used as a basis for pay differences on the same job and level of responsibility, may be seen as internally inequitable. Thus, it is essential, although often difficult, to balance carefully the four elements of job content and to place them in order of priority.

External Equity

Employees see their compensation as externally equitable when they believe that their total compensation is about equal to that which they would receive by performing the same job under the same conditions for another employer in the same labor market. The conditions include such factors as employee benefits, stability of employment, physical environment, commuting distance, and even the human relations environment in which the work is performed.

---

1. The sections on a firm's external competitiveness and internal and external compensation equity are adapted from the American Society for Personnel Administration and the American Compensation Association, *Elements of Sound Base Pay Administration* (1981), p. 2.

Figure 7-2   Average Hourly and Weekly Earnings: Selected Industries

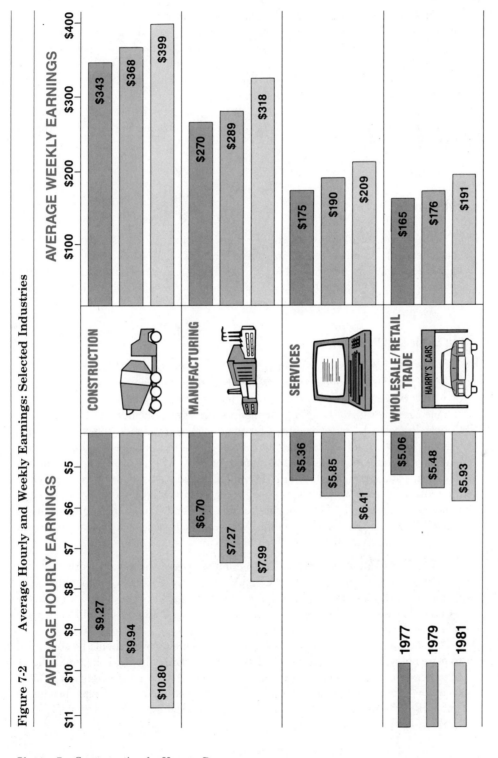

AVERAGE HOURLY EARNINGS

AVERAGE WEEKLY EARNINGS

CONSTRUCTION
$9.27
$9.94
$10.80
$343
$368
$399

MANUFACTURING
$6.70
$7.27
$7.99
$270
$289
$318

SERVICES
$5.36
$5.85
$6.41
$175
$190
$209

WHOLESALE/RETAIL TRADE
HARRY'S CARS
$5.06
$5.48
$5.93
$165
$176
$191

1977
1979
1981

SOURCE: U. S. Department of Labor, *Monthly Labor Review* (October, 1982), p. 67.

The concept of external equity will face some changes in the 1980s for both hourly and salaried employees. Recent slowdowns in business and the competition for jobs among the unemployed masses are expected to produce the smallest pay raises in a decade. Many employees will not get their annual raises that until recently were granted almost automatically. Today companies are looking at what they have to pay to be competitive rather than what they should pay to protect employees from inflation. Furthermore, since 1982, millions of employees have been asked to give up cost-of-living pay increases, vacation time, and other benefits in order to keep their jobs.

Federal Legislation

Legislation, regulations, executive orders, and judicial decisions have a significant impact on compensation management. Two laws that are currently in the spotlight are the Fair Labor Standards Act and the Equal Pay Act. The former is primarily concerned with wages based on hourly rates. On the other hand, the latter deals with discriminatory practices in setting wage rates.

Fair Labor Standards Act

The Fair Labor Standards Act (FLSA), also known as the Wage and Hour Act of 1938, placed a floor under the wages of labor and a ceiling on the number of hours of work per week for workers in private industry whose products enter interstate commerce. Referring to the FLSA the night before signing the bill into law, President Roosevelt declared, "Except perhaps for the Social Security Act, it is the most far-reaching, the most far-sighted program for the benefit of workers ever adopted." This may have been an overstatement, as a major problem with the FLSA was its limited coverage. It was estimated that only 11 million workers, about one fifth of the labor force, were covered by the FLSA. Now most exemptions to the FLSA have been remedied. Currently the FLSA applies to industries and firms in the nonagricultural sector accounting for 85 percent of all U.S. workers. Recent changes have extended it to retail and service fields.

The Pros of Minimum Wages. The **minimum wage** is the lowest hourly rate that can be paid to workers covered by the FLSA. Originally it was 25 cents per hour. The maximum workweek, above which time-and-a-half rates had to be paid, was originally 44 hours but was soon reduced to 40 hours. As Table 7-1 shows, the minimum wage rate since January 1, 1981, has been $3.35 per hour.

Those in favor of minimum wage laws argue that employers should be compelled to pay employees the wage rates needed for a fair standard of living. Labor unions have been active in pushing for higher minimum wages. At the present, organized labor favors *indexing* (or tying) minimum wages to manufacturing wages. As manufacturing wages rise, the minimum wage would go up, thus establishing a higher floor under factory pay.

Table 7-1   Minimum Wage Standards Established under the Fair Labor Standards Act, 1938-1981

Legislation	Hourly Rate	Effective Date
Act of 1938	$ .25	Oct. 24, 1938
	.30	Oct. 24, 1939
	.40	Oct. 24, 1945
Amendments of:		
1949	.75	Jan. 25, 1950
1955	1.00	Mar. 1, 1956
1961	1.15	Sept. 3, 1961
	1.25	Sept. 3, 1963
1966	1.40	Feb. 1, 1967
	1.60	Feb. 1, 1968
1974	2.00	May 1, 1974
	2.10	Jan. 1, 1975
	2.30	Jan. 1, 1976
1977	2.65	Jan. 1, 1978
	2.90	Jan. 1, 1979
	3.10	Jan. 1, 1980
	3.35	Jan. 1, 1981

SOURCE: Employment Standards Administration, Division of Evaluation and Research, 1977.

The Cons of Minimum Wages. Of all the factors involved in the problem of youth employment, none has been more extensively debated than the effects of the minimum wage. Those who oppose the upward trend in minimum wages argue that it does not benefit the unskilled, especially teenagers. There is strong evidence that the minimum wage cuts deeply into the number of full-time jobs available for youth by forcing them out of the better full-time jobs and into part-time jobs that pay lower hourly rates.

As we noted in Chapter 6, overall teenage unemployment has been running about 20 percent, with twice this level among black teenagers. Also, some basic industries, such as steel, autos, and rubber, are undergoing profound structural changes. Economists estimate that as many as 200,000 employees will never be rehired by these old industries. For these employees, especially the older ones, minimum-wage jobs that offer little security and few benefits may become a permanent condition. Thus, some economists argue for a youth differential, or *teenwage,* that would run about 15 percent under the minimum wage for adults.

Equal Pay Act

As an amendment to the Fair Labor Standards Act of 1938, the Equal Pay Act of 1963 requires equal pay for similar work. *Similar work* refers to jobs that require equal skill, effort, and responsibility and which are performed under similar working conditions. However, there are four exceptions, or *affirmative defenses,* to equal pay for similar work. Unequal pay for similar work can be based on: a seniority system, a merit system, a system which measures earnings or quality of production, or any factor other than sex.

A prime issue of the 1980s that is concerned with equal pay among men and women doing similar work is the theory of **comparable worth.** This issue has been brought before the Supreme Court of the United States for a ruling. Women often are seen as victims of wage discrimination because they generally hold "women's jobs" that have been assigned lower wages than those held mainly by men. For example, should matrons who guard women prisoners and perform some clerical duties be paid less than male correction officers who guard male prisoners?

It has been argued that the two main reasons for the practice of paying lower wages to jobs traditionally held by women are profit and prejudice. Those who favor the theory of comparable worth argue that jobs should be based on their intrinsic value and not simply on the supply and demand for the jobs. They maintain that federal law requires women to get equal pay for women's jobs that are comparable in importance, skill, and responsibility to men's jobs. Opponents of this issue say that it is too complex and that judges should not have to determine whether jobs are "comparable." Moreover, they argue that the application of comparable worth across the job market would be financially devastating to the economy. Thus, the issue of comparable worth is proving to be a thorny and volatile aspect of the Equal Pay Act, and it must be considered in setting up a basic pay structure.

Forms of Wage Payment

It is difficult to discuss base pay without also discussing forms of wage payment, as these are closely related. In fact, they influence each other. There are many forms of wage payment, just as there are many pay plans. Established industry or management-union practices often determine which combination will be used. Three common forms of payment for base pay are discussed in this section.

Straight Salary

A straight salary, which is the simplest form of wage payment, may be expressed in terms of a stated amount per day, week, month, or year. Straight-salary plans may or may not provide for deductions for absence or tardiness according to the policies of the companies using them. There is little in this system other than the possibility of a salary increase to serve as an incentive to an employee to work harder on the job.

Time Wages

This form of wage payment is made on the basis of stated rates per hour or per day worked, without regard to quantity or quality of output. If an employee whose hourly rate is $5 works 8 hours, he or she receives a total wage of $40. Under the Fair Labor Standards Act, employers must pay time-and-a-half for overtime. Many union contracts also provide double-time for work on Sundays and holidays. Except for the overtime feature and the possibility that poor work may lead to being fired, there is little incentive in this form of wage payment.

Shift Premium

A type of time wages occurs when a higher rate is paid to workers on the afternoon shift (swing shift) or the night shift (graveyard shift). This form of wage payment is called the shift premium plan. Appearing during World War II when additional pay was used to get employees to work these shifts, this plan has continued in many industries.

WAGE INCENTIVES

An employee's performance is based upon both ability and motivation, or the "will to do." Employee productivity could depend on the manager's skill in tapping this will to do, thus promoting the effective and efficient use of all the human resources in the organization. Three financial ways of encouraging performance throughout the organization are by giving wage incentives that go beyond the base pay to individual employees, work groups, and executives.

Incentives for Individual Employees

Two commonly used wage incentives for individual employees are the piece-rate plan and the commission plan. These wage incentive plans often have a minimum level built into them so that they include, in effect, both a base pay and an incentive pay.

Piece-Rate Plan

The piece-rate plan involves payment at a stated rate per piece produced. Thus, if the piece rate for a given part is 20¢ and a worker produces 250 pieces in a day, the worker will be paid $50.00. In many plants, workers have a day or hourly rate that becomes effective whenever they are not doing piece work. This allows for time used in setting up the machine, sharpening tools, waiting for stock, and so on. Also, most piece-rate plans specify a standard task that the workers must perform before they can begin to receive the incentive pay.

Commission Plan

The commission plan is used with salespersons and is, in effect, a piece-rate system. The salesperson's salary is a commission that is paid for each unit of product that he or she sells. The commission may be either a certain sum of money per unit, or it may be a percentage of the value of the item sold.

Since some companies pay only on a commission basis, a salesperson who fails to sell anything during any given period receives no pay for that time. Other companies pay a basic salary plus commissions. A number of firms give their salespersons drawing accounts, which are chargeable against commissions earned. For example, a salesperson who has a drawing account of $200 a week might, during a four-week period, earn $1,500 in commissions. A common method of handling this situation is to pay this person $200 weekly for the first three weeks, and then at the end of the fourth week to pay $200 plus $700 ($1,500 commissions minus $800 drawings). If, however, commissions for the four weeks are less than $800, say $700, this salesperson would receive only $100 at the end of the fourth week.

A number of firms use a guaranteed drawing account. This operates in the same manner as the regular drawing account except that at the end of a pay period, such as four weeks, if a salesperson's commissions are less than the total drawings, the debt is canceled and the person starts with a clean slate. Thus, a guaranteed drawing account is quite similar to a salary.

Bonus Plan

Bonuses usually are related to length of service rather than to output. Therefore, they are more a form of wage payment than a performance incentive. Sometimes bonuses are used as a mild form of incentive in banks, offices, and other businesses where it is hard to maintain records of each person's production. Bonuses may lead employees to stay with the company, but beyond this they have little incentive value.

Incentives for Work Groups

A group incentive plan covers groups of employees who exceed their performance goals. Sometimes group representatives work with compensation managers to establish, monitor, and improve the group incentive plans. These plans vary from company to company, but the three best-known group incentive plans are: gains-sharing plans, profit-sharing plans, and employee stock ownership plans.

Gains-Sharing Plans

Economists have long argued that compensation systems in the United States, particularly those included in long-term union contracts, respond too slowly to changes in business cycles. They further argue that what is needed is a gains-sharing plan that rewards improved performance. If gains-sharing were built in to long-term contracts, this would make compensation more sensitive to economic conditions.

Probably the most famous type of gains-sharing plan is the **Scanlon Plan,** which links employees' extra earnings to the company's sales. A steelworker named Joe Scanlon developed this plan in the 1930s and then promoted it in several companies over the next 20 years. Under the Scanlon Plan bonus payments are based on a ratio of the total labor cost to the total production value (monthly sales, plus or minus the inventory changes). Assume, for example, that the ratio of the total labor cost to the total production value is 50 percent. Labor will share in whatever savings it makes to reduce the 50 percent ratio. The plan is not a form of profit sharing since employees benefit from reduced labor costs regardless of a firm's profit.

The Scanlon Plan is more than a system of bonuses tied to productivity. It is also a style of management designed to give employees some control over the jobs by encouraging them to make suggestions and participate in decisions affecting them. As such, it also forces management itself to grow and develop increasing professional competence.

The Dana Corporation, TRW, Colt Industries, Continental Oil, and Midland-Ross are among the many companies experimenting with the Scanlon Plan. It is estimated that 1,500 to 2,000 companies use various kinds of gains-sharing plans to tie compensation to some measure of company performance. Two other plans are the **Rucker Plan,** which bases the pay on the value added in manufacturing, and the **IMPROSHARE Plan,** which bases the bonus payments on the number of employee-hours required in production.

Profit-Sharing Plans

Sometimes seen as an employee fringe benefit, profit sharing is a bonus to employees based on the size of a company's profit. It is handled through cash payments or through the distribution of company stock. Unlike group incentive plans, profit sharing is tied to company profits rather than to standards of performance. Thus, profit sharing is an expense of doing business. As one may guess, employees often begin to rely on this bonus as a built-in part of their wages, and they are not happy to lose this when profits are not available for distribution. Nevertheless, profit sharing is thought to encourage production, lower labor turnover, and sometimes increase resistance to pressures for unionization.

Employee Stock Ownership Plans

Since the 1950s, **Employee Stock Ownership Plans (ESOPs)** have been advocated as a means for companies to give their employees a share in ownership. The originator of the ESOP concept is Louis Kelso. He called his theory "two-factor economics" to recognize the importance of capital, along with labor, as factors that create wealth. ESOPs were not widely recognized until 1974, when Senator Russell B. Long became an ESOP advocate. As chairman of the Senate Finance Committee, Senator Long got an amendment building ESOPs into the Pension Reform Act.

There are many versions of ESOPs, and some are used for purposes other than what Kelso had in mind. In Kelso's version, the ESOP is designed to promote the "capitalist revolution" by allowing workers to use corporate credit to buy a piece of the business in which they work. Figure 7-3 shows how an ESOP is set up.

With an ESOP, the employees have no personal liability for the company's loan but still have the chance to accumulate a wealth-producing asset—the company's stock. The employees' investment is the time and effort they put into their jobs to make the business profitable. The advantage to the employer is that the ESOP raises new capital and the company can deduct both interest payments and repayments of principal from its taxable income.

ESOPs have proven to be no fable, as large and smaller companies are finding them a rich source of capital financing. Of course, there are some drawbacks to ESOPs. These plans are not necessarily incentives to greater productivity and less absenteeism

Figure 7-3   Basic Steps in an Employee Stock Ownership Plan

1.
A company forming an ESOP borrows, say, $1 million from a bank.

2.
The loan, which is guaranteed by the company, is used by the ESOP to buy $1 million of stock from the company at fair market value.

3.
To repay the loan, the company makes annual tax-deductible "contributions" to the ESOP, and the ESOP gives this to the bank.

4.
The stock goes into an *Employee Stock Ownership Trust* (ESOT) which administers accounts for each employee, with stock being allocated on some mix of earnings and length of service.

unless they are coupled with nonfinancial motivators such as sincere two-way communication between workers and management. Also, an employee's paycheck and at least part of his or her retirement nest egg in the form of company stock are in the same basket. Nevertheless, ESOP supporters argue that employees who belong to ESOPs can emerge with substantial assets after a normal working career with a company. Hallmark Cards, Gamble-Skogmo, Ralph M. Parsons (worldwide construction) Company, Amsted Industries, and Arrow Metal Products Company are just a few of the companies using this approach.

Incentives for Executives

Compensation incentives for high-level executives increasingly are linked to long-range performance. Many companies now are using long-term income plans (LTIs), which allow executives to set measurable internal standards of performance and to gauge their productivity by these standards. Three important performance-related incentive plans for executives are: incentive stock options, performance shares, and stock appreciation rights. In addition to performance-related rewards, executives also receive various fringe benefits and perquisites that are granted to the lower echelon of employees which are discussed later in this chapter.

Incentive Stock Options

Almost dead in the 1970s, stock options for executives are coming to life in a big way as a result of the Economic Recovery Act of 1981. A key type of stock option permitted by this act is the **Incentive Stock Option (ISO),** which is a *qualified* option that is eligible for tax benefits. An ISO basically gives an executive the right to pay today's price for a block of shares in the company at a future time. After exercising the option, the executive must hold the shares for at least a year. Under the new law, the executive does not have to pay any tax on the exercised options until the shares are sold. Then the gain on up to $100,000 worth of options a year will be taxed at the capital gains rate of 20 percent. By contrast, *unqualified* options are taxed at personal income rates as soon as they are exercised, and for most executives that means a 50 percent tax rate.

Performance Shares

The ISO usually doesn't stand alone as an incentive for corporate management. There is a trend toward combining ISOs with some kind of performance share, or performance unit. Using performance shares, a company promises to award an executive free stock or a cash bonus if some long-term performance goal is met. Honeywell, for example, uses growth in earnings per share as its performance guideline. Ralston Purina bases its performance shares on earnings goals over four-year periods. Performance shares are popular because they are straightforward plans based on performance, not on the stock market; and there is nothing for the executive to buy.

Stock Appreciation Rights

With a **Stock Appreciation Right (SAR),** an executive can ignore the stock option and take a cash bonus equal to the value of the stock's appreciation over a span of time. The SAR is a popular item and its use is expected to spread. Some companies resist SARs because, unlike the stock options, SARs come out of company earnings.

FRINGE BENEFITS

Let's say an employee makes $300 a week in gross pay. Take-home pay, after deductions, comes to about $260. But to the employer, the cost of that employee is $390 a week! Why is this? It's because of **fringe benefits** which, in broad terms, are benefits of all kinds given to employees apart from their regular pay. Fringe benefits are important elements in the total compensation package for employees at all levels.

Cost of Fringe Benefits

Before World War II, fringe benefits amounted to a little "extra" added to the wages. In 1923, for example, fringes amounted to 3 percent of the total payroll. But these fringes grew to 15 percent by 1953 and 24 percent by 1973. Now they amount to around 30 percent of the wages. This means that an employee in private industry earning $12,000 a year actually receives about $15,600. The typical firm now pays about $5,600 per employee in annual fringe benefits.

Scope and Trends of Fringe Benefits

Figure 7-4 gives some idea of the scope and type of fringe benefits. For most working Americans, fringes tend to be fairly ordinary. About 15 percent of these fringes, which are part of the payroll, is in the form of wages paid for time off such as paid vacations, holidays, and rest periods. About 20 percent is outside the payroll in the form of group health and life insurance, company benefit plans, and miscellaneous employee benefits.

Higher-level executives in the "over-$50,000" income bracket, however, lean toward special nonpayroll benefits that reflect executive status and are not taxable as current income. These are called executive perquisites or "perks." While companies are steering away from some of the more extravagant perks, such as club memberships and personal use of the company airplane, the number of firms offering at least some noncash benefits is rising. Some executives look toward perks as a bridge to a high standard of living that reflects a successful career, but that has been eroded by inflation.

The scope of fringe benefits constantly changes. Three current trends in fringe benefits are: reductions in employee benefit costs, flexible or "cafeteria" benefit programs, and employee assistance programs.

Reduction in Employee Benefit Costs

After years of steady increases in fringe benefits, more companies have found that, in the face of shrinking profits and heavy competition, cost cutting must become a major corporate aim. This cost cutting includes reductions to wage and benefit packages that cover health plans, vacations, and pensions. When will the fringe binge

---

Figure 7-4   **Some Miscellaneous Fringe Benefits**

Some Worker Fringes	Some Executive Perquisites
• Price discounts on firm's products	• Extensive executive physical exams
• Free trips for employees of airlines, railroads, etc.	• Special parking
• Christmas gifts	• Spouse traveling on company business
• Employee cafeterias	• Use of company cars
• Company picnics, Christmas parties	• Luncheon club memberships
• Recreational facilities for free use by employees	• Country club memberships
• Legal advice	• Extended vacations
• Annual medical checkups	• Use of company airplanes
• Low-interest loans to buy company stocks or for other purposes	• Use of company apartments
• Generous travel reimbursement for company business	• Executive dining rooms
• Tuition reimbursement for approved educational programs	• Financial counseling, estate planning, and income tax preparation
	• Sabbatical leaves
	• Personal protection (bodyguards)
	• Season tickets for various events
	• Executive development programs

come back? Probably not until five years or so after the economy is moving again. This trend is like a person going on a diet. Companies don't want to get benefit-heavy again because it's so hard to cut back.

Flexible Benefits

An increasingly popular way to cut fringe benefit costs is to offer a **flexible or "cafeteria" benefits plan.** With this plan, employees are given a package of benefits that include basic and optional items within certain limits. Basics might include modest medical coverage, life insurance, and vacation pay. Then employees can use credits to choose among additional benefits. Under American Can Company's program, for example, employees earn credits based on length of service and salary to "buy" benefits to supplement a basic package. Thus, to participate in a new day-care program, employees would have to shift credits from another benefit such as vacations. In this way employees, often with varying life-styles, get flexibility; and the employer gets a cost ceiling on benefits.

Employee Assistance Programs

Employee counseling services that deal with personal problems such as alcoholism, drug abuse, absenteeism, family troubles, legal tangles, or anything that might detract from an employee's job performance are provided in Employee Assistance Programs (EAPs). Some companies use staff psychologists, and some use outside counseling services on a yearly contract basis. Executives and rank-and-file employees are proving to be equally in need of EAPs. Some managers may see EAPs as money-wasting fads. But Control Data Corporation estimates that its EAP saves ten times its cost through increased productivity.

In addition to these newer trends in fringe benefits, many companies offer more common and long-standing benefits such as pension plans and unemployment benefits.

Pension Plans and ERISA

The product of almost a decade of legislative wrangling, the 247-page Employee Retirement Income Security Act (ERISA) was signed into law by President Ford on Labor Day, 1974. The purpose of the Act is to make sure that the 45 million employees who are covered by over 300,000 private pension plans receive benefits from those plans in accordance with their credited years of service with the employer. In 1964, for instance, the collapse of the Studebaker Corporation's pension plan followed the plant closing. The benefits of 8,500 Studebaker workers were virtually erased.

In 1974, ERISA set up the Pension Benefit Guarantee Corporation (PBGC) to insure private pension plans. The PBGC, a self-financing department within the Department of Labor, guarantees within limits the payment of vested pension benefits in the event that a pension plan is terminated. Premiums of between 50 cents and $2.60 per participant are paid to the PBGC on a yearly basis, depending on the type of pension plan. If a large corporate plan went under, PBGC could handle immediate costs. Then PBGC could go to Congress and arrange premium increases for its members.

In addition to the protection of private pension plans, there are tax advantages for the individuals covered by ERISA. In effect, an employee can defer paying taxes on a portion of his or her total compensation until the pension money is withdrawn at retirement. At that time, the individual probably will be in a tax bracket lower than the bracket he or she was in during the years of major earnings.

About half of American employees now have some kind of pension coverage, and about 70 percent in the 40–44 age bracket will be getting pension benefits by the time they retire. This group will collect pension checks from a variety of plans which include defined-benefit plans, defined-contribution plans, Individual Retirement Accounts, Keogh Plans, and salary reduction plans.

Defined-Benefit and Defined-Contribution Pension Plans

A **defined-benefit plan** provides for a fixed benefit or at least a fixed method of determining benefits. Contributions to this type of pension plan vary over the years. A **defined-contribution plan** works the opposite way: contributions are fixed, but the actual amount of the benefits is not known before retirement.

IRAs and Keogh Plans

At the time of ERISA, only individuals who were not covered by a pension plan on their job were eligible for Individual Retirement Accounts (IRAs), a tax-deferral pension plan. As of January, 1982, the Economic Recovery Tax Act liberally changed the IRA picture. Today anyone can have an IRA, whether or not he or she is covered by other pension plans. The Act raised the maximum a person can deduct for income-tax purposes from $1,500 to $2,000 a year, or $2,250 for a person whose spouse is not employed. Payroll-deduction IRAs can give smaller companies a workable, uncomplicated retirement plan at almost no cost to these companies. The new **Simplified Employee Pensions (SEPs)** can provide a company-funded retirement plan with relatively little red tape. Under a SEP-IRA, the maximum tax-deferred contribution is $15,000 or 15 percent of total compensation each year, whichever is less.

Keogh Plans are for self-employed persons or those who own part of a business which is not incorporated. Participants in the older Keogh Plan could contribute the lesser of $7,500 or 15 percent of annual income into a tax-deferred retirement plan. In 1982 the allowable contributions were raised to $15,000 and will jump to $30,000 in 1984.

Salary Reduction Plans

Many employers are convinced that salary reduction plans are better pension plans for employees than payroll-deduction IRAs for two reasons. First, salary reduction plans let employees save more than the $2,000 yearly limit for IRAs. Second, these plans permit employees to withdraw their money early in an emergency without having to pay a penalty. Salary reduction plans go by a variety of names, including cash or deferred arrangements (CODAs) and 401 (k)s, after the section of the Internal Revenue Code that authorizes them. A **salary reduction plan** allows employees to put 10 percent, or even more, of their salaries into a company profit-sharing or savings plan. For tax purposes, the money is treated as a form of company contribution to a thrift plan. This means lower federal and social security taxes for the wage earner. Therefore, the higher an employee's pay, the greater the advantages from a salary reduction plan.

Vesting Rights and Pension Portability

Vesting rights are rights that employees have to pension benefits. After a stated time, the pension benefits legally belong to them and cannot be taken away even if they leave their employers. Most rights are vested in about ten years. However, the new SEP-IRAs are immediately 100 percent vested.

Pension portability refers to the transferability of a pension when a person changes jobs. Voluntary pension portability is one of the most important and least understood tax breaks in ERISA. Where the former and current employers are willing to cooperate, the transfer of pension funds may be made directly between their plans within 60 days without tax or capital-gains penalties. This is called a *tax-free rollover*. If the employee leaves a company to become self-employed, the IRA can be used. At present there remains a serious lack of portability between pension plans. For instance, no workable scheme exists for transferring pension credits between defined-benefit plans. This lack of portability exposes workers to serious potential losses in the value of their pension benefits if they should decide to change jobs.

Pensions and Social Security

Most older Americans believe that security in their later years rests on a three-legged stool of Social Security, private pensions, and savings (see Figure 7-5). Of these

---

Figure 7-5   The Three-Legged Retirement Stool

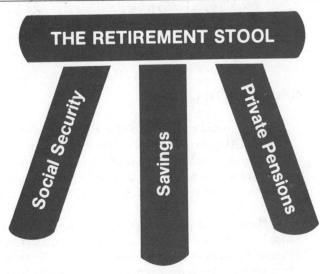

"legs," Social Security has been the most important to them. Figure 7-6 shows that the Social Security System consists of three programs which are financed through separate trust funds.

The Social Security program is becoming increasingly shaky in its ability to cover the current level of benefits being paid. Furthermore, inflation has a way of wiping out much of the purchasing power of personal savings on deposit in banks. With two of the three legs of the retirement stool wobbly, people are looking more carefully at their private pension programs. Some pension programs, such as the SEP-IRA, can be integrated with Social Security contributions at work. Integration means reducing an individual's pension payments by the amount being paid into Social Security.

Figure 7-6   The Three Programs of the Social Security System

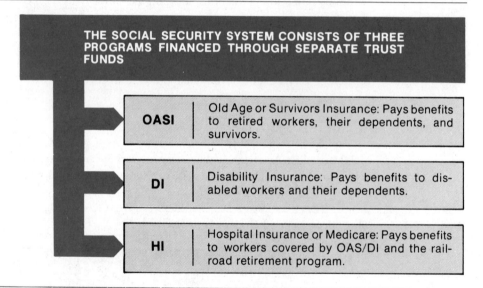

Unemployment Benefits

As we noted earlier, in 1982 the unemployment rate was at its highest level in more than 41 years. A number of benefits exist to tide over people who lose their jobs. These benefits include: state unemployment insurance, extended state and federal unemployment benefits, supplemental unemployment benefits, guaranteed annual wages, and Trade Adjustment Assistance. The extent of these benefits is summarized in Figure 7-7.

Normally the payments of unemployment benefits come from state and federal trust funds that are fed by taxes on employers. Most benefits are not funded to cover extended periods of unemployment. By 1983, 20 states and territories had to borrow from the federal government to pay unemployment benefits because their special funds were broke.

Figure 7-7   Five Types of Unemployment Benefits

STATE UNEMPLOYMENT INSURANCE
Averages about $95 a week and lasts for as long as 26 weeks.

EXTENDED STATE AND FEDERAL UNEMPLOYMENT BENEFITS
For up to 13 weeks, when the jobless rate in the state reaches 4.5 percent of insured workers. Financed by state and federal governments.

SUPPLEMENTAL UNEMPLOYMENT BENEFITS
Commonly called SUB and limited chiefly to unions in auto, steel, and rubber industries. Uses funds from state, federal, and company sources. For each hour worked, employers pay about 5 cents into a SUB fund.

GUARANTEED ANNUAL WAGES
Employer agrees to pay eligible workers a guaranteed wage for 48 out of 52 weeks regardless of business profits. Usually GAWs are tied to SUB programs.

TRADE ADJUSTMENT ASSISTANCE
Under the 1974 Trade Act, employees are eligible for special government assistance in cash and job searches when it is proved that jobs were lost to imports.

SUMMARY   In years past, employee compensation was simply a matter of setting pay policies based on the supply and demand for labor and the practices of competitors. Fringe benefits and work incentives were a relatively minor part of the total pay package. Today a well-designed compensation system includes base pay, performance-related incentives, and fringe benefits. The rates for base pay must recognize the need to be competitive in the marketplace for human resources; internal and external equity in compensation; and federal legislation such as the Fair Labor Standards Act and the Equal Pay Act. Forms of wage payment, such as straight salary, time wages, and shift premium, are closely related to decisions on base pay.

Incentive programs reflect the performance of individuals, groups, and executives. Piece-rate pay and commissions provide incentives for individual performance. Better-known group incentive programs include the Scanlon Plan, profit sharing, and Employee Stock Ownership Plans (ESOPs). Executive incentive plans are starting to emphasize long-term performance. These plans include Incentive Stock Options, performance shares, and Stock Appreciation Rights (SARs).

Fringe benefits now comprise about 30 percent of a person's total compensation. This is down from about 35 percent in 1978, as corporate cost-cutting has reduced pension packages. Two trends in fringe benefits are flexible or "cafeteria" benefits plans and employee assistance programs (EAPs). Fringe benefits also may include pension plans, social security, guaranteed annual wages, and executive perquisites or "perks." Executive perks lean toward nontaxable items.

BACK TO THE CHAPTER OPENER

1. What main aspects of wage systems could be included in the bargaining over compensation?
2. What factors other than job skill relate to the concept of internal wage equity?
3. What types of executive incentives could be used to reward high-level performance?
4. Why do executives sometimes prefer executive perquisites to fatter paychecks?

BUSINESS TERMS

salary	140	
compensation equity	142	
minimum wage	144	
comparable worth	146	
Scanlon Plan	148	
Rucker Plan	149	
IMPROSHARE Plan	149	
Employee Stock Ownership Plans (ESOPs)	149	
Incentive Stock Option (ISO)	151	
Stock Appreciation Right (SAR)	151	

fringe benefits	151
flexible or "cafeteria" benefits plan	153
defined-benefit plan	154
defined-contribution plan	154
Simplified Employee Pensions (SEPs)	154
salary reduction plan	154
vesting rights	155
pension portability	155

QUESTIONS FOR DISCUSSION AND ANALYSIS

1. Should the level of skill required for a task be the main factor in setting the pay for that task? Explain.
2. Why do you think unions generally oppose youth wage differentials, or "teenwages," which are set below the minimum-wage level?
3. Should a female clerk in, say, a retail fabric shop get paid about the same as a male clerk in a bike shop? Discuss.
4. Presumably a worker does "a fair day's work for a fair day's pay." Why then are wage incentive plans often used?
5. Discuss some ways in which ESOPs might be abused or used in ways other than what Louis Kelso preaches.
6. Why is the Incentive Stock Option (ISO) considered a long-term incentive?
7. What is the main difference between performance shares and Stock Appreciation Rights (SARs)?
8. Do you see any arguments that could be used against Employee Assistance Programs (EAPs)? Discuss.
9. Should pensions be provided as a reward for loyalty or as a matter of an employee's rights? Explain.
10. Should the Internal Revenue Service tax the employee's fringe benefits? Explain.

1. Some people argue that the minimum wage is a reasonably good tool for p'
poor workers from unconscionably low wages, helping to relieve poverty, and '
ing purchasing power in the economy. Others argue that because of the u
effects of the minimum wage, these benefits do not necessarily result. The
the minimum wage to the $3.35 level in 1981 have received special atter
because of the high level of unemployment in the economy. Many economists feel tha
the minimum wage has had a major disemployment effect on teenagers, especially on
black youth.

Talk with the managers of three fast-food franchises, preferably with a mixed ethnic
and racial work force, and determine what effect the $3.35 minimum wage has had
on the following:

a. The number of hours teenagers work.
b. The mix of age levels employed.

Give a short oral report in class on whether you feel teenagers have benefited from the
minimum wage.

2. Corporate employee fringe benefits traditionally have been designed to fit the needs of
an employee who is the sole breadwinner of a family. Now, the work force is characterized by a greater variety of family and behavior patterns than before, and new types
of benefits may be needed to better accommodate the variety of family patterns
and life-styles.

Prepare a short written report indicating the following:

a. Four trends in family behavior and work patterns that you feel may be changing
the way of life that the traditional benefits were designed to serve.
b. How new compensation/benefit packages could be designed to make them better
fit current needs.

3. Paula Morton, president of a relatively large manufacturer of solar equipment, could
hardly believe what she had just been told. She thought that Harry Harlow, one of her
best supervisors, would be delighted with the offer she had just made to move him into
a salaried, middle-management job as general foreman. But Harlow turned down the
offer. As he explained it, he would have to take a pay cut if he were promoted! He said,
"The top managers in the company have their bonuses, and the hourly employees have
their cost-of-living increases. The white-collar people in the middle have neither. As a
middle manager, I would be making less than some of my subordinates. Why should
I work longer hours with more pressure if there is nothing in the paycheck to make
it worthwhile?"

Morton reasoned with him that the combination of recession and inflation was
holding down pay raises in the industry and, for the time being, was blurring the
financial line between bosses and subordinates. Therefore, at that time, getting ahead
didn't necessarily mean getting more money. "That's easy for you to say," Harlow
replied, "but I still notice the new wing of plush executive offices and a lot of nice cars
in the executive parking area." Morton was annoyed by that reasoning, but she realized
that Harlow was right in pointing out that supervisors should earn a premium in salary
over their subordinates. But she wondered how this wage differential could be accomplished without changing the entire wage structure in the company, especially in the
current economically depressed period.

Prepare a two-page report suggesting a more imaginative payroll package for Morton
to offer Harlow.

Upsurge in Concessionary Bargaining

Rome had its legions. The Green Bay Packers had Vince Lombardi. And Jimmy Hoffa and Walter Reuther had their industry-wide contracts. These massive bargaining agreements, which typically include uniform provisions for dozens of employers, helped give organized labor its nationwide clout. But, lately, hard-pressed companies in such industries as automobiles, rubber, steel and trucking have been demanding—and getting—significant concessions from individual bargaining units. The major victim: big labor's hallowed master contracts. "By the mid-Eighties these nationwide arrangements will be gone," says Audrey Freedman, a Conference Board labor expert.

So far, employers have been getting concessions only in last-resort cases. "It's being done when the company may have to do something radical like closing the plant forever," says Donald DeScenza, an analyst at Donaldson, Lufkin & Jenrette. "The workers are faced with the prospect of not being able to get any other work or having to move thousands of miles. That's an upheaval." Freedman, however, thinks the present give-backs are only the beginning...

"The whole union movement is based on the premise that with great numbers there is great strength," says DeScenza. "Without the master contract, you no longer have that." That's why even though master agreement breakouts may be on the upsurge, they usually don't come without a fight from organized labor...

Though erosion of nationwide bargaining clearly weakens labor's leadership, the change isn't solely to the employers' benefit. Some companies, as the history of the coal industry indicates, actually prefer centralized negotiating with a strong union. Such bargaining can make it easy to minimize competition. Plant-by-plant bargaining also opens up a Pandora's box of complications. "Can you imagine negotiating rent in a major apartment house separately for each occupant?" asks Richard Hayden of Goldman, Sachs.

On the other hand, individual contracts will clearly weaken labor's position during a strike. That's when enormous union leverage can cripple an entire industry at once, and this threat can minimize an employer's bargaining strength...

The most important effect of the current erosion of bargaining power, however, has to do with productivity. Centralized labor negotiations, quite simply, breed inefficiency. "Having a universal wage when people are manufacturing different things in different markets with different cost structures just doesn't make sense," Freedman concludes. As today's competitive pressures are proving, master contracts may be a luxury that neither unions nor management can afford.

SOURCE: Adapted from Anne Field, "Labor's Love Lost," *Forbes* (September 14, 1981), p. 70. Reproduced with permission.

Labor-Management Relations

Objectives:

- Identify and discuss four mileposts of modern union growth.
- Explain three bargaining tools and tactics of labor.
- Explain six bargaining tools and tactics of management.
- Distinguish among mediation, conciliation, and arbitration.
- Identify and discuss four key federal labor laws.
- Identify five unfair management practices under the Wagner Act.
- Identify six unfair labor practices under the Taft-Hartley Act.
- Distinguish among collective bargaining, coalition bargaining, and concessionary bargaining.
- Explain the three main elements in concessionary bargaining.
- Discuss nine challenges to union solidarity.

The first successful sit-down strike was directed by a Master of Arts from Harvard University. Clearly, strike leader George Edwards had not expected to go from Harvard to the work force at Kelsey-Hayes Wheel Corp. in Detroit. The Great Depression that put him and others like him on production lines also motivated them to help relieve the hardships they shared with other workers. Beside them worked radicals of various stripes, eager to forge a labor movement capable of remaking society. Together workers, ideologists, and displaced potential executives and professionals created the big industrial unions. In some cases, they rejuvenated the old-line craft unions.

Edwards was a member of labor, as the term **labor** applies broadly to the human factor in the production and distribution of goods and services. Usually labor-management relations are concerned with the issues and matters arising through the collective action of employees, especially between company managers and the unions with which they deal. This bargaining relationship is relatively recent, however, as the labor union movement in the United States has had an uneven history of acceptance.

THE EMERGENCE AND GROWTH OF ORGANIZED LABOR

In 1789 the British consul in America reported to London that a "series of centuries" would have to elapse before a people "possessing so strong a natural disposition" to agriculture as the Americans would undertake manufacturing on a large scale. His estimate proved wrong. America's abundant resources, expanding territory and transportation systems, and growing population led to a factory system by 1825. This system spread from New England to New York and Philadelphia, and to the new states beyond.

Beginnings of Organized Labor

The growth of organized labor was erratic during the early history of our country. However, three important labor associations were formed in this early period: benevolent societies, mutual aid societies, and trade unions.

Benevolent Societies

Even before the Declaration of Independence, skilled artisans in handicraft and domestic industries joined together in benevolent societies. They did this primarily to provide members and their families with financial assistance in the event of serious illness, debt, or death of the wage earner. Although these early associations had few of the characteristics of present-day labor unions, they did bring workers together to deal with problems of mutual concern.

Labor ardently supported George Washington and his Federalist party. Workers in the early 1790s, convinced that "importations were highly unfavorable to mechanic improvement," backed the Federalist tariff policy. Skilled workers—also known as craftsmen, artisans, or mechanics—received 75 to 100 percent higher wages than the unskilled, who fared poorly in this period. Laborers, railroad workers, stevedores, and seamstresses—who made up nearly 40 percent of the urban working class—received $1 or less per day at the turn of the century.

Mutual Aid Societies

By the end of Washington's second term in 1796, "mutual aid" or "journeymen" societies of skilled workers began to emerge in Northeastern cities. These included painters, carpenters, and shoemakers (or "cordwainers," as they were called). Some of these societies went beyond mutual aid with their economic demands. These demands included various forms of minimum wages and the equivalent of a closed shop (although that term was not then used). Their objectives were backed by various forms of strikes or "turnouts." This was the beginning of the trade unionism movement.

Trade Unions

The first trade union, or the merging of separate journeymen's societies in different crafts, took place in New York City in 1833. New societies were formed in most major urban cities. Their central interests were wages and hours, and their characteristic tool was the strike. This movement was essentially a city-by-city phenomenon. When industrial production soared in the mid-1800s, skilled workers found their position increasingly uncertain. As recently as the late 1800s, workers labored ten hours a day, six days a week. Premium pay for overtime, paid vacations and holidays, and retirement benefits were almost unknown. The status of unions and the conditions of work have improved greatly since then.

Modern Union Growth

Labor's dramatic past helped to cast its present form. This can be seen in four mileposts of modern union growth: the Noble Order of Knights of Labor, the American Federation of Labor (AFL), the Congress of Industrial Organizations (CIO), and the combined AFL-CIO.

Knights of Labor

The Noble Order of the Knights of Labor was founded in 1869 by Uriah S. Stephens as a small local union of Philadelphia garment makers. At first it functioned as a secret society because of widespread bitterness against unions. By 1886 it claimed over 700,000 members throughout the country. The Order had a broad aim: the replacement of a competitive society by a cooperative one. More specifically, its program called for the eight-hour day, equal pay for equal work by women, abolition of convict labor and child labor, public ownership of utilities, and the establishment of cooperatives. Reliance was placed on educational and political methods rather than on collective bargaining to achieve these goals.

This orientation led to an internal clash in the organization with stronger craft unions who wanted to bargain for the basic goals of higher wages and improved working conditions. In 1881, several craft unions left the Knights to form the Federation of Organized Trades and Labor Unions, which became the American Federation of Labor in 1886.

American Federation of Labor

Samuel Gompers was elected the first president of the AFL in 1886. Gompers, born in 1850, came as a boy with his parents to America from the Jewish slums of

London. He entered the cigar-making trade and became a leader of his labor union and of the national Cigar Makers Union. Except for one year, Gompers was president of the AFL until his death in 1924. The AFL under Gompers's leadership pursued the goals of "pure and simple" unionism and a better life for workers. In Gompers's words:

> ...We want more schoolhouses and less jails; more books and less arsenals; more learning and less vice; more constant work and less crime; more leisure and less greed; more justice and less revenge; in fact, more of the opportunities to cultivate our better natures...[1]

AFL membership reached 4 million by 1920. Total union growth was slowed by the Great Depression of the early 1930s, but it started to revive under the New Deal labor legislation covered later in this chapter. Figure 8-1 shows the growth of the labor movement since 1930.

Figure 8–1 Union Membership in the United States, 1930–1982 (In Numbers and Proportions of the Labor Force)

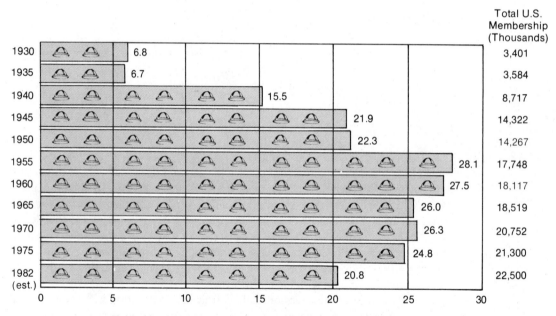

Union Membership as a Percentage of Total U.S. Labor Force

SOURCE: U. S. Department of Commerce, *Statistical Abstract of the United States: 1982–1983* (103d ed.; Washington, DC: U. S. Government Printing Office, 1982).

---

1. Lane Kirkland, "The Opportunity to Cultivate Our Better Natures" (an editorial), *The AFL-CIO American Federationist* (January, 1981), p. 1.

Part II • Management and Organization of Human Resources

Around 1934, an internal struggle developed in the AFL over the question of whether unions should be organized to include all workers in an industry, or only specific crafts or occupations. Efforts at compromise and conciliation failed. In 1938, nine unions expelled from the AFL formed the Congress of Industrial Organizations.

Congress of Industrial Organizations

John L. Lewis, then president of the United Mine Workers, was elected to head the CIO. Lewis was born in Iowa in 1880 of Welsh immigrant parents. He became a coal miner and then, in 1920, president of the United Mine Workers.

AFL-CIO

A new era in American labor history opened in December, 1955, with the formation of the AFL-CIO. The merger of the two federations, rivals since 1935, brought into one organization unions representing approximately 16 million workers, or between 85 and 90 percent of the membership claimed by all unions in the United States. George Meany, former AFL president, was elected president. Walter Reuther, former CIO president, became head of a newly created Industrial Union Department and a vice-president of the AFL-CIO. Meany was a plumber by trade, and Reuther was an automotive toolmaker.

The AFL-CIO marriage had its problems. The United Auto Workers (UAW) became increasingly critical of the way the AFL-CIO handled such problems as unemployment and poverty, civil rights, and foreign policy issues. These differences, plus a personality conflict between Meany and Reuther, contributed to the split in the labor movement which resulted in the formation of the Alliance for Labor Action (ALA) in 1968. The Alliance's charter members — then the two largest unions in the country — were the Teamsters and the United Auto Workers. In May, 1970, Walter Reuther died in an airplane accident, and the ALA later disbanded.

George Meany retired in 1979, at the age of 85, and died in 1980. Lane Kirkland succeeded George Meany as AFL-CIO president in 1979. The United Auto Workers, led by president Douglas A. Fraser, rejoined the AFL-CIO in 1981.

There are a number of independent unions that are not affiliated with the AFL-CIO. The AFL-CIO merger, nevertheless, reflects the fact that the two basic types of unions in this country are the craft union and the industrial union. Craft unions are organized according to crafts or trades such as painters, plumbers, machinists, and teamsters. Industrial unions are organized according to mass-production industries such as steel workers, clothing workers, and automobile workers.

LABOR GOALS AND BARGAINING

The aims of labor are both political and economic. Yet organized labor has been weakened politically and economically by years of slow decline and especially by the recent harsh economic downturn. Thus, organized labor faces an uphill battle in its efforts to protect past gains and achieve current goals. We will cover some traditional goals of labor and the types of bargaining and tactics that labor uses to achieve its goals.

Later in the chapter we will emphasize the impact of concessionary bargaining on the goals and practices of organized labor.

Goals of Organized Labor

The labor movement is in a period of change and upheaval. However, several goals and practices — some new, some old — remain high on labor's list. These include: employment security, higher wages, seniority rights, union security or recognition, checkoff of union dues, and fringe benefits.

Employment Security

Employment security is a union goal that guarantees workers a steady lifetime job or income. It is clearly the emerging central issue for unions, passing even the traditional push for higher wages. Steelworkers, for example, have made great strides toward lifetime security for members. The centerpiece of the United Steelworkers' plan is the "rule of 65," a provision for special pensions for workers between the ages of 45 and 55. Under this plan a worker with at least 20 years of service and who is at least 45 years of age — thus the number 65 — could receive a regular pension plus a $300 monthly supplement. This amounts to a wage of more than $600 a month until age 62 or until the company finds a worker suitable long-term employment. Such employment may require worker relocation.

Figure 8-2 shows the main issues in employment security. The steelworkers' plan is fairly ambitious, and today a steelworker must be employed before the plan can

---

Figure 8–2   Some Key Issues in Employment Security for Unions

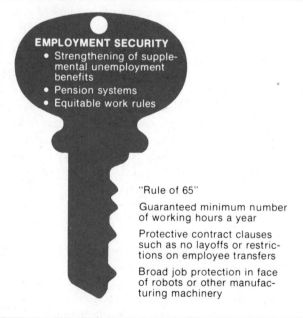

EMPLOYMENT SECURITY
- Strengthening of supplemental unemployment benefits
- Pension systems
- Equitable work rules

"Rule of 65"

Guaranteed minimum number of working hours a year

Protective contract clauses such as no layoffs or restrictions on employee transfers

Broad job protection in face of robots or other manufacturing machinery

---

work. It seems clear that some form of employment security will remain a goal in both private- and public-sector bargaining.

Higher Wages

Unions have played a major role in the long, slow movement toward higher wages and shorter hours since the early days of the Industrial Revolution. However, as long as employment and plant closings remain high, management will be demanding wage concessions. For example, some managements are now trying to divert some cost-of-living increases (COLAs) to pay for other benefits. Furthermore, in efforts to keep plants open, many local unions have negotiated concessions on wages, benefits, and work rules, thus eroding nationwide wage patterns.

Seniority Rights

Next to the union card, seniority is the union worker's most valued possession. **Seniority rights** are based on the length of service on the job and affect decisions about layoffs, rehiring, transfers, and promotions.

For many minority groups, the union seniority tradition of "last-hired-first-fired" has meant that gains made in hiring them are nearly wiped out when economic hard times hit and layoffs begin. Unions argue that minorities also need the long-run protection of jobs on the basis of job longevity, and that *phantom security* (unearned) given to compensate for past discrimination in hiring is unfair if used to replace workers with longer job service.

A U.S. appeals court has held that antidiscrimination goals cannot take precedence over workers' seniority rights in layoffs without a specific say-so from Congress. In other words, such a remedy must be prescribed by the legislature and not by judicial decree.

Union Security or Recognition

Union security is organized labor's goal to have management recognize a union as the sole negotiating unit, or bargaining agent, of its employees. To unions, it means compulsory unionism as covered by clauses in collective bargaining agreements. There are many types of union security clauses and agreements that provide varying degrees of union security. The main types are presented in Figure 8-3.

A recent but little-publicized arrangement is the **custom contract** negotiated by closed or union building-trades shops in the face of wage competition from open shops. The custom contract usually relates to smaller jobs where open shops are more active. It reduces wages, fringe benefits, and the number of work classifications that must be observed.

Checkoff of Union Dues

The term **checkoff** refers to the collection of union dues by the employer through payroll deductions. Provisions for this collection are found in the labor agreement between the union and the management.

Figure 8–3   Main Types of Union Security Clauses and Agreements

Security Clause	Description
• Closed shop	• Employers may hire only persons who are union members, and all employees must remain members in good standing as a condition of employment. Closed shops are illegal under the Taft-Hartley Act, but some *referral unions*, such as "hardhat" construction trade unions, get around this through the use of union *hiring halls* from which employers may get their workers. Coercion of employers to use hiring halls is illegal, but various forms of coercion are hard to detect.
• Union shop	• Employees must join the union within a certain period of time, usually 30 days, and remain a union member during the employment. Right-to-work laws now ban the union shop in 20 states.
• Open shop	• Sometimes a confusing term. An *open shop* often means no union or no union contract. An *open shop contract* means that both union and nonunion workers may be employed.
• Merit shop	• A nonunion or "open" shop in the construction industry.
• Agency shop	• Employees for whom the union negotiates as the bargaining unit must pay union dues, but they do not have to join it. Some states forbid the agency shop.
• Maintenance of membership arrangement	• Workers need not belong to a union to get the job, but those who do become union members must continue this membership to retain their jobs.
• Project agreement	• Construction unions agree to loosen work rules and perhaps reduce wage rates for a specific job. These usually contain no-strike clauses.

Fringe Benefits

Over the past 40 years unions have gained for their members such fringe benefits as pensions, employee insurance, hospitalization, and coverage for visits to physicians, dentists, psychiatrists, and vision specialists. About a million American workers and their families are covered by prepaid legal insurance plans to provide advice about wills, divorces, and some kinds of lawsuits. Today, however, many fringe benefits are being adjusted downward in labor-management negotiations.

Collective and Coalition Bargaining

When a company becomes unionized, **collective bargaining** takes the place of individual bargaining. The union becomes the bargaining agent for its members and, in some cases, for nonunion employees.

Why Collective Bargaining?

Collective bargaining benefits both workers and management. For the workers, the collective bargaining agreement between the company and the union sets up the expected conditions of work and the procedures to be used in dealing with employee complaints or grievances. For management, the collective bargaining agreement covers the steps involved in dealing with the union representatives on work issues and interpreting clauses in the agreement. Union negotiators are expected to bargain more skillfully than could most individual workers.

Coalition Bargaining

In companies where several unions have contracts, some unions have joined together in the bargaining process. This is known as **coalition bargaining, coordinated bargaining, or conglomerate bargaining.** The unions argue that coalition bargaining is necessary to balance the strength of industrial conglomerates. But other parties fear that this maneuver may result in a superstrike, with disruption of production and possible large-scale violence.

BARGAINING TACTICS AND TOOLS

In Japan, wages traditionally are raised at the start of the new business year, April 1. This leads to the spring labor offensive known as "shunto." Over a period of weeks, or even months, millions of unionists stage sporadic strikes, go-slows, workshop rallies, and street marches. Usually one key industry, such as steel or automaking, settles. This creates a precedent upon which other industries in the economy negotiate, depending on the economic health of individual companies.

In the United States, as in Japan, the success of labor-management bargaining varies from year to year and contract to contract. When bargaining goes roughly, however, American labor and management may turn to various tactics and tools to achieve their goals.

Labor's Tools

The lifeblood of trade unionism in the United States has always been the representation of members in negotiations with employers. Since World War II, the trend has been toward the peaceful resolution of disputes. The strike, however, continues to play a role in collective bargaining, as Figure 8-4 wryly suggests. Other tactics include pickets and boycotts.

Strikes

A **strike or walkout** is a temporary refusal by employees to continue their work until their demands are met by management. In early 1937, the newly-formed United Auto Workers used the sitdown strike as a new tactic to force GM to recognize the UAW as the workers' bargaining agent. This was successful, but not without bloody conflicts with police officers and company-hired strikebreakers. Figure 8-5 describes various kinds of strikes, including the sitdown strike.

Figure 8–4

THE WALL STREET JOURNAL

"Another setback—the mediators just went out on strike."

SOURCE: From *The Wall Street Journal*, April 27, 1979, p. 18. Permission—Cartoon Features Syndicate.

Figure 8–5   Various Kinds of Strikes

Type of Strike	Description
• Sitdown strike	• Workers come to work but refuse to work or leave their work stations until their demands are met. These are illegal in some states and now seldom used.
• Slowdown strike	• Workers continue to work, but at a slower pace. On an individual basis, this is called *goofing-off,* or *soldiering on the job.*
• Jurisdictional strike	• A union tries to force an employer to use its workers instead of workers from another union in disputes over who should do which work. Most jurisdictional strikes are unfair labor practices under the Taft-Hartley Act.
• Wildcat or outlaw strike	• Workers go on strike without the official consent of the union, thus violating the terms of the contract.
• Sympathy strike	• Workers go on strike as a union strategy to support the grievances of some other group of striking workers, rather than because of their own grievances.

Pickets

Picketing consists of posting one or more persons at the gates of a struck plant to block or harass persons trying to enter the plant. Picketing also informs the public that a strike is in progress. *Mass picketing* occurs when a large number of strikers block the gates. It is generally put down by the courts as a type of mob rule. *Common situs* ("common sites") picketing is a key goal of construction unions. Recent attempts to legalize this practice would allow a striking construction union to picket an entire building site even though it is striking against only one subcontractor. If these picket lines were honored, a single striking union could close down an entire construction project. In the construction industry, common situs picketing is the name for a secondary boycott.

Boycotts

A **boycott** takes place when union members refuse to purchase products from companies whose employees are on strike or where some condition prevails to which the union is opposed. This type of boycott is called a *primary* boycott. A *secondary* boycott exists when workers apply these tactics against a handler who sells the goods of a struck or nonunion plant. The Taft-Hartley Act prohibits certain types of secondary boycotts, including common situs picketing.

Boycotts today are growing in use and complexity as a union tool. For example, there often is a thin line between a secondary boycott and a product boycott. A *product* boycott involves picketing or other efforts of an informational nature not intended to affect a store's business. Its purpose is to turn customers away from the boycotted product to others not opposed by labor.

A recent type of boycott is the *interlocking directorate* boycott. This boycott was first used by the Amalgamated Clothing and Textile Workers Union (ACTWU) against J. P. Stevens & Company. The union's goal was to isolate Stevens from the rest of the business and financial community. Various tactics were involved in this two-way maneuver. In one instance the ACTWU forced Manufacturers Hanover Corporation to drop from its board of directors an outside member, the chief officer of J. P. Stevens. In another case the union forced the resignation of Avon's chief executive from J. P. Stevens's board by threatening a boycott of Avon's products.

Management's Tools

Over a period of time, management's bargaining tactics have included lockouts; blacklists; injunctions; yellow-dog contracts; mutual aid pacts and strike insurance; and, recently, antilabor management consultants.

Lockouts

In 1979, trucking firms across the nation locked their doors after the Teamsters Union called a series of selective strikes. A **lockout** is an employer's refusal to allow the workers to enter the plant to work. It may take place for many reasons, including an employer's resentment of employees' actions or simply to prevent in-plant efforts to organize a union.

Blacklists

A **blacklist** is a secret list of names of persons thought to be union agitators or sympathizers. It is compiled by employers' associations and is circulated among the members of the association for the purpose of denying employment to the listed persons. Blacklisting is an unfair labor practice under a ruling of the National Labor Relations Board.

Injunctions

An **injunction** is a court order that aims to restrain the union from interfering with a plant's production, usually at the time of a strike. It is usually secured by the employer. At one time injunctions were issued against almost all forms of strike activity, but in recent years they have been restricted to mass picketing, acts of violence, or damage to the employer's property.

Yellow-Dog Contracts

A **yellow-dog contract** is an agreement signed by workers, usually as a condition of securing jobs. In this agreement, they promise not to join a union while working for the employer. The Norris-LaGuardia Act outlawed this type of contract.

Mutual Aid Pacts and Strike Insurance

Employers' **mutual aid pacts (MAPs) and strike insurance** allow the managements of struck firms to hold out over long strikes. For at least 30 years, these tools have paid benefits to struck companies. Mutual aid pacts have been used in the air transport industry and the railroads. Strike insurance was first used in the publishing and printing industries in 1953.

Anti-Union Management Consultants

For about 20 years, the use of anti-union management consultants by employers has been growing. The primary function of these specialists is to defeat unionization, whether in an organizing campaign, bargaining on a contract, or in a campaign to decertify a union as a bargaining agent.

Anti-union management consultants provide a variety of services which might include union "prevention," management and supervisor training, devising employee compensation programs, and other functions aimed at optimizing employer-employee relations and minimizing union influence. These steps help employers create work environments designed to resist unionization.

Methods of Settling Labor Disputes

Successful labor relations are measured by the degree to which disputes between management and workers are effectively settled. Successful dispute settlement often requires the help of an outside third party or agency to bring the two sides together. The main methods used to settle labor disputes are mediation and conciliation, and arbitration.

Mediation and Conciliation

In mediation, an impartial third party tries to move both sides to agreement without using coercion. Conciliation and mediation are often used interchangeably. In a strict sense, **conciliation** means that the mediator tries to get the parties to agree to offers freely made by either side. In **mediation**, the mediator also offers suggestions *not* put forth by either side in an attempt to reach agreement.

The Taft-Hartley Act set up a Federal Mediation and Conciliation Service (FMCS) in 1947 to provide assistance to labor and management in settling contract disputes. The use of the FMCS is voluntary, and the disputing parties do not have to accept the solutions. The National Board of Mediation, established by the Railway Labor Act, mediates labor disputes in the railroad industry.

Arbitration

In **arbitration**, both parties to a dispute agree to submit the dispute to a third party for a binding decision. Arbitration has a long history in our concept of justice, but its application to labor disputes is rather new. Old English law books refer to agreements to arbitrate commercial disputes in 1224. Arbitration was thus viewed as a means to avoid the delays and costs of the legal system of the English courts.

In labor relations, arbitration was also adopted to avoid going through the slow, costly, and complex court system, as well as the costly alternative of a strike. More than 90 percent of major U.S. labor agreements have grievance arbitration provisions.

When disputing parties freely agree to arbitrate, *voluntary* arbitration takes place. But they must abide by the decision, or award, of the arbitrator. When arbitration is required by law for the resolution of disputes, it is known as *compulsory* arbitration.

LABOR LEGISLATION

Labor legislation has come to play a key part in the relative bargaining strengths of labor and management, and both groups have become politically active through lobbyists and political action committees (PACs). By law, corporations and labor unions may create and run "separate, segregated" political funds through collections from members and employees. The money collected is given to candidates friendly to the goals of the union or company. However, unions and corporations alike are barred from using their own money for political purposes.

The AFL-CIO's Committee on Political Education (COPE) is the best known and most active political action committee in the country. Corporate PACs have generally been less active than those of labor but are growing rapidly. In this section, four key federal labor laws are discussed. These are the Davis-Bacon Act, National Labor Relations Act, Labor-Management Relations Act, and Labor-Management Reporting and Disclosure Act. Also discussed are two important federal laws that are pending and some aspects of state labor legislation.

Davis-Bacon Act

The Davis-Bacon Act was depression-era legislation that regulates wage rates for government construction projects. Enacted in 1931, this Act states that federal construction project wages must be based on prevailing local wages. The Davis-Bacon Act was designed to prevent contractors from paying substandard wages to cheap, transient labor, and thus be able to underbid local employers. Since 1931 the law has expanded to include many federally assisted construction projects such as highways, sewers, housing, transportation systems, recreational facilities, and airports. The federal assistance totals about $35 billion a year. Also, some 40 states have enacted "little Davis-Bacon laws" covering state projects. Now, however, many employers feel that workers paid under Davis-Bacon rules receive wages that are much higher than the average compensation. So, as noted later in this chapter, the Act is ripe for repeal or change.

National Labor Relations Act

In 1935, Congress passed the National Labor Relations Act, commonly known as the Wagner Act because of its sponsorship by Senator Wagner of New York. The purpose of this law was to help workers organize unions that were free from employer domination and to secure recognition for these unions from their employers. Employees were given the right to self-organization; to form, join, or assist labor organizations; to bargain collectively through representatives of their own choosing; and to engage in concerted activities for the purpose of collective bargaining or other mutual aid or protection. The specific provisions of the Wagner Act included a list of five so-called unfair labor practices in which employers were forbidden to engage. These are listed in Figure 8-6.

A National Labor Relations Board (NLRB) consisting of three members who were not to be affiliated with either labor or industry was established. The NLRB was empowered to prevent employers from engaging in any of the listed unfair labor practices. It conducts elections among the employees to determine the representatives who will bargain collectively for them with the employers. The Act also provided that representatives designated for collective bargaining should be the exclusive representatives of the employees in matters of wages, hours of work, and other conditions of employment.

Labor-Management Relations Act

In the years following the Wagner Act, many members of Congress became convinced that the Wagner Act had gone too far in favor of the unions, which had

Figure 8–6   Unfair Labor Practices

Unfair for Management (Wagner Act)	Unfair for Labor (Taft-Hartley Act)
1. To interfere with, restrain, or coerce employees in their collective bargaining or self-organizing activities.	1. A union may not coerce employees into joining a union (except in the case of a union shop) nor employers in the selection of their representatives for collective bargaining or handling employee grievances.
2. To dominate or interfere with the formation or administration of any labor organization or to contribute financially to its support.	2. A union may not try to force employers to discriminate against an employee except in the case of a union shop where the employee has not paid union dues and the initiation fee.
3. To discriminate in conditions of employment against employees for the purpose of encouraging or discouraging membership in any labor organization.	3. If a union has been certified as the bargaining agent for the employees, it cannot refuse to bargain collectively with the employer.
4. To discharge or otherwise discriminate against an employee who has filed or given testimony under the Act.	4. A union is not permitted to engage in secondary boycotts or jurisdictional strikes, or to force assignment of certain work to certain unions.
5. To refuse to bargain collectively with the chosen representatives of the employees.	5. A union may not charge excessive fees under union shop agreements.
	6. A union may not require an employer to pay for work that is not performed.

grown big and powerful during World War II. Accordingly, the Labor-Management Relations Act (Taft-Hartley Act) was enacted in 1947 as an amendment to the Wagner Act to restore the balance in labor relations. Most of the Wagner Act's major provisions were amended or modified by the Taft-Hartley Act.

A notable feature of the Taft-Hartley Act is that it contains a list of unfair labor practices in which unions cannot engage. These are also shown in Figure 8-6. Section 14(b) of this Act is especially important as it permits states to pass legislation forbidding the union shop (see "State Labor Legislation" on pages 177–178).

Labor-Management Reporting and Disclosure Act

Also known as the Landrum-Griffin Act, the Labor-Management Reporting and Disclosure Act of 1959 was brought about by the findings of the McClellan Committee of the U.S. Senate. In almost three years of investigation and hearings, the Committee developed clear and impressive evidence of racketeering, employee coercion, and financial irresponsibility in certain unions.

There are two basic parts to the Landrum-Griffin Act: a code of conduct providing certain rights to union members and imposing certain obligations on union officers, and amendments to the Taft-Hartley Act restricting certain picketing and boycott practices. Some specific points of this Act are listed in Figure 8-7.

1. Every union must file a detailed annual financial report with the Secretary of Labor and make the information in it available to members.
2. Employers and labor relations consultants must report annually to the Secretary of Labor on all payments made or received to influence employees on labor matters.
3. The financial and "conflict of interest" activities of union leaders must be disclosed.
4. Theft or embezzlement of union funds is a crime.
5. Union officers must be bonded by American companies.
6. New regulations are established for the election of union officers.
7. The NLRB is permitted to refuse jurisdiction over certain types of cases.
8. *Organizational picketing* (when a union places pickets outside a firm it is unsuccessfully trying to organize) is prohibited.
9. Certain aspects of secondary boycotts are eliminated.
10. The non-Communist affidavit clause of the Taft-Hartley Act is eliminated.

Pending Federal Labor Legislation

Two possible and important changes in federal labor legislation are the repeal of the Davis-Bacon Act and the enactment of a domestic-content law for new cars sold in the United States.

Repeal of the Davis-Bacon Act

Figure 8-8 shows the main pros and cons of the Davis-Bacon Act. There is considerable feeling today that the Act no longer serves its original purpose and that it adds to the federal deficit and inflation. Thus, the Act appears ripe for repeal or a major revision.

Figure 8–8   Pros and Cons of the Davis-Bacon Act

Backers Claim That the Act:	Opponents Claim That the Act:
1. Forces contractors paying union wages to be efficient.	1. Forces contractors to pay unrealistically high wages.
2. Allows government to benefit from the work of highly skilled workers.	2. Means high wages that discourage small firms from bidding on federal projects.
3. Keeps workers from being victimized and exploited by employers.	3. Is inflationary.
	4. Discriminates against minorities, women, and young people, as fewer trainees are used.
	5. Gives the Labor Department too much say in setting regional wage rates.

Enactment of a Domestic-Content Law

Labor unions once favored free trade and did not favor protectionist measures, as they feared trade wars with other countries. But in the face of the growing fleet of foreign cars on our highways and the growing unemployment of American workers, labor unions now are pushing for laws to require automakers who sell in the United States to use a minimum of American-made parts of up to 90 percent.

If enacted, this bill would halt a trend of American automakers buying parts abroad. It would also force foreign car companies to build more plants in the United States or cut their exports. Labor unions argue that domestic-content legislation would create between 500,000 and 1,000,000 jobs in autos, steel, glass, electronics, and other supplier industries.

State Labor Legislation

In addition to federal labor legislation, laws affecting organized labor have been enacted by several states. Among these are laws outlawing the closed shop; banning strikes by public employees and employees of public utilities; forbidding jurisdictional, sit-down, and sympathy strikes; and prohibiting compulsory unionism. The Taft-Hartley Act permits states to outlaw the closed shop and maintenance of membership. As Figure 8-9 shows, 20 states now have so-called **right-to-work laws.** These laws

---

Figure 8–9   The 20 States with "Right-to-Work" Laws

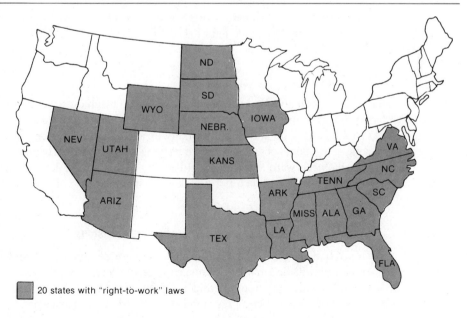

20 states with "right-to-work" laws

---

stipulate that no one shall be required to join a union in order to secure or to retain a job. Although these right-to-work laws do not prohibit union activity, labor opposes them as a drain on union power in collective bargaining.

CURRENT LABOR ISSUES AND TRENDS

The American labor movement today is a product of the character and aspirations of workers as they have collectively sought to improve wages, hours, working conditions, and generally to work toward a better life for all. Just as labor's past has been a prelude to its present, some insight into future labor-management relations can be gained by noting the major issues and trends that the labor movement faces today. These issues and trends include the growth of concessionary bargaining, the emergence of minority and women unionists, and various challenges to union solidarity.

Growth of Concessionary Bargaining

In 1981 and 1982 some major automobile companies in the United States asked their employees for hundreds of millions of dollars in wage and benefit cuts. This launched the era of **concessionary bargaining** in which managers are more aggressive in trying to get union agreements that make union wages and benefits respond to the employer's competitive needs. Concessionary bargaining may rewrite the whole pattern of collective bargaining in America. Three key aspects of concessionary bargaining are: give-backs, participation of union workers in profits and decisions, and the weakening of industrywide national union contracts.

Give-Backs

The term **give-backs** refers to the giving up by unionized employees of hard-won pay hikes, fringe benefits, or work rules that hamper productivity. The scope of give-backs is wide and covers workers in airline, auto, rubber, steel, and trucking companies. Some observers see give-backs as a long-term loss of power for the unions. Union officers warn that they are only doing what has to be done to save jobs and that union cooperation should not be taken for granted.

Participation of Union Workers in Profits and Decisions

When unions make concessions, they are certain to demand trade-offs that employers will find hard to live with over the long run. However, it appears that a trend is under way from the usually adversary management-worker relationship to a more cooperative one. A key trend is increased labor-management communication, with workers' representatives having a say in management decision making and sharing responsibility for improved productivity. When workers trade give-backs for participation in management's decisions, they can be seen as investors in the company. Unions will have to think about how they represent workers who are also investors, as this is a new role for the American labor movement.

Weakening of Industrywide National Union Contracts

Concessionary bargaining appears to be creating a basic change in labor relations—the weakening of industrywide national union contracts that have set the pattern of bargaining for 30 years. These national contracts have tended to go for increased pay and benefits regardless of economic conditions. Now, an increasing number of companies and unions are modifying national contracts to fit local situations such as potential plant closing. Some experts contend that concessionary bargaining is a short-term trend that is not especially important to long-term union-management relations. Others believe that the new forms of collaboration between bosses and workers may transform industrial relations.

Emergence of Minority and Women Unionists

The present American trade union movement faces pressures from within its ranks as well as in its collective bargaining. It is being challenged by both blacks and women. Both groups vow to win better representation within their unions and to move toward such goals as equal pay, job security, and equal opportunity for better job slots.

Black Unionists

For black persons, the struggle for job rights has been linked to the struggle for civil rights. This is clearly evidenced in the life of A. Philip Randolph, who was a champion for his own union, the Sleeping Car Porters, and for the rights of all humanity. As Bayard Rustin put it:

> For 70 years, A. Philip Randolph was a central figure in the American struggle for trade union and civil rights. His life reflects an awesome constancy: he opposed the separatist and elitist movements of Marcus Garvey and W. E. B. DuBois in the 1920s just as effectively as he did the separatist and "black capitalism" panaceas of 40 years later. Widely known for his gentle and dignified bearing, he was nonetheless an iron-willed radical whose great gifts as a leader stemmed from his own understanding of the human condition.[2]

A. Philip Randolph died on May 16, 1979. Because of people like him, the successes of the United States civil rights movement gave a boost to labor's try for job

---

2. Adapted from Bayard Rustin, "In Memory of A. Philip Randolph," *The AFL-CIO American Federationist* (June, 1979), pp. 18–22.

equality. One of their major efforts is the Coalition of Black Trade Unionists (CBTU), established in 1972. There are about 3 million blacks in unions, comprising roughly 15 percent of union memberships. About one-third of all blacks eligible for union cards have been organized, but few blacks have advanced to top union positions. For example, more than 20 percent of the United Steelworkers' 1.4 million members are black. But it was only in 1976 that Leon Lynch was appointed vice-president of the union, becoming the first black person to hold a top office in the union since its beginning.

Some CBTU goals are: to work for the election of a Congress that will fight for minority programs, to offset the impact of economic downturns on the black worker and community, and to continue its organizing efforts.

Women Unionists

The first collective action of black working women in American history was taken by laundresses of Jackson, MS in 1866. The Women's Trade Union League was created in the early 1900s to educate women workers about the advantages of union membership, to support their demands for better working conditions, and to acquaint the public with the serious exploitation of women workers — many of them in "home industries" or industrial sweatshops. But by and large the labor movement in its first century was comprised of men. Now steps are being taken by the AFL-CIO and by women activists to expand the role of women workers in trade unions and in union offices.

Women in the AFL-CIO. Women comprise about 30 percent of the 14 million members of the AFL-CIO, and unions are looking to women workers for new union growth in the 1980s. Lane Kirkland, in one of his first steps as head of the AFL-CIO, created a special committee to report on ways women and minorities can be given an expanded role in organized labor. Furthermore, in 1980 the AFL-CIO elected the first woman to its executive council.

Coalition of Labor Union Women. Women workers are taking steps to help themselves. During the founding convention of the Coalition of Labor Union Women (CLUW) in 1974, its leaders charged that roughly one out of every five union members is a woman. There are about 4.5 million women in U.S. unions, but women are poorly represented on union boards. However, the members of the CLUW do not reject existing trade unionism. Rather, they are aiming for such goals as equal pay, day care, and improved working conditions for women workers by remaining within the union movement and making it move their way.

Both the CBTU and the CLUW could become a threat to the AFL-CIO and to labor generally if they bring together their closely related causes. Top union officials are worried that the labor movement could evolve into a two-tiered union movement of traditional unions and special-interest blocs with contradicting objectives and positions.

Women Office-Worker Groups. The nation's women office workers are banding together these days to overcome their low status, low pay, and poor career opportunities in the ranks of American business. They are organizing into unions and into a loose confederation of office-worker groups. The largest group, Women Employed's (WE), was formed in 1973. Other groups include "Nine-to-Five," "Women Working," and "Women Organized for Employment." In addition, white-collar unions are going after both men and women engineers, computer programmers, and draftspersons. These organizing efforts almost certainly will mean higher costs for employers.

Other Challenges to Union Solidarity

The essence of the labor movement is solidarity, as shown in the first stanza of the trade union anthem in Figure 8-10. But solidarity is becoming harder for organized labor to maintain. On almost every front, things have gone awry for labor—for example, declining membership, threatened wages and benefits, and downside influence with government. Now union leaders are trying to pull organized labor out of the rut. Some of the pressure points to watch in labor-management relations in the 1980s, in addition to concessionary bargaining and the activities of minority and women unionists, are outlined in Figure 8-11.

These issues and trends have not gone unnoticed by corporate employers of all sizes. As a result, management increasingly is resisting unionization activities and union demands at the bargaining table. Despite these trends, however, business students should recognize the contributions of unions. Because of the threat of unionization, many workers in nonunion shops receive union pay and benefits without paying union dues. Unions have taken stronger stands than business corporations in opposing federal wage and price controls. Unions generally understand our freedoms and have been a positive force in shaping foreign policy. These, along with the historical contributions of unions to the welfare of workers, are powerful arguments for healthy unionism. Nevertheless, management now is tightening up its labor re-

---

Figure 8–10   "Solidarity Forever" (To the Tune of "The Battle Hymn of the Republic")

When the union's inspiration through the workers' blood shall run,
There can be no power greater anywhere beneath the sun.
Yet what force on earth is weaker than the feeble strength of one
But the union makes us strong.
Solidarity forever, solidarity forever,
Solidarity forever, for the union makes us strong.

Figure 8–11   Other Challenges to Union Solidarity in the 1980s

 NEW LEADERSHIP. In order for labor organizations to meet their many problems, they will need leaders who are bright, flexible, and able to build strong grass-roots support.

 THE ROBOT AGE. Efficient, sophisticated "steel-collar workers" may usurp countless blue-collar jobs.

 DECLINE IN USE OF STRIKES. Unions are less able to mount strikes, and managements are more inclined to try breaking them.

 DEREGULATION OF MOTOR TRANSPORT INDUSTRY. Nonunion companies are encouraged to expand operations and routes into areas that were previously covered by union truckers under strict ICC rules that provided monopolistic controls on shipping routes and kept shipping rates and wages uniformly high.

 THE "SOUTHERN STRATEGY" AND ORGANIZING THE SUN BELT. In 1976, union leaders accused General Motors of a *Southern Strategy* to build non-union plants in the South. Since 1976, more companies and jobs have shifted to the Sun Belt. Weakened by job losses in the North, unions need organized support in the South; but the South generally rejects unions.

 THE GENERATION GAP IN UNIONS. Younger members often demand better treatment on the job and are equally angry about authoritarian bosses in plants and unresponsive bureaucrats in unions. The younger workers sometimes are described by senior workers as *silver platter unionists* because they have inherited established unions. Sometimes they are called *slot-machine unionists* because they want instant benefits without supporting the union.

 PENSIONERS' RIGHTS. While unions continue, in the face of concessionary bargaining, to fight for higher wages and benefits demanded by younger workers, they are being pressed by their growing ranks of retirees and older workers to protect pensions against erosion by inflation.

lationships in order to make productivity the uppermost issue in bargaining. Business and union managers clearly are entering a new and challenging era of labor-management relations in which old patterns are dropping away and new patterns are yet to be set.

SUMMARY   The forerunners to modern labor unions were benevolent societies, mutual aid societies, and trade unions. The activities of these groups varied widely in goals and effectiveness, but they did help set the scene for the growth of modern labor as noted by four important union mileposts: the Noble Order of the Knights of Labor, the American Federation of Labor (AFL), the Congress of Industrial Organizations (CIO), and the combined AFL-CIO.

The labor movement has been weakened politically and economically by the recent economic downturn and now is in a period of upheaval and change. However, the following goals of labor still hold: employment security, higher wages, seniority rights, union security or recognition, checkoff of union dues, and expanded fringe benefits.

Management and labor employ various tactics and tools in dealing with each other. Key labor bargaining tactics include strikes, picketing, and boycotts. Management's tools over time have included lockouts; blacklists; injunctions; yellow-dog contracts; mutual aid pacts and strike insurance; and, recently, the use of anti-union management consultants. Sometimes an outside third party or agency is used to bring both sides together. Various ranges of third-party involvement are seen in such methods as mediation, conciliation, and arbitration.

Both labor and management are concerned with labor legislation, as this has a great impact on their relative bargaining strengths. Major labor legislation since the 1930s includes the Davis-Bacon Act, the National Labor Relations Act (Wagner Act), the Labor-Management Relations Act (Taft-Hartley Act), the Labor-Management Reporting and Disclosure Act (Landrum-Griffin Act), and state labor legislation which includes right-to-work laws.

In pursuing its goals, labor is coming face-to-face with the new era of concessionary bargaining in which hard-pressed employers push for concessions, or give-backs, in wages and benefits. In return for give-backs, labor is asking for participation in profits and management decisions. Concessionary bargaining also appears to be weakening industrywide national union contracts.

In addition to concessionary bargaining, labor faces other challenges to its solidarity. These challenges include the emergence of minority and women unionists, the need for new leadership, competition from robots, decline in the use of strikes, deregulation of the motor transport industry, the "Southern strategy," facing the generation gap in unions, and demands for pension protection.

BACK TO THE CHAPTER OPENER

1. What is concessionary bargaining?
2. What are two other kinds of bargaining in addition to concessionary bargaining?
3. What are give-backs?
4. In addition to give-backs, what are two other main elements in concessionary bargaining?
5. The lifeblood of unionism is solidarity. How does the national union contract relate to solidarity?

BUSINESS TERMS

labor	162	lockout	171
employment security	166	blacklist	172
seniority rights	167	injunction	172
union security	167	yellow-dog contract	172
custom contract	167	mutual aid pacts (MPAs) and	
checkoff	167	strike insurance	172
collective bargaining	168	conciliation	173
coalition bargaining,		mediation	173
coordinated bargaining,		arbitration	173
or conglomerate bargaining	169	right-to-work laws	177
strike or walkout	169	concessionary bargaining	178
picketing	171	give-backs	178
boycott	171		

QUESTIONS FOR DISCUSSION AND ANALYSIS

1. What was the difference between the benevolent societies and the mutual aid societies?
2. What is the difference, if any, between employment security and union security?
3. Discuss whether it is possible for workers to be loyal both to their employers and to their unions.
4. Do you think strikes by public employees and employees in public utility industries should be allowed where shutdowns may endanger the public welfare? Explain.
5. Why might it be difficult to distinguish between a secondary boycott and a product boycott?
6. Unions seem to be far more concerned about the use of anti-union consultants than about other management tools and tactics. Why do you think this is so?
7. What is the difference, if any, between conciliation and mediation?
8. If you were a blue-collar steel worker with ten years' service, how would you feel if your employer asked for give-backs in wages and fringe benefits?
9. The current move by labor unions to concessionary bargaining is dictated by the sheer need to save members' jobs and to survive. But it also includes some trends that may become permanent features of industrial relations in the United States. Name four union or company measures that may result in workers identifying more strongly with the economic performance of the companies that employ them.
10. What effects may concessionary bargaining, especially worker participation in profits and management decisions, be likely to have on managerial accountability for company performance?

PROJECTS, PROBLEMS, AND SHORT CASES

1. Frank Vessidini was scowling as he joined some fellow assembly-line supervisors for coffee in their corner of the shop cafeteria. "What's the matter, Frank?" Phil Colwell asked. "You look all shook up!"

   "For ten years I looked forward to being a supervisor in this company, Phil. Now, after being a supervisor for two years, I'm beginning to think that we're really getting the works!"

Shelly Minami joined the conversation. "I'll go along with that, Frank. Not only do we get paid less than some of the union members we used to work with, but now we're caught between management and the workers in the layoffs around here. I really don't know whether we are white- or blue-collar employees, but I do know that we don't have many people on our side when it comes to pay or job protection."

"And what about the new merit system?" Colwell muttered. "Now the bosses are saying that seniority doesn't count much any more and that they want to keep the people who do the job best regardless of seniority."

"That rating system stinks," Minami retorted. "I'm convinced that the bosses are playing games with our ratings to give low scores to the people they want out! I wonder how difficult it would be to rejoin our old union or to organize a supervisors' union or some kind of bargaining group? I think we need some protection from those idiots upstairs!"

Discuss the following:

a. How unusual would you guess the plight of the supervisors in this incident to be today?

b. Can supervisors join the same union that their subordinates are in?

c. What can higher-level managers do to head off union-organizing activities among supervisory personnel?

2. Public-employee unionists are among the fast-growing segments of the union movement. But it now is clear that in 1981 the Professional Air Traffic Controllers Organization (PATCO) found itself in a strike that left the union bankrupt and cost 12,000 workers their jobs. This topic is covered in the article "How Safe Are Our Airways?" in the August 24, 1981 issue of *U.S. News & World Report.* Review this article and present a verbal report to the class on PATCO's four strategic errors that doomed the strike from the start.

3. The recent economic downturns in our society, along with the shift from basic industries to high-tech and service industries, have contributed to a period of uncertainty and change in labor-management relations. Many unions are struggling to establish a new niche in this changing scene. Even some unionists are asking themselves if unions are still necessary, although union officials are quick to point out how workers have benefited and continue to benefit from collective bargaining and the protection of a union contract.

Have unions been a positive force in our society? Interview the following parties in your community:

a. A member of a trade union who is over 40 years old.

b. A member of a trade union who is less than 25 years old.

c. A business manager who is over 40 years of age.

Based on these interviews and your own perceptions, prepare a written report on whether workers would be better off today if there had never been an American trade union movement. Summarize your conclusions in a short verbal report to the class.

III. Production and Productivity

Chapter 9. *American Productivity*
10. *Production and Manufacturing Systems*
11. *Materials Management*

Photo courtesy of The Graphic Expression, Inc.

Boosting Our Sagging Productivity

...Why has American productivity gone into reverse? What can be done to change that trend? More than 350 experts from business, labor, government and the academic world met recently at the American Productivity Center in Houston, Tex., to discuss these questions. *U. S. News & World Report* talked with conference delegates from this country and abroad. Following is a sampling of their comments.

THOMAS VANDERSLICE, President, General Telephone & Electronics Corporation.... We've got to raise the level of new investment in plant and equipment and speed the diffusion of new technology. All this is going to require patience. We didn't get into this productivity decline in a single year, and it's going to take a few years to turn things around.

KOHEI GOSHI, Chairman, Japan Productivity Center. The most important reason for Japan's sustained high growth in productivity is the cooperative attitude between management and labor. That includes our lifetime-employment system. Once a person is employed, he pretty much stays with his company for a whole working career. He entrusts his entire life to the corporation. He shares his prosperity with the company. We in Japan have learned much from the U. S. about industrial engineering. But we have mixed that technique with more emphasis on the human side. Both the U. S. and Europe need to do that...

AMITAI ETZIONI, Director, Center for Policy Research, Columbia University.... The single most important factor for the U. S. in the 1980s is whether the country will dedicate itself to reindustrialization. If society is preoccupied with nonwork, nonproductive matters, it sets a counterproductive context...

ROBERT C. PEW, President, Steelcase, Inc. We commissioned a survey to find out how office workers felt about their workplaces. One thing came out clearly: These workers said they could be more productive, given the right tools and the proper office environment. But they wanted to be involved in decisions on how to work more efficiently. Somewhere between 50 and 70 percent of our total U. S. work force is in offices, not on production lines. So we need to give more attention to the working environment of service employees and white-collar workers.

EDWARD O. VETTER, management consultant. ...I agree that in this country we've let our hardware run down and that we suffer from archaic tax laws. But a lot of businessmen have let those things become an excuse for failing to do a good human-relations and labor-relations job within the constraints of existing depreciation regulations and union rules. The average American worker is a damn good one; he wants to do as good a job as possible.

SOURCE: Adapted from "How to Stop Sag in Productivity—Experts' Ideas," a copyrighted article in *U. S. News & World Report* (July 28, 1980), pp. 57–58.

9

American Productivity

Objectives:

- Explain why productivity is important to job opportunities.
- Explain the relationship of productivity to inflation.
- Distinguish between partial productivity and total productivity.
- Discuss six reasons for the decline in American productivity.
- Discuss three key steps to improving American productivity.
- Define quality of work life.
- Define William Ouchi's Theory Z.
- Identify 13 steps in Theory Z.
- Identify the seven elements in the 7-S model.
- Explain how Quality Circles work.

It has been said that if all the economists in the world were positioned in a line, head-to-toe, they would not reach from here to an agreement! But, surprisingly, economists who may agree on nothing else are nearly unanimous on two points. First, it seems clear that economic matters will dominate the 1980s. While specific headlines may center on energy, defense, and politics, underlying all these will be our ability to improve our productivity—to obtain more output per unit of input.

The second point is that, over the long pull, productivity gains are the best weapons against economic ills such as inflation, high interest rates, rising unemployment, and a general decline in our standard of living. Therefore, we should understand the importance of productivity to ourselves and our nation, the measures of productivity, the reasons for our declining productivity, and the steps we can take to improve our productivity.

WHY PRODUCTIVITY IS IMPORTANT

Why is productivity so important to our well-being? The basic reason is that **productivity** is a measure of the efficiency with which a person, business, or entire economy produces goods and services. It is a key indicator of a nation's economic vigor. As such, it has a great deal to do with the American ideals of opportunity, social justice, and the continuing problem of inflation.

Productivity and Opportunity

Most of us would like to be richer, or at least improve our present standard of living. Even more basically, however, many people in our society would like to find a decent, entry-level job — a steady, modern job that offers a chance to advance in one's work. This is called a **primary job.** A **secondary job,** on the other hand, is a temporary, dead-end job, where one does grubby work with inefficient processes and bosses.

A growing, dynamic economy is the key to primary jobs and higher standards of living. Only in a growing economy are entry-level jobs available without having to pull someone else off the ladder. And a dynamic, expanding economy tends to be an efficient, productive economy. In contrast, in a stagnant economy the number of jobs are not expanding. We have a sort of "zero-sum" situation where, for one person to get ahead, another must be pushed to the bottom of the ladder.

Productivity and Social Justice

Many people in our society are not employed in the mainstream of our economic activity. These include young persons, old persons, physically disadvantaged persons, and persons who don't have the ability or training to work steadily. Yet these groups still have the right to live the promise of American life.

The programs that help these groups are planned on the basis of an expanding economy. In a limited-growth economy there are great gaps in the quality of life for various groups in society. And, as we have noted, for one person to prosper, another's quality of life will be reduced. We need sustained, private-sector growth with millions of new jobs every year simply to have an adequate tax base to keep our social programs going. For everyone to be better off, the economy must grow.

Productivity and Inflation

Inflation is an economic condition that reduces the purchasing power of money. It is caused by an excess economic demand relative to our ability to supply goods and services. This excess demand results in a rise in the general level of prices and a reduction of what a dollar will buy. Thus, inflation clearly is related to our cost of living—how much we can buy with every dollar we spend. This suggests that there are demand and supply sides to the problems of dealing with inflation.

Demand Side of the Problem

Many economists agree that inflation is caused by excess economic demand. Demand becomes excessive when it is far greater than our output of goods and services. But demand, by itself, would not be a critical factor if people did not have the money or credit to pay the higher prices for the goods and services brought about by the gap in demand and output. This excess demand does become a critical factor when more money and credit are made available to the would-be consumers. The chief culprit here is the Federal Reserve Board's willingness to pump more money into the economy. This is done through such means as printing money, raising the level of government-spending programs, and adjusting the amount and terms under which funds are made available to banks.

Supply Side of the Problem

When people want more out of an economic system than they put in, an inflationary gap develops. In the face of this gap, there are three ways for a family to improve its actual standard of living. It can put more family members to work, each family member can work longer hours, or working family members can increase their productivity. The last course is best, not only for families but also for the United States economy. The ways to improve productivity are discussed in the last part of this chapter.

Both Sides of the Problem

A reduction in the rate of inflation requires a reduction in excessive demand for goods and services. Demand will not be excessive and prices will not rise rapidly if the Federal Reserve Board (Fed) limits the money supply and if our output is more clearly balanced with our economic demands. Productivity is the key to upgrading our output of goods and services while holding prices down.

THE MEASURES OF PRODUCTIVITY

In general, the concept of productivity refers to a comparison of the output of a production process with one or more of its inputs. Thus, productivity may mean different things in different situations. For example, we can measure the productivity of a cornfield in terms of bushels of corn yielded per acre; the productivity of an automobile in terms of miles run per gallon; or the productivity of a light-bulb factory in terms of light bulbs produced per worker. Although productivity may be measured in many ways, the two most commonly used measures are partial productivity and total productivity.

Partial Productivity

The most familiar reports of productivity refer to output compared with the input of just *one* of the several factors of production. This one factor is labor. **Labor productivity** is a measure of output per employee-hour and is called **partial productivity** because it involves a single input.

In a factory, labor productivity is measured by dividing the total output by the number of employee-hours needed to produce that output. If the output goes up while the number of employee-hours remains unchanged, the labor productivity is said to have increased. Figure 9-1 shows productivity growth in terms of manufacturing output per employee-hour for selected countries between 1973 and 1980.

Unfortunately there is a major drawback to measuring productivity in terms of only one element of input such as labor. Although labor is an essential input in the production of most outputs, it is *not* the sole input. An increase in the ratio of light bulbs produced per worker says nothing about the reasons for this change in productivity. Neither does the increase indicate the importance of the other factors of production involved. Actually the increase reflects the *joint* effect of a number of elements such as changes in workers' skill levels, changes in technology, capital investment per worker, layout and flow of materials, managerial skills, and energy resources.

Figure 9-1   Manufacturing Productivity Growth Rates, 1973-1980

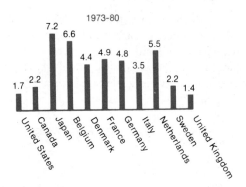

SOURCE: American Productivity Center.

Total Productivity

To find the causes for the change in productivity in the light-bulb factory, we need to know more about the other factors that go into making the light bulbs. This involves measuring **total productivity** (or total-factor productivity), the output relative to nonhuman inputs as well as human ones. This measure relates output to an entire set of resources used in the production process by assigning a weight to each resource based on its relative importance to the production process.

Measuring total productivity allows managers to isolate reasons for changes in levels of production. But it also requires great effort in terms of paperwork and performing the needed measurements. Thus, the general analysis of productivity usually focuses on the performance of only one major factor—labor.

OUR DECLINING PRODUCTIVITY

The American economy has not been well over the past 15 years. It has been trying to shake off various viruses such as inflation, high interest rates, and rising unemployment. Underlying these factors has been the disease of declining productivity. And some feel that the disease has reached a crisis level.

Productivity Since 1948

Even if some people don't feel that the disease of slowing productivity has reached a crisis level, it should be obvious to even the most optimistic observer that the patient's pulse has been weakening. Figure 9-2 shows the productivity growth rates for major sectors of the American economy since 1948. Note that productivity growth in the seventies, especially since 1973, has been extremely sluggish. From 1948 to 1965, the productivity of American private business grew 3.2 percent a year. This was followed by a 2.4 percent growth rate from 1965 to 1973, a 0.8 percent growth rate from 1973 to 1979, and a minus growth rate from 1979 to 1980. Since 1980, the rate of productivity growth has been just about zero.

Reasons for the Decline

There is a long list of possible causes for the recent decline in productivity. Of the list, the following factors often are mentioned: lagging capital investment per worker, decline in research and development, changing composition of the work force, energy problems, environmental costs, and employee attitudes.

Lagging Capital Investment per Worker

Labor is not the only input into the production process. Capital—in the form of buildings, tools, or machines—must also be used. The proportion of capital investment that each worker has to work with is called the **capital-labor ratio.** This ratio has a lot to do with what the worker can produce. As Figure 9-3 indicates, productivity

Figure 9-2   **Labor Productivity Measures of the U.S. Economy[1] (By Sector-Selected Period, 1948-1980)**

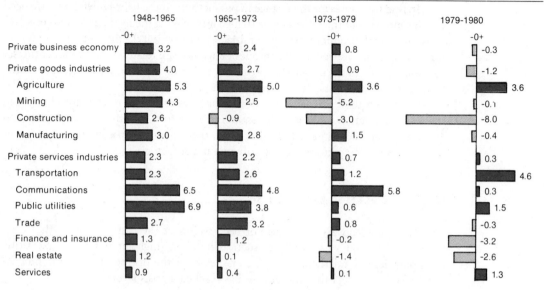

	1948-1965	1965-1973	1973-1979	1979-1980
Private business economy	3.2	2.4	0.8	-0.3
Private goods industries	4.0	2.7	0.9	-1.2
Agriculture	5.3	5.0	3.6	3.6
Mining	4.3	2.5	-5.2	-0.1
Construction	2.6	-0.9	-3.0	-8.0
Manufacturing	3.0	2.8	1.5	-0.4
Private services industries	2.3	2.2	0.7	0.3
Transportation	2.3	2.6	1.2	4.6
Communications	6.5	4.8	5.8	0.3
Public utilities	6.9	3.8	0.6	1.5
Trade	2.7	3.2	0.8	-0.3
Finance and insurance	1.3	1.2	-0.2	-3.2
Real estate	1.2	0.1	-1.4	-2.6
Services	0.9	0.4	0.1	1.3

[1]Average annual growth rate, real GDP/hour.

SOURCE: American Productivity Center.

Figure 9-3   **International Comparison of Investment and Productivity Growth, 1971-1980**

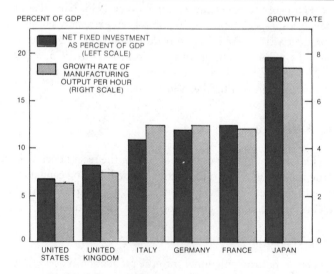

SOURCE: *Economic Report of the President* (Washington, DC: U.S. Government Printing Office, February, 1983), p. 82.

is more likely to increase rapidly in countries where this ratio is high than in countries where it is low. Figure 9-3 compares the percentage of net fixed investment to growth rate of manufacturing output per hour among six countries. Note that fixed investment in the United States has not been growing as fast as that of the other countries. One reason for the lack of capital investment, or capital formation, in the United States is that Americans are saving far less of their money than are citizens of other industrialized countries (see Table 9-1). The choice between current consumption and current savings and investment is one of the most critical decisions confronting our society. To the extent that people are willing to save and to put off present consumption (economists call this the propensity to save), these savings can be devoted to new capital investment. The lack of capital investment may reinforce a vicious cycle in which poor productivity results in lower profits. This, in turn, further discourages capital investment needed to insure future productivity growth.

Table 9-1 **Comparisons of Ratios of Savings to Disposable Personal Income, Major Industrialized Nations**

Period	United States	France	F. R. Germany	Italy	Netherlands	United Kingdom	Japan	Canada
1970	7.4	16.7	14.6	21.6	14.0	9.0	18.1	5.3
1975	7.7	18.6	16.4	23.2	14.5	12.7	22.5	10.9
1976	5.8	16.0	14.7	22.9	14.6	11.8	22.4	10.0
1977	5.0	16.9	13.6	22.5	12.6	10.5	21.1	9.8
1978	4.9	17.8	13.7	23.8	12.3	12.4	20.1	10.3
1979	4.5	16.7	14.2	n.a.	11.4	13.8	n.a.	10.5

SOURCE: American Productivity Center.

Decline in Research and Development

Investment in research and development (R&D) as a percent of gross national product has steadily declined in the United States while it has risen in many other countries such as Japan, West Germany, and the Soviet Union. Figure 9-4 shows that R&D expenditures in the United States accounted for about 3 percent of the GNP in the mid-1960s but then declined to just slightly over 2 percent by 1978. Most of this drop was brought about by reductions in military and space-related research. Some funds for R&D were used to deal with problems of safety, health, and the environment. While many of these problems need to be met, the diversion of funds away from *industry-specific R&D* results in fewer innovative ways to produce more and better goods with less labor.

Changing Composition of the Work Force

Productivity tends to decline when the percentage of inexperienced workers in the work force increases. This is true because new workers lack work experience and

Figure 9-4   National R&D Expenditure as Percentage of GNP (1953 and 1961-1980)

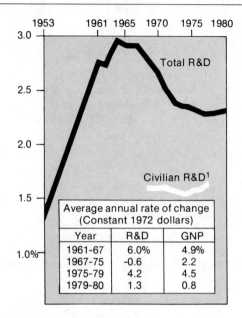

¹Excluding federally funded defense and space programs.

SOURCE: American Productivity Center.

Figure 9-5   The Baby Boom over Time: Population Growth by Age, 1950-1990

	Total	Under 5 yrs.	5-13 yrs.	14-17 yrs.	18-24 yrs.	25-34 yrs.	35-44 yrs.	45-54 yrs.	55-64 yrs.	65+ yrs.
					(percent change)					
		The Baby Boom¹								
1950-1955	9.0	13.1	24.5	9.5	-6.9	1.0	5.9	8.2	9.2	17.2
1955-1960	8.9	9.6	18.0	21.3	7.7	-5.6	5.7	9.0	6.9	14.8
1960-1965	7.5	-2.5	8.5	26.2	25.8	-2.0	0.9	6.1	9.3	10.7
1965-1970	5.4	-13.5	2.5	12.4	21.7	12.6	-5.3	6.7	9.3	8.9
1970-1975	4.2	-7.4	-8.7	6.4	11.8	22.2	-1.4	2.0	6.0	11.6
1975-1979	3.3	-1.4	-8.4	-3.9	6.1	13.3	10.2	-3.4	5.9	10.0
1980-1985	4.8	17.4	-3.6	-8.7	-5.5	10.2	22.0	-1.1	2.5	9.5
1985-1990	4.6	3.4	11.9	-11.3	-9.7	3.1	16.6	12.7	-4.4	9.2

¹These are the age groups most affected by the baby boom, defined here as persons born in the years 1946 to 1961.

SOURCE: Lynn E. Browne, "Why the Mini-Skirt Won't Come Back." *New England Economic Review* (November/December, 1981), p. 18.

skills to make them highly productive. Also, the task of training the newcomers takes some time and effort from the experienced workers.

During the 1960s and 1970s, the participation rate (percent) of newcomers in the work force increased for two different reasons. First, the postwar baby boom of the 1940s and 1950s led to many young people entering the work force in the 1960s and 1970s (see Figure 9-5). Second, during the past 20 years, women started seeking work outside the home in record numbers. Many argue that this surge of inexperienced or unskilled workers has contributed to our declining productivity. However, as the participation rate of untrained employees levels off and the younger workers mature, the work force will become relatively more experienced. These changes are expected to have a positive effect on productivity in the 1980s.

Energy Problems

Shortages and higher prices of energy in the United States may have reduced output per employee-hour in recent years. An example is the shift in demand for products such as polyester fabrics. To make these fabrics, large amounts of high-priced energy and petroleum-based basic materials, or *feedstocks*, are required. The costs of adjusting to such a change and shifting to other products may show up in the form of lower productivity growth. Another example is the shift in consumer usage of electrical energy as a result of oil price hikes in the mid-1970s. This led to the underutilization of power-generating capacity.

Also, higher energy prices may have reduced productivity growth by encouraging firms to substitute manual labor for machines that use electrical energy. This shift from *energy-intensive* machines to *labor-intensive* production methods usually reduces the average output per employee-hour.

Environmental Costs

Industry has had to invest hundreds of millions of dollars in nonproductive equipment to protect the environment. Though governmental regulations may produce a cleaner environment and a safer workplace, they do not result in the production of more goods and services.

Environmental regulations may also affect productivity by reducing the profitability of some types of capital investments. For example, if an operation requires heavy pollution-control costs to comply with the law, the return on the revenue-producing part of the operation must be enough to cover these added costs. Environmental regulations, therefore, may have slowed our productivity growth in recent years.

Employee Attitudes

Employee motivation is probably the most controversial of the possible reasons for our declining productivity growth. Some believe that our positive attitudes toward work have declined and that these attitudes have been replaced by boredom and a rejection of the work ethic, as Figure 9-6 suggests.

Figure 9-6   Decline of the Work Ethic

THE WALL STREET JOURNAL

"As far as the seven deadly sins go, I can't get very excited over 'sloth'."

SOURCE: From *The Wall Street Journal,* June 5, 1980, p. 24. Permission—Cartoon Features Syndicate.

Others argue that the work ethic has always had its ups and downs and that older workers have always complained that the younger generation is lazy. Regardless of one's feelings about this situation, there are hopeful signs for the 1980s. Students now seem more job-oriented, and some companies are putting greater emphasis on both employee motivation and supervisor training.

STEPS TO IMPROVE OUR PRODUCTIVITY

Indeed, the 1980s are a decisive decade. The United States has been losing the international-trade war because foreign competitors have been producing some goods that are not only better than ours, but also cheaper. If we fail to come to grips with our productivity problems, the United States will wind up taking a back seat to more disciplined countries such as West Germany and Japan.

Yet the forces of decline can be stemmed. If United States industry stays ahead in capital formation, technology, and management, it will stay ahead in world markets. This challenge involves many factors. However, three important actions are among the keys to halting our declining productivity. These are: to increase savings and investments in capital goods and R&D, to develop a long-term management perspective, and to upgrade management-employee relations.

Increase Savings and Investments

Most economists agree that investment is needed to increase productivity and economic growth. They also agree that saving is necessary for investment to take place. Therefore, it is important to understand the relationship between savings and investments.

Savings

To economists, saving means nonconsumption. There are basically two things that can be done with the income earned by all persons in a nation during a given year: spend it now for consumer goods or services, or save it.

The thrift motto "A penny saved is a penny earned" may at one time have characterized the savings habit in the United States. Unfortunately that is no longer the case because consumption-oriented Americans drop far behind the Europeans and Japanese in their rates of saving.

Whenever the ratio of savings to income falls, business suffers. This is part of our problem today — the savings rate in the United States dropped to less than 5 percent of disposable personal income in 1979 (refer to Table 9-1 on page 195). Historically American consumers have spent about 92 percent of the income they receive and have saved 8 percent of it. Business firms typically borrow that remaining 8 percent from the capital market. The firms use these funds, along with their retained earnings, to finance new projects. In turn, the projects provide jobs, income, and goods and services to American consumers.

If most people spent all the income they receive, there will be little or nothing left for investment in new factories, productive equipment, and homes. Therefore, the Yankee incentive to save should be restored if the United States is to be pulled out of its economic doldrums. To encourage savings the Economic Recovery Tax Act of 1981, among other things, provided for the following:

> . . . The Individual Retirement Account (IRA) provisions in the tax code were extended to cover the entire working population. Working individuals are now permitted to make a yearly tax deductible contribution of $2,000 to finance consumption during retirement. Taxes are only paid when the funds plus accumulated interest are withdrawn from the IRA. Private estimates suggest a substantial response to this legislation, with about $10 billion placed in IRAs during 1982. . .
>
> The 1981 tax legislation also provided for an interest exclusion starting in 1985, allowing individuals to exclude 15 percent of their net interest income up to a limit of $3,000. This will also raise the return to savings and spur capital formation. Extending the exclusion to dividends as well as interest payments would reduce the tax bias favoring debt over equity as a source of corporate finance.
>
> The 1981 tax act also raised the return to saving by reducing the top marginal rate on capital gains from 28 percent to 20 percent. This reform partially compensates for the serious distorting effect of inflation on the measurement of capital gains.[1]

---

1. *Economic Report of the President* (Washington, DC: U.S. Government Printing Office, February, 1983), p. 88.

Investments

The sluggish growth of business investments has been a disappointment in recent years. Vigorous business investment is important, not only to support business recoveries but also to increase the productive capacity of the economy. Investment is critically needed in two areas: capital goods and R&D.

Investment in Capital Goods. Americans are still the most potentially productive workers in the world. But when outmoded machinery and insufficient capital result in our achieving less than our full potential, then American industry and every American worker are handicapped. Today the average plant in the United States is 20 years old as compared to 12 years for Germany and 10 years for Japan.

To encourage more investment in modern plants and equipment, two key actions can be taken with regard to tax policy and depreciation allowances. For tax purposes, business firms could be allowed to depreciate their present plant and equipment on the basis of replacement value instead of historical, noninflated costs. This would increase the cash flow of corporations and provide funds for modernization. Further easing of the depreciation allowances could be done by shortening the suggested service lives of capital assets.

Investment in R&D. Research and development are the "seed corn" for this nation's industrial sector. R&D spawns innovation, technology, new industries, and new jobs. Unfortunately R&D in the United States reached its peak in 1964. Table 9-2 shows that nearly 40 percent of the patents now issued in the United States are to non-United States citizens!

Productive R&D can be fostered by taking the following steps:

Table 9-2		Percent of U. S. Patents Granted to Foreign Inventors, 1966-1978			
Year	Total Foreign	West Germany	Japan	United Kingdom	All Other
1966	20.1	5.8	1.6	3.9	8.8
1969	25.4	6.7	3.2	4.7	10.8
1972	31.1	7.7	6.9	4.2	12.3
1975	35.1	8.4	8.8	4.2	13.7
1978	38.0	8.9	10.5	4.2	14.4

SOURCE: American Productivity Center.

1. Allow flexible depreciation for equipment and special-purpose structures used in R&D.
2. Allow flexible depreciation for purchased patents and secret processes.
3. Clarify antitrust policy so that large companies can work together more closely on new technology.
4. Develop institutions and programs to promote the rapid diffusion of advanced technology throughout our economy. Both the Japanese and West Germans have such institutions.

Perhaps the greatest barrier to R&D is the unwillingness of managers with a short-term orientation to take risks and to maintain a long-run climate of support for innovation.

Develop a Long-Term Management Perspective

While our competitors have been seeking to optimize their market position and competitiveness over the long term, we have been increasingly preoccupied with immediate results. Instead of formulating policies that strengthen the American industrial system, for decades we have milked it for short-term benefits.

American managers have been trained to have a fixation for consistent, short-term profit growth. Their compensation arrangements usually reward growth over a period as short as one year. They are often pitted in competition within the same company against the most successful divisions, which may be on different development cycles. Furthermore, they are expected to maintain consistently high returns on both sales and investment. Why has this come about? Mainly because individual stockholders and large institutional stockholders of American corporations want performance, not explanations. They want financial results now, as measured against current market standards.

Simply turning on the faucets for capital goods and R&D, although important, is not enough. To make these steps work, we need chief executives who are rewarded for solid, long-term results. These persons should have a great awareness of the human and economic penalties for the short-term management of long-range problems. They should aim toward the gradual creation of an overall strategic plan that integrates specific productivity projects into a solid, long-term program. This plan may encompass such points as capital investments, training, technical innovations, reorganization, and as we shall see in the next section, worker involvement in management's decisions.

Upgrade Management-Employee Relations

Workers have been prime targets for criticism because productivity figures often are based on national output per worker. Older generations tend to bemoan what they see as a loss of the work ethic among younger workers. And American managers tend to think that increased efficiency comes not from the effort or commitment of workers, but from better technology and well-educated managers who provide the necessary guidance.

This approach has focused managerial attention on increasing output per worker at the production-line level, often by automating assembly lines to turn out more goods with fewer human hands. While many assembly-line improvements are needed, American managers have been accused of throwing more capital and technology at the productivity problem rather than facing up to the need for new managerial techniques and attitudes. For example, direct labor accounts for about 12 percent of the American manufacturing sales dollar. Yet a whopping 80 percent of sales revenue is tied to areas directly controlled by management!

Aim for a High-Quality Work Life

The bad news for business managers is that their own poor performance is largely responsible for productivity problems. The good news is that they can do much to correct the problem of poor productivity. But they cannot do it alone. Managers must make use of workers' brains as well as hands. This calls for a participatory process in which workers gain a voice in decision making at the shop-floor level. A workable participatory management program requires a change in attitude throughout the company, and this must be supported from the top. This change of attitude is reflected in the current interest in the quality-of-life concept. There are various definitions of **quality of work life (QWL),** but perhaps the best definition is that of Charles Bisanz, a consultant to the Northwestern Bell Co.: "It is not a solution devised by management so much as it is a decision by management to share responsibility with employees in devising solutions."[2] Evidence is growing that QWL programs can meet the twin goals of increasing job satisfaction and of improving quality and productivity.

The success of QWL requires changes in the attitudes and practices of managers and workers about the quality of relationships in an organization. Two popular books provide insights as to what this effort requires. These are *Theory Z: How American Business Can Meet the Japanese Challenge* by William G. Ouchi and *The Art of Japanese Management: Applications for American Executives* by Richard T. Pascale and Anthony G. Athos.

On Theory Z. In his book, *Theory Z,* Ouchi writes that old plants and equipment are not, by themselves, the cause of the American economic problem. The cause seems to be the way American organizations treat their workers. Ouchi's theme is that American organizations can draw on the success of the Japanese without imitating

---

2. Charles G. Burck, "Working Smarter," FORTUNE (June 15, 1981), p. 73. © 1981 Time Inc.

them because there are specific principles of organizations that have little to do with national cultures, but much to do with organizational cultures. In effect, **Ouchi's Theory Z** can be defined as a way of managing people — a style that focuses on a strong company philosophy, a distinct corporate culture, long-range staff development, and consensus decision making.

Ouchi lays out 13 steps that would help a United States company in shifting to a participative, integrated work force. These steps are listed in Figure 9-7. However,

Figure 9-7   Going from A to Z: The 13 Steps

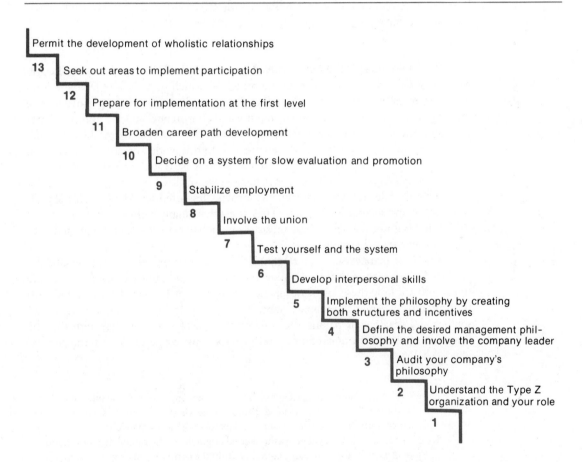

- Permit the development of wholistic relationships
- 13 Seek out areas to implement participation
- 12 Prepare for implementation at the first level
- 11 Broaden career path development
- 10 Decide on a system for slow evaluation and promotion
- 9 Stabilize employment
- 8 Involve the union
- 7 Test yourself and the system
- 6 Develop interpersonal skills
- 5 Implement the philosophy by creating both structures and incentives
- 4 Define the desired management philosophy and involve the company leader
- 3 Audit your company's philosophy
- 2 Understand the Type Z organization and your role
- 1

SOURCE: Reprinted from *Theory Z: How American Business Can Meet the Japanese Challenge* by William G. Ouchi, Ph. D., copyright © 1981, by permission of Addison-Wesley Publishing Co., Reading, MA.

in practice, the steps will not follow the exact sequence in the list. These steps are intended as a guide rather than as a "cookbook approach" to management. Our challenge, then, is to refocus American corporate organizational culture to include technology and the coordinating and organizing of people.

According to Ouchi, a **Theory Z organization** is one that:

1. Has a policy of long-term employment along with an investment in training.
2. Has a policy of thorough evaluation and careful promotions.
3. Plans career development across functional areas.
4. Uses quantitative analysis to enhance decisions rather than to control them.

Ouchi has studied several successful United States companies which include Eli Lilly, Rockwell International, Dayton-Hudson, Hewlett-Packard, and Intel. His study shows how these companies exhibit definite "Z" tendencies.

On *The Art of Japanese Management.* In their book, *The Art of Japanese Management*, Pascale and Athos show how the principles which underlie the Japanese form of management also appear in outstanding American firms. Two keys to participative management seem to be: managerial stability and consistency, and the ability to integrate all viewpoints and activities in an organization. To achieve all these, the **7-S model** for organizational performance has been created. In this model, organizational success occurs when the seven S's in Figure 9-8 are carefully activated over the long run.

Although American managers have focused on strategy, structure, and systems for some time, Pascale and Athos fault them for paying less attention to the *soft S's* of staff, style, skills, and superordinate goals. They stress that simply being effective at each of the seven S's is not enough. These must be individually effective and integrated with one another in a cohesive way.

American managers recognize that differences between the American and Japanese cultures require different managerial practices and philosophies. But they are starting to ask how these levers of Japanese management can best be integrated with the strengths of American management. This interest in Japanese managerial philosophies and practices is paving the way for the use of some Japanese terms in the literature of American organization and management. Some of these terms are explained below.

1. *Mikoshi.* In **mikoshi** management, Japanese company executives avoid outward displays of strong leadership. Instead, they favor giving assignments to subordinates and then encouraging and stimulating the subordinates' performance.
2. *Nemawashi.* The term **nemawashi** referred originally to the careful digging around the root of a tree before it is transplanted. Within the context of management, *nemawashi* means "root-digging" persuasion by somebody who takes the lead and carefully maneuvers others to align with the idea or position, thus obtaining a consensus.

Figure 9-8   The 7-S Model

● Strategy	● Plan a course of action leading to the allocation of a firm's scarce resources, over time, to reach identified goals.
● Structure	● Characterization of the organization chart (i.e., functional, decentralized, etc.).
● Systems	● Proceduralized reports and routinized processes such as meeting formats.
● Staff	● "Demographic" description of important personnel categories within the firm (i.e., engineers, entrepreneurs, M. B. A.s, etc.). "Staff" is *not* meant in line-staff terms.
● Style	● Characterization of how key managers behave in achieving the organization's goals; also the cultural style of the organization.
● Skills	● Distinctive capabilities of key personnel or the firm as a whole.
● Superordinate Goals	● The significant meanings or guiding concepts that an organization imbues in its members.

SOURCE: Richard T. Pascale and Anthony G. Athos, *The Art of Japanese Management: Applications for American Executives* (New York: Simon & Schuster, 1981), p. 81. Copyright © 1981 by Richard Tanner Pascale and Anthony G. Athos. Reprinted by permission of Simon & Schuster, a Division of Gulf & Western Corporation.

3. *Ringi.* The **ringi** system is an organized method for obtaining formal approval by superiors of a plan initiated at lower levels in the organization. Under this consensus decision-making system, people at various levels become involved in the decision-making process. Thus, the plan enjoys wide exposure and negotiation as it works its way up to the top executive.

4. *Uzekara.* The term **uzekara** refers to the careful preparation of the factory "dish" for the reception of new management techniques and programs. In other words, it takes the place of simply imposing management's decisions on the organization in a one-way, authoritarian manner.

Establish Quality Circles

There are many variations of participative decision making at the lower levels of an organization. These are found in job enlargement, in autonomous work groups, in ombudspersons, in facilitators, and especially in Quality Circles (QCs). Quality Circles are becoming an important technique for upgrading the quality and quantity of an organization's work and are rapidly growing in use.

Nature of Quality Circles. A Quality Circle is a group of eight to ten workers and supervisors who are generally involved in related work. They meet regularly on company time to identify, analyze, and solve product-quality and production problems, as well as to improve general operations. Often a personnel specialist trains the workers in elementary data gathering and statistics. The circle members learn how to talk the language of management and to present their ideas to executives. Figure 9-9 shows how Quality Circles work.

The QC reflects a basic shift to a new outlook on worker participation in decision making. Oddly enough, the idea for QCs came not from Japan, but from American business consultants. After World War II, the Japanese picked up the idea as a means of improving the quality of their products. Today eight million Japanese workers are involved in QC systems.

Figure 9-9   How Quality Circles Work

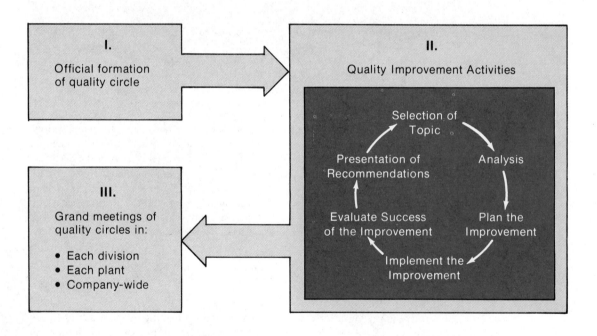

Use of Quality Circles. The first United States firm to adopt the full QC concept was Lockheed Missile and Space Company of Sunnyvale, CA. Now well over 300 American corporations are using the concept in an effort to achieve higher quality and productivity. General Motors has over 100 Quality Circles operating in its various automotive divisions. QCs also can be found in supermarkets, banks, and government offices.

Many business organizations in the United States will change greatly in the 1980s. The emphasis on QWL at all levels in the organization suggest the coming of numerous nontraditional organizational forms and relationships in the American business scene. These changing organizations will reflect the many efforts by management to harmonize and integrate company and employee goals between organizational levels and across horizontal divisions. It is becoming clear that an upgraded QWL means more than the use of fads or gimmicks. It is a state of mind that involves everyone from the president to the production trainee in thinking about new and better ways to improve quality and productivity.

SUMMARY

Productivity growth in the United States has slowed dramatically in the past 20 years. Since the late 1960s, productivity in the private sector has risen only about half as much as it did during the two decades following World War II. Slower productivity growth means fewer good jobs, a slower growth of real incomes, and higher inflation.

Although the slowdown in productivity is clear, the reasons for the slowdown are complex. Six reasons were pinpointed in this chapter. These are: lagging capital investment per worker, decline in research and development, changing composition of the work force, energy problems, environmental costs, and worker attitudes.

America must come to grips with its productivity problems in the 1980s. The actions that must be taken to achieve a higher-quality work life include increasing savings and investments, developing a long-term management perspective, and upgrading management-employee relations. This requires a decision by management to include employees in decisions that affect them.

In facing up to this challenge, American managers can draw from successful practices of Japanese managers without necessarily imitating everything that is done in the Japanese organizational culture. A good starting point in this effort is to consider both Ouchi's Theory Z type of organization and management and the 7-S model for organizational performance. Finally, the Quality Circle that has been highly successful in Japan reflects a basic shift toward manager-employee participation in decision making. The goal of Quality Circles is higher quality and productivity in goods, services, and all phases of an organization's operations.

BACK TO THE CHAPTER OPENER

1. How does net fixed investment, as a percentage of Gross Domestic Product, differ in the United States from that of other industrialized nations?
2. How does the emphasis on the human side of productivity in Japan differ from that of many companies in the United States?
3. What percentage of American personal income goes into savings to be reinvested? How does this compare with other industrialized nations?
4. How does management-worker participation in decision making relate to the concept of the quality of worklife?
5. Does the United States invest more or less in R&D in comparison to other industrialized nations?

BUSINESS TERMS	productivity	190	Ouchi's Theory Z	203
	primary job	190	Theory Z organization	204
	secondary job	190	7-S model	204
	inflation	191	mikoshi	204
	labor productivity	192	nemawashi	204
	partial productivity	192	ringi	205
	total productivity	193	uzekara	205
	capital-labor ratio	193	Quality Circle	205
	quality of work life (QWL)	202		

QUESTIONS FOR DISCUSSION AND ANALYSIS

1. Is persistent inflation caused mainly by federal tax policies? Explain.
2. Is labor the single most important factor in productivity?
3. Six reasons for our declining productivity were noted in the chapter. What other reasons can you give?
4. Why do people in Japan save more of their income than people in the United States?
5. The bulge from the postwar baby boom will be felt in the work force until 1990 or so. In which age bracket will the baby boom be mainly felt in 1984?
6. Should we expect any more baby booms in the future? Explain.
7. Should industry have to invest heavily in "nonproductive" equipment to protect the environment? Explain.
8. This chapter notes three key actions to halting productivity decline. Name at least five background variables or determinants that will help shape the actions to be taken and the future course of productivity.
9. What is the difference between the soft S's and the hard S's in the 7-S model?
10. Would some workers in a Quality Circle hesitate to express their ideas if some of their bosses are also in the Circle?

PROJECTS, PROBLEMS, AND SHORT CASES

1. Ed Wiggins shook his head as he scanned the weekly production figures for his company, which makes brake linings and automotive gaskets. "Those workers just can't seem to get up to the production levels of a couple of years ago," he muttered to himself. "You'd think that with layoffs and the unemployment rate the people who are working would bust themselves to do a job." His gaze turned to a magazine article he had cut out regarding Chinese factory workers. It praised the ingenuity and self-reliance of Chinese workers and their ability to jerry-build machinery to substitute for modern machinery. "My machines may not be the newest," he mused, "but I bet those Chinese factory workers could make them sing. Let's face it—American workers are just dragging their feet!"

Prepare a report indicating the following:

a. Whether you feel American workers are dragging in productivity.
b. What other factors Wiggins should consider with regard to productivity.

2. Young people often take a negative view of business profits. Prepare a short report indicating why teenagers may have a special stake in business profits. (Hint: What is the relation of profit to productivity and innovation?)

3. Quality Circles are not limited to production activities. They are found in many types of organizations and can deal with any aspect of operations that may improve organizational performance. Start a Quality Circle with five to seven class members. The QC should be comprised of members who vary as much as possible in age, sex, and ethnic or racial background. It might meet about half an hour per week on its own time and should focus on problems within the department or school that can be handled on a factual rather than an emotional basis. The QC should prepare a short report and make a verbal presentation to the class by the end of the course.

Fame in the Factory

Armed with an MBA from Columbia, Peter Smith landed a prestigious job in General Signal's mergers and acquisitions department, where he worked closely with the chairman. But when he heard that the company was creating a post as director of manufacturing services, he volunteered and got the job. "My peers were aghast," he says.

Smith had his reasons: "There's enormous excitement in manufacturing. You transform raw materials into something of value and deal with a spectrum of people you'd never come across."

In 1977 Smith was appointed manufacturing vice president of Regina, a $50-million unit that makes floor-care appliances. An erratic performer, the operation had gone through three vice presidents in five years. Smith found the production floor grueling. "The first thing I noticed was the extraordinary pace," he says. "We worked at a run all day. Manufacturing is unlike any other discipline in the need for immediate decisions."

At age 29, Smith was General Signal's youngest vice president and the company's first MBA assigned to manufacturing. The union wanted to test his style. "I had only been there a few weeks when a worker struck a supervisor. This was punishable by a one-day suspension or termination. I terminated her on the spot. We had a severe lack of shop-floor discipline."

Smith believes most manufacturing problems arise when management doesn't talk with the workers. "People will flood you with ideas if you let them." He cites his experience with a switch-assembly operation where workers had to twist together five pairs of wires, cap them with nuts, and stuff them into a vacuum-cleaner handle. "We had quality problems with the nuts falling off, and the workers had to wear Band-Aids on their fingers. One suggested we use a switch with push-in connections instead, but the materials cost would double. I calculated how much more productivity we would need to offset the cost and asked the union to help me prove we could get it by using the new switch." The change cut the rejection rate, formerly 20%, to less than 1%. In three years at Regina, Smith reduced the cost of assembling a vacuum cleaner from $1.56 to 88 cents and generated savings of $12 million.

He continues to be attentive to workers' ideas in his current job as president of BIF, a General Signal unit that makes water-treatment equipment. Alfred Malo, 59, a lathe operator, praises Smith for laying off 150 white-collar workers. "There used to be five of them for every one of us," Malo says. "Peter got it down to three to one. I can tell the difference in the parking lot." Smith insists that production workers be well rewarded: "If they help us make money, we have to give a little back to them. The guys in the office can't always get *all* the gravy."

Smith hasn't done badly for himself in manufacturing. His income has more than quintupled in six years; at 33 he is the company's youngest president and is besieged with job offers. "There was no way I could have proved how important I was to the company had I stayed in finance," he says. "In manufacturing there is a clear connection between your skills and the company's profit. If the scrap rate is 5% of materials costs and you get it down to 2%, you can get a 30% improvement in profit without adding a dollar in sales. Nobody else in the company can do that."

10 *Production and Manufacturing Systems*

Objectives:

- Distinguish between production and manufacturing.
- Identify three basic factors that influence the design of a manufacturing system.
- Distinguish between standard and custom products.
- Discuss the two basic orientations, or focuses, of manufacturing organizations.
- Distinguish between mass production and the assembly line.
- Discuss how total quality control differs from conventional quality control.
- Identify six categories of simple and automated machinery.
- Distinguish between programmable machines and industrial robots.
- Define CAD and CAM.
- Discuss five questions managers must deal with prior to using robots in their factory system.

The word production often is used in the sense of making things. In fact, to many persons production *is* manufacturing. However, **manufacturing** is simply a special form of production by which raw and semifinished materials are processed and converted into finished products needed by consumers. In a broader and more basic sense, **production** is the transformation of inputs from human and physical resources into outputs desired by consumers. These outputs may be either goods or services. So, although a large restaurant is not considered to be a manufacturer, it is also engaged in production. In fact, there are many service companies engaged in production.

Examples are printing, cleaning and laundering, fast-food, and health-care organizations. The production of services often is called **operations management.**

Effective production of goods and services requires innovation. When most people hear the word innovation, they think about new or better products. However, new products may not be as significant as another form of innovation — **process innovation** — which means skill and care in the way managers organize the processes of production. For example, according to James Harbour, an automotive consultant in Detroit:

> Better factory layouts and more flexible use of workers enables Japanese auto makers to assemble a small car with approximately 15 man-hours of labor, compared to as much as 30 hours for American products. If the entire production process is considered from iron ore to finished vehicles. . . a host of other cost advantages give Japanese car makers a $2,500 cost edge over U.S. manufacturers in the production process. . .[1]

Car makers are not the only companies that are giving increased attention to process innovation. Across the country top-level managers are saying that manufacturing and production operations have been neglected for too long. These managers now are recognizing that the best-conceived strategic plans or marketing analyses are useless if products are too costly to produce or too shoddy to sell. They are beginning to see that when a company effectively aligns its factory planning and management to its corporate objectives, it is likely to do better at raising productivity, developing new technology, and making better products.

Thus, we now are entering an era in which production and corporate management are becoming recommitted to one of the basics of business: making a better product faster and cheaper. This effort is important because the great bulk of assets used in manufacturing companies — capital invested, people employed, and management time — is allotted to the production function of the business rather than to marketing or finance. This situation is true also in service firms.

In this chapter we will deal mainly with manufacturing. To be effective in process innovation, the production manager will have to cope with the complexities of computer-aided machines and factory systems. We will first cover the basic concepts in production and manufacturing, and then move on into the exciting and challenging world of automated factory processes.

BASIC FACTORS IN MANUFACTURING SYSTEMS

The ability of a company's manufacturing system to reinforce corporate strategy is determined by a number of decisions over a long period of time. Some basic, long-run decisions affecting the design of manufacturing systems are:

---

1. Amal Nag, "U.S. Car Industry Has Full-Sized Problems in Subcompact Market," *The Wall Street Journal*, January 7, 1983, pp. 1, 8. Reprinted by permission of *The Wall Street Journal,* © Dow Jones & Company, Inc. (1983). All Rights Reserved.

1. *Location of the production facility.* Where will the factory be located in reference to nearness of markets, closeness to adequate supplies of labor and materials, environmental pollution controls, and other factors?
2. *Layout of the facility.* How shall the factory be arranged so that its operations are efficiently carried on?
3. *Selection of equipment and processes.* What equipment will be purchased so that goods or services may be produced at minimum cost?
4. *Production design of items processed.* In what form (pattern, style, quality) will goods and services be made?
5. *Job design.* How shall the human work of production be subdivided among people in view of skill, health, and costs involved?

Each of these decisions has various possible answers. Furthermore, the decisions are interrelated. So, where should one start? A primary factor that bears on the above points is the nature of the product to be produced. Thus, a major set of manufacturing decisions concerns matching the company's choice of equipment and processes with its products' characteristics. As Figure 10-1 notes, the type or character of the product determines the basic manufacturing organization and orientation. These factors, in turn, are reflected in the types of production processes to be used.

Figure 10-1   Three Basic Factors in the Manufacturing System

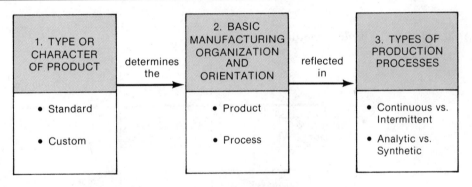

Type or Character of Product

Decisions regarding the design of a manufacturing system, small or large, will be based primarily on the type or character of the product. The two main classifications of manufactured products are standard products and custom products.

Standard Products

Items that are produced by manufacturers to their own specifications are called standard products. The manufacture of these items is called standard manufacture. Examples of standard products are television sets, toothbrushes, and automobiles.

If standard products carry the manufacturer's brand name, they are called proprietary products. The manufacturer of a proprietary product may produce under a brand name for three types of users: the general public (e.g., Valvoline motor oil); a specific segment of the public that uses the product in specialized occupations or hobbies (e.g., Nautilus health equipment); or original equipment manufacturers that require components or subassemblies (e.g., Dana axle asemblies).

Custom Products

A custom product is made to the customer's specifications and design, sometimes with customer-owned tooling. This specific product is sold only to the one customer. The manufacture of these items is called custom manufacture, and the custom manufacturer usually specializes in certain processes, materials, or subassemblies. Examples of custom products are tailor-made clothing and specialized machine tools.

Manufacturing Organization and Orientation

The organization for manufacturing depends on the complexity of the products manufactured and the size of the company. In a large company the manufacturing organization has such divisions as engineering, production control, inspection, and purchasing. The division heads report to the manufacturing manager. Figure 10-2

Figure 10-2   A Manufacturing Organization

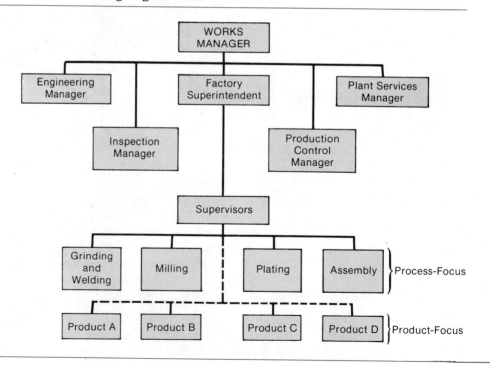

shows the organization of manufacturing in a medium-size firm that makes a fairly simple product. Note that the inspection manager is independent of the factory superintendent and the production control manager. This gives inspection the independence it needs to do its job without unnecessary pressure from competing interests.

Process- and product-focuses are the two basic manufacturing orientations. The manufacturing organization in Figure 10-2 has a process-focus. Process-focused organizations typically are dedicated to producing a variety of products with various specialized processes. They require a large staff with heavy centralized authority to coordinate the processes and the product mix. If the manufacturing organization in Figure 10-2 had a product-focus, it would be charted as shown by the dotted lines. In such an organization each product group is essentially an independent small company where authority is highly decentralized. Thus, a company's manufacturing orientation is a key characteristic that helps to shape its policies, control systems, managerial attitudes, and competitive strategies.

Types of Production Processes

The type of products a company produces, along with its basic manufacturing orientation in making these products, will have a bearing on the types of production processes used. Two major classifications of production processes are based on the length of production run (continuous v. intermittent) and on the nature of the processes used to make the final product (synthetic v. analytic).

Continuous v. Intermittent Production Processes

In a continuous process, production runs for long periods of time. Sometimes machines perform the same operations for months or years, and often the entire operation relies on the machines to keep running. Automobiles and petroleum are produced by a continuous process.

An intermittent (or batch) process involves short production runs on various products. Machines are shut down often for retooling. Most job shops fit this category. A job shop has certain equipment and facilities, such as a foundry or machine tools, that allow it to take on a variety of jobs within a broad specialty. Steel production often is a batch-process activity, with huge furnaces and rolling mills strung out over large spaces. A smooth flow of production requires close cooperation between departments and between workers and supervisors within departments.

Synthetic v. Analytic Production Processes

Synthetic and analytic production processes are based on the nature of the process rather than the length of production runs. In a synthetic process, basic parts, components, or chemicals are combined to form a final product. Examples are the manufacture of dinnerware or steel. In some instances, as in the manufacture of electrical appliances, materials are assembled without undergoing physical or chemical change. Synthetic process is sometimes called the assembly process, especially when a mass-production assembly line is used.

The analytic (or disassembly) process is one in which a basic material or substance is broken down into a number of other final products. Lumber milling and meat dressing are examples of this. If the lumber and meat products are first disassembled and then combined (pressed, finished, etc.) into other products such as plywood or pressed ham, this analytic process is called a fabrication process. The analytic process also is sometimes called a converting process, as in the textile field.

MASS PRODUCTION AND THE ASSEMBLY LINE

When most people think about modern American manufacturing, they don't think about the production processes discussed previously. Instead, the mass-production assembly line naturally comes to mind. Furthermore, most people don't realize that the use of mass-production assembly lines involves two separate concepts: mass production and the assembly line. **Mass production** is the effective combination of three factors: specialized labor, machine power, and interchangeable parts. The combination of the first two factors — specialized labor and machine power — brought about the factory system developed in Europe. However, the third factor — the idea of interchangeable parts — came about in this country. It was conceived by Eli Whitney for his rifle manufacturing plant about 1800. Today large industrial organizations throughout the world use the mass-production system to meet the needs of mass markets.

The assembly line is only one aspect of mass production, which is broadly defined in Figure 10-3. Assembly lines, however, vary widely in their uses and characteristics. Figure 10-4 shows some important differences among assembly lines.

In the 1920s Charlie Chaplin's *Modern Times* viewed the assembly line as the height of the battle between humans and technology. Today most negative reports about assembly lines seem to come from their use in automobile manufacturing, with its huge size and unrelenting pace. So, for many years, mass production and the assembly line have been seen both as models of crushing monotony and as vital models of efficiency, enabling industry to achieve high-speed, low-cost production. However, many factory workers may never return to the shop to continue their love-hate relationship with the assembly line. Later in the chapter we will see that mass production and the assembly line are being changed radically by the era of the automated factory.

THE ON-GOING PRODUCTION FUNCTION

Even a carefully established production system needs attention given to its daily operations. Steps must be taken to maintain and improve the reliability and efficiency of operations and to control the quantity and quality of output. To do this, production managers deal with such activities as work improvement, production control, maintenance of equipment, and quality control.

Figure 10-3   Five Aspects of Modern Mass Production

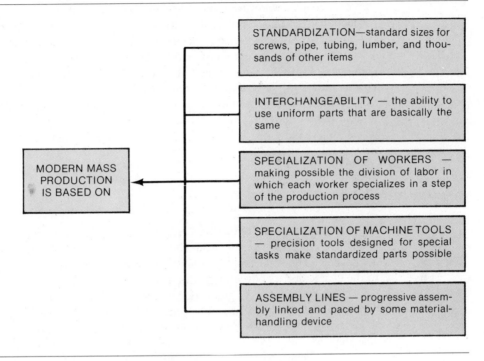

Figure 10-4   Differences Among Assembly Lines

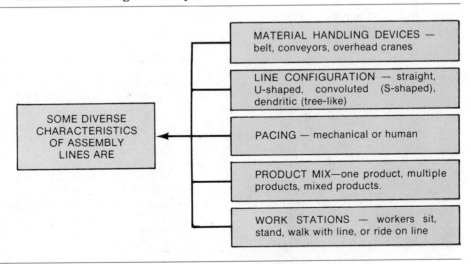

Work Improvement

The goal of work improvement is the reduction of effort, time, and cost in production operations. This involves understanding each operation in the production system, studying details of each work step, and finding better ways to perform the tasks. Work improvement seeks to answer these questions: Can some part of the work be eliminated? Can some parts of the task be combined? Can the sequence of work steps be changed? Can the operation be simplified?

Work improvement relies on such techniques as motion study and time study to help answer the above questions. Motion study aims at finding the most effective series of motions to do a job. Time study deals with the time these motions should take.

Production Control

The objective of **production control** is to coordinate all the elements in the production process—workers, machines, tools, and materials—into a smoothly operating whole. The details of the various systems of production control differ according to the characteristics of the industries in which they are used.

There are two types of production control: order control and flow control. Order control is used by shops that produce only to customer orders. Flow control is used in shops that produce for stock and fill customers' orders from finished goods inventories. The steps in both types are similar. The four basic steps in production control are described in Figure 10-5. These are: planning, routing, scheduling, and performance follow-up and control.

Figure 10-5   Four Basic Steps in Production Control

Step	Description
• Planning	• The order for a customer or for stock is broken into its parts. A *bill of materials* lists the parts and subassemblies needed for the order. The various parts and materials are requisitioned from inventory, manufactured in-house, or purchased from outside sources.
• Routing	• Routing determines the path the work will take through the shop, the sequence of operations to be performed, and who will perform them.
• Scheduling	• Scheduling involves setting up the timetables for the work as it goes through various fabrication processes. The timetables are followed on *master schedules* for the entire order, on *weekly department schedules* for each department's part of the order, and on *load ahead schedules* showing future work for the departments.
• Performance follow-up and control	• Various follow-up routines and reports are prepared. These include such items as actual versus expected departmental performance, flow of parts and materials, and the level of scrap and rejected pieces.

Maintenance of Equipment

Modern factories are highly mechanized. Machine failure may result in the loss of many employee-hours of productive labor or even in the shutdown of the plant. Preventing breakdown of major equipment is a prime responsibility of a production manager. **Maintenance** includes all the activities involved in keeping machinery and equipment working at a desired level of reliability. **Reliability** is the probability that a production system or piece of equipment will function properly for a specified time.

Three methods of attaining a satisfactory level of equipment reliability are: establishing a repair facility, using preventive maintenance, and providing redundancy. The company that uses its own people and equipment to provide repair service can usually shorten downtime — the time during which the machine is inoperative. Also, a repair facility is necessary for preventive maintenance, which depends on periodic inspections and systematic care of machinery.

If the cost of downtime is high and preventive maintenance is difficult and expensive, a company may turn to redundancy to avoid downtime and shutdowns. **Redundancy** is the use of a backup system so that breakdowns will not stop the operations. For example:

> Perhaps the ultimate in redundant systems is a computer Raytheon Corporation is designing for an Air Force satellite. As the computer can't be serviced by human technicians, but is supposed to have a 95% chance of working for at least five years in space, it has built-in spare circuit boards, processors, logic chips and a program that constantly makes sure everything is working. The "heal thyself" computer automatically transfers functions from malfunctioning parts. Even if it is knocked out by an enemy killer satellite, a set of permanently wired instructions will send out requests for new instructions. If it gets them, it can reorganize the remaining working parts of the computer piece by piece until a new computer arises, phoenix-like, from the debris of the old.[2]

Back on earth many firms, such as banks, are building backup systems to run when their computers fall victim to fire, power failure, sabotage, and the like. These backup systems include such methods as linking clusters of microprocessors in fail-safe modules that can switch work back and forth, creating additional space into which backup computers could be moved, and joining groups of computer users who agree to back each other up.

Because of the decreasing size and cost of silicon microprocessor chips and the self-diagnostic programs that now can be built into the chips, some computers now have **parts redundancy**. These features will allow computers to diagnose their own problems and keep on running even if major parts fail.

---

2. William M. Bulkeley, "Self-Servicing Machines Fast Becoming Reality, Offering the Appeal of Reliability at Lower Cost," *The Wall Street Journal,* August 13, 1979, p. 6. Reprinted by permission of *The Wall Street Journal,* © Dow Jones & Company, Inc. (1979). All Rights Reserved.

Quality Control

No area of production is more important to the United States than the area of quality control, and U.S. industry now is pushing itself to meet the new world standards set by the Japanese. America's leadership in quality has been eroding for years. Reports one writer:

> "There's no question that the Japanese have set new world standards," says Robert E. Cole, who has worked in Japanese factories and now directs the University of Michigan's Center for Japanese Studies. "Their best factories are better than our best factories."[3]

The answer to Japanese competition lies in learning from Japan, just as Japan learned from others how to improve the quality of its products. Interestingly, Japan learned mainly from an American statistician, Dr. W. Edwards Deming, who helped launch quality control in Japan 30 years ago. "A measure of his esteem is the award given annually for the Japanese person or group that has made the greatest contribution to improving quality in the past year. It's known simply as the Deming Award."[4]

Conventional methods of **quality control** involve setting and monitoring standards of manufacturing. However, the Deming approach to quality control differs greatly from conventional methods. In conventional methods, such as those used in the auto industry until recently, massive quantities of parts made were inspected and the defective parts were thrown away. The Deming approach to quality control, sometimes called **total quality control or process control**, takes the position that mass inspection is outmoded. Instead, reliance is placed on statistical techniques to control a product's quality, uniformity, and cost at every stage of the manufacturing process.

Another important difference between the conventional and the Deming approaches to quality control is that Dr. Deming insists that management—not workers—is responsible for at least 85 percent of all poor-quality parts. According to one observer:

> Many factors—poor machines, poor maintenance, poor material, poor engineering, poor environment, or poor workers—can cause the production of defective parts. But the boss has the ultimate responsibility for the defects, because he usually puts these elements into the system and only he can change them if poor parts result.[5]

The revolution in quality control goes far beyond the basics we have discussed, and the exact approach will vary between companies and between nations. Clearly, however, Dr. Deming's ideas are receiving widespread attention and application in the United States, as the importance of product quality cannot be overemphasized in today's highly competitive world.

---

3. Jeremy Main, "The Battle for Quality Begins," FORTUNE (December 29, 1980), p. 28. © 1980 Time Inc. All rights reserved.
4. Joseph M. Callahan, "US Automakers Now Heed Teacher of Quality Control," *The Christian Science Monitor,* December 23, 1981, p. 15.
5. Joseph M. Callahan, Christian Science Monitor News Service, "Deming System: Better, Cheaper Automobiles?" *Rocky Mountain News,* January 9, 1982, p. 2-A.

TOWARD THE AUTOMATED FACTORY

The manufacturing industry in the United States is in the midst of a transition period as profound as those periods that followed the introduction of the steam engine and electricity. Today the new technology is based on computers and **robotics**, the use of robots in production and manufacturing. As these technologies work their way through the economy, supplier-customer relationships are being altered and the traditional types of production processes are falling prey to automated factory systems. We soon will begin to see basic products, such as automobile engines, being redesigned so that they are even more compatible with the use of automated machinery.

Many industries have a large investment in earlier technologies, and changing over to new technology is difficult. However, a robot revolution is sweeping Japan and is leading the industrialized world into a high-technology future. By 1986 or so, the extent of this revolution will be far clearer than it is now. However, it is already clear that automated manufacturing is here to stay and that companies will have to speed up the automation of their manufacturing operations in order to remain competitive. We will discuss some basic aspects of this factory transition in terms of simple and automated machines and systems, and of managing automated factories.

Simple and Automated Machines and Systems

The term **automation** applies to the control of machine tools by computers. If the computer can make the necessary adjustments to the machine's operation by itself, the system is called closed-loop control. If the computer must signal an operator to reset the machine, the system is called open-loop control. Despite the revolution in automated production processes that is upon us, it is clear that many terms and concepts relating to this revolution mean different things to different people. For example, much of what the Japanese call robots are simply mechanical arms that can perform basic, repetitive jobs in a factory, such as lifting objects and placing them elsewhere. In the United States these devices are classified as automated machines rather than robots.

Sometimes, however, it is difficult to determine where a nonrobotic machine ends and a robot begins. The goal of this section is to sort out some basic types of simple and automated machines in order to appreciate the nature and scope of the automated era of manufacturing. We will cover six basic categories: simple machines, programmable or instructible machines, reprogrammable industrial robots, sensory robots, mechatronic systems, and CAD/CAM systems. These categories are briefly summarized in Figure 10-6.

Simple Machines

The simple machine, such as a drill press or a grinder, is an extension of muscle power just as robots are mechanical simulators of such basic human functions as picking, grasping, or lifting. One writer notes that "the Greeks were the first to

Figure 10-6 Summary Description of Simple and Automated Machines and Systems

Type	Description	Examples
SIMPLE MACHINES	• Simulate human functions through the mechanisms of a lever, wheel, screw, wedge, or pulley	• Drill press, jointer
PROGRAMMABLE OR INSTRUCTIBLE MACHINES	• Perform relatively inflexible series of tasks through electromechanical instructions	• Lathe run by punched-tape instructions, assembly-line canning
REPROGRAMMABLE INDUSTRIAL ROBOTS	• Perform series of tasks plus a totally different job through electronic instructions	• Robot spray-painting bicycle frames, assembling dashboards for autos
SENSORY ROBOTS	• Perform tasks and react to changes in environment through artificial senses created by sophisticated computer software	• Welding robot that can adjust automatically to different product configurations such as various auto bodies in an assembly line
MECHATRONIC SYSTEMS	• Make new products and production processes by integrating mechanical and electronic machines	• Redesigning of a light bulb and of machines and assembly lines to achieve an "intelligent" automated system
CAD/CAM SYSTEMS	• Design and analyze products through mathematically based computer graphics (CAD), and make products through computer-controlled machines (CAM) to achieve an automated factory system	• Designing and testing properties of nose cones for missiles, communicating designs directly to machine tools or robots through robotics language

categorize the simple machines into five groups: the lever, the wheel, the screw, the wedge, and the pulley. These mechanisms form the basis of all machinery."[6]

Programmable or Instructible Machines

A **programmable or instructible machine** can do a series of tasks when a set of instructions is fed into it by the human who controls it. A typical programmable machine is the assembly-line bottle-capper. It continues to put on bottle caps in the same way until stopped. Another example is the numerically controlled (NC) machine tools of the 1950s. Controlled by a magnetic- or punched-tape, these tools perform specific tasks such as boring cylinders in automobile engine blocks.

---

6. Lee Edson, "Slaves of Industry," *Across the Board* (July/August, 1981), p. 8.

Reprogrammable Industrial Robots

No matter how complex a programmable machine may be, the reprogrammable industrial robot differs from it in one important way. The **reprogrammable industrial robot** not only can be programmed to do the sequence of tasks required for a job, but also it can be reprogrammed to do a different job. Thus, the industrial robot is far more flexible than the programmable machine.

The reason a robot can be reprogrammed and go beyond the capabilities of the simple machine or the programmable machine lies in its electronic brain, called a microprocessor. The microprocessor can be defined as "a device that crowded the central element of a computer, its arithmetic and logic circuits, onto the same [silicon] chip."[7] In other words, a microprocessor is a computer on a chip. Microprocessors are the heart of the microcomputers that lead the robots through their functions.

There are many kinds of industrial robots. Simple *pick-and-place robots* are mechanical manipulators that have limited freedom of movement and generally are used to pick up something from one spot and move it to another. A *servo robot* goes beyond the pick-and-place robot; it can be reprogrammed by physically leading its arm through new tasks, such as spraypainting coatings on appliance panels. In the more advanced computerized robot, instructions are transmitted electronically instead of by physically leading the robot through the new routine. For example, in welding auto bodies, the computerized robot can be reprogrammed for a particular sequence of body styles in the assembly line. Thus, computer programming is the key to turning robots into flexible, reprogrammable assemblers. Figure 10-7 shows a Cincinnati Milacron industrial robot that can be reprogrammed to handle various tasks. The Cincinnati Milacron reprogrammable robot shares three things in common with other robots: an arm or manipulator which does the work, a power supply which provides the energy to handle the job, and a control system to direct the robot's efforts.

Sensory Robots

The advanced **sensory or "smart" robots** integrate one or more artificial senses with sophisticated computer software. Vision is their chief sense, but sensory robots also hear and touch. That is, they react to sound and force. Sensory robots can perform locomotion, manipulation, sensing, and communication with humans or with other robots. An example of a sensory robot would be a roving plant sentry robot with a built-in minicomputer that reacts to changes in its environment. In the assembly line, an example of a sensory robot would be the auto-painting robot equipped with magnetic and optical sensors that allow it to adjust to different body styles.

Mechatronic Systems

The term mechatronics is an English word coined by the Japanese to refer to smart robot assembly systems. **Mechatronics** involves the linking of mechanical devices with the electronics of computerized robots to produce new hybrid machines and processes

---

7. James Cook, "The Molting of America," *Forbes* (November 22, 1982), p. 165.

Figure 10-7   An Industrial Robot

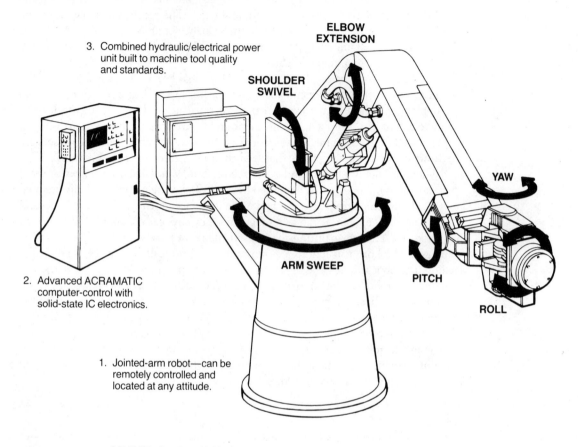

3. Combined hydraulic/electrical power unit built to machine tool quality and standards.

ELBOW EXTENSION

SHOULDER SWIVEL

2. Advanced ACRAMATIC computer-control with solid-state IC electronics.

YAW

ARM SWEEP

PITCH

ROLL

1. Jointed-arm robot—can be remotely controlled and located at any attitude.

SOURCE: Courtesy of Cincinnati Milacron.

that contain the best features of both types of machinery. Mechatronics goes beyond individual robots to include the entire robotics system. In a robotics system, production lines are modified to suit the machines and robots that will be used. In addition, the product itself may be redesigned so that smart robots can be used to make it. This process also is called making the products and production processes "intelligent."

CAD/CAM Systems

In 1981, IBM entered the robotics market with a one-armed programmable robot system attached to the IBM personal computer. However, IBM is pursuing not only the robot market. As one analyst puts it: "What's at stake here is the whole computer-aided design and computer-aided manufacturing industry. That's up for grabs today because there aren't any standards yet."[8] What are computer-aided design (CAD) and computer-aided manufacturing (CAM) and why are these important?

The term CAD/CAM refers to a system which uses both a process and machines in an effort to apply mathematics to product design and manufacturing. As we previously pointed out, numerically controlled (NC) machines stand between simple machines and the more flexible industrial robots. Now, CAD linked to NC machines is what CAD/CAM mainly means, although CAD/CAM has no precise definition.

Computer-Aided Design (CAD). The **CAD** of CAD/CAM, according to an analyst, "is basically designing, drafting, and analyzing with computer graphics displayed on a screen."[9] The underlying principle of CAD is to take a three-dimensional design, such as the shape of an airplane wing, and then trace it and store the image in a computer memory in the form of an almost infinite number of mathematical points in space. For example:

> Boeing's new jet transport, the 767, was largely designed through the use of mathematical representations inside a computer. Parts and assemblages displayed on the screen could be fitted, analyzed, and subjected to simulated stresses before they existed in tangible form. That saved time and improved design as well.[10]

Computer-Aided Manufacturing (CAM). The **CAM** in CAD/CAM refers to the computerized control of production machines. Computer-aided machines "range from machine tools running on punched-tape instructions to robots that can be reprogrammed to perform any of a variety of industrial tasks."[11]

Computer-Integrated Manufacturing (CIM). Experts want to extend CAD/CAM concepts toward the ultimate CAD/CAM vision of the totally automated factory. Sometimes the label CAD/CAM implies full computerization, but it also means different things to different users. As a result, some experts in industrial automation use the term **CIM** (Computer-Integrated Manufacturing) to describe the automated factory in which computer-assisted designs can be translated directly into machine-tool or robotics language which, when fed into a computer, permits manufacturing machines to be run at any location. In addition, overall management control programs would monitor and direct all these activities.

Mechatronics, discussed earlier in this chapter, is a big step in the direction of CIM. Regardless of the term used, manufacturing managers will have to analyze and

---

8. Susan Chace, "IBM Unveils a Programmable Robot Unit That Can Be Tied to Its Personal Computer," *The Wall Street Journal,* February 26, 1982, p. 10. Reprinted by permission of *The Wall Street Journal,* © Dow Jones & Company, Inc. (1982). All Rights Reserved.

9. Gene Bylinsky, "A New Industrial Revolution Is on the Way," FORTUNE (October 5, 1981), p. 106. © 1981 Time Inc. All rights reserved.

10. *Ibid.,* p. 109.

11. *Ibid.,* p. 107.

understand the complex and detailed needs of every aspect of their operations before these operations can become a computer-integrated manufacturing facility.

Managing Automated Factories

The robot revolution is in its early stages, but it is rapidly building up steam. Automated machines and processes are seen by some industrial planners as the answer to American industry's basic problem — stagnation in productivity — which we discussed in Chapter 9. As observed in an article:

> Not only can the robot work three shifts a day, but it takes no coffee breaks, does not call in sick on Monday, does not become bored, does not take vacations or qualify for pensions. . . it is immune to government and union regulations on heat, fumes, noise, radiation, and other safety hazards. . . (and) the typical robot costs $40,000. . . and it can still be paid for and operated at $4.80 an hour; the worker often costs $15 to $20. That is the formula for a gold rush.[12]

In a joint forecast by the American Society of Manufacturing Engineers and the University of Michigan, the following predictions were made:

1. By 1985, 20 percent of the labor in the final assembly of autos will be replaced by automation.
2. By 1987, 15 percent of all assembly systems will use robotic technology.
3. By 1988, 50 percent of the labor in small-component assembly will be replaced by automation.
4. By 1990, the development of sensory techniques will enable robots to approximate human capability in assembly.[13]

Such forecasts, however, assume that American managers will be ready for the introduction and effective use of automated machines and processes. This may be an optimistic assumption with regard to managing technological transition periods and creating a working environment for the effective use of robots. Three long-term issues that managers must deal with as a basis of effective technological management are:

1. Which technology to pursue and when to pursue it.
2. How to manage the transition from one technology to the other.
3. How to prepare the corporation for technological change.[14]

Once the robotic technology is determined, one expert suggests that there is no point in introducing robots unless the managers can answer "yes" to each of the following questions:

---

12. "The Robot Revolution," *TIME* (December 8, 1980), pp. 73–74. Copyright 1980 Time Inc. All rights reserved. Reprinted by permission from *TIME*.
13. *Ibid.*, p. 83.
14. Richard N. Foster, "A Call for Vision in Managing Technology." Quoted from the May 24, 1982 issue of *Business Week* by special permission.

1. Are workers closely observing standard work procedures?
2. Are the right materials delivered to the right place at the right time?
3. Are quality control standards applied to all components and procedures, including accuracy and tolerance in component size?
4. Are production machinery, jigs, and tools maintained properly?
5. Do workers properly operate stand-alone machine centers, transfer presses, and the like?[15]

The correct technology must be chosen. But even the correct technology is only as effective as the environment in which it will be used. Robotics and automated processes will not simply happen. Rather, they will require an innovative, long-term perspective on the part of corporate and production management.

SUMMARY

Production and manufacturing often are thought to mean the same thing. However, production, in its broad usage, pertains to the transformation of resources into goods and services. Manufacturing is a form of production relating to the processing and converting of resources into finished goods needed by consumers.

The two main types of production processes are based on the length of the production run (continuous or intermittent) and on the nature of the processes (analytic or synthetic). The production processes used reflect the type of products (standard or custom) and the manufacturing orientation (product-focused or process-focused).

Mass production and the assembly line are well-known features of modern American manufacturing. Mass production involves effectively combining specialized labor, machine power, and standardized parts. The assembly line is only one aspect of mass production. It may vary on the basis of the type of material handling devices used, the configuration of the line, pacing, product mix, and the nature of the work stations.

Once a manufacturing production system is set up, steps must be taken to maintain and improve its operation. These on-going steps include the areas of work improvement, production control, equipment maintenance, and quality control.

The big news in production and manufacturing is the use of automated machines and processes. The nature and scope of this revolution in manufacturing is just beginning to take shape, and it is expected to affect every aspect of our industrial activity. Automated machines include programmable or instructible machines, reprogrammable robots, and advanced sensory robots. Automated processes include mechatronics and the use of computer-assisted design (CAD) and computer-assisted manufacturing (CAM). These machines and processes are leading American industry into the era of the fully automated factory. However, these major innovations are not a substitute for good workers and managers. It will be the job of corporate and production managers to carefully deal with technological change and provide an overall working environment for the effective use of robotics and automated processes.

---

15. Kenichi Ohmae, "Steel Collar Workers: The Lessons from Japan," *The Wall Street Journal,* February 16, 1982, p. 24. Reprinted by permission of *The Wall Street Journal,* © Dow Jones & Company, Inc. (1982). All Rights Reserved.

1. How does manufacturing relate to production?
2. What type of manufactured product is a Regina floor-care appliance?
3. What is the basic manufacturing orientation or focus of the Regina and BIF divisions of General Signal Corporation?
4. How might the types of machines and processes used today to make floor-care appliances differ from those of five years ago?
5. How might the era of automated machines and factories make a difference in what kind of educational business background a factory manager should have?

BUSINESS TERMS

manufacturing	211	robotics	221
production	211	automation	221
operations management	212	programmable or instructible	
process innovation	212	machine	222
mass production	216	reprogrammable industrial	
production control	218	robot	223
maintenance	219	sensory or "smart" robots	223
reliability	219	mechatronics	223
redundancy	219	CAD (Computer-Aided Design)	225
parts redundancy	219	CAM (Computer-Aided	
quality control	220	Manufacturing)	225
total quality control or		CIM (Computer-Integrated	
process control	220	Manufacturing)	225

QUESTIONS FOR DISCUSSION AND ANALYSIS

1. Explain why a large supermarket is considered to be engaged in production.
2. What kinds of production processes would likely be used in standard manufacture and in custom manufacture?
3. Can research and development be described as synthetic or analytic processes? Explain.
4. Would an automobile manufacturer use order control rather than flow control? Why?
5. Give an example, other than those in the text, of the use of redundancy in a production system.
6. In what basic way does total quality control differ from conventional quality control?
7. Why, would you guess, did Japanese automakers practice Dr. Deming's statistical quality control long before American automakers did?
8. What is the basic difference between a programmable machine and an industrial robot?
9. How does mechatronics differ from CAD/CAM and Computer Integrated Manufacturing?
10. Do you think the era of automated factory processes will lead to the dehumanization of manager-employee relationships? Explain.

PROJECTS, PROBLEMS, AND SHORT CASES

1. Zapp Corporation, an electronics manufacturer, was faced with a parts defect rate of more than three times that of its Japanese competitors. Despite pressure on the quality control department to become more effective, the problem persisted. In desperation, Zapp's CEO called in a consultant in quality control. The consultant recommended a top-to-bottom quality control program. A key step in this program was a training

program for the top 60 managers in the corporation, from the CEO on down, including courses in quality control.

"What a bum rap," fumed Sheila Herbert, manager of financial planning and analysis and one of the top 60 executives. "We've got a quality control department and a plant manager. Let those people handle the problem. I've got my own work to do. I can't pass off my problems on the plant personnel, so why should I have to suffer for their problems?"

Prepare a report defending the consultant's recommendation of the quality control training program for the top managers.

2. A large and modern cafeteria today may offer a choice of a dozen vegetables, a dozen main dishes, and two dozen desserts. A key managerial skill is focused on creating an even flow between the steam table and the kitchen. This is especially true for the "hot spot"—the spot right under the nose of the customer. Just about anything in the hot spot is expected to sell.

Visit a large public cafeteria and prepare an oral report on the following:

a. How the flow of food is handled.

b. Which items are placed in the "hot spot" and which are farther from the customer's reach.

3. Consult current issues of such periodicals as *Business Week, Forbes,* and *Fortune* in your school library and prepare a portfolio of reproductions of at least five advertisements or articles that describe recent advances in production procedures. These could include such items as machine tools, automation, machinery, new inventions, and electrical controls.

Write a brief report on your findings, estimating the probable importance of each item to the field in which it will be used.

Managing Material Requirements Planning

"I started with steel filings in my shoes," says Oliver W. Wight, 51, perhaps the most successful of an expanding group of consultants who are helping business apply computers to the tricky task of managing inventories. In his first job after college, as an inventory clerk for Raybestos-Manhattan, he picked up the no-nonsense manner of the shop floor. That may well be the secret of Wight's success.

For most purchasing agents and production chiefs, the computer is an intimidating machine. Ollie, as everyone seems to call him, has developed a patter that translates "material requirements planning," the newest technique of inventory control, into something that sounds less threatening: "Whata you gonna make? What does it take to make it? Whata you got? Whata you gotta get?" He repeats the refrain several times an hour at educational seminars and in videotaped presentations that he shoots in a studio near his home overlooking Laké Sunapee in rural New Hampshire.

Wight was making $25,000 a year as a manufacturing-education manager for IBM when he quit in 1968 to strike out on his own. The Wight companies now gross over $5 million a year.

Recently he started a consulting service that evaluates the roughly 100 software packages now available to companies without the resources or the inclination to develop their own inventory-control systems. Such packages, coupled with increasingly cheap computer power, have brought sophisticated inventory management within reach of even small manufacturing companies. "The small companies are doing better than the giants," Wight says.

In big companies, senior management is so far removed from production that it often doesn't realize that many other standard procedures may have to be altered if the enterprise is to benefit from changing to a system that meshes production scheduling and inventory control. Teaching top executives how to use material requirements planning is now his most important endeavor, says Wight, because their insights will ultimately determine whether this managerial tool lives up to its potential for improving productivity.

SOURCE: "A Plain Teacher of a New Art," in Lewis Beman, "A Big Payoff from Inventory Controls," FORTUNE (July 27, 1981), p. 79. © 1981 Time Inc. All rights reserved.

Materials Management

Objectives:

- Distinguish among purchasing, procurement, and materials management.
- Discuss the two main elements of materials management.
- Describe six purchasing policies.
- Describe the six basic steps in ordering and receiving materials.
- Explain the role of value analysis.
- Distinguish between materials control and inventory control.
- Distinguish among order-point analysis, material requirements planning (MRP), and the Kanban system.
- Identify ten functions of the traffic department.
- Explain the strengths and weaknesses of six modes of external transport.
- Explain the role of the freight forwarder.

Concerned with the rising costs of purchasing, transportation, distribution, and inventory, the new president of a domestic billion-dollar industrial company told a meeting of division managers:

> We are buying, shipping, and inventorying something like $400 million worth of materials. Who do we have in charge of these costs and assets? . . . In our 25 divisions, we do not have one purchasing, production control, or distribution manager who is promotable to general management levels. . .

Now if you really want to get scared, you should remember that we spend $12 million a year on new product R&D. Do you know the easiest way to bomb a new product? Poor materials management—you can't get the right materials, or the quality is off, or you can't get the product through the factory, or you can't coordinate transportation and distribution to get the product into the hands of the customer.[1]

This president was not alone in his recognition of the growing importance of materials management in this era of inflation, disinflation (slowing down of price increases), and resource scarcity. When inflation rages, businesses are able to pass on to consumers the price increases from their suppliers. However, in periods of disinflation, there are no excessive price increases to pass on to consumers. Instead, businesses should look to sound cost controls and efficiency in managing their operations.

THE EVOLUTION OF MATERIALS MANAGEMENT

Purchasing may be defined as the buying of materials and supplies. Over the past 30 years, purchasing has evolved from little more than a routine clerical job to a major function that is recognized as having a great impact on the success of most companies. The term **procurement** is a step up from basic purchasing. It is often used in business and government activities to describe the combined functions of purchasing, inventory control, and traffic control. Recently the term **materials management** has developed out of the expanded scope of purchasing and procurement. Materials management includes all the activities relating to the acquisition, control, and movement of materials and supplies used in the production of a firm's finished products.

Materials Management Organizations

There are various types of materials management organizations. Some types emphasize physical distribution, including inventory control and traffic control. Others may be supply-oriented, with an emphasis on purchasing and inventory control. Still others may be manufacturing-oriented, emphasizing activities that take place in the flow of materials from one process or location to another.

Materials Managers

Materials managers are specialists who control a company's material requirements by deciding what to buy, how much to buy, how to schedule shipments, and how to keep inventories at proper levels. These managers also may be called logistics managers, physical distribution managers, supply managers, and so on. Materials managers are professionals who occupy high levels in an organization. As Figure 11-1 shows,

---

1. Reprinted by permission of the *Harvard Business Review*. Excerpts from "Materials Managers: Who Needs Them?" by Jeffrey G. Miller and Peter Gilmour (July/August 1979). Copyright © 1979 by the President and Fellows of Harvard College; all rights reserved.

Figure 11-1   Reporting Relationships in Traditional v. Materials Management Organizations

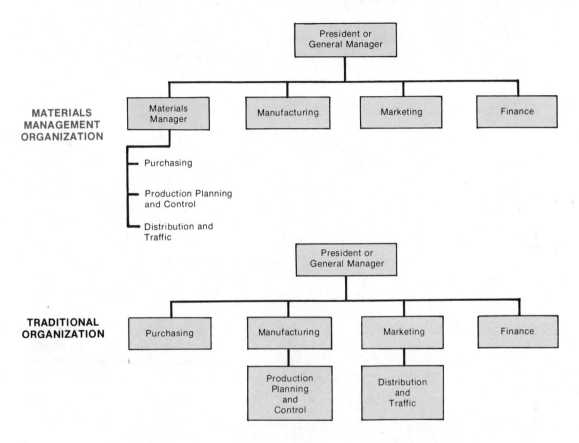

SOURCE: Reprinted by permission of the *Harvard Business Review.* An exhibit from "Materials Managers: Who Needs Them?" by Jeffrey G. Miller and Peter Gilmour (July/August, 1979). Copyright © 1979 by the President and Fellows of Harvard College; all rights reserved.

reporting relationships in a materials management organization differ from those in more traditional organizations. In the latter, the purchasing manager may report to the president; the production planning and control manager may report to the manufacturing manager; and the distribution and traffic manager may report to the marketing manager.

Not all companies use the materials management approach. But three basic conditions that have brought about the need for materials management organizations and managers in many companies are the following:

1. Wide economic swings between inflation and disinflation.
2. Deregulation of air, rail, and truck transport.
3. Use of the computer in dealing with the complexities caused by the first two conditions mentioned above.

Despite the variety of organizational tasks and managerial titles in a materials management organization, the use of this approach covers two basic areas: purchasing and distribution management. These two areas are discussed in the rest of this chapter.

NATURE AND FUNCTIONS OF PURCHASING

The department of a business that buys the needed materials for production is the purchasing department. The typical corporate purchasing department today is responsible for spending over half of every dollar that its company receives. Importantly, every dollar saved in purchasing is a new dollar of profit as compared, for example, with a dollar of sales that, because of tax payments, contributes only a small amount to profit. Each department in a business should have certain goals to accomplish. The four prime goals of purchasing are:

1. Buying the proper products for the purpose required.
2. Having the materials available at the time they are needed.
3. Securing the proper amount.
4. Paying the right price.

Until the mid-1970s, the purchasing function was being steadily decentralized along with other corporate operations. Then acute resource shortages began to occur and companies discovered that they needed all the buying power they could muster. This led to a recentralization of purchasing for greater buying leverage.

Organization of the Purchasing Department

The head of the purchasing department is usually called the purchasing manager or **purchasing agent.** In small plants the purchasing agent and a clerk or two may comprise the purchasing department. In larger plants there may be a specialized group of buyers working under the purchasing agent, who may hold the position of General Purchasing Agent or, perhaps, Vice-President of Purchasing (or Materials Management). Figure 11-2 indicates both the internal structure and the position of the purchasing department in a company of average size.

While most professionals seem to be becoming more specialized, purchasing managers must continually broaden their outlook. Not only are they looking for the best buy today, but also they are making sure that there are supplies for the future. This means that they participate in top-level discussions about the acquisition and development of raw materials sources, as well as about capital expenditures. In a number of large companies, the purchasing manager has a *sourcing* manager who keeps track of the worldwide availability of materials. This activity includes checking with suppliers

Figure 11-2   Organization of a Purchasing Department

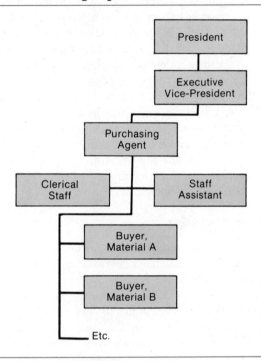

to find out where raw materials are coming from and what the suppliers are doing to ensure their availability. Careful planning to meet future needs for materials is becoming a major factor in corporate earnings.

Purchasing Policies

As explained in Chapter 5, a policy is a broad guideline that says something about how goals will be attained. Purchasing policies are especially important in the face of fluctuating material prices and material availability. Many companies face the need to strengthen policies, systems, and procedures for various areas of purchasing and materials control, including the policy areas discussed below.

Manufacturing v. Buying

The decision to purchase or to make a certain part required in manufacturing a product is called a **make-or-buy decision.** For example, a computer manufacturer may decide either to make its own microchips or to buy a company that makes them in order to assure itself a supply of this item. Purchasing managers should be alert to changes in a company's demand and supply of various products and should provide top managers with information needed to make wise make-or-buy decisions.

Hand-to-Mouth v. Forward Buying

If a firm follows a policy of **hand-to-mouth buying,** it orders small amounts at frequent intervals. **Forward buying** involves orders for larger amounts placed less frequently. There is no sharp line between the two policies, but purchasing departments tend to follow either one or the other, depending on market prices. If prices tend to fluctuate widely and often, hand-to-mouth buying probably will minimize the risk of loss through inventory depreciation. On the other hand, if prices tend to be relatively stable over longer periods of time, the company may make larger purchases with longer intervals between orders.

Another factor affecting the choice between these two policies is the amount of capital tied up in inventories of materials and parts. In recent years the trend has been toward rapid use, or turnover, of inventories. Rapid turnover of inventories results in savings in storage space; minimizes risk of inventory spoilage, damage, and theft; and releases capital for other uses.

Contract Purchasing

In **contract purchasing** a company makes an agreement with its suppliers, or vendors, to have materials delivered over a long period of time. There are two reasons for this practice: to protect the supply and to take advantage of low prices prevailing at the time of the contract. Also, corporate purchasing managers view national contracts to cover the various materials needs of all divisions as the single most effective way to control future material costs.

Purchasing agents usually prefer to negotiate fixed-price contracts. However, there are times when change becomes more unpredictable, thus making it difficult to accurately forecast price and supply. One way to spread the risk between seller and buyer is to make a *flexible price agreement* (FPA). There are four basic types of flexible price agreements:

1. *Delivery price:* The price is determined at time of delivery.
2. *Renegotiated:* Predetermined price with rights to renegotiate the price with extreme changes in conditions.
3. *Escalator:* Price fixed for set period and then escalated after the period expires.
4. *Cost plus:* Purchaser agrees to pay cost and an additional percentage above cost.[2]

As you can see, the idea of an FPA is that the seller and the buyer agree to determine the price of an item or service at the time of delivery or for a set period, or agree to renegotiate the price when there are extreme changes in market conditions. Thus, under unfavorable market conditions, FPAs permit price negotiations with reasonable terms for both the buyer and the seller.

---

2. Adapted from Dale Varble, "Flexible Price Agreements: Purchasing's View," © 1980 by the Regents of the University of California. Reprinted from CALIFORNIA MANAGEMENT REVIEW, Volume XXIII, No. 2, pp. 45 to 46, by permission of the Regents.

Speculative Purchasing

Normal purchasing is based on the anticipated need for certain items. **Speculative purchasing,** or market purchasing, goes beyond the normal needs in the amounts ordered and prices paid. There are various reasons for this practice: anticipation of higher prices for the items needed; fear of strikes against a major supplier; or perhaps the chance to make a quick profit on excess inventories when the prices go up. Because of its risky nature, speculative purchasing is not a normal policy in most companies.

Reciprocal Buying

Reciprocal buying means that a company buys from customers who, in turn, buy from that company. For example, a producer of motor trucks might buy coal only from a coal company that uses its trucks for delivery. This practice has been condemned as uneconomical and wasteful, and it is now illegal when restraint of trade can be shown. The arguments against it are that it narrows the field of suppliers with the result that the buyer pays higher prices and possibly fails to procure the exact goods required. The main argument in favor of reciprocal buying is that it helps to hold customers—a rather persuasive factor. Most firms recognize the value of ethical dealing with their suppliers as well as with their customers. The National Association of Purchasing Management has developed a set of rules known as the Principles and Standards of Purchasing Practice to which its members adhere (see Figure 11-3).

Use of Sealed Bids

Sometimes an order is awarded on the basis of sealed bids. The purchasing agent provides prospective vendors with information concerning specifications and quantities needed. The vendors submit sealed, written offers on or before the date when the sealed bids are opened. The offers are compared, and the order is given to the lowest bidder who can meet the specifications. The sealed bid procedure is common in governmental agencies at all levels and is growing in private businesses, schools, and hospitals.

A new type of bidding program was started by General Motors in 1982 for the 1983 model year. As one newspaper article explains it:

> In the past, each GM plant typically ordered its steel requirements from among a group of a dozen or so integrated steelmakers, often paying the producers' published list prices...(now) GM plants will submit a list of their steel requirements...to GM headquarters in Detroit. There, the automaker will compile a master list of steel needs that will be sent out to various integrated steelmakers for bids in the coming months.[3]

The bidding system of General Motors is not based on price alone. It takes into account each steelmaker's quality record, location, and prices. The system is aimed at selecting the most efficient steel producers as GM's long-term suppliers.

---

3. Amal Nag, ''GM Is Adopting Bidding System for Buying Steel,'' *The Wall Street Journal*, March 23, 1982, p. 3. Reprinted by permission of *The Wall Street Journal*, © Dow Jones & Company, Inc. (1982). All Rights Reserved.

Figure 11-3   Principles and Standards of Purchasing Practice Advocated by the National Association of Purchasing Management

LOYALTY TO HIS COMPANY
JUSTICE TO THOSE WITH WHOM HE DEALS
FAITH IN HIS PROFESSION

*From these principles are derived the N. A. P. M.
standards of purchasing practice.*

1. To consider, first, the interests of his company in all transactions and to carry out and believe in its established policies.
2. To be receptive to competent counsel from his colleagues and to be guided by such counsel without impairing the dignity and responsibility of his office.
3. To buy without prejudice, seeking to obtain the maximum ultimate value for each dollar of expenditure.
4. To strive consistently for knowledge of the materials and processes of manufacture, and to establish practical methods for the conduct of his office.
5. To subscribe to and work for honesty and truth in buying and selling, and to denounce all forms and manifestations of commercial bribery.
6. To accord a prompt and courteous reception, so far as conditions will permit, to all who call on a legitimate business mission.
7. To respect his obligations and to require that obligations to him and to his concern be respected, consistent with good business practice.
8. To avoid sharp practice.
9. To counsel and assist fellow purchasing agents in the performance of their duties, whenever occasion permits.
10. To cooperate with all organizations and individuals engaged in activities designed to enhance the development and standing of purchasing.

WE SUBSCRIBE TO THESE STANDARDS

Purchasing Functions

Purchasing departments, often along with engineering, marketing, and production, may perform a wide variety of functions from company to company. The purchasing agent selects the company's suppliers, conducts negotiations, prepares specifications, places orders for goods and services, inspects incoming shipments, maintains balanced inventories, and also arranges for building repairs and externally supplied maintenance services. Moreover, the purchasing agent is responsible for the continuing evaluation of vendor effectiveness. Many of these activities will be found in two of the main purchasing functions: ordering and receiving materials, and value analysis.

Ordering and Receiving Materials

Figure 11-4 shows the basic steps in the process of ordering and receiving materials. These steps are described in detail below.

Establishing Specifications. Industrial purchasing relies on descriptive details, or material specifications, established by the purchaser. These specifications usually come from the engineering staff. Many industrial goods have industrywide standards that are commonly recognized and accepted by all users. Nuts, bolts, washers, raw cotton, lumber, and many other finished or semifinished goods fall into this category. In specifying these items, the purchasing department simply indicates the industry grades desired.

Recognizing Need and Activating the Purchase. The actual purchasing process is initiated by a purchase requisition which is issued by a stock control clerk when the stock of an item falls to a set level. Orders for standardized or frequently purchased items may be placed upon receipt of the requisition. In the absence of industry standards, or when an item is not often purchased, the purchasing agent may send letters of inquiry to several prospective vendors inviting their bids.

Selecting the Vendor. Over the course of time purchasing agents and buyers build up a knowledge of the markets for the materials they purchase. Buyers are expected to know about the vendors with whom they deal — their products; their terms, prices, and discounts; the quality of their goods; their delivery reliability; and anything else that will help buyers perform their purchasing functions more effectively.

Placing and Following Up the Order. To place an order most companies complete a formal purchase order specifying a description of the goods wanted, the unit prices, the quantities desired, discount terms, shipping instructions, and the order number. To make certain that orders will be delivered on time, many firms use an order

Figure 11-4   Steps in Ordering and Receiving Materials

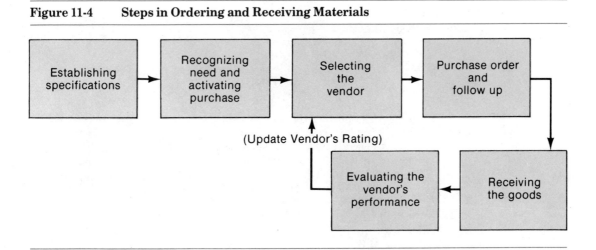

follow-up system designed to inform the purchasing agent of the current status of all outstanding orders.

Receiving the Goods. When the goods arrive, the receiving clerk checks them against a copy of the purchase order to verify that the order provisions have been met. If the shipment is correct in quantity, quality, and price, the goods are sent to stock and the vendor's invoice is certified for payment. If there are any discrepancies between the order and the shipment, the purchasing department must work this out with the vendor or shipper.

Evaluating the Vendor's Performance. Finally, the department's records are updated to reflect the vendor's current performance. Few businesses can be top performers all the time, but consistent performance within an acceptable range is a vendor's best advertisement.

Value Analysis

Value analysis involves a systematic appraisal and examination of products and parts to see if any cost-saving changes in design, materials, or processes can be made and to make sure the products or parts fulfill their functions at the lowest possible cost. It starts with the question: "What is this item worth?" Now, with the possibility of material shortages, another question being asked is: "How available is this part in the form we need?" Value analysis may take many approaches, but questions similar to those in Figure 11-5 are usually found in value analysis checklists to see if maximum value is being gained for each dollar spent for a product or service.

The terms "value analysis" and "value engineering" are often used synonymously, although some authors prefer to define value engineering as the application of value analysis techniques in the engineering sphere of responsibility. Both terms are valid, for value analysis or value engineering is a team effort (often referred to as VA/VE) involving representatives of engineering, production, and marketing, as well as pur-

---

Figure 11-5   Value Analysis Checklist

Value Analysis Checklists Usually Include the Following Kinds of Questions:

√Can the item be eliminated?
√Does it need all of its features?
√Can the weight or any features be reduced?
√Can a standard item be substituted for it?
√Are closer tolerances specified than are necessary?
√Is unnecessary machining performed on the item?
√Are the finishing requirements finer than necessary?
√Can the packaging or shipping requirements be reduced?
√Will another dependable supplier supply it for less?
√Is anybody buying it for less?

chasing. In this team effort the purchasing department questions engineering specifications, and the engineering department questions purchasing practices and policies such as awarding orders based solely on price.

DISTRIBUTION MANAGEMENT

Distribution management emphasizes the control of total costs of transportation, warehousing, inventory control, protective packaging, and materials handling. It seeks to achieve its objectives by a detailed analysis of the costs through all the stages of distribution—from the raw state to finished goods in the hands of customers. Distribution managers today must be flexible and able to react quickly to changes in supplies, services, and other cost factors. They also must develop distribution strategies that support the company's overall corporate goals. Basic areas that distribution managers are concerned with are: materials control, inventory control, materials movement, and modes of external materials transport.

Materials Control

Materials control is a system of records and procedures designed to inform management of the quantity and location of materials that are in the plant. It provides a record of the transfer of materials from one department to another and of the manufacturing processes through which the materials pass, and it serves as the authority for this movement. It also is important as a source of cost data for the cost accounting department.

Whenever materials move from one place to another within the plant, records are adjusted to reflect this transfer and to fix the responsibility for their custody. Identifying tags accompany all goods to allow accurate checking. The use of computers is growing rapidly in materials control, as the location and quantity of each item can be quickly stored in computers and retrieved or monitored as needed. Assembly lines now can plug into word processors to automatically order parts and materials as needed. And *bar-code scanners,* similar to those at checkout counters of supermarkets, now are being used in some firms for keeping track of materials.

Inventory Control

Most businesses cannot operate effectively without some stock of goods on hand. Generally companies must order goods ahead of customer demand. If a company does not maintain adequate inventories of merchandise or finished goods, customer relations are hurt, the reputation of the company as a dependable source of supply is damaged, and sales are lost. A manufacturer who does not avoid inventory shortages of raw materials and semifinished goods finds that the flow of production is interrupted, that machines and equipment are not fully utilized, and that costs are increased.

On the other hand, if inventories clearly exceed customer demand, funds that could be used for other purposes are tied up, storage costs are increased, and inventories are likely to suffer deterioration, obsolescence, or theft. It is the goal of **inventory control** to find the optimum level of stock to keep on hand under conditions of changing market demand, production requirements, and financial resources.

For example, Atlanta-based Oxford Industries is a supplier of mid-priced apparel to such large retailers as Sears Roebuck & Co. and J. C. Penney Company. In 1982, Oxford achieved the fastest growth in its history by a move from unbranded merchandise into its own higher-priced designer-label clothing. How did Oxford's CEO, J. Hicks Lanier, go about controlling inventory in the face of the need to keep up with the fast-changing trends in consumer taste in the fashion business? As *Business Week* explains it:

> Lanier has imposed strict controls on inventories. The presidents of Oxford's 10 divisions must "borrow" funds from headquarters at 2% above the prime rate for any inventories greater than the company's target levels. The cost of this loan is counted against each division's profits—and against each president's bonus. "We really are getting our message across from top to bottom," says Vice-President for Finance R. William Lee, Jr.[4]

As British economist John Maynard Keynes pointed out four decades ago, many business decisions are not based mainly on careful mathematical calculations, but rather on "animal spirits"—outbursts of spontaneous optimism. Three systems that inventory control managers may use in place of "animal spirits" to meet their goals are: order-point analysis, material requirements planning, and the Kanban approach.

Order-Point Analysis

The rise and fall of a company's inventory of goods on hand, or its inventory cycle, has two periods: the period in which the goods are ordered and received and the period in which they are used in production or sold. Figure 11-6 illustrates an inventory cycle.

We can apply a simple inventory control situation to the diagram in Figure 11-6. Suppose that Company X has annual sales of 20,800 units and that the sales are made uniformly throughout the year at the rate of 400 units a week. The units can be obtained from a dependable supplier in carload lots of 400 units. It takes one week to place and process an order and one week to deliver the order from the supplier to Company X. Lead time is therefore two weeks. If an order is placed for 400 units on the first day of the first week of the inventory cycle, the goods will be available for use on the first day of the third week. By the beginning of the fourth week, the inventory will be depleted. Therefore, if an out-of-stock condition is to be prevented, a second order must be placed at the beginning of the second week. This cycle of ordering and using goods must be regularly repeated throughout the year.

---

4. "Oxford: A Venture into Designer-Label Clothes Spruces up Earnings by 90%," *Business Week* (June 21, 1982), p. 68.

Figure 11-6 **The Inventory Cycle**

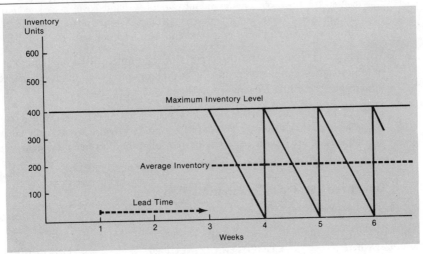

The **average inventory** carried over the period of this regular cycle is equal to the minimum inventory plus one-half of the order quantity. In this situation there was no minimum inventory, or safety stock. The average inventory of 200 units obviously is between the minimum and maximum levels of inventory. If the safety stock were set at 200 units, the maximum inventory would be 600 units and the average inventory 400 units. Thus, management may view the minimum inventory as the basic level necessary to provide uninterrupted production or good customer service. Maximum inventory is the level it can afford to carry in view of the costs involved.

Material Requirements Planning

In the example above, the demand for goods was based on a historically even production schedule and the supply of goods was regular and dependable. However, such demand and supply conditions do not always come about in actual practice. Checks against future requirements must be made to avoid reorders based only upon past experience and practice. Developing materials forecasts from historical data can be risky, particularly when marketing or product engineering plans may change the sales mix or product design.

The use of the computer and mathematical inventory control programs has given materials managers greater understanding of the relationships that exist among material requirements, carrying costs, order costs, lead times, and safety stocks. An inventory control system that offers these capabilities is called **material requirements planning (MRP).** This system exists in various degrees of complexity. As two experts have observed:

In a sense, material requirements planning is simply a computer program for production. It enables management to time in the most efficient way the ordering and manufacturing of components and subassemblies that make up completed products. In a broader sense, however, it represents a complete set of related activities that begin with forecasting and order entry and end with feedback from the shop floor.[5]

Figure 11-7 shows the three parts of a complete MRP system. Notice that the system requires careful planning, costly computer programs, and feedback on performance. According to some observers:

> MRP imposes a strict discipline on manufacturing personnel, which often comes as a severe shock after loose "seat of the pants" methods. It is virtually impossible to implement MRP without observing the following outcomes: informal systems are

Figure 11-7   The Three Parts of a Complete MRP System

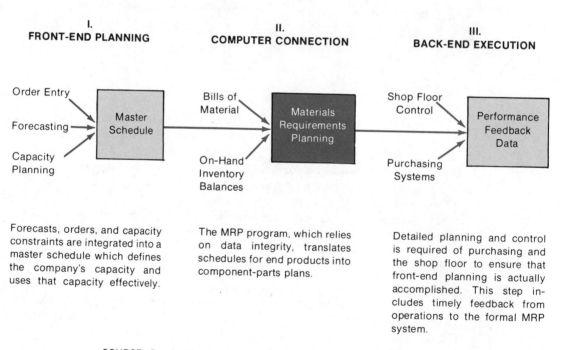

I.
FRONT-END PLANNING

II.
COMPUTER CONNECTION

III.
BACK-END EXECUTION

Order Entry → Master Schedule
Forecasting →
Capacity Planning →

Bills of Material → Materials Requirements Planning
On-Hand Inventory Balances →

Shop Floor Control → Performance Feedback Data
Purchasing Systems →

Forecasts, orders, and capacity constraints are integrated into a master schedule which defines the company's capacity and uses that capacity effectively.

The MRP program, which relies on data integrity, translates schedules for end products into component-parts plans.

Detailed planning and control is required of purchasing and the shop floor to ensure that front-end planning is actually accomplished. This step includes timely feedback from operations to the formal MRP system.

5. Reprinted by permission of the *Harvard Business Review*. Excerpt from "Planning Your Material Requirements" by Robert W. Hall and Thomas E. Vollmann (September/October, 1978). Copyright © 1978 by the President and Fellows of Harvard College; all rights reserved.

formalized; semi-independent functions are interrelated; job descriptions are created, eliminated, or changed; power and authority relations are changed; and performance becomes more visible.[6]

Some basic differences between order-point analysis and MRP are summarized in Figure 11-8.

Figure 11-8   Summary of Differences Between Order-Point and MRP Systems

In an Order-Point System	In a Material Requirements Planning System
1. Inventory purchases are based on historical need for parts.	1. Inventory purchases are based on the projected end products.
2. Parts are purchased independently of each other.	2. Parts are purchased in a time-phased sequence that reflects their dependency on each other and the end product.
3. *How much* to order is emphasized.	3. *When* to order is emphasized.
4. Inventory purchases assume relatively uniform usage and gradual depletion of inventory.	4. The average usage assumption is rejected in situations of uneven demand and supply.
5. Inventory control is a clerical procedure.	5. Inventory control is computerized and action-oriented.
6. The need for some safety stock on all items is assumed.	6. The inventory level is based on current bills of materials for projected end products.

Kanban: A Japanese Approach to Inventory Control

In the 1920s, Henry Ford set up the Rouge Industrial Complex to concentrate all aspects of his auto production in a single location. However, after World War II, the entire auto industry decided to scatter its final-assembly plants around the country. In the eyes of auto companies' managements, there may have been a good reason for this decision. According to *Business Week,* "Ford Chairman Caldwell speculates that 30 years ago auto executives may have deliberately spread their plants around the country to keep their newly unionized workers dispersed as much as possible."[7]

Today, years after World War II, Henry Ford's vision of an integrated auto-making complex is a reality — in Toyota City! Located in central Japan, Toyota City is the site of 8 of Toyota's 10 factories and most of the shops of its suppliers. This concentration of supplier and assembly operations, as envisioned by Henry Ford, allows Toyota's factories to keep on hand only the parts needed for immediate production. Fresh orders for parts are delivered directly to the assembly areas only when needed. This inventory control system is a key aspect of a broader system called the **Kanban**, or "just in time," system. The Kanban system involves a close relationship among suppliers, assembly

---

6. James F. Cox, Robert W. Zmud, and Steven J. Clark, "Auditing an MRP System," *Academy of Management Journal* (June, 1981), p. 389.
7. "U.S. Auto Makers Reshape for World Competition," *Business Week* (June 21, 1982), p. 88.

workers, and managers that emphasizes quality control as a necessary condition to the virtual absence of inventories at Toyota's factories.

Kanban and Suppliers. Kanban puts pressure on suppliers to improve the quality of their own products because they know the factory has no stockpiled parts to fall back on if some parts are defective. Says one manufacturing executive at Hewlett-Packard: "Kanban requires almost 100 percent perfect parts and a relationship of intimacy and trust with the vendor."[8]

In order to develop a close working relationship with suppliers, Toyota gives its business to about 250 suppliers. (This compares with about 3,000 suppliers with whom American automakers may deal.) In return, Toyota's suppliers do all or most of their business with Toyota.

Kanban and Workers. Lean inventories require mutual trust between management and workers on the line. In a typical American factory, inspection is done in steps along the assembly line. In the Kanban approach, parts are inspected when they come in. The only further inspection is made by workers in their own areas of operations. At Toyota, each worker can signal the assembly line to stop at any time. The workers are expected to use this signal whenever anything seems wrong with the operation of the line or when defects are spotted in the product. Thus, the Kanban system implies workers' responsibility for quality — to correct one's own errors or to pinpoint the errors of other workers as soon as possible.

Implications of Kanban. American automakers find it hard to change their system of manufacturing cars, and not all aspects of Kanban can be adopted in the United States. In fact, American companies will become most effective by combining their own strengths with those Japanese techniques that are most desirable. But if American automakers and other companies wish to close the gap between inventory and quality control among themselves and among international competitors, they may take the following steps:

1. Develop closer working relationships with suppliers and reduce the number of suppliers in order to boost quality and trim costs.
2. Expect some suppliers to move near the assembly plants they service.
3. Involve workers more deeply in quality improvement which permits leaner inventories.
4. Redesign automobiles and other products for ease of manufacturing and quality control, as well as for sales appeal.

Kanban means more than inventory and quality control. It is part of an overall system based on a close, long-term relationship of trust and responsibility among managers, suppliers, and workers. This relationship results in a constant effort to improve all aspects of production.

---

8. Marilyn Chase, "U.S. Microelectronics Firms Study Japan for Secrets of Quality and Productivity," *The Wall Street Journal,* June 30, 1981, p. 12. Reprinted by permission of *The Wall Street Journal,* © Dow Jones & Company, Inc. (1981). All Rights Reserved.

Materials Movement

Materials management is concerned not only with the purchase, storage, and control of materials, but also with **materials movement.** Materials movement includes efforts to minimize the costs and delays associated with the internal handling of materials and the external transport of goods to and from the company.

Internal Materials Handling

Methods and processes of internal materials handling usually are designed by engineering specialists as part of the production system. The in-house methods used in handling materials are determined by the nature of the materials, layout of the factory, and type of product made. Each industry has its special materials handling problems. However, some basic internal materials handling devices include gravity-feed and mechanical conveyor belts, overhead conveyors, pipelines, forklift trucks, and driverless tractors that operate by chain-driven mechanisms through slots or tracks in the floor.

External Materials Transport

External shipment of materials comes under the traffic function. The basic function of the traffic department is to secure delivery of materials and parts at the least possible transportation costs and to ship the finished goods by the most efficient means. Traffic departments are established in larger companies to handle the specialized traffic function, and these are directed by a traffic manager. Figure 11-9 shows the main functions of the traffic department.

The management of traffic affects many other departments. The processing or manufacturing departments expect an adequate flow of materials scheduled at the right time. Careful scheduling of inbound and outbound shipments is required in controlling the size of inventories. The traffic department helps the purchasing department make the most desirable decisions from the standpoints of transportation costs and services. As will be noted, this requires great skill.

Modes of External Materials Transport

Freight transportation was never too popular with business students aiming to make their mark in American industry. To build a product and sell it often seemed more exciting than how to get it from place to place. This may not be the case much longer. The changes rolling down the pike for the once-routine freight transportation industry promise to make it a more competitive and dynamic business. For example, the deregulation of air, truck, and rail transport has introduced greater complexity and competition into much of the U.S. freight transportation marketplace. In addition, we find a trend toward mergers of transportation companies and the greater use of *intermodal* shipments — shipments that use various modes of transport rather than a single mode. This trend means greater diversity in the alternative choices of transportation, terms of service, and rates that must be considered. Transportation is now

Figure 11-9   Main Functions of the Traffic Department

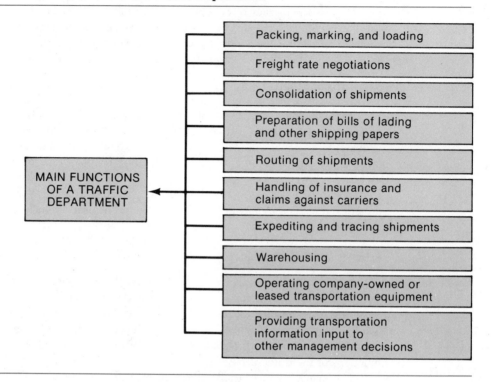

becoming an exciting growth area, and it holds a much greater potential for an exciting business career than a few years back.

The main modes of materials transport are described in the remainder of this chapter. Their main strengths and weaknesses are summarized in Figure 11-10. However, as we have noted above, external materials transport must increasingly be thought of more as an intermodal system than as the selection of a single mode of transport from among various alternatives.

Surface Transport: Rails

In 1973 the nation's major railroads hauled more than 1.5 billion tons of freight. Ever since, they have been trying to get back to that record level. But various factors are working against higher rail freight traffic. These include continuing shortages of freight cars, deterioration of railroad tracks and roadbeds, obsolete terminals, and restrictive work rules which prevent real productivity increases without automation.

Rail delivery time has become more erratic, but not all types of freight are equally sensitive to rail service. Railroads inherently are the cheapest form of land transportation for large loads over long distances, and they remain an important form of transport in the United States. Trains in the United States move shipments of more than half of our coal; new autos and auto parts; iron, steel, and primary metals; lumber and wood used in the country; chemicals; household appliances; and wheat and other food grains.

The recent deregulation of railroads promises to make the rail network even more efficient and competitive. The Staggers Act of 1980 enables railroads to:

1. Alter rates, within certain ranges, without seeking government approval.
2. Legalize contracts with customers that guarantee rates and services, usually in exchange for large volumes of business.
3. Abandon unprofitable lines and to enter new markets.
4. Merge into larger super railroads.

On the other side of the deregulation coin, railroads can no longer jointly set prices. Now they must compete in terms of services offered, reliability of rail car supply, speed of service, and the like. Railroad rates generally are expressed in rates per 100 pounds or per ton from the point of origin to the destination. A distinction is made in the rates applicable to goods shipped in carload lots (CL) and those shipped in less

Figure 11-10   Strengths and Weaknesses of Various Transportation Modes

Method	Strengths	Weaknesses
• Railroads	• Low cost for moving a wide variety of goods over long distances Maintain fairly reliable schedules Rail system has wide coverage	• Usually not speedy Deliveries often infrequent to any one point Wide variations in dependability Shortages of special shipping cars
• Trucks	• Great flexibility and adaptability as to points served and goods carried Short hauls are relatively inexpensive Usually a speedy method Can be combined with rail service	• Often more expensive than rails on long hauls Lack of uniformity in truck regulations Trucks can be polluters
• Waterways	• Great flexibility in moving a wide variety of goods, especially in pre-loaded containers Low cost for high-bulk items	• Slow, and deviates from established delivery schedules Water transportation may be seasonal
• Pipelines	• Moves high number of units per unit of time Dependable and safe	• Pipeline construction is very costly Inflexible, and limited purposes Needs processing or other transportation facilities at end of line
• Airplanes	• Speedy between major cities Less damage to goods and fewer stolen goods	• Relatively high costs and low flexibility as to goods that can be economically flown per transportation dollar Lack of terminals in smaller cities

than carload lots (LCL). LCL rates are generally between 15 and 30 percent higher than the rates for carload shipments.

The effects of railroad deregulation are beginning to be felt in three ways. Competition among railroads and from motor carriers has intensified, mergers have accelerated, and intermodal shipments have become more common. Some railroads will not survive. But deregulation should be a positive factor for rail transport over the long run.

Surface Transport: Motor Trucks

Who moves America's economy? Twenty years ago there was little doubt about it — the railroads hauled a vastly larger proportion of the nation's freight than any other transportation mode. But this is no longer true. As Figure 11-11 shows, the trucks keep gaining even though they burn four times more fuel than trains to move a ton of freight. Many analysts feel that the lines in Figure 11-11 will cross before 1990. Motor-carrier managements have a greater degree of flexibility in handling their employees than railroad managements. Also, railroads must maintain their own tracks and roadbeds.

For relatively short hauls up to 300 miles, motor trucks compete well with railroads. They are of particular importance to communities with little or no railroad service. Also, about 75 percent of all food in the United States moves to market on interstate highways. Trucking rates vary. They may be either lower or higher than railroad rates.

Part of the traditional distinction between rail and truck transportation has been blurred by innovations and by the deregulation of trucks and rails. For example, national coverage of railroads combined with the local flexibility of trucks is provided by *piggy-back* service — a long-haul movement of either trucks and trailers on railroad flatcars (TOFC) or of containers on flatcars (COFC). A recent innovation in piggyback intermodal service is the RoadRailer, developed by Bi-Modal Corp. This is a piggyback-style truck trailer that rides on truck tires over the highway and then lets down railroad wheels to travel on tracks. The use of RoadRailers by railroads cuts the use of diesel fuel compared with conventional TOFC trains. However, RoadRailers are heavier on an individual basis than conventional highway trailers. Also, RoadRailers cannot be mixed into the same train with conventional rolling stock.

In the long run, the changes that occur in the railroad industry may be influenced as much by trucking deregulation as by rail deregulation. The Motor Carrier Act of 1980 lifts many controls over truck rates. The Act makes it easier for new companies to enter the business, for existing companies to expand into new territories and routes, and for all truckers to vary their prices according to costs and market forces. For example, the Act frees contract carriers from a previous ICC rule limiting them to only eight customers. Thus, these carriers will be able to compete on a lower-cost basis with unionized carriers. Figure 11-12 shows the four main ICC categories of motor carriers. The ICC regulates common and contract carriers according to the commodities they carry. Therefore, private and exempt carriers generally may not carry regulated commodities on a for-hire basis.

Figure 11-11   Trucks v. Trains: Percentage Volume of Domestic Intercity Freight Traffic

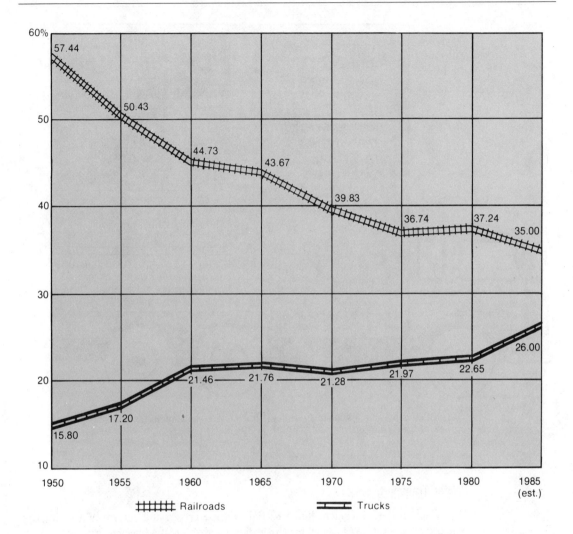

SOURCE: U. S. Bureau of the Census, *Statistical Abstract of the United States: 1982–1983* (103d ed.; Washington, DC: U. S. Government Printing Office, 1982), p. 607.

Rail and motor-carrier deregulation encourages the growth of intermodal piggyback service, which lets shippers take advantage of the economies offered by different transport modes. Although trucks and railroads still compete among themselves and with each other, collaboration will be increasingly important to growing intermodal services and innovations.

Figure 11-12   Four Categories of Motor Carriers

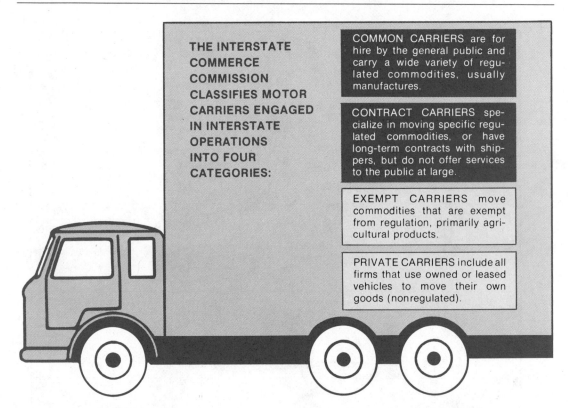

THE INTERSTATE COMMERCE COMMISSION CLASSIFIES MOTOR CARRIERS ENGAGED IN INTERSTATE OPERATIONS INTO FOUR CATEGORIES:

COMMON CARRIERS are for hire by the general public and carry a wide variety of regulated commodities, usually manufactures.

CONTRACT CARRIERS specialize in moving specific regulated commodities, or have long-term contracts with shippers, but do not offer services to the public at large.

EXEMPT CARRIERS move commodities that are exempt from regulation, primarily agricultural products.

PRIVATE CARRIERS include all firms that use owned or leased vehicles to move their own goods (nonregulated).

SOURCE: Adapted from William J. Kahley, "Trucking Deregulation in the Southeast," *Economic Review of the FRB of Atlanta* (July, 1982), p. 39.

Water Transport: Barges

Back in 1847, President James K. Polk vetoed a rivers and harbors bill, saying that the use of general taxes to pay for the projects wasn't justified because the entire U.S. populace wouldn't benefit. But a young Congressman from waterways-minded Illinois named Abraham Lincoln led a legislative override of the veto. That signaled what was to be a long history of generous federal policy toward inland waterways. Now all that is changing. A fuel tax of 4 cents a gallon for barge traffic imposed in 1980 may be boosted to over 30 cents by 1985.

Since the early years of our nation, the waterways of the country—rivers, the Great Lakes, and the coastline routes—have been important in the transport of certain kinds of freight. This includes goods of large bulk and low value such as coal, grain, oil, lumber, sugar, cotton, and corn. Barges carry about 40 percent of grain exported from this country. The main traffic way is the Mississippi River and its major tributaries. Another major waterway, the 250-mile Tennessee-Tombigbee (Tenn-Tom) Waterway, is scheduled for completion in 1986. It is a massive undertaking and connects the Port of Mobile, AL to the Tennessee River.

Water transport is the cheapest but also the slowest method of moving goods. However, considerable versatility in water transport modes has been developed, and the barge industry is profitable and fast-growing. For example, the specially built LASH (Lighter-Aboard SHip) freighters gather up to 90 fully loaded barges, called "lighters," of about 300 tons and carry the barges overseas. Congested harbors can be avoided by loading or offloading the barges at a river's mouth, where they can penetrate far inland along the waterway.

Water Transport: Ships

By most measures, the Port of New York and New Jersey was the number-one port in the country, in terms of dollar value of exports and imports handled, from 1800 to 1977. By 1978, however, it was passed up by the Port of New Orleans, as shown in Figure 11-13. One reason for New Orleans's growth has been its efforts to upgrade its containerization facilities. Another reason is the population growth in the south-eastern part of the United States. The Port of New Orleans also handles the heavy barge traffic flowing down the Mississippi River.

Figure 11-13   The Nation's Busiest Seaports

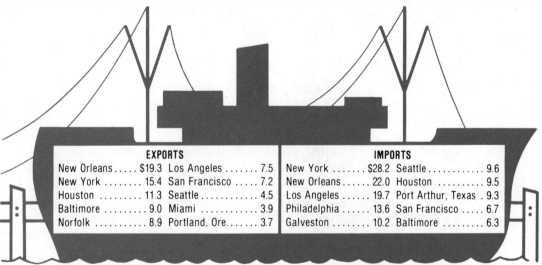

EXPORTS		IMPORTS	
New Orleans $19.3	Los Angeles 7.5	New York $28.2	Seattle 9.6
New York 15.4	San Francisco 7.2	New Orleans 22.0	Houston 9.5
Houston 11.3	Seattle 4.5	Los Angeles 19.7	Port Arthur, Texas . 9.3
Baltimore 9.0	Miami 3.9	Philadelphia 13.6	San Francisco 6.7
Norfolk 8.9	Portland, Ore 3.7	Galveston 10.2	Baltimore 6.3

SOURCE: Data (in billions of dollars) are taken from Eugene Carlson, "Southern Ports Are the Busiest," *The Wall Street Journal,* May 25, 1982, p. 27. Reprinted by permission of *The Wall Street Journal,* © Dow Jones & Company, Inc. (1982). All Rights Reserved.

Containerization is the most significant maritime technological innovation since the changeover from sail to steam. It is the shipping of cargo in large aluminum or steel boxes. These boxes have doors at one end and measure 8 feet across, 8 feet high, and come in sizes of 10-foot lengths up to 40 feet. The use of containerships, built to carry the pre-loaded containers, is growing rapidly. On the other hand, the number of United States flag conventional or breakbulk vessels, in which cargo is handled in nets or slings, has been declining since World War II.

Containerization is only one of several technological developments in preloading that have made shipping more capital-intensive in the past 15 years. LASH shipping was mentioned with regard to barges. Another innovation is *Ro/Ro,* or "Roll on-Roll off" shipping, where freighter ships are built with traffic ramps and trucks are driven on board to detach and leave their trailers or containers. Sometimes it is called *fishyback* freight. Pallet ships, another innovation, have cargo loaded on portable platforms.

In all, the spread of container-related innovations has greatly expanded the types of goods traditionally transported by ships. The most recent type of ship is called the Supercarrier. It handles both containerized and noncontainerized cargoes. The Supercarrier can be recognized by a ramp that sticks straight up from the stern of the vessel when it is at sea. When the ramp is let down, it can reach over 160 feet to allow cargo to be loaded and unloaded. This allows the Supercarrier to operate in ports that lack modern loading facilities.

Another boost to shipping, in addition to innovations in containers and ships, comes from Free-Trade Zones (FTZs). FTZs are tax-free areas, mostly within seaports, which are exempted from normal customs duties so as to encourage foreign shipping and investment in the United States. The more the FTZs are used, the more services that can be provided by the FTZ ports.

Pipelines

A network of about 170,000 miles of pipelines is used to transport crude petroleum, natural gas, and even coal in slurry form (a mixture of pulverized coal and water). The Port of New York, for example, cannot accommodate large oil tankers, and the dredging costs to achieve this are too high. It is probable that offshore tanker terminals will be built instead, and the petroleum transported to shore by pipeline.

If the cost of building a pipeline is to be justified, there must be continuous processing of the material transported. Therefore, companies that own pipelines consider them to be extensions of their productive facilities rather than transportation devices. While pipelines have the disadvantages of governmental regulation and inflexible routes, they have a distinct long-run cost advantage over transportation by railroad or motor carrier.

Air Transport: Airfreight

Airfreight has been taking off in recent years at a pace that seems unstoppable. Revenue from it has risen more than 40 percent just since the mid-1970s and is growing at a faster pace than passenger revenue.

Individuals and businesses are cutting days of shipping time by jetting everything from doctoral theses and racehorses to computers and auto parts. While speed is the major lure, other reasons, such as security (shippers say gems and furs are far easier to trace and control in air travel) and convenience, are growing in importance. Another important factor is the rising cost of warehousing duplicate inventories, such as computer parts, all around the country. Many firms are finding it more economical to airfreight the parts when they are needed.

The capacity of wide-bodied jets means that almost anything can go by air. A DC-10 can carry more than 100,000 pounds of small packages. On the other hand, American Airlines has flown a single shipment of a 47,000-pound ship reduction gear from New York to Los Angeles.

The small-package market (packages under 70 pounds) is the center of the airfreight industry. This category once was almost dismissed by some people in the airfreight business as lacking the growth and profit potential to be worth the effort. Now 90 percent of all packages sent by air weigh less than 100 pounds.

Well-known airfreight companies include Federal Express Corp., Emery Air Freight Corp., Airborne Freight Corp., Burlington Northern Air Freight, and Purolator Courier Corp. Tiger International is strong in heavy cargo. (The U.S. Postal Service, with its Express Mail, also is part of the airfreight picture.) Recently most of these companies have been acquiring their own aircraft rather than relying solely on space in commercial airliners. The next major move in airfreight may be joint ventures with European companies to expand the routes and to get some help in dealing with customs barriers.

Freight Forwarders

The freight forwarder is discussed last because it overlaps the other modes of transport. A **freight forwarder** is a broker for companies that ship in less-than carload, truckload, or airplane-load lots. This person combines these broken lots into full loads and ships them at carload rates. The forwarder's profit comes from the difference between the carload rate the forwarder pays and the rate charged to the customer. For the customer, the skill of the forwarder results in faster and less expensive service than is usually possible through ordinary LCL shipments.

Companies may also be freight forwarders. The airfreight companies we just discussed are in this category. Airfreight forwarders have established themselves in the small-package area with the ability to guarantee overnight delivery with door-to-door service. As some freight-forwarding companies become more intermodal, their roles probably will overlap with the role of individual brokers.

As we have seen, external materials transport is one important aspect of distribution management. Furthermore, distribution management is a basic area within materials management. Not every organization has the management sophistication and computer capabilities to adopt an integrated system of physical distribution. Nevertheless, it seems clear that today's materials manager or distribution manager has an increasingly complex job. Thus, this person will not be simply a purchasing, traffic, or materials specialist. Rather, materials managers will need to be dynamic, broad-gauge professionals who can draw on the skill, technological knowledge, and professional competence of many specialists.

SUMMARY   In recent years the functions of purchasing, procurement, and materials management have become increasingly important to manufacturing organizations. Importantly, every dollar saved in purchasing contributes a new dollar to the company's profit picture. Procurement is a step up from basic purchasing and usually includes inventory control and traffic control. Materials management includes all of the activities relating to the acquisition, control, and movement of a firm's materials and supplies. Two basic areas in materials management are purchasing and distribution management.

Purchasing is usually done by a purchasing department. The head of this department is usually called the purchasing manager or purchasing agent. Policy areas that are important to purchasing managers include: making or buying parts and equipment, hand-to-mouth buying, forward buying, contract purchasing, speculative purchasing, reciprocal buying, and using sealed bids.

The functions performed by purchasing departments vary widely from company to company. However, most of these departments perform two main activities: ordering and receiving materials, and value analysis.

The four basic areas in distribution management are materials control, inventory control, materials movement, and modes of external materials transport. Materials control informs management of the quantity and location of materials in the plant. Two systems of inventory control are: order-point analysis, based on historical buying practices and needs; and material requirements planning, based on the interdependent relationship of parts and materials, anticipated production, and the sale of end products. Another approach to inventory is found in the Japanese "Kanban," or "just-in-time," system. Kanban includes quality and inventory control. It is based on a close, long-term working relationship of trust and responsibility among a company's managers, workers, and suppliers.

Materials movement involves the transport of materials in-house or outside the company. External materials movement comes under the traffic function, often directed by a traffic manager. The main modes of external materials transport are: rails, trucks, barges, ships, pipelines, and airplanes. However, external materials transport increasingly is based on the use of an intermodal system rather than of a single mode.

Materials management is growing in scope and complexity, and the effective materials manager can make important contributions to the success of a company.

BACK TO THE CHAPTER OPENER

1. In which of two basic areas of materials management does inventory control belong?
2. How does inventory control differ from materials control?
3. How does material requirements planning differ from order-point analysis?
4. What type of inventory control system do Japanese automakers use?
5. How may the deregulation of air, rail, and truck transport affect material requirements planning?

BUSINESS TERMS				
purchasing	232	value analysis	240
procurement	232	distribution management	241
materials management	232	materials control	241
materials managers	232	inventory control	242
purchasing agent	234	average inventory	243
make-or-buy decision	235	material requirements planning	
hand-to-mouth buying	236	(MRP)	243
forward buying	236	Kanban	245
contract purchasing	236	materials movement	247
speculative purchasing	237	containerization	254
reciprocal buying	237	freight forwarder	255

QUESTIONS FOR DISCUSSION AND ANALYSIS

1. Why is a purchasing dollar saved more important to the profit picture than a sales dollar?

2. What basic impact will GM's new bidding program likely have on GM's relationships with its steel suppliers?

3. How are value analysis (VA) and value engineering (VE) similar? How do they differ?

4. In what kind of organization might materials managers be called distribution managers?

5. What is the basic difference between traditional inventory control (based on the inventory cycle order point) and material requirements planning?

6. Is Kanban basically an inventory control system? Explain.

7. If you were the owner of a small interstate trucking company, would you see the deregulation of trucking, rail, and air transport as good for your business? Why or why not?

8. What is the difference between piggyback and fishyback freight service?

9. Indicate the methods of transportation that you would select for each of the following products:

   a. Coal — in large amounts from Cleveland, OH to Buffalo, NY.
   b. Petroleum — on a regular basis for a distance of 90 miles.
   c. Expensive suits — from Chicago to New York.
   d. A computer — from Minneapolis to London.

10. Why should freight forwarders be able to do enough transporting better than regular shippers to justify the use of their forwarding services?

PROJECTS, PROBLEMS, AND SHORT CASES

1. Gil Harrigan, purchasing agent for a utility company, returned from a utility trade association meeting with a new-found zeal for trimming inventories. The speaker at the meeting emphasized the need to keep lean inventories regardless of the economic picture. "Let the suppliers carry your inventory," he was told at the meeting. "Don't buy anything until it's absolutely necessary."

   Soon afterward, Harrigan placed an order for a utility truck rack that was made to carry special utility company equipment to construction sites. He was told by the vendors that they no longer stocked that item on a regular basis because of inventory costs and cutbacks. However, a more expensive rack could be provided within a week, or the regular rack could be special-ordered and shipped in.

"What's wrong with our suppliers?" Harrigan complained as he hung up the phone. "Doesn't anybody want to stock anything anymore? How can we trim our inventory if our suppliers don't do their job?"

"Maybe your suppliers also go to trade meetings," his secretary muttered to herself.

Prepare a report to Harrigan suggesting more steps to take to keep this type of problem from occurring in the future.

2. Ramona Waldo, president of Spray-Rite, noticed that sharply higher raw material costs were eroding the profits on a line of compressors the company made. She ruled out the possibility of charging higher prices for the compressors because of competition and a slow economic climate, and she concluded that the company had better start cutting costs wherever possible.

Various steps were taken, almost on a panic basis. The salespersons were asked to fly coach and rent only compact cars. Office personnel worked staggered shifts so that the WATS line could be used in dealing with customers in various parts of the country. A close watch was even kept on such relatively minor items as office supplies and the length of coffee breaks.

In a meeting of department heads, held to discuss cost-cutting measures, the product engineering manager suggested that these measures were all right as temporary steps but that the company really needed a continuing program to redesign its products and pursue cheaper production costs.

"No, sir!" Waldo stated emphatically. "Whatever we do, we're not going to cheapen our products and jeopardize our reputation!"

a. What do you think of Waldo's response?
b. What do you think of the company's cost-cutting program?
c. What other steps might the company take to save on factory and material costs?

3. The deregulation of rail, truck, and air transport companies has forced these companies to rethink their personnel needs and policies as competition for new markets heats up. Discuss with the materials manager or the human resources manager at a trucking company, rail company, or airline company what characteristics or skills the company now looks for in traffic staff and other functions that were not so important before deregulation. Share your findings with the class in a 10-minute oral report.

IV. Marketing

Chapter 12. Marketing Management
       13. Products and Their Distribution
       14. Personal Selling and Advertising
       15. Prices and Pricing Policies
       16. International Business

Wine, Baubles, and Glamour Are Used to Help Lure Female Consumers to Ford's Showrooms

Women head 21 million U.S. households—more than 25% of the total—and the Ford Motor Co., Dearborn, Mich., is making a concerted effort to make those potential car buyers comfortable in its dealers' showrooms.

Toward that end, Ford is in the middle of an experiment in the Dallas and San Diego markets to find a better way to sell to women. The $500,000 experiment, which will continue into 1983, involves showroom parties at which invited female consumers sip wine, receive a gold bracelet as a gift, and peruse the new models in a no-pressure setting.

The female car buyer was a rarity 15 years ago, according to Marilyn J. King, Ford's manager of contemporary markets, North American automotive operations. By 1972 they accounted for 21% of new car purchases, and that figure has climbed to 40% today—a market potentially worth $35 billion.

The Dallas-San Diego experiment is part of the effort to develop a "comfortable buying process for women," King said, a process devoid of the traditional high-pressure tactics associated with car buying.

"When they go into a dealership, many women feel intimidated by the technical aspects," she said. "We want to create an ideal environment for women in which they're not hassled or hustled.

"They don't want to be patronized by salesmen who call them 'dear' or 'honey' and suggest they bring their husband or father with them the next time they come to the showroom. They want technical information about the cars, and they want to be treated like a man would be treated."

The showroom parties appear to be a hit in Dallas, where more than 500 women turned out for one of them. Engraved invitations, wine and cheese, and beautiful models all lend a touch of class to the events.

"At nice luncheons, women enjoy having another woman come along to model clothes for them," King said. "Our thought was to duplicate that." Another possibility might be to have male models at the showroom parties, she said.

Salesmen are admonished not to try to sell any cars to the women in attendance. That would be contrary to the ambience Ford is trying to create, she said; besides, the hard sell just won't work with today's better-educated consumer.

"It's a new process for our salespeople," King said. "Car salespeople have not been held in high esteem in the past, but I think that's going to change.

"More professionalism is being introduced in sales, and I think we'll see women getting involved in the field. The stereotype of men knowing about cars may be true, but women are very good at interpersonal relations, and personality is the key to car sales, not gender."

More than 100 cars have been sold in Dallas as a result of the parties, a modest figure considering the investment made but well worth it if it gives Ford an edge in marketing its vehicles to the projected 57 million working women by 1990.

The Dallas-San Diego experiment is only a small part of the company's total effort to reach contemporary consumers, she said. "Rather than look at a mass market as we did in the past, we're trying to fine-tune both our marketing and the way we do business.

"There are many things we're doing to isolate people's needs. We are conducting focus groups all over the country, and top management has organized a product evaluation panel of female employees who represent a cross-section of American women."

SOURCE: "Wine, Baubles, and Glamour Are Used to Help Lure Female Consumers to Ford's Showrooms," *Marketing News* (August 6, 1982), p. 1. Reprints from *Marketing News*, published by the American Marketing Association.

Marketing Management

Objectives:

- Understand the marketing concept and explain why marketing is important in our economy.
- Explain how the marketing system creates intangible satisfactions.
- Explain the importance of the eight basic marketing functions.
- Explain how the marketing mix can be used to develop a marketing strategy.
- Understand the differences between market segmentation and product differentiation.
- Explain how the uncontrollable factors in the marketing environment affect a marketing manager.
- Identify the different types of buying motives.
- Understand the six stages in the buying process.
- Identify the research activities that are frequently conducted by a marketing research department.
- Explain the three basic ways to gather primary data.

When Carleton College, a small liberal arts school in Northfield, MN, had a problem with declining enrollments, school officials turned to marketing.[1] College administrators decided to market their school in the same manner as Procter & Gamble markets its Tide; General Motors, its Chevrolets; and I.B.M., its computers. Carleton

---

1. Lawrence Ingrassia, "College Learns to Use Fine Art of Marketing," *The Wall Street Journal*, February 23, 1981, p. 25.

conducted marketing research to find out the needs and interests of prospective students. Then, the school developed interesting and creative mailings that were sent to high school students. One research finding showed that prospective students thought the Minnesota climate was too cold and barren. Carleton proceeded to turn the winter season into an advantage by picturing spirited cross-country skiers and the beauty of winter in a promotional brochure.

As indicated by the Carleton College story, marketing is not merely another business practice. Marketing helps to sell services, persons, and ideas as well as soap, shoes, and soft drinks. Museums and public television stations use carefully developed marketing programs to raise funds. National political candidates conduct extensive marketing campaigns to gain support. The AFL-CIO and the U.S. Chamber of Commerce are employing marketing techniques to influence our attitudes toward labor and business.

In our fast-paced, competitive society, a complete marketing study is necessary for the successful introduction of a new good or service. The organization that is production-oriented is concerned about its ability to sell existing goods. The organization that is marketing-oriented is concerned about creating goods and services that satisfy consumer needs. This is the essence of the marketing concept. The three distinct elements that comprise the **marketing concept** are: satisfaction of consumer needs, coordination of all activities in support of marketing, and achievement of organizational objectives through customer satisfaction.

An organizational objective of most businesses is to attain a certain level of profit. Service organizations, however, generally have objectives that are appropriate for their operations. In the previous example, Carleton College had an objective of obtaining a large number of applicants so it could continue a selective admissions policy.

The significance of the marketing concept for a business was first described in the 1952 annual report of General Electric:

> The concept introduces the marketing man at the beginning rather than at the end of the production cycle, and integrates marketing into each phase of the business. Thus, marketing through its studies and research will establish for the engineer, the design and manufacturing man, what the customer wants in a given product, what price he is willing to pay and where and when it will be wanted. Marketing will have authority in product planning, production scheduling, and inventory control, as well as in sales distribution and servicing of the product.

MARKETING AND ITS IMPORTANCE

Marketing has been defined as "the human activity directed at satisfying needs and wants through exchange processes."[2] In the past this activity has been aimed mainly at satisfying physical needs such as food, shelter, and clothing. In recent years this activity has been expanded to satisfy our desire for a better quality of life.

---

2. Philip Kotler, *Marketing Management* (4th ed.; Englewood Cliffs, NJ: Prentice-Hall, Inc., 1980), p. 21.

For example, marketing programs have been developed for energy conservation and environmental protection.

In our economy the basic importance of marketing is highlighted by examining three factors: employment in marketing, the number of marketing establishments that exist, and marketing costs.

Employment in Marketing

In the early 1980s, the number of employees in retailing was nearly 16 million; in wholesaling, 3.8 million; and in selected services, 8.0 million. These numbers totaled nearly 28 million, which represented over 28 percent of all individuals employed in this country.

Number of Marketing Establishments

The scope of marketing is measured by the number of establishments engaged in distributive activities. Also to be included is the number of organizations that support marketing such as transportation firms, finance companies, advertising agencies, and advertising media. The *1977 Census of Business* lists the following number of establishments: retail, 1,855,000; wholesale, 383,000; and selected services, 1,835,000. Thus, the total of marketing establishments is 4,073,000.

Marketing Costs

Marketing costs are the costs of the marketing process, and they emphasize the contribution of marketing to our economy. A historic study of distribution costs indicated that the consumer dollar is allocated as follows:[3]

Cost of production		41.1%
Cost of marketing		
Retail costs	19.2	
Wholesale costs	10.7	
Manufacturers' marketing costs	13.9	
Transportation costs	13.4	
Other marketing costs	1.7	58.9
Total costs		100.0%

Other studies indicate that the proportion of marketing costs in the selling price of a consumer product ranges from 42 to 59 percent. If costs are a measure of importance, then the marketing process should be considered to be as economically significant as the manufacturing process.

---

3. Paul W. Stewart and J. Frederic Dewhurst, *Does Distribution Cost Too Much?* (New York: The 20th Century Fund, 1939), pp. 117–118.

MARKETING AS A PRODUCTIVE SYSTEM

Both marketing and manufacturing are systems, or processes. A difference between the two systems is that the satisfactions provided by marketing are intangible while those provided by manufacturing are tangible. As Figure 12-1 shows, the manufacturing system creates **form utility,** which is the satisfaction derived from a physical change in the product. On the other hand, the marketing system creates other consumer utilities through costly marketing activities that may be performed during the marketing process. Thus, transportation creates **place utility,** and product storage creates **time utility.** Promotion creates both **possession utility** and **information utility.** For example, a refrigerator manufactured by General Electric Company in Louisville, KY has no value to a consumer shopping in Denver, CO. Value is created when the refrigerator is transported (place utility) to a dealer's store in Denver. Consumers desire to make their selection from among the various models displayed and stored (time utility) in the dealer's showroom. The dealer uses extensive advertising (information utility) to inform the consumer about the refrigerator and personal selling (possession utility) to complete the transaction.

Figure 12-1   Creation of Consumer Utilities

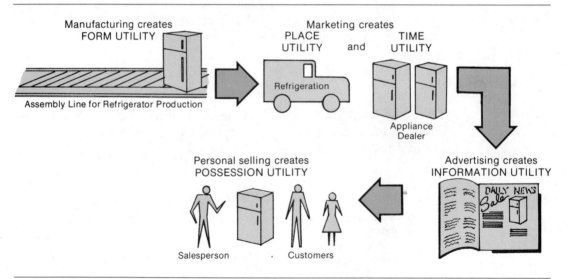

MARKETING ORGANIZATION STRUCTURE

The objectives of a firm determine the structure of its organization. Typical organizations are difficult to diagram since no two companies, even in the same industry, have identical corporate objectives. The General Electric organization differs from Westinghouse Electric, and the General Motors structure differs from Ford Mo-

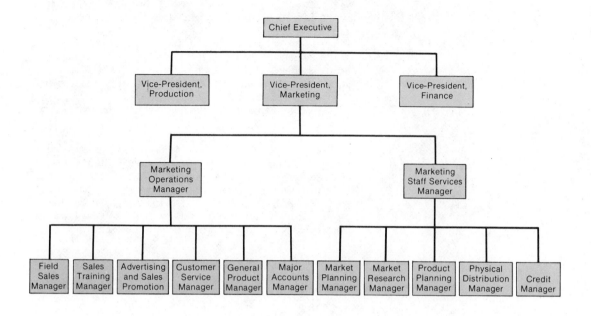

tors. Figure 12-2 shows the marketing organization of a representative business which has adopted the marketing concept.

Marketing, along with production and finance, is one of the three major functional areas of business. The marketing function is headed by the vice-president of marketing or the marketing manager, who frequently is responsible to the chief executive of the firm. Figure 12-3 provides a profile of the typical chief marketing executive.

Marketing activities, however, often are grouped under a marketing operations manager and a marketing staff services manager. This separate grouping lessens the number of individuals who report directly to the vice-president of marketing and permits staff specialization.

Marketing Operations

The activities for which the marketing operations manager is responsible are field sales, sales training, advertising and sales promotion, customer service, product management, and major accounts. The field sales manager, through an extensive sales organization, has charge of all the salespersons in the organization. Training programs on basic selling, product features, and company policies are developed and conducted for the salespersons by the sales training manager. Advertising and sales promotion

Figure 12-3   **Typical Chief Marketing Executive**

Stature:	Vice-president, reporting to the president, with both line and staff authority.
Responsibility:	Direct control of marketing planning, market research, general marketing, sales promotion, corporate and product advertising, and new product planning.
Compensation:	Total compensation of $139,710.* Stock option, automobile, and town and country club memberships.
Mobility:	17 years tenure with employer, less than 5 years in the position, and 2 previous employers.
Origins:	Born in Midwest, 50 years old.
Education:	Bachelor's degree in liberal arts, as likely to have attended a midwestern state school as one of Ivy League; almost one in four has a graduate degree, most often an MBA.
Expertise:	Previous experience in direct sales, staff marketing, advertising/promotion, and market research; considers ability to contribute to top management decisions and skill in motivating employees as major contributions to success as chief marketing executive.

*Total compensation has been updated to reflect 1980 average.

SOURCE: *Profile of a Chief Marketing Executive* (New York: Heidrick and Struggles, 1976), p. 3.

programs which complement and intensify the selling activity are prepared by the advertising and sales promotion manager. The customer service manager tries to correct consumer complaints about product defects. Most multiproduct companies utilize product managers who are responsible for developing and marketing specific product lines. The individual product managers report to the general product manager. In many large firms certain key or major accounts are handled by the major accounts manager at corporate headquarters rather than by salespersons in the field.

Marketing Staff Services

The marketing staff services manager is responsible for market planning, marketing research, product planning, physical distribution, and credit service. The market planning manager tries to find the best markets or customers for the company's products. Collecting, analyzing, and interpreting marketing data are the major activities of the marketing researcher. The product planning manager designs and creates new products to satisfy the ever-changing needs of consumers. The main task of the physical distribution manager is to minimize the storage and transportation costs for a product and to maximize product availability to consumers. To encourage sales the credit manager must provide a variety of credit plans for prospective customers.

MARKETING FUNCTIONS

Marketing functions are those inescapable economic activities which are found throughout the marketing system. The marketing system includes eight basic marketing functions which are divided into three major categories:

1. Exchange
$$\begin{cases} 1. \text{ Buying} \\ 2. \text{ Selling} \end{cases}$$

2. Physical Distribution
$$\begin{cases} 3. \text{ Transportation} \\ 4. \text{ Storage} \end{cases}$$

3. Facilitating
$$\begin{cases} 5. \text{ Financing} \\ 6. \text{ Marketing research and information} \\ 7. \text{ Risk taking} \\ 8. \text{ Product standardization and grading} \end{cases}$$

Buying and selling are concerned with the exchange of goods from seller to buyer. The transportation function is concerned with the movement of goods from the place of production to the point of consumption. The storage function provides for the storage of goods until they are needed by consumers. Finance, marketing research and information, risk taking, and product standardization and grading are the functions that aid in the performance of the other functions.

The marketing functions must be performed at some point in the marketing process. Even though the responsibility for the performance of a function may be shifted from one point to another within the process, the function cannot be eliminated. For example, if a seller of refrigerators would not deliver the appliance to the buyer's home, the buyer would have to perform this transportation function.

As the marketing functions are shifted within the marketing system, companies develop different operating policies and varying cost structures. A firm manufacturing a retailer-branded lawn mower for a large retail chain, such as Sears, performs no mass advertising and incurs no other promotional costs. The promotional activities for the lawn mower and their costs are assumed by Sears. In contrast, Lawn-Boy produces and distributes its own brand of lawn mower and operates differently. Lawn-Boy needs an advertising budget and an advertising department in order to gain brand identity.

MARKETING MIX

Marketing mix refers to the combination of decision elements in a company's marketing program. The combination is determined and controlled by marketing executives. The decision elements of marketing which are commonly identified as the four P's are:[4]

1. *Product.* Concerned with product planning, development, modification, branding, and packaging decisions.

---

4. The four P's were popularized by E. Jerome McCarthy, *Basic Marketing* (7th ed.; Homewood, IL: Richard D. Irwin, Inc., 1981), p. 42.

2. *Place.* Concerned with decisions to determine which marketing establishments can be linked together most effectively in transferring product ownership from producer to consumer.
3. *Promotion.* Concerned with communicating to consumers and the related personal selling, advertising, and sales promotion decisions.
4. *Price.* Concerned with decisions regarding price determination, general and specific pricing policies, supply and demand relationships, and legal restrictions.

Marketing Strategy

Marketing functions and marketing mix are two different concepts. The marketing functions are inescapable activities in the marketing process. The marketing mix combines with the marketing activities to form purposeful marketing plans or strategies. In developing a marketing strategy, the combination of decision elements in the marketing mix is influenced by such factors as the market to be served, competition, marketing legislation, nonmarketing costs, structure of distribution, and demand.

Use of Different Marketing Strategies

The cosmetics industry illustrates how different marketing strategies can be developed by altering the marketing mix of a firm. Many cosmetic manufacturers, such as Coty and Maybelline, market through wholesalers who distribute to retailers. These manufacturers price competitively and promote extensively to consumer media, such as television, magazines, and newspapers. They do this to stimulate a grass-roots consumer demand for their products.

In contrast, the marketing mix for Avon cosmetics is entirely different. Avon has carved a niche for itself in the cosmetics industry by catering to the person who desires to purchase a quality product directly from a salesperson. Although Avon advertises in the mass media, the bulk of its promotional expenditures is for commissions paid to a large direct sales force. These salespersons knock on household doors and announce, "Avon calling."

Market Segmentation and Product Differentiation

Market segmentation and product differentiation are complementary marketing strategies. Basically, market segmentation is a product development strategy, while product differentiation is essentially a promotional strategy.

When the market for a product is divided into two or more homogeneous groups of consumers, and variations of the product are developed to satisfy each group, **market segmentation** has occurred. Market segmentation allows a marketing manager to develop a strategy that will be responsive to the needs of a unique market sector.

Adequacy, measurability, and accessibility are the conditions that must be met for a strategy of market segmentation. Sales from the market segment should be large enough to justify the marketing effort directed to the segment. A firm that desires to sell a low-calorie salad dressing should be able to ascertain the adequacy of the market for the product. Life insurance industry statistics showing the number of overweight persons in this country would be a measure of this market. Assuming the market is adequate and measurable, management should decide if the prospective customers are accessible. Magazines directed to weight-watchers and morning television programs that feature exercise sessions inform individuals about the low-calorie product. Figure 12-4 is a food ad that is directed to calorie-conscious consumers.

Bases of Segmentation

As Figure 12-5 shows, markets are segmented on any of the following bases: geographic, demographic, psychographic, or behavioristic. For many years marketing

---

Figure 12-4   Ad Directed at Calorie-Conscious Consumers

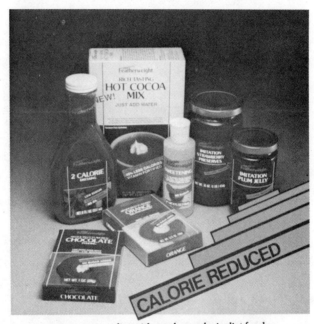

SOURCE: Chicago Dietetic Supply, La Grange, IL. Reproduced with permission.

Figure 12-5   Major Segmentation Variables and Their Typical Breakdowns

Variables	Typical Breakdowns
Geographic	
Region	Pacific, Mountain, West North Central, West South Central, East North Central, East South Central, South Atlantic, Middle Atlantic, New England
County size	A, B, C, D
City or SMSA size	Under 5,000, 5,000–19,999, 20,000–49,999, 50,000–99,999, 100,000–249,999, 250,000–499,999, 500,000–999,999, 1,000,000–3,999,999, 4,000,000 or over
Density	Urban, suburban, rural
Climate	Northern, southern
Demographic	
Age	Under 6, 6–11, 12–19, 20–34, 35–49, 50–64, 65+
Sex	Male, female
Family size	1–2, 3–4, 5+
Family life cycle	Young, single; young, married, no children; young, married, youngest child under six; young, married, youngest child six or over; older, married, with children; older, married, no children under 18; older, single; other
Income	Under $3,000, $3,000–$5,000, $5,000–$7,000, $7,000–$10,000, $10,000–$15,000, $15,000–$25,000, $25,000 and over
Occupation	Professional and technical; managers, officials and proprietors; clerical, sales; craftsmen, foremen; operatives; farmers; retired; students; housewives; unemployed
Education	Grade school or less; some high school; graduated high school; some college; graduated college
Religion	Catholic, Protestant, Jewish, other
Race	White, black, oriental
Nationality	American, British, French, German, Scandinavian, Italian, Latin American, Middle Eastern, Japanese
Social class	Lower-lower, upper-lower, lower-middle, upper-middle, lower-upper, upper-upper
Psychographic	
Life style	Straights, swingers, longhairs
Personality	Compulsive, gregarious, authoritarian, ambitious
Behavioristic	
Purchase occasion	Regular occasion, special occasion
Benefits sought	Economy, convenience, prestige
User status	Nonuser, exuser, potential user, first-time user, regular user
Usage rate	Light user, medium user, heavy user
Loyalty status	None, medium, strong, absolute
Readiness stage	Unaware, aware, informed, interested, desirous, intending to buy
Marketing-factor sensitivity	Quality, price, service, advertising, sales promotion

SOURCE: Philip Kotler, *MARKETING MANAGEMENT: Analysis, Planning, and Control*, 4th Edition, ©1980, p. 199. Reprinted by permission of Prentice-Hall, Inc., Englewood Cliffs, New Jersey.

managers have been aware of and have reacted to geographical differences in markets. For example, the management of one chain of shoe stores locates all of its retail stores in the broad-belted temperate zone of the midwestern United States. This eliminates the need to merchandise shoes that appeal to customers in either more southern or northern regions.

Demography is the study of vital and social statistics such as births, deaths, marriages, and population fluctuations. Socioeconomic variables, such as age level, family size, income, and occupation, are types of demographic data often used to classify markets. Recognizing the need to attract the growing adult market, Disney World in Florida opened a $1 billion Experimental Prototype Community of Tomorrow (EPCOT), which demonstrates the future of technology. Noting the large growth in the teenage market, Gerber Products is attempting to persuade this group to think of baby foods as tasty desserts.

Segmenting markets by identifying individuals who share the same type of lifestyle or personality traits is called **psychographic market segmentation.** For example, automobile manufacturers market life-styled automobiles ranging from sporty two-seaters to roomy station wagons. Retailers market tweeds and traditional apparel to those with conservative tastes.

Behavioristic market segmentation classifies consumers according to their response, knowledge, or attitude about a good or service. For example, consumers use toothpaste for a variety of reasons, including decay prevention, whiter teeth, and fresher breath. Consumers can be divided according to their loyalty to a product or store. Retailers frequently offer special sales and other promotions to their loyal customers.

Product Differentiation

The effort by marketing managers to secure some control over the demand for a product by promoting distinctions between their products and those of competing sellers is called **product differentiation.** Promotional efforts, such as advertising and packaging, are used to shift consumer demand toward a firm's product. Examples of those who are quite skilled in the use of this strategy are producers of detergents such as Cheer, Tide, All, and Dash.

Application of Segmentation and Differentiation

The first step a firm takes when planning to introduce a new product is to research the needs of the prospective markets. The next step is to develop a product that satisfies the requirements of a particular market. If the company has executed its market segmentation strategy successfully, its product may be unique to this market sector. Polaroid, which was protected by various patents, was able to retain the instant camera market to itself for 28 years after the camera's introduction in 1948. Timex, which pursued a policy of mass-marketing inexpensive watches, dominated its market for a long time. Levi Strauss was the dominant producer in the denim jeans market for many years.

As a new product becomes accepted and its sales increase, other manufacturers enter the marketplace with competitive products. These competitors effectively reduce the market share held by the original firm. For example, in 1970, Levi Strauss had over a 50 percent market share in a jeans market that accounted for $950 million at wholesale. By 1980, competition had eroded Levi's market share to 30 percent in a much larger market that was worth $4.2 billion at wholesale.

In an effort to recapture its original share of a particular market segment, the initial producer develops additional products for its market. These new products, which contain few important physical differences from the original product, are differentiated from the latter through mainly promotional and brand changes. When faced with competition, Polaroid, Timex, and Levi Strauss all introduced slightly differentiated products in order to maintain a dominant position in their respective markets. Thus, a strategy of product differentiation often follows one of market segmentation.

When sales of a product begin a steady decline, a firm must make a decision either to modify extensively or to drop the line. To justify the redesign of a product, a company must determine whether a sufficient need exists. After spending nearly five years in building and equipping new factories in the mid-1970s, Polaroid introduced the technically complex SX-70 as its major product. In the 1980s, Timex is changing its product mix so that mechanical watches that accounted for 90 percent of its line in the 1970s will account for only 30 percent by the mid-1980s. Replacing them will be more stylish and technically advanced digital and quartz watches. Levi Strauss is currently introducing new upscale women's and men's product lines such as the Levi's Young Misses line and the Levi's Tailored Classics line for men. These lines should help the firm to win back some of its market share.

UNCONTROLLABLE FACTORS IN THE MARKETING ENVIRONMENT

Marketing managers make their decisions within a social, economic, and political environment. Although they cannot control this environment, they seek as much information as possible about it. This information helps them make more suitable decisions. In the long run the decisions of marketing managers modify their environment. In the short run, however, they do not significantly change the environmental influences surrounding them. There are five uncontrollable marketing factors which are particularly significant to a marketing manager. They are competition, marketing legislation, nonmarketing costs, structure of distribution, and demand.

Competition

"Macy's won't tell Gimbels, but Gimbels always knows" is a familiar story in retailing. A marketing manager should be knowledgeable about the pricing, promotion, product, and place policies of all competitors. Some firms develop marketing intelligence systems in an effort to gather knowledge for better decision making. A major portion of the intelligence activity is devoted to accumulating information about competition. Important sources of intelligence for the marketing manager of a firm include:

1. The firm's salespersons.
2. The company's suppliers.
3. Government sources.
4. Trade associations.
5. Industry and competing company publications.
6. Marketing research.
7. Expert opinions.
8. Rumors.

Marketing Legislation

Since marketing managers must make decisions within the scope of the law, they must have a knowledge of marketing legislation. Managers should also understand the laws so that the effect of their decisions upon public policy and social welfare can be evaluated. The body of marketing laws is designed to protect the buyer from the seller, protect the seller from the buyer, and protect one competitor from another. The dominant American conviction is that uncontrolled competition among firms is an economic liability. Consequently, the bulk of marketing legislation is concerned with competition. To maintain some influence on marketing legislation at all levels of government, companies join trade associations and employ public relations personnel and lobbyists.

Nonmarketing Costs

In most cases the decisions made by a marketing manager have an impact on both marketing and nonmarketing costs. For example, a managerial decision is made to employ an additional 50 salespersons in an effort to intensify coverage in all major markets. This involves not only additional marketing costs, but also extra manufacturing costs. The expense of manufacturing the additional products which are needed because of the intensified selling effort are *nonmarketing* costs. Although both costs are affected by the managerial decision, only the employment of additional salespersons is controllable by the marketing executive. Cost accountants and financial planning committees help marketing managers recognize how their decisions affect costs in other areas such as production and finance.

Structure of Distribution

The structure of distribution refers to the alternative channels of distribution that are available to move goods from producers to consumers. A channel of distribution is the path taken in the transfer of title to a good from producer or manufacturer to the final user. The structure of distribution is considered to be an uncontrollable marketing factor since the manufacturer must typically choose the firm's channel from among those in existence. For example, a new manufacturer of electric garbage disposal units may desire to grant an exclusive franchise to appliance wholesalers in large metropolitan areas. An investigation shows, however, that the desired wholesalers are already handling competitive lines and that they do not care to add any additional lines. The manufacturer considers selling directly to appliance retailers, but a cost analysis reveals that this type of selling is not economically feasible. The attention of the manufacturer then turns to searching for other types of middlemen to handle the firm's line. The manufacturer finally decides to use hardware wholesalers to provide the needed distribution.

Studies of market potential, distribution cost analyses, and the application of mathematical models guide the marketing manager in selecting the most efficient distribution channel.

Demand

Demand refers to the potential sales volume for a product or service in a given period of time. In order to forecast demand, a marketing manager should be conscious of population trends, income patterns, and buying behavior of consumers.

Population Trends

Population is the underlying market factor for consumer demand. From 1900 to 1980, the population in the United States grew from 76 million to 230 million — an increase of 203 percent. Rather than looking at total population, however, it is more significant for a marketing manager to segment the population by age groups, geographical location, and income.

As illustrated in Figure 12-6, during the 1980s the population bulge will be moving through the young adult age group into the relatively older age bracket. Between 1946 and 1964, 76 million people were born — which is nearly one-third of the U.S. population. Since young adults are an important market for household furnishings, fashion goods, and recreational items, any decrease in their number has considerable impact in the marketplace.

Another recent trend has been the movement of population from some northern states to the South. Between 1970 and 1980, population in the Sun Belt states grew 22.5 percent while the remainder of the states had only a 5.5 percent increase. Individuals are drawn to the Sun Belt states by employment prospects, an appealing climate, and an attractive social environment. In 1980, for the first time the center of population moved west of the Mississippi River. Also, population has been shifting from the cities and their suburbs to small communities. From 1970 to 1980, population increased faster in nonmetropolitan areas (15.8 percent increase) than in metropolitan areas (9.8 percent increase). Older persons who live on pensions and fixed incomes often seek to retire in small communities that are not troubled by high property taxes, traffic congestion, and rising crime rates. In addition, recent innovations in production technology, transportation, and communications have been important factors in the growth of rural employment.

Income Patterns

The aggregate amount for spending and saving in this country during a particular period of time is called **disposable personal income.** This amount is a prime factor in

Figure 12-6   Projected Changes in Population, 1980–1990

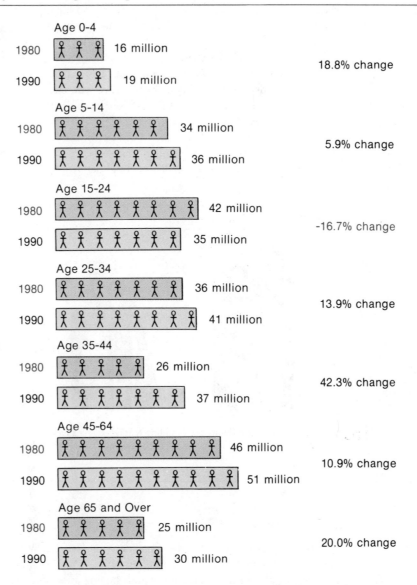

Age 0-4
1980   16 million   18.8% change
1990   19 million

Age 5-14
1980   34 million   5.9% change
1990   36 million

Age 15-24
1980   42 million   -16.7% change
1990   35 million

Age 25-34
1980   36 million   13.9% change
1990   41 million

Age 35-44
1980   26 million   42.3% change
1990   37 million

Age 45-64
1980   46 million   10.9% change
1990   51 million

Age 65 and Over
1980   25 million   20.0% change
1990   30 million

SOURCE: U.S. Bureau of the Census, *Current Population Reports, Population Estimates and Projections*, Series P-25, No. 707.

determining consumer demand. Personal income is the most important source of consumer purchasing power. Other sources include credit and wealth.

Most families spend the greatest part of their income on necessities such as food, housing, clothing, and basic transportation. The income available after necessities have been purchased and a certain living standard has been met is called **discretionary income.** A family's discretionary income is dependent upon family size, composition of the family, total income, social environment, and life-cycle stages. As the income of a family increases, the discretionary portion usually has more than a proportionate rise. For example, families in the $25,000-and-up income bracket spend over four times more for education than those in the $8,000 to $9,999 bracket.

In recent years the dual-earner families have created a growing market for many consumer goods. As displayed in Figure 12-7, the added income of a working wife pushes the median family income to $26,879. This is 28 percent higher than the income of the "All families" category and 42 percent greater than that of families with wives not in the paid labor force. Because of the importance of convenience to dual-earner families, they are excellent markets for goods and services related to easing child care, food preparation, and household activities.

Figure 12-7   Family Income, 1980

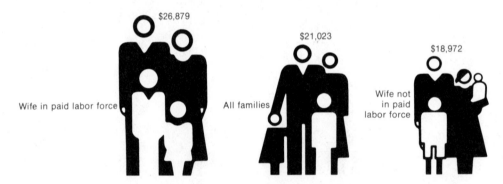

SOURCE: "Dual-Earner Families: Doubling Marketers' Pleasure," *Sales & Marketing Management* (October 26, 1981), p. 43, S&MM Survey of Buying Power—Part II. Copyright 1981.

Buying Intentions

Since consumers make the final decision on the products and brands to be purchased, it is important for a marketing manager to have an understanding of buying intentions and consumer behavior. Family buying intentions are measured periodically by organizations such as the Survey Research Center of the University of Michigan. Industrial buying intentions are determined by the McGraw-Hill Survey of industrial expenditures and the Securities and Exchange Commission Survey of capital investments. Models of consumer behavior constructed by behavioral scientists help the marketing manager understand the buying activities of consumers. Since an understanding of consumer behavior is vital to the marketing manager, this topic is explored in more depth in the next section.

CONSUMER BEHAVIOR

A knowledge of consumer behavior has helped many companies in successfully marketing their products. Listerine mouthwash was introduced with the advertising headline, "Always a bridesmaid but never a bride." Much of the success of Virginia Slims cigarettes is due to its promotional appeals which are directed to the modern or liberated woman. Many individuals drive a Cadillac because it is an easily recognized symbol of prestige.

Both psychological (or intrapersonal) forces and social (or interpersonal) forces influence consumer behavior. The psychological forces arise from within an individual and affect his or her mental process. These forces include motivation, perception, learning, attitudes, and personality. The social forces are the elements in the external environment that interact on an individual and direct her or his buying behavior. These elements are culture, social class, reference groups, and family.

Buying Motives

Because of the importance of motivation in the buying process, we will examine several types of buying motives. Buying motives are difficult to classify since they are closely allied to one another, are capable of being classified into numerous groupings, and overlap in meaning. A **buying motive** is aroused when bodily energy is activated and selectively directed toward satisfying a need. Maslow's hierarchy of needs, which was presented in Chapter 5, represents one set of buying motives. Maslow theorizes that individuals buy to satisfy the following order of needs: physiological, safety, social, esteem, and self-fulfillment. The following discussion identifies several other categories of buying motives.

Rational and Emotional Motives

Socially approved reasons for buying are called *rational* buying motives. In general, they tend to economize the money and time spent for a good or service. These motives include dependability, low price, economy in use, money gain, and convenience. The promotions for most industrial goods use rational buying motives.

Emotional buying motives relate to a person's psychological drives. Some critics disapprove of these motives since these do not reduce the long-run costs for a product and may appear wasteful. Such motives include prestige, individuality, conformity, comfort, pleasure, creativity, and emulation. The "Reach Out and Touch Someone" advertising by the Bell System (see Figure 12-8) is an example of emotional appeal. The entire cosmetic industry is based on emotional selling appeals. Charles Revson, the late legendary founder of Revlon cosmetics, often stated that the purpose of the cosmetic industry is to sell hope.

Dormant and Conscious Motives

Dormant buying motives are unknown and unrecognized by consumers until these are brought to their attention. Homemakers may not be aware of a need for a micro-

Figure 12-8   An Emotional Buying Appeal

"Nobody else even laughed, but I knew you'd love it."

Reach out and touch someone.   Ⓐ Bell System

SOURCE: Courtesy of American Telephone & Telegraph Company, Long Lines Division, April, 1983.

wave oven until they see one demonstrated and talk with friends who have them. *Conscious* buying motives are known and clearly recognized by the consumer without exposure to any marketing effort. The seven-year-old is absolutely conscious of the need for a dirt bike because a friend down the street already has one.

Patronage Motives

Patronage motives attract buyers to a particular vendor. These motives are different from those that attract buyers to a certain product. Vendors can use patronage motives that appeal to their particular market. For example, K mart employs low prices, wide assortments, and self-service to appeal to its customers. Saks Fifth Avenue uses fashion merchandise, numerous customer services, and attractive stores to attract wealthy patrons.

Buying Process

Once individuals become conscious of their needs, they seek need-satisfying behavior. This behavior is evidenced by the different decision stages that a consumer goes through over a period of time. Since these stages tend to overlap one another, it often is hard to tell where one stage stops and the next one begins. As illustrated in Figure 12-9, the six stages in the buying process are:

1. *Problem recognition.* When dissatisfaction with goal attainment exceeds a minimum level of tolerance, the recognition of a problem occurs.
2. *Initial interest.* Promotional activities arouse an initial interest in a general class of goods or services.
3. *Conviction to act.* The underlying buying motives stimulate a definite commitment to buy.
4. *Search for alternatives.* Product information is sought from formal sources, such as advertisements and salespersons, and from informal sources such as users of the product and opinion leaders.

Figure 12-9   Forces and Steps in the Consumer Buying Process

---

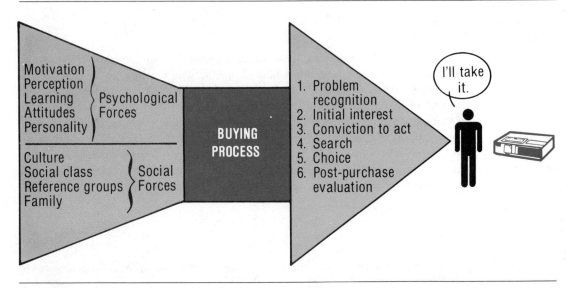

---

5. *Choice of products and sources.* Attention shifts from interest in a general product class to the selection of a specific good or service.

6. *Post-purchase evaluation.* As a result of post-purchase doubt, a consumer searches for information on the correctness of his or her purchase action.

MARKETING RESEARCH

The American Marketing Association defines **marketing research** as "the systematic gathering, recording, and analyzing of data about problems relating to the marketing of goods and services."[5] This definition adequately describes the processing of the data, but additional knowledge is needed about the type of facts to be assembled. Data are gathered and analyzed for the controllable marketing factors (product, place, promotion, and price) and the uncontrollable marketing factors (competition, marketing laws, nonmarketing costs, structure of distribution, and demand). The purpose of the data gathering is to improve decision making within the marketing system. Procter & Gamble annually surveys 1.5 million individuals in connection with about 1,000 marketing research projects.

The following research activities are conducted often by a marketing research department:

1. Developing market and sales potentials.
2. Establishing a firm's share of total industry sales.
3. Determining market and customer characteristics.
4. Constructing sales analyses.
5. Developing competitive product studies.
6. Determining the acceptance of new products.
7. Developing short-range sales forecasts.

Sources of Data

Both internal and external data gathered by or for a firm for its use are known as **primary data**. If these facts are published or otherwise released, they are known as **secondary data** to other users. Secondary data are widely used in marketing research because of the enormous quantities of data available, frequently without cost, from government and private agencies. Some government sources include the U.S. Census reports, the yearly *Statistical Abstract of the United States*, the *Survey of Current Business*, the *Federal Reserve Bulletin*, and the *Monthly Labor Review*. Private sources of secondary information are publications issued by newspapers and magazines, trade journals, trade associations, private agencies, and colleges and universities.

---

5. Committee on Definitions, *Marketing Definitions: A Glossary of Marketing Terms*, published by the American Marketing Association, 1960, pp. 16–17.

Data-Gathering Methods

The marketing researcher has three basic ways to gather primary data: observation, survey, and experiment. The purpose of the research and the availability of money, time, and personnel influence the selection of the data-gathering method.

Observation

The observation technique relies on viewing and/or noting the activities of the respondents. Since consumers are unaware that their actions are being observed, it is assumed that they act in a normal manner. A difficulty with this technique is that it does not explain the reasons, attitudes, and behavior behind the action. A study on the frequency of shoplifting utilized personal observation. A total of 226 customers were followed from the time they entered the store to the time they departed. The observers reported that 23 individuals (or 10 percent) stole merchandise.

Survey

In the survey method the researcher gathers facts directly from a sample of respondents. Surveys are used most often to gather primary data. Such data may be collected by mail, by telephone, or by personal interview. As shown in Figure 12-10, a marketing researcher evaluates these three survey techniques on the following criteria:

1. Flexibility.
2. Length of questionnaire.
3. Accuracy.

4. Speed.
5. Cost per response.
6. Cost of administration.

A new and important form of personal interviewing is the **focus group**, which involves interviewing 8 to 12 persons at the same time in order to probe attitudes and

Figure 12-10   Factors to Evaluate in Choosing Among Three Survey Techniques

Factors to Evaluate	Mail	Telephone	Personal Interview
Flexibility of the interview	none	high	high
Length limitation of questionnaire	moderate	moderate	long
Assurance of accurate, unbiased response	high	moderate	moderate
Speed of collecting information	slow	fast	moderate
Overall cost per response	moderate	low	high
Cost of interviewer administration	low	moderate	high

obtain group interaction. Focus groups are most effective in the early stages of a marketing research project. This is because the groups develop ideas and generalizations that can be tested further with larger sample sizes in personal interviews. Marketing researchers often obtain interviewing space in a shopping center and draw focus groups from a cross section of shoppers.

In the late 1970s, when General Electric was tied for fourth place in microwave oven sales, it conducted several focus-group sessions to determine consumer attitudes toward its products. A conclusion from the sessions was that consumers dislike these bulky ovens cluttering their countertops. As a result, in 1979 the company introduced the "Spacemaker" microwave that fits over the range in place of the exhaust hood. Within a year the strong sales from this product helped General Electric to capture 16 percent of the market and move to the number-one position in microwave sales.

Experiment

In the experimental method, a controlled experiment is conducted to assess the impact of a new product, packaging, promotion, store layout, or other marketing practice. One type of experiment that is used to measure changes in sales involves both a control group and a test group. In the control group, all of the important factors that affect the outcome of the experiment are held constant. In the test group, one of the factors is varied. For example, K mart conducted an experiment by changing the layout in a test store and then comparing its sales per square foot to other stores that maintained their old layout. The Ford Motor Co. also has measured consumer response to different advertisements for the same car through the experimental method.

There are several drawbacks with the experimental technique. It is costly and requires trained researchers. In addition, if marketing decisions must be made rapidly, the process is too slow. In some cases the inability to control all the variables except the one being tested creates another difficulty.

SUMMARY   In our fast-paced, competitive society most firms have adopted the marketing concept. This concept includes three distinct elements: satisfaction of consumer needs, coordination of all company activities in support of marketing, and achievement of organizational objectives through customer satisfaction.

The basic importance of marketing in our economy is indicated by employment in marketing, the number of existing marketing establishments, and marketing costs. Marketing is a productive system that provides intangible satisfactions, or utilities, to consumers. The performance of costly marketing activities creates place, time, possession, and information utilities.

A typical marketing organization is headed by a marketing manager, who is often responsible to the chief executive of a firm. Reporting to the marketing manager are a marketing operations manager and a marketing staff services manager. The marketing operations manager is responsible for the sales activities, and the marketing staff services manager is responsible for many of the nonselling activities. The eight major economic activities that must be performed in the marketing process are known as marketing functions.

Marketing mix refers to the combination of decision elements in a company's marketing program. These are product, place, promotion, and price. By altering the marketing mix of a firm, different marketing strategies can be developed. Market segmentation and product differentiation are two different but complementary marketing strategies. Market segmentation is a product development strategy, while product differentiation is a promotional strategy.

Marketing managers operate within a social, economic, and political environment. Since the environmental influences are generally uncontrollable by marketing managers, they are referred to as uncontrollable marketing factors. These factors include competition, marketing legislation, nonmarketing costs, structure of distribution, and demand.

Both psychological (or intrapersonal) forces and social (or interpersonal) forces influence consumer behavior. This behavior is evidenced by the different decision stages that a consumer experiences. These stages are problem recognition, initial interest, conviction to act, search for alternatives, choice of products and sources, and post-purchase evaluation.

The purpose of marketing research is to improve decision making within the marketing system. Much of the research is centered upon the controllable elements of the marketing mix and the uncontrollable factors in the marketing environment. Marketing researchers employ observation, survey, and experiment as basic data-gathering methods.

BACK TO THE CHAPTER OPENER

1. Is Ford practicing the marketing concept?
2. What is the difference between market segmentation and product differentiation?
3. Does the female car-buying market satisfy the conditions that must be met for a strategy of market segmentation?
4. What are the uncontrollable factors in the marketing environment that are significant to a marketing manager at Ford?
5. How can Ford most effectively use its focus groups?

BUSINESS TERMS

marketing concept	262	psychographic market segmentation	271
marketing	262	behavioristic market segmentation	271
form utility	264		
place utility	264	product differentiation	271
time utility	264	disposable personal income	274
possession utility	264	discretionary income	276
information utility	264	buying motive	277
marketing functions	267	marketing research	280
marketing mix	267	primary data	280
market segmentation	268	secondary data	280
demography	271	focus group	281

1. How can a nonprofit organization, such as your school, use the marketing concept? Explain.
2. Would you expect marketing costs to be greater in some industries than in others? Explain.
3. Assume that you are the vice-president of marketing for Kellogg cereals. Because of budget cuts, you are asked to eliminate the four least essential marketing positions shown in Figure 12-2 on page 265. Which four would you eliminate?
4. Which would be the most important decision element ("P") in the marketing mix for a manufacturer of home computers?
5. Which is the more important strategy for marketing managers: market segmentation or product differentiation? Explain your answer.
6. How can psychographic market segmentation be used to market automobiles or toothpaste?
7. How can General Motors obtain information about the new car models that will be introduced by competitors?
8. How will the population trends of the 1980s affect the types of goods and services that are marketed?
9. Are emotional buying motives more wasteful and less legitimate than rational buying motives? Discuss.
10. How can the experimental method of gathering data aid Procter & Gamble in choosing a package design for a new detergent?

1. Select three product advertisements that are directed to specific market segments. Identify the appeals that direct each ad to a particular geographic, demographic, psychographic, or behavioristic market segment. Are there any other market segments that would be attracted to the advertised products? If so, identify the specific segments for each of the products.
2. Bring into class two advertisements that contain rational buying motives and two that contain emotional buying motives. In each case indicate the specific appeal, such as dependability or prestige, that is stressed in the ad. For each of the ads, can you think of any other appeals that would be as effective as the ones used? Explain.
3. The Burpee Baby Products Company is a medium-sized producer of baby food and baby products such as bibs, rattles, and pacifiers. In its 45 years of existence, the company's product line has changed little. In the past, the ability of the company to utilize its present plant and equipment determined the type of new items to be produced.

   In recent years, management has become concerned about the decreasing birthrate. Any decrease in the number of babies reduces the potential market for the company's products. This development has led the company to adopt the marketing concept. Management now recognizes the need to develop new products based upon marketing research studies. To implement the marketing concept, management is planning to reorganize the marketing department. This department is headed currently by a sales manager who is responsible to the company president. An advertising manager, a credit manager, a physical distribution manager, and six salespersons report directly to the sales manager. There are no other positions in the marketing department.

a. Draw a revised and broadened marketing organization chart for the Burpee Baby Products Company, showing each marketing position. Describe the specific duties of each position.

b. Should the company continue to be concerned about a downward trend in the birthrate? Provide statistics on births during the decade of the 1970s and make an assumption about the trend of the birthrate during the 1980s. Identify the sources for your answers. (Hint: The *Statistical Abstract of the United States* or the U. S. Bureau of the Census, *Current Population Reports* will be helpful.)

The Video Game Sales War

Everyone, it seems, is trying to enter the home video game business, bringing forth a profusion of new game-playing machines and games.

Where there was once little more than Space Invaders, there are now such games as Space Raiders, Space Wars, Space Battle, Spacechase, Space Fury, Space Cavern, Space Hawk and Space Vultures, not to mention Communist Mutants From Space....

The profusion of entrants is not surprising. Home video game cartridges, which sell for $20 to $25 apiece, have been one of the fastest-growing areas of consumer electronics, accounting for an estimated $1.2 billion in sales last year.

Yet the market has been controlled by a handful of companies. Last year there were four manufacturers of video game devices—Atari, Inc., Mattel Electronics, Magnavox, and Astrovision, now called Astrocade. Then, there was one company, Activision, that concentrated on game software for the Atari system—that is, the cartridges of instructions that make the game work....

This year there appear to be another half-dozen producers of game machines. They include Coleco Industries, a toy and game company, the Emerson Radio Corporation and Commodore International Ltd....

The entries come as there is growing Wall Street speculation that the business of making devices— essentially, microcomputers dedicated to the sole function of playing video games—is slowing down. One threat to these machines, which range in price from $150 to $300, are inexpensive personal computers that play games as well as perform other, more computer-like things.

Many analysts, however, among them Michele Preston, with Cyrus J. Lawrence, Inc., reject that notion. She said that while there were 4.5 million game machines sold last year, some eight million will be sold this year, representing a gain of 70 percent. Only eight million households, or about 10 percent of the nation's total, have games....

Even if the overall business is still growing, the crowded field is sure to reduce profits. "They can't all have prosperity at the same time," said Harold Vogel, an analyst with Merrill Lynch.

The newcomers are expected to have a tougher time entering the market, if only because retailers will be hard-pressed to find shelf space to carry all the competing products.

"There is a fairly narrow funnel at the retail level," said Josh Denham, president of Mattel Electronics.

Competitors say the weakness of the market leader, Atari, which has 70 percent of the installed machines, is the relatively poor quality of its graphics. Its home video version of Pac-Man, despite the hoopla surrounding its release, disappointed consumers used to the more refined arcade version.

By emphasizing superior features, others think they can make inroads on Atari's market. Mattel and Magnavox have introduced audio attachments to their games....

For its part, Atari is introducing a more expensive game, priced at $300, about twice that of its existing units. Another company, the Arcadia Corporation of Santa Clara, Calif., is planning to sell a $70 "supercharger" that would upgrade the quality of Atari's existing game....

SOURCE: Andrew Pollack, "The Video Game Sales War, Newcomers Flood Market," *The New York Times,* June 9, 1982, p. D1. © 1982 by The New York Times Company. Reprinted by permission.

Products and Their Distribution

Objectives:

- Explain the meaning of the term "product."
- Distinguish between industrial goods and consumer goods.
- Identify the three major categories of industrial goods.
- Identify the three major categories of consumer goods.
- Recall some of the major areas for product-policy decisions.
- Describe the various stages in the life cycle of a product.
- Recognize the most frequently used channels of distribution for consumer goods.
- Identify the four factors that are considered by management in selecting a channel of distribution.
- Distinguish between wholesaling and retailing.
- Identify the major types of wholesalers and retailers.

The former promotional slogan of Hush Puppies shoes was "Hush Puppies are dumb."[1] Until the company changed its product line, this slogan was all too apt. With the price for pigskin about half the price for cowhide, you would think that this cost advantage would have spurred the sales of Hush Puppies. Not so, however! The difficulty was that the styles of the shoes had not been changed since they were introduced in 1957. Because of the company's unexciting products, only 45 percent of

---

1. Subrata N. Chakravarty, "Old Dog Learns New Tricks," *Forbes* (August 17, 1981), p. 64.

Hush Puppies sales were to women. This was of great concern to the company because women spend twice as much on shoes as men do. Another disturbing statistic was that the average buyer of Hush Puppies was age 50.

The solution to this problem of stagnating sales was to completely restyle the company's lines. Some open-toed shoes and others with moderate heels were added to their women's lines. The company enlarged its product mix by introducing new styles that were fabricated from cowhide and man-made materials. By the early 1980s, the average age of Hush Puppies customers was pushed down to the mid-30s, and 59 percent of its sales was to women. These needed changes in the product line dramatically increased the company's sales and earnings.

To consumers, a product is more than a physical combination of pigskin, vinyl, and glue. A **product** is a bundle of satisfactions or utilities. Consumers consider their shoes as an effective means of protecting their feet, but they also view them as attractive additions to their wardrobe. When consumers buy their shoes, they are purchasing all of the intangible and psychic values associated with the shoes, as well as the tangible product.

TYPES OF GOODS

All goods can be placed into one of two broad categories: industrial goods or consumer goods. **Industrial goods** are sold primarily for use in producing other goods or in rendering services.[2] **Consumer goods** are used by ultimate consumers or households. These are in such form that they can be used without further commercial processing.[3] Because of their use by both individual consumers and industrial consumers, goods such as tires and typewriters fall into both categories.

Industrial Goods

Industrial goods generally are classified according to their use in a business. On this basis there are three major categories of industrial goods. One category is unprocessed and processed materials entering directly into the production process such as raw materials, semimanufactured goods, and parts. A second grouping, MRO items, is composed of maintenance, repair, and operating supplies used to support the production process. Capital goods, the final classification, consist of machinery and equipment utilized to form the product.

Consumer Goods

Consumer goods usually are characterized by the shopping effort required to obtain the goods. As Figure 13-1 shows, consumer goods are classified into three

---

2. Reprinted from Committee on Definitions, *Marketing Definitions: A Glossary of Marketing Terms,* published by the American Marketing Association, 1960, p. 14.
3. *Ibid.,* p. 11.

Figure 13-1   Characteristics of Classes of Consumer Goods

Characteristics	Convenience	Shopping	Specialty
• Time and effort devoted by consumer to shopping	• Very little	• Considerable	• Cannot generalize. May go to nearby store and exert minimum effort, or may have to go to distant store and spend much time.
• Time spent planning the purchase	• Very little	• Considerable	• Considerable
• How soon want is satisfied after it arises	• Immediately	• Relatively long time	• Relatively long time
• Are price and quality compared?	• No	• Yes	• No
• Price	• Low	• High	• High
• Frequency of purchase	• Usually frequent	• Infrequent	• Very infrequent
• Number of retailing outlets handling the goods	• As many as possible	• Few	• Few; often only one in a market
• Type of promotion	• Effective use of mass advertising	• Effective use of personal selling	• Use of personal selling and word-of-mouth

SOURCE: From *Fundamentals of Marketing,* 6th edition, by William J. Stanton. Copyright © 1981 by McGraw-Hill Book Company. Used with permission of McGraw-Hill Book Company.

categories. **Convenience goods** are goods that are bought by the consumer after little shopping effort, purchased frequently, bought by habit, and sold in numerous outlets. Generally convenience goods, such as candy bars (Hershey), cigarettes (Salem), and milk (Borden), have low unit prices. Goods that are bought after comparing the features of several brands, purchased infrequently, and sold in a limited number of selected outlets are known as **shopping goods.** Usually shopping goods have a higher unit price than convenience goods. Examples of shopping goods are men's suits (Palm Beach), automobiles (Chevrolet), and furniture (Bassett). **Specialty goods** are goods bought by the consumer after a special shopping effort, purchased very infrequently, and sold in a few exclusive outlets. Generally specialty goods carry a high unit price; but since no substitutes are considered, price is not a major consideration. Fine jewelry (Tiffany necklace), prestige automobiles (Jaguar), and expensive perfume (Jean Patou's Joy) are examples of specialty goods.

Since not every consumer relates to a product the same way, the buying habits of the majority of consumers determine the classification for a particular good. As the buying habits of consumers change over time, goods shift from one classification to another. The usual shift is from the specialty, to the shopping, to the convenience goods category. For example, in 1950, the black and white television consoles of Zenith and RCA that sold for $700 to $800 were specialty goods. By 1960, the $300 to $400 table model receivers that were available from a variety of manufacturers were considered to be shopping goods. In the 1980s, the small portable sets that sell for under $100 and are available in drugstores and supermarkets are treated by many consumers as convenience goods.

PRODUCT POLICIES

Product policies guide management in developing new products and in modifying or eliminating existing products. The product policies of a firm should be compatible with the policies of the remaining three P's (place, promotion, and price) in a firm's marketing mix.

New Product Development

The success of a product depends on the proper development and management of the product. It has been estimated that a single product failure in the food and drug lines may cost from $75,000 in test markets to $30 million after a nationwide introduction. A study by the advertising agency of Dancer-Fitzgerald-Sample indicates that 98 percent of all new food products failed to attain $15 million in annual sales, which it considers a measure of success. As Figure 13-2 shows, even the windshield wiper experienced difficulty in obtaining acceptance by automobile manufacturers. In many

---

Figure 13-2   Difficulty in Obtaining Product Acceptance

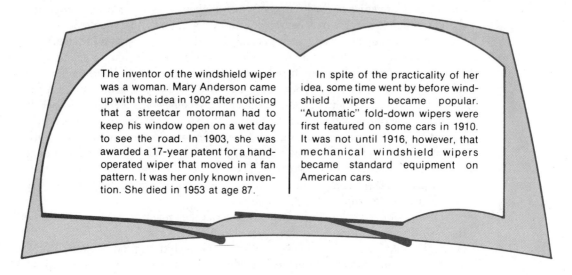

The inventor of the windshield wiper was a woman. Mary Anderson came up with the idea in 1902 after noticing that a streetcar motorman had to keep his window open on a wet day to see the road. In 1903, she was awarded a 17-year patent for a hand-operated wiper that moved in a fan pattern. It was her only known invention. She died in 1953 at age 87.

In spite of the practicality of her idea, some time went by before windshield wipers became popular. "Automatic" fold-down wipers were first featured on some cars in 1910. It was not until 1916, however, that mechanical windshield wipers became standard equipment on American cars.

SOURCE: *Parade* (June 27, 1982), p. 20. Reproduced with permission.

Figure 13-3   **Some Consumers Still Buy Products in Their Decline Stage**

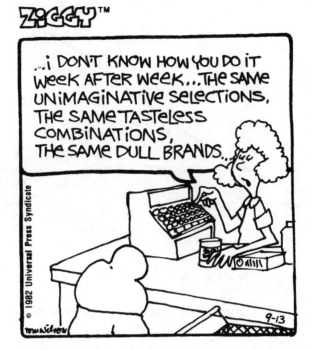

companies a product planning manager, product planning committees, or project groups are responsible for new product development.

Stages of a Product Life Cycle

In an earlier period of our economy, products had a relatively long life cycle. But since the 1970s the changing life-styles of consumers, technological advances, and competitive responses have shortened the life cycle of products. The A. C. Nielsen research firm has determined that a new consumer product has less than three years of sales growth before it begins to lose its share of the market. Figure 13-3 shows that some individuals continue to buy a product even after most consumers have deserted it for others.

As shown in Figure 13-4, there are five stages in a **product life cycle:**

1. Introduction stage.
2. Growth stage.
3. Maturity stage.

Figure 13-4   Product Life Cycle

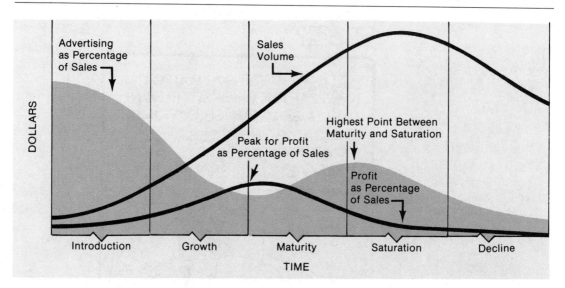

NOTE: The broken time line indicates that different products move through the stages at varying speeds.

SOURCE: Adapted from *Management of New Products* (New York: Booz, Allen & Hamilton), p. 4.

4. Saturation stage.
5. Decline stage.

In certain instances a product in the decline stage can be recycled. New features, positioning, and new uses contribute to the recycling of a product. For example, when Crest changed its toothpaste flouride mixture, the toothpaste was promoted as an advanced-formula product with improved cavity protection. Hazel Bishop increased its sales of cosmetics by positioning its products to price-conscious women. Arm & Hammer greatly enlarged its market for baking soda by promoting it as a versatile deodorant.

Example of a Product Life Cycle

The color television market illustrates the movement of a product through its life cycle. In the late 1950s the color television market was in the introduction stage. Since RCA was the major brand in the market, buyers of a color receiver generally purchased an RCA. Recognizing its dominant market position, RCA promoted heavily to create consumer demand for color television.

During the early 1960s, the color television market moved into the growth stage. Although RCA sales and profits increased, new competitors began entering the market. Prices remained high with console models selling for $500 or more. By 1965 nearly 10 percent of American homes had color television sets.

In the late 1960s the color television market reached maturity. Companies such as Zenith, Magnavox, Admiral, Sears, General Electric, and Motorola moved in on RCA's market. Mass production and new technology lowered prices. Less expensive consoles and table models opened sales to new segments of the market. In 1970, 42 percent of all American families were enjoying color television.

By 1979, with nearly 90 percent of American homes having color television, the market approached the saturation stage. With strong foreign and domestic competition, the growth in sales slowed. Small portable models priced under $350 became popular. RCA began differentiating its product from competing products by promoting its ColorTrak System.

In the 1980s a recycling of the color television receiver is occurring. From sales of 10.2 million sets in 1980, volume is expected to expand to 12 to 14 million by 1985. Color television sets are being used as home entertainment and information centers. Cable channels, videodisc and videocassette players, video games, stereophonic broadcasting, home computers, and large-screen projectors have contributed to moving the product back into the growth stage.

Product Line and Product Mix

Multiproduct firms often market a complete line of products. A **product line** is a group of closely related products. These products either satisfy a class of needs, are used together, are sold to the same customer groups, are marketed through the same type of outlets, or fall within given price ranges.[4] General Electric markets a complete product line of major appliances, as shown in Figure 13-5. By marketing all products

---

Figure 13-5   General Electric's Major Appliance Line

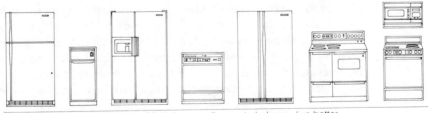

GE has over 100 kitchen appliances to help you live better.

SOURCE: General Electric Major Appliances Division, Louisville, KY. Reproduced with permission.

---

4. *Ibid.*, p. 18.

in a line using the same promotions, the same sales force, and the same type of outlets, a firm may achieve significant economies of operation.

The **product mix** of a company is the combination of its product lines. For example, the product mix of General Electric includes major appliances, portable appliances, jet engines, electric motors, medical equipment, and missile and radar systems. By spreading its sales over a broad product base, a company reduces the adverse effect of a sales decline in a single product line.

Planned Obsolescence

As fashions shift and technology advances, new products cause old ones to become obsolete. Critics have charged that businesspersons seeking the sales of new products purposely plan for the phasing out of old products — a practice referred to as **planned obsolescence.** These charges often are aimed at the automobile industry. This criticism probably overstates the influence of product promotion and understates the influence of our cultural and value systems on product acceptance.

Brands and Trademarks

Firms frequently use **brand names**, such as Pepsi Cola or Ivory soap, to identify their products and to distinguish them from competing goods. Several alternative branding policies are available to a firm. A brand, such as Lawn-Boy, promoted and distributed by a manufacturer, is known as a **national or manufacturer's brand.** When a middleman, such as a wholesaler or a retailer, sponsors a brand, it is called a **private or dealer's brand.** Most of the merchandise offered by Sears carry Sears' private brands such as Craftsman, Kenmore, or Kings Road. Private brands permit a middleman to obtain closer control of the marketing effort and to avoid direct product competition with other merchants.

A brand may serve as a company trademark, but a **trademark** can be a word, name, symbol, or any combination of the three that provides a unique company identification. Some of the trademarks of American companies are depicted in Figure 13-6. Brands and trademarks may be registered for 20 years with the U. S. Patent Office and may be renewed indefinitely for 20-year periods. In some instances a trademark becomes so closely associated with a product that it loses its exclusive protection and becomes available for general use. The terms aspirin, escalator, zipper, shredded wheat, and cellophane were once registered trademarks that are now in the public domain.

Labels

Labels on a product or package should provide information which will help the consumer make a buying decision. By using words, letters, or numbers, a grade label specifies the quality of a good. *Prime* is the highest quality designation for beef, *Grade A* identifies the best quality of canned corn, and *Number 1* indicates the top grade of

Figure 13-6   Trademarks of American Companies

SOURCE: Reproduced by permission of Motorola, Inc.; Consolidated Foods Corporation; Tenneco, Inc.; Nabisco Brands, Inc.; Grand Union Co.; and United Airlines.

wheat. An informative label furnishes data on the care, use, and preparation of the product. The Federal Trade Commission, recognizing the importance of informative labeling, requests manufacturers to place permanent care instructions on the labels of all textile apparel. A descriptive label lists the important attributes of a product. Nutritional labeling, which the Food and Drug Administration requires for some products, is a form of descriptive labeling.

DISTRIBUTION POLICIES

In the early history of our country when markets were small and compact, producers sold directly to final consumers. As markets grew and the distance between major markets increased, a system of middlemen—both at wholesale and at retail—evolved between producers and the final consumers.

Channels of Distribution

The routes that goods take in their progress from producers to consumers are known as **channels of distribution**. Each middleman in the channel needs to work closely with all other middlemen to move goods from producers to consumers in the least expensive and most efficient manner.

Channels for Consumer Goods

In the most direct channel of distribution for consumer goods, no middlemen are involved. The producer sells directly to the consumers (see Figure 13-7). This channel is used by many house-to-house selling firms, such as Fuller Brush and Avon Products, and by some producers who distribute by mail order such as the Franklin Mint Corporation and the Columbia Record Club.

Figure 13-7   Producer to Consumers

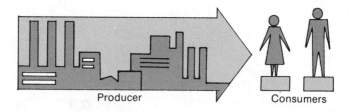

In another channel, producers sell to retailers, who in turn sell to consumers (see Figure 13-8). This channel is the path taken by goods handled by department stores and chain stores.

Figure 13-8   Producer to Retailer to Consumers

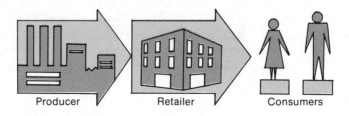

In a third channel the wholesaler enters the picture between the producer and the retailer (see Figure 13-9). This is the traditional way by which goods have been

Figure 13-9   Producer to Wholesaler to Retailer to Consumers

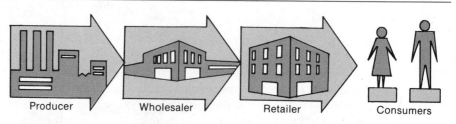

distributed in this country. It is still the main system for goods that reach the consumer through small independent retailers such as grocers, druggists, hardware dealers, or apparel stores.

Producers may adopt any one or more of these channels to have their goods reach as many final consumers as possible. Many producers sell directly to the chains and large independent stores and at the same time utilize wholesalers to reach the small independent retailers. The channel of distribution pattern then would be the following:

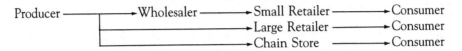

Channels for Industrial Goods

The major difference between the channels of distribution for industrial goods and for consumer goods is that a retailer is not usually in the industrial channel. The two commonly used channels in industrial marketing are illustrated in Figure 13-10.

The first of the two channels in Figure 13-10 may include manufacturers' branch offices with or without stocks for delivery to customers. Frequently a manufacturer's salesperson fills customers' orders directly from the factory. Thus, they work from a branch office without stock. Examples of manufacturers who have branch offices without stock are IBM and Otis Elevator Company.

Figure 13-10   Channels for Industrial Goods

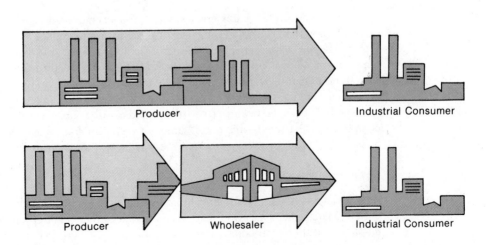

Channel Decisions

The initial step in deciding which channels of distribution are to be used for a product is to determine the customers for the product. Because of the many customers to be reached and the complexity of our distribution system, products often are marketed through more than one channel. In selecting a channel, managers must consider the following four factors: market, channel member, product, and environment.

Market Factors

In addition to whether a good is directed to the consumer or industrial market, there are several other market factors that determine channel selection. If the product is sold in large quantities to customers in a densely concentrated market, such as New York or Chicago, a short channel of distribution may be utilized. There may be many consumers in a concentrated market; but if these consumers buy in small quantities, a longer channel is necessary. A longer channel often is used when customers are spread over a wide area.

Channel Member Factors

An understanding of the capabilities and motivations of each channel member — from manufacturer to consumer — helps to explain the development of distribution channels. For example, financially strong manufacturers who desire to retain complete control of their marketing efforts may shorten the channel for their products by performing some or all of the middlemen's activities. The motivations of middlemen influence channel selection, too. Some retailers, such as large department stores, often desire to buy directly from producers.

Product Factors

Because of certain characteristics, some products move through shorter channels of distribution than others. Perishable items, such as fresh produce and dairy products, typically require a short channel of distribution. Goods which are custom designed for a specific use, such as large electrical transformers or computer installations, commonly have a short channel of distribution. The expense of physical handling requires a short channel for products such as coal and concrete blocks, which have a low cost relative to their bulkiness. A manufacturer who markets either an expensive product or a complete product line is able to sell directly to retailers and bypass wholesalers. This is because the direct selling expenses are a relatively low percentage of total sales.

Environmental Factors

Social, economic, and political forces often alter the planned channels of distribution. Management may find that certain middlemen do a better job than others in marketing to the urban poor. During an economic recession, manufacturers seek the least expensive way to get their products into the hands of consumers. In some cases this may mean changing or eliminating certain middlemen.

WHOLESALING

Wholesaling includes all the marketing activities of firms that sell to retailers, industrial firms, and all other commercial users. In other words, wholesaling includes all sales transactions except those made to the ultimate consumer, which are known as retailing. The scope of wholesaling is seen in Table 13-1 which shows the number, sales volume, and operating expenses of selected types of wholesalers.

Table 13-1   **Number, Sales Volume, and Operating Expenses for Total Wholesale Trade and Selected Types of Wholesalers in the United States, 1977**

	Establishments (Number)	Sales ($1,000)	Operating Expenses as Percentage of Sales
Wholesale trade, Total	382,837	1,258,400,268	9.4
Merchant wholesalers, Total	307,264	676,057,580	12.7
Groceries and related products	37,960	182,905,391	8.3
General-line groceries	3,178	41,038,862	6.8
Voluntary group wholesalers	459	12,527,811	6.2
Retailer cooperative wholesalers	214	11,346,788	5.8
Other general-line wholesalers	2,505	17,164,263	8.0
Manufacturers' sales branches and offices, Total	40,521	451,854,912	6.0
Merchandise agents, brokers, and other functional middlemen, Total	35,052	130,487,776	4.6

SOURCE: U. S. Department of Commerce, *1977 Census of Wholesale Trade,* Vol. II, *Geographic Area Statistics,* pp. 8, 10.

Reasons for Wholesaling

Wholesaling performs a necessary marketing service in our competitive, profit-motivated economy. A large number of producers in many different areas must move their products to widely scattered industrial consumers and retailers. Figure 13-11 shows why wholesalers may be able to do this more economically than producers. It is less costly for a producer of packaged cereals to sell through 3,200 grocery wholesalers than directly to nearly 179,000 grocery retailers.

The services offered to manufacturers by wholesalers are:

1. Establishing a strong contact with retailers.
2. Storing for the manufacturer.
3. Dividing large shipments into smaller quantities.
4. Assuming the credit risk.
5. Providing transportation economies.

Figure 13-11   Reasons for Wholesaling

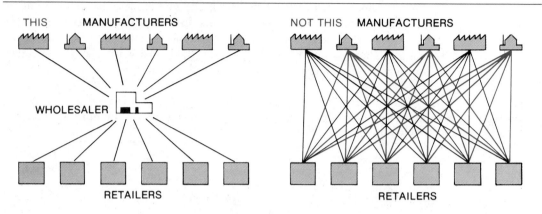

The services performed for retailers by wholesalers include:

1. Serving as a purchasing agent for retailers.
2. Storing for the retailer.
3. Assembling goods from numerous suppliers.
4. Maintaining balanced stocks.
5. Providing prompt delivery services.
6. Financing the retailer.
7. Furnishing promotional and managerial assistance.

Merchant Wholesalers

Merchant wholesalers are wholesale establishments that buy and sell merchandise on their own account. They take title to the goods which they handle, and they face all the risks of owning these goods. When the bulk of their business is to industrial users, they are known as industrial distributors. Merchant wholesalers are commonly classified by the line of goods handled or by the functions performed.

By Lines of Goods Handled

Based upon the lines of goods handled, there are three types of merchant wholesalers. The general-merchandise wholesaler handles a variety of goods in diverse lines such as health and beauty aids, home furnishings, clothing, hardware, and automobile accessories. This type of wholesaler often serves rural general stores, variety stores, or small department stores. The general-line wholesaler markets a single line of goods, such as hardware or groceries, and typically sells to retailers who limit themselves to the wholesaler's line of goods. For example, hardware wholesalers sell to hardware retailers and grocery wholesalers distribute to grocery retailers. A specialty wholesaler carries an assortment of goods in a part of a general line. There are plumbing supply distributors selling only the plumbing part of the hardware line, and there are frozen-food distributors marketing only the frozen-food segment of the grocery line.

By Functions Performed

Merchant wholesalers usually are categorized as either service (or full-function) wholesalers or limited function wholesalers. Service wholesalers extend a broad range of services to their customers. Limited-function wholesalers limit their services and functions, thus reducing their costs.

Service Wholesalers. Among the types of merchandise handled by service wholesalers are groceries, drugs, hardware, and dry goods. Their principal customers are retailers. Most general merchandise, general line, and specialty wholesalers operate as service wholesalers. A rack jobber, or rack merchandiser, who supplies supermarkets with nonfood items, such as health and beauty aids, housewares, records, magazines, and greeting cards, is a unique type of service wholesaler. Rack jobbers typically warehouse their merchandise, install their own display racks, replenish store inventories, and price their goods.

Limited-Function Wholesalers. Limited-function wholesalers include drop shippers, wagon distributors, and cash-and-carry wholesalers. The nature of the product and the desire to reduce the costs of distribution are two reasons for using these middlemen. Drop shippers, or desk jobbers, operate mainly in the lumber and coal industries where the product is bulky. They take orders, contact suppliers, and have suppliers ship the goods directly to the customer. A wagon or truck distributor, who uses a truck as a warehouse, sells perishable items such as fruits, vegetables, tobacco, and candy to supermarkets and restaurants. A cash-and-carry wholesaler keeps operating expenses low by using self-service and central checkouts and by eliminating credit and delivery service.

Functional Middlemen

The term **functional middlemen** is used for the group of wholesalers who do not take title (become the legal owners) to the goods which they sell. They are in business for themselves and negotiate purchases and sales in domestic and international trade on behalf of their clients, who do take title to the goods. These middlemen usually receive commissions or fees. They may or may not take possession of the goods involved. An additional activity that some of them perform for their clients is furnishing marketing information. The important wholesalers in this classification are: manufacturers' agents, selling agents, merchandise brokers, commission merchants, and auction companies.

Integrated Wholesaling

Manufacturers' sales branches and chain store warehouses are forms of *integrated wholesaling*. This type of wholesaling occurs when two or more typically separate business activities, such as manufacturing-wholesaling and wholesaling-retailing, are combined under one ownership. In establishing sales branches, manufacturers move forward in the channel of distribution. In establishing chain-store warehouses, retailers move backward in the channel. Manufacturers with financial and managerial capability, such as Goodyear and General Electric, often establish wholesale branches as a means of gaining greater control over the marketing of their products. For chain organizations, such as Kroger and Safeway, the chain-store warehouse is a collection point for goods to be shipped to their retail stores.

RETAILING

The activity that involves selling consumer goods to ultimate consumers for their own use is known as **retailing**. The marketing institutions in this field are called retailers. Figure 13-12 shows the percentage of retail stores, retail sales, and population in each of the continental 48 states. The sales and profits as a percentage of sales for the ten largest retail firms in the United States are shown in Table 13-2.

Retailers are classified by lines of goods handled, by ownership, by geographic location, and by type of operation.

Table 13-2 **The Ten Largest Retailing Companies Ranked by Sales, 1981**

Rank		Sales (In Thousands of Dollars)	Net Income as Percentage of Sales	Number of Employees
1	Sears, Roebuck (Chicago, IL)	27,357,400	2.4	337,400
2	Safeway Stores (Oakland, CA)	16,580,318	0.7	157,411
3	K mart (Troy, MI)	16,527,012	1.3	280,000
4	JCPenney (New York, NY)	11,860,169	3.3	187,000
5	Kroger (Cincinnati, OH)	11,266,520	1.1	127,271
6	F. W. Woolworth (New York, NY)	7,223,241	1.1	139,800
7	Lucky Stores (Dublin, CA)	7,201,404	1.3	66,000
8	American Stores (Salt Lake City, UT)	7,096,590	0.9	64,000
9	Federated Department Stores (Cincinnati, OH)	7,067,673	3.7	120,800
10	Great Atlantic & Pacific Tea (Montvale, NJ)	6,989,529	Loss	60,000

SOURCE: "FORTUNE Magazine's Directory of the Fifty Largest Retailing Companies," FORTUNE (July 12, 1982), p. 140. © 1982 Time Inc.

Figure 13-12   Retail Map of the United States

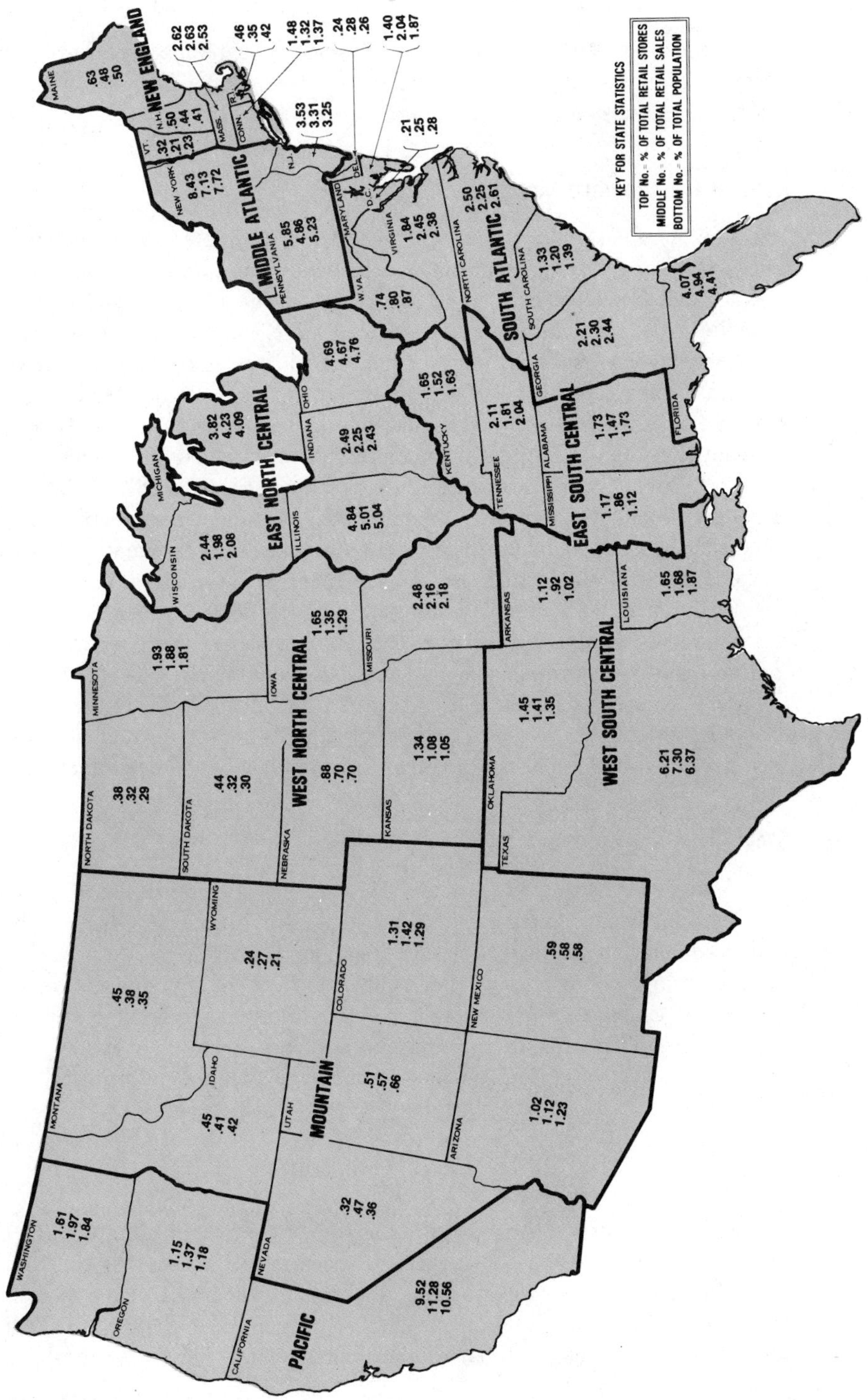

SOURCE: *1982 Retail Map of the United States* (New York: Audits and Surveys, Inc., 1981-1982). Reproduced with permission.

By Lines of Goods Handled

The extent of the lines of goods handled by a retailer frequently determines operating policies and practices. Based on the lines of goods handled, three classes of stores are general-merchandise, single-line, and specialty.

General-Merchandise Stores

The large variety of goods which they offer characterizes **general-merchandise stores**. One type, the general store, is usually found in sparsely populated rural areas. It is a small nondepartmentalized store that carries a wide range of staple goods, including groceries, clothing, dry goods, hardware, and sporting goods. The Hudson Bay Company of Canada and the Northern Commercial Company of Alaska continue to operate many general store-trading post combinations. A department store, which is a large departmentalized establishment handling a wide variety of shopping goods, is usually the dominant store in a community. Macy's in New York is the world's largest store, with over one million square feet of selling space. In 1879, F. W. Woolworth established the first 5 and 10 cent store which, after many decades of price inflation, is more aptly called a limited-price variety store. Nearly 90 percent of these stores are operated by retail chains such as Woolworth and Newberry.

In the mid-1950s, discount stores, which sold a mix of hard and soft goods at relatively low markups, appeared on the retailing scene. These stores advertised extensively, minimized free customer service, maximized use of self-service, utilized relatively inexpensive facilities, and emphasized discount prices. By the 1980s, having adopted many of the operating policies of department stores, numerous discounters such as K mart and Zayre now want to be called low-priced department stores.

Single-Line Stores

A **single-line store**, which may carry a variety of merchandise in several related lines, is usually recognized by its most important line. Single-line establishments include grocery, appliance, drug, hardware, and sporting goods stores. Scrambled merchandising, where a retailer carries lines of goods traditionally stocked by another retailer, has caused the identity of many single-line stores to become blurred. Grocery supermarkets which handle a variety of nonfood items often exhibit this blurred identity. In some Kroger supermarkets, nearly 60 percent of the shelf space is devoted to nonfood items.

Specialty Stores

A **specialty store** offers a depth of assortment in one portion of a line of goods. Specialty stores, such as meat markets and dairy stores, are directly competitive with single-line stores such as supermarkets. In some lines of trade, such as books, records, and automobiles, practically all the establishments are specialty stores. Most retail service establishments, such as beauty salons, bowling alleys, and theaters, are specialty operations.

By Ownership

A retail establishment is either independently owned or is a unit in a chain organization. Chains account for 47 percent of retail sales, but they operate only 18 percent of all retail stores.

Independents

Most stores that are individually and usually locally owned, such as grocery, drug, shoe, and hardware stores, are **independents**. The typical independent retail store is a small operation usually managed by the owner or owners as a proprietorship or partnership. These stores are usually thinly financed. As a general rule they buy through wholesalers and do little advertising or aggressive selling. In every community, however, these are capable independents whose methods are up-to-date and whose profits reflect their ability.

Chain Stores

Two or more stores in the same general line of business which are centrally owned and managed by a corporate chain are known as **chain stores**. Fifty percent of the following types of establishments are operated by chains: department stores, discount stores, limited-price variety stores, grocery stores, and women's ready-to-wear stores. The advent of suburban shopping centers in the 1950s and their reliance on strongly financed tenants, such as chains, has increased the number and strength of chain organizations. The increase in chain-store sales and establishments as a percentage of total retail sales and establishments is shown in Figure 13-13.

Chain organizations customarily centralize many of their activities, permitting specialization and efficiencies in operation. They commonly practice central buying, whereby most of the merchandise for the stores is purchased in large quantities by a central office rather than by each store. Many chains, particularly those in the grocery and drug fields, maintain chain-store warehouses. Suppliers ship in large quantities to these warehouses. A warehouse serves as a supply center for the units in a chain. Other centralized activities include installing uniform accounting systems for all stores, operating a real estate department, preparing store advertising, and training prospective store managers.

Voluntary Chains

There are two types of **voluntary chains**: those sponsored by independent wholesalers and those promoted by groups of cooperating retailers who establish and own the wholesale operation that serves them. The voluntary chain practices, which closely resemble those of the corporate chain, have permitted thousands of independent retailers to achieve operating economies. The strength of the voluntary chains lies in the cooperative spirit of the members. By the same token, their principal weakness lies in the lack of positive control within the group. Voluntary chains are found mainly in the grocery, variety goods, and automobile accessory lines. IGA food stores, Ace Hardware, and Western Auto dealers are members of voluntary chain organizations.

Figure 13-13   Chain-Store Sales and Establishments as a Percentage of Total Retail Sales and Establishments

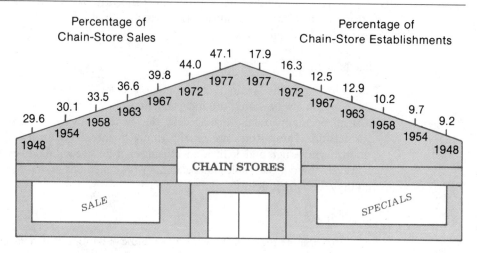

SOURCE: U. S. Bureau of the Census, *Statistical Abstract of the United States: 1982–1983* (103d ed.; Washington, DC: U. S. Government Printing Office, 1982), p. 801.

By Geographic Location

Until 1950 nearly all major retailers in a city were located in the downtown area. Since the 1950s, many retailers have followed the consumer to the suburbs and located in planned shopping centers. These **planned shopping centers** are carefully designed, constructed, and managed by developers who lease space to a variety of retailers. Over one-third of all retail sales in the United States is accounted for by the 24,000 planned shopping centers that exist today.

Shopping centers have been classified into three different types: the neighborhood center, the community center, and the regional center.

Neighborhood Shopping Center

The shopping center which generally serves 7,500 to 20,000 people living within a 6- to 10-minute drive is the neighborhood shopping center. The major store in the center—and the prime traffic generator—is a supermarket. The other stores in the center, which may include a drugstore, hardware store, bakery, and beauty shop, offer convenience goods and services.

Community Shopping Center

A market of 20,000 to 100,000 people living within a 10- to 20-minute drive is handled by the community shopping center. The dominant store is generally a small department store or a large variety store. A majority of the stores stress shopping goods such as clothing and appliances.

Regional Shopping Center

Over 100,000 consumers are served by the regional shopping center, and some of these consumers may drive long distances to get to the center. Often the center is an enclosed mall with a department store at each end as its major tenants. The three-story, 2.2-million-square-foot Woodfield Mall in Schaumburg, IL, which is shown in Figure 13-14, contains 235 stores and is located on a site nearly as large as the Vatican City.

By Type of Operation

Although the majority of retailers stock a wide variety of goods and operate from a store, there are some merchants who are nonstore retailers. Their *nonstore* operations include house-to-house selling, mail-order houses, and vending machines.

House-to-House Selling

Since 1960, the desire of many consumers for the convenience of shopping in their own homes has resulted in the success of aggressive new house-to-house selling organizations such as Amway and Avon. Older firms, such as Fuller Brush and Electro-lux, remain in the field, too. In many communities Green River Ordinances restrict house-to-house selling. These laws reflect both the fear of local merchants and the suspicion of householders toward house-to-house selling.

Mail-Order Houses

Mail-order houses sell and deliver goods by mail. They make use of catalogs, media advertising, direct mail, and the telephone to attract customers. Most mail-order firms are quite small operations that sell specialty housewares, foods, and apparel. These specialty retailers, such as L. L. Bean and Land's End, account for nearly two-thirds of all catalog sales. Originally the mail-order house served the rural consumer who lacked adequate retailing facilities. In recent years the large firms, such as Sears and Penney's, have attracted the convenience-oriented urban consumer by accepting telephone orders.

The ease of in-home shopping, the rise in discretionary consumer income, and the use of the computer to identify target markets are factors that have contributed to the increased use of catalogs by a variety of retailers. Lane Bryant, which caters to fuller-figure women, mails nearly 15 million seasonal catalogs to its customers each year. Bloomingdale's, the trendy New York department store, issues a new catalog each month. Sears now publishes 19 different specialty catalogs for its various customer segments. These catalogs are more productive and less expensive for Sears than its massive general catalog, which costs four dollars each to print and mail.

Figure 13-14   Woodfield Mall in Schaumburg, IL

SOURCE: Courtesy of the Taubman Company, Inc., Troy, MI.

Vending Machines

Although vending machines date back to the 1880s, their greatest growth has come in recent years. Vending machines permit the sales of small convenience items to be made at times and in places where another type of retailing is not possible. In a recent year Americans spent an average of $65.59 in vending machines, and the machines generated total sales of $13.8 billion. Cigarettes, coffee, candy, and soft drinks account for nearly 80 percent of their volume.

SUMMARY

A product is more than a combination of steel, aluminum, plastic, and other components; it is a bundle of satisfactions or utilities for the consumer. The two broad categories of products, or goods, are industrial goods and consumer goods. Industrial goods are primarily used in producing other goods or in rendering services. There are three major types of industrial goods: unprocessed and processed materials; maintenance, repair, and operating supplies; and capital goods. Consumer goods are used by ultimate consumers or households. They can be used without further commercial processing. The three major categories of consumer goods are convenience goods, shopping goods, and specialty goods.

Some of the important product-policy decisions are concerned with new product development, product line and product mix, planned obsolescence, brands and trademarks, and labels. A new product has a definite life expectancy. The five distinct stages in a product life cycle are: introduction, growth, maturity, saturation, and decline. Many firms develop a product line of closely related products. A widely criticized product policy is planned obsolescence.

The routes that goods take in their progress from producers to consumers are known as channels of distribution. The three most often used channels of distribution for consumer goods are: producer to consumers, producer to retailer to consumers, and producer to wholesaler to retailer to consumers. In selecting a channel of distribution, managers evaluate factors concerning the market, channel member, product, and environment.

Wholesaling includes all the marketing activities of firms that sell to retailers, industrial firms, and all other commercial users. A major type of wholesaler is the merchant wholesaler, who takes title to the goods he or she handles. A form of merchant wholesaler is the limited-function wholesaler, who restricts services and functions. Another important type of wholesaler is the functional middleman, who does not have title to the goods that she or he sells.

Retailing involves the sales of products to ultimate consumers for their own use. Retailers are classified on the basis of lines of goods handled, ownership, geographic location, and type of operation.

BACK TO THE CHAPTER OPENER

1. Is a home video game a convenience, shopping, or specialty good?
2. When the article was written, at what stage of the product life cycle was a home video game?
3. Are national brands more important than private brands in the home video game business?
4. What are the two most important channels of distribution for home video games?
5. Based on the lines of goods handled, what is the classification of retailers who handle only home computers and home video games?

BUSINESS TERMS				
product	288	trademark	294
industrial goods	288	channels of distribution	295
consumer goods	288	wholesaling	299
convenience goods	289	merchant wholesalers	300
shopping goods	289	functional middlemen	301
specialty goods	289	retailing	302
product life cycle	291	general-merchandise stores	304
product line	293	single-line store	304
product mix	294	specialty store	304
planned obsolescence	294	independents	305
brand names	294	chain stores	305
national or manufacturer's brand	294	voluntary chains	305
private or dealer's brand	294	planned shopping centers	306

QUESTIONS FOR DISCUSSION AND ANALYSIS

1. Can industrial goods be placed into convenience, shopping, and specialty goods categories? Explain.
2. Are the sales of industrial goods more likely to be seriously affected by a business recession than the sales of consumer goods? Explain.
3. Are there any goods that ever shift over time from the category of convenience, to shopping, to specialty goods?
4. How will the marketing mix of a moped (motorized bicycle) manufacturer change as the product moves through the various stages of its life cycle?
5. The Timex Corporation is a major producer of inexpensive watches. Timex executives plan to add a new product line, and they ask you for your recommendation. What line would you suggest they add? Explain.
6. Why isn't planned obsolescence as important in the automobile industry today as it was 20 years ago?
7. Shouldn't a wholesaler be present in the channel of distribution for all consumer products?
8. Why should discount stores now want to be known as low-priced department stores?
9. Will the three types of shopping centers that are mentioned in the text continue to be constructed in the future? What other types will be developed?
10. By the year 2000, what new forms of retailing do you see? What are your reasons for suggesting these new forms?

PROJECTS, PROBLEMS, AND SHORT CASES

1. Procter & Gamble, Revlon, and Xerox are companies that have added new product lines in recent years. Answer the following questions on these three companies:

   a. From library sources, such as *Moody's Industrials* or Standard and Poor's finance manuals, identify the major product lines for each of the three companies.
   b. Are all of the product lines which are handled by each company complementary to each other? Explain.
   c. If you could recommend that each of these companies add one new product line, what line would you recommend for each? Explain your answer.

2. Identify a neighborhood, a community, and a regional shopping center with which you are familiar. What are the features that caused you to designate each center as one of the three types? Draw the design of each center, showing its entrances and the location

of its dominant stores. Are the dominant stores in each center located correctly in order to obtain the most efficient consumer traffic flow? Explain.

3. In the early 1960s the huge Du Pont chemical company developed a synthetic leather called Corfam. At that time, vinyl substitutes were being used in place of leather for inexpensive shoes. Although Corfam was a type of vinyl, Du Pont positioned the product as a high-priced, quality alternative to leather. The cost structures of leather and Corfam were very similar. An advantage of Corfam was its durability and long life. Another important feature was that it could be processed into a variety of textures, including alligator hide. A drawback to the new product was that it did not breathe like leather, causing the wearer of Corfam shoes to experience hot, soggy feet. Another disadvantage was the inflexibility of the material.

In order to gain consumer acceptance for Corfam as a quality product, Du Pont permitted only the producers of high-priced, prestige shoes to use the material in their shoes. Du Pont spent millions of dollars promoting Corfam to the public and building its quality image, to no avail.

Despite the aggressive promotional efforts of this giant company, the sales of Corfam peaked rapidly and started declining. Finding that Corfam was not accepted as a quality substitute for leather in fine shoes, Du Pont approached the manufacturers of low-priced shoes to use it. They balked, however, because it was much higher priced than plain vinyl and it lacked the softness of leather. After eight years of mediocre sales, Du Pont finally closed its Corfam production facilities and sold them to Poland. Corfam was dubbed the Edsel of the shoe industry!

For Poland, which had been very dependent on leather imports, the Corfam operation proved to be a very wise purchase. The Poles, with the help of DuPont, made several product improvements in Corfam, including better breathability and more flexibility. During the 1970s the price of leather rose rapidly. By the early 1980s the price of leather was about 20 percent more than Corfam. For the Poles these developments meant an expanded and profitable market for Corfam. The once-shunned material is now being exported into the United States, where it is being used in shoes and other products. One of the exciting new applications for Corfam is in the semiconductor industry, where it is used in the manufacture of silicon chips. Perhaps, as a result of the Polish success with Corfam, jokes about Americans are now being told in Poland!

a. Was Du Pont justified in closing its Corfam line after only eight years of production?

b. What are some of the mistakes that were made by Du Pont in developing and marketing Corfam?

c. Prepare an illustration showing the movement of Corfam through its life cycle at the time that it was being marketed by Du Pont. Show the sales curve and the width of each stage in the life cycle.

d. Should the shoe manufacturers who are using the imported Corfam from Poland advertise that their shoes are made with Corfam?

Lots of Hoopla About Three Little Words as Coca-Cola Kicks off New Ad Campaign

Outside the Civic Center (in Atlanta), klieg lights scan the sky, glancing off 30-foot-tall balloons of Coke cans and bottles. Inside, conductor Robert Shaw and 35 members of the Atlanta Symphony Orchestra are poised to rise on a hydraulic stage in the midst of a multimedia blizzard.

The live musical prelude, overdubbed with a full orchestra in wraparound stereo, is a short takeoff on Beethoven's Fifth, and it builds to a crescendo as images from 35 Xenon slide projectors, Eidophor television projectors, and interlocked 35mm and 16mm film projectors bounce off walls, standard screens and 20 giant balloon screens suspended from the ceiling. A cast of 100 singers and dancers gyrates in the aisles and on the auditorium's stage. . . .

The fanfare came with the unveiling last night of eight little television commercials that mark the beginning of the company's new ad campaign. "Coke and a smile" is out; "Coke Is It" is in.

Most people won't care one way or the other. But to soft-drink types, all this is serious business. Coke already has lavished millions of dollars on the fledgling campaign, and if the 2,500 or so representatives of Coke bottlers who saw it last night like it well enough, they and Coke will pour hundreds of millions of dollars into it over the next few years.

It's doubtful that many Americans will escape "It" even for the next few days. Tonight at 9:15, for example, Coke will run ads simultaneously on all three major networks and reach an estimated 96 million viewers by the end of the evening. Coke won't specify how much all this costs, except to say that 1982 ad expenditures will be the highest in the brand's history, and that the company believes "It" is the most expensive introduction in the history of soft-drink advertising.

"Coke Is It" may or may not beat the recently launched "Pepsi's got your taste for life" in the hearts and minds of consumers, but in extensive market pretesting it's already whipped a number of other proposals at McCann-Erickson, Coke's ad agency. Also-rans include "You've got a Coke comin' to you"; "Just like you, Coke comes through"; "Coke makes it better"; and "Goin' all out, goin' for Coke." . . .

The lyrics to "Coke Is It" strongly address the issue of taste, an area in which Pepsi has been successfully pounding away at Coke for years with its "Pepsi challenge" commercials featuring taste tests in which consumers choose Pepsi.

Coke is it! The biggest taste you've ever found, Coke is it!. . .The most refreshing taste around reads one line. Another version seems to return to the "It's the real thing" strategy believed by many Coke executives to have been the most successful counter to Pepsi: *It's the way that you feel when you know—it's real—Coke is it!*

"We said: We're going to be going into other industries, so let's get a campaign that reemphasizes that we're a soft-drink company," says Mr. Goizuetta, the chairman (of Coca-Cola). "The agency's charter was to capture our corporate strategy in the campaign, and they've done it in three words." . . .

It isn't always easy to say why a company like Coke decides to change a campaign . . . . But in this case it seems clear that recently installed management at Coke wasn't especially happy with the advertising it inherited from its predecessors.

SOURCE: John Huey, "Lots of Hoopla About Three Little Words as Coca-Cola Kicks Off New Ad Campaign," *The Wall Street Journal*, February 5, 1982, p. 29. Reprinted by permission of *The Wall Street Journal,* © Dow Jones & Company, Inc. (1982). All Rights Reserved.

Personal Selling and Advertising

Objectives:

- Explain the differences among personal selling, advertising, and sales promotion.
- Distinguish among the different types of salespersons, and identify the three ways of organizing a sales force.
- Explain the seven steps in the sales process.
- State some typical advertising objectives, and explain the usefulness of the AIDA formula.
- Describe the differences between product advertising and institutional advertising.
- Distinguish among primary, selective, mass, class, and cooperative advertising.
- Compare the features of the five major advertising media by examining their basic characteristics.
- Describe the services of an advertising agency.
- Identify the major complaints against advertising and the answers to these complaints.
- Describe the steps that have been taken to protect the public from the more harmful types of advertising.

After nearly eight years of development, in 1982 Eastman Kodak launched a spectacular promotional campaign for its new disc camera.[1] Trade sources indicated that Kodak spent nearly $40 million to introduce the camera, which ranged in price

1. Gay Jervey, "Largest-Ever Ad Launch for Kodak Disc," *Advertising Age* (March 8, 1982), p. 10.

from \$45 to over \$100. This was the largest expenditure for an ad campaign in the 101-year history of the company.

Kodak relied heavily on network television in order to reach 95 percent of the population at least 18 times prior to the week before Christmas, 1982. Because of the need to inform consumers about the many unusual features of the camera, Kodak employed lengthy 90-second commercials in addition to the shorter 30- and 60-second ones.

In magazines, such as *People, Sports Illustrated, TV Guide,* and *Time*, Kodak used four-color ads with extensive copy that extolled the virtues of the disc camera. In an effort to reach 60 percent of the households, Kodak placed four-color ads in the Sunday newspaper supplements. For a cooperative advertising program with retailers, the company produced four different television commercials. As a result of this extensive promotional campaign, the introduction of the disc camera was the most successful one in Kodak history.

Promotional activities have contributed greatly to the creation of an affluent society. In developing a promotional strategy, management commonly uses three basic forms of promotion: personal selling, advertising, and sales promotion. **Personal selling** is the oral presentation in a conversation with one or more prospective purchasers for the purpose of making sales.[2] **Advertising** refers to any paid form of nonpersonal presentation and promotion of ideas, goods, or services by an identified sponsor.[3] **Sales promotion** is identified as those marketing activities, other than personal selling, advertising, and publicity, that stimulate consumer purchasing and dealer effectiveness. This includes displays, shows and exhibitions, demonstrations, and various other nonrecurring selling efforts.[4] In most firms the expenditure for personal selling is usually greater than the expenditure for advertising. A Federal Trade Commission study revealed that, for all manufacturing, the average advertising expense in media was 1.2 cents of each sales dollar. The average total selling expense, which includes all advertising and personal selling expenses, was 6.7 cents of every sales dollar.

PERSONAL SELLING

"Nothing happens until someone sells something," is a slogan of the Sales and Marketing Executives Club. Although a product may be properly planned, priced, and distributed, there is no return to the company until the product is sold. In a survey of 400 company presidents, there was common agreement that personal selling is the most important aspect of marketing.

---

2. Reprinted from Committee on Definitions, *Marketing Definitions: A Glossary of Marketing Terms*, published by the American Marketing Association, 1960, p. 18.
3. *Ibid.*, p. 9.
4. *Ibid.*

Types of Salespersons

Just as there are many kinds of doctors, such as in medicine, philosophy, and jurisprudence, there are many kinds of salespersons. The salesperson in the hosiery department at Sears differs greatly from the IBM salesperson who sells a computer installation to a large bank. Depending upon the degree to which they solve problems for their customers, the duties of salespersons range from simple clerking to creative selling, as depicted in Figure 14-1.

A truly creative salesperson obtains, analyzes, and evaluates information from a prospective customer. This information is then incorporated in the sales presentation. Although found in all types of selling situations, creative selling frequently occurs in industrial selling, particularly in the sales of complicated installations and equipment. Creative salespersons who employ engineering knowledge in their sales presentations are known as sales engineers. Another type of creative selling is performed by the service salesperson who sells the benefits of intangibles such as stocks, bonds, and insurance.

An account representative is a type of salesperson found in many industries such as wholesaling, foods, and apparel. The account representative's job is to maintain cordial relationships and obtain new orders from old customers. A manufacturer's salesperson who promotes a product to those influencing its sale to the ultimate consumer is known as a missionary salesperson. Often a manufacturer who uses a wholesaler-to-retailer-to-consumer channel of distribution employs missionary sales-persons to call directly upon retailers. Their mission is to inform retailers about the selling features of a product. They do not secure orders for a manufacturer's product; they leave this assignment to the wholesaler's salespersons. A missionary salesperson who is employed by a pharmaceutical manufacturer, such as Eli Lilly or Upjohn, to explain the benefits of the firm's products to prescribing physicians is known as a detailer.

Figure 14-1   Continuum Showing the Types of Salespersons

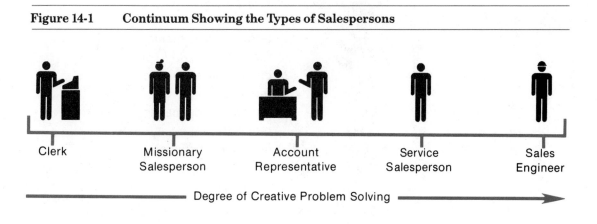

Sales Organizations

A sound organization structure is required for the effective management of the sales activity. Often a sales force is organized on one or more of the following bases: geographic, product line, or customer.

Geographic Sales Organization

The most common method of organizing a sales force is by geographic areas. A geographic sales organization is particularly appropriate for firms which distribute a broad product line over a wide geographic area. A major advantage is that management is able to respond rapidly to serve its customers and to meet competition. The disadvantages relate to the costs and the complexity which arise from the geographic dispersion of the sales force. Many companies use counties as a basis for their sales territories. Pulsar Time, Inc., however, uses television market areas because television is its most important form of advertising. Roche Laboratories divides its territories by zip-code areas. As Figure 14-2 shows, some large organizations with national distribution may have as many as four layers of sales management and 600 salespersons. The line of advancement for an ambitious salesperson with managerial hopes is a gradual climb through these levels of sales management.

Product Line Sales Organization

When a firm markets two or more full lines of products, the sales force is often a product line sales organization. Since the activities of a salesperson are limited to a

---

Figure 14-2   Levels of Sales Management

- 600 salespersons
  report to
- 100 territory sales managers
  report to
- 20 district sales managers
  report to
- 4 regional sales managers
  report to
- 1 field sales manager

---

particular product line, the individual becomes a specialist in that line. A disadvantage of this form of organization is the duplication of selling and administrative effort. The General Foods Corporation sales force is divided into six product divisions: beverages and breakfast foods, main meal and dessert foods, frozen foods, powdered soft drinks, coffee, and pet foods.

Customer Sales Organization

A third way in which the sales force is organized is by type of customer. A customer sales organization best illustrates the organizational application of the marketing concept since it places the focus of the sales effort on serving the customers' needs. The use of several sales forces to serve different customer groups often increases a company's marketing and administrative expenses. In the early 1980s, IBM shifted from a product line sales organization to a customer-based one. The data processing, general systems, and office products groups were combined into two new customer divisions: one that serves existing customers and another that prospects for new customers. Under the old product line sales organization, there was intense competition among the different IBM divisions for sales of data processing equipment to the same customers.

Steps in the Sales Process

A well-organized sales effort follows a step-by-step plan that should be flexible enough to meet most selling situations. As Figure 14-3 shows, the seven steps in the sales process are: prospecting, preapproach, approach, presentation, trial close, answering objections, and close.

Prospecting

In order to replace old customers and acquire new ones, a salesperson needs to conduct systematic prospecting. Prospecting is the activity which develops new sales leads. Sources of prospects include friends, business associates, present users, and paid informers known as *bird dogs*. For example, an insurance salesperson effectively used the Welcome Wagon service to obtain the names of prospects at $1.85 per name. In some instances, salespersons practice cold canvassing, which involves contacting completely unknown individuals.

Preapproach

After the prospects have been identified, a preapproach investigation determines if the prospects qualify as potential customers. Another purpose of the preapproach is to gather information which will permit a salesperson to tailor the sales presentation to the prospect. This use of the information builds a salesperson's self-confidence and increases sales effectiveness. In the life insurance industry, salespersons say that for every ten qualified prospects contacted, three will be willing to talk seriously and one will buy a policy.

Figure 14-3   Seven Steps in the Sales Process

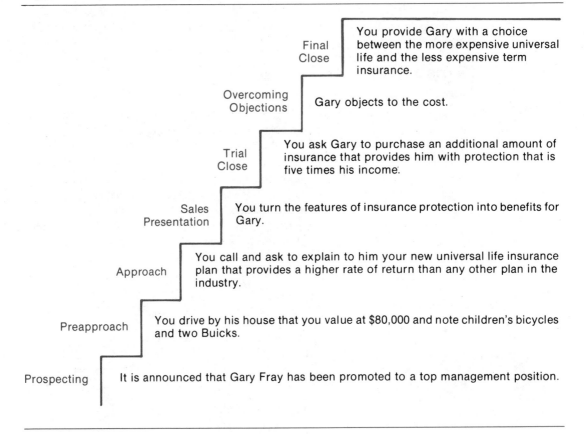

Final Close — You provide Gary with a choice between the more expensive universal life and the less expensive term insurance.

Overcoming Objections — Gary objects to the cost.

Trial Close — You ask Gary to purchase an additional amount of insurance that provides him with protection that is five times his income.

Sales Presentation — You turn the features of insurance protection into benefits for Gary.

Approach — You call and ask to explain to him your new universal life insurance plan that provides a higher rate of return than any other plan in the industry.

Preapproach — You drive by his house that you value at $80,000 and note children's bicycles and two Buicks.

Prospecting — It is announced that Gary Fray has been promoted to a top management position.

Approach

In the approach, the salesperson attempts to capture the prospect's attention and interest. The approach is especially important since it provides the prospect with the first impression of the salesperson. If the salesperson is successfully received, he or she can proceed with the sales presentation.

Presentation

The **sales presentation** is the key element in the selling process. In the presentation a salesperson demonstrates to the prospect how the product features produce customer benefits. Some companies provide prepared, or canned, sales presentations for their salespersons. Generally the most effective presentations are the ones which are adaptable to a prospect's situation. Through questioning, a salesperson is able to identify a problem confronting the prospect. The salesperson then indicates how the product can provide a solution to the problem.

Trial Close

A trial close is used during a presentation to see if the prospect has made a mental commitment to purchase. By gauging a prospect's reaction during the presentation, a salesperson receives some indication of the prospect's willingness to buy. In some instances a single trial close may lead to a sale; in other cases several trial closes may be necessary.

Answering Objections

The presence of objections is often viewed as a favorable factor since it indicates that the prospect is attempting to resolve various questions as he or she moves toward a purchase decision. Some objections, however, may just be excuses for not buying. Knowledgeable salespersons are aware of the usual objections they will encounter and are ready to respond to them. Commonly expressed objections relate to:

1. Product features.
2. Product cost.
3. Need for the product.
4. Timing of the purchase.
5. Seller of the product.

Close

Whenever a prospect expresses a definite interest in the product, the salesperson should close. Several effective closing techniques are utilized by successful salespersons. These include the *assumptive* close where the salesperson asks a final question such as "To which address do you want this shipped?" Another type of close is the *choice* close where the salesperson poses a question such as "Would you prefer to pay cash or use credit?" A third type of close occurs when a salesperson overcomes a final objection. A statement may be made to the prospect such as "Will you agree that if we can resolve this final objection, you will complete the purchase?" A fourth common type of closing involves presenting a summary of the product benefits and then asking for the order.

Telemarketing

In order to reduce the cost of a sales call—which in 1981 was $178 for an industrial sales call—an increasing number of sales presentations are being made over the telephone. As consumers, we have all been contacted over the telephone by individuals selling magazine subscriptions or insurance. Now, through **telemarketing**, the telephone is rapidly becoming a major communication medium for industrial selling. Numerous large firms have established telemarketing centers that permit them to engage in a carefully planned program of telephone selling.

ADVERTISING

For years American businesses have recognized the importance of advertising. Procter & Gamble, which first advertised its products in 1882, is now spending $671.8 million annually on advertising. As indicated in Table 14-1, the top ten advertisers spend over $4.1 billion annually on advertising. The importance of advertising in stimulating competition was demonstrated by a Federal Trade Commission rule that freed optometrists to advertise the price of glasses and contact lenses. As a result of the increased competition, the price of glasses rose by only half as much as the Consumer Price Index in a recent period and only by one-third of the price for health-related goods and services.

Table 14-1 **The Top Ten National Advertisers of 1981 in Major Media**

Rank	Company	Total Expenditures
1	Procter & Gamble	$ 671,800,000
2	Sears, Roebuck & Co.	544,100,000
3	General Foods Corp.	456,800,000
4	Philip Morris, Inc.	433,000,000
5	General Motors Corp.	401,000,000
6	K mart Corp.	349,600,000
7	Nabisco Brands	341,000,000
8	R. J. Reynolds Industries	321,300,000
9	American Telephone & Telegraph Co.	297,000,000
10	Mobil Corp.	293,100,000
	TOTAL	$4,108,700,000

SOURCE: Reprinted with permission from the September 9, 1982 issue of *Advertising Age*. Copyright 1982 by Crain Communications, Inc.

Objectives of Advertising

An advertising manager for a company needs to set forth carefully the specific objectives of its advertising. Some typical advertising objectives are:

1. *To provide information*. By advertising its toll-free reservation number, Holiday Inn provides information to prospective travelers.
2. *To create interest*. Polaroid attracted interest in its Sun Cameras and its 600 speed instant film by offering free "smile insurance" with the claim that one should get 10 good shots for 10 earnest tries.
3. *To persuade*. Through a series of advertisements stating, "We're the Best GM Ever," General Motors attempted to persuade consumers that it's a leader in technology, quality, and fuel economy.
4. *To generate immediate sales*. When Macy's department store advertises a pre-holiday sale of women's coats, it wants to generate immediate sales.

5. *To establish a favorable image*. The Hallmark Greeting Card Company desires to establish a favorable company image by sponsoring the "Hall of Fame" television specials.

Tasks of Advertising

To help accomplish the objectives of advertising, it is appropriate to use the AIDA formula. **AIDA** is derived from the first letter in each of the major tasks of advertising: to attract Attention, to draw Interest, to create Desire, and to get Action. The AIDA formula is appropriate for all promotional efforts and helps in accomplishing the objectives of advertising. The use of AIDA is illustrated by the Digital Systems ad in Figure 14-4 on page 323.

Types of Advertising

The two basic types of advertising are product advertising and institutional advertising. **Product advertising** is designed to sell one or more definite, identified products. It usually highlights their good qualities, satisfaction-giving features, or prices. **Institutional advertising** is created for the purpose of getting some message across to the public.

Product Advertising

Within the general category of product advertising are several subtypes. *Primary* advertising is intended to stimulate an interest in and a desire for a certain class of goods. Frequently the good is some new type of product that has just come on the market or an established product that is seeking to expand its market. Figure 14-5 on page 324 is an illustration of primary advertising that was prepared by the American Dairy Association to expand the demand for butter during its most important consumption periods—November and December. *Selective* advertising is supposed to direct consumers toward the purchase of a particular brand of good such as a Ford Escort or a Brooks Brothers' suit. In the dairy industry, Land O'Lakes Foods does extensive advertising for its brand of butter (see Figure 14-6 on page 325).

Mass advertising is advertising that appeals to a cross section of people. As shown in Figure 14-7 on page 326, Bridgestone Tires used golfer Lee Trevino in a successful advertising campaign because of his wide familiarity to the general public. *Class* advertising, on the other hand, is directed at special groups of people, such as industrial purchasing agents or college students. (Figure 14-4 on page 323, showing the use of AIDA, also illustrates class advertising that is directed to prospective purchasers of computer systems.) The Votrax ad in Figure 14-8 on page 327 is aimed at product designers and product managers who have a use for voice synthesizers. The McDonald's ad in Figure 14-9 on page 328 focuses on black consumers.

A form of product advertising where the costs of advertising are shared by manufacturers and their middlemen is **cooperative advertising.** Most cooperative advertising agreements provide the suppliers with some control over how the co-op funds will be spent. In some instances the supplier prepares a complete ad for the retailer, who simply adds the store name and inserts the ad in the local media. Figure 14-10 on page 329 shows an interesting co-op ad that is sponsored by a retailer and its supplier of consumer-credit service.

Institutional Advertising

By means of institutional advertising a firm may announce a change in location, the adoption of a new policy, or anything else that might be of general interest to its customers. Another form of institutional advertising exists when several advertisers issue a joint advertisement for their mutual benefit. Figure 14-11 on page 330 illustrates an effective institutional ad by Phillips Petroleum for the support of United States diving.

Publicity is favorable information about a product or institution that is supplied to the advertising media. It usually appears in editorial or news form. Since publicity has no media costs, it is not really a form of advertising. The Thanksgiving Day parade in New York sponsored by Macy's is a form of publicity.

Advertising Media

Advertising media are the different types of vehicles, or devices, by which advertising reaches its audience. These include newspapers, television, direct mail, radio, magazines, and other media. Table 14-2 reveals that the total advertising expenditures in all media for 1981 were over $61.3 million.

Table 14-2   Advertising Volume in the U. S. in 1980 and 1981

Medium	1980 Millions of Dollars	1980 Percentage of Total	1981 Millions of Dollars	1981 Percentage of Total	Percentage of Change
Newspapers	15,541	28.5	17,420	28.4	+12.1
Magazines	3,149	5.8	3,533	5.8	+12.2
Farm publications	130	0.2	146	0.2	+12.2
Television	11,366	20.9	12,650	20.6	+11.3
Radio	3,702	6.8	4,212	6.9	+13.8
Direct mail	7,596	13.9	8,871	14.3	+15.6
Business publications	1,674	3.1	1,841	3.0	+10.0
Outdoor	578	1.1	650	1.1	+12.5
Miscellaneous	10,744	19.7	12,087	19.7	+12.5
TOTAL	54,480	100.0	61,320	100.0	+12.6

SOURCE: Reprinted with permission from the March 22, 1982 issue of *Advertising Age.* Copyright 1982 by Crain Communications, Inc.

Figure 14-4   Use of AIDA Formula in Advertising

Source: Digital Systems
Digital Systems' Ad Objective:

To get accounting firms to make inquiries, this full-color ad was prepared by Dodson, Craddock & Born Advertising as one in a series of three scheduled in two trade journals. Total production cost for this ad — minus the separations — was about $350. Ad costs were minimal because the agency president and vice-president posed as airline passengers (no residuals), and the agency art director shot the picture. For that perfect shot, Eastern Airlines in Pensacola, FL held up passenger boarding for three minutes! It also provided the aircraft at no charge.

Total advertising for Digital Systems consisted of six ads each in the two trade journals, plus direct mail on a light scale. During the 12-month period this series ran, sales more than doubled that of the previous year!

Figure 14-5   Example of Primary Advertising

Source: American Dairy Association
American Dairy Association's Ad Objective:

With margarine advertising expenditures exceeding $32 million annually, the American Dairy Association — spending less than $1 million — needed a compelling proposition to maintain a competitive presence for butter. Noting that margarine's strategy was based on tasting as good as butter, D'Arcy-

MacManus & Masius/Chicago ran this 4-color national print ad during butter's most important consumption period, November – December, when consumers seek quality for special meals. This creative strategy literally turned around the margarine taste claims with a strong statement of butter's quality and superiority, plus a competitive call to action, served up with mouth-watering appetite appeal.

When the flavor really counts.

Figure 14-6　Example of Selective Advertising

Source: Land O' Lakes, Inc.
Land O' Lakes' Ad Objective:

Land O' Lakes, Inc., ran a series of four-color ads in which the entire copy consisted of "When the flavor really counts." The copy was terse because the brand is so well known. Both the elegance of the photography and the brevity of copy position the brand as a leader. The most important element in the ad is the plate of vegetables which tempts the reader. The photograph says, "Look how this butter complements the cooking." Then the reader's eyes swing back to the package, which has a very strong design element. Finally, the reader's eyes are pulled to the farm, which identifies with the brand's very strong rural heritage. The advertising is meant both to reinforce brand loyalty and to encourage infrequent butter users to choose the brand.

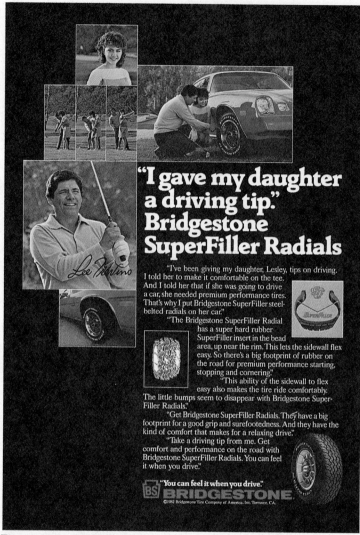

Figure 14-7   Example of Mass Advertising in Magazines

Consumer print advertisement provided by Bridgestone
    Tire Company of America, Inc., Torrance, CA
Bridgestone Tire Co.'s Ad Objective:

In 1981 the Bridgestone Tire Co. brought a new radial car
tire to market in the U.S.A. Because of advanced materials
technology and innovative engineering, this was a genuine
"breakthrough product." The creative strategy called for telling
a complicated and highly technical story in simple terms in a
memorable way. Lee Trevino was selected as the most
appropriate spokesperson because he is well known to the

general public and to the golfing fraternity, he had not been
overused for other product endorsements, and his personal
charm and wit were an added bonus. Trevino's message to the
public was, "You can feel it when you drive."

The first objective of the campaign was to increase the level
of brand awareness of Bridgestone among licensed male
drivers. A post-campaign survey showed that awareness was
increased from 52% to 70%. By the close of 1981, unit
shipments were 168% ahead of the prior year—a figure that
was 138% of the company's sales goal.

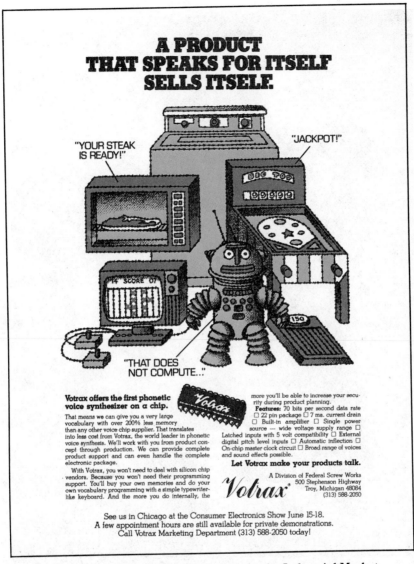

Figure 14-8 Example of Class Advertising to the Industrial Market

Source: Votrax
Votrax's Ad Objective:

The Challenge: To stimulate product designers and product managers to explore the possibility of adding voice capability to their products via a phonetic voice synthesizer on a chip. Votrax's ability to offer a very large vocabulary with over 200% less memory makes adding voice far more practical and cost-effective than most designers previously believed it to be.

The Solution: This award-winning three-color advertisement proved to be an exceptionally effective vehicle for getting our message across. The headline quickly identified sales opportunities, and it was later used on a variety of collateral pieces for the company. Body copy was targeted directly to the audience — chock-full of benefits to be gained by dealing with Votrax for complete product support.

Figure 14-9   Example of Class Advertising to the Consumer Market

Source: McDonald's Corporation
McDonald's Ad Objective:

McDonald's wants the black consumer to "wake up" to the idea of having a good hot breakfast at "Mickey D's." This ad illustrates all the reasons why they should: good hot food, fast service, and even a chance to spend a few minutes with friends before work. The flexibility and spontaneity that McDonald's offers in the morning are very strong selling points. Black consumers represent a very important segment of McDonald's breakfast business, and this ad is designed to keep them coming back for more.

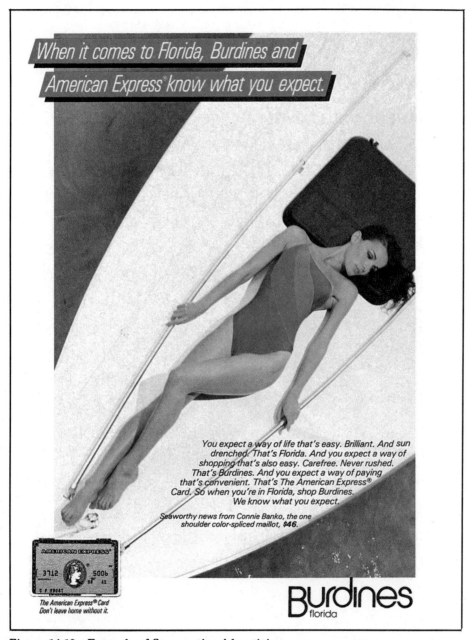

Figure 14-10   Example of Cooperative Advertising

Source: Burdines and American Express
Burdines' and American Express's Ad Objective:

One of the immediate benefits of this cooperative ad between Burdines and American Express is the financial one — that of sharing expenses for production and page placement which are substantial. Through these ads, Burdines wished to establish itself as the leading store for swimwear in the country. What better place than a Florida store to buy swimsuits!

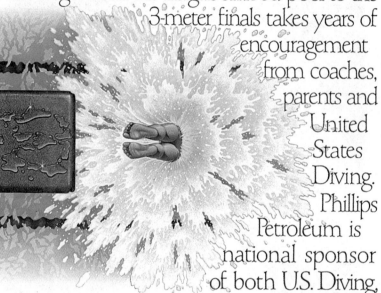

It's a long way down to the top.

It starts with bellyflops and bruises. Over fifty practice dives a day. Every morning from age 7. And to get from the neighborhood pool to the 3-meter finals takes years of encouragement from coaches, parents and United States Diving. Phillips Petroleum is national sponsor of both U.S. Diving, and U.S. Swimming. Giving thousands of eager young athletes a very important chance for glory. Because it takes a lot of getting to the bottom to make it to the top.

Figure 14-11   Example of Institutional Advertising

Source: Phillips Petroleum
Phillips Petroleum's Ad Objective:

Phillips Petroleum wanted to create greater visibility and support for United States diving competition. The advertisement was designed to extol the character-building aspects of the amateur sport and encourage other corporations to sponsor sports that lead to the Olympics.

Media have several basic characteristics. These characteristics are:

1. *Minimum cost*. The lowest possible cost of placing an ad in a medium.
2. *Cost per thousand (CPM)*. The cost to the advertiser of reaching 1,000 prospects in a medium. This cost is computed as follows:

$$\text{cost per thousand} = \frac{\text{cost of medium to advertiser} \times 1,000}{\text{number of prospects reached}}$$

3. *Geographic selectivity*. The ability of a medium to deliver the advertiser's message to a particular geographic area such as a designated city or metropolitan community.
4. *Interest selectivity*. The capacity of a medium to deliver the advertiser's message to groups of consumers who are interested in the advertised product.
5. *Flexibility*. The ability of the advertiser to change the message shortly before the ad is to appear.
6. *Reach*. The total number of prospects that come into contact with the advertiser's message.
7. *Frequency*. The total number of similar advertising messages that a prospect encounters.

Figure 14-12 relates these basic characteristics to the major advertising media.

Newspapers

Newspapers, which are the most popular advertising medium, have low minimum costs and CPM. Rather than measuring the cost per thousand prospects, newspapers

Figure 14-12   Characteristics of Major Advertising Media

Basic Characteristics	Newspapers	Television	Direct Mail	Radio	Magazines
Minimum cost	Low	Very high	Low	Low	High
Cost per 1,000 prospects	Low; uses milline rate	Moderate	High	Low	Moderate
Geographic selectivity	High	National—low Local—high	Very high	High	National edition—low Regional edition—high
Interest selectivity	Low	Low	Very high	Moderate	General interest—low Specific interest—high
Flexibility	High	Low	High	High	Very low
Reach	High	High	Dependent on mailing list	Moderate	Low
Frequency	Related to ad insertions	Related to number of commercials	Related to number of mailings	Related to number of commercials	Related to interval of publication

use a *milline rate* and measure cost per million readers. The cost per million readers is typically $8 to $12. The milline rate is computed as follows:

$$\text{milline rate} = \frac{\text{cost of one newspaper line} \times 1{,}000{,}000}{\text{number of prospects reached}}$$

For example, the milline rate for the St. Louis Post-Dispatch is:

$$\frac{\$2.75 \times 1{,}000{,}000}{236{,}888 \text{ circulation}} = \$11.61$$

Newspapers are quite selective from a geographical standpoint. They permit advertisers to pinpoint their advertising to the metropolitan areas that they wish to reach. From the standpoint of interest selectivity, most newspapers reach all economic and social levels of people and have a general rather than a special appeal. A favorable characteristic of newspaper advertising is its flexibility or timeliness. In most cases changes in advertising copy can be made within a few hours of the time the paper goes to press. This permits advertisers to follow with great speed any national or local event, the weather, or changes in their own internal situations. For instance, the St. Louis Post-Dispatch desires to receive advertising copy 48 hours prior to publication.

Since nearly 80 percent of all adults read a daily newspaper, the reach for newspapers is high. A newspaper provides an advertiser with the ability to reach immediately nearly all of a particular market. The frequency of a newspaper ad is directly related to the number of times the ad is inserted in the paper. The more times the ad is inserted, the more frequently a reader can see it.

Television

Television, with its immense social and cultural impact, is the second most important advertising medium. Procter & Gamble, which is the largest television advertiser, produces nearly 1,000 commercials annually. Because the advertising rates for television are proportional to the audience reached, the cost for network television is considerably higher than for spot, or local, television. **Spot television** is the purchase of time on a local station. The media cost for a 30-second commercial on network television in prime time generally runs about $75,000. Based on adult viewers, the CPM for a 30-second spot announcement on television is $2.47. The St. Louis CBS affiliate, KMOX-TV, typically charges $2,500 for a 30-second spot during prime evening time. This is equivalent to a charge of $6.02 for every 1,000 adults reached. Compared to other media, television has a moderate cost per thousand.

Because of the dominance of nationwide networks in television programming, actual geographic selectivity is limited to locally produced shows and spot commercials. Interest selectivity is in conflict with the quest for large viewing audiences by television networks. High audience ratings attract advertisers to a network. Numerous amply financed advertisers are needed to sponsor the many costly television shows. For example, it cost $250,000 to sponsor a 30-second commercial during the 1984 Olympics in Los Angeles. Certain programs provide some interest selectivity, such as the Saturday morning cartoons, the afternoon "soap operas," the evening news, and sports events.

The average 30-second commercial, which costs $45,000 to $60,000 to produce and takes 16 weeks to complete, does not lend itself to flexibility. Commercials and shows originating at the local level, however, may retain the dimensions of timeliness and flexibility.

The reach for television advertising is fairly high. Nearly 82 million households have at least one television set and more than half of these homes own more than one set. Cable television reaches 23.7 million, or 29 percent, of these households. On the average, television households view over 49.5 hours of television per week.[5] As more messages are added to an advertiser's schedule, the reach and frequency increase. Frequency, however, grows at a slower rate than reach. This occurs because each successive announcement reaches a large number of different viewers rather than the same viewers. Because of the need for accurate estimates of reach and frequency, the A. C. Nielsen Company has developed a widely used audience-measuring system for television.

Direct Mail

The third most often used advertising medium — direct mail — takes a number of different forms. Postcards, letters, catalogs, folders, and booklets are commonly used. Although direct mail involves no time or space costs, it entails expenses for production and printing, mailing lists, and distribution. This form of advertising has a low minimum cost which makes it a suitable medium for small businesses. On a cost per thousand basis, however, direct mail is an expensive advertising medium. If 20-cent postage is used, the mailing cost alone for 1,000 pieces is $200.

The basis of all direct-mail advertising is the mailing list. Lists may be compiled from a variety of sources and may be classified almost endlessly. Through the choice of the list, direct-mail advertising can be made extremely selective as to both geographical location and consumer interests. Depending somewhat upon the elaborateness of the copy, this medium can be changed or discarded entirely until the copy is actually sent. There are many companies that compile and classify lists of businesses and consumers. A typical list can be purchased from these companies for $30 to $50 per thousand names. The more specialized lists command a higher price.

The reach of direct mail is entirely dependent upon selection of the mailing lists. A very specialized mailing list which may be appropriate for some businesses restricts the reach. The frequency is determined by the number of mailings that are made to the individuals on the list. As the frequency of mailings increases, it becomes more difficult for a prospect to ignore a direct-mail promotion.

Radio

Radio is the fourth most popular advertising medium. This medium has a low minimum cost and a low cost per thousand. Radio commercials can be produced very

---

5. A. C. Nielsen Company, *1982 Nielsen Report on Television* (1982), pp. 3, 7.

simply and inexpensively. The ability to purchase spot announcements on a single station minimizes an advertiser's media costs. The cost per 1,000 listeners for spot radio based on adult listeners is $1.28 for a 30-second commercial. The dominant radio station in St. Louis, KMOX, charges $235 for a 30-second spot during the morning driving time. This charge amounts to $1.44 for every 1,000 prospects reached.

Radio is an excellent medium for territorial selectivity because advertisers can select just those stations that broadcast into the areas that they wish to reach. Interest selectivity, on the other hand, is somewhat less certain because the makeup of the listener group for any one program cannot be determined with any great degree of accuracy. Radio advertising is exceedingly flexible because it is possible to change the copy if necessary even while a program is in progress. This permits advertisers to tie their messages to sudden events.

Radio does a better job of delivering frequency than reach for advertisers. Radio listenership tends to be concentrated among a small number of heavy listeners. This concentration results in the same audience receiving a frequent repetition of commercials.

Magazines

Magazines are the fifth most important advertising medium. Magazine advertising requires a substantial investment from advertisers. A full-page, four-color ad in *Time* costs nearly $86,000; in *Reader's Digest*, about $98,000. Even a full-page, four-color ad in *Motor Trend*, a specialized publication, costs almost $22,000. On a cost per 1,000 basis a full-page, four-color ad in *Reader's Digest* runs $5.22. Overall, magazines average a moderate $9.72 cost per thousand for a full-page, four-color ad. Since most magazines have nationwide coverage, they are an important medium for national advertisers such as Ford, RCA, and Philip Morris.

For advertisers with limited geographic distribution, regional editions of magazines, such as *Time, Newsweek,* and *Reader's Digest*, are available. A full-page, four-color ad in the *Reader's Digest* regional edition that includes St. Louis is about $20,600 — or $10.16 per 1,000 circulation. Regional editions provide advertisers with access to smaller markets without requiring them to pay for circulation in areas where their products are not sold.

Since the general-interest magazines reach a wide variety of individuals, they are effective media for products with a wide appeal.

Magazine advertising lacks flexibility. Often there is a long lapse of time between the deadlines for advertising copy and date of publication. This period is sometimes great enough to make the themes of the insertions out of date by the time they reach the readers. *Reader's Digest* requires nine weeks and *Time* requests seven weeks for four-color advertisements to be submitted before the date that they will reach the readers.

The reach and frequency of magazine advertising are low. Except for the general-interest publications, few magazines have circulations that reach more than a few million readers. Even *Time* has a circulation of only 4.6 million copies. A firm can increase the reach of its magazine advertising by adding to its advertising schedule different magazines with little audience duplication. Since most magazines are weekly or monthly publications, the frequency of an advertiser's message is restricted to these time intervals.

Other Advertising Media

Other common advertising media include: business papers, which circulate only among members of a particular profession or industry; outdoor advertising, which consists of billboards and signs; transportation advertising, which is found in buses, taxis, and subways; point-of-purchase aids, such as display racks, demonstrations, and product samples; and advertising specialties, which include calendars, matchbooks, pencils, and other items containing an advertising message.

The Advertising Agency

An **advertising agency** is an organization equipped to undertake all phases of the preparation and execution of advertising for its clients. It handles the complete advertising campaign, which includes writing copy, creating art work, and selecting and making contracts with the media. Such secondary activities as product and market research, designing of packages and labels, and consultation of marketing matters generally are among the services of the larger agencies. Practically all national newspaper, television, and magazine advertising is produced by agencies. The specialized talents of such agencies enable them to perform these functions better than the advertisers could.

Figure 14-13 shows the organization of a typical advertising agency on the basis of the functions performed. Table 14-3 identifies the top ten advertising agencies in the United States in terms of billings. **Billings** represent the total of all advertising space, time, and service charges billed to clients.

The principal method for compensating agencies is a 15 percent commission paid by the media on the basis of the space or time cost of the advertising placed by their clients, the advertisers. For example, assume that an agency acting for a client buys space that costs $30,000 in a magazine. The magazine bills the agency for $30,000 less the 15 percent commission of $4,500 — or a net of $25,500. The agency in turn bills the client for the full $30,000. When the $30,000 is paid by the client, the agency keeps $4,500 and remits $25,500 to the magazine. Over the past several years, however, some agencies have switched to another form of compensation — the service charge, which is composed of charges for materials, services, and a fair profit. Such agencies view the service charge as a fairer method than commission.

Criticisms of Advertising

Since advertising is in the public view, it is subject to extensive criticism. Many of the expressions of disapproval are criticisms of our competitive enterprise system. Certain critics set themselves up as authority figures and attempt to judge the correctness of advertising for everyone. Some of the frequently heard complaints about advertising and the responses to these complaints are:

Figure 14-13   A Typical Advertising Agency Organization Chart by Functions

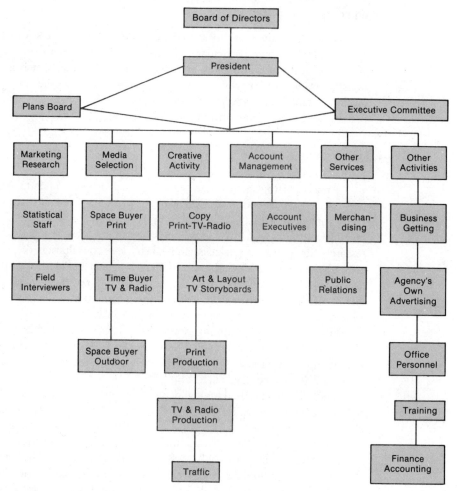

SOURCE: American Association of Advertising Agencies.

1. Complaint: Much advertising is merely competitive and stresses minor differences in products.
   Response: Competitive advertising is a reflection of our competitive economic system. What appear to be minor product differences to some are important product features to others.
2. Complaint: Advertising makes the advertised goods cost more than if they were not advertised.
   Response: In many cases advertising develops a mass market for a product. This permits a manufacturer to use mass production techniques that reduce the costs of the product.

Table 14-3   **The Top Ten Advertising Agencies in the United States Ranked by World Billings, 1982**

Rank		World Billings (000,000)	U. S. Billings (000,000)	Total Employees
1	Young & Rubicam	$2,511.7	$1,645.4	7,025
2	Ted Bates Worldwide	2,374.0	1,555.8	5,041
3	J. Walter Thompson Co.	2,315.2	1,115.4	7,443
4	Ogilvy & Mather	2,151.0	1,179.7	7,010
5	McCann-Erickson Worldwide	1,841.4	550.3	5,850
6	BBDO International	1,605.5	1,050.5	3,583
7	Leo Burnett Co.	1,487.4	919.8	3,498
8	Saatchi & Saatchi Compton Worldwide	1,302.6	510.9	1,140
9	Doyle Dane Bernbach	1,235.0	920.0	2,986
10	Foote Cone & Belding	1,195.9	853.9	3,888

SOURCE: Reprinted with permission from the March 16, 1983 issue of *Advertising Age*. Copyright 1983 by Crain Communications, Inc.

3. **Complaint:** Certain advertisements are in poor taste or offensive to the public.
   Response: Occasionally some advertisers have exceeded the bounds of good taste for some segments of the public. Both advertising agency executives and media representatives strive to prevent the appearance of any advertisement that provokes displeasure.

4. **Complaint:** Many advertisements are false or misleading.
   Response: Reputable advertisers do not intentionally mislead consumers. Most advertisers carefully check their copy for truthfulness. Many conduct tests to make certain that consumers perceive an ad exactly as it was intended.

5. **Complaint:** Advertising causes people to buy things that they do not really need.
   Response: The needs of individuals are never completely fulfilled. After their basic needs are met, individuals seek additional self-satisfying goods. Advertising informs the consumer of the availability of these goods.

6. **Complaint:** Advertising creates monopolistic power.
   Response: One cannot generalize that large-scale advertising creates monopolistic power. Rather, the situation for each product should be analyzed on the basis of factors such as capital requirements, lack of product and/or marketing ability, prospective earnings, and failure to have a line of related products.

Ensuring Truth in Advertising

Many advertising groups, government agencies, and consumer organizations have taken steps to protect the public and businesspersons from some of the more harmful types of advertising. Figure 14-14 summarizes the major industry and government regulations that assist in ensuring truth in advertising.

Figure 14-14   Industry and Government Regulations That Ensure Truth in Advertising

Industry Self-Regulation	**Government Regulation**

Better Business Bureaus
   National Advertising Division
   National Advertising Review Board
Trade Practice Rules
Advertising media ethical standards
	Federal regulation
	   Federal Trade Commission
	   Wheeler-Lea Act
	   Food and Drug Administration
	   Federal Communications
	     Commission
	State regulation
	   "Printers' Ink" Statute

Industry Self-Regulation

There are several forms of self-regulation in the advertising industry. Better Business Bureaus attempt to police misleading ads in local media. The weapons for the 155 local bureaus have been twofold—adverse publicity for the offending firms and recourse to the federal courts when false advertising is sent through the mails. In recent years the Council of Better Business Bureaus has established a National Advertising Division (NAD). The NAD reviews and evaluates all challenges to the truth and accuracy of national advertising brought by outside sources or initiated by its own monitoring program. Any appeals from the decisions of the NAD go before the National Advertising Review Board (NARB). The NARB is a five-member judicial panel that is drawn from the major advertising trade associations.

Recognizing that false or misleading advertising reflects unfavorably on all members of the trade, some industries, such as the Cosmetic and Toilet Preparations Industry, have developed Trade Practice Rules. These rules, established with the assistance of the Federal Trade Commission, usually prohibit false advertising, misbranding, and deception by any member of the trade. Advertising media provide self-regulation, too. Nearly all media have certain minimum ethical standards for acceptable advertising. The Radio Code and the Television Code of the National Association of Broadcasters establish the basic standards for broadcast media.

Government Regulation

The two principal federal agencies for fighting fraudulent advertising are the Federal Trade Commission (FTC) and the Food and Drug Administration (FDA). When the FTC was formed in 1914, it was empowered only to prevent firms from competing unfairly against each other. In 1938 the Wheeler-Lea Act gave the FTC expanded authority to prevent firms from engaging in unfair or deceptive practices against the general public. This authority permits the FTC to ban the false advertising of foods, drugs, and cosmetics. The Federal Food, Drug, and Cosmetic Act of 1938 assigned to the FDA the power to prohibit the false labeling and deceptive packaging of foods, drugs, and cosmetics.

The FTC has the power to order corrective ads and to impose refunds to customers in cases where goods were sold by deception. In a major case, the STP Corporation was fined $500,000 and spent another $200,000 publishing retractions of its claims that STP reduced oil consumption by up to 20 percent. In another celebrated case, Listerine was required to advertise that the product does not really prevent colds or sore throats or lessen their severity.

The FTC supports consumer groups in the use of counteradvertising. This type of message counteracts product claims and advertising themes which raise controversial issues. The agency is requiring advertisers in selected industries, such as automobiles and appliances, to provide proof of certain advertising claims.

Another federal agency that has indirect influence over advertising on television and radio is the Federal Communications Commission (FCC). The FCC has established policies on the types of products that can be advertised and on the content of ads. Its authority stems from its power to license television and radio stations.

In 1911, *Printers' Ink*, a former advertising trade paper, set forth for the state legislatures a model statute that was designed to control false or misleading advertising in intrastate commerce. As a result, 44 states have adopted some form of a *"Printers' Ink" statute*. The value of many of these state statutes has been lessened by poor enforcement.

Consumer Actions

Various consumer groups have been successful in getting deceptive or distasteful advertising changed. The ban on television cigarette advertising can be attributed partially to consumer advocates. A group of concerned parents, called Action for Children's Television, carefully evaluates the quality of commercials that are directed at children. In the early 1980s, in response to efforts by the Coalition for Better Television and the National Coalition on Television Violence, Procter & Gamble withdrew sponsorship from 50 network television programs. The company indicated that it would refuse to sponsor shows that contain excessive sex, violence, and profanity.

SUMMARY   In developing a promotional strategy, three basic forms of promotion are available: personal selling, advertising, and sales promotion. Selling involves personal contact with a prospective customer. The duties of salespersons range from simple clerking to creative selling. A sales force usually is organized on one or more of the following bases: geographic, product line, or customer. Most personal selling efforts consist of the following seven steps: prospecting, preapproach, approach, presentation, trial close, answering objections, and close.

Nonpersonal communications with customers include the following types of advertising: product, institutional, primary, selective, mass, and class. Some typical advertising objectives are to provide information, create interest, persuade, generate immediate sales, and establish a favorable image. The tasks of advertising are illustrated by the AIDA formula. These tasks are to attract attention, draw interest, create desire, and get action. Cooperative advertising is a special form of advertising that involves the sharing of advertising costs between manufacturers and their middlemen.

On the basis of advertising expenditures, the five top media are newspapers, television, direct mail, radio, and magazines. An advertiser can determine when to use each medium by evaluating its various characteristics. Practically all national newspaper, television, and magazine advertising is produced by advertising agencies for their clients.

Critics incorrectly charge that advertising is merely competitive, makes goods cost more, is in poor taste, is false or misleading, causes people to buy unneeded goods, and creates monopolistic power. Advertising is basically a reflection of our competitive economic system. The advertising industry, government, and consumer groups have all taken steps to protect the public and businesspersons from the more harmful types of advertising.

BACK TO THE CHAPTER OPENER

1. What is the advertising objective of the "Coke Is It" campaign?
2. Are the "Coke Is It" television commercials examples of product or institutional advertising?
3. How could Coca-Cola use cooperative advertising?
4. Why does Coca-Cola use extensive television advertising?
5. Why does Coca-Cola use an advertising agency?

BUSINESS TERMS

personal selling	314	institutional advertising	321
advertising	314	cooperative advertising	321
sales promotion	314	publicity	322
sales presentation	318	advertising media	322
telemarketing	319	spot television	332
AIDA	321	advertising agency	335
product advertising	321	billings	335

QUESTIONS FOR DISCUSSION AND ANALYSIS

1. Why do pharmaceutical companies use missionary salespersons?
2. Isn't a customer sales organization always more effective than a product line sales organization?
3. What is an attention-getting approach for a salesperson of home computers? of gas home furnaces? of a home fire alarm system?
4. Should salespersons anticipate objections and answer them in their sales presentations or should they wait until the objections are brought up by prospects?
5. Can you name any other advertising objectives in addition to those listed in the text?
6. Recommend the best advertising medium for each of the following advertisers, and provide the reasons for your choices:

   a. An operator of a winter ski resort.
   b. A publisher of college textbooks.
   c. A manufacturer of microwave ovens.
   d. An operator of a beauty salon.
   e. A bottler of a popular soft drink.

7. Is reach more important than frequency in advertising by a department store? by a producer of toothpaste?
8. How do the characteristics of cable television as an advertising medium differ from over-the-air network television?
9. Who should accept the blame for false advertising—the advertising agency that prepared the ad or the advertiser? Discuss.
10. What is the best means of ensuring truthfulness in advertising?

1. Choose a well-known product with which you are familiar and prepare a step-by-step sales plan. To enhance your accuracy gather as much information as possible about the product. Include in your plan the following steps:
   a. Prospecting.
   b. Type of information for the preapproach.
   c. Approach.
   d. Sales presentation.
   e. Trial close.
   f. Anticipating and answering of objections in the presentation.
   g. Close.

2. Select a magazine ad for soft drinks and one for automobiles.
   a. Compare and contrast the appeals in the two ads.
   b. Suggest other appeals that could be effectively used in each ad.
   c. Do the ads conform to the AIDA formula?

3. In the late 1970s, Maxwell House coffee changed its advertising strategy and permanently retired Cora, its affable, middle-aged spokeswoman. Cora first appeared in television commercials in 1972 as a competitive response to Folger's Mrs. Olson. The role for both Cora and Mrs. Olson in commercials was to instruct frustrated housewives on how to prepare a satisfying cup of coffee for their husbands. Because this advertising depicted husbands who had been unhappy with their coffee, some critics contended that the commercials projected a poor image for coffee generally and discouraged coffee drinking.

   Recognizing that coffee consumption in the United States was declining, Maxwell House was very sensitive to this criticism of its commercials. In 1962, nearly 75 percent of the adult population drank coffee. By 1978, only 59 percent of the population were coffee drinkers. The downturn in coffee consumption was very noticeable in the young adult market.

   A Maxwell House spokesperson indicated that the company wanted to shift its advertising direction from attempting to capture a large share of the coffee market to increasing the size of the overall market. Toward this end the advertiser prepared light, entertaining commercials that stressed the pleasure of drinking coffee throughout the day. These commercials were directed particularly to young adults, who often substitute colas or other beverages for coffee.

   Although some other coffee marketers were surprised by the altered advertising strategy of Maxwell House, the coffee producer felt comfortable with its new campaign. The Maxwell House brand was not being neglected in its new approach, for in a 30-second commercial the brand name was mentioned up to eight times. Because Maxwell House enjoyed a 38 percent share of overall coffee sales, a large number of any new coffee drinkers would probably become Maxwell House customers.

   Executives of Folger coffee disagreed with the advertising strategy of their major competitor. They stated that they would continue to promote their brand rather than pursue a campaign that would broaden the market for all coffee producers. Folger accounted for nearly 22 percent of the coffee market.

   a. Can a single advertiser increase the primary demand for an established product category such as coffee? Do you believe that Maxwell House has embarked on the correct advertising strategy?

   b. Explain how the other major advertising media, in addition to television, could be used to promote Maxwell House coffee.

   c. Do you believe that Maxwell House uses an advertising agency? What would be the advantages of an advertising agency to this coffee producer?

Pricing of Products Is Still an Art, Often Having Little Link to Costs

Although merchants of just about everything devote a great deal of time and study to determine what prices to put on their products, pricing often remains an art. In some cases, it does involve a straightforward equation: material and labor costs plus overhead and other expenses, plus profit, equal price. But in many other cases the equation includes psychological and other factors so subtle that pricing consultants, themselves high-priced, are retained to help assay what the market will bear.

One such firm is Management Decision Systems Inc., Waltham, Mass., which uses consumer surveys and computer models to help manufacturers determine the most marketable price on products. The firm usually measures consumer reaction to two different prices on the same product. It usually discovers that the lower price is preferred, but, as in the case of Fleischmann's gin, not always. "The higher you price certain products, like a Mercedes-Benz, the more desirable they become," says Gerald Katz, an MDS vice president.

To decide prices, manufacturers usually weigh costs and prices on similar products, and then, as an apparel maker puts it, "take a good guess." Herbert Denenberg, a promoter of consumer causes in Philadelphia and former Pennsylvania state insurance commissioner, says that "everybody thinks people go about pricing scientifically. But very often, the process is incredibly arbitrary."

At its 20 factory outlet stores, Cowden Manufacturing, a subsidiary of Interco Inc., St. Louis, prices jeans at just $9.86. Why the 86 cents? "When people see $9.99 they say, 'That's $10,'" says James McAskill, Cowden's general sales manager. "But $9.86 isn't $10. It's just psychological."

Higher prices seem to suggest higher quality. The relation is dubious. The price on a higher quality product may be considerably higher than the product's extra quality. In 1979, University of Iowa professor Peter C. Reisz tried to relate the prices of 679 brands of packaged foods with their quality ratings as determined over 15 years by Consumers Union. His conclusion: "The correlation between quality and price for packaged food products is near zero."

Marketing men, however, sense that consumers are buying more than a mere commodity when they buy some goods. A $100 bottle of perfume may contain $4 to $16 worth of scent. The rest of the price goes for advertising, packaging and profit. Such perfume sells. "Women are buying atmosphere and hope and the feeling they are something special," says Henry Walter Jr., chairman of International Flavors & Fragrances Inc., a major scents manufacturer. "There are very few people who are willing to settle for what will satisfy pure needs."

Low prices also sell. Or so J. C. Penney Co., the big retailer, hopes in the case of its bargain $13.50 "plain pockets" jeans and its $18 leisure shirts with fox emblems. Penney does more than concede that the clothes are knockoffs of Levi Strauss and Co.'s $17 jeans and Lacoste's $23 alligator shirts. It *insists* that they are practically identical. Levi Strauss asserts that the Penney jeans are inferior. Lacoste executives decline to dignify the question by discussing it . . . .

SOURCE: Jeffrey H. Birnbaum, "Pricing Products Is Still an Art, Often Having Little Link to Costs," *The Wall Street Journal,* November 25, 1981, p. 25. Reprinted by permission of *The Wall Street Journal,* © Dow Jones & Company, Inc. (1981). All Rights Reserved.

Prices and Pricing Policies

Objectives:

- Identify several typical pricing objectives of a firm.
- Recognize the different types of cost approaches and market approaches used in determining selling prices.
- Understand the differences between markup on cost and markup on retail.
- Identify several of the more prominent pricing policies.
- Explain when a skimming-the-cream pricing strategy is more appropriate than a penetration-pricing strategy.
- Explain the differences between the unfair-trade laws and the Robinson-Patman Act.
- Explain the equilibrium theory of pricing.
- Illustrate the concepts of elastic demand and inelastic demand.
- Understand why firms in oligopolistic industries adopt similar pricing structures and maintain stable prices.
- Explain the usefulness of the Consumer Price Index and the Producer Price Indexes.

When RCA introduced its videodisc player that was priced at $499, the company anticipated strong sales and high profits. After all, the units were several hundred dollars cheaper than videotape players that were selling for over $800. The expected sales did not occur, however, and a year and a half later RCA had lost two-thirds of its original 8,000 videodisc dealers. RCA had forecast that, by 1990, between 30 and 40 percent of all homes would own a videodisc player. Because of competition for the consumer's time and money from other video sources, other market analysts suggested that a more realistic forecast was less than 10 percent.

A pleasant marketing surprise for RCA was the large number of videodisc albums that were being purchased by videodisc owners. About 30 albums were being bought annually by each of these owners. Armed with this knowledge, RCA dramatically changed its pricing strategy. Company officials decided to follow the pricing approach of the giant razor-blade producer, Gillette, that makes its profits on replacement blades rather than on razors. RCA slashed its videodisc player price from $499 to $299 and sales zoomed. At the same time, the company vigorously expanded its profitable offerings of new albums.

Many other companies are faced with pricing situations that are similar to the RCA experience. Price is an important element in the marketing mix of most firms. The use of prices expedites the buying and selling of goods and services. This chapter examines some of the major pricing considerations that confront businesspersons.

PRICING OBJECTIVES

The pricing objectives of a firm should reflect both its specific marketing objectives and its broader company objectives. Figure 15-1, which was derived from a landmark study of pricing objectives in large companies, illustrates the pricing goals in ten major American corporations. This study and other research reveal that typical pricing goals include:

1. *Obtaining a target return on investment.* Alcoa, the large aluminum producer, prices its products so the earnings from sales yield a 20 percent return on investment after taxes.
2. *Stabilizing prices.* Standard Oil of Indiana wants to stabilize prices and avoid ruinous price wars.
3. *Maintaining or increasing market share.* Sears seeks to increase its market share in the communities in which it is located.
4. *Meeting or reducing competition.* Because competition is the essence of our enterprise system, Goodyear's pricing goal of meeting competitive prices is reasonable.
5. *Promoting the product line.* General Electric seeks to promote through pricing its entire line of major appliances.
6. *Serving a desired market segment.* RCA offers different television sets to different market segments at different prices.
7. *Optimizing profits.* Companies, such as IBM and Procter & Gamble, attempt to optimize their profits over the long run. Short-run profit maximization may cause a company to focus narrowly on the profit that can be achieved on each transaction.

APPROACHES IN DETERMINING PRICES

The two basic approaches in determining selling prices are the cost approach and the market (or competitive) approach. In the cost approach, management sets a price after determining the product cost. In the market approach, a price is established by referring to the current market price for similar items.

Figure 15-1   Pricing Goals of Ten Selected Industrial Corporations

Company	Principal Pricing Goal	Collateral Pricing Goals
Alcoa	20% on investment (before taxes); higher on new products (about 10% effective rate after taxes)	a. Promotive policy on new products b. Price stabilization
American Can	Maintenance of market share	a. "Meeting" competition (using cost of substitute product to determine price) b. Price stabilization
A&P	Increasing market share	a. General promotive (low margin policy)
DuPont	Target return on investment—no specific figure given	a. Charging what traffic will bear over long run b. Maximum return for new products—"life cycle" pricing
General Electric	20% on investment (after taxes); 7% on sales (after taxes)	a. Promotive policy on new products b. Price stabilization on nationally advertised products
General Foods	33⅓% gross margin ("⅓ to make, ⅓ to sell, and ⅓ for profit"); expectation of realizing target only on new products	a. Full line of food products and novelties b. Maintaining market share
Goodyear	"Meeting competitors"	a. Maintaining "position" b. Price stabilization
Sears, Roebuck	Increasing market share (8–10% regarded as satisfactory share)	a. Realization of traditional return on investment of 10–15% (after taxes) b. General promotive (low margin policy)
Standard Oil (Indiana)	Maintenance of market share	a. Price stabilization b. Target return on investment (none specified)
Union Carbide	Target return on investment	a. Promotive policy on new products; "life cycle" pricing on chemicals generally

SOURCE: Adapted from Robert F. Lanzilotti, "Pricing Objectives in Large Companies," *American Economic Review,* Vol. 48 (December, 1958), pp. 924-927.

Cost Approach

Since all firms desire to set a price which will cover their costs and make a profit, some type of cost approach is used by the majority of businesses. The various cost approaches include markup on total costs, rate-of-return pricing, variable cost pricing, break-even analysis pricing, and average cost pricing.

Markup on Total Costs

All types of businesses — manufacturers, wholesalers, and retailers — often arrive at their selling prices through the use of markup percents. Markups are expressed as percents of either the cost or the selling price. A **markup** should cover the cost of handling the article to be priced, a portion of the firm's expenses, and a certain amount of profit. The costs and markups for a small car as it moves from the assembly line to the showroom are illustrated in Figure 15-2.

Figure 15-2   Costs and Markups for a Small Car

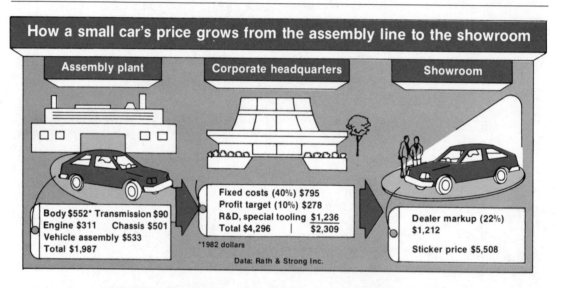

How a small car's price grows from the assembly line to the showroom

Assembly plant

Corporate headquarters

Showroom

Body $552* Transmission $90
Engine $311   Chassis $501
Vehicle assembly $533
Total $1,987

Fixed costs (40%) $795
Profit target (10%) $278
R&D, special tooling $1,236
Total $4,296 | $2,309

*1982 dollars

Data: Rath & Strong Inc.

Dealer markup (22%) $1,212

Sticker price $5,508

When the markup percent is based on cost, multiply the markup percent by the cost to obtain the dollar markup. When the markup percent is based on selling price, multiply the markup percent by the selling price to obtain the dollar markup. Figure 15-3 shows the basic formula, and variations of it, for finding the selling price, the markup percent, and the cost. It also shows how markup as a percent of selling price (or retail) can be converted into markup as a percent of cost — or vice versa. Table 15-1 gives selected markup percents based on selling price and their equivalents as markup percents based on cost.

The following example shows how to determine the selling price of an item with a cost of $60 and a desired 40 percent markup on selling price. By referring to Table 15-1, you will note that the equivalent markup percent of cost is 66.7 percent. Then compute as follows:

Figure 15-3   Formulas for Markup Calculations

Formulas		Examples
Cost (C) + Dollar markup (M) = Selling price (SP)		$60 + $ 40 = $100
C	= SP − M	$60 = $100 − $40
M	= SP − C	$40 = $100 − $60
M% on SP	= M ÷ SP	40% = $40 ÷ $100
M% on C	= M ÷ C	66.7% = $40 ÷ $60

To convert markup as a percent of selling price into markup as a percent of cost, or vice versa, the two formulas shown below are useful:

Formulas	Examples
$\dfrac{\text{M\% on SP}}{100\% - \text{M\% on SP}} = \text{M\% on C}$	$\dfrac{40\%}{100\% - 40\%} = 66.7\%$
$\dfrac{\text{M\% on C}}{100\% + \text{M\% on C}} = \text{M\% on SP}$	$\dfrac{66.7\%}{100\% + 66.7\%} = 40\%$

Table 15-1   Retail Price Markup Table

How to Use This Table: Find the desired markup percent based on selling price in the column at the left. Multiply the cost of the article by the corresponding percent in the column at the right. Add this amount to the cost in order to determine the selling price.

Desired Markup Percent (Based on Selling Price)	Equivalent Percent of Cost	Desired Markup Percent (Based on Selling Price)	Equivalent Percent of Cost
5.0	5.3	20.0	25.0
6.0	6.4	25.0	33.3
7.0	7.5	30.0	42.9
8.0	8.7	33.3	50.0
9.0	10.0	35.0	53.8
10.0	11.1	37.5	60.0
12.5	14.3	40.0	66.7
15.0	17.7	42.8	75.0
16.7	20.0	50.0	100.0

$$\textit{Step 1.} \quad \text{Cost} + \text{Dollar markup} \;\; = \text{Selling price}$$

$$\textit{Step 2.} \quad \$60 \; + (\$60 \times 66.7\%) = \text{Selling price}$$
$$\$60 \; + \$40 \qquad\qquad = \$100$$

$$\textit{Check:} \quad \text{Markup \% on Selling price} \times \text{Selling price} = \text{Dollar markup}$$
$$40\% \qquad\qquad\qquad\qquad \times \$100 \qquad = \$40$$

If the desired 40 percent markup is based on cost, the selling price is determined as follows:

$$\textit{Step. 1.} \quad \text{Cost} + \text{Dollar markup} \;\; = \text{Selling price}$$

$$\textit{Step 2.} \quad \$60 \; + (\$60 \times 40\%) = \text{Selling price}$$
$$\$60 \; + \$24 \qquad\qquad = \$84$$

Rate-of-Return Pricing

By using the rate-of-return pricing method, a firm can achieve a target return on investment. The desired rate of return may be attained through either a low net profit and a high volume or a high net profit and a low volume. The two approaches may yield similar results since the return from the sales of five items for a profit of one dollar each is equivalent to the sale of one item for a profit of five dollars. Discount department stores follow the former approach, while traditional department stores adhere to the latter approach. If the unit sales of a product can be estimated, then a selling price can be determined which will achieve the desired return on investment.

Variable Cost Pricing

Management generally desires a selling price that covers variable costs, fixed costs, and a profit. Circumstances may arise, however, where only covering variable costs is used as a basis for pricing a product. **Variable costs** are the escapable, or out-of-pocket, costs such as labor and materials which are incurred only when units are produced. **Fixed costs** are the inescapable costs, such as plant, equipment, and other overhead expenses, which are present regardless of the number of units produced.

A manufacturer who produces both a national brand and a private brand often uses variable cost pricing to determine the selling price for the private brand. The manufacturer already has the plant and equipment to produce its own national brand. It needs only to add another shift of workers and to purchase additional materials in order to produce the private brand. If the manufacturer can sell the private-brand item at a price greater than the variable cost, the additional markup received is a contribution to the fixed costs. The use of variable cost pricing provides a partial explanation of why private-brand goods are often lower priced to the consumer than similar national-brand goods. Using variable pricing, Figure 15-4 illustrates the computation of a manufacturer's costs for a private-brand refrigerator and for a national-brand one.

Break-Even Analysis Pricing

The **break-even point** for a product is the volume of sales needed to cover its total variable and fixed costs. When sales move beyond the break-even point, profits begin

Figure 15-4   **Using Variable Cost Pricing in Computing a Manufacturer's Costs for a Private-Brand Refrigerator and for a National-Brand Refrigerator**

Costs Allocated to Each Unit	Private-Brand Refrigerator (e.g., Sears Kenmore)		National-Brand Refrigerator (e.g., Whirlpool)	
Variable costs				
Labor	$ 75		$ 75	
Materials	115		115	
Total variable costs		$190		$190
Fixed costs				
Plant	$ 0		$ 25	
Equipment	0		40	
Other overhead expenses	0		35	
Total fixed costs		$ 0		$100
Profit		$ 10		$ 10
Total unit cost		$200		$300

to generate rapidly. Break-even analysis is intended primarily to furnish management with information concerning the outcome of different combinations of prices, costs, and quantities. Its major importance is not in price determination, but in comparing alternative prices in reference to their effect on the break-even point. After its near brush with bankruptcy, Chrysler rigorously cut its costs and reduced its break-even point from the sales of 2.5 million cars in 1981 to 1.2 million units in 1982.

A break-even chart, which is displayed in Figure 15-5, uses straight lines to show the relationships among total sales, total costs, variable costs, and fixed costs. It assumes that variable costs vary proportionally with sales and that fixed costs will not vary regardless of sales volume. In Figure 15-5 the following assumptions are made: Selling price of a unit is $100; variable costs are 60 percent of sales, or $60 a unit; and the monthly fixed costs are $50,000. The chart shows that total costs equal total sales when sales reach the break-even point of 1,250 units. If less than this number of units is produced, the company suffers a loss. When more than 1,250 units are sold, the company makes a profit.

Another method to determine the break-even point is by using the following formula:

$$\text{Break-even point in units} = \frac{\text{Fixed costs}}{\text{Price per unit} - \text{Variable cost per unit}}$$

Figure 15-5   A Break-Even Chart

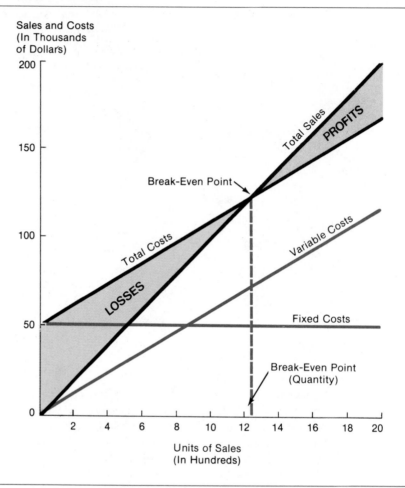

By substituting the data in the preceding example, the calculation for the break-even point is:

$$1,250 \text{ units} = \frac{\$50,000}{\$100 - \$60}$$

Average Cost Pricing

The average cost is determined by dividing total costs by the total units sold. Total cost is composed of both variable and fixed costs. In determining a price based on average cost, management assumes that forecasted sales will be similar to past sales. If actual sales are less than the forecast, the fixed costs may not be completely covered and losses may occur. On the other hand, if sales are much larger than the forecast, profits will be greater than expected. Suppliers to the government often submit sealed bids that are determined by the average cost pricing method.

Some electric utilities have adopted a form of pricing that reflects the average cost of producing power at different periods during the day. This type of pricing is called *time-of-day pricing.* Under time-of-day pricing a utility charges its customers increased rates during the peak daytime periods and reduced rates during the off-peak evening periods. For example, an industrial customer may be charged three times as much to run a welding machine at 2:00 p.m. as to run it at 11:00 p.m. This type of pricing has been adopted by utilities as an energy-saving method.

Market or Competitive Approach

Although management desires to cover its costs, market or competitive factors may exert strong influences on pricing. The basic market approaches include: prevailing or customary prices, price of substitute products, what the traffic will bear, and price leadership.

Prevailing or Customary Prices

If a particular price for a product becomes accepted, a manufacturer may be compelled to price the product at the prevailing or customary price. Working backward from the selling price, the manufacturer is forced to determine the costs. Many producers of standardized products conform to established prices. Candy bars and soft drinks are usually sold for a customary amount which is a multiple of five, such as 25, 30, or 35 cents. In many instances, producers either adjust the size of the product or make quality adjustments in order to maintain the prevailing price. For example, over a 23-year period Hershey altered the weight of its basic chocolate bar 14 times while changing its price only 3 times. On the other hand, in an effort to hold down prices the Wilber Chocolate Co. substituted cheaper vegetable fat for cocoa butter in its chocolate chips and powder.

Price of Substitute Products

In instances where a new product can be substituted for an older product, the price of the older product often will determine the price of the new product. This is a form of cross-elasticity of demand. In the carpet industry the different synthetic fibers, such as olefin, Kodel, Dacron, and nylon, may be substituted for one another. Consequently, all of these fibers have similar pricing structures.

What the Traffic Will Bear

The phrase "what the traffic will bear" has a rather unpleasant sound since it implies excessively high profits. Nevertheless, it is a rather widely used indicator of the upper limits to the prices that may be set by sellers. Sellers who know their market are aware of the price limits above which they cannot go and retain their customers. What the traffic will bear reflects the attitude of the users of the product toward its value to them. Thus, a special instrument that will aid a surgeon in performing a difficult operation might be worth $100, even though it might cost only $15 to produce. Football fans are willing to pay a "what the traffic will bear" price for prized tickets to the NFL Super Bowl held every January.

Price Leadership

In many business fields there are certain acknowledged leaders. Although these leaders apparently set their prices without much regard for the other members of the trade, their price moves are followed quickly by competitors. To a considerable extent the United States Steel Corporation in the steel business and the various Standard Oil companies in the field of gasoline and oil have been price leaders. The reasons for this price leadership are usually prestige, size, aggressiveness, and prominence.

PRICING POLICIES

Carefully designed pricing policies provide assurance that uniform pricing decisions will be made within a firm. Product managers, sales managers, and others are involved in determining prices in a large organization with several product lines. Several of the more prominent pricing policies that will be discussed include: high prices, competitive prices, and low prices; skimming versus penetration pricing; odd prices; delivered prices; price lining; unit pricing; one price versus varying price; leader pricing and bait pricing; and discount pricing.

High Prices, Competitive Prices, and Low Prices

A seller caters to different segments of the market by choosing either a high price, a competitive price, or a low price policy. Some firms produce a quality product and charge a high price in the hope that it will become known as the "Cadillac of the industry." As shown in Figure 15-6, Rolex follows a prestige price policy by pricing its watches at $7,950 and $5,750. Stimorol chewing gum follows a similar pricing policy and proudly proclaims that it is a chewing gum for the rich (see Figure 15-7). Many manufacturers and merchants, such as Sears and JCPenney, price their products competitively to appeal to the majority of American consumers. Some sellers, such as discount department stores, use low prices as their principal sales appeal.

Skimming *v.* Penetration Pricing

Skimming the cream pricing is a high pricing policy generally associated with a product in the initial stages of its life cycle. If a high price will not necessarily restrict demand or result in the emergence of potential competitors, a skimming policy may

Figure 15-6   **Prestige Pricing for Watches**

SOURCE: Courtesy of Tiffany & Co., New York, NY.

be quite appropriate. Du Pont has found price skimming to be very successful when introducing new specialty products.

Penetration pricing, a type of low pricing policy, is used by some firms to secure a dominant position for a new product in the market. When a new product is introduced into a highly competitive market, penetration pricing is the most appropriate pricing strategy. This type of pricing discourages potential competition. When Commodore introduced its new electronic quartz digital wristwatch, it priced the watch at a low $7.95 (only a thousandth of the price of the $7,950 Rolex watch in Figure 15-6). A company spokesperson indicated that the purpose of the modest price was to achieve in electronic watches the same dominant market position that Timex obtained in traditional watches.

Figure 15-7   Prestige Pricing for Chewing Gum

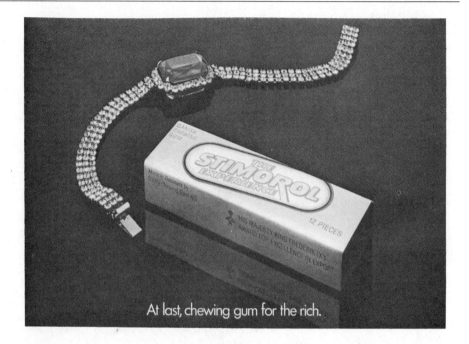

At last, chewing gum for the rich.

SOURCE: Reproduced with permission of Dandy Confectionary, Inc., White Plains, NY.

Odd Prices

One school of merchandising thought (see Figure 15-8) believes that $2.95 is a more appealing price than $3, that 19 cents will sell more goods than 20 cents, and that $99.95 is more effective than $100. For example, Sears ends many of its prices with either $0.95 or $0.99. The underlying theory of this odd-price policy is that $1.99 makes the prospective buyer think of $1 plus some cents, rather than of a price slightly less than $2.

Delivered Prices

Some manufacturers adopt the policy of establishing their prices on what is called a "delivered basis." This means that the price quoted to buyers is **f.o.b. (free on board) destination**. It includes all transportation costs and is the price that buyers must pay to take delivery of the goods at their receiving docks or the freight terminal in their cities.

Opposed to this plan is the practice of quoting **f.o.b. shipping point (or factory)**. In this case the seller places the goods on a common carrier at the factory loading dock and all further transportation charges over and above the quoted price are paid by the buyer. The pricing of automobiles is an example of this latter policy. Figure 15-9 illustrates these two forms of f.o.b. pricing.

Price Lining

By limiting the prices for their goods to a few specific pricing points, retailers adopt a policy of **price lining**. Edward A. Filene, founder of Boston's Filene's department store, advocated only three major price points for each class of merchandise. For example, in men's sport coats there would be only three price points: $79.95, $89.95, and $99.95. The advantages cited for a policy of price lining are that it simplifies consumer buying decisions, makes the retail buyer's job easier, and produces more rapid stock turnover.

Figure 15-8   Example of Odd Pricing

SOURCE: Drawing by Mankoff; © 1982. The New Yorker Magazine, Inc.

Figure 15-9   Illustration of f.o.b. Pricing for a Product with an $80 Cost and a $20 Transportation Charge

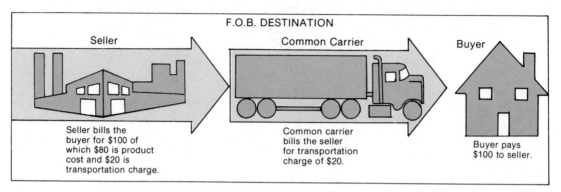

F.O.B. DESTINATION

Seller

Common Carrier

Buyer

Seller bills the buyer for $100 of which $80 is product cost and $20 is transportation charge.

Common carrier bills the seller for transportation charge of $20.

Buyer pays $100 to seller.

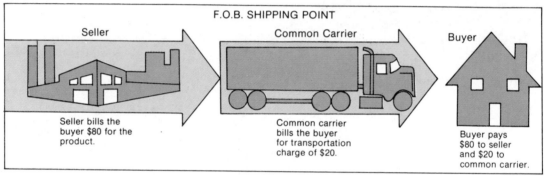

F.O.B. SHIPPING POINT

Seller

Common Carrier

Buyer

Seller bills the buyer $80 for the product.

Common carrier bills the buyer for transportation charge of $20.

Buyer pays $80 to seller and $20 to common carrier.

Unit Pricing

Unit pricing, which is being practiced by many supermarkets, involves stating the price of a product in terms of units of measure such as ounces, pounds, or quarts. Several states, such as Connecticut, Maryland, and Massachusetts, require unit pricing for certain foods. New York City passed unit pricing legislation after a group of homemakers was sent to supermarkets to determine the best buy on 14 products. These shoppers made the incorrect choice 40 percent of the time!

One Price *v.* Varying Price

Most retailers use the **one-price policy**, where the established price applies to all comers and is not subject to haggling by individual customers. At other distribution levels, however, this policy does not always hold true. Although some manufacturers and wholesalers follow it rather rigidly, many others may lower their prices from time to time in favor of particular purchasers. This flexibility of price may come about because of the superior bargaining skill of certain buyers or because of the size of their purchases.

A **varying-price policy** has the effect of enabling large buyers to secure lower prices than their smaller competitors. To prevent this practice from placing small buyers at too great a disadvantage, the Robinson-Patman Act was passed by Congress. This Act forbids certain types of pricing practices that favor large buyers.

Leader Pricing and Bait Pricing

Both leader pricing and bait pricing are examples of promotional pricing policies. In **leader pricing**, a high-demand good, such as most convenience goods, is priced low and promoted highly to attract customers into a store. The leader item may be sold at cost or even below cost, making it a **loss leader**. Once a customer is in the store to purchase a leader item, there is a good chance that he or she will make numerous unplanned purchases.

Bait pricing involves advertising a low-priced model of shopping goods, such as furniture or appliances, to lure customers into a store. Once the customers are in the store, a salesperson attempts to persuade them to purchase higher-priced models. In many cases the compensation plan for the retail sales personnel strongly encourages them to trade a customer up from the bait model to a more expensive product. When the Federal Trade Commission becomes aware that the "bait and switch" practice (when the low-priced model used as bait is not available) is being used, the Commission orders retailers to discontinue its use. In the past, Sears was accused by the FTC of using this practice to sell sewing machines and other home appliances.

Discount Pricing

Sellers who elect to pursue a varying-price policy have two principal methods by which they may put this plan into effect: through simple price concessions and by means of a discount policy. An example of the first method is the lowering of a price of $1.50 per unit to $1.35. A form of price concession that has become common during business downturns is the temporary price rebate. A **rebate** permits a seller to maintain the product's original selling price while still providing a price concession to stimulate sales. Manufacturers often have consumers contact them directly to obtain the rebate. The manufacturers are then assured that the consumers are receiving a price concession regardless of the retailer's price.

A **discount** may be defined as a reduction in price made by a seller to a buyer. Some retailers, including several major gasoline retailers, offer discounts to consumers who pay with cash rather than with a credit card. Trade discounts, quantity discounts, and cash discounts are often offered by sellers to buyers in commercial transactions.

A **trade discount**, which is based on the list price of the product, recognizes the different functions performed by wholesalers and retailers. The list price is usually the price paid by the consumer. For example, if the list price, which is frequently the price charged the retail customer, is $45 and the trade discount is 33$\frac{1}{3}$ percent, the wholesaler's price to the retailer is $30. Figure 15-10 illustrates the procedure and purpose of a trade discount.

A **quantity discount**, which may be either cumulative or noncumulative, is often granted to buyers who order in large quantities. Presumably the large sales which occur as a result of this policy save the vendors storage, shipping, and billing costs. Cumulative quantity discounts often are given to buyers who make two or more purchases from a vendor. The noncumulative type is applicable only to single purchases. Table 15-2 shows how noncumulative quantity discounts are usually presented to purchasers.

Sometimes both a trade discount and a quantity discount are granted to a retailer. The net price to the retailer is calculated in two steps in the following example:

$$
\begin{array}{ll}
\text{List price} & = \$45 \\
\text{Trade discount} & = 33\frac{1}{3}\% \\
\text{Quantity discount} & = 5\%
\end{array}
$$

Step 1. List price	=	$45.00
Less trade discount ($33\frac{1}{3}\% \times \$45$)	=	$-15.00
Price with trade discount	=	$30.00
Step 2. Price with trade discount	=	$30.00
Less quantity discount ($5\% \times \$30$)	=	$-\ 1.50
Net price to retailer	=	$28.50

A **cash discount** is an inducement offered by the seller to encourage buyers to pay their bills within a short time after the goods have been delivered. The most common cash discount is 2/10, net 30. This means that if the invoice is paid within 10 days after its date, the buyer may deduct 2 percent from the amount of the invoice. Otherwise, the full amount is due in 30 days.

Figure 15-10   Illustration of the Procedure and the Purpose of a Trade Discount Provided by a Wholesaler to a Retailer

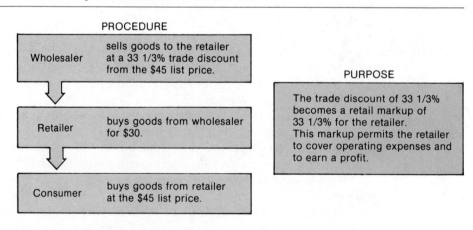

Table 15-2   Example of a Noncumulative Quantity Discount Pricing Schedule for Mimeograph Paper

Mimeo Bond No. 1 Sulphite White	Quantity of Sheets				
	1,000	5,000	15,000	50,000	200,000
	Cost per 1,000 Sheets				
8½ × 11 — 16 lb.	10.36	5.70	4.53	3.96	3.65
8½ × 11 — 20 lb.	12.35	6.79	5.40	4.72	4.35
8½ × 14 — 16 lb.	13.19	7.25	5.77	5.05	4.65
8½ × 14 — 20 lb.	15.70	8.64	5.87	6.00	5.53

PRICE LEGISLATION

Federal price-control plans were put into effect during the periods of World War II, the Korean War, and the post-Vietnam War. These controls were intended to prevent prices from rising under the stress of an unbalanced supply-demand situation. The federal government, aside from persuasion and threats, presently limits its price-control activities to providing support prices for certain agricultural and dairy commodities.

There are both state and federal pricing laws. The state laws are categorized as unfair-trade laws (with some variations on this title). The major federal legislation on pricing is the Robinson-Patman Act.

Unfair-Trade Laws

Unfair-trade laws are used in nearly half the states under such titles as unfair-trade practices act, unfair-sales act, unfair-practices act, unfair-sales practices act, and fair-sales act. Under these laws, sellers — producers, wholesalers, and retailers — are forbidden to sell goods at less than their cost plus, in many states, certain specified percentage markups. These laws have been called "anti-loss-leader" laws since the form of price cutting against which they were enacted has been the loss leader. Several states have similar laws applicable only to specific commodities such as cigarettes, dairy products, gasoline, bakery products, and alcoholic beverages.

During the depression of the 1930s, many states passed so-called **fair-trade laws.** Under these laws manufacturers of branded goods could execute contracts with retailers specifying a minimum price for these goods. In the mid-1970s, as an anti-inflation move, Congress passed legislation that ended all fair-trade pricing.

Robinson-Patman Act

When the Robinson-Patman Act was passed by Congress in 1936, small businesses were pressing legislators for laws against price-cutting by chain stores. Between 1920 and 1930, chain operators had dramatically increased their share of total retail sales from 5 to 30 percent. Many individuals felt that there was a need to curtail all unjustified cost practices conducted by large chain organizations. In fact, the Robinson-Patman Act was initially referred to as the anti-A & P act, since one of the most famous cases under the Act involved the A & P food chain. The major provision of the Act makes it unlawful for a seller to sell similar goods at different prices to different buyers where the effect may be to lessen competition or to create a monopoly. For example, it would be illegal for Procter & Gamble to sell a case of Tide to a Kroger store for $70 when it sells the same item to a competing Safeway store for $50.

PRICING THEORIES

Economists have advanced several theories of pricing. These theories explain how the price of a commodity is set, the movement of prices, and why the price level is where it is at any one time.

Equilibrium Theory

The **equilibrium theory of prices** is based upon the assumptions of pure competition. This theory assumes that two forces operate in the field of price — supply and demand. These forces bring about a price (equilibrium point) at which the quantity demanded by buyers equals the quantity that sellers are willing to supply.

The theory further assumes that if the current price for a commodity is found to be above the theoretical equilibrium point, two events will occur to force the price downward. The higher price will discourage would-be buyers, thereby reducing the quantity demanded. In addition, the higher price and greater profit opportunities will attract new producers into the field, whose added products will increase the quantity supplied. The effect of this decreased demand and increased supply will be to reduce the price, probably below the equilibrium point. When this takes place, the results are the reverse of the previous condition. The lowered price then attracts buyers, increasing the quantity demanded. In addition, the lower price and the diminished profit opportunities force some high-cost producers to leave the field. As a result, the quantity of supply is reduced. This brings about an upward movement of price toward the equilibrium point.

Figure 15-11   Graphic Illustration of the Equilibrium Theory

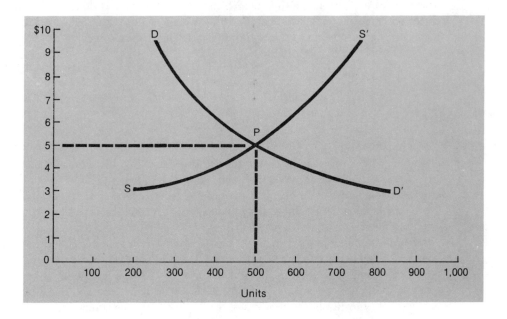

Figure 15-11 shows a graphic representation of the operation of the equilibrium theory. Curve *D-D'* represents the quantities of the product that could be sold at the various price levels. Curve *S-S'* represents the quantities that sellers would be willing to supply at different price levels. Point *P*, where 500 units would be demanded at $5 each, portrays the point of equilibrium where demand and supply are equal.

Demand Elasticity

Demand elasticity refers to the effect that a change in the price for an item has on the quantity demanded. If changing the price of an article produces a significant alteration in the quantity demanded, it has demand elasticity, or an elastic demand. Likewise, if a price change does not bring about a significant difference in the quantity demanded, the article has inelasticity of demand. The assumption is, of course, that the quantity demanded will move in the opposite direction from price. During the 1970s, when gasoline prices increased and consumer demand for it decreased, the elasticity of demand for this fuel was demonstrated. The classic example of demand inelasticity for a product is salt. Regardless of the price of salt, people use a fixed amount.

Monopoly

The presence of a monopoly implies the complete control of the price by the monopolist and the absence of competition. In the business world at large, there are very few pure monopolies. Those which do exist, such as the public utilities, are subject to governmental regulation that greatly curtails their freedom to set prices.

Oligopoly

In an industry where a few large firms are dominant, all products are similar, and total demand is relatively inelastic, oligopolistic pricing occurs. Firms in such industries as steel, aluminum, and automobiles are confronted with this type of pricing. Because companies in an oligopolistic industry experience an inelastic demand, they usually adopt similar pricing structures and maintain stable prices. These companies realize that price cutting triggers vigorous price competition and reduces profitability. In many cases a major firm in an oligopolistic industry assumes price leadership and maintains stable prices. Since a price-cutting firm in an oligopolistic industry experiences no significant increase in demand or market share, promotional or service competition often replaces price competition. Some critics contend that the pricing policies of firms in oligopolistic industries effectively reduce competition.

Monopolistic Competition

In the case of certain agricultural products, there is little if any difference between the products of different producers. Thus, competition is based mainly on price. This situation is probably as close to the economists' concept of pure competition as is to be found in our economic system. Most other small and medium-size producers create dissimilar products by making changes in packaging, promotion, taste, or appearance. These producers are engaged in monopolistic competition. The markets for candy bars, cosmetics, and clothing are characterized by this form of competition. A Snickers is different from a Hershey bar, and Revlon's Charlie perfume is distinctive from Coty's Sophia fragrance.

PRICE INDEXES AND TRENDS

The federal government prepares several commonly accepted measures of the general price level. These include the monthly Consumer Price Index and the Producer

Price Indexes, which are used widely as a reflection of inflationary or deflationary trends in the economy.

Consumer Price Index

The **Consumer Price Index (CPI)**, which is prepared monthly by the U. S. Department of Labor, is a widely used measure of the changes in the purchasing power of the dollar. Prices for the thousands of goods and services that represent the CPI are gathered by 350 data collectors in 85 urban areas across the country. Changes in this index are the basis for the automatic wage adjustments, known as escalator clauses, that are incorporated into numerous labor-management contracts. Labor Department officials estimate that a 1 percent increase in the CPI triggers over a $1 billion increase in incomes. In addition, the CPI often is used to adjust the following payments: welfare, private pensions, rent on commercial buildings, Social Security, and alimony. Beginning in 1985, personal income tax brackets, the zero bracket rate, and the personal exemption will be altered annually based on the increase in the CPI. Figure 15-12 shows the changes in the CPI from 1972 to 1982.

Figure 15-12   Annual Increases in the Consumer Price Index, 1972–1982

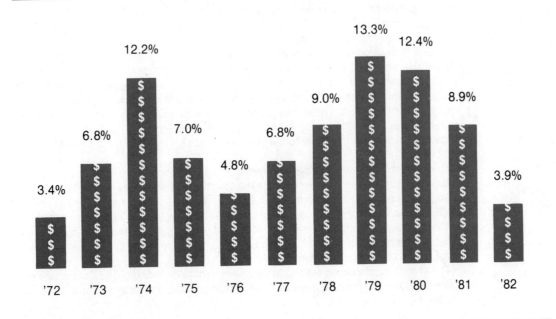

Producer Price Indexes

The average price changes received in primary markets by producers of commodities that are in various stages of processing are measured by the **Producer Price Indexes**. There are indexes for finished goods, intermediate or semifinished goods, and crude materials. The finished goods price index has become the most important one and is often referred to as the Producer Price Index (PPI). This index measures the price changes of goods, such as automobiles, farm equipment, and machine tools, that are ready for sale to the ultimate user. It serves as a rough indicator of the prices that consumers will be paying for goods at the end of the production and distribution process. The PPI is used by many industries as a benchmark for adjusting long-term sales contracts and by economic forecasters, market analysts, and government agencies.

SUMMARY   The typical pricing objectives of companies include: obtaining a return on investment, stabilizing prices, maintaining or increasing market share, meeting or reducing competition, promoting the product line, serving a desired market segment, and optimizing profit. Managers use either the cost approach or the market approach in determining their selling prices. The cost approaches include: markup on total costs, rate-of-return pricing, variable cost pricing, break-even analysis pricing, and average cost pricing. The basic market approaches consist of: prevailing or customary prices, price of substitute products, what the traffic will bear, and price leadership. The markup method is the customary way for wholesalers and retailers to arrive at the selling prices. Markup covers the cost of handling, a portion of the firm's expenses, and a certain amount of profit. A markup is expressed as a percent of an item's cost or selling price.

Several of the prominent pricing policies that are followed by firms include: high prices, competitive prices, and low prices; skimming versus penetration pricing; odd prices; delivered prices; price lining; unit pricing; one price versus varying price; leader pricing and bait pricing; and discount pricing. The most important state laws that affect pricing are the unfair-trade laws. These laws prohibit goods to be sold at less than their cost plus, in many states, a specified percentage markup. The major federal pricing legislation is the Robinson-Patman Act. This law forbids certain types of price discrimination that reduce competition.

The equilibrium theory of prices assumes that the price for an item is established where the quantity demanded by buyers equals the quantity that sellers are willing to supply. If changing the price of an item produces a significant alteration in the quantity demanded, there is demand elasticity. If a price change does not bring about a significant difference in the quantity demanded, there is an inelasticity of demand. Firms in an oligopolistic industry experience an inelastic demand situation. This situation causes such firms to resist price cuts and to maintain stable prices.

The impact of inflation is measured by government price indexes. The Consumer Price Index measures the price changes in thousands of goods and services that are purchased by typical Americans. The Producer Price Indexes measure the average price changes for finished goods, intermediate or semifinished goods, and crude materials.

BACK TO THE CHAPTER OPENER

1. What are the differences between the cost approach and the market approach to pricing?
2. Why does a company use a markup-on-total-cost approach to pricing?
3. Why isn't there always a close correlation between the quality and the price of an item?
4. What is the underlying theory of an odd-price policy?
5. Why are private brands, such as certain JCPenney merchandise, often priced lower than similar national brands?

BUSINESS TERMS

markup	346	loss leader	357
variable costs	348	bait pricing	357
fixed costs	348	rebate	357
break-even point	348	discount	357
skimming the cream pricing	352	trade discount	357
penetration pricing	353	quantity discount	358
f.o.b. (free on board) destination	354	cash discount	358
f.o.b. shipping point (or factory)	355	unfair-trade laws	359
price lining	355	fair-trade laws	359
unit pricing	356	equilibrium theory of prices	360
one-price policy	356	demand elasticity	361
varying-price policy	357	Consumer Price Index (CPI)	363
leader pricing	357	Producer Price Indexes	364

QUESTIONS FOR DISCUSSION AND ANALYSIS

1. Is the cost approach to pricing more important than the market approach for perfumes? for hydraulic presses? for men's suits?
2. Should all retailers use the combination of low net profit and a high volume to attain a desired return on investment? Explain.
3. Could a manufacturer use variable cost pricing for all of its products? Discuss.
4. How could break-even analysis be used to establish your college tuition? What are some of the costs that would need to be known?
5. Explain how you would determine the price for a new toothpaste that was guaranteed to prevent cavities.
6. Is an odd-price policy used more effectively with shopping goods than with specialty goods?
7. Why do most retailers follow a one-price policy while manufacturers often follow a varying-price policy?
8. What groups lobby for the passage of state unfair-trade laws?

9. How would federal price controls affect the equilibrium theory of prices?
10. The Consumer Price Index often is used to make upward adjustments in wages, pensions, and other payments. Do these upward adjustments result in inflationary increases in the index? Explain.

PROJECTS, PROBLEMS, AND SHORT CASES

1. Using a markup table, formulas for markup calculations, or formulas for calculating discounts, compute the answers to the following problems:

   a. Markup on cost is 40 percent; cost is $30. Find the retail selling price.
   b. Markup on cost is 25 percent; retail price is $15. Find the cost.
   c. Markup on retail price is 40 percent; cost is $70. Find the retail price.
   d. Markup on retail price is 35 percent; retail price is $75. Find the cost.
   e. A sportswear producer receives from a retailer an order for 250 jackets. Each jacket sells for a list price of $80. The retailer receives from the producer a 45 percent trade discount and an additional 5 percent quantity discount on all items when the order exceeds 100 units. How much should the retailer pay to the producer?
   f. A retailer buys $2,000 worth of goods; the terms are 2/10, net 60. The invoice is dated June 11 and is paid on June 20. How much should be remitted to the seller?

2. This project involves both odd pricing and price lining. Visit a store that handles several different lines of men's and women's clothing. From these lines select three lines, such as suits, pants, and shirts, which would be appropriate for this project. Then prepare a written report that fully explains the answers to the following questions:

   a. Is an odd-price policy followed in each of the lines? When an odd-price policy is followed, what are the most frequently used odd prices?
   b. Is a policy of price lining followed in each of the lines? When price lining is followed, how many price lines are there and what are the prices? If price lining is not followed in any of your three lines, find in the store a merchandise line where price lining is applied and indicate the price lines.

3. In 1982, the battle of the overnight package deliveries began. The giant United Parcel Service (UPS) challenged the smaller Federal Express, Emery Air Freight, and Purolator Courier by offering overnight delivery of commercial packages at rates that undercut competition by up to 50 percent. For many years, UPS has been a fierce competitor of the U. S. Postal Service's parcel post operation. UPS operates 55,000 trucks, deals with over 500,000 shippers daily, and handles about 6 million packages each day. To compete effectively with the three smaller but established airfreight carriers, UPS purchased 16 second-hand Boeing 727s and established a sorting center in Louisville, KY.

   For its new overnight service, UPS developed a pricing strategy that took into consideration its present investment in equipment and operations. Because its drivers were already picking up packages from thousands of customers for truck delivery, UPS could easily gather additional packages for overnight air delivery. This would minimize collection costs for the new activity. The prices for its airfreight business were established so that they reflected only the extra costs of providing the new service.

   Happily for its competitors, there were some limitations associated with the new UPS service. Overnight delivery would be provided by UPS in only the major 24 metropolitan markets. The other carriers served many more cities. Because UPS trucks were not radio-equipped, shippers would need to schedule a day in advance their deliveries with the carriers. Shippers who were unable to determine their next day's shipping requirements would not find the UPS service very useful.

With the announcement of the UPS entry into the overnight delivery market, concerned officials at both Federal Express and Emery Air Freight prepared strategies to combat the new competitor. They were particularly interested in maintaining their high-volume accounts and blunting the pricing edge of UPS.

a. What type of pricing approach is UPS following for its overnight delivery service? Aren't those shippers who use only UPS truck service in those 24 cities served helping to pay for the airfreight service? Discuss.

b. What type of pricing approaches and policies can the other overnight carriers use in order to meet the UPS competition?

The Camaro and Firebird Go International

Giant General Motors has embraced the "less is more" school of thought not only for its new cars but for new markets.

The Chevrolet Camaro and Pontiac Firebird debuted in January as sleek, low-chrome, aerodynamic sporty coupes sans their hot-rod image of old. Clean, uncluttered lines were the design story. The Camaro is going abroad as the Camaro Z28-E (for export) into markets so small as to be scorned before. "For Chevrolet, export is good business. If we can see orders for 50,000 or 60,000 cars, that might be just the kind of business we need to keep a plant running. I hope to develop business overseas," said Robert Stempel, Chevrolet general manager and recently in charge of European-sourced GM vehicles.

"It means extra work on our part, tailoring the car to the country. My experience in Europe has been that a lot of the competition does a lot of work for a lot smaller market. It's good business and we have to learn to do the same thing," Mr. Stempel said.

The Camaro Z28-E is being marketed in Europe, the Middle East, and Japan for starters as part of GM's "It's another world" ad campaign for U.S.-built cars. The North American Vehicles Overseas division, based in Detroit, is the guiding hand. "The car is outfitted especially for overseas markets as a luxury, sport touring car," said John F. Beck, NAVO vp. It's the first to come off U.S. assembly lines as a NAVO export vehicle. Campaigns for other GM vehicles started last fall, using cars modified only for legal and safety requirements. Camaro gets such overseas tricks as clear plastic headlamp covers, foldaway sport mirrors, license plate pockets that will hold various sizes of license plates, an engine oil cooler as standard equipment, and an engine set up to run on leaded gas. It uses a U.S. Z28 front and a Berlinetta (tricolor tail lamps) rear end.

Camaro fits into the umbrella theme of "It's another world" and the tag "The new Americans from General Motors." Print ads show a drawing of the car against a Cape Canaveral background with astronaut boots in the foreground.

Copy says, "The design of the Z28-E is both pleasing to the eye and impervious to the wind. Its sport/touring suspension will gracefully handle anything from a one-lane cobblestone to a six-lane autobahn. Its 5.0 liter V8 engine will do everything a 5.0 liter V8 should do. And its interior could only come from General Motors. Very comfortable, very complete—and very American."

SOURCE: Reprinted with permission from the March 22, 1982 issue of *Advertising Age*. Copyright 1982 by Crain Communications, Inc.

International Business

Objectives:

- Discuss the basic reasons why nations trade.
- Distinguish between absolute advantage and comparative advantage.
- Describe the cultural differences among countries that affect international trade.
- Identify the methods that companies use to engage in international trade.
- Discuss the importance of GATT.
- Discuss the roles of the Eximbank and of DISCs.
- Indicate four forms of protectionism.
- Describe three forms of economic integration.
- Distinguish between balance of payments and balance of trade.
- Evaluate the role, motives, benefits, and criticisms of multinational corporations.

Spartanburg, which is nestled in the northwest corner of South Carolina near the Blue Ridge Mountains, appears to be a typical small American city of 46,000 residents. It differs from many American cities, however, because it is the host to more than 40 foreign companies from 9 different countries. These companies have invested more than $1.8 million in the local economy, and they employ over 4,000 local workers.

The major reason for this international aspect of Spartanburg is that the city is in the heart of the textile industry. Nearly 80 percent of all U.S. textile mills are within a 200-to-250-mile radius of the city. The community is at the crossroads of two major interstate highways and has good rail and air transportation facilities. When the

Milliken textile mill in Spartanburg bought new machinery in the late 1950s, the purchases were made from Swiss firms. Because of the excellent opportunities for business from other nearby mills, the Swiss companies built plants in Spartanburg. Soon other firms from Germany, France, Austria, Italy, The Netherlands, England, Japan, and Canada arrived in order to share in a growing market for textile machinery. Because of the foreign participation in the city's economy, some observers have suggested that Spartanburg be renamed Euroville or Europeville!

Wherever there are profitable markets in the world, businesses will develop to serve them. With reductions in tariff barriers and advances in communications and transportation, these businesses may be multinational companies rather than solely domestic companies. This chapter focuses on why and how world trade is conducted and describes the development of multinational companies.

WHY NATIONS TRADE

When the Japanese sell us Toyotas and we sell them IBM computers, trade occurs. The goods and services that we purchase from another country are called imports. Those that we sell to another country are called exports. To the United States, exports are very important for two reasons: (1) one out of every six U. S. manufacturing jobs is directly tied to exports, and (2) 40 percent of U. S. agricultural production is shipped overseas. Figure 16-1 shows that Canada, Japan, and Mexico are the major trading partners of the United States. Although the climate for trade among nations is sometimes hostile and unstable, the United States, like many other countries, continues to pursue global trade for economic, political, and other reasons.

Economic Reasons

In Chapter 1 we noted that our capitalistic enterprise system is based on specialization and division of labor. Countries work the same way. Just as workers specialize by combining their talents and training with the available natural and capital resources, so countries specialize on the basis of their unique characteristics. These include energy supplies, climate and soils, transportation advantages, material resources, managerial talents, and labor skills. Thus, each nation can produce a wide variety of goods and services with different levels of efficiency and cost. The goods and services it actually chooses to produce depend on its absolute and comparative advantages.

Absolute Advantage

A nation has an **absolute advantage** over other nations in the production of a good or service if:

1. It happens to be the sole producer of a good through some natural monopoly or pure luck, or
2. It is able to produce the good more cheaply than other nations can.

Figure 16-1　Major U. S. Trading Partners

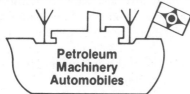

Country	U.S. Imports 1980 ($ billions)	Country	U.S. Exports 1980 ($ billions)
1. Canada	41.5	1. Canada	35.4
2. Japan	30.7	2. Japan	20.8
3. Mexico	12.6	3. Mexico	15.1
4. Saudi Arabia	12.6	4. United Kingdom	12.7
5. Germany, F. R.	11.7	5. West Germany	11.0
6. Nigeria	11.1	6. Netherlands	8.7
7. United Kingdom	9.8	7. France	7.5
8. Libya	8.6	8. Belgium and Luxembourg	6.7
9. Taiwan	6.9	9. Saudi Arabia	5.8
10. Algeria	6.6	10. Italy	5.5

SOURCE: *Twenty-Fifth Annual Report of the President of the United States on the Trade Agreements Program, 1980–1981,* p. 24.

In the past the United States had an absolute advantage in the production of ships, steel, and consumer electronics because it was able to produce them more cheaply than any other country. However, this absolute advantage has long been lost to Japan. In turn, Japan has also lost its absolute advantage in the production of textiles to other producers in the Orient.

Comparative Advantage

Will a nation that enjoys an absolute advantage in a wide range of goods and services specialize in the production and trade of all these items? Not necessarily, because international trade is a two-way street. The theory of **comparative advantage** assumes two points:

1. A nation will produce only those goods that it can make more cheaply than another.
2. A nation will not produce those items that can be bought more cheaply elsewhere.

The theory of comparative advantage recognizes the basic point that, if we do not buy some goods from other countries, they will not have the money to buy goods from us. It encourages a country to produce and export those goods that provide a decidedly productive advantage. When each country specializes in certain goods that it can produce most efficiently and cheaply, a net gain in international trade results.

In order to demonstrate the theory of comparative advantage, let us assume that the United States and Egypt both produce wheat and cotton and that both countries have the same amount of land available for the production of these two crops. As illustrated in the left side of Figure 16-2, when the two countries produce their own supplies of wheat and cotton, no trade occurs. In this situation the United States produces wheat on half of its available land and cotton on the other half. The wheat yields $100 million in revenues and the cotton yields $80 million for total revenues of $180 million. Egypt follows a similar division for its land. Its wheat crop generates $40 million and its cotton generates $60 million for total revenues of $100 million. The revenues for both countries from the two crops total $280 million.

When the United States and Egypt specialize in their most efficiently produced crop, trade occurs. As shown in the right side of Figure 16-2, in a trading environment the United States would place all of its land into wheat and might realize revenues of $200 million. Egypt would produce only cotton and might earn revenues of $120 million. This application of the theory of comparative advantage would increase the total revenues generated by the two crops to $320 million—a gain of $40 million.

As will be noted later in this chapter, the theory of comparative advantage has not been working well in recent years. Industrially advanced nations have turned

Figure 16-2   Example of Comparative Advantage

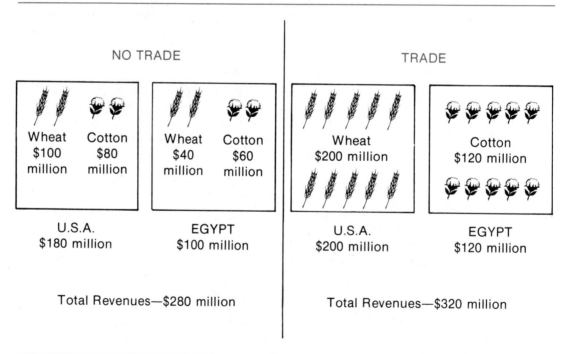

increasingly to trade barriers to equalize the cost differences of goods produced at lower costs by other countries. Furthermore, developing countries think that the comparative advantage doctrine holds back their industrial progress.

Political Reasons

There is a saying, "The sight of the gallows clarifies the mind." Without a doubt, the prospect of severe trade disruptions leads some countries to reexamine their aggressive tendencies. Therefore, many people feel that the expansion of world trade among many countries is an important step toward world peace. For the United States, the Arab oil embargo in 1973 and 1974 left little doubt that the security of the United States and its democratic partners is linked with the economic health and political stability of the developing world.

In some countries, such as West Germany and Japan, there is close cooperation between government and business. Government policies and diplomacy include major efforts to support and expand trade relationships. Unfortunately American business has not enjoyed consistent and stable support. In fact, the U. S. State Department is known more for its occasional successes than for the establishment of enduring, effective relationships throughout the world. American executives abroad have had to wear the cloaks of diplomats at times to fill this gap.

Why isn't the Soviet Union with a large area and 270 million persons an important market for foreign automobile manufacturers? It is because this communist country has a very closely controlled economy, and the state determines the types of goods that will be available to consumers. An automobile is not one of those goods! The form of government — democracy, socialism, or communism — that a country has influences the character of its international trade. For example, the U. S. has been able to develop a vigorous trade relationship with democratic West Germany, but a very weak one with communist East Germany.

The governments of some countries have a stated policy to develop strong domestic industries. Although this is often cited as being an obstacle to trade, in some cases it promotes trade. In their efforts to enlarge their own basic industries, they become excellent customers for American heavy equipment and sometimes even complete cities! For example, the Caterpillar Tractor Company sells half of its products overseas. The Bechtel Corporation, the largest U. S. construction and engineering company, has been employed by the Saudi Arabian government to supervise the construction of Jubail, a complete industrial city that will house 300,000 people (see Figure 16-3).

Other Reasons

Toyota, Nissan, and Honda aggressively market their automobiles in the United States because our country represents the largest market in the world for automobiles. Factors that affect the importance of a country as a desirable market include: population, consumer incomes, and the availability of facilities for transportation, commu-

Figure 16-3   A New City in Saudi Arabia

SOURCE: *Aramco World Magazine* (November/December, 1982).

nication, energy, banks, and middlemen. Figure 16-4 shows the wide range in per capita income among countries.

Figure 16-5 shows that over 55 percent of the world's population live in the 7 countries that contain more than 100 million people. Of these seven countries, the United States and Japan experience high standards of living and large appetites for consumer goods. The other five countries have lower standards of living and more limited consumer expenditures. Although mainland China contains over a billion people, low consumer income prevents it from being a strong market for automobiles. On the other hand, China has become a growing market for Coca-Cola and other low-priced convenience goods.

In numerous less developed nations, a large gap in income exists between a few quite wealthy individuals and a vast number of very poor people. This unequal distribution of income results in the existence of two widely divergent markets. The wealthy consumers purchase Rolls Royces and Mercedeses, and the less fortunate ones are lucky to be able to buy new shoes or sandals.

Figure 16-4   Per Capita Incomes of Countries

Countries[1] with per capita incomes of—

Less than $300: Afghanistan, Bangladesh, Benin, Bhutan, Burma, Burundi, Cape Verde, Central African Republic, Chad, China, Comoros, Cuba, Ethiopia, Gambia (The), Guinea, Guinea-Bissau, Haiti, India, Madagascar, Malawi, Maldives, Mali, Mauritania, Mozambique, Nepal, Niger, Pakistan, Rwanda, Sierra Leone, Somalia, Sri Lanka, Tanzania, Uganda, Upper Volta, Western Samoa, Zaire

$300-$699: Angola, Bolivia, Botswana, Cameroon, Congo (People's Republic of the), Djibouti, Dominica, Egypt (Arab Republic of), El Salvador, Equatorial Guinea, Ghana, Grenada, Guyana, Honduras, Indonesia, Kenya, Lesotho, Liberia, Mongolia, Morocco, Nigeria, Papua New Guinea, Peru, Philippines, Sao Tome and Principe, Senegal, Solomon Islands, St. Vincent, Sudan, Swaziland, Thailand, Togo, Tonga, Vanuatu,[2] Yemen Arab Republic, Yemen (People's Democratic Republic of), Zambia, Zimbabwe.

$700-$2,999: Albania, Algeria, Antigua, Argentina, Bahamas, Barbados, Belize, Brazil, Chile, Colombia, Costa Rica, Cyprus, Dominican Republic, Ecuador, Fiji, French Guiana, Guadeloupe, Guatemala, Iraq, Ivory Coast, Jamaica, Jordan, Kiribati, Korea (Democratic People's Republic of), Korea (Republic of), Macao, Malaysia, Malta, Mauritius, Mexico, Namibia, Nicaragua, Oman, Pacific Islands (U. S. Trust Territory of the), Panama, Paraguay, Portugal, Puerto Rico, Romania, St. Kitts-Nevis, St. Lucia, Seychelles, South Africa, Suriname, Syrian Arab Republic, Tunisia, Turkey, Uruguay, Venezuela, Yugoslavia.

$3,000-$6,999: Bahrain, Bulgaria, Channel Islands, Czechoslovakia, French Polynesia, Gabon, German Democratic Republic, Gibraltar, Greece, Guam, Hong Kong, Hungary, Ireland, Isle of Man, Israel, Italy, Martinique, Netherlands Antilles, New Caledonia, New Zealand, Poland, Reunion, Saudi Arabia, Singapore, Spain, Trinidad and Tobago, United Kingdom, USSR, Virgin Islands (U. S.).

$7,000 and over: American Samoa, Australia, Austria, Belgium, Bermuda, Brunei, Canada, Denmark, Faeroe Islands, Finland, France, Germany (Federal Republic of), Greenland, Iceland, Japan, Kuwait, Libya, Luxembourg, Netherlands (The), Norway, Qatar, Sweden, Switzerland, United Arab Emirates, United States.

[1]Democratic Kampuchea, Iran, Lao People's Democratic Republic, Lebanon, and Viet Nam are excluded in the aggregation.
[2]Formerly New Hebrides, which became independent on July 31, 1980.

SOURCE: The World Bank, *1980 World Bank Atlas*, p. 4.

CONDUCTING WORLD TRADE

Although General Motors and General Electric are large multinational companies with operations around the globe, there are numerous smaller companies that engage in international trade. Because 95 percent of the world's population and two-thirds of its purchasing power are located outside the United States, it is important

Figure 16-5   Countries with Population over 100 Million

	Country	Population (In millions)	
1.	China	⚲⚲⚲⚲⚲⚲⚲⚲⚲⚲	1,027
2.	India	⚲⚲⚲⚲⚲⚲	680
3.	Russia	⚲⚲	266
4.	United States	⚲⚲	229
5.	Indonesia	⚲	151
6.	Brazil	⚲	122
7.	Japan	⚲	117

for American firms to be present in foreign markets. However, before we explain the different methods by which a company may engage in international trade, we might first consider some important factors that U. S. companies often fail to study before they sell products to a foreign country. These factors are concerned with differences in language, in values and attitudes, and in political climate.

Cultural Differences to Observe

When introducing Coca-Cola into the Chinese market in 1920, the company used a group of Chinese symbols that when spoken sounded like Coca-Cola. However, when read, these symbols meant, "a female horse fattened with wax." Upon reentering the Chinese market in the 1970s, Coca-Cola used a series of Chinese characters that translates into "happiness in the mouth." This critical problem of proper translation is only one of many cultural differences facing American corporations overseas.

Culture is the total pattern of human behavior that is practiced by a particular group of people. Because of their cultural heritage, businesspersons in each country conduct their business activities differently. As indicated in Figure 16-6, a variety of factors contribute to the culture of a society. Our discussion, however, will be limited to the differences in language, values and attitudes, and political climate.

Differences in Language

An understanding of the language of another country is important to the success of conducting business in that country. Advertisements, package labels, and operating manuals must communicate the correct message about a product. In addition to the strict dictionary definitions, there are slang or suggested meanings to some words, too. As previously cited, Coca-Cola had a translation problem in China. Pepsi Cola experienced a somewhat similar difficulty in Germany. To the surprise of Pepsi officials,

Figure 16-6   Factors Contributing to the Culture of a Society

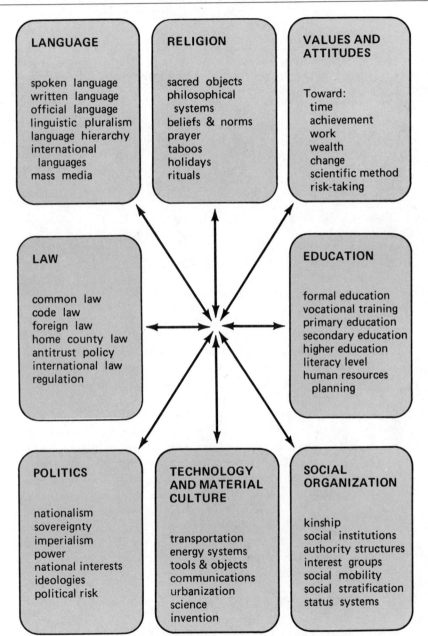

LANGUAGE

spoken language
written language
official language
linguistic pluralism
language hierarchy
international
 languages
mass media

RELIGION

sacred objects
philosophical
 systems
beliefs & norms
prayer
taboos
holidays
rituals

VALUES AND ATTITUDES

Toward:
 time
 achievement
 work
 wealth
 change
 scientific method
 risk-taking

LAW

common law
code law
foreign law
home county law
antitrust policy
international law
regulation

EDUCATION

formal education
vocational training
primary education
secondary education
higher education
literacy level
human resources
 planning

POLITICS

nationalism
sovereignty
imperialism
power
national interests
ideologies
political risk

TECHNOLOGY AND MATERIAL CULTURE

transportation
energy systems
tools & objects
communications
urbanization
science
invention

SOCIAL ORGANIZATION

kinship
social institutions
authority structures
interest groups
social mobility
social stratification
status systems

SOURCE: Vern Terpstra, *Cultural Environment of International Business* (Cincinnati, OH: South-Western Publishing Co., 1978), p. xiv.

its "Come Alive with Pepsi" slogan, when translated into German, meant "coming alive from the grave." Several other examples of translation difficulties are shown in Figure 16-7.

Figure 16-7   Translation Bloopers

American Term	Foreign Translation
• "Nova"—the name of a Chevrolet compact car.	• In Spanish, "No va" means "it doesn't go."
• "Software"—the term for computer programs.	• In Indonesia, this term means "underwear," "tissue," or "computer junk."
• "Body by Fisher"—the car bodies built by General Motors.	• In Flemish, this slogan means "Corpse by Fisher."
• "Fiera"—an inexpensive Ford truck sold in developing countries.	• In Spanish, the truck's name means "ugly old woman."
• "Mist-Stick"—a hair curling iron produced by Sunbeam Corp.	• In German, this brand name means "manure wand."

Differences in Values and Attitudes

The values and attitudes of many foreign cultures are much different from ours. Most American businesspersons move rapidly and want quick responses to their business requests. In some cultures the decision process that generates responses is very slow and complex. For example, in Japan the need for a group consensus slows the decision-making process. In the Latin American countries many business activities are halted at midday for a siesta.

Sometimes transactions are delayed because a seller does not know whom to contact. An American businessperson once spent six months in eastern Europe seeking the individual who had the authority to negotiate a particular contract! In some countries, business transactions can be hastened by contacting the proper individuals. This is the case in the Middle East, where American companies often use intermediaries. A Saudi Arabian agent declared that over a six-year period he expedited sales of $11.5 billion and received $575 million in commissions for his service.

Sometimes outright payments to political figures are necessary in order to obtain business. American businesspersons have frequently remarked that the 1977 law that makes bribes to foreign officials illegal has placed them at a competitive disadvantage in foreign markets.

Differences in Political Climate

The political climate of a country affects a foreign company's ability to operate in that country. Some governments, such as India, closely control the operations of a foreign business within their countries. For example, rather than disclosing to the Indian government its well-kept secret formula for making Coca-Cola, the Coca-Cola firm discontinued its operations there. In communist nations, such as Russia and

China, the government determines the types of goods that will be made available to the public. Therefore, in order to operate in communist and socialist countries, a foreign business often must form a partnership with the host government.

Regardless of a country's form of government, a foreign business wants an environment that is relatively free of political and social unrest. Political turmoil has resulted in the kidnappings and deaths of some American business executives in certain Latin American nations. In Iran, a movement away from the Western culture back to the strict Moslem society resulted in the takeover of many "immoral" American businesses.

Nationalism, which is a country's effort to preserve its economic and political independence, is another problem that often confronts a business operating overseas. Nationalism causes a country to take over a foreign-owned business and operate it. Between 1970 and 1974, for example, 34 nations took over $1.2 billion worth of American property and investments overseas. Included in these were the properties of most American oil companies that were operating in the Middle East.

Finally, no country will permit foreign companies unlimited access to its markets and a major voice in determining its economic policies. Even friendly Canada is enforcing legislation that restricts American investments. For example, its government is "Canadianizing" its oil and gas industry by reducing foreign ownership from 72 percent in 1975 to 55 percent in 1981, with an eventual goal of 50 percent by 1990.

Another aspect of the political differences among countries relates to law. Each country has its own legal requirements covering such areas as finance, marketing, personnel, construction, and ecology. Many nations have legislated that the measurements for imported goods be based on the metric system. This forces American manufacturers who engage in international trade to change all of their measurements to meters, grams, and liters.

Methods of Conducting International Trade

There are several methods of conducting international trade. Among these are: exporting, licensing, joint ventures, management contracts, wholly owned manufacturing operations, and cartels. Each company must evaluate its own situation and choose the most appropriate method.

Exporting

Selling goods produced in one country to another country is called **exporting**. This method entails a minimum financial risk and a great deal of business flexibility for a firm. Government statistics indicate that 60 percent of all American firms engaged in exporting employ fewer than 100 workers. By broadening its sales base to other countries, a firm can reduce the sales peaks and valleys that are caused by domestic seasonal and economic factors.

Some firms shift their export activities to a professional exporter who either buys the goods outright or sells them on a commission basis in overseas markets. For example, the American Whirlpool Corporation uses the Japanese Sony trading company to export certain product lines to Japan.

Licensing

Under a licensing agreement, a firm in one country permits a firm in another country to use its patents, trademarks, and technical processes to manufacture and market a product. **Licensing** involves shifting the technology and property rights from one company to another. For a medium-size firm, licensing is an inexpensive and rapid way to penetrate a foreign market. The firm that obtains the license may already be operating in that foreign market. Because licensing increases the technology and earnings base of a country, it may be welcomed in a country that is usually hostile to foreign investments.

A disadvantage of licensing is that it may establish a potential competitor for the firm that provides the licensing technology. For example, in the food processor business a French company, Robot-Coupe, had an agreement to manufacture the Cuisinart food processor for sale in the American market. Robot-Coupe eventually became disenchanted with the arrangement and is now producing a food processor under its own name and directly competing with Cuisinart.

Joint Ventures

Under a joint venture, a foreign firm and one established in a host country share the ownership and control of a third company in the host country. For example, Xerox initiated a joint venture with the Rank organization in England and formed Rank-Xerox, which was given the rights to manufacture and market all Xerox products outside North America.

Compared with operating a wholly owned business in a foreign country, a joint venture spreads the capital and management requirements among two or more companies that each contribute their expertise to the operations. Another benefit is that a joint venture lessens the probability of an unfriendly takeover by the host country. When a foreign firm combines with a well-known domestic company in the host country, the resulting joint venture often is accorded favorable status by the host country. A major objection to a joint venture is that, by sharing responsibilities, a firm loses absolute control over its operations.

Management Contracts

Some firms enter a foreign market by entering into management contracts with an overseas company or government. These agreements call for a company to assume the complete operation and management of a business in return for a fee. For example, Sears, Roebuck designed and is managing several department stores in South American countries without any ownership interest in the units.

A management contract is sometimes the result of the takeover of a foreign business by a host country. When the host country finds that it does not have the expertise to handle the operations, it asks the foreign firm to come back and run its former business. In the early 1970s when the Middle Eastern countries took over the American oil companies operating on their lands, they were forced to contract with the American companies to keep their oil fields producing.

Wholly Owned Manufacturing Operations

For a variety of reasons, some companies establish wholly owned manufacturing operations in foreign countries. Low-cost labor caused Coleman Products to construct a plant in Mexico where it pays workers $1.04 an hour, compared to a $20 wage-and-benefit package paid to American workers. Because of the high cost of transporting its products, Coca-Cola has established bottling plants around the world. As indicated in the discussion of protectionism later in this chapter, high tariffs, nontariff barriers, and other protectionist policies encourage companies to manufacture in foreign countries.

Cartels

Another way to conduct international trade is through a cartel. A **cartel** is formed when a group of companies or countries handling similar goods join together in an effort to control the market for these goods. Members of the cartel generally agree to restrict production, maintain prices, establish exclusive sales territories, and sometimes to engage in centralized selling and distribution of profits. For example, in the early 1970s the Organization of Petroleum Exporting Countries (OPEC) was very effective in raising oil prices from $2.70 to over $30.00 a barrel. OPEC, which is composed of many of the major oil producing countries, is an example of a worldwide cartel.

PROMOTING WORLD TRADE

What do Marco Polo, Christopher Columbus, Henry Ford II, and Ray Kroc (founder of McDonald's) have in common? All of them have sought to expand overseas trade. The commercial travels of Marco Polo in the Old World and Christopher Columbus in the New World are well known. Less known is that Ford Motor Co. typically receives 40 percent of its revenues and much more than 40 percent of its profits from overseas operations. And McDonald's, as American as apple pie, operates over 1,000 outlets in 25 countries that generate over 15 percent of its income.

General Agreement on Tariffs and Trade (GATT)

During the depression years of the 1930s, industrial nations raised tariff barriers to protect their own producers. For example, in 1930 the United States passed the Smoot-Hawley Tariff Act. The initial intention of this Act was to protect only agriculture. However, powerful interests extended the Act to impose high protective tariffs on many other products. Other countries followed with similar measures. This caused a tariff war which blocked world trade and contributed to the roots of World War II.

To prevent a similar breakdown in trade after World War II, the General Agreement on Tariffs and Trade (GATT) was established in Geneva in 1948 by 23 countries. GATT rules for world trade are the results of negotiations to encourage mutual tariff concessions and to promote increases in the exports and imports of participating nations. However, GATT does not rigidly bind its member nations. Article 19 of GATT provides that countries can impose tariff measures when their domestic industries are threatened by imports of specific products. Today 88 countries responsible for more than 80 percent of the world's trade are members of GATT. Numerous nonmembers also apply GATT rules. World trade has grown nine times in volume since GATT was established in 1948.

A major goal of GATT is to provide all member nations with nondiscriminating or equal treatment in regard to tariffs, customs regulations, and taxes. Thus, all members are accorded the **most-favored-nation (MFN) treatment**. For the United States this means that the imports from all foreign countries that have signed MFN commercial treaties with the U. S. are treated alike. Because of MFN treaties, communist Rumania pays the same low tariffs on imports into the U. S. as democratic Australia.

Kennedy Round

In an effort to lower trade barriers, the Trade Expansion Act of 1962 was passed during John F. Kennedy's administration. This Act authorized President Kennedy to negotiate multilateral tariff reductions up to 50 percent on an across-the-board basis, rather than on an item-by-item basis. It also opened the Kennedy Round of tariff negotiations held within GATT from 1964 to 1967. Fifty-four countries participated in the Kennedy Round, which covered 400,000 tariff headings. An average tariff reduction of 35 percent was achieved on nonagricultural items.

Tokyo Round

In 1979, after more than five years of bargaining, the Tokyo Round of trade negotiations by the GATT members was concluded. The final agreement was a broad package of tariff cuts and international codes meant to lower nontariff trade barriers. Over an eight-year period, world tariffs were to be reduced an average of 33 percent on nearly 5,700 items.

Geneva Meeting

In 1982, in an atmosphere of worldwide recession and increasing trade protectionism, the GATT nations met in Geneva, Switzerland, to recommit themselves to a liberal open trading policy. This was a difficult goal in a world where trade volume was stagnant in the two previous years. If the future will prove that the Geneva meeting slowed the erosion in the trading system until the world recovered from a deep recession, history will accord it a success.

Free-Trade Zones

A **free-trade zone** is an area in a country where foreign goods can be stored, processed, or assembled without being subject to tariffs until they are moved to another part of the country. If the goods are exported directly from the free-trade zone to another country, no tariffs are paid. Only about 1 percent of U. S. international trade passes through its free-trade zones. On a global basis, however, a substantial 9 percent of international trade flows through the several hundred free-trade zones throughout the world.

Italy's Olivetti Co., for example, is assembling typewriters from imported components in a free-trade zone in Harrisburg, PA. By operating in the free-trade zone, Olivetti saves 88 percent of the normal duties on components. A free-trade zone that is involved in international banking is described in Figure 16-8.

Figure 16-8   A Free-Trade Zone for International Banking

New York has a unique free-trade zone that permits American banks to have "foreign branches" within the United States. Nearly 100 U. S. and foreign banks plan to open offices in this free-trade zone for international banking. The banks in the zone are limited to international transactions such as making foreign loans and accepting foreign deposits. However, they can service the foreign subsidiaries of American companies, too.

This unusual free-trade zone is a response to American taxes and stringent banking regulations. These factors have kept American banks from being competitive in overseas markets and have caused several New York banks to open "shell" branches in areas such as the Bahamas and the Cayman Islands. Because the paperwork for these branches was processed in New York, the state contended that it should receive state and local taxes from the branches. The banks convincingly argued that the payment of these taxes would force them out of business. This is because the profit margins on international banking transactions are very narrow, and over half of the business of these banks is in the international area. Listening to the bankers' appeals, the Governor of New York and the State Superintendent of Banks advocated a free-trade zone for international banking. They recognized that the zone could create thousands of new jobs and cause the return of hundreds of billions of dollars that were deposited in overseas banks. In 1981, with the approval of the New York State Legislature and the Federal Reserve system, the first international banking zone became a reality.

SOURCE: Adapted from Robert A. Bennett, "A Free-Trade Zone for Banks Opening in New York," *The New York Times*, December 3, 1981, p. A1. © 1981 by The New York Times Company. Reprinted by permission.

U. S. Export-Import Bank

The International Monetary Fund and the World Bank (see Chapter 20, pages 505-506) are important organizations that assist in financing international trade. Specific export help to American firms is extended through the U. S. Export-Import Bank (Eximbank), an independent federal agency set up in 1934. The Eximbank's main purpose is to advise U. S. exporters and to finance export trade that commercial banks don't want to handle. It does this by making direct loans to the exporters and their customers. Eximbank also provides insurance against certain types of political and commercial risks to American exporters who sell on credit to overseas buyers. In addition, the Eximbank loans funds to commercial banks to aid them in financing exports.

DISCs

Since 1972, our tax code has allowed certain U. S. exporters to defer federal income taxes on one-half of their export profits by forming special corporations known as Domestic International Sales Corporations (DISCs). The tax deferral continues as long as the corporation reinvests the deferred taxes in export business. This tax deferral was given to DISCs to offset the huge export tax subsidies granted by other countries to their exporters. DISCs have provided an effective boost to U. S. exports. For example, over 10,000 DISCs were formed by the end of 1980. Approximately 75 percent of U. S. exports are channeled through DISCs, and about 300,000 U. S. jobs are associated with these exports.

Trading Companies

Firms that buy and sell goods from many different foreign companies and assist in financing and forming business combinations that compete for international contracts are called **trading companies**. For example, Mitsui & Co. and Mitsubishi Corp. are two of the eight large Japanese trading companies that handle a major share of Japan's exports and imports. In fact, in 1981 the U. S. offices of these two giant traders handled nearly 10 percent of all American exports to other countries!

Countertrade occurs when a foreign company or country pays for its imports by exchanging them for its own goods and services. It is a form of the oldest type of trade — barter. The growing use of countertrade by foreign companies is now forcing the organization of U. S. trading companies. For example, General Electric (GE), which is the largest U. S. exporter, established the General Electric Trading Co. with offices in 30 countries to handle its countertrade operations and to market the products of other noncompeting companies abroad. In one complex arrangement, GE had to purchase Swedish products in return for a contract to supply jet engines for a new Swedish fighter plane. In turn, the GE Trading Co. found buyers for the Swedish products. Sears, Roebuck & Company has established a trading company that is selling its management services to foreign companies and arranging trade between foreign firms. In 1982, legislation was passed that allows bank holding companies to establish export trading companies.

U. S. corporations, however, have been hindered in their efforts to form trading organizations. U. S. antitrust laws and the Foreign Corrupt Practices Act of 1977 restrict American trading companies from operating with as much freedom as their massive Japanese counterparts.

PROTECTIONISM AND ECONOMIC INTEGRATION

Unfortunately many nations often see the promotion of an open international trading system as an action against their own national interests. This may lead individual nations to consider some form of **protectionism**, which advocates government economic protection for domestic producers through restrictions on foreign competitors. Or groups of nations may band together and turn to some form of economic integration to protect their regional interests.

Two conditions give rise to demands for protectionism. First, as markets evolve, countries lose their competitive advantage in some products and gain it in others. However, the firms in industries that have lost markets to competitors suffer from having their capital locked in place. Also, their workers have specialized skills that make shifting to new industries a costly problem. Their demands for protection from imports are often more loudly voiced than the demands of consumers for lower prices. The costs of such protection may greatly exceed the benefits. It may cost the public $50,000 to $60,000 annually to protect a domestic job that pays a worker only half that amount in wages and benefits. Most citizens are probably unaware of these costs because they are spread among all 50 states and 230 million individuals. Thus, the public does not usually resist protectionism measures.

An example of a protectionist measure was a "domestic auto content" bill that was introduced in Congress in 1982 and strongly supported by the United Auto Workers. The bill would require all cars sold in this country to have a certain percentage of U. S. parts. This percentage would begin at 20 percent and increase to 90 percent, based on sales volume. Figure 16-9 shows that even today's American-made cars are built with many foreign-made parts.

Second, economic slack abroad adds to world trade tensions because it provides an incentive for some foreign producers to increase the volume of their exports by cutting prices or subsidizing exports in the U. S. market. Selling abroad at less than home prices is called **dumping**, and this goes against GATT rules. When countries are found guilty of subsidizing exports into the U. S., punitive duties can be levied against these countries.

In the early 1980s, two international trade controversies occurred in the steel industry. One involved dumping and the other related to government subsidies. The dumping case attracted wide attention when Mitsui & Co., the huge Japanese enterprise, admitted it sold steel in the U. S. at prices lower than it had stated on certain official documents. The firm agreed to pay $11.2 million in penalties—the largest settlement in the history of the Customs Service. In a case involving government subsidies, the U. S. International Trade Commission ruled that subsidized steel imports from six European countries severely injured the American steel industry. In some cases a foreign government was paying as much as 40 percent of the cost of a company's steel production.

Forms of Protectionism

By defining "pure wool" as 97 percent wool, Belgium effectively restricts the importation of French wool, which is 85 percent wool. This is one example of the

Figure 16-9   Made in America with Foreign Parts

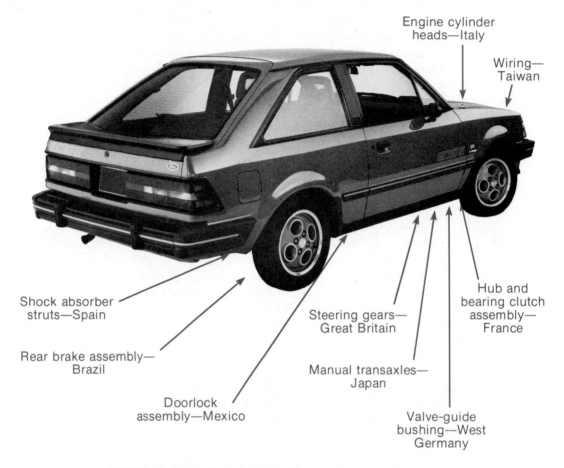

Engine cylinder heads—Italy

Wiring—Taiwan

Shock absorber struts—Spain

Rear brake assembly—Brazil

Doorlock assembly—Mexico

Steering gears—Great Britain

Manual transaxles—Japan

Valve-guide bushing—West Germany

Hub and bearing clutch assembly—France

SOURCE: Ford Motor Co. Reproduced with permission.

many forms of protectionism. Perhaps the four most widely practiced forms are tariffs, quotas, "orderly marketing" arrangements, and nontariff trade barriers.

Tariffs

The taxes imposed by a nation on imported goods are called **tariffs**. Wherever foreign imports threaten to do damage to a domestic industry, a loud hue and cry arises for some form of protection—often tariffs. Although GATT has successfully reduced numerous tariffs, many still exist and effectively restrict trade.

Tariffs may be based on the quantity of the imported goods, their value, or a combination of quantity and value. A *specific* tariff, which is used mainly for staple commodities, is assessed on a certain quantity of goods such as $.20 per bushel. An *ad valorem* tariff, which is used primarily for manufactured products, is based on the percentage value of a good such as 2 percent duty on its stated value. A *compound* tariff is a combination of the specific and ad valorem duties such as $.20 per pound and 2 percent on the value of the good.

Quotas

A **quota** is a strong form of protectionism because it sets a specified ceiling on the volume of imports no matter how noncompetitive the domestic prices become. Figure 16-10 shows more examples of quotas established by the United States, Great Britain, and Italy.

Figure 16-10   **Some Quotas Set to Protect Domestic Industries**

Country	Annual Quotas
United States	• Specialty steel imports limited to 151,000 tons • Shoes from Taiwan and Korea limited to 155 million pairs
Great Britain	• South Korean television sets limited to 35,000 units • Suits from Rumania limited to 384,000 units
Italy	• Motorcycles from Japan limited to 18,000 units

Orderly Marketing Arrangements

Market-sharing arrangements negotiated between importing and exporting countries are known as **orderly marketing arrangements**. For example, Great Britain and Japan have a "gentlemen's agreement" that Japan will have no more than 10 percent of the British auto market. The arrangement between France and Japan limits Japanese autos to no more than 3 percent of the French market.

Nontariff Trade Barriers

Japan, which is an extremely protectionist nation, guards its markets by many nontariff and nonquota trade barriers. **Nontariff trade barriers (NTBs)** are defined broadly as measures other than tariffs or quotas, public or private, that distort trade flows. For example, Japan's many-layered distribution system is largely controlled by giant trading companies. After the numerous middlemen take their cuts, a U. S. refrigerator can cost the consumer in Japan up to $1,000. Also, the Japanese government keeps changing its standards in the "testing" of imported automobiles. The U. S. government has published a 300-page listing of NTBs that are effectively used by 138 countries to restrict textile imports. Several other examples of nontariff barriers are shown in Figure 16-11.

NTBs generally have the effect of interfacing with and preventing the normal working of competitive forces. They also have the effect of directing more of a

Figure 16-11   Examples of Nontariff Barriers

- Government participation in trade

- Specific limitations on trade

- Standards

- Charges on imports

- Use of specific customs office

- The Canadian government grants export subsidies on Michelin x-radial steel-belted tires.
- The Philippine government sets arbitrary and excessive valuations and long delays; the Egyptian government insists that dubbing of foreign motion pictures must be done in Egypt.
- The Australian government insists that margarine be pink-colored.
- The Lebanese government imposes landing charges, wharf dues, handling dues, and storage dues on all imports.
- The French government requires that all imports of Japanese video recorders pass through a single, understaffed customs office at Poitiers.

SOURCE: U. S. Department of Commerce.

country's income to the protected domestic firms and workers than if these barriers did not exist. From the standpoint of the seller, it is often the uncertainty created by these barriers, as well as the effect of these barriers that restricts access to foreign markets, that are important. The recent demands that the United States should retaliate against the foreign NTBs have contributed to protectionist attitudes in Congress.

Forms of Economic Integration

The adoption of a common economic policy by a group of nations is called economic integration. Some nations agree on *preferential* tariffs, which are lower tariffs on identical commodities that are imports from a particular group of nations. An example is the preferential tariff treatment that British Commonwealth members enjoy in trading with Great Britain. Other nations may form **free-trade associations** where goods flow freely among member countries without being subject to tariffs. The European Free Trade Association, which is composed of Austria, Iceland, Norway, Sweden, Switzerland, Portugal, and Finland (associate member), is a good example. Nations may go one step further by forming a **customs union**, where they agree not only to abolish trade restrictions among themselves, but also to adopt common policies regarding trade outside the union. The two major free-world trading communities are the European Common Market, whose status most nearly approaches that of a customs union, and the Association of Southeast Asian Nations (ASEAN). Other important trading communities include the Central American Common Market (CACM) and the Latin American Free Trade Association (LAFTA).

The European Common Market

The European Common Market began as the European Coal and Steel Community in 1950. Its six original members were Belgium, France, West Germany, Italy, Luxembourg, and The Netherlands. Added later were Great Britain, Denmark, Ireland, and Greece. In 1957, the six original members signed the Treaty of Rome in which they agreed to establish the European Common Market and to expand the common import duties and economic policies they believed to be beneficial for them.

The original force that brought the European Common Market together was the need for a united stand in economic negotiations with a strong United States. Today, the European Common Market is concerned about its ability to trade profitably with the eastern European countries and the Asian nations, too. Figure 16-12 compares the gross national product and population of the European Common Market with the three leading industrial nations of the world.

Figure 16-12   GNP and Population of the European Common Market and Leading Industrial Nations

---

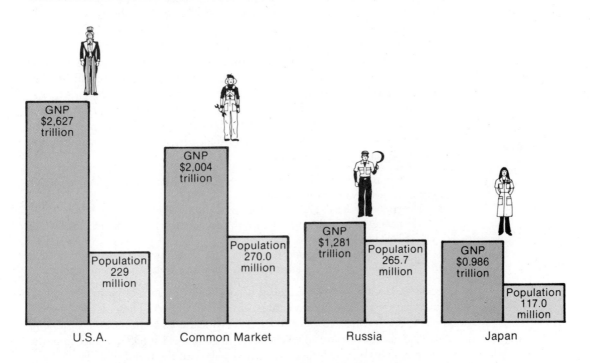

SOURCE: *1982 Hammond Almanac* (Maplewood, NJ: Hammond Almanac, Inc., 1982). Adapted with permission.

Association of Southeast Asian Nations

If you're wearing rubber-soled shoes these days, you're probably walking on a little piece of Southeast Asia. Eighty percent of the world's rubber and 60 percent of its tin are produced by the 260 million people in 5 noncommunist countries that comprise ASEAN. They are Thailand, Singapore, Malaysia, Indonesia, and the Philippines.

INTERNATIONAL PAYMENTS AND BALANCE OF TRADE

A country's **balance of payments** refers to the difference between total payments to and total receipts from foreign nations during a given time. Its **balance of trade** refers to the difference between the monetary values of its merchandise imports and exports. A country that exports more goods than it imports has a favorable balance of trade. One that imports more goods than it exports has an unfavorable balance of trade.

A country could have an unfavorable balance of trade, but a favorable balance of payments. This is because the payments for trade or goods are only a portion of the total expenditures that are made to other countries. The other major payments made are for long-term investments, foreign and military aid, and travel abroad. In the early 1980s the United States had an unfavorable balance of trade but a favorable balance of payments. This condition existed because the surplus in the U. S. nontrade accounts (service accounts) was greater than the deficit in its trade account (goods only). This situation is depicted in Figure 16-13.

From the 1870s to 1970, U. S. sales abroad—with the exception of a few years—exceeded purchases. Then, starting in 1971 the U. S. trade position weakened and it began experiencing an annual balance-of-trade deficit. Factors that contributed to this declining trade position included:

1. An increase in U. S. labor costs, giving rise to a greater demand for less expensive imports made with cheaper labor.
2. The growing value of raw material imports, particularly petroleum.
3. The failure of our trading partners to provide meaningful access to their markets for U. S. products.
4. The lack of aggressive export policies by American firms.
5. The use of an American dollar that was overvalued relative to other currencies.

Because the U. S. also experienced a continuous balance-of-payments deficit, our trading partners began accumulating a surplus of dollars. These dollars were in excess of the amount needed to conduct trade with the U. S. In order to dispose of these excess dollars, a country could exchange them for gold at $35 an ounce from the U. S. Treasury. This exchange process worked well until the hoard of dollars held by other nations exceeded the U. S. stock of gold. To avoid the loss of all of our gold, in 1971 President Nixon suspended the conversion of dollars into gold.

Without the dollar's being pegged to a specific amount of gold, it became a floating currency (see Chapter 20, page 504). The value of a floating currency is

Figure 16-13   U. S. Balance of Payments, 1980

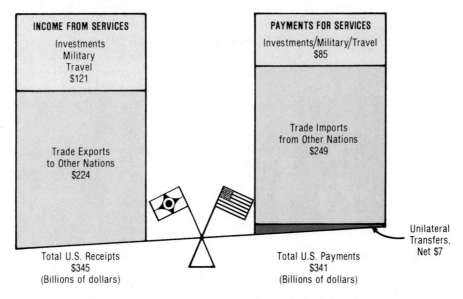

SOURCE: U. S. Department of Commerce, Bureau of Economic Analysis.

determined by its supply and demand in foreign exchange markets. Like wheat, corn, or any other commodity, the dollar's "price" is established in the marketplace.

The following illustration shows the effects of a floating currency on international trade. Let's assume that the U. S. dollar is worth 300 yen (Japanese currency) over a certain period of time. During this time, a Japanese good with a price of 1,500 yen costs an American buyer the equivalent of $5.00 ($1 = 300 yen). Then the Japanese increase their exports to the United States without a corresponding increase in imports from the United States. As a result, the Japanese obtain a large supply of U. S. dollars. Because the supply of U. S. dollars in Japan exceeds the demand for them, the value of the U. S. dollar declines to 250 yen. Now, the Japanese good with a price of 1,500 yen costs an American buyer $6.00 ($1.00 = 250 yen). When it costs more dollars to buy Japanese goods, the United States will reduce the imports of those goods.

MULTINATIONAL CORPORATIONS

For the past thirty years, the world's business has been changing from *international* trade, based on countries exporting to and importing from others, to multinational trade. In *multinational* trade, companies invest directly in plants in other countries and maintain some degree of control over those plants.

Since 1960, American direct investments overseas have risen rapidly. Foreign direct investments in the United States are increasing fast, too. These include direct investments in such well-known U. S. companies as Stouffer Foods, Howard Johnson, Cutter Laboratories, Baskin-Robbins, Clorox, Bantam Books, Magnavox, A&P food chain, Saks Fifth Avenue, and the Marshall Field stores.

The main vehicle for the recent growth in world trade is the multinational corporation. In the United States, multinationals emerged in the 1850s. They grew rapidly, and by 1900 about 1 of the then-existing 50 largest corporations had significant overseas operations. As shown in Table 16-1, when the sales of multinational com-

Table 16-1 **Gross National Product of Nations and Gross Annual Sales of Multinational Corporations (In Billions of U. S. Dollars)**

1. United States	$2,626.5	31. Argentina	$56.7
2. Soviet Union	1,280.6	32. Nigeria	54.3
3. Japan	986.1	33. Austria	53.4
4. West Germany	642.4	34. BRITISH PETROLEUM	52.2
5. China, People's Republic	592.0	35. Venezuela	51.0
6. France	508.1	36. Denmark	50.7
7. Italy	302.9	37. South Africa	47.9
8. United Kingdom	297.9	38. STANDARD OIL OF CALIF.	44.2
9. Brazil	251.5	39. Iran	43.6
10. Canada	235.3	40. South Korea	42.4
11. Mexico	138.0	41. Norway	40.4
12. India	137.4	42. Turkey	39.5
13. Australia	132.7	43. Hungary	39.4
14. Poland	124.9	44. FORD MOTOR	38.2
15. Spain	114.8	45. Iraq	35.6
16. EXXON	108.1	46. Finland	33.4
17. East Germany	99.6	47. China, Republic of Taiwan	32.5
18. Netherlands	99.4	48. STANDARD OIL OF IND.	29.9
19. Sweden	92.3	49. Bulgaria	29.8
20. Romania	89.3	50. ENI	29.4
21. Belgium	85.1	51. Greece	29.3
22. Czechoslovakia	85.0	52. IBM	29.0
23. Saudi Arabia	83.8	53. Philippines	28.8
24. ROYAL DUTCH/SHELL GROUP	82.3	54. Thailand	28.5
25. Yugoslavia	72.3	55. GULF OIL	28.2
26. Switzerland	64.6	56. Algeria	27.9
27. MOBIL	64.5	57. ATLANTIC RICHFIELD	27.8
28. Indonesia	63.1	58. GENERAL ELECTRIC	27.2
29. GENERAL MOTORS	62.7	59. Columbia	26.3
30. TEXACO	57.6	60. Egypt	24.1

NOTE: The GNP of countries is for 1980, and the sales of the MNCs are for 1981.

SOURCE: *1982 Hammond Almanac* (Maplewood, NJ: Hammond Almanac, Inc., 1982), p. 190; and "The 50 Largest Industrial Companies in the World," FORTUNE (August 23, 1982), p. 181.

panies are compared to the gross national products of countries, 12 multinational firms rank among the top 60 "countries" of the world.

Multinational Defined

A **multinational corporation (MNC)** that is truly international in ownership and management has:

1. Direct investments in manufacturing or other facilities in other countries.
2. Global management that coordinates and interchanges technology, production, sales, and distribution among its subsidiaries and the parent company.

Some individuals include in the definitions of an MNC the criteria that 20 percent of its sales should come from abroad. Table 16-2 shows the top 25 MNCs by sales. Interestingly, 14 of them are U. S.-based companies. Multinational corpora-

---

Table 16-2   **The 25 Largest Industrial Companies in the World (Ranked by Sales)**

Rank	Company	Headquarters	Sales ($000)	Net Income ($000)
1	Exxon	New York	108,107,688	5,567,481
2	Royal Dutch/Shell Group	The Hague/London	82,291,728	3,642,142
3	Mobil	New York	64,488,000	2,433,000
4	General Motors	Detroit	62,698,500	333,400
5	Texaco	Harrison, NY	57,628,000	2,310,000
6	British Petroleum	London	52,199,976	2,063,272
7	Standard Oil of California	San Francisco	44,224,000	2,380,000
8	Ford Motor	Dearborn, MI	38,247,100	(1,060,100)
9	Standard Oil (Ind.)	Chicago	29,947,000	1,922,000
10	ENI	Rome	29,444,315	383,234
11	International Business Machines	Armonk, NY	29,070,000	3,308,000
12	Gulf Oil	Pittsburgh	28,252,000	1,231,000
13	Atlantic Richfield	Los Angeles	27,797,436	1,671,290
14	General Electric	Fairfield, CT	27,240,000	1,652,000
15	Unilever	London/Rotterdam	24,095,898	800,379
16	E. I. du Pont de Nemours	Wilmington, DE	22,610,000	1,401,000
17	Francaise des Pétroles	Paris	22,764,032	175,807
18	Shell Oil	Houston	21,629,000	1,701,000
19	Kuwait Petroleum	Safat (Kuwait)	20,586,871	1,690,312
20	Elf-Aquitaine	Paris	19,666,141	682,316
21	Petróleos de Venezuela	Caracas	19,659,115	3,316,040
22	Fiat	Turin (Italy)	19,608,480	N. A.
23	Petrobrás (Petróleo Brasileiro)	Rio de Janeiro	18,946,056	831,215
24	Pemex (Petróleos Mexicanos)	Mexico City	18,804,190	40,790
25	International Telephone & Telegraph	New York	17,306,189	676,804

SOURCE: "The 50 Largest Industrial Companies in the World," FORTUNE (August 23, 1982), p. 181. © 1982 Time Inc.

---

tions are different not only because of their diverse operations but also because of their degree of ownership, size, geographic distribution, management philosophies, and many other variables. Their activities may range from making thimbles in Mexico to exploring for oil off the coast of Africa, from wholly owned U. S. subsidiaries to plants in which the U. S. ownership is very limited, and from huge factories to small sales outlets.

Role of MNCs

In recent years, as nations have more clearly defined their goals and priorities, they have been confronted by multinational corporations that flow through boundaries, sometimes establish controversial policies, and occasionally frustrate the national efforts. Thus, the question of national and commercial authority and power arises. Who has final control over the actions of the multinational subsidiary — the parent or the host country? Who decides whether capital and profits flow freely from one subsidiary to another? Who decides whether a plant closes or stays open?

Motives of MNCs

Criticisms of the motives of multinational corporations by some industry and labor groups abound. These criticisms have tended to oversimplify the motives for investing abroad or have sometimes implied suspect or hostile motives in certain investments. If one were to inquire into the motives for foreign investment by multinational companies, the following might be typical:

1. A need to get behind tariff walls to safeguard the company's export markets.
2. Greater efficiency and responsiveness by producing in the local market as compared with exporting to it.
3. The possibility of lower production costs which make it cheaper to produce components abroad.
4. The fear that competitors going abroad may capture a lucrative foreign market or may, by acquiring cheaper sources of supply, threaten the domestic position of the company.
5. A need to diversify product lines to avoid fluctuations in earnings.
6. A desire to assist licensees abroad who may need capital to expand their operations.
7. A desire to avoid home country regulations such as antitrust laws in the United States.
8. The ability to move funds from one country to another in order to minimize the cost of borrowed funds or to take advantage of exchange rates.

In general, the basic forces that lead corporations to invest abroad are the search for profit and the fear of losing foreign markets to foreign or domestic competitors.

Benefits from MNCs

MNCs are visible symbols of each nation's dependence upon other nations. Their presence offers several advantages to their host countries — particularly when these countries are developing nations. The MNC with its resources of capital, managerial skills, and technology can assist in developing the resources of a host country. Saudi Arabia, Nigeria, and Venezuela have been greatly strengthened economically by the presence of multinational oil companies. MNCs also bring the latest technological advances to a host country. For example, ITT, a large diversified American corporation, has its four most sophisticated research centers in Germany, France, Spain, and England. MNCs are able to broaden economic opportunity within a host country by locating plants in depressed regions, as they have done in southern Italy. They are a stabilizing factor in the search for world peace. When markets are relatively free and countries are economically dependent on each other, the probability of armed conflict is lessened.

Criticisms of MNCs

Because of the impact of MNCs on international trade, critics of MNCs would like to see them more closely controlled. Many of the criticisms occur because an MNC is seeking to maximize its profit on a global basis while a host country is interested in maximizing the welfare of its citizens. Within the United States the MNCs have been accused of exporting jobs and employing cheap foreign labor instead of American workers. In numerous cases, however, the MNCs increase employment by building overseas factories that require American parts and equipment. A government study over a ten-year period revealed that MNCs increased the number of U. S. employees by 31 percent while companies operating solely in the U. S. showed employment gains of only 12 percent.

MNCs have been accused of not paying their proper share of U. S. income taxes. Because an MNC's tax payments are split between the U. S. and the host country, it does not pay as much U. S. taxes as a company operating solely in the U. S. In a recent year, out of three dollars earned, Mobil Oil returned two dollars to foreign governments around the world.

Some critics contend that the MNCs are insensitive to the needs of a host country and its citizens. It should be noted that the MNC establishes operations where there are resources or markets. They add to the host country's gross national product, increase employment, and aid its balance of payments. Most MNCs employ local citizens and assist in their training. In addition, the MNC has been condemned for exploiting the resources of host countries. However, the investment and risks taken by an MNC in extracting mineral or other materials contribute greatly to the economic development of the country. The host country receives from the MNCs royalties, taxes, technology, management skills, and worker incomes.

Finally, the MNCs have been criticized for engaging in unethical practices such as bribing foreign officials and intervening in the politics of foreign countries. For example, United Brands made payoffs to certain Latin American officials in order to obtain low taxes on banana exports, and ITT assisted the opposition party in Chile in order to depose a leftist government. Although unethical activities are pursued by only a few businesspersons, the adverse publicity from these actions damages the reputation of all businesses. In defense of these actions, the MNCs have stated that they are following accepted practices in other countries and are trying to protect their investments. To eliminate any further misconduct by American MNCs, in 1977 the U. S. Congress passed the Foreign Corrupt Practices Act.

SUMMARY   Nations trade primarily for economic and political reasons. Although a nation may have an absolute advantage over other nations in the production of a good or service, trade can take place if the theory of comparative advantage is followed. This theory states that a nation will produce only those goods that it can make more cheaply than another nation could. Population, consumer incomes, and the availability of transportation, communications, energy, and commercial services are factors that affect the importance of a country as a desirable market.

Cultural differences which include language, values and attitudes, and political climate affect international trade transactions. A company that plans to engage in international trade must evaluate its own situation and choose the most appropriate method. Possibilities include exporting, licensing, joint ventures, management contracts, wholly owned manufacturing operations, and cartels.

Since World War II, trade negotiations and various export promotion and market development programs have been helpful in expanding world trade. The General Agreement on Tariffs and Trade (GATT) was negotiated by the major trading nations to encourage mutual tariff concessions and to promote increases in the exports and imports of participating nations. Export help to American firms is extended through the U. S. Export-Import Bank (Eximbank), an independent federal agency set up in 1934. Since 1972, our tax code has allowed certain U. S. exporters to defer federal income taxes on half of their export profit by forming special corporations known as Domestic International Sales Corporations (DISCs). Trading companies, which have been used for many years by the Japanese, are now being established by U. S. firms. These companies buy and sell goods from many different firms and assist in financing and forming business combinations that compete for international contracts.

When nations see the promotion of an open trading system as an action against their own national interests, they often consider some form of protectionism which includes tariffs, quotas, orderly marketing arrangements, and nontariff barriers. In some instances groups of nations may band together and turn to some form of economic integration, such as preferential tariffs, free-trade associations, and customs unions, to protect their regional interests. The European Common Market is the best known example of a customs union.

A country's balance of payments refers to the difference between its total payments to foreign nations and its total receipts from foreign nations. Its balance of trade refers to the difference between the money values of its imports and exports. In several recent years the U. S. has had an unfavorable balance of trade, but a favorable balance of payments.

When a firm operates in several countries out of a parent country and it has global ownership and management, it is a multinational corporation (MNC). The basic forces that motivate an MNC are the search for profit and the fear of losing foreign markets to foreign or domestic competitors. The MNC, with its resources of capital, managerial skills, and technology, can assist in developing the resources of a host country. Because of their impact on international trade, according to critics, MNCs should be more closely controlled. Much of the conflict occurs because an MNC is seeking to maximize its profit on a global basis while a host country is interested in maximizing the welfare of its citizens.

BACK TO THE CHAPTER OPENER

1. Why can't the exact model of an American car be exported overseas?
2. Why don't the overseas plants of General Motors produce the Chevrolet Camaro and the Pontiac Firebird?
3. What are the difficulties that General Motors encounters in creating advertisements which will be seen in the overseas markets?

BUSINESS TERMS

absolute advantage	370	dumping	385
comparative advantage	371	tariffs	386
exporting	379	quota	387
licensing	380	orderly marketing arrangements	387
cartel	381	nontariff trade barriers (NTBs)	387
most-favored-nation		free-trade associations	388
(MFN) treatment	382	customs union	388
free-trade zone	382	balance of payments	390
trading companies	384	balance of trade	390
protectionism	385	multinational corporation (MNC)	393

QUESTIONS FOR DISCUSSION AND ANALYSIS

1. Name an item in which the United States enjoys an absolute advantage and an item in which the U. S. has an absolute disadvantage.
2. Should American companies be prohibited by the U. S. government from selling certain types of products overseas?
3. Why is an effective communication system essential for dealing with commercial credit in international business transactions?
4. When a company markets overseas, what actions can it take to avoid unforeseen cultural problems?
5. Is a joint venture always better than a licensing arrangement for a company that engages in international trade?
6. If free-trade zones reduce tariff collections in a country, what is the advantage of having them?
7. Are tariffs a stronger form of protectionism than quotas?
8. Why are countries willing to enter into orderly marketing arrangements with each other when it would seem that some parties to this agreement would have little to gain?
9. Is the balance of trade a more important statistic for a country than its balance of payments?
10. Should a multinational company that is operating in a totalitarian country actively press for more human rights in that country?

PROJECTS, PROBLEMS, AND SHORT CASES

1. Recently foreign car manufacturers have greatly increased their share of the American car market. Using reference sources such as the *Business Periodicals Index*, prepare a paper on the following topics:

   a. The reasons why Americans buy foreign cars.
   b. The advantages that foreign car producers have over American car producers.
   c. The steps that U. S. car producers can take to regain a greater share of the U. S. car market.

2. Choose any three of the American multinational companies shown in Table 16-1 on page 392. Then indicate on a map the countries in which the three operate. Accompany this map with a list of the major product lines that are produced in these countries by the three companies. Helpful sources for this assignment include *Moody's Industrials* and corporate annual reports.

3. A recent article in *Newsweek* magazine about multinational corporations prompted the following discussion between college senior Ted Pauley and his classmate, Jill Herm.

"If I had the opportunity to be employed by a multinational firm, I don't know if I would accept the job," pondered Ted. "Somehow, they just don't seem moral! You hear about their unethical practices and how they take advantage of the foreign consumer."

"Why," countered Jill, "do you think these companies have double standards and operate differently overseas than in this country? After all, according to everything I've learned, U. S. corporate regulations are the toughest in the world. In fact, the restrictions make it difficult for some of our giant companies to compete against the lesser-controlled foreign biggies."

"Well, you may have a point," responded Ted softly. "But," with his voice rising, "there's more to it than just honoring the letter of the law. A company should express a genuine concern for the citizens of the country in which it's operating. Any company that has sales in the billions of dollars throughout the world can become a powerful moral force that can benefit society."

"Whoa, Ted!" admonished Jill. "You're expecting too much from these firms. After all, they were established to make a profit for their stockholders — not to take on the role of a moralist and preach the good word around the world. Lay off, man, you're coming down too hard on the multinational!"

"Jill, let me recite a few things that I've read about these companies and their overseas activities. Then you tell me whether they're acting right or wrong," Ted responded tartly. "Although some American companies have shut down their operations in South Africa, others, such as IBM, are still there. How can pressure be exerted on South Africa to get rid of its apartheid (separating blacks and whites) policies until all companies move out? Nestlé, a Swiss multinational, has been marketing in some less-developed countries a powdered baby formula that needed the addition of water. The problem was that much of the water in these countries is polluted. And, of course, it's been proven that companies such as Gulf Oil and Lockheed made under-the-table payments to foreign representatives in order to obtain business in those countries. Now can you really say that these companies acted ethically?" queried Ted.

a. Should there be more than just an economic relationship between a multinational company and a host country? Explain.

b. What are the benefits that a multinational company can bring to a developing country?

c. Provide responses to Ted about the issues that he raises in regard to the actions of IBM in South Africa, of Nestlé and its baby formula, and of Gulf Oil and Lockheed making under-the-table payments to foreign representatives. In order to prepare informed responses, you may want to draw from sources in other books or in the *Business Periodicals Index*.

V. Accounting and Finance

Chapter 17. Accounting and Financial Statements
18. Long- and Short-Term Financing
19. Security and Commodity Exchanges
20. Money and Banking
21. Risk Management and Insurance

Courtesy Merchants National Bank, Allentown, Pa.

Accounting Firm's Road to Success

In the early days the going was precarious, Thomas A. Mahoney recalls. Back in 1969, starting out alone, he founded his own accounting firm.

Several months later Arnold L. Cohen joined Mr. Mahoney, and the combination became Mahoney, Cohen & Company, which is still the firm's name. "Mahoney & Cohen — it sounds more like a vaudeville act than an accounting firm," Mr. Mahoney said in a recent interview. "Nobody knew us. We were Brand X. At the beginning, we took any business we could lay our hands on. It was a scramble to survive."

Mr. Mahoney has come a long way, he acknowledges. During the firm's first few years, the clients of Mahoney, Cohen were mostly "highly leveraged apparel companies," which translates as Seventh Avenue garment makers in hock to their teeth . . . It now has about 100 corporate or institutional clients, along with some 300 individuals for whom it provides tax work and advice. Mr. Mahoney declines to identify his clients, but the list reportedly contains several leading fashion designers, including Ralph Lauren and Diane Von Furstenberg.

Among other businesses, Mahoney, Cohen handles law firms, restaurants and publishing houses . . . And while most of the firm's work is for corporations, it gets some business from such organizations as the United States Tennis Association and even a Cherokee Indian tribe in North Carolina.

For the most part, however, its clients are smaller private companies — and that is by design. "The private firms, usually with revenues of $1 million to $50 million a year, are our market," said Mr. Cohen, a former financial vice president of the Puritan Fashions Corporation, a producer of women's apparel.

At Mahoney, Cohen's level, an accountant tends to be a jack-of-all-trades, a general practitioner, not only auditing but also giving management and tax advice.

"Most of the companies we work for don't have a treasurer or financial executive," Mr. Mahoney said. "So we offer sort of a rent-a-financial-vice-president service."

Like the accounting profession's Big Eight Firms, which have hundreds of partners and thousands of staff members, Mahoney, Cohen audits its clients by the strictures of "generally accepted accounting principles." Yet the financial statements of private companies are mainly intended for the demanding eye of a different audience — banks and other lenders, along with a handful of shareholders, not the Securities and Exchange Commission, which monitors publicly held companies.

Banks and small accounting firms commonly work together hand-in-glove. At the start, sometimes banks referred a troubled apparel company to Mr. Mahoney, who was once a vice president with John P. McGuire & Company, a commercial finance company active in the garment district. (Before that, he was an audit manager at Arthur Young & Company, one of the Big Eight.) Such a referral would give Mr. Mahoney an assignment as a consultant. If the company survived, he was often asked to be its auditor, too.

Nowadays much of the firm's new business results from client recommendations. "A satisfied client talks to his friend at the country club, and your phone rings — that's how your business grows," Mr. Mahoney said. "You slowly, carefully build a reputation, and eventually that pays off."

Accounting and Financial Statements

Objectives:

- Identify different types of accountants.
- Explain the three accounting steps that precede an interpretation of the results.
- Identify and describe the sequence of the accounts used in preparing an income statement.
- Identify and describe the sequence of the accounts used in preparing a balance sheet.
- Explain the purpose of the statement of changes in financial position.
- Calculate several types of financial ratios.
- Explain the meaning of the results obtained from an analysis of the financial statements.
- Discuss the purpose and types of audits.
- Distinguish between regular budgeting and zero-base budgeting.
- Identify the groups that establish standards and rules in the accounting field.

An owner of a privately held corporation wanted to obtain capital and expand by making a public stock offering. An investment banker reviewed the corporation's financial statements and judged the company as financially sound with good growth potential. The cautious investment banker, however, indicated that in order to enhance the sales of its stock, the company should be audited by one of the prestigious "Big Eight" accounting firms.

The owner accepted this valuable counsel and set up interviews with a partner from each of the "Big Eight" firms. Several weeks later the owner happily contacted the investment banker and announced that the selection process had been completed. The owner indicated that a thorough study of the capabilities of each firm had been conducted. Curious about the criteria used for the selection, the investment banker asked the owner how the choice was made. The owner responded that during the interviews each accountant was asked the seemingly simple question: "What does two plus two equal?" All but one of the respondents hastily answered, "Why four, of course." The one that was selected, however, stopped for a moment, pondered, and slowly replied, "What number did you have in mind?"[1]

Because of the reliance of accountants on **generally accepted accounting principles (GAAP)**, the conversation cited above should never have taken place. These principles are broadly defined standards that accountants follow in preparing financial statements. Accountants operate within reasonably defined limits in order to achieve uniformity in statement preparation. The annual report of every large corporation contains an accountant's message that is similar to the one in Figure 17-1 from the General Motors' report. This message assures the reader that the company's financial statement was prepared in conformity with generally accepted accounting principles applied on a consistent basis.

What is the nature of this business activity that furnishes us with guidelines for the handling of financial information? **Accounting** may be defined as the recording, classifying, and summarizing of business transactions, and the interpretation of this compiled information. Examples of business transactions are buying and selling goods, meeting payrolls, borrowing money, and paying taxes. Fortunately these transactions

Figure 17-1   Accountant's Report for General Motors

──────────────────── **ACCOUNTANTS' REPORT** ────────────────────

**Deloitte
Haskins + Sells**

1114 Avenue of the Americas
New York, New York 10036

CERTIFIED PUBLIC ACCOUNTANTS

General Motors Corporation, its Directors and Stockholders: February 7, 1983

We have examined the Consolidated Balance Sheet of General Motors Corporation and consolidated subsidiaries as of December 31, 1982 and 1981 and the related Statements of Consolidated Income and Changes in Consolidated Financial Position for each of the three years in the period ended December 31, 1982. Our examinations were made in accordance with generally accepted auditing standards and, accordingly, included such tests of the accounting records and such other auditing procedures as we considered necessary in the circumstances.

In our opinion, these financial statements present fairly the financial position of the companies at December 31, 1982 and 1981 and the results of their operations and the changes in their financial position for each of the three years in the period ended December 31, 1982, in conformity with generally accepted accounting principles applied on a consistent basis.

Deloitte Haskins & Sells

SOURCE: *General Motors Annual Report 1982*, p. 24

───────────────

1. Abraham J. Briloff, *Unaccountable Accounting* (New York: Harper & Row, 1972), pp. 1–2.

can be measured in dollars and cents. This common denominator makes possible an accounting system.

An accounting system is an absolute necessity for any business. Management cannot make intelligent decisions without knowing, for example, its cash balance, how much is owed to and by the firm, and whether operations are profitable. Outsiders are also interested in the financial summaries prepared from adequate accounting records. Taxes are paid on the income reported, investors decide whether to become stockholders, and banks and suppliers make credit decisions based on financial statements.

TYPES OF ACCOUNTANTS

Accountants employed by businesses are known as industrial accountants. The owner of a small business may keep its accounting records or use part-time help. Other firms, however, have at least one accountant or bookkeeper on their payrolls. Larger firms have an accounting department in which the industrial accountants are known by their specialized activities such as cost accountants, internal auditors, tax accountants, or budget accountants. Figure 17-2 shows the organization of the accounting department of a large manufacturing concern.

Another category of accountants consists of governmental accountants, who work for the local, state, or federal government. Federal agencies, such as the Internal Revenue Service (IRS), the Federal Bureau of Investigation (FBI), and the General Accounting Office (GAO), employ governmental accountants.

To the financial community, public accountants are the most important category. Public accountants are independent firms who offer their services to the public. If they have complied with state certification rules, which include passing a rigorous examination, they are called **certified public accountants (CPAs)**. If they have not fulfilled certification rules, they are known in most states as public accountants (PAs). Most

Figure 17-2   Organization Chart for an Accounting Department

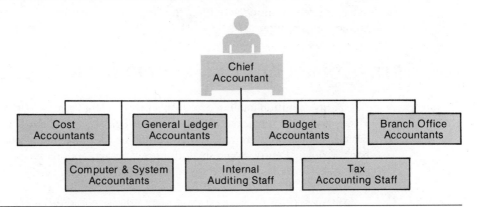

corporations have their books audited annually by CPA firms. The ranks within a CPA firm are illustrated in Figure 17-3. As indicated earlier, these firms certify the accuracy of corporate financial statements, which are usually available to the general public, and their attached certificate carries a great deal of weight. So, CPA firms employ exceptionally able professionals, maintain complete independence from the firms they audit, and adhere to a high order of ethical standards.

Figure 17-3   Ranks Within a CPA Firm

Rank	Years with Firm	Duties
• Partner	10+	• Relationship with client; overall responsibility for audit; signs audit opinion and management letter; billing and collection of fees.
• Manager	6-9	• Supervisor of audit; helps senior plan audit program and time budgets; reviews working papers, audit opinion, and management letter.
• Senior	3-5	• In charge of the audit on the job; holds costs and time within budget; directs and reviews work of the juniors.
• Assistant (or Junior)	0-2	• Performs detailed audit procedures; prepares working papers, documenting work accomplished.

SOURCE: Scott/Page/Hooper, AUDITING: A SYSTEMS APPROACH, 1982, pg. 12. Reprinted with permission of Reston Publishing Company, a Prentice-Hall Co., 11480 Sunset Hills Road, Reston, VA 22090.

The eight CPA firms with the largest number of partners, clients, offices, and the highest revenues are known as the "Big Eight," as shown in Table 17-1. Each of these firms is a limited partnership that has over 1,400 partners and 100 worldwide offices. Their clients account for an overwhelming 94 percent of all sales, profits, and employment in the United States and pay 90 percent of the corporate income tax. The legal department at the "Big Eight" firm of Touche Ross & Co. qualifies as the largest "law firm" in the world. Through expansion of their international operations and their management consulting activities, the "Big Eight" have become huge multinational business organizations.[2]

BASIC STEPS IN ACCOUNTING PROCEDURES

As its definition implies, accounting involves four basic steps which are shown in Figure 17-4: recording, classifying, summarizing, and interpreting. In the first step, business transactions are recorded in chronological order into a journal, which is a book of original entry. Some small firms rely on pen-and-ink records, but others use adding machines, cash registers, and computers.

---

2. Mark Stevens, *The Big Eight* (New York: Macmillan Publishing Co., Inc., 1981), pp. 8–9.

Table 17-1   Scope of the "Big Eight"

Firm	Home Office	1981 World Revenues (In Millions)	Number of Partners	Major Clients
Coopers & Lybrand	New York	$998	2,010	AT&T, Firestone, Kroger, Gulf Oil
Peat, Marwick, Mitchell & Co.	New York	$979	1,931	Xerox, Penney, General Electric, Safeway
Arthur Andersen & Co.	Chicago	$973	1,400	General Dynamics, Texaco, ITT, General Telephone
Price Waterhouse	New York	$850	1,613	IBM, Exxon, Du Pont, Goodyear
Ernst & Whinney	Cleveland	$807	1,600	Coca-Cola, Time Inc., Bank of America, McDonnell Douglas
Deloitte, Haskins & Sells	New York	$800	2,000	General Motors, Monsanto, TWA, Procter & Gamble
Arthur Young & Company	New York	$800	1,944	McDonald's, American Airlines, Mobil, Lockheed
Touche Ross & Co.	New York	$704	1,979	Sears, Prudential, RCA, Greyhound

The next step is the classification of transactions. By a process known as posting, the entries in the journal are transferred to a ledger, which is a book of accounts. Each account brings together all transactions affecting one item such as cash or sales. At stated periods—monthly, quarterly, semiannually, or annually—the ledger accounts are totaled, or balanced. These accounts provide the basic information for financial statements.

Summarizing, the third step, is done by constructing the financial statements. The income statement and the balance sheet are the principal ones prepared at regular intervals. Since these statements are the result of and the reason for much of the work done by an accounting department, they will be examined in some detail. Other financial statements that may or may not be required (cost of goods manufactured schedule, capital statement, retained earnings statement, and statement of changes in financial position) will be illustrated and discussed briefly.

The final step in accounting procedures is to interpret the data contained in the financial statements. The fact that a business may or may not have been operated at a profit is of vital concern, but this one figure fails to tell the whole story. For example, a bank may be willing to extend a loan to a firm that has a strong financial structure despite recent operating losses. Judicious use of such borrowed funds might correct conditions so that future business operations would be profitable. On the other hand, a firm may be headed for financial trouble even though it is currently operating profitably. Thus, the interpretation of financial statements will also be explained in detail.

Figure 17-4   Four Basic Steps in Accounting Procedures

STEP 1
Recording

	DATE	DESCRIPTION	POST. REF.	DEBIT	CREDIT	
1	1983 Dec. 1	Cash		300000		1
2		L. A. Eason, Capital			300000	2
3		Original investment				3
4		in employment agency.				4

JOURNAL   PAGE 1

STEP 2
Classifying

ACCOUNT L. A. Eason, Capital   ACCOUNT NO. 311

DATE	ITEM	POST REF	DEBIT	DATE	ITEM	POST REF	CREDIT
				1983 Dec. 1		1	300000

STEP 3
Summarizing

Hunt Taxi Corporation
Balance Sheet
August 31, 1983

Assets		
Cash		$665000
Supplies		25000
Equipment	$1250000	
Less accumulated depreciation	35000	1215000
Total assets		$1905000
Liabilities		
Accounts payable		$45000
Capital		
Capital stock	$1800000	
Retained earnings	60000	
Total capital		1860000
Total liabilities and capital		$1905000

STEP 4
Interpreting

	1984	1983
Net income..	$91,000	$76,500
Preferred dividends..	9,000	9,000
Remainder—identified with common stock	$82,000	$67,500
Shares of common stock outstanding	50,000	50,000
Earnings per share on common stock	$1.64	$1.35

FINANCIAL STATEMENTS _____

Compared to the balance sheet, which is static, the income statement is dynamic. This means that the income statement reflects summaries of operations over a period of time, while the balance sheet is a picture of the business at a given instant of time. Both of these statements are prepared at the same time, and the net income (or loss) shown on the income statement is reflected in the capital section of the balance sheet.

The Income Statement

The **income statement** summarizes the incomes and expenses of a business for a stated period of time such as a year, six months, a quarter, or a month. It shows such information as the total merchandise purchased and sold, expenses incurred, and miscellaneous sources of income. Other names given to this statement are profit and loss statement, operating statement, income summary, and income account.

Figure 17-5 presents an income statement for Jordan's Book Store, a proprietorship. Each major section of this income statement is labeled with a number and is explained below.

1. Revenue from Sales

The major source of income for most firms is the sale of merchandise. The sales figure includes the amounts paid by customers and the amounts they have agreed to pay if sales have been made on account. It is a total for the year or for a shorter period of time if statements are prepared more often. The value of merchandise returned by, and/or price reductions granted to, customers must be subtracted from this total. The resulting figure is called net sales.

2. Cost of Merchandise Sold

The **cost of merchandise sold** represents the purchase price of the merchandise that was sold by the firm during the year. The steps used to arrive at this figure are the ones shown on the income statement. Purchases–adjusted for returns, allowances, and discounts–are added to the merchandise on hand at the beginning of the year to obtain the total cost of all the merchandise that might have been sold. From this total cost the inventory figure at the end of the year is subtracted to obtain the cost of merchandise sold.

The beginning and ending inventories are usually determined by a physical count. A value is attached to each item in stock on the inventory date. There are two commonly used valuation policies: FIFO and LIFO. **FIFO** stands for "first in, first out." It assumes that items first acquired or produced, such as raw materials, parts, finished goods, and merchandise, are priced out ahead of similar items that were acquired later. **LIFO**, or "last in, first out," assumes that the most recent prices paid for these items will be used in pricing out inventories used or sold. Currently LIFO is more popular because higher recent costs reduce profits. As a result, companies save taxes and can reinvest these savings or put them to other uses. General Motors uses LIFO to value

Figure 17-5   An Income Statement

JORDAN'S BOOK STORE
Income Statement
For Year Ended December 31, 1984

1. Revenue from sales:			
Sales		$440,650	
Less: Sales returns and allowances		8,100	
Net sales			$432,550
2. Cost of merchandise sold:			
Merchandise inventory, January 1, 1984		$ 86,310	
Purchases	$284,300		
Less: Purchases returns and allowances	$7,860		
Purchases discount	3,100	10,960	
Net purchases		273,340	
Merchandise available for sale		$359,650	
Less: Merchandise inventory, December 31, 1984		78,400	
Cost of merchandise sold			281,250
3. Gross profit on sales			$151,300
4. Operating expenses:			
Selling expenses:			
Sales salaries	$ 42,100		
Advertising expense	14,400		
Store supplies expense	2,170		
Depreciation expense—store equipment	3,240		
Miscellaneous selling expense	5,150		
Total selling expenses		$ 67,060	
General expenses:			
Office salaries	$ 18,150		
Office supplies expense	1,320		
Taxes expense	6,200		
Depreciation expense—building	6,000		
Depreciation expense—office equipment	2,310		
Insurance expense	2,450		
Uncollectible accounts expense	2,000		
Miscellaneous general expense	1,700		
Total general expenses		40,130	
Total operating expenses			107,190
5. Income from operations			$ 44,110
6. Other income:			
Dividends on stock		$ 300	
Other expense:			
Interest expense		6,980	6,680
7. Net income			$ 37,430

most of its domestic inventories. If GM had used the FIFO method in 1981 for valuing its U. S. inventories, they would have been worth $1.9 billion more.[3]

The value of purchases (merchandise, raw materials, or parts) is obtained from the ledger account to which have been posted all the invoices covering the various shipments received. Purchases returns and allowances are computed according to the same pattern indicated above for sales; purchases discounts are merely price reductions granted to the firm.

Sally Jordan, the proprietor whose income statement is shown in Figure 17-5, sells books and office supplies. She purchases all the merchandise that she has available for sale. By contrast, manufacturing firms produce their goods from raw materials and/or semifinished goods that they purchase. In this case the line "Net purchases" in the income statement would be replaced with "Schedule No. 1—Cost of goods manufactured"; and the term "finished goods inventories" would replace "merchandise inventory." Figure 17-6 shows a *Schedule of Cost of Goods Manufactured* for the Creviston Manufacturing Company.

3. Gross Profit on Sales

The difference found by subtracting the cost of merchandise sold from the net sales is termed the **gross profit** on sales. For business firms that have substantial operating expenses, the gross profit on sales should be one third or two thirds of the total sales figure. In the retail industry the gross profit on sales is known as the gross margin and reflects the average overall markup percentage on goods sold. The gross profit or gross margin must be adequate to cover the operating expenses of the business and to provide a net income.

4. Operating Expenses

All of the costs that a business firm incurs in its normal operations are grouped under the classification of operating expenses. Operating expenses are usually subdivided into selling expenses and general or administrative expenses. Selling expenses are incurred as a direct result of the sales activities of the firm. Such items as salaries of salesclerks, advertising, store supplies used, depreciation on store equipment, and delivery costs are examples of selling expenses. The advantage of separating these expenses from general expenses is that the total for one year compared with the total for another year may be significant. If total selling expenses have increased, it is then possible to locate the cause or causes for the increase in individual items.

Office salaries, rent, taxes, insurance, office supplies used, depreciation on buildings and office equipment, and the cost of bad debts resulting from uncollectible account sales are examples of general expenses. They are costs connected with the general operation of the business.

---

3. *General Motors Annual Report 1982,* p. 20.

Figure 17-6   A Schedule of Cost of Goods Manufactured

CREVISTON MANUFACTURING COMPANY
Schedule No. 1 — Cost of Goods Manufactured
For Year Ended December 31, 1984

Work in process, January 1, 1984			$ 29,000
Raw materials:			
Inventory, January 1, 1984		$ 61,000	
Purchases	$184,900		
Less: Purchases returns & allowances	2,500		
Net purchases		182,400	
Total cost of materials available for use		$243,400	
Less: Inventory, December 31, 1984		70,000	
Cost of materials placed in production		$173,400	
Direct labor		152,000	
Factory overhead:			
Indirect labor	$ 14,800		
Repairs	12,000		
Heat, light, and power	19,600		
Depreciation — machinery & equipment	25,350		
Factory supplies expense	10,400		
Patents expense	7,250		
Insurance expense	3,600		
Total factory overhead		$ 93,000	
Total manufacturing costs			418,400
Total work in process during year			$447,400
Less: Work in process inventory, December 31, 1984			34,800
Cost of goods manufactured			$412,600

5. Income from Operations

The difference found by subtracting the total operating expenses from the gross profit on sales is the income from operations. If there are no other income or expense items, this figure is also the net income. But most businesses do have nonoperating incomes and costs. In some instances the total operating expenses may exceed the gross profit on sales. Should this occur, the difference between these two amounts would be known as the loss from operations.

6. Other Income and Other Expense

Other income and other expense are of a financial, rather than an operating, nature. They are also known as nonoperating income and expense or financial income and expense. The most common example of other income is interest received. Interest paid on notes, mortgages, and bonds is an example of other expense. Other income and other expense are added to or subtracted from the income from operations.

7. Net Income

The final figure on an income statement and the one that represents the result of all operations of a business, both operating and nonoperating, is the net income (or net earnings) or net loss. It is the most interesting single figure on an income statement and is frequently referred to as the **bottom line** (see Figure 17-7).

Income statements for unincorporated and incorporated businesses are identical except for the determination of the net income for corporations. As legal entities they must pay income taxes, assuming that operations have been profitable. Consequently, an income statement for a corporation might end as follows:

Net earnings before income taxes	$1,764,580
Income taxes	820,160
Net earnings	$ 944,420

Figure 17-7   **The Bottom Line**

THE WALL STREET JOURNAL

"Just give me the bottom line."

SOURCE: From *The Wall Street Journal,* November 12, 1980, p. 24. Permission—Cartoon Features Syndicate.

The Balance Sheet

The **balance sheet** lists a firm's assets, liabilities, and capital as of the close of business on a specific date–usually the end of a month, a quarter, or a year. The firm's

assets include cash on hand and in banks, accounts owed by its customers, inventories on hand, buildings, equipment, and land owned. Its **liabilities** consist of the claims of its creditors against its assets. **Capital** is the ownership interest in the business and consists of the original and subsequent funds invested by the owner or owners, plus profits retained in the business. The word "capital," when used in this sense, is also called net worth, proprietorship, or owner's equity. Corporations more often use the term stockholders' equity or shareholders' equity.

Since all the assets of a business are subject to claims by its creditors and owners, total assets should equal the total claims of creditors and owners. The statement that assets equal liabilities plus capital is known as the **balance-sheet equation** and is expressed as follows:

$$Assets = Liabilities + Capital$$

or

$$Assets - Liabilities = Capital$$

The balance-sheet equation stresses that a business has an entity of its own in showing the amount of its obligation to its owner or owners.

Figure 17-8 shows the balance sheet for Jordan's Book Store, whose income statement is shown on page 408. Note that the three major classifications — assets, liabilities, and capital — have been divided into subclassifications. Assets are classified as current assets, fixed assets, investments, and intangible assets. Liabilities are classified into current liabilities and long-term liabilities. Each major section of this balance sheet is numbered for easy reference.

1. Current Assets

Cash and other assets that will be converted into cash or used within a short time are **current assets**. The maximum length of time for conversion into cash is usually one year. If merchandise is sold on open-book account or for notes, it can be assumed that the accounts receivable or notes receivable will be collected in less than one year from the date of the sale. Such items as office supplies on hand will be used within a year, and insurance currently prepaid will expire in the months ahead.

2. Fixed Assets

Assets that are intended for use rather than for sale and that are expected to last beyond one year are **fixed assets**. For example, land for a building site may last forever. Although automobiles or trucks may not last more than three to five years, such assets are sold when they are no longer useful to the firm. They are not purchased for the purpose of selling them to customers.

With the exception of land, fixed assets deteriorate in value with use and the passage of time. Because it is desirable to show both the original cost of a fixed asset and its reduced value year by year, two separate figures are required. The accumulated depreciation is increased each year until it equals the value of the asset. At that time, if the estimate of the useful life of the asset was accurate, its balance-sheet value will

Figure 17-8   A Balance Sheet

JORDAN'S BOOK STORE
Balance Sheet
December 31, 1984

Assets

1. Current assets:

Cash		$ 14,080
Accounts receivable	$ 28,340	
Less: Allowance for doubtful accounts	3,200	25,140
Merchandise inventory, December 31, 1984		78,400
Store supplies		1,560
Office supplies		1,270
Prepaid insurance		930
Total current assets		$121,380

2. Fixed assets:

Store equipment	$ 32,400		
Less: Accumulated depreciation	8,300	$ 24,100	
Office equipment	$ 23,100		
Less: Accumulated depreciation	7,040	16,060	
Building	$150,000		
Less: Accumulated depreciation	30,000	120,000	
Land		9,000	
Total fixed assets			169,160

3. Investments:

Stock in Steelcraft, Inc.	5,000

4. Intangible assets:

Goodwill	7,500
Total assets	$303,040

Liabilities

5. Current liabilities:

Notes payable	$ 14,000	
Accounts payable	33,900	
Taxes payable	2,680	
Total current liabilities		$ 50,580

6. Long-term liabilities:

Mortgage payable	90,000
Total liabilities	$140,580

Capital

7. Sally Jordan, capital	162,460
Total liabilities and capital	$303,040

be zero because the accumulated depreciation is subtracted from the original value. The asset will then be discarded or sold for its scrap value.

3. Investments

Stocks or bonds of other organizations that are purchased by a firm for income or for other reasons are investments. It is unusual for a proprietorship to list investments because stocks and bonds normally are purchased by a person rather than by a business. In the example of Jordan's Book Store, it made an investment in Steelcraft, Inc., to obtain an exclusive territorial dealership for its line of steel desks, chairs, and filing cabinets.

4. Intangible Assets

When assets that are purchased have no physical substance but have some other value, such as a legal right, they are known as **intangible assets**. The most common of these is **goodwill**. This is the price paid for an operating business above the net fair value of its assets over its liabilities. This premium reflects the good name, trade connections, or earning capacity of the business.

5. Current Liabilities

Debts that are owed and payable within a short time are classified as **current liabilities**. Amounts owed to trade creditors—such as purchases of merchandise on open-book account—are due in 30, 60, or 90 days, depending upon the terms of the transaction. Amounts owed to banks and employees are other common current liabilities. Liabilities that will come due and be payable within one year after the date of the balance sheet should be treated as current liabilities.

6. Long-Term Liabilities

Debts that will not be due for several years are called **long-term liabilities**. Examples of long-term liabilities are monies borrowed by selling bonds and long-term notes, as well as mortgages payable. The sum of long-term liabilities and current liabilities represents the amount of capital that has been secured from outsiders for use in the business.

7. Capital

If a business is a proprietorship, a single line shows the amount of capital as of the date of the balance sheet. This amount is supported by a **capital statement** that shows changes which have taken place since the date of the previous balance sheet. Figure 17-9 presents the capital statement for Jordan's Book Store.

If a business is a partnership, the interests of all partners are shown in the capital section of the balance sheet. For example, if Cook, Dapper, and Chan own and operate a partnership under the name of the Cook Drug Company, the capital section of the balance sheet for this firm might appear as follows:

Figure 17-9   A Capital Statement

JORDAN'S BOOK STORE
Capital Statement
For Year Ended December 31, 1984

Capital, January 1, 1984		$143,030
Net income for the year	$37,430	
Less: Withdrawals	18,000	
Net increase in capital		19,430
Capital, December 31, 1984		$162,460

R. D. Cook, capital	$ 68,400
P. M. Dapper, capital	35,250
E. C. Chan, capital	19,800
Total capital	$123,450

The supporting capital statement for a partnership would be similar to that of a proprietorship, except that it would show changes that had taken place in each partner's capital account.

On corporate balance sheets the individual interest of each stockholder is not shown even though the company may have only one, two, or three owners. Instead, dollar values for the different types of stock outstanding, paid-in surplus, and the amount of retained earnings are shown. The stockholders'-equity section of a balance sheet for a corporation with both preferred and common stock outstanding might appear as follows:

Preferred stock	$ 500,000
Common stock	1,200,000
Paid-in surplus	2,435,000
Retained earnings	14,177,236
Total stockholders' equity	$18,312,236

Instead of a capital statement, a **retained earnings statement** for a corporation presents the details of changes that have taken place in its capital account during the year. Figure 17-10 shows such a statement for the Creviston Manufacturing Company.

Statement of Changes in Financial Position

The **statement of changes in financial position** shows the sources that provided working capital, what this working capital was used for, and the components of the resulting increase or decrease in working capital. **Working capital** is the dollar difference between the total current assets and the total current liabilities. As Figure 17-11

Figure 17-10   A Retained Earnings Statement

CREVISTON MANUFACTURING COMPANY
Retained Earnings Statement
For Year Ended December 31, 1984

Balance, January 1, 1984		$3,486,750
Net income for the year		649,000
Total		$4,135,750
Less: Cash dividends:		
Preferred stock	$300,000	
Common stock	200,000	500,000
Balance, December 31, 1984		$3,635,750

Figure 17-11   A Statement of Changes in Financial Position

CREVISTON MANUFACTURING COMPANY
Statement of Changes in Financial Position
For Year Ended December 31, 1984

Sources of working capital:		
Net income	$649,000	
Depreciation	38,400	
Sale of subsidiary	750,000	$1,437,400
Application of working capital:		
Cash dividends paid	$500,000	
Purchases of property, plant, and equipment	277,400	
Reduction in long-term debt	620,000	1,397,400
Increase in working capital		$ 40,000
Changes in working-capital components:		
Increase (decrease) in working capital		
Current assets:		
Cash	$ (1,800)	
Receivables	14,300	
Inventories	36,700	
Prepaid expenses	2,100	$ 51,300
Current liabilities:		
Accounts payable	9,400	
Taxes payable	1,900	11,300
Increase in working capital		$ 40,000

shows, the customary major source of working capital is the net income of the business. Another source of working capital — depreciation — reduces net income but does not require an outlay of cash during the current year. Other sources include the sale of securities and unneeded assets. Working capital is commonly used to pay dividends, retire long-term debt, and acquire additions to property, plant, and equipment.

The difference between the sources of working capital and its uses will either increase or decrease the amount on hand the previous year. To show in detail the effect on each current asset and current liability, the increase or decrease from figures reported a year ago is shown in the lower portion of the statement.

INTERPRETATION OF FINANCIAL STATEMENTS

Only after the income statement, balance sheet, and any other desired statements are prepared can the final basic step of interpretation be performed. By means of percentages, ratios, and other techniques, it is possible to analyze the financial status of a business. Figure 17-12 shows a partial analysis of a balance sheet and the related income statement. The various accounts in financial statements offer many possibilities for interpretation. Comparisons with previous statements or with those of competing firms can be made, too.

The financial ratios of a firm are important to its creditors — particularly suppliers and financial institutions. Prior to dealing with a firm, suppliers often analyze its financial ratios in order to determine its debt-paying ability. Dun & Bradstreet (D&B), a large financial-reporting organization, computes the average financial ratios for numerous lines of trade (see Table 17-2). By comparing the D&B ratios with the ratios of a prospective customer, a supplier can evaluate the prospect's financial strength. Robert Morris Associates, which is the national association of bank loan and credit officers, also publishes financial data and ratios for nearly 300 lines of business. Bankers judge the financial strength of a commercial-loan applicant by comparing the applicant's financial data with the Robert Morris data.

Some of the most useful ratios for analyzing financial statements are explained below and calculated for Jordan's Book Store, whose financial statements have been illustrated.

Current Ratio

The **current ratio** is found by dividing the total current assets by the total current liabilities. This ratio is very important to the owners and to short-term creditors because the current assets are a source of funds to pay current liabilities. An acceptable minimum current ratio is usually 2 to 1. The fact that current assets sometimes shrink in value whereas current liabilities do not explains the need for $2.00 of current assets for every $1.00 of current liabilities.

By referring to the balance sheet on page 413, the current ratio for Jordan's Book Store is:

Figure 17-12   Partial Analysis of Financial Statements

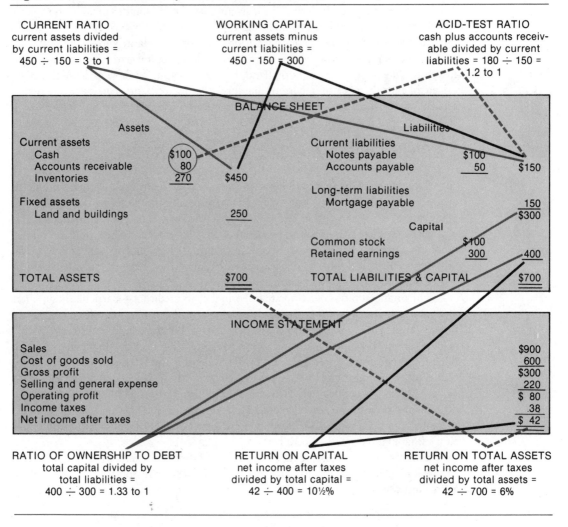

CURRENT RATIO
current assets divided
by current liabilities =
450 ÷ 150 = 3 to 1

WORKING CAPITAL
current assets minus
current liabilities =
450 - 150 = 300

ACID-TEST RATIO
cash plus accounts receivable divided by current
liabilities = 180 ÷ 150 =
1.2 to 1

BALANCE SHEET

Assets			Liabilities		
Current assets			**Current liabilities**		
Cash	$100		Notes payable	$100	
Accounts receivable	80		Accounts payable	50	$150
Inventories	270	$450			
			Long-term liabilities		
Fixed assets			Mortgage payable		150
Land and buildings		250			$300
			Capital		
			Common stock	$100	
			Retained earnings	300	400
TOTAL ASSETS		$700	**TOTAL LIABILITIES & CAPITAL**		$700

INCOME STATEMENT

Sales	$900
Cost of goods sold	600
Gross profit	$300
Selling and general expense	220
Operating profit	$ 80
Income taxes	38
Net income after taxes	$ 42

RATIO OF OWNERSHIP TO DEBT
total capital divided by
total liabilities =
400 ÷ 300 = 1.33 to 1

RETURN ON CAPITAL
net income after taxes
divided by total capital =
42 ÷ 400 = 10½%

RETURN ON TOTAL ASSETS
net income after taxes
divided by total assets =
42 ÷ 700 = 6%

$$\frac{\text{Current assets}}{\text{Current liabilities}} = \frac{\$121,380}{\$50,580} = 2.4 \text{ to } 1$$

Acid-Test Ratio

The **acid-test ratio** is a refinement of the current ratio in that it determines the ability of a firm to meet its current debt on very short notice. It recognizes that the conversion of merchandise inventory into cash takes more time than is true for other current assets. To find the acid-test ratio, divide the total cash and net receivables by

Table 17-2   Dun & Bradstreet Key Business Ratios

Line of Business (and number of concerns reporting)	Current Assets to Current Debt	Net Profits on Net Sales	Net Profits on Tangible Net Worth	Net Profits on Net Working Capital	Net Sales to Tangible Net Worth	Net Sales to Net Working Capital	Collection Period	Net Sales to Inventory	Fixed Assets to Tangible Net Worth	Current Debt to Tangible Net Worth	Total Debt to Tangible Net Worth	Inventory to Net Working Capital	Current Debt to Inventory	Funded Debts to Net Working Capital
	Times	Percent	Percent	Percent	Times	Times	Days	Times	Percent	Percent	Percent	Percent	Percent	Percent
5531 Auto & home supply stores (53)	2.72	4.04	15.94	25.84	7.51	8.88	•	6.8	15.2	45.9	101.6	102.0	61.0	21.5
	1.79	1.41	8.21	11.27	4.54	6.39	•	5.8	27.6	105.0	166.2	123.0	95.3	53.0
	1.38	0.47	2.33	3.68	3.18	4.86	•	3.8	53.3	185.8	290.0	179.4	146.3	111.2
5641 Children's & infants' wear stores (41)	4.44	4.46	17.03	19.83	7.12	9.47	•	5.6	5.9	32.4	68.5	88.5	32.0	26.2
	2.66	2.45	9.06	11.35	4.95	5.14	•	4.3	21.7	61.0	103.6	113.0	51.0	41.7
	1.79	0.44	0.92	1.59	3.04	3.17	•	2.9	45.4	116.0	186.5	162.5	84.2	78.7
5611 Clothing & furnishings men's & boys' (223)	4.52	4.64	15.49	20.51	5.68	6.24	•	6.3	7.5	22.4	45.0	69.3	36.3	10.8
	2.75	2.21	7.14	8.26	3.49	4.19	•	4.4	16.5	47.5	88.1	92.4	61.8	28.1
	1.84	0.48	1.54	2.07	2.38	2.69	•	3.1	37.2	90.3	153.1	131.1	93.0	52.0

SOURCE: Dun & Bradstreet Corporation, *Key Business Ratios* (New York, 1981). By permission of Dun & Bradstreet Credit Services, a company of The Dun & Bradstreet Corporation.

the current liabilities. If the firm owns marketable securities purchased on a temporary basis, these may be added to the cash and net receivables. An acceptable minimum acid-test ratio is 1 to 1.

Using information from the balance sheet on page 413, the acid-test ratio for Jordan's Book Store is:

$$\frac{\text{Cash + Accounts receivable (net)}}{\text{Current liabilities}} = \frac{\$14,080 + \$25,140}{\$50,580} = .8 \text{ to } 1$$

Whereas Jordan's current ratio was comfortably in excess of the 2 to 1 minimum, its acid-test ratio falls short of the 1 to 1 acceptable minimum. This indicates an area in which Sally Jordan should take corrective action.

Inventory Turnover

A retail firm must always try to "turn over," or sell, its present stock of salable goods as rapidly as possible before it loses its maximum value. The frequency with which this move is accomplished is called the **inventory turnover**, which is a measure of efficiency.

The preferred method of determining the turnover of merchandise inventory is to divide the cost of merchandise sold by an average monthly inventory. In the case of Jordan's Book Store, only the beginning and ending inventories are available for averaging. Its inventory turnover would be calculated in two steps:

Step 1.　$\$86,310 + \$78,400 = \$164,710$
　　　　　$\$164,710 \div 2 \qquad = \$ 82,355$, average inventory

Step 2.　$\dfrac{\text{Cost of merchandise sold}}{\text{Average inventory}} = \dfrac{\$281,250}{\$82,355} = 3.4 \text{ turns}$

For a retail grocery store, 3.4 would be a poor turnover; but for a book and office supply store it is excellent. A comparison with previous years' turnovers and with similar stores of the same size would be helpful.

Ratio of Ownership to Debt

Practically every business is financed by a combination of funds secured from its owners and its creditors. The **ratio of ownership to debt** shows the relative proportion of capital secured from these two sources. A mark of conservative financing is substantial ownership on the part of the proprietors or stockholders. This means that the ownership equity is large enough to absorb extensive and continued losses, and there is less danger of insolvency.

To find the ratio of ownership to debt for Jordan's Book Store, divide Sally Jordan's capital account by total liabilities, as follows:

$$\frac{\text{Capital}}{\text{Total liabilities}} = \frac{\$162,460}{\$140,580} = 1.2 \text{ to } 1$$

This is an unsatisfactory ratio, as proprietors ought to contribute at least twice and preferably three times as much capital as is secured from creditors. Assuming the continued profitability of the firm, a conservative policy on withdrawing these profits should improve this ratio.

Rate of Return on Capital

Individuals invest their own funds in a business to obtain a return on their investments. Because of the risks involved in running a business, the rate of return should be higher than that obtained from an identical amount invested in conservative securities. Also, although a proprietor may devote full time to the business, a personal salary is not included as an operating expense.

As shown in the capital statement on page 415, Sally Jordan's investment in her business was $143,030 at the beginning of the year and $162,460 at the end of the year. An average of these two amounts is $152,745. The **rate of return on capital** is calculated by dividing the net income by the average investment. For Jordan's Book Store this rate is:

$$\frac{\text{Net income}}{\text{Average investment}} = \frac{\$37,430}{\$152,745} = .245 \text{ or } 24.5\%$$

A rate of return on capital of almost 25 percent is very good, but it must be remembered that this includes the personal service rendered by Sally Jordan to her store.

Rate of Return on Total Assets

Another measure of a firm's efficiency is the **rate of return on total assets**. To find this ratio, divide the net income after taxes by the total assets. The income statement for Jordan's Book Store shows no taxes paid. So, its rate of return on total assets is:

$$\frac{\text{Net income}}{\text{Total assets}} = \frac{\$37,430}{\$303,040} = .124 \text{ or } 12.4\%$$

This rate of return on assets must be considered very good as Sally Jordan would find it difficult in most years to obtain this yield by investing the same amount in securities. Also, this rate should be higher than the rate she pays for borrowed capital.

Earnings per Share of Common Stock

A dollar-and-cents figure that is frequently shown in the printed annual reports of corporations and widely used by security analysts is the **earnings per share** of common stock, or EPS. EPS is computed by dividing the amount available to common stockholders by the number of shares of common stock outstanding.

EPS cannot be computed for Jordan's Book Store, which is a proprietorship, or for partnerships. However, it can be calculated for the Creviston Manufacturing Company, whose retained earnings statement is shown on page 416. Assuming that this corporation has 800,000 shares of common stock outstanding, Creviston's EPS is computed as follows:

Net income	$649,000
Less: Preferred-stock dividends	300,000
Income available to common stockholders	$349,000

$$\frac{\text{Income available to common stockholders}}{\text{Number of common-stock shares outstanding}} = \frac{\$349,000}{800,000} = \$0.44, \text{ EPS}$$

AUDITS

Since the Equity Funding scandal of the early 1970s, there has been greater interest in auditing the activities of companies. In the Equity Funding case, 50 percent of the policies listed on the books of its life insurance subsidiary were nonexistent. Thus, the reinsurers who bought dummy policies from Equity for millions of dollars were defrauded.

A **financial audit** is a periodic examination and evaluation of the accounting records of a firm. It is commonly an *external* audit conducted by persons outside the organization, usually CPAs. They examine the financial records of the firm mainly for the benefit of creditors, investors, and government agencies. They examine the accounting transactions of the firm in accordance with generally accepted auditing standards. When deviations are found, the auditors suggest various corrective actions. Since so many measures of performance are based upon financial information, accurate financial records are necessary for these audits. The Securities and Exchange Commission requires that publicly owned corporations have an audit at the time they file their registration statements to go public, and annual audits thereafter.

Government auditors engage in external audits, too. The purpose of their audits is to determine whether an organization is complying with various governmental regulations. For example, auditors at the Internal Revenue Service check income tax returns. Those at the General Accounting Office audit firms that have government contracts, and those at the Federal Deposit Insurance Corporation examine bank transactions.

The *internal* audit is an independent-opinion activity conducted by employees within the organization. Internal auditors review the efficiency of the organization's policies, procedures, and controls. In addition, they determine the reliability of the data that are generated by the organization.

A special kind of audit—the corporate social audit—defines corporate social responsiveness and was described in Chapter 2.

BUDGETS

All large companies and governmental units, such as school districts, use budgets as an aid in management planning and control. A **budget** is a written plan of action in numerical form, covering a specific period of time, against which actual performance may be compared. The purpose of a budget is to establish goals, develop a plan that achieves these goals, and provide periodic comparisons to determine whether the goals are being met. The customary coverage for an operating budget is a year, which is then broken down into quarters or months.

Budget Preparation

Within a company, budgets typically are prepared for: sales, sales expense and advertising, production, all major departments, cash, and estimates of the financial statements. All the activities of a business depend primarily on the volume of sales. Thus, the first step in the preparation of a company budget is to establish the sales budget. All the other departmental budgets, such as the production budget, are then set up on the basis of their relation to the sales budget.

Budgetary Control

Budgetary control is achieved by the use of forms, such as the one illustrated in Figure 17-13. They show the budget figures for a period of time, such as a month, with a space for inserting actual performance reports as soon as they are compiled. A comparison between the planned and actual results indicates how well each department and the entire organization are doing in measuring up to its budgeted figures. Any variations will be noted and corrective steps, if required, can be taken. For example, if sales in a certain territory are running below the budget, the sales manager can get in touch with the salespersons in that area to discover the cause of the trouble.

Zero-Base Budgeting

In traditional budgeting a manager simply adds to or subtracts from a previous year's budget to arrive at a new one. In recent years a new budgeting concept called **zero-base budgeting (ZBB)** has been adopted by some firms. In industry, ZBB was first used in 1969 at Texas Instruments. Zero-base budgeting requires the budget requests to be justified in detail from scratch—or zero—each year. A manager must be able to show why any money should be spent at all.

Figure 17-13   Budgetary Control Statement Indicating Variations from a Budget

REED'S DEPARTMENT STORES
Income Statement with Variations from Budget
For Month Ended January 31, 1984

	January Budget		January Actual		January Variation
Sales		$264,000		$271,000	$+7,000
Cost of merchandise sold:					
Merchandise inventory, Jan. 1	$ 66,700		$ 65,100		$−1,600
Purchases	190,000		194,000		+4,000
Merchandise available for sale	$256,700		$259,100		$+2,400
Merchandise inventory, Jan. 31	75,000		70,000		−5,000
Cost of merchandise sold		181,700		189,100	+7,400
Gross profit on sales		$ 82,300		$ 81,900	$− 400
Operating expenses:					
Selling expenses:					
Sales salaries	$ 26,000		$ 27,500		$+1,500
Advertising	9,000		10,200		+1,200
Delivery expense	3,200		3,400		+ 200
Misc. selling expenses	2,000		2,350		+ 350
Total selling expenses	$ 40,200		$ 43,450		$+3,250
General expenses:					
Office salaries	$ 9,000		$ 9,175		$+ 175
Rent	3,600		3,600		0
Taxes	2,000		2,000		0
Insurance	1,300		1,300		0
Misc. general expenses	900		830		− 70
Total general expenses	$ 16,800		$ 16,905		$+ 105
Total operating expenses		$ 57,000		$ 60,355	$+3,355
Net income from operations		$ 25,300		$ 21,545	$−3,755
Other expense:					
Interest expense		300		250	− 50
Net income		$ 25,000		$ 21,295	$−3,705

In ZBB, projects are ranked and priorities are assigned. As a result, some projects are either eliminated, budgeted at a reduced level, budgeted at a similar level, or increased. ZBB attacks duplication and vested interests that have escaped serious review under the traditional budgeting methods. When the state of Georgia adopted ZBB, it discovered that seven different state agencies had the responsibility for the education of deaf children!

STANDARDIZATION AND REGULATION

Accounting is not an exact science despite the impression given by amounts shown in exact dollar terms. Many entries involve judgments such as how fast to depreciate a factory building or whether to use FIFO or LIFO in valuing inventories. Many such decisions can have a substantial bearing on the stated earnings of a business. Gains can be turned into losses, and vice versa. In order to reduce the areas in which figures can be manipulated, strenuous efforts have been made in recent years to require more uniformity in accounting procedures.

The most important group in the area of standardization is the Financial Accounting Standards Board (FASB). Established in 1973 by the American Institute of Certified Public Accountants (AICPA) and four other professional groups, the FASB establishes principles that CPA firms follow in auditing their clients. The process of establishing these principles is depicted in Figure 17-14. In specialized areas several

---

Figure 17-14   How Accounting Principles Are Established

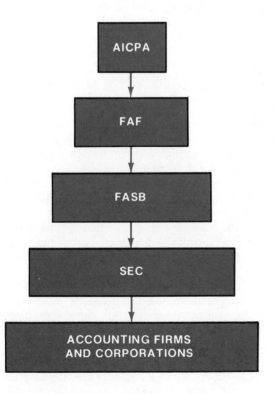

The American Institute of Certified Public Accountants Board of Directors appoints the trustees of the FAF.

The Financial Accounting Foundation Board of Trustees appoints the members of the FASB, which consists of 7 members with 4 coming from public accounting.

The Financial Accounting Standards Board establishes accounting principles and determines the procedures to be used in formulating them.

The Securities and Exchange Commission evaluates and accepts the accounting principles established by the FASB as those satisfying the requirements of the federal securities acts.

All accounting firms and publicly held corporations use the FASB accounting principles, as accepted by the SEC, in reporting financial information to the public.

---

committees of various accounting societies attempt to establish standards. Notable among these is the Auditing Standards Division of the American Institute of CPAs.

Of the positions taken by the Financial Accounting Standards Board, two have had the widest impact. The Statement of Financial Accounting Standards No. 8 requires firms operating overseas to show gains and losses in converting foreign currencies into American dollars. The Statement of Financial Accounting Standards No. 14 requires corporations engaged in several different types of businesses to provide information by industry, as well as by geographic areas. In Figure 17-15, this information is depicted for the General Foods Corporation.

In general, the Securities and Exchange Commission accepts the accounting principles proposed by the FASB. The Office of the Chief Accountant is the major accounting and auditing authority for the SEC. It formally establishes the accounting rules that determine the structure and content of the financial statements that are filed with the SEC.

SUMMARY

Accountants follow generally accepted accounting principles (GAAP) in establishing accounting systems for businesses. Small firms may be able to keep financial data confidential, but large companies publish their statements at least annually. In order to gain acceptance of these figures by the public, these corporations have their books audited by a firm of CPAs, who certify the accuracy of the statements.

One of the major financial statements prepared by an accounting department is the income statement. It summarizes results for a period of time, frequently a year, and ends with a single figure showing a net income or net loss. This is the so-called bottom line, which is the most important figure to outsiders who are interested in the company. The other major financial statement is the balance sheet. It depicts the financial situation of the business at a specific moment in time. It shows what is owned and what is owed, with the difference being the book value of the ownership equity. Another statement that is commonly prepared is the statement of changes in financial position. This shows the sources and uses of working capital for a period of time such as a year.

After the financial statements are prepared, it becomes possible to analyze the results. Ratios, percentages, and turnovers can be calculated. Some of these are of considerable interest to outsiders, but all should prove valuable to management.

There are both external and internal audits, depending on who is conducting the audit. An external audit is conducted by either independent CPAs or government auditors who are not employees of the firm being audited. An internal audit is an independent-opinion activity conducted by the employees within an organization.

A budget is a written plan of action in numerical form, covering a specific period of time, against which actual performance may be compared. In zero-base budgeting, projects are ranked and priorities are assigned. As a result, some projects are either eliminated, budgeted at a reduced level, budgeted at a similar level, or increased.

The most important group that standardizes accounting procedures is the Financial Accounting Standards Board. It establishes the accounting principles that CPA firms follow

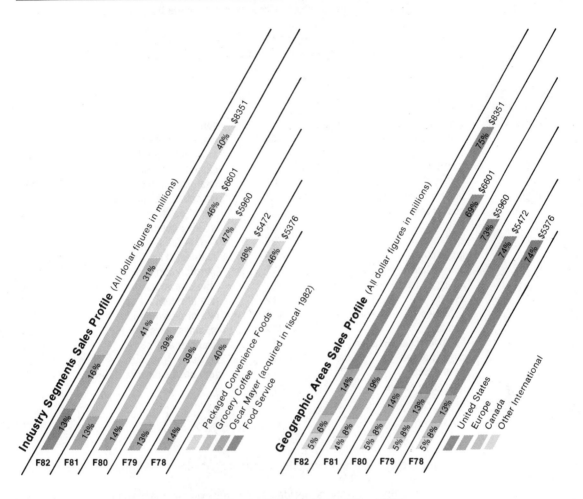

SOURCE: *General Foods Corporation Annual Report/Fiscal 1982.*

in auditing their clients. In general, the Securities and Exchange Commission accepts the accounting principles proposed by the FASB. The SEC formally establishes the accounting rules that determine the structure and content of financial statements.

1. What types of accountants are employed by Mahoney, Cohen & Company?
2. Is Mahoney, Cohen & Company a member of the "Big Eight"?
3. What is meant by "generally accepted accounting principles"?
4. What are the three major types of financial statements that Mahoney, Cohen & Company prepares for its clients?
5. Because it is a small accounting firm, should Mahoney, Cohen & Company be expected to adhere to the principles established by the FASB for auditing clients?

BUSINESS TERMS

generally accepted accounting principles (GAAP)	402
accounting	402
Certified Public Accountants (CPAs)	403
income statement	407
cost of merchandise sold	407
FIFO	407
LIFO	407
gross profit	409
bottom line	411
balance sheet	411
assets	412
liabilities	412
capital	412
balance-sheet equation	412
current assets	412
fixed assets	412
intangible assets	414
goodwill	414
current liabilities	414
long-term liabilities	414
capital statement	414
retained earnings statement	415
statement of changes in financial position	415
working capital	415
current ratio	417
acid-test ratio	418
inventory turnover	420
ratio of ownership to debt	420
rate of return on capital	421
rate of return on total assets	421
earnings per share (EPS)	422
financial audit	422
budget	423
zero-base budgeting (ZBB)	424

QUESTIONS FOR DISCUSSION AND ANALYSIS

1. Why are the generally accepted accounting principles (GAAP) so important in the accounting profession?
2. Assume that a business decided to operate without maintaining any accounting records. What types of problems would it encounter?
3. Are the CPAs who audit the books of a corporation more important to the corporation than the industrial accountants who keep the books?
4. Explain the basic differences between an income statement and a balance sheet. Which is more important to the creditors of a company?
5. Is the so-called bottom line the most important figure shown on any of the financial statements?
6. Is it possible that a firm with a poor reputation could legitimately show goodwill on its balance sheet?
7. What financial ratios of a company would a stockholder use to judge the efficiency of its management?
8. Should all organizations—large and small—periodically submit to a financial audit?

9. How can a budget be both a planning and a control tool for an organization?
10. Should the accounting profession be permitted to establish its own set of standards and regulations?

1. Using the information concerning Lamont's Menswear given below, prepare the following financial statements:

a. Lamont's Menswear, owned and operated by Kevin Lamont, had the following account balances at the end of December 31, 1984. From this information prepare an income statement using Figure 17-5 on page 408 as a guide for the proper format.

Sales	$300,000	Depreciation expense—	$ 3,500
Sales returns and	10,000	store equipment	
allowances		Office salaries	22,000
Merchandise inventory,	60,000	Uncollectible accounts	2,500
January 1, 1984		expense	
Purchases	170,000	Depreciation expense—	2,000
Purchases returns and	4,000	office equipment	
allowances		Depreciation expense—	4,500
Purchases discount	7,000	building	
Merchandise inventory,	65,000	Taxes expense	5,000
December 31, 1984		Insurance expense	5,500
Sales salaries	30,000	Miscellaneous office	1,500
Advertising expense	10,000	expense	
Store supplies expense	3,000	Interest expense	2,500

b. Lamont's Menswear had the following additional account balances at the end of December 31, 1984. From this information prepare a balance sheet using Figure 17-8 on page 413 as a guide for the proper format.

Cash	$ 22,000	Store equipment	$ 35,000
Accounts receivable	37,000	Accumulated depreciation,	7,000
Allowance for doubtful	5,000	store equipment	
accounts		Office equipment	20,000
Merchandise inventory	65,000	Accumulated depreciation,	4,000
Store and office supplies	7,800	office equipment	
Prepaid insurance	1,200	Notes payable	11,000
Building	80,000	Accounts payable	10,500
Accumulated depreciation,	12,000	Taxes payable	5,500
building		Mortgage payable	30,000
Land	8,000	Kevin Lamont, capital	200,000
Goodwill	9,000		

c. Lamont's Menswear had the following additional account balances at the end of December 31, 1984. From this information prepare a capital statement using Figure 17-9 on page 415 as a guide for the proper format.

Kevin Lamont, capital	$180,000	Kevin Lamont, drawing	$ 24,000
January 1, 1984			

2. Information for the year ended December 31, 1984, from the books of the Value Rite Hardware Store is presented below. From this information compute the following ratios:

    a. Current ratio.
    b. Acid-test ratio.
    c. Inventory turnover.
    d. Ratio of ownership to debt.
    e. Rate of return on capital.
    f. Rate of return on total assets.
    g. Earnings per share of common stock.

Current assets	$200,000	Current liabilities	$ 80,000
Cash	35,000	Total liabilities	90,000
Receivables	45,000	Capital, January 1, 1984	285,000
Merchandise inventory, January 1, 1984	70,000	Capital, December 31, 1984	330,000
		Cost of merchandise sold	510,000
Merchandise inventory, December 31, 1984	120,000	Net income	42,750
Total assets	420,000		

Number of shares of common stock outstanding = 21,375

3. Lori Fryberg operated a successful women's apparel store in Barre, VT. The store offered a broad assortment of moderate-priced clothing that was directed toward the working woman. Although Fryberg did not carry shoes, she often was requested by her customers to stock them. At the time they purchased their apparel, many women wanted to buy matching shoes. As a result of these requests, Fryberg decided to add a shoe salon to her store. In the back of her store was a storage room that could be easily converted into a shoe salon.

When a shoe retailer in a nearby city decided to end his business, Fryberg was presented with the opportunity to purchase his remaining stock of women's shoes. Fryberg carefully examined these shoes and determined that they would very nicely complement her apparel lines. She was able to buy the entire stock for $26,000, which was only 50 percent of the original cost to the shoe retailer. She believed that over a period of time she could realize about $70,000 to $85,000 from the sale of the shoes. Fryberg agreed to pay cash for the shoes by the end of 30 days.

Because Fryberg rented her building, she had little invested in fixed assets. Before she added the shoes to her inventory, her balance sheet showed the following current assets and current liabilities:

Current assets:		Current liabilities:	
Cash	$ 6,000	Accounts payable	$20,000
Accounts receivable	42,000	Notes payable	16,000
Merchandise inventory	36,000		$36,000
	$84,000		

The addition of the shoe salon would increase her merchandise inventory to $62,000 and her accounts payable to $46,000. In order to pay for the shoes within the 30-day period, Fryberg sought a loan for $26,000 from a local bank. To her amazement the loan application was rejected because, with the loan, her current ratio would be less than 2 to 1 and her acid-test ratio would be below 1 to 1. At a conference with the bank loan officer, she was informed that her loan request would be granted if she could attain the acceptable financial ratios.

What actions should Fryberg take in order to attain the proper financial ratios for her business? (Assume that she does not seek any other credit or capital financing.)

Booming Markets Spur Flood of New Brokers

Ronald M. Schwartz, vice president at Merrill Lynch, Pierce, Fenner & Smith in charge of training and development, remembers "when you had to shoot a cannon down Wall Street" to find a prospective stock broker.

Today, with the financial markets booming, potential brokers are pouring onto Wall Street in numbers unmatched since the "go-go" years of the late 1960s.

Most brokerage firms report applications far in excess of their training needs. Bache Halsey Stuart Shields, for example, gets 700 to 1,000 applications a month for a program that accepts 50 to 60 trainees. E. F. Hutton turns away 15 applicants for every one it takes.

According to the National Association of Securities Dealers (N. A. S. D.), about 12,000 people took the General Securities Examination (G. S. E.) in 1980, up from 9,000 in 1979. Based on a 1,700-test-per-month average so far this year, the number of new brokers licensed in 1981 could clear 20,000.

The average broker's gross sales were up 30 percent in 1980, to an average of nearly $150,000, according to industry estimates. Although earnings vary from firm to firm, brokers average 30 to 35 percent of gross sales. Experienced brokers are paid through commission. New brokers generally receive a small salary as well.

Essentially, a broker is trained in two phases. First, three months of study in the branch office for the G. S. E., a mandatory certification test administered by the N. A. S. D. and the New York Stock Exchange; second, a plane flight to company headquarters — usually New York — for a four-week "in-house" program.

The home office programs are "like boot camp," according to Mr. McGough, who perhaps appropriately is a former Marine Corps drill instructor. "These people will be out making a living in a very short time, so we hit them with everything at once. We put it to them. It's one of those situations where regardless of what they do, they're wrong."

The bulk of the work at most training programs involves the acquisition of product knowledge, as well as an understanding of compliance laws, Securities and Exchange Commission regulations, and various trading codes. A small staff of four or five gives most of the rudimentary lectures.

Guest lecturers address topics ranging from macroeconomic analyses to warnings on the dangers of wearing a screaming yellow bow tie. (One firm, for example, includes on its agenda visits from psychologists and business fashion experts, in addition to lectures on economics from the dean of Dartmouth's Tuck School of Business.)

All training departments stress that nobody can acquire an exhaustive familiarity with 60 to 120 different types of investments in a little less than a month. Accordingly, each firm has areas of primary emphasis. At Hutton, for example, the stress is placed on stocks, syndicates, municipal bonds and taxable investments, and some "easy options stuff." Areas such as commodities, financial futures and life insurance are too complicated, and the trainee is left to learn about them at the branch office.

Estimates at most firms put the cost of a training program, including salary and accommodations, at between $20,000 and $25,000 a trainee.

SOURCE: "Booming Markets Spur Flood of New Brokers," *The New York Times,* April 2, 1981, pp. Y27, Y33. © 1981 by The New York Times Company. Reprinted by permission.

Long- and Short-Term Financing

Objectives:

- Explain which types of financing are appropriate to obtain circulating and fixed capital.
- Describe the general features that are common to all bond issues.
- Distinguish between preferred and common stock.
- Itemize three features that might be advantageous to the purchaser of a preferred stock.
- Explain why common stocks are the most popular type of investment.
- Describe how an investment banking company functions to assist corporations in securing long-term financing.
- Discuss the role of mutual funds.
- Identify the five types of short-term debt available to businesses.
- Identify the common types of assets used as collateral for short-term loans.
- Explain why an effective rate of interest is usually much higher than a nominal rate.

The full conversion to fuel-efficient cars is stretching the financial resources of the American automobile industry. A former Secretary of Transportation has indicated that the cost of the conversion will run about $70 billion, the largest privately funded investment program in history. Nearly $20 billion of this cost will be for the plants and equipment that are necessary for producing new parts and components.[1] The mag-

---

1. William G. Mecklenburg and Stanley R. Klion, "Where Is the Money Going to Come From?" *World,* published by Peat, Marwick, Mitchell & Co., No. 3 (1981), p. 7.

nitude of these huge amounts is demonstrated when you consider that the total asset value of giant General Motors is $40 billion. Just to spend $1 billion a year requires the expenditure of $1,900 a minute! A major question facing the automobile industry is, where will all of this money come from?

All businesses, small ones and industry giants, require financing in order to own necessary assets. As described in Chapter 17, these assets are classified on a balance sheet as current assets, fixed assets, investments, and intangible assets. Current assets include items that are constantly in motion as inventories are sold, receivables are collected, and cash is received and paid out. Because of this constant turnover, current assets are also called **circulating capital**. The other types of assets are far more stable and constitute the **fixed capital** of the firm.

The distinction between the two types of capital is important. Short-term financing is best suited for circulating capital needs. Long-term financing is appropriate for acquiring fixed capital and for financing a permanent supply of working capital. The purchase of land and buildings, for example, should be financed with funds from lenders who do not expect to be repaid for a number of years or with funds from the owners of the business. On the other hand, a business may borrow money from a bank on a 90-day note to buy merchandise that will be sold in less than 90 days because the receipts from the sale of these goods should easily provide the cash needed to repay the loan. A basic financial principle is to finance long-term needs with long-term sources of funds and short-term needs with short-term sources of funds.

A factor in the bankruptcies of the Miracle Mart discount-store chain and the W.T. Grant variety-store organization was the attempt to finance their store expansion programs with short-term financing. These retailers would purchase their inventories on 60- to 120-day credit terms from suppliers. Within 30 days of receipt, however, the inventory would be sold to their customers. Instead of paying their suppliers with the available money, the retailers would use the funds to finance the development of new stores. Then, they would begin the "purchase inventory on credit — sell the inventory — invest in new stores" cycle over again. This method of financing store expansion (long-term needs) with accounts payable (short-term sources) worked well until the business downturn in the early 1970s caused a sudden decrease in consumer spending. No longer could the inventories be sold in 30 days or even 60 or 120 days! Merchandise suppliers demanded their payments; but the retailers, having no funds available, were forced into bankruptcy.

The proper use of long- and short-term financing is essential for the survival and growth of a business. Because of their importance, the various financial instruments and institutions involved in long- and short-term financing are described in this chapter.

LONG-TERM FINANCING

Long-term financing includes loans that usually mature in ten years or more, and all funds that are contributed by the owners. The long-term liabilities and capital sections of the balance sheet comprise the areas of long-term financing. Long-term liabilities frequently are referred to as *debt capital*. "Capital" is more accurately identified as *equity capital* because it includes the funds originally contributed by the owners plus all net profits allowed to remain in the business. Long-term financing opportunities for small businesses are limited mainly to loans against fixed assets. Proprietorships, partnerships, and many small corporations must rely heavily on equity capital.

The existence of large corporations is based on their ability to sell stocks and bonds to the public. The evidence of ownership in corporations consists of **stock certificates** (see Figure 18-1) that show, among other things, the name of the owner, number of shares, and type of stock. Stocks do not have a maturity date. All corporations must issue stock as it alone represents ownership. On the other hand, a **bond** (see Figure 18-2) is a debt of the issuing corporation which matures at a stated future date and on which the corporation pays interest annually or semiannually. Although some corporations do not issue bonds, the public utility industry does acquire over half of its capital from bonds. This is possible because utility companies have a constant stream of earnings from which they can pay their debts. Figure 18-3 shows the cycle of long-term financing through the sale of stocks and bonds.

Figure 18-1   A Stock Certificate

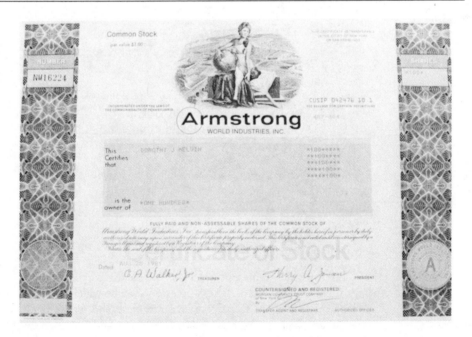

General Features of Bonds

Bonds may have both general features and specific features. All bond issues sold by industrial firms, railroads, public utilities, and financial institutions have the general features described below.

Figure 18-2   A First Mortgage Bond

Provision for Trustee

Bonds, which represent a debt of the issuing corporation, are usually held by a large number of investors. These investors may be widely scattered over the country and may need someone to safeguard their interests and act in their behalf should action be required. Such a person is known as a *trustee* and is chosen by the corporation at the time the bond issue is sold. Today a trust company or large bank usually serves as a trustee.

The duties of the trustee are included in the legal agreement under which the bonds are issued, called the **indenture**. Under it the trustee certifies that the bonds are genuine, holds any collateral that may be used as security for the issue, and collects money from the corporation to pay the interest and repay the principal. In addition to these specific duties, the trustee makes sure that all provisions of the indenture are carefully followed during the lifetime of the issue.

Various Denominations

Most industrial, railroad, financial, and public utility bonds are issued in units of $1,000. The dollar value printed on a bond is called its face value, or denomination. Sometimes the denominations of part of the bond issue will run higher, such as $5,000, $10,000, and $50,000 units. Or the denominations may be in lower amounts, usually $500 or even down to the $100 level. If bonds have a face value of less than $500, they are frequently referred to as *baby bonds*. Regardless of the denomination, the price of a bond is quoted in terms of a ratio to 100 with fractions in eighths, quarters, or one half. For example, a $1,000 industrial bond quoted at 101¾ would cost $1,017.50.

Figure 18-3   Cycle of Long-Term Financing

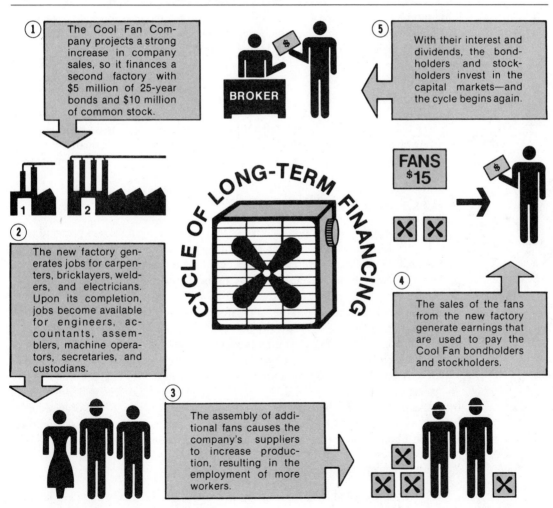

1. The Cool Fan Company projects a strong increase in company sales, so it finances a second factory with $5 million of 25-year bonds and $10 million of common stock.

2. The new factory generates jobs for carpenters, bricklayers, welders, and electricians. Upon its completion, jobs become available for engineers, accountants, assemblers, machine operators, secretaries, and custodians.

3. The assembly of additional fans causes the company's suppliers to increase production, resulting in the employment of more workers.

4. The sales of the fans from the new factory generate earnings that are used to pay the Cool Fan bondholders and stockholders.

5. With their interest and dividends, the bondholders and stockholders invest in the capital markets—and the cycle begins again.

BROKER

FANS $15

Maturity Dates

Bonds must be repaid at some future date. The length of time between the issue and the repayment dates varies considerably, but practically all bonds will run for at least 10 years and may not mature for as long as 100 years. As bonds provide long-term financing, a period shorter than 10 years would hardly be satisfactory. Common lives of bond issues are 20, 30, and 40 years.

Evidence or Lack of Evidence of Ownership

A *registered bond,* such as the one in Figure 18-2, shows the name of the owner on the face of the security. The issuing corporation keeps a record of the owner of a registered bond and mails interest checks to that person. Registered bonds protect their owners against loss since these cannot be sold without a proper signature.

A *coupon bond* (see Figure 18-4) shows no evidence of the owner. The issuing corporation does not know who holds the coupon bond and pays interest to the party who presents the dated coupons which are clipped from the bond. Thus, coupon bonds are easier to sell and are preferable for use as security for a bank loan.

Special Features of Bonds

Practically every bond issue is different in some respect from one issued by another company or from another series that is sold by the same company. Usually there is a descriptive phrase which indicates the bond's special features. These features are described below.

Type of Security Offered

People who invest in bonds usually expect some type of security as protection in case the bond issuer finds it impossible to live up to the terms of payment of interest or principal. Bonds usually run for a long period of time, and a bond issuer that is prosperous today may fall on hard times before the maturity date of the issue. Some of the common types of security offered to bondholders are real estate mortgages, chattel mortgages, stocks and bonds of other companies, or merely the excellent credit standing of the bond issuer.

Bonds backed by mortgages on real property are *real estate mortgage bonds.* Bonds that are backed by movable property that is pledged are called *chattel mortgage bonds.* When the chattel mortgage is on rolling stock of railroads such as engines, freight cars, and passenger coaches, such bonds are called *equipment trust certificates.* Bonds backed by stocks or bonds of other companies are *collateral trust bonds.* If the only security backing a bond issue is the good name of the issuer, the bonds are known as **debenture bonds.** All bonds issued directly by the federal government are debenture bonds.

Method of Repayment

At the time a bond issue is sold, buyers are informed as to how the debt is to be discharged. There are two common methods of repayment. One is to issue bonds that

Figure 18-4   A Coupon Bond

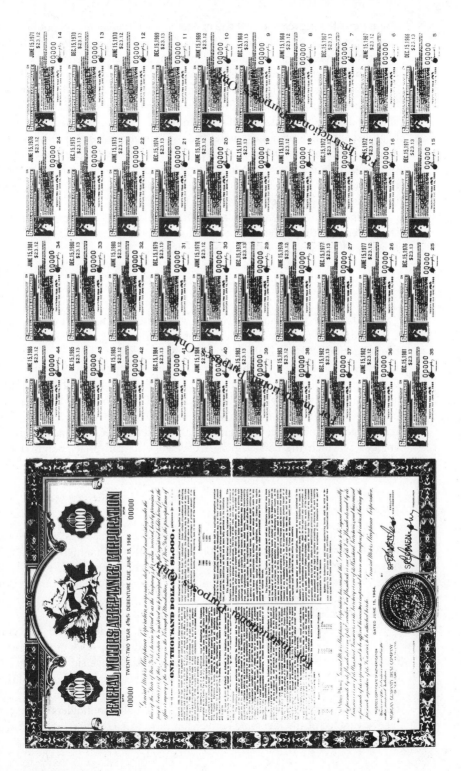

mature in different years so that the impact of the full amount will not be felt at a given date. Such bonds are known as serial bonds. For example, a 20-year, $100 million issue might run for 10 years without any bonds maturing. At the end of the eleventh year and annually for the remaining life of the bonds, $10 million in bonds are retired.

Another method of repayment is to establish a sinking fund. Under this plan the bond issuer deposits annually with the trustee an amount of money that will equal the amount due at the expiration of the bond issue. For the same 20-year, $100 million bond issue in the previous example, the issuer might deposit $5 million a year with a trustee. At the end of 20 years, the deposits would amount to the face value of the total issue. Actually the size of the yearly deposits could be smaller because funds already received by the trustee are invested elsewhere and are earning interest. Bonds issued under this plan are called sinking-fund bonds.

Some corporations, particularly railroads and public utilities, expect to liquidate their debt by retiring one bond issue with the proceeds received from another issue. Bonds sold this way are called refunding bonds.

Terms of Callability

Although bonds must be retired when they mature, it may be desirable for the bond issuer to liquidate the debt at an earlier date. To make this possible, in the indenture a clause is inserted which provides that the bonds can be called, or redeemed, at the option of the issuer according to previously announced terms. The call price of the bonds is generally higher than their original face value. For example, a 40-year bond issue might not be callable for 10 years but may be called between 10 and 20 years at a premium of $75 for each $1,000 bond; between 20 and 30 years, each bond might be called at a premium of $50 and, thereafter, at its face value. The exact amount at which the bond can be redeemed is its **call price.** Bonds that have this special feature are called **callable or redeemable bonds.**

Terms of Convertibility

As an investment, bonds appeal to insurance companies, savings banks, and individuals who desire a stated rate of return coupled with a high degree of safety. To attract buyers who desire some speculative possibilities as well, some bond indentures provide for the exchange of bonds into common stock of the same issuer at the option of the holder during the life of the bond issue. Such bonds are known as **convertible bonds.**

A typical convertible feature would allow the holder of a $1,000 bond to exchange it for 25 shares of common stock. If the common stock of the issuer is selling for $30 per share at the time the bond issue is sold, the conversion privilege is obviously of no value. However, if the stock advances to $50 per share, the bond will rise in value to about $1,250. Assuming a call could be made by the issuer at $1,050, the bondholders would do well to convert promptly. And if all bondholders of the corporation take advantage of the favorable conversion ratio, the corporation's bond redemption problem is solved.

Types of Preferred Stocks

There are two basic types of stock: preferred and common. Some firms have never sold any preferred stock. Others have issued several separate preferred series. **Preferred stocks** show a stated rate of return that, when paid, is known as a dividend. Because of the stated dividend rate and other possible features, such as convertibility, some investors feel that preferred stocks occupy a middle ground between bonds and common stocks. This viewpoint has no legal justification since preferred stocks are a form of ownership rather than of debt. The stated return on a preferred stock is not owed until dividends are declared by the board of directors. The number of shares to be authorized and a brief description of the type or types of preferred stock that may be issued are contained in the original application for a charter or might, at a later date, be added by a charter amendment.

The name "preferred stock" indicates that such shares have preference over common stock. Without exception, preferred stockholders receive dividends *before* common stockholders. Sometimes the board of directors of a corporation may *pass the dividend*, which means that dividends are not declared. The board cannot pass the dividend and yet declare a common-stock dividend. Also, preferred stockholders receive any remaining funds ahead of common stockholders in a corporate liquidation.

Cumulative or Noncumulative

Dividends on preferred stock are usually declared on a quarterly basis. If a dividend is passed by the board of directors, is the dividend forever lost to the preferred stockholders? For *cumulative* preferred stock the dividends omitted in previous periods must be declared before any dividends are declared for common stockholders. For *noncumulative* preferred stock such omissions do not need to be paid in a future period.

Participating or Nonparticipating

As stated earlier, preferred stocks have an established dividend rate. For example, this stated rate might be $6 a year per share. When the firm is particularly successful, however, some preferred stockholders may share equally with the common stockholders in the firm's high earnings. *Participating* preferred stock allows its owners to receive more than the stated return. *Nonparticipating* preferred stock limits its owners to the annual dividends stated at the time of issue.

Callable or Noncallable

Like some bond issues, *callable* preferred stock provides in the original agreement for a call price at which these stocks may be redeemed at the option of the issuer. *Noncallable* preferred stock means that no callable price was provided for in the original agreement. The only way the issuer can call in outstanding preferred stock of this type is to buy the shares on the open market. If some owners of such stock refuse to sell, their shares will remain outstanding as long as the corporation is in existence.

Convertible or Nonconvertible

Preferred stocks, particularly if they are nonparticipating, may not be overly attractive to investors. The lack of assurance that the dividend will be declared more than offsets the slightly higher yield of preferred stock in comparison with that of bonds issued by the same corporation. To induce investors to purchase a preferred-stock issue, the contract may include a clause providing for conversion of the preferred stock into common stock at the option of the stockholder. If a preferred stock selling for $100 a share is convertible into four shares of common stock which is quoted at $22 a share, there is no value to the conversion privilege. Should the selling price of the common stock rise beyond $25, the preferred stock will increase in value. At some point the preferred stockholder might decide to convert if the yield on four shares of common is higher than the yield on one preferred share.

Par or No-Par

The stated value printed on the face of a stock certificate, preferred or common, is known as its par. All shares of stock which are issued with printed stated values are classified as par stock. If a par is not stated, the stock is no-par stock. As far as stockholders are concerned, however, there is practically no difference in value between par and no-par stocks.

When the preferred stock has a par value, for example $100 a share, the dividend rate is given as a percentage such as 5 percent. Also, the stock may be sold at a premium or discount (above or below par). If the stock has no par value, the dividend rate must be stated in terms of dollars, such as a $5 preferred stock. For example, the VLI Corporation has a 7 percent convertible preferred-stock issue outstanding, while Integrated Resources, Inc., has a $3.03 cumulative convertible issue outstanding.

Voting or Nonvoting

Common law holds that since stock represents ownership, all stock is entitled to vote. In the case of preferred stocks, this privilege is frequently removed or restricted by the contract under which it is issued. It is a right that is sacrificed in return for securing other favored treatment.

If preferred stock does not have regular voting power (one vote for each share), it may have voting privileges on special matters. For example, preferred stock may vote when a bond issue is proposed that might jeopardize the favored position of the preferred stock. Or the preferred stock may have voting rights when a stated number of quarterly preferred dividends have been passed by the board of directors.

One Issue or Several Issues

Some corporations, notably public utilities, have more than one issue of preferred stock outstanding. Because each issue was originally sold on different dates in different years under varying market conditions, the stated rate of return is different for each series. For example, the Commonwealth Edison Company, a Chicago-based electric company, has 16 different issues of preferred stock outstanding.

Common Stocks

Common stocks represent ownership and are the least complicated of all securities used for long-term financing. No dividend rate is ever stated on them. They cannot be convertible, participating, cumulative, or callable. Voting rights of common stock are rarely restricted. Common stockholders take the greatest risks but stand to make the maximum gain if the corporation is successful.

Common stocks can be of the par or no-par variety. Many corporations have issued common stock with such low par values as $1 to reduce incorporation fees, annual franchise payments, and the tax on the transfer of shares. Occasionally a corporation will issue Class A and Class B common stock with voting rights denied to one of the classes.

This brief description of common stocks might lead to the conclusion that they are relatively unimportant when just the reverse is true. Most corporations secure more than one-half of their capital from stock issues. Usually the percentage of capital secured from common stock far exceeds the preferred-stock figure. Some companies have had common stock outstanding and have been paying dividends for over 100 years, as Figure 18-5 shows.

A study of Figure 18-6, which highlights the major differences between stocks and bonds, will give the reasons why most corporations rely on stocks rather than on bonds for long-term financing.

Long-Term Financial Institutions

The only financial institutions that are exclusively concerned with the long-term capital needs of business are investment banking companies. Other financial institutions described in this chapter normally render only indirect assistance although they are essential parts of the long-term capital picture.

Investment Banking Companies

The primary function of an **investment banking company** is to act as a financial middleman and market newly issued securities for corporations that have long-term capital needs. The "merchandise" that bankers, such as The First Boston Corporation and Lehman Brothers Kuhn Loeb, purchase from corporations for subsequent sale to investors consists of bonds, preferred stocks, and common stocks.

Suppose the Stoddard Manufacturing Company decides to construct and equip a new factory building. The firm calculates that it must raise additional capital funds of $50 million. If the company decides to obtain these funds from an issue of mortgage bonds, the problem of selling these securities to the public would be extremely difficult if it is unfamiliar with this field of finance. An investment banking company can be contacted and, if it agrees to market the bonds, the entire problem is solved as far as the manufacturing company is concerned. Assuming that the investment banking company believes that it can sell the bonds at par, it might agree to buy them for $49,600,000. The discount of $400,000 represents the investment banking company's gross profit, called the *spread.*

Figure 18-5   Oldest Stocks Paying Annual Dividends

Dividends Began In	Stock	Dividends Began In	Stock
1784	Bank of New York Co., Inc.	1867	Connecticut General Corp.
1784	First National Boston Corp.	1868	American Express Co.
1791	Industrial National Corp.	1872	Equimark Corporation
1813	Citicorp	1874	INA Corporation
1813	First Nat'l. State Bancorporation	1875	First Int'l. Bancshares, Inc.*
1827	Chemical New York Corp.*	1877	Stanley Works*
1840	Morgan (J. P.) & Co., Inc.	1879	Cincinnati Bell, Inc.*
1848	Chase Manhattan Corporation	1880	Bancal Tri-State Corp.*
1851	Connecticut Natural Gas Corp.*	1881	American Tel. & Tel. Co.*
1851	Manhattan Life Corp.	1881	Corning Glass Works
1852	Bay State Gas Co.*	1881	Security Pacific Corp.
1852	Manufacturers Hanover Corp.	1882	Bell Canada*
1852	Washington Gas Light Co.*	1882	Diamond International Corp.
1853	Cincinnati Gas & Electric Co.	1883	Carter-Wallace, Inc.
1853	Continental Corporation	1883	Chesebrough-Pond's, Inc.
1856	Scovill, Inc.	1883	Exxon Corporation
1863	Pennwalt Corporation	1883	Reece Corporation
1863	Singer Company	1885	Consolidated Edison Co.
1865	Irving Bank Corp.*	1885	Eli Lilly and Company
1866	First Atlanta Corp.	1885	UGI Corporation
1866	Travelers Corporation*	1886	Hackensack Water Co.

*Unbroken quarterly record since the 19th century.

SOURCE: *New York Stock Exchange Fact Book, 1982*, p. 28. Reproduced with permission.

Figure 18-6   Major Differences Between Stocks and Bonds

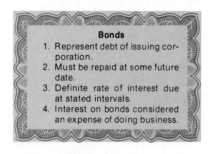

Bonds
1. Represent debt of issuing corporation.
2. Must be repaid at some future date.
3. Definite rate of interest due at stated intervals.
4. Interest on bonds considered an expense of doing business.

Stocks
1. Represent ownership in corporation.
2. No obligation to repay although sometimes stock is retired.
3. Unless and until dividends are declared, no return paid to stockholders.
4. Dividends considered a distribution of profits.

If the Stoddard Manufacturing Company decides to sell stock rather than bonds, a similar procedure would be followed, except that an additional complication would exist. Prior to selling shares of stock through the investment banking company, Stoddard's existing stockholders might have to give up their right to subscribe to new stock issues.

If the issue to be marketed is not too large for an investment banking company, this institution may handle the entire transaction through its central office and branches. If the issue is too large for one firm or if the risk is too great, other investment banking companies may be invited to participate in handling the transaction. Thus, an underwriting syndicate is formed. Figure 18-7 shows an advertisement for an underwriting syndicate that was formed to market a bond issue.

Brokerage Firms

In finance and real estate, brokers are persons who buy and sell for others and charge a commission for their services. In finance a number of brokers frequently join together to form a brokerage firm. A member of a brokerage firm is officially known as a *registered representative* since he or she has been required to pass examinations and to register with the National Association of Securities Dealers.

The chief activity of a brokerage firm is to serve its clients by buying and selling securities that have previously been issued and are currently outstanding. This is different from an investment banker, who handles only newly issued securities, although large brokerage firms also function as investment banking companies. Because brokerage firms exist, long-term securities are more attractive to investors than they would otherwise be. Investors are more willing to buy a new issue when they know there is a market for it. Also, brokerage firms will lend limited amounts to those who buy securities from them, thereby increasing the amount of money entering the long-term financing area. The number of offices and salespeople and the amount of capital of the leading brokerage firms are shown in Table 18-1.

In recent years the large brokerage houses have broadened their offerings and have become diversified financial department stores. These organizations often provide a variety of financial services ranging from stocks, bonds, options, commodities, and mutual funds to life insurance, mortgages, money-market funds, pensions, consumer loans, and credit cards. Among the firms that have evolved into investment advisers and offer these services are Dean Witter Reynolds, Prudential-Bache Securities, Shearson/American Express, Paine Webber, E. F. Hutton, and Merrill Lynch, Pierce, Fenner & Smith. Some brokerage houses have merged with larger organizations and have obtained additional capital, managerial talent, and financial products. Shearson Loeb Rhoades was acquired by American Express, a major credit card company. The Bache Group was merged into the Prudential Insurance Company, the largest insurer in the country. Dean Witter Reynolds was purchased by Sears, Roebuck, the giant retailing and insurance complex.

Trust Companies

Financial institutions that specialize in acting as trustees for business firms and individuals are called trust companies. In today's financial world most trust companies

Figure 18-7   **An Underwriting Syndicate of Investment Banking Companies**

This announcement is neither an offer to sell nor a solicitation of offers to buy any of these securities.
The offering is made only by the Prospectus and the related Prospectus Supplement.

NEW ISSUE   January 21, 1983

1,000,000 Shares

Republic Steel Corporation

$5.25 Cumulative Convertible Preferred Stock
($50 stated value)

The $5.25 Cumulative Convertible Preferred Stock is convertible into Common Stock of the Company at any time, unless previously redeemed, at a conversion price of $19.15 per share, subject to adjustment in certain events.

Price $50 Per Share
plus accrued dividends, if any, from date of issue

Copies of the Prospectus and the related Prospectus Supplement may be obtained in any State in which this announcement is circulated only from such of the undersigned as may legally offer these securities in such State.

The First Boston Corporation   **Merrill Lynch White Weld Capital Markets Group**
                                          Merrill Lynch, Pierce, Fenner & Smith Incorporated

Bear, Stearns & Co.	**Blyth Eastman Paine Webber** Incorporated	**Dillon, Read & Co. Inc.**
Donaldson, Lufkin & Jenrette Securities Corporation	**Drexel Burnham Lambert** Incorporated	**Goldman, Sachs & Co.**
E. F. Hutton & Company Inc.	**Kidder, Peabody & Co.** Incorporated	**Lazard Frères & Co.**
Lehman Brothers Kuhn Loeb Incorporated	**Prudential-Bache** Securities	**L. F. Rothschild, Unterberg, Towbin**
Salomon Brothers Inc	**Shearson/American Express Inc.**	**Smith Barney, Harris Upham & Co.** Incorporated
Warburg Paribas Becker A. G. Becker	**Wertheim & Co., Inc.**	**Dean Witter Reynolds Inc.**
Alex. Brown & Sons	**Oppenheimer & Co., Inc.**	**Thomson McKinnon Securities Inc.**
Butcher & Singer Inc.		**Janney Montgomery Scott Inc.**
Legg Mason Wood Walker Incorporated		**Moseley, Hallgarten, Estabrook & Weeden Inc.**
Tucker, Anthony & R. L. Day, Inc.		**Wheat, First Securities, Inc.**

SOURCE: First Boston Corporation, New York, NY. Reproduced with permission.

Table 18-1   The Leading Financial Brokerage Firms

In Offices			In Salespeople			In Capital		
1	Merrill Lynch	476	1	Merrill Lynch	8,600	1	Merrill Lynch	$969.5
2	Edward D. Jones	307	⌠2	E. F. Hutton	4,000	2	Shearson	469.9
3	Dean Witter	295	⌡2	Dean Witter	4,000	3	E. F. Hutton	448.0
4	E. F. Hutton	275	3	Shearson	3,495	4	Dean Witter	274.1
5	Shearson	266	4	Paine Webber	3,400	5	Bache	251.9
6	Paine Webber	234	5	Bache	2,907	6	Paine Webber	243.2
7	Bache	195	6	Thomson-McKinnon	1,494	7	Drexel Burnham	134.2
8	A. G. Edwards	176	7	A. G. Edwards	1,325	8	Kidder Peabody	112.4
9	Thomson-McKinnon	132	8	Smith Barney	1,320	9	A. G. Edwards	99.9
10	Smith Barney	92	9	Kidder Peabody	1,058	10	Smith Barney	94.7
			10	Drexel Burnham	736			

NOTE: Figures are for 1980. Capital is in millions of dollars.

SOURCE: William M. Reddig, "Edward D. Jones, Country Broker," *The New York Times,* February 21, 1982, p. F4. © 1982 by The New York Times Company. Reprinted by permission.

also operate as commercial or savings banks, and the majority of large commercial banks maintain a trust department. Consequently, the functions of a trust company frequently are carried out by a department of a larger financial institution.

As explained on page 436, trust companies serve as trustees for bond issues. As trustees for issues of stock, they frequently function as a *transfer agent* by recording changes in ownership following each sale of shares. For large corporations with thousands of outstanding shares of stock which are traded daily on exchanges, such as Ford Motor Co. and IBM, the service of a transfer agent is usually a necessity.

Investment Companies

Investment companies must not be confused with investment banking companies, for these two types of financial institutions are totally different. **Investment companies** are organizations that sell shares to individuals and other investors and then use the cash received to purchase securities of other firms as their only assets. The holdings of some investment companies, called the *portfolio,* are diversified among bonds, preferred stocks, and common stocks. Others concentrate on only one type of security or industry, such as a municipal bond fund and a high-technology industry fund. As shown in Figure 18-8, investment companies provide a method by which a person can invest indirectly in many different securities.

There are two main types of investment companies: closed-end and open-end. *Closed-end* investment companies issue shares only when first organized. Later these shares are traded on a security exchange or on the over-the-counter market. *Open-end* investment companies sell shares at any time and in any quantity. They are

Figure 18-8 Portfolio of an Investment Company

INVESTMENTS OWNED As of March 31, 1982

Common Stocks

	SHARES	%(1)
AEROSPACE		
United Technologies Corp	40,000	65%
AGRICULTURAL MACHINERY		
Deere & Company	30,000	42
APPAREL AND TEXTILES		
Brown Group Inc	15,900	18
AUTOMOTIVE AND ACCESSORY		
General Motors Corporation	80,000	1.46
BANKS AND FINANCE		
BankAmerica Corp	97,000	79
Citicorp	60,000	58
Morgan (J. P.) & Company Inc	51,000	1.22
Northwest Bancorporation	50,000	47
		3.06
BROADCASTING		
CBS Inc	45,000	81
BUILDING		
Armstrong World Industries	50,000	33
Owens-Corning Fiberglas Corp	52,000	42
		75
CHEMICALS		
American Cyanamid Company	10,000	12
Dow Chemical Co	60,000	62
du Pont (E. I.) de Nemours & Company	70,000	1.04
Eastman Kodak Company	75,000	2.43
Freeport-McMoRan Inc	53,850	39
Hercules, Inc	30,000	26
Monsanto Company	26,000	72
Stauffer Chemical Company	100,000	88
Union Carbide Corporation	15,000	31
		6.77
COMMUNICATIONS		
American Telephone and Telegraph Company	103,000	2.58
COSMETICS		
Avon Products, Inc	60,000	64
Chesebrough-Pond's Inc	50,000	80
Gillette Company	60,000	91
		2.35

	SHARES	%(1)
DRUGS AND MEDICAL SUPPLIES		
Abbott Laboratories	100,000	1.29%
American Home Products Corp	70,000	1.08
American Hospital Supply Corp	40,200	75
Becton, Dickinson & Company	15,000	28
Bristol-Myers Co	20,000	49
Lilly, Eli & Co	53,000	1.34
Merck & Co. Inc	50,000	1.60
Pfizer, Inc	40,000	91
SmithKline Beckman Corp	30,000	89
Upjohn Company	30,000	62
Warner-Lambert Company	60,000	61
		9.86
ELECTRIC AND ELECTRONICS		
General Electric Company	81,000	2.28
Maytag Company	20,000	22
Sperry Corporation	50,000	62
		3.12
ELECTRIC UTILITIES		
Central & South West Corporation	60,000	41
Commonwealth Edison Company	40,000	37
Duke Power Company	80,000	80
Florida Progressive Corporation(1)	60,000	1.29
Florida Power & Light Company	180,000	82
Gulf States Utilities Company	114,400	64
Houston Industries Inc	60,000	51
Illinois Power Company	10,000	09
Middle South Utilities, Inc	100,000	58
South Carolina Electric & Gas Co	75,000	53
Virginia Electric & Power Co	120,000	68
		6.72
FOODS AND BEVERAGES		
Coca-Cola Company	70,000	1.02
Dart & Kraft Inc	40,000	90
General Foods Corp	40,000	60
Heinz (H. J.) Company	70,000	91
Nabisco Brands, Inc	30,000	43
		3.86
FOREST PRODUCTS		
Georgia-Pacific Corp	20,000	15
International Paper Company	70,000	1.02
Weyerhaeuser Company	30,000	35
		1.52
GAS UTILITIES		
Tenneco, Inc	40,000	49
Texas Eastern Corp	30,000	58
Texas Gas Transmission Corp	30,000	35
		1.42

(1) Formerly Florida Power Corp

	SHARES	%(1)
GROCERY CHAINS		
Safeway Stores, Incorporated	50,000	65%
HOUSEHOLD PRODUCTS		
Colgate-Palmolive Company	49,000	40
Procter & Gamble Company	38,000	1.40
		1.86
INDUSTRIAL MACHINERY		
Dresser Industries, Inc	20,000	20
INSURANCE		
Connecticut General Insurance Corp	35,000	79
Continental Corporation	60,000	72
St. Paul Companies, Inc	50,000	1.06
Travelers Corporation	100,000	2.25
		4.82
NONFERROUS METALS		
Aluminum Co. of America	20,000	22
INCO. Limited	45,000	24
		46
OFFICE EQUIPMENT		
International Business Machines Corporation	430,000	11.41
NCR Corp	20,000	37
Xerox Corporation	30,000	50
		12.28
OIL SERVICE		
Schlumberger Ltd	50,000	95
PETROLEUM		
Exxon Corporation	270,400	3.37
Gulf Oil Corporation	101,000	1.44
Mobil Corporation	130,000	1.27
Royal Dutch Petroleum Company	120,000	1.73
Standard Oil Company of California	60,000	82
Standard Oil Company (Ohio)	40,000	58
Standard Oil Company (Indiana)	85,000	1.38
Texaco, Inc	85,000	1.13
Union Oil Company of California	80,000	1.09
		12.81
RAILROADS AND EQUIPMENT		
ACF Industries Incorporated	40,000	61
Burlington Northern Inc	35,000	70
Norfolk & Western Railway Company	50,000	1.04
Santa Fe Industries	50,000	57
Southern Railway Company	90,000	1.18
Union Pacific Company	85,000	1.40
		5.50

	SHARES	%(1)
RETAIL TRADE		
Federated Department Stores, Inc	69,000	1.30%
K mart Corp	115,000	90
May Department Stores Company	35,000	42
Penney (J. C.) Inc	50,000	76
Sears, Roebuck and Co	230,000	5.32
RUBBER		
Goodyear Tire & Rubber Company	40,000	38
SERVICES		
Hospital Corporation of America	25,000	33
STEEL		
Inland Steel Company	29,000	28
United States Steel Corporation	30,000	31
		59
TOBACCO		
Philip Morris, Inc	40,000	84
Reynolds (R. J.) Industries, Inc	40,000	81
		1.65
MISCELLANEOUS		
Eastern Gas & Fuel Associates	25,000	22
TOTAL COMMON STOCKS		93.49%

Preferred Stock

	SHARES	%(1)
Crocker National Corp. $2.1875 Conv	35,000	.32%

Bonds

	PRINCIPAL AMOUNT	%(1)
GOVERNMENTS		
U. S. Treasury Bills		
Due 4/8/82	$1,500,000	66%
Due 4/22/82	1,000,000	44
Due 5/13/82	4,000,000	1.75
Due 5/20/82	5,000,000	2.18
TOTAL U. S. GOVERNMENTS		5.03%
TOTAL INVESTMENTS		98.84%
CASH, RECEIVABLES, ETC., NET		1.16
NET ASSETS		100.00%

(1) Approximate percentage of net assets

SOURCE: Dividend Shares, Inc., New York, NY. Reproduced with permission.

commonly called **mutual funds** and are the most important type of investment company. Their shares are not traded on a security exchange or over the counter. Whenever they desire, however, people owning the stock of a mutual fund can sell it back to the fund. The mutual fund industry, including money-market funds, has total assets of nearly $300 billion and includes over 21 million shareholders. Among the well-known mutual funds are Investors Diversified Services, the Price Rowe Funds, and the Value Line Funds.

Other Long-Term Financial Institutions

Other financial institutions which have substantial sums to invest in long-term financing are savings banks, savings and loan associations, insurance companies, foundations, and pension funds. Savings banks and savings and loan associations specialize in mortgage loans on residences but also give loans to businesses for building offices, warehouses, and stores. Insurance companies are interested primarily in bonds. In some instances they will purchase an entire issue amounting to millions of dollars in what is called *private placement*. Such a private placement saves the corporation in need of long-term financing the cost of using an investment banking company. Foundations and pension funds purchase stocks as well as bonds.

SHORT-TERM FINANCING

The items in the current-liabilities section of a balance sheet are sources of short-term financing. These items are debts that have a maturity date of less than one year. Examples are amounts owed for goods purchased on credit terms, outstanding loans from banks that are due within one year, and accrued payables such as amounts owed for salaries or taxes.

Unlike long-term financing, which remains stable for month after month, short-term financing involves day-by-day changes. Constant financial management is required, which is usually provided by a treasurer or controller. This officer must plan to have cash available to meet debts as they come due. At the same time, having more cash on hand than is necessary means a loss of interest income that could be earned on these surplus funds. The complexity of the job of a financial manager can be appreciated, in part, by examining the various types of short-term obligations available.

Types of Short-Term Debt

There are several types of short-term debt. Five that are discussed in this chapter are: open-book accounts, notes payable, commercial drafts, bank acceptances, and commercial paper. The distinctions among these types and their proper uses will be explained. Of these, the most common types of short-term debt are open-book accounts and notes payable to a commercial bank.

Open-Book Accounts

When a firm buys materials, equipment, supplies, and merchandise from a supplier with the implied obligation to pay the invoice at a later date, an **open-book account** is entered on the books of both companies. Between 85 and 90 percent of all business transactions in the United States involving the sale and purchase of goods use an open-book account. Although not usually thought of as a loan, the net effect is that the seller is financing the buyer for the period of time between the receipt of the goods and the payment of the bill. In transactions between retailers and consumers the term *charge accounts* replaces open-book accounts.

The smooth flow of business transactions in this country could not be maintained without the use of open-book accounts. The manufacturer buys raw materials on credit terms, converts them into finished goods, and sells them to wholesalers on open account. The wholesaler sells the merchandise to retailers without requiring immediate payment, and retailers may do likewise in their sales to consumers. When consumers pay for their purchases, the cash received permits the retailer to pay the wholesaler, who in turn can pay the manufacturer.

Credit Terms. The length of time granted to manufacturers for settling open-book accounts is usually longer than that extended to the wholesaler — and so on to the retailer and consumer. This is because of the added amount of time needed for the flow of goods from maker to user. For example, raw materials may be sold to the manufacturer on credit terms of 90 days; the manufacturer may extend 60-day credit to the wholesaler; the wholesaler may allow the retailer 30 days; and the retailer expects customer charge accounts to be paid once a month. Actually credit terms vary by industries and by different suppliers. Granting more liberal credit terms may be one of the elements of competition.

Frequently the maximum length of the credit terms is not used because the seller allows the purchaser a cash discount. As described in Chapter 15, if an invoice carries the terms 2/10 net 30, the buyer can deduct 2 percent if the account is paid within 10 days after the date of the invoice. This saving is so substantial that many firms have a policy of taking advantage of every cash discount offered.

Credit Information. Most established businesses have a good reputation for prompt payment of their accounts, and sellers are willing to ship goods to them on an open-book account basis. New firms do not have this advantage and, in some cases, older firms are not acquainted with the credit reputations of new customers. In these circumstances a business wishing to obtain credit usually furnishes the name of its bank and invites creditors to verify its financial responsibility.

There are also credit-rating agencies to whom a supplier can turn to check on the desirability of shipping goods on open account. Of these, Dun & Bradstreet, Inc., (D&B) is outstanding. This is a nationwide mercantile credit-rating agency that lists thousands of large and small business organizations in its publications. An example of a D&B business information report is shown in Figure 18-9. Another organization that operates on a national and international basis is Equifax, Inc. It specializes in individuals rather than business firms. In many cities there are mercantile credit interchange bureaus and retail credit bureaus. Most of these belong to the National

Figure 18-9 **A Dun & Bradstreet Business Information Report**

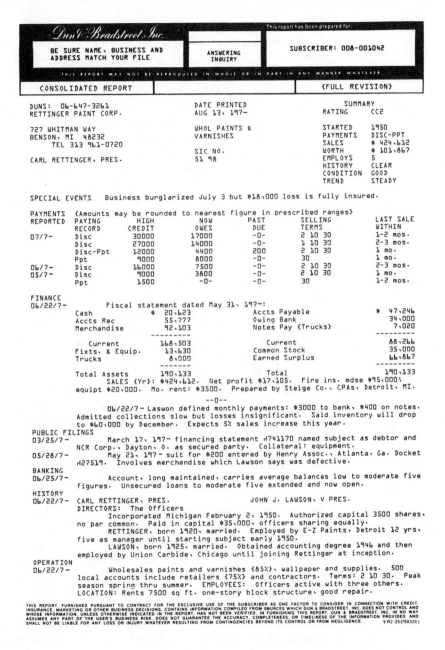

SOURCE: Dun & Bradstreet Corporation, New York, NY. Reproduced with permission.

Credit Interchange System or the Associated Credit Bureaus of America so that information between bureaus is available on a nationwide basis.

Notes Payable

Next to the use of open-book accounts as a source of short-term debt capital is the use of notes that are payable to commercial banks or to individuals or firms. An example of a note payable is a **promissory note,** a written instrument in which the maker promises to pay to the party named a definite sum of money at a determinable future date. The *maker* is the signer of the note and eventually becomes the one who pays the note. The bank or individual or company in whose favor the note is drawn is the *payee.* Most promissory notes bear interest at a rate that is stated on the face of the instrument. As used in short-term financing, most notes have a maturity date of from one to six months. Figure 18-10 shows a promissory note.

The words "pay to the order of" which appear on a promissory note make it possible for the payee to pass the note to a third party by signing on the reverse side of the instrument. Such a signature is known as an endorsement, and the note qualifies as a **negotiable instrument.**

Figure 18-10   A Promissory Note

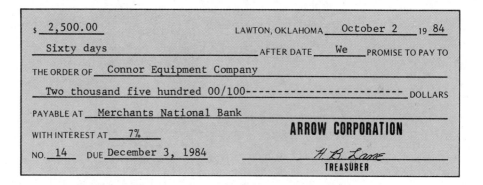

Business Loans from Commercial Banks. If a firm wishes to borrow $100,000 from a bank for 90 days or 3 months, it will sign a note payable to the bank for this amount and insert the rate of interest the bank agrees to charge. Assuming that this rate is 8 percent, the total cost of borrowing $100,000 for one-fourth of a year would be $8,000 ÷ 4 = $2,000. The bank may subtract this amount from the face of the note, in which case the borrower will receive $98,000 instead of $100,000. Interest deducted in advance by a bank is called a **bank discount.**

Some business firms, anticipating that they may need to borrow at some indefinite future time, submit information to their banks covering such items as financial statements, names of officers and directors, and certain details about their operations. If an investigation by the bank seems to warrant making a loan, the firm will be notified that the bank has granted a line of credit for a specified amount such as $25,000 or

$500,000. The obvious advantage in having established a line of credit is the advance knowledge of how much can be borrowed quickly at any time the need arises. For example, the Macy department store organization has lines of credit with banking institutions of $547 million which are used mainly to support the commercial paper issued by the Macy Credit Corporation.[2]

Installment Purchase of Equipment. Notes payable are also used in connection with purchases of machinery and equipment on an installment basis. Although the bulk of installment buying is done by consumers, businesses also purchase such items as delivery trucks, drill presses, and other forms of heavy machinery on an installment basis. This involves a down payment and the signing of a note specifying monthly payments, which may extend over a period as long as three years.

The payee of an installment sales contract may hold the note or, as is more likely, sell it to a **sales finance company.** This is a financial institution that buys installment sales contracts from dealers who have sold merchandise to consumers. In this respect a sales finance company differs from other types of loan companies that make loans directly to consumers payable on an installment basis.

Loans from Governmental Agencies. Some states have created corporations that make loans to encourage businesses to locate or expand within their boundaries. Federal agencies, such as the Small Business Administration (SBA), the Disaster Loan Corporation, and the Commodity Credit Corporation, also make loans. The SBA guarantees or makes loans to small businesses that are unable to obtain funds elsewhere at reasonable interest rates. The Commodity Credit Corporation specializes in making loans to farmers who use harvested crops as collateral. Federal banks also are helpful to selected groups such as rural and consumer cooperatives.

Commercial Drafts

A **commercial draft** is a credit instrument similar to a promissory note except that it is made by the person who is to receive the money. The party who makes the draft, usually a business firm, is the *drawer.* The draft is sent either to the *drawee,* the person who is obligated to the drawer, or to the drawee's bank. Upon acceptance of the draft, the drawee writes his or her name across the face of the instrument. Commercial drafts may be *time* drafts, which indicate the length of time on the face of the draft; or they may be *sight* drafts, which means that the drawee pays upon presentation of the draft. A time draft that arises in connection with a shipment of merchandise is known as a **trade acceptance.**

Commercial drafts sometimes are used by manufacturers to sell a sizable quantity of goods to a customer who is either unknown or who has a doubtful credit standing. The procedure is to take the sequential steps in making a cash-on-delivery shipment by freight as shown in Figure 18-11. The shipper obtains a receipt called an order bill of lading from the freight company at the time the goods are shipped. When this document is used, the freight agent at the destination cannot release the goods until the order bill of lading is presented. The shipper attaches a sight draft to the order bill

---

2. *Macy's Annual Report* (July 31, 1982), p. 15.

Figure 18-11   Sequential Steps in Making a Cash-on-Delivery Shipment by Freight

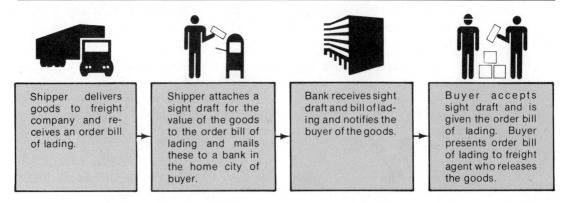

| Shipper delivers goods to freight company and receives an order bill of lading. | Shipper attaches a sight draft for the value of the goods to the order bill of lading and mails these to a bank in the home city of buyer. | Bank receives sight draft and bill of lading and notifies the buyer of the goods. | Buyer accepts sight draft and is given the order bill of lading. Buyer presents order bill of lading to freight agent who releases the goods. |

of lading and mails both papers to the customer's bank. To obtain delivery of the shipment, the customer must accept the sight draft by paying it. The order bill of lading is given to the customer, who can then obtain the goods from the freight company.

Bank Acceptances

Bank acceptances are arrangements for short-term financing which allow a borrower to obtain from a bank only those funds that are actually needed at the time of need. For example, assume that the Ross Manufacturing Company wishes to buy some raw materials. Before ordering these, the company arranges with its bank to accept drafts drawn against the bank for the goods to be purchased. The bank issues letters of credit, which indicate that it will accept the drafts. The Ross Manufacturing Company then sends the letters of credit to the producers of the raw materials, instructing them to send the bills of lading to the bank and to draw on the bank for the purchase price. When the materials arrive, the bank accepts the drafts. In order to obtain the bills of lading, the Ross Manufacturing Company must sign a note in favor of the bank.

Commercial Paper

In the financial world **commercial paper** refers to unsecured promissory notes that well-known corporations sell on the open market. These notes are issued in denominations of $5,000, $10,000, and $25,000. They amount in total to a substantial sum, run from two to six months, and are sold to commercial-paper houses. In turn, the commercial paper is sold to such buyers as industrial corporations, pension funds, and financial institutions. Only large corporations with an unquestioned credit standing, such as the Macy Credit Corporation and the General Motors Acceptance Corporation, can use this source of short-term financing. For example, the Macy Credit Corporation usually has about $90 million of commercial paper outstanding.[3] The

3. *Ibid.,* p. 6.

advantages of using commercial paper are that money can be borrowed at a lower rate of interest than would be charged by a bank and that the borrower can secure more funds than most banks are willing or legally able to lend.

Security for Short-Term Loans

In some instances firms are required to pledge assets as security (or collateral) for short-term loans. Sometimes they voluntarily offer the collateral because they might benefit from a lower interest cost. The common types of assets used as collateral are: accounts receivable, inventories, movable property, and other assets.

Accounts Receivable

Accounts receivable are the open-book accounts owed to a firm by its customers. These are used as security in two ways: by pledging and by factoring.

Pledging. When pledging assets, the borrowing firm allocates a selected number of its accounts receivable to the lending agency in return for a loan of 75 to 80 percent of their total value. The borrower promises to forward all cash received as payment for these accounts receivable until such time as it has repaid its loan plus interest. Customers of the borrowing firm are not aware that their accounts have been pledged as security for a loan. Furthermore, the lending agency can collect from the borrowing firm even if the firm's customers default, or fail to pay their debts. Financial institutions that make short-term loans on pledged accounts receivable include commercial banks and commercial finance companies such as the General Electric Credit Corporation.

Factoring. In factoring, accounts receivable are purchased outright by an institution known as a **factor**. The factor takes title to the accounts and collects them. It also charges the borrowing firm a service fee and interest on the loan. Customers of the borrowing firm must be informed of the sale of their accounts so that they will make their payments to the factor—the new owner of the receivables. In the event of customers' default, factors cannot collect from the borrowing firm. Numerous firms operate both as commercial finance companies and as factors.

Inventories

Inventories may be used as collateral in several ways. When the lending agency has a lien (legal right to hold property) on all of the inventories of the borrower, such a lien is known as a **floating lien.** This is a weak method because the borrower retains physical possession of the inventories and is free to sell them.

A more common method of inventory financing involves the use of a warehouse receipt. The owner of goods that are stored in a bonded public warehouse receives a **warehouse receipt** which specifies that the goods will be released to the person who rented the space—or to order of bearer—upon payment of the storage charges. The wording of this receipt makes it negotiable and allows firms to pledge their stored goods as collateral for a loan. For example, assume that the Amos Candy Company buys 100 tons of sugar on terms of 2/10 net 30. The shipment arrives and is stored in a bonded public warehouse. The Amos Candy Company is issued a warehouse receipt and endorses it in favor of its bank as collateral for a promissory note. The cash received from the bank allows the candy company to pay the invoice for the sugar within the discount period. When the promissory note is due, the candy company will have to pay it or sacrifice the right to have its warehouse receipt returned. If the candy company defaults on the note, its bank will sell the sugar to other users.

Movable Property

The most widely used form of security for short-term loans is movable property such as automobiles and trucks, equipment, supplies, and even livestock if ownership of animals is involved in the business. To obtain a loan secured by movable property, the borrower signs both a note that specifies the terms of repayment and a financing statement. A financing statement isn't necessary when pledging durable goods such as automobiles, trucks, and mobile homes, as a certificate of title is issued for each of these. The lending institution keeps physical possession of title certificates until the loan is repaid, thus preventing the borrower from selling the pledged property.

Other Assets

Marketable securities, such as stocks and bonds, may be assigned to a bank as security for a loan. If the need for funds will last only a month or two, it may be preferable to borrow against marketable securities rather than to sell them to raise the cash needed. Another asset that can be used as security is the cash surrender value of life insurance policies carried on the lives of partners or executives of a company. The insurance company involved will loan an amount equal to the cash surrender value of the policies.

Cost of Short-Term Financing

It is sound financial management to secure short-term funds at the lowest possible cost. The least expensive method of borrowing is the use of the open-book account. Even when overdue, a borrower usually pays no interest on open-book accounts. Generally the rate on interest-bearing obligations is affected by money-market rates and by the amount of risk assumed by the lender. The lowest charge, called the **prime rate,** is the interest rate quoted by large city banks on loans made to their most creditworthy customers. The variation in the prime rate in recent years is depicted in Figure 18-12.

In computing borrowing costs, business firms and consumers need to be aware of the difference between nominal and effective rates of interest. The **nominal rate of interest** is that stated on the instrument used in connection with the loan which does not take into account any finance charges. The **effective rate of interest,** or the annual percentage rate (APR), is the true interest cost, which is higher than the nominal rate.

The effective rate on loans repayable on an installment basis is almost double the nominal rate because interest is calculated on the full amount of the loan for the entire borrowing period despite the gradual reduction of the actual amount owed. To illus-

Figure 18-12   Variations in the Prime Rate

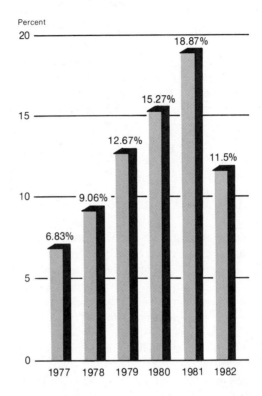

NOTE: All rates are annual averages except 1982, which is an end-of-year rate.

SOURCE: Federal Reserve Board.

trate, assume that a business buys a new pickup truck for $7,000. The business turns in an old truck as a down payment of $1,000 and makes a loan for the remaining $6,000. It agrees to repay the loan of $6,000 at a nominal interest rate of 8 percent a year, in monthly installments for 2 years. The monthly payment is calculated as follows:

$$2 \times (\$6,000 \times .08) = \$960 \text{ (nominal interest for 2 years)}$$
$$\$6,000 + \$960 = \$6,960 \text{ (actual size of the loan)}$$
$$\$6,960 \div 24 = \$290 \text{ (monthly installment)}$$

To approximate the effective rate of interest, the following formula can be used:

$$E = \frac{2 \times p \times f}{a(n + 1)}$$

where E = effective rate of interest

p = number of payments in a year

f = cost of the loan in dollars

a = amount of the loan

n = number of installment payments

Substituting the facts given in the example for the letters in the formula, the approximate effective rate of interest is 15.36 percent:

$$E = \frac{2 \times 12 \times \$960}{\$6,000(24 + 1)} = \frac{\$23,040}{\$150,000} = .1536 = 15.36\%$$

Short-Term Financing Institutions

Several specialized financial institutions that aid the short-term financial needs of businesses have been described in connection with the types of loans they offer. These include sales finance companies, commercial-paper houses, commercial finance companies, factors, and governmental agencies. Used much more frequently, and more important by far, are the services provided by commercial banks. Commercial banks are financial institutions that not only make loans to businesses, but also render several other services.

Without question the most important service rendered by banks to businesses and individuals is the checking account. A check is a negotiable instrument signed by the bank's customer, directing the bank to pay to the person or business named the amount of money specified. With the exception of cash sales at the retail level, checks are used in practically all business transactions. Other services of a commercial bank that are relevant to short-term financing include handling the conversion of foreign currencies; collecting notes, drafts, and bond coupons; renting safe-deposit boxes; and preparing and mailing dividend checks.[4]

In recent years federal regulators have permitted banks to offer new high-interest-rate accounts that attract investors who want high yields and safety of principal. These accounts are not subject to federally imposed interest-rate ceilings and are insured by the FDIC up to $100,000. They are a response to the high-yielding money-market funds that are being offered by investment companies and brokerage houses and that were draining savings away from banks. A **money-market fund** is a type of mutual fund that consists of short-term money-market securities. Examples of these securities are commercial paper, bank acceptances, Treasury bills (part of the short-term debt of the U.S. government), and certificates of deposit (issued by savings institutions in exchange for a minimum deposit over a specified time).

---

4. The role of commercial banks is more completely described in Chapter 20.

SUMMARY
Businesses must be financed. This requirement is divided between the need for long-term funds and an equally important need for short-term funds. The distinction between the two types of financing is important because each one uses completely different legal instruments and financial institutions.

Long-term financing includes debt with a maturity of at least ten years and investments made by the owners. Proprietorships, partnerships, and small corporations are limited to mortgaging assets owned in securing debt capital. Large corporations are able to issue bonds. These debt instruments usually have a minimum face value of $1,000, mature in 20 to 40 years, and pay interest semiannually to their owners. Frequently security is offered to protect the bondholders, although some firms issue debentures, which are unsecured bonds. The conversion privilege of bonds adds the spice of speculation to an otherwise conservative investment.

The ownership equity in corporations is represented by preferred and common stock. Preferred stock ranks ahead of common stock but usually pays only a fixed rate of return. Common stocks are a residual type of ownership. If the firm prospers, common stockholders receive the maximum return on their investments.

Although several types of financial institutions assist in the long-term financing area, investment banking companies are the most important. These institutions market bonds and stocks for corporations, sometimes by forming a syndicate. They sell these securities to individuals and banks, but the larger purchasers of such securities are mutual funds, trusts, pension funds, insurance companies, foundations, and savings institutions.

Short-term financing is all debt, and this debt has a maturity of less than a year. The vast majority of short-term financing needs are met by using open-book accounts or by borrowing from a commercial bank. Open-book accounts normally do not involve an interest charge. Other short-term financing instruments are commercial drafts, bank acceptances, and commercial paper.

Some type of collateral is frequently required for promissory notes, commercial drafts, and bank acceptances. Accounts receivable, inventories, and movable property are the most common assets offered. If the collateral pledged is adequate, the rate of interest charged may be less. Frequently, however, the effective rate is so much higher than the nominal rate that it becomes very expensive to borrow short-term funds.

In the short-term financing area there are several specialized financial institutions. Among the most widely used institutions are sales finance companies, commercial finance companies, and factors. But more important than any of these specialized companies are commercial banks. In addition to making loans and rendering many other services to business, banks offer checking accounts without which it would be impossible for most businesses to function. To attract investors who want high yields, banks offer money-market funds.

BACK TO THE CHAPTER OPENER

1. What is the difference between an investment banking company and a brokerage firm?
2. What types of securities are sold through brokerage firms?
3. Why are brokers important in the financial markets?
4. Do brokers handle more than one type of financial obligation from the same company?
5. Do brokers sell the stock of mutual funds?

BUSINESS TERMS

circulating capital	434	promissory note	452
fixed capital	434	negotiable instrument	452
stock certificates	435	bank discount	452
bond	435	sales finance company	453
indenture	436	commercial draft	453
debenture bonds	438	trade acceptance	453
call price	440	bank acceptances	454
callable or redeemable bonds	440	commercial paper	454
convertible bonds	440	factor	455
preferred stocks	441	floating lien	455
common stocks	443	warehouse receipt	455
investment banking company	443	prime rate	456
investment companies	447	nominal rate of interest	456
mutual funds	449	effective rate of interest	456
open-book account	450	money-market fund	458

QUESTIONS FOR DISCUSSION AND ANALYSIS

1. If a firm borrows money to increase its circulating capital, would its working capital be increased?
2. Why does a bond issue require the use of a trustee while a stock issue does not require one?
3. Do real estate mortgage bonds and chattel mortgage bonds always offer to bondholders superior protection over debenture bonds?
4. What method of bond repayment would offer the most security to a bondholder?
5. If a company is on the edge of bankruptcy and has a great need for additional capital, would its management prefer to issue common stock or bonds?
6. Why would a company desire to issue preferred stock rather than additional common stock?
7. Does an investment banking company function primarily as a bank or as a marketing organization?
8. Are all promissory notes negotiable instruments?
9. Discuss the attitude a customer might take toward a supplier that sold all of its accounts receivable to a factor.
10. If interest is not charged on open-book accounts, why would a firm ever borrow money to finance merchandise purchases?

PROJECTS, PROBLEMS, AND SHORT CASES

1. The capital stock outstanding of the Nelson Corporation consists of the following:

    Preferred stock: 1,000,000 shares, par value $100 per share, 10 percent, cumulative, nonparticipating
    Common stock: 2,000,000 shares, no-par

    Through 1981, dividends were paid on both classes of stock. But in 1982, net profits after taxes were only $4,000,000, so the board of directors passed the dividends. In 1983, profits increased to $9,000,000 and the board declared a dividend of $5 a share on the preferred stock. In 1984, profits increased sharply to $20,000,000 and the board of directors wished to resume dividend payments on the common stock. Calculate the maximum per-share dollar distribution available to the common stockholders in 1984, assuming that all profits earned in 1982, 1983, and 1984 are paid out.

2. When Kelly Edwards purchased a new $9,000 car for her business, she received a trade-in allowance of $3,000 which she used as a down payment. She agreed to pay the bank $212 a month for 3 years, or a total of $7,632 in installment payments. Her payments were based on a nominal interest rate of 9 percent a year. Using the formula on page 458, compute the effective rate of interest that she paid.

3. Prepare a report that compares and contrasts the sources of long-term and short-term financing for a public utility, such as Commonwealth Edison, and an industrial corporation such as General Motors. Note the proportion of total debt and long-term debt to stockholders' equity. Identify the types of stock that are outstanding in each company. Indicate the composition of the current and fixed assets in each organization and specify which debt instruments you believe are used to finance the different assets.

4. A group of ten civic leaders in Midland, TX determined that, in an effort to draw additional industry to the community, an industrial park was needed. After exploring several alternative financing arrangements, the ten individuals decided to incorporate and develop the park as a profit-making venture. Land would be purchased, streets would be paved, utility services would be provided, and several shell buildings would be erected on the park site. The investing group believed that the availability of their attractive facilities, combined with a "Move to Midland" promotional campaign, would attract industrial firms to the city.

A careful analysis of the financial aspects of the park revealed that it would cost $14,850,000. Before proceeding with the project, the 10 individuals felt that they must raise $15,000,000. Each member of the group pledged to invest $500,000 in the stock of the corporation. Several local banks agreed to loan a maximum of $1,000,000 for 1 year at 10 percent interest with a provision that the note could be renewed year by year if a minimum of $100,000 was paid annually on the principal.

Develop for the industrial park a financial plan that shows the type and amounts of financial obligations and the financial institutions that could be used to provide the remainder of the required financing. Assume that the ten civic leaders would like to retain control of the corporation. Justify your decisions in regard to the debt and/or equity used, as well as the financial institutions employed.

The First Woman Trader on the Midwest Stock Exchange

Kim Brown's trading career in Chicago during the mid-1970s represents one of the highlights of the fifty-year history of the K. J. Brown & Company, a Muncie, Indiana-based brokerage firm.

In the summer of 1971, she secured a position with the Chicago commodities firm of Louis Ritten and Company as a "runner" for its orders on the Chicago Board of Trade. "Runners are low-paid individuals who simply carry customer's orders between the exchange post and the individual brokers," Kim recalls. "Trading opened at 9 A. M. and closed at 1:20 P. M.; so once the market closed, I'd do clerical work for the Ritten firm."

Ritten officials advised her to enroll in the Chicago Grain Institute courses which she ultimately passed to become a licensed commodities broker. "In my first year in Chicago, I was working as a runner during the market hours, doing office work in the afternoons, and then going to school at night," Kim explains. "All I lived and breathed was the market."

In the spring of 1972, Kim wanted experience with the stock market and left the Ritten firm to join The Illinois Company, a prominent Chicago-based NYSE firm. By that time, she had passed all of the grain marketing courses of the Chicago Board of Trade. Her duties with The Illinois Company included serving as a secretary and licensed grain broker for the firm. "This was my first experience at bringing clients into the markets," Kim recalls.

In early 1973, Kim changed positions once again. She joined the correspondent and arbitrage unit of E. F. Hutton and Company on the floor of the Midwest Stock Exchange. In her new capacity, she worked as a phone clerk and as an assistant to the Hutton floor broker.

Back in Muncie, her father, Kenneth "Bud" Brown, president of K. J. Brown & Company, was keeping track of the progress Kim was making in Chicago. Always looking for talented brokers, Bud realized that Kim could give the firm its own floor broker in the heart of Chicago's financial district, if she became a stock exchange member and passed the various exchange requirements. In the summer of 1973, Kim returned to Muncie to prepare herself for becoming a stock exchange member and floor broker.

Several obstacles stood in the way of Kim's taking her eventual position for the firm at the MSE. First, she needed to pass several stock exchange examinations which would qualify her as a trading member. Subsequently passing the licensing examinations, Kim qualified as a registered representative and a registered principal with the firm. She also passed the examination by the Midwest Stock Exchange. Second, the Exchange itself carries regulations regarding its trading members. "New members need to be approved by the entire MSE membership," Kim recalls. "Since I knew many of the members and they were familiar with my work, I didn't expect to encounter any problems there." . . .

On January 19, 1974, she went to the Midwest Stock Exchange and began her first day as an active trader.

"As I walked in the door, the doorman said, "Kim, the news media is waiting to interview you!" Around the exchange floor there were film crews and television cameras that surrounded me all day. It was pretty clear that from this point on, everything I did was going to be watched, either by other women who were looking for their first opportunity to trade or by male brokers who were going to be evaluating my work."

SOURCE: E. Bruce Geelhoed, *Bringing Wall Street to Main Street: The Story of K. J. Brown & Company, Inc., 1931–1981* (Muncie, IN: Ball State University Bureau of Business Research, 1982), pp. 45, 47, 49. Reproduced with permission.

19 Security and Commodity Exchanges

Objectives:

- Identify two national and seven regional security exchanges.
- Explain each of 11 items appearing in stock quotations as printed in *The Wall Street Journal*.
- Describe the procedure followed in buying or selling shares of stocks on the New York Stock Exchange.
- Distinguish between quotations for stocks and bonds.
- Distinguish between quotations for industrial bonds and government bonds.
- Explain how speculators can sell stocks they do not own.
- Contrast state and federal regulations on the sales of securities.
- Explain the operation of the over-the-counter market for securities.
- Distinguish between a call and a put on an options exchange.
- Explain how hedging is used in the futures market to protect the legitimate manufacturing profit of a processor.

"I feel like we're preachers spreading the gospel," declared Dennis H. Rowland, vice-president for finance of Imagic, a medium-size producer of home video games. Rowland made this statement as he and several other company executives armed with impassioned speeches, a slide presentation, and game samples toured the country seeking funds for their growing company. The goal was to convince investment bankers and the public to buy 2.7 million shares of stock which would raise $40.5 million for the company.[1]

When the stock market rallies, many companies offer new stock issues to the public. Company officials are hopeful that eager buyers will gobble up the issues and fatten the company treasury. If the new issue holds a promise of high returns, it can be sold at a high price-earnings ratio to an enthusiastic public. It is not unusual for an initial public offering of stock to sell at 40 times annual earnings compared with the average price-earnings ratio of 13 for the Dow Jones Industrial Average of stocks!

Once in the hands of the public, over-the-counter trading occurs in the issued securities. Eventually a company may grow and mature to the point where it meets the requirements for listing on a major stock exchange. This is a long-term goal of many companies because a listing ensures the company of a continuous and active market for its stock.

Since a knowledge of the methods used for the exchange of securities and certain commodities is important to students of business, this chapter focuses on the operations of the markets in which they are traded. Stocks and bonds are traded on organized security exchanges, over the counter, or on option exchanges. Commodities are traded at organized commodity exchanges.

ORGANIZED SECURITY EXCHANGES

A **security exchange**, commonly called a stock exchange, is an organization that provides facilities for its members to buy and sell listed securities. Stocks and bonds that have been approved for trading on a security exchange are called **listed securities**.

The chief function of a security exchange is to provide a convenient means by which individuals and organizations can buy or sell outstanding securities of well-known corporations. A security exchange is not a source of capital to the corporation that has its stocks and bonds listed. The listed securities are stocks and bonds that previously have been sold to investors and are now being resold. Sales that take place on an exchange are between such diverse security holders as individuals, corporations, banks, insurance companies, pension funds, investment trusts, churches, hospitals, trust funds, and endowment funds.

For every buyer there must be a seller. The statement that "everybody is buying stocks" merely means that the demand is greater than the supply, which results in higher prices. When an investor thinks a stock will go up in price and wishes to buy at that time, he or she would not be able to do so if a holder of the same stock did not believe it was a good time to sell. Conversely, even in a severely depressed market there is always a buyer if a seller is willing to accept the buyer's offering price.

National and Regional Security Exchanges

In the United States we have two national security exchanges and seven regional security exchanges. The most important of these are the New York Stock Exchange

---

1. "Going Wild over Going Public," *Business Week* (December 6, 1982), p. 100.

(also called the Big Board), the American Stock Exchange (also called Amex or Curb Exchange), and the regional Midwest Stock Exchange in Chicago. The other regional exchanges are the:

1. Boston Stock Exchange
2. Philadelphia-Baltimore-Washington Stock Exchange
3. Cincinnati Stock Exchange
4. Intermountain Stock Exchange
5. Spokane Stock Exchange
6. Pacific Stock Exchange

The New York Stock Exchange (NYSE) is the most famous and largest of the security exchanges (see Figure 19-1). There are 1,366 seats on the NYSE. A seat is a membership, and its owner can buy and sell securities for his or her own account or for others. A membership can be transferred if the prospective buyer has been approved by the board of directors of the NYSE. A seat on the NYSE sold for as much as $625,000 in 1929 and for as little as $17,000 in 1942. A recent price was $285,000.[2]

The NYSE lists approximately 2,200 stocks of 1,565 companies and over 3,100 bonds of slightly more than 1,000 companies.[3] Almost every sizable industrial company is represented on the NYSE, as it accounts for 87 percent of the volume of all stocks sold through security exchanges.[4] On a normal trading day, about 60 million shares of stock in more than 1,300 corporations are bought and sold at the NYSE. Since mid-1982, there have been many days when over 100 million shares have been traded.

To qualify for listing on the NYSE, a corporation must obtain approval from the Securities and Exchange Commission (SEC) and meet the following NYSE standards:

1. It must have a minimum of 1,000,000 shares publicly owned.
2. It must have a minimum of 2,000 stockholders, each owning at least 100 shares.
3. Its annual earnings should exceed $2½ million currently and $2 million for each of the previous two years.
4. Its net tangible assets must have a minimum value of $16 million.
5. The market value of its publicly held shares, which is adjustable, must be at least between $8 and $16 million depending upon market conditions.

Daily stock quotations are listed in *The Wall Street Journal* under the headings "NYSE–Composite Transactions" and "Amex–Composite Transactions." These quotations include trades on the Midwest, Pacific, Philadelphia, Boston, and Cincinnati regional stock exchanges and are reported by the National Association of Securities Dealers, Inc., (NASD) and the Intermarket Trading System Network (Instinet). An examination of Table 19-1 shows the relative trading importance of the different exchanges, including the NASD and the Instinet. Figure 19-2 shows how stock quotations appearing in *The Wall Street Journal* and other financial news sources provide a considerable amount of information about the preceding day's activity for each stock listed. For illustrative purposes, Figure 19-2 shows the trading information for the common stock of Avon Products, Inc., as reported on one day in January, 1983.

---

2. *New York Stock Exchange Fact Book, 1982*, p. 55.
3. *Ibid.*, p. 32.
4. *Ibid.*, p. 14.

Figure 19-1   On the Floor of the New York Stock Exchange

SOURCE: Courtesy of Edward C. Topple, New York Stock Exchange Staff Photographer.

Trading Procedures

The initial step in the buying and selling of stocks on an exchange is to send the order to the trading floor of the exchange. Here it is given to a member of the exchange who is known as a **commission broker**. On the floor are a number of video display locations called trading posts at which specified stocks are bought and sold. When a customer places an order to buy 100 shares of Eastman Kodak Company common stock, for example, the member locates the post at which Kodak is traded and makes an offer to buy under the terms specified by the customer. Figure 19-3 shows the different types of orders that an investor may place with a stockbroker.

Table 19-1   Trading Volume in the Different Exchanges

	1981 Number of shares	1982 Number of shares
New York Stock Exchange	11,853,740,000	16,460,000,000
American Stock Exchange	1,343,000,000	1,343,000,000
Midwest Stock Exchange	700,830,000	983,988,000*
Pacific Stock Exchange	451,591,000	593,559,000*
NASD	319,081,000	484,651,000
Philadelphia Stock Exchange	215,000,000	320,690,000
Boston Stock Exchange	74,406,000	98,843,000
Cincinnati Stock Exchange	47,226,000	59,839,000
Instinet	17,125,000	34,300,000

*11 months of 1982.

SOURCE: "Big Board, OTC Volumes Set Highs in '82 as Trading Surged in Last Five Months," *The Wall Street Journal,* January 3, 1983, p. 17. Reprinted by permission of *The Wall Street Journal,* © Dow Jones & Company, Inc. (1982). All Rights Reserved.

**Figure 19-2   Explanation of Stock Quotations
Reported Daily in Financial Papers**

52 weeks		Stocks	Div.	Yld. %	P-E Ratio	Sales 100s	High	Low	Close	Net Chg.
High	Low									
31¾	19⅜	Avon	2	6.3	10	2320	u32⅛	31⅝	31¾	+¼
(1)	(2)	(3)	(4)	(5)	(6)	(7)	(8)	(9)	(10)	(11)

(1) The highest price paid for Avon common stock during the preceding year.
(2) The lowest price paid for Avon common stock during the preceding year.
(3) The abbreviated company name is used.
(4) The indicated annual dividend per share. If the stock quoted is preferred, the letters "pf" are shown preceding the dividend figure. If the quotation is for warrants, the letters "wt" are used. If a small letter appears after the dividend, it refers to a footnote that should be consulted in a section of the paper titled "Explanatory Notes."
(5) The current annual yield which is computed by dividing the dividend by the closing price.
(6) The price-earnings ratio which is obtained by dividing the current price of a share by the annual earnings per share.
(7) The number of shares sold, expressed in 100-share lots. The illustration shows that 232,000 Avon common shares were sold.
(8) The highest price at which shares changed hands during the day. The letter "u" indicates a new high.
(9) The lowest price at which shares changed hands during the day.
(10) The closing price per share for the day.
(11) The change from the closing price for the previous day.

Figure 19-3   **Types of Orders to Buy or Sell Stocks**

Type of Order	Terms of the Order
Round lot	Buy or sell 100 shares, the conventional trading unit.
Odd lot	Buy or sell fewer than 100 shares.
Market order	Buy or sell at the best price when the order reaches the trading floor.
Limit order	Specify the price at which the stock is to be bought or sold.
Fill or kill order	Cancel the limit order if it cannot be executed.
Good-till-canceled order	Limit order is good until canceled.
Stop order	Sell at a specified price when investor anticipates a possible drop in stock price in order to limit losses or protect profits.
MIP order	Buy under the NYSE Monthly Investment Plan under which stock can be bought on a monthly or quarterly basis, with a minimum investment of $40 a quarter.

Odd-lot orders are placed with **odd-lot dealers** who buy and sell less than a round lot (100 shares) of stock. By grouping several odd-lot orders, odd-lot dealers may be able to buy one or more round lots which are distributed to the several buyers. Because odd-lot dealers buy and sell from their own stock holdings, they are not really brokers. On the NYSE, the Exchange serves as the dealer for odd-lot transactions. Some large brokers, such as E. F. Hutton and Dean Witter Reynolds, act as odd-lot dealers for their own customers.

When a limit order at $60 a share, for example, is placed and the stock is selling at $62, the member leaves the order with another broker who is known as a specialist. A **specialist** spends most of the time at one post and concentrates on a limited number of securities (see Figure 19-4). The specialist will make a memorandum of the customer's order and, if at a later time in the day or at a later date an offer is made to sell at $60, the limit order will be executed.

A Sample Transaction. Assume that Mrs. Elizabeth Morrow lives in a suburban area of Chicago. She has decided to buy 50 shares of American Telephone & Telegraph common stock. Assume that a neighbor, James Riley, is employed as a stockbroker by E. F. Hutton, which has offices in many cities, including Chicago. Mrs. Morrow telephones Riley and places a limit order at $61. Riley teletypes this order to New York, where it is routed to the NYSE and delivered to Laura Gray, a member on the trading floor who is associated with E. F. Hutton.

Gray goes to the post at which AT&T is traded. Because Mrs. Morrow placed an odd-lot order, Gray turns this order over to an odd-lot specialist operating at the post. At this particular moment AT&T has dipped to 60¾. So, the odd-lot specialist buys 100 AT&T shares and allocates 50 to Gray. The news is transmitted to Chicago, and Riley notifies Mrs. Morrow accordingly. This transaction is depicted in Figure 19-5. A seller of AT&T stock would have gone through a similar process. The machinery for buying or selling stocks is well established, and transactions are completed in a relatively short time.

Consolidated Tape and Composite Quotation Systems. How did Mrs. Morrow decide on a buying price of $61 a share? She may have been following the daily reports in the newspaper. Or her stockbroker may have recommended the stock as a good buy at this price. If Mrs. Morrow had been in the Chicago office of Riley's brokerage firm, she could have watched the electronic tape of the NYSE on a video display machine. The tape shows actual transactions on the Big Board by means of electric letters and numbers, about the size of those on electric basketball scoreboards, that move from right to left.

Figure 19-6 shows a small segment of the consolidated tape as its appears on a screen. The stock of each company is represented by a unique symbol. Below the symbol is the per-share price in round lots. For sales up to 100 shares, the sales will be printed without any quantity. Sales of 200 to 9,900 shares will be indicated by printing the number of units (with the last two digits dropped) followed by an "s," and then the

Figure 19-4	Function of a Stock Specialist

A public shareholder would like to be sure that he or she can buy or sell shares whenever she or he wants to and at the best possible price. When no public buyer or seller appears on the other side, however, the market in a stock can evaporate, unless a market maker steps in to buy or sell for his or her own or the firm's account. At the exchanges, specialists and other registered market makers perform this function, as dealers do in over-the-counter markets; and some large brokerage houses have begun making their own markets in certain stocks.

At the NYSE, the specialist function is defined to include "effective execution of commission orders" and "maintenance, insofar as reasonably practicable, of a fair and orderly market on the Exchange" in assigned stocks. The market is considered fair if it is free of manipulative and deceptive practices and if it avoids giving any market participants undue advantages; it's considered orderly if trading prices are continuous (showing little or no change) from sale to sale and if large amounts of buying or selling interest can be accommodated without significant price changes.

In the course of going about his tasks, the specialist may act as an agent for other brokers or as a dealer for her or his own account; in fact, however, he or she acts as a dealer in only about a quarter of all trades. (There is some double counting here, since the specialist as dealer is handling the same stock twice—once as a buyer and once as a seller.) For the other three-quarters, the specialist is involved as an auctioneer—arranging bids and offers at the daily opening and otherwise bringing public orders together.

The specialist must meet the responsibilities and eligibility requirements outlined in the specialist job description and must conform to a code of acceptable business practices. Based on the job description and the code, specialists are evaluated quarterly by the floor brokers they serve. The evaluation questionnaires provide the principal information used by the NYSE Allocation Committee, which assigns stocks to specialists and, when necessary, reassigns them.

SOURCE: John J. Mulhern, "The National Stock Market: Taking Shape," *Business Review* (Federal Reserve Bank of Philadelphia, September/October, 1980), p. 7.

Figure 19-5   Steps in a Stock Transaction

Mrs. Morrow contacts broker Riley to place a limit order for 50 shares of AT&T at $61.

Riley teletypes the order to broker Gray on the trading floor of the NYSE.

Broker Gray goes to the AT&T post and gives the order to an odd-lot specialist in AT&T.

Odd-lot specialist buys 100 AT&T shares and allocates 50 to broker Gray.

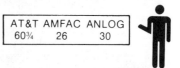

Broker Gray notifies broker Riley, who notifies Mrs. Morrow that she has bought 50 shares of AT&T stock.

price. Sales of 10,000 or more shares are always printed with all the digits. Figure 19-6 is read from right to left as follows:

> 25,300 shares of Clorox Co. common at 24¼
> 100 shares of Superior Oil common at 30¾
> 9,800 shares of PayLess Drug Stores common at 26¼
> 100 shares of Pan Am World Airways common at 5⅛

At the present time almost all security brokers have on their desks a computer terminal that is a part of a composite quotation system. The terminal permits the display of price quotations and trades for stocks on all the major exchanges and the over-the-counter markets. The system is programmed to supply information on 90 percent of the transactions within 90 seconds.

Figure 19-6   A Consolidated Ticker Tape Segment

Price Variations and Averages

As Figure 19-6 shows, stock prices are quoted in eighths, quarters, and halves. In Chapter 18 we noted that bond prices are quoted in relationship to 100 regardless of the bond's denomination. Government bonds, however, are an exception as they are quoted in thirty-seconds such as $98^{24}/_{32}$ for a $1,000 bond. For convenience in printing, this quotation usually is shown as 98.24 but the bond will cost $987.50 ($98\frac{3}{4}$).

To judge whether the stock market is up or down, averages are published in the financial pages of newspapers and aired on radio and television. The best-known is the Dow Jones Industrial Average (DJIA), which is based on only 30 corporations, which are listed in Figure 19-7. The history of the DJIA is related in Figure 19-8. Standard & Poor's index uses 425 industrials, 25 rails, and 50 utilities. Since 1966 the NYSE has issued an average based on all of its stocks. Also, each trading day the NYSE makes a report every half hour on the number of cents an average share has gained or lost.

Averages for the over-the-counter market, which is discussed on pages 477–478, are also released daily. Bond averages are likewise reported; again, the best-known is the Dow Jones, which is based on 40 issues.

Costs of Trading

Whether they are buying or selling, customers of a brokerage firm pay a commission for services rendered. Commissions charged by members of the NYSE vary by the

Figure 19-7   Thirty Stocks Used in Dow Jones Industrial Average

Alcoa	General Electric	Owens-Illinois
Allied Corporation	General Foods	Procter & Gamble
American Brands	General Motors	Sears, Roebuck
American Can	Goodyear	Standard Oil of California
American Express	Inco Ltd.	Texaco
American Telephone	IBM	Union Carbide
Bethlehem Steel	International Harvester	U.S. Steel
Du Pont	International Paper	United Technologies
Eastman Kodak	Merck & Co.	Westinghouse Electric
Exxon Corporation	Minnesota Mining & Manufacturing	Woolworth

Figure 19-8   What's a Dow Jones?

NEW YORK—Ask any dozen people on the street to identify Charles Henry Dow and you're likely to get vacant stares.

But combine the name with that of Edward D. Jones and the recognition factor should soar.

Dow and Jones, a couple of newspaper reporters from New England, teamed up 100 years ago to compile and sell investment information to stockbrokers. From their partnership was born the Wall Street Journal and an enduring phrase—the Dow Jones industrial average.

Today, the index they pioneered is the world's most widely quoted measure of stock market ups and downs. It gauges the course of American capitalism on a continual basis.

In recent months, as the market has staged its most vigorous short-term advance ever, the words "Dow Jones average" have resounded over the airwaves of radio and television and have repeatedly adorned the front pages of the nation's newspapers.

Critics of the venerable Dow average insist that it and its 30 component parts are an inadequate indicator of what's happening on a stock exchange that lists more than 1,500 stocks and in a market with several thousand.

No matter. The Dow perseveres.

New and more sensitive indexes appear. But the Dow keeps attracting the attention.

"The Dow is the oldest market indicator," said William M. LeFevre, vice president of Purcell, Graham and Co. and one of the Dow's ardent champions. "It has become ingrained in the minds of investors and the news media."

SOURCE: James Russell, "Enduring Partnership," *Muncie Star,* December 19, 1982, p. C12. Reprinted by permission of Knight-Ridder Newspapers.

amount of money involved and by the number of shares in the transaction—odd lot, single round lot, or multiple round lots. For many years brokers charged uniform commission rates, but since May 1, 1975, these rates have been competitive. In general, the commission a customer pays for a single round lot will amount to more than 1 percent but less than 2 percent of the purchase or sale price. For example, one firm charges $77.50 for executing an order for 100 shares of stock selling for $50 a share.

In addition to commissions, some states levy a small tax on the transfer of shares. Also, the Securities and Exchange Commission charges the seller a fee of 1¢ for each $300 or fraction thereof of the money involved. These costs are relatively minor.

Speculative Transactions

In every market one finds investors and speculators. An investor is one who buys securities in order to hold them on a more or less permanent basis. The speculator hopes to make a profit buying and selling them within a few weeks, days, or within the trading hours of a single day. Speculators who buy stocks in anticipation of a rise in price are known as **bulls**. Those who sell, expecting the market to go down in the days or weeks ahead, are known as **bears**.

Short Selling. As illogical as it may seem, a bear often sells shares he or she does not own by borrowing them, usually from a broker. The borrowed shares may be owned by the broker or may be shares that the broker is holding for a customer. This market operation is known as **short selling**. The bear sells today expecting to buy, or "cover the short sale," within a relatively short time after the market goes down to a price at which a profit can be made.

For example, Dick Mayes, a speculator, borrows from a broker 1,000 shares of 3M stock and sells these shares through this broker at $55 on a Monday morning. Sometime between Monday and the following Friday the 3M shares become available at $53½. Mayes covers the short sale by buying 1,000 shares at $53½. As a result, he makes a profit of $1,500 minus the costs of trading. However, if the 3M shares go higher than $55, Mayes will incur a loss. When Mayes buys 1,000 shares to replace those borrowed, his loss is the amount that the stock has increased in value.

Margin Trading. A speculator can also increase profits by buying stocks on a margin. In **margin trading,** a buyer pays only a portion of the purchase price and borrows the balance from a broker or a bank. Margin requirements—or the portion that should be paid in cash—are determined by the Federal Reserve Board, and these have varied from as high as 100 percent to as low as 40 percent. In addition, the NYSE requires a customer to deposit at least $2,000 in cash or its equivalent in securities before opening a margin account with a member firm. As of 1983, the margin requirement was 50 percent.

For example, assume that the current margin requirement is 50 percent. A speculator who has only $10,000 to invest can buy 200 shares of a stock selling at $100 by borrowing the other $10,000 from a broker. If the stock rises to $115, the speculator can sell the 200 shares and make a profit of $3,000 minus commissions, taxes, and interest on the money borrowed. But if the stock price declines, the broker will require an additional deposit for protection against loss. If the margin trader cannot put up the additional deposit, the broker will sell the 200 shares no later than when the price drops to $50 to protect the loan. And the speculator's original $10,000 investment will be lost.

From the foregoing discussion it might appear that speculators are using stock exchanges as a type of gambling casino. Although there is some truth in this, speculators render a real service to investors and to the exchanges. They not only keep the market active but also hold price variations between sales of a particular stock to fractions of a point. Speculators are one important reason why an investor can always find a buyer or a seller for a stock or bond listed on an exchange.

Role of Security Exchanges

When a corporation sells stocks and bonds directly to the public or through investment banking companies, it is said to be using the *primary market* (first-time sale). Sales of these securities at a securities exchange take place in what is known as the *secondary market* (resale of outstanding securities). Without the secondary market it would be difficult for the primary market to function. Maintaining a free market, with stock prices established at all times by the forces of supply and demand, makes listed securities more desirable than unlisted ones. Listed stocks and bonds can be used as collateral for bank loans or as security for collateral trust bonds. Estates are easier to appraise to the extent that they contain listed securities. Without these advantages, investors and speculators would not be willing to buy the securities offered in the primary market.

For a corporation large enough to qualify, it is a matter of some prestige to have its stocks and bonds listed on an exchange. Table 19-2 shows the NYSE-listed companies with the largest number of stockholders. The chances are good that the number of stockholders will increase after listing, thus helping the corporation's sales and certainly making it easier for the "in group" to retain control. Of even greater importance is the added bargaining power a corporation has with an investment banking company when negotiating for the sale of additional securities.

Security exchanges have provided a marketplace where individuals can invest their savings at a relatively low commission charge. Whenever the United States is in a period of inflation, the purchasing power of the dollar declines. Although there is no perfect hedge against inflation, over the long run common stocks do tend to increase in value when consumer prices go up. This happens because corporations increase their prices to offset higher costs of labor and materials to such an extent that their profits also increase proportionally.

Finally, individuals can feel confident about the reliability of their brokers. The Securities Investor Protection Act of 1970 insures customers of a brokerage firm against losses which are caused by the insolvency of the broker. In 1980 the limits of the protection were increased to $500,000 per customer, except claims for cash which are limited to $100,000 per customer.[5]

Table 19-2   NYSE-Listed Companies with the Largest Number of Stockholders

Company	Number of Stockholders	Company	Number of Stockholders
American Telephone & Telegraph	3,055,000	American Electric Power	340,000
General Motors	1,122,000	Gulf Oil	302,000
Exxon Corporation	776,000	Mobil Corporation	292,000
International Business Machines	742,000	Commonwealth Edison	275,000
General Electric	502,000	Philadelphia Electric	267,000
General Telephone & Electronics	476,000	Pacific Gas & Electric	255,000
Texaco, Inc.	384,000	Standard Oil of California	247,000
Sears, Roebuck	354,000	du Pont de Nemours	243,000
Southern Company	351,000	Tenneco, Inc.	238,000
Ford Motor	342,000	United States Steel	236,000

SOURCE: *New York Stock Exchange Fact Book, 1982,* p. 35. Reproduced with permission.

---

5. Securities Investor Protection Corporation, "An Explanation of the Securities Investor Protection Act of 1970 as Amended Through 1980" (1980), p. 1.

Regulation of Security Sales and Exchanges

In the early part of the twentieth century, less than half a million people owned corporate stocks and bonds. Because there were no effective regulations to cover security sales, unscrupulous promoters committed many security swindles. When an aroused public finally demanded legislation to curb these swindles, both the states and the federal government enacted appropriate laws.

State Regulation

In 1909, the United States Post Office secured the passage of a law that made it a criminal offense to use the mails to defraud. This law, however, did not prevent crooked security salespersons from operating in various cities and communities. In 1911, Kansas became the first state to pass a law regulating security sales. While considering the bill, a member of the legislature remarked that some promoters would sell stock in the "blue sky" itself. Today the laws regulating security sales that have been passed in most states are known as **blue-sky laws.** These blue-sky laws frequently cover the following items:

1. New security issues must be registered with an appropriate state official.
2. Dealers, brokers, and salespersons must obtain annual licenses.
3. Individuals charged with fraud in connection with the sale of stocks and bonds are prosecuted.

Federal Securities Act of 1933

The Securities Act of 1933, which controls the interstate sale of securities, has been called the "information law" because full disclosure of relevant financial facts is its major requirement. This is accomplished by requiring a company to:

1. File a registration statement, which contains extensive details about the company and the proposed issue of securities.
2. Prepare a condensed version of the registration statement, called a prospectus, which must be furnished to each prospective buyer of the stocks or bonds offered for sale (see Figure 19-9).

Since 1934 the enforcement of this law has been under the jurisdiction of the Securities and Exchange Commission. The SEC is given 20 days after the registration statement has been filed to issue a stop order if it believes that the proposed offering should not be made to the general public. Even if a stop order has not been issued, the SEC does not guarantee the correctness of the information supplied.

Federal Securities Exchange Act of 1934

The Securities Exchange Act of 1934 is notable because it established the powerful SEC. The major provisions of the Act are:

1. Every corporation whose stock is listed on one of the national exchanges is required to file a registration statement with the SEC. Furthermore, this statement must be kept up-to-date by the filing of annual reports.

Figure 19-9   Example of a Prospectus

$20,000,000

CRIME CONTROL, INC.

10% Convertible Subordinated Debentures due November 1, 1997

Interest Payable May 1 and November 1

The Debentures are convertible into shares of Common Stock of the Company at a conversion price of $18 per share, subject to adjustment in certain events. On November 4, 1982, the closing bid and asked prices of the Company's Common Stock in the over-the-counter market as reported by NASDAQ were $15 and $15¾ per share, respectively.

The Debentures are redeemable at the option of the Company, in whole or in part, on or after November 1, 1984, at the redemption prices set forth herein. Sinking fund payments of $2,000,000 annually commencing November 1, 1988, are calculated to retire 90% of the issue prior to maturity.

The Debentures will be subordinated to all Senior Debt (as defined) of the Company. As of September 30, 1982, the Company's Senior Debt was approximately $20,600,000. See "Capitalization".

THESE SECURITIES HAVE NOT BEEN APPROVED OR DISAPPROVED BY THE SECURITIES AND EXCHANGE COMMISSION NOR HAS THE COMMISSION PASSED UPON THE ACCURACY OR ADEQUACY OF THIS PROSPECTUS. ANY REPRESENTATION TO THE CONTRARY IS A CRIMINAL OFFENSE.

	Price to Public(1)	Underwriting Discounts and Commissions(2)	Proceeds to Company(1)(3)
Per Debenture	100%	3.75%	96.25%
Total	$20,000,000	$750,000	$19,250,000

(1) Plus accrued interest from November 1, 1982, to date of delivery.

(2) The Company has agreed to indemnify the Underwriters against certain liabilities under the Securities Act of 1933. See "Underwriting".

(3) Before deducting expenses of the Company estimated at approximately $325,000.

The Debentures are being offered by the Underwriters subject to prior sale and when, as and if delivered to and accepted by the Underwriters, and subject to approval of certain legal matters by counsel. It is expected that delivery of the Debentures will be made against payment therefor on or about November 12, 1982, at the offices of Thomson McKinnon Securities Inc., One New York Plaza, New York, New York.

Thomson McKinnon Securities Inc.

The date of this Prospectus is November 5, 1982.

SOURCE: Thomson McKinnon Securities, Inc., New York, NY. Reproduced with permission.

---

2. Practically all of the security exchanges, both national and regional, were classified as national and placed under the jurisdiction of the SEC.

3. The determination of margin requirements is under the control of the Federal Reserve Board.

4. Any practice that is an attempt to manipulate the securities market is prohibited.

5. Proxy statements are subject to scrutiny to make sure that they are truthful and not misleading.

6. Corporate officers who own 10 percent or more of the stock of a company listed on a national exchange must list their holdings with the SEC and must not sell the company's securities on a "short" basis. Any profits made by them through the

purchase and sale of the company's securities completed in less than six months must be paid to the company.

In addition to laws covering specific details, the SEC has issued numerous rulings in furthering its authority to regulate security sales in the United States. For example, listed corporations are required to have an annual audit by an independent accounting firm and to publish an annual report. A recent ruling that has affected corporations with all, or almost all, "insider" directors specifies that the board must have an audit committee consisting of at least three "outside" directors.

OVER-THE-COUNTER MARKETS

Purchases and sales of outstanding public and corporate securities that do not take place on an organized security exchange are made in **over-the-counter markets**. The bonds and stocks that are traded over the counter (OTC) are known as **unlisted securities**. In contrast to the approximately 4,700 different issues of stocks and bonds traded on all security exchanges, there are about 50,000 different OTC bonds and stocks. These include U.S. government and other public bonds and notes, most corporate bonds, mutual funds, foreign securities, bank stocks, insurance stocks, and industrial and public utility stocks that do not qualify for listing on an exchange.

Unlike the technique used on security exchanges where brokers meet face to face, security dealers who function in the OTC market make a public announcement that they "make a market" in unlisted securities on the basis of bid and asked prices. The bid prices are those that would-be buyers of OTC securities are willing to pay. The asked prices are those at which would-be sellers are willing to sell the bonds or stocks they own. These security dealers, who can be either investment banking companies or brokers or both, usually carry an inventory of different unlisted bonds and stocks. Their gross profit is the difference between bid prices and asked prices. Figure 19-10 shows and explains how over-the-counter quotations are published in financial pages.

Figure 19-10   Over-the-Counter Quotations

Stock & Div.		Sales 100s	Bid	Asked	Net Change
ABankrs Ins	.50	297	10⅞	11	+⅛
(1)	(2)	(3)	(4)	(5)	(6)

(1) Name of corporation.
(2) Annual dividend per share if the company pays a dividend.
(3) Number of round lots traded the previous day.
(4) Closing per-share price offered by a would-be buyer.
(5) Closing per-share price of a would-be seller.
(6) Difference between the closing bid and asked prices of today and of the previous trading day.

In the past, one of the problems that faced security dealers operating in the OTC market was the difficulty of obtaining bid and asked prices at the moment when a customer wished to buy or sell. Telephone calls made to market-making brokers were a partial solution, as were the daily reports of the National Quotations Bureau, a commercial service for subscribers. In 1971 the National Association of Securities Dealers, a trade association to which most brokerage firms belong, began operating automated quotations known as NASDAQ (National Association of Securities Dealers Automated Quotations). This is a computerized communications system that provides constant information on approximately 3,500 of the larger companies that are traded over the counter. A broker equipped with a desk-top quotation terminal can obtain up-to-the-second information on any of the stocks on line in the central computer.

Regulation of OTC Markets

In 1938, Congress passed the Maloney Amendment to the Securities Exchange Act which authorized investment banking companies to form associations for the purpose of self-regulation. The only association ever formed under this authority was the NASD. This nonprofit corporation is composed of broker and dealer members who have been required to pass a qualifying examination as Registered Representatives or Principals. These members are also required to subscribe to extensive and detailed Rules of Fair Practice.

The Third and Fourth Markets

Sometimes transactions in listed securities take place off the organized exchange on which the bond or stock is listed and thus become a part of the over-the-counter market. When large blocks of listed securities are traded off the floor of the exchange with a brokerage firm acting as an intermediary between two institutional investors, the transaction is said to take place in the **third market**. The same transfer of securities without the use of an intermediary broker is referred to as the **fourth market**. This market evolved because institutions can save the brokerage fee by dealing with each other.

DEVELOPMENT OF A NATIONAL MARKET SYSTEM

In 1975 the Securities and Exchange Commission mandated the securities industry to develop a **national market system (NMS)** that would encourage nationwide competition in securities trading. The NMS would be a computerized trading system that would link the organized stock exchanges and the over-the-counter market so buyers and sellers could execute their orders at the best competitive price. Lately, the SEC has been evaluating the merits of two different types of NMS in order to establish the most efficient one.

One of the experimental systems is the *Intermarket Trading System* (ITS) that began in 1978. The ITS involves the composite quotation system and a network of computers in each security exchange. It allows a broker on the floor of a particular exchange to route a customer order to another exchange when the price of the security involved is better at the other exchange. By checking the quotes that are displayed on the composite quotation system, a floor broker can determine which exchange has the best price for a particular stock. Then, using the computer at his or her exchange, the broker can route the order to the exchange with the best price.

ITS continues the use of security exchanges for trading purposes while allowing a customer to buy or sell a security at the best competitive price. This system, however, does not guarantee that orders are directed to the exchange with the best price. Expressing his displeasure with this form of an NMS, the president of a large brokerage house declared that the system is as far from the concept of an automated, efficient marketplace as a tom-tom is from a communications satellite.

In 1982 the SEC approved the use of an updated electronic network that links the stock exchanges and the over-the-counter market for trading in certain actively traded stocks. The network permits customers to execute orders through brokers and obtain the best price on the trade, regardless of the location of the market used. Under this plan brokers obtain the most competitive price on an exchange, but they are able to conduct trades for their customers away from an exchange, too.

The other experimental type of NMS is the completely automated market that is being conducted by the all-electronic Cincinnati Stock Exchange. In this system, brokers route all of their orders through computer terminals in their offices. A central computer matches all of the buy and sell orders, securing automatically the best price for a customer. Some industry observers believe that in the future all of the stock exchanges will be merged into one large computerized operation. Because of the great impact an all-electronic market would have on the activities of the NYSE, its officers have been hesitant to adopt the concept.[6]

OPTION MARKETS

Stock options traded on an **option exchange** give the holder the privilege of buying or selling a named stock at a specified price within a stated time period. These options should not be confused with stock options which are granted to corporate executives and are issued by a corporation. Stock options traded on an option exchange are provided by brokers, speculators, and investors.

The only exchange devoted exclusively to trading options is the Chicago Board Options Exchange (CBOE). Organized in 1973, it was the first option market. Now, the American Stock Exchange, the Pacific Stock Exchange, the Philadelphia Stock Exchange, and the Midwest Stock Exchange (merged into the CBOE in 1980) are also engaged in options trading. Only a limited number of corporations are represented in each market. The total number of different common-stock issues in all options markets is about 300.

---

6. Robert C. Klemkosky and David J. Wright, "The Changing Structure of the Stock Market: The National Market System," *Business Horizons* (July/August, 1981), pp. 10–20.

An option to buy is known as a **call**. An option to sell is a **put**. The price at which the option can be exercised is known as the **striking price**. This is always a price ending in 5 or 0; and 3 or 4 striking prices are available. Options mature quarterly, ending on the third Saturday of the month. If a speculator buys both a put and a call for the same stock, usually with different expiration dates, the transaction is known as a **spread**.

Individuals use the option markets to make large profits with a relatively small outlay of cash. For example, assume that in December a speculator believes that Exxon stock, which is being quoted at $50, will increase sharply in price over the next few months. The speculator therefore purchases a call at $50 with the option cost of $2.75 a share. This means that for $4,950 the speculator acquires the right to buy 1,800 shares ($4,950/$2.75 = 1,800) of Exxon stock at $50 until the expiration date of the option. If the price of Exxon stock increases to, say, $60 a share within the option period, the speculator can exercise the call and make a profit. The market value of 1,800 shares at $60 is $108,000; at $50, it is $90,000. Therefore, the difference between these two market values of 1,800 shares is $18,000 ($108,000 less $90,000). If the call is exercised, the speculator makes a profit of $13,050 ($18,000 less $4,950, the cost of the option). If the stock fails to advance or perhaps declines during the option period, the call will not be exercised and the speculator loses the option cost of $4,950.

During 1981, 57.6 million option contracts were traded on the CBOE, representing options on almost 5.8 billion shares of stock, which was 52 percent of the volume traded on the NYSE.[7] Options quotations are reported on a daily basis in *The Wall Street Journal*. Figure 19-11 shows an excerpt of listed options quotations, and Figure 19-12 gives an explanation of these quotations.

COMMODITY EXCHANGES

A **commodity exchange** is an organized market for a selected list of commodities. In general, these products are produced in large quantities by thousands of suppliers and can be stored. Such products as wheat, corn, soybeans, sugar, wool, cotton, oats, rye, silver, lead, gold, zinc, tin, rubber, coffee, and cocoa are examples of commodities traded on exchanges. In addition, some livestock and vegetables are listed on certain commodity exchanges.

The oldest and best known commodity exchange is the Chicago Board of Trade, on which grains, soybean meal and oil, silver, plywood, iced broilers, and steers are traded (see Figure 19-13). Other exchanges handling grains are located in Minneapolis, Kansas City (MO), and Winnipeg, Canada. The leading exchanges that handle cotton, wool, cocoa, rubber, hides, and potatoes are located in New York City. There are also overseas markets, notably the London metals markets.

---

7. Chicago Board Options Exchange, *Market Statistics—1982*, p. 20.

Figure 19-11   Listed Options Quotations

Chicago Board

Option & NY Close	Strike Price	Calls—Last			Puts—Last		
		Jan	**Apr**	**Jul**	**Jan**	**Apr**	**Jul**
Alcoa	25	6	7¼	r	1-16	¾	¾
31½	...30	1 15-16	4	4⅛	7-16	1⅝	2⅛
31½	. 35	¼	1½	1¾	r	5¾	4¾
Am Exp	.65	r	4¾	7½	r	r	r
Am Tel	. 50	13	14	s	r	⅛	s
63¾	... 55	9	9½	9⅝	1-16	⅜	¾
63¾	... 60	3⅝	5⅛	6¼	3-16	1⅜	2⅜
63¾	... 65	½	2¼	3¼	1 15-16	3¼	4¾
Atl R	30	17¼	17¾	r	r	r	r
47¾	... 35	13	12¾	r	r	¼	⅞
47¾	... 40	7¾	8¾	8¾	1-16	⅞	2
47¾	... 45	3	4½	6	⅜	2⅛	r
47¾	...50	11-16	2⅜	3¾	3	4½	r
47¾	... 55	1-16	1⅛	2¼	r	r	r
Avon	 20	r	9¼	r	r	r	r
29⅜	... 25	4¾	4⅞	6⅛	1-16	½	2
29⅜	... 30	9-16	1⅝	2⅝	1¼	r	3
BankAm	.20	1 3-16	1 15-16	2⅞	5-16	1⅛	r
20¾	... 25	1-16	9-16	13-16	r	r	r
20¾	... 30	r	r	⅜	r	r	r

r—Not traded. s—No option offered. o—Old.
Last is premium (purchase price).

SOURCE: *The Wall Street Journal*, January 7, 1983. Reprinted by permission of *The Wall Street Journal*, © Dow Jones & Company, Inc. (1983). All Rights Reserved.

Figure 19-12   Explanation of Listed Options Quotations

	Option & NY Close	Strike Price	Calls-Last			Puts-Last		
			Jan	**Apr**	**Jul**	**Jan**	**Apr**	**Jul**
(1)	Alcoa	25	6	7¼	r	1-16	3/4	3/4
	31½	30	15-16	4	4 1/8	7-16	1 5/8	2 1/8
	(2)	**(3)**	**(4)**	**(5)**	**(6)**	**(7)**	**(8)**	**(9)**

(1) Name of corporation—Alcoa.
(2) Closing price for the day of Alcoa on the NYSE composite listing.
(3) The striking price.
(4) Cost per share for January contract to buy.
(5) Cost per share for April contract to buy.
(6) Cost per share for July contract to buy; "r" indicates there is no trade.
(7) Cost per share for January contract to sell.
(8) Cost per share for April contract to sell.
(9) Cost per share for July contract to sell.

Figure 19-13   On the Floor of the Chicago Board of Trade

SOURCE: Courtesy of the Chicago Board of Trade.

Transactions at Commodity Exchanges

Trading on a commodity exchange is conducted by members of the exchange, who are usually brokers or partners in brokerage firms. Individuals who wish to make a purchase or sale on a commodity exchange proceed in much the same manner as in buying or selling shares of stock. A broker, who might be the same person used to buy securities, is contacted. The broker's firm probably holds a membership on the commodity exchange. The commission charged varies with the commodity and quantity and is generally reasonable.

On a commodity exchange there are two markets: spot and futures. The **spot market** is the cash market. A buyer in the spot market usually expects delivery of the commodity and the seller usually owns the product sold. In the **futures market** contracts for purchase or sale call for delivery some months in the future. However, actual delivery is rarely made, as the buyer of a contract will normally close the account by selling a contract. The original seller of a contract follows a reverse procedure.

A Sample Futures Transaction

In December, Jose Diaz believes that corn is underpriced, as it is selling at $3.00 a bushel. Diaz instructs his broker to buy 10,000 bushels for May delivery. (In this transaction Diaz is taking a *long position*; if he had contracted to sell May corn, he would have taken a *short position*.) The margin requirement for trading in commodities is commonly about 10 percent. Therefore, the broker would probably require Diaz to make a deposit of no less than $3,000.

Diaz follows the market and is pleased when, in March, May corn is selling for $3.75 a bushel. At this time he instructs his broker to sell a contract for 10,000 bushels at $3.75 and to use this contract to cancel his December purchase contract. Thus, on an investment of $3,000, Diaz makes a profit of $7,500 ($37,500 less $30,000), minus commissions.

If the price of corn had gone down to $2.70 a bushel, Diaz would have been forced to cover his May sale unless he supplied additional cash to increase his margin account. In any event, he would have had to buy another contract no later than May.

A Sample Hedging Transaction

The main useful purpose of the futures market is to protect the legitimate manufacturing profit of a processor who uses one of the commodities traded on an exchange. This is called **hedging**. It becomes necessary because the selling price of the processed product tends to follow the cash price of the raw material despite the time gap between purchase of the raw material and sale of the finished product. For example, Procter & Gamble hedges in soybeans and lard, and Black & Decker is involved in the futures market in metals. The classic example of a hedging transaction involves wheat. This is because flour sells in close relationship to the day-by-day price of wheat rather than on the basis of the cost of wheat that may have been purchased two or three months earlier for conversion into flour.

A typical hedging transaction, illustrated in Figure 19-14, might work in the following manner. On February 1 the ABC Milling Company buys 100,000 bushels of wheat in the spot market at $5.00 a bushel. The cost of processing the wheat is $200,000. When converted into flour, it is worth $750,000 in the current market. This means that the company expects to make a profit of $50,000 ($750,000 less $700,000). As a hedge, on February 1 the company also sells a futures contract on 100,000 bushels of wheat at $5.00 for May delivery. This provides adequate time to convert the wheat bought on the same day into flour ready for sale by April. However, by March the price of wheat declines to $4.00 a bushel, and the company finds that it cannot sell the flour in April for more than $650,000. This means an overall loss of $50,000 on its purchase of February 1. So, the company buys another futures contract for 100,000 bushels of wheat for $400,000 to offset the contract sold on February 1. This results in a profit on the February 1 sales contract of $100,000. This profit of $100,000, less the $50,000 loss on the April sale of flour, allows the company to earn the $50,000 that it originally hoped to make on its manufacturing operations.

Figure 19-14   A Hedging Transaction

Cash Transactions		Futures Transactions	
February 1		February 1	
Purchased 100,000 bushels of wheat @ $5.00 per bushel	$500,000	Sold May contract 100,000 bushels @ $5.00	$500,000
February and March			
Paid manufacturing costs	200,000	In April	
Total cost of flour	$700,000	Purchased May contract 100,000 bushels @ $4.00 to	400,000
In April		offset Feb. 1 sale	
Sale of flour	650,000		
Loss on sale of flour	$ 50,000	Profit on futures transactions	$100,000

Profit on futures transactions	$100,000
Less loss on sale of flour	50,000
Net profit	$ 50,000

Regulation of Commodity Exchanges

The commodity exchanges are regulated by the Commodity Futures Trading Commission (CFTC). This agency was created by the Congress in 1974 to take over the inadequate supervision that had been exercised by the Commodity Exchange Authority. Despite the Authority's limited jurisdiction over futures trading in only 20 agricultural commodities, it had issued several rulings that the CFTC has continued. For example, units of trading were established for sugar at 50 tons, for cotton at 100 bales, and for grains at 5,000 bushels. Daily price variations had been set at 20 cents a bushel for wheat and soybeans, and 2 cents a pound for cocoa. A speculator was limited to ownership of 2,000,000 bushels of one grain or 30,000 bales of cotton. In general, the CFTC has the authority to oversee the markets for commodity futures in much the same manner as the SEC watches over the stock and options exchanges.

SUMMARY   The American public can buy and sell a wide variety of stocks, bonds, options, and commodities in established markets. Most individuals need to use a broker and pay a commission for services rendered. Regardless of the buyer's or seller's motive, the government regulates the markets to insure fair play.

The best known of the security markets is the New York Stock Exchange, where nearly 60 million shares of stock change hands each trading day. Its daily activity is reported at length in the financial pages of almost all metropolitan newspapers. The ease of buying either a round lot or odd lot is one of the reasons why over 32 million people in the United

States are stockholders. In recent years the securities industry has been experimenting with the development of a national market system that would encourage nationwide competition in securities trading.

In order to avoid manipulation and other methods of sharp dealing in securities, the federal government established the Securities and Exchange Commission in 1934. The SEC has extensive authority over all security exchanges. Stockholders benefit from the SEC regulations that require corporations to publish annual reports and to have annual audits by independent CPA firms.

Many corporations do not have their securities listed on the NYSE or other stock exchanges. It is necessary to use the over-the-counter market when buying or selling unlisted securities. By means of an electronic communications network, it is possible to secure bid and asked prices on approximately 3,500 different unlisted issues at all hours during a working day.

The newest entries into the buying and selling of stocks are the option markets. The Chicago Board Options Exchange is the only exchange that deals exclusively with options although options are also traded on some stock exchanges. By means of a call or a put, speculators have the opportunity to reap large profits or, conversely, to lose their entire investment.

An entirely different kind of market is the commodity exchange. In most instances buyers or sellers of futures contracts neither expect delivery nor expect to deliver the commodity bought or sold. Rather, they buy or sell a second contract at a later date to offset the first contract. Processors of commodities use commodity exchanges to hedge their manufacturing profits, but most transactions at these exchanges are between speculators. The federal government established the Commodity Futures Trading Commission in 1974 to eliminate unfair practices and outright fraud in commodity markets.

BACK TO THE CHAPTER OPENER

1. What is the function of a stock exchange?
2. What are the major stock exchanges in this country?
3. What are the steps in trading a stock through a broker on a stock exchange?
4. How would the development of a national market system affect the Midwest and other regional stock exchanges?
5. What is the difference between a stock exchange and a commodity exchange?

BUSINESS TERMS

security exchange	464	third market	478
listed securities	464	fourth market	478
commission broker	466	national market system (NMS)	478
odd-lot dealers	468	option exchange	479
specialist	468	call	480
bulls	472	put	480
bears	472	striking price	480
short selling	472	spread	480
margin trading	473	commodity exchange	480
blue-sky laws	475	spot market	482
over-the-counter markets	477	futures market	482
unlisted securities	477	hedging	483

1. In what ways is a stockholder better off by owning shares of a listed stock rather than an unlisted stock?
2. What is the significance of the price-earnings ratio in stock quotations?
3. Is the odd-lot dealer more useful than the specialist in the stock market?
4. Is the Dow Jones Industrial Average more helpful to investors than to speculators in the stock market?
5. How are competitive commission rates on purchases and sales of stock an improvement over uniform commission rates?
6. Is there any difference between gambling and speculating in the stock market?
7. Purchasers of automobiles, furniture, and homes can usually borrow from 80 to 100 percent of the purchase price. Why is the margin on stocks sometimes at 100 percent and usually no lower than 50 percent?
8. Why would it be difficult for the primary market to function without the secondary market in securities?
9. Is trading on an option exchange more speculative than futures trading on a commodity exchange?
10. Why don't all companies utilizing a raw material that is listed on the futures market use hedging to protect their legitimate manufacturing profits?

**PROJECTS,
PROBLEMS,
AND
SHORT
CASES**

1. Refer to a current issue of *The Wall Street Journal* or a metropolitan newspaper and itemize the following information:

   a. Closing average, DJIA.
   b. Closing price per share of American Telephone & Telegraph Co. $4 preferred stock.
   c. High for the year of International Business Machines common stock.
   d. Closing quotation of Exxon bonds, 6s due in 1997.
   e. Bid price for Standard Register stock.
   f. Asked price for Dart Drug stock.
   g. Put price for Eastman Kodak Co. stock, lowest per-share price, first maturity.
   h. Cash price for a bushel of corn.
   i. Closing price for December futures, Chicago Board of Trade wheat.

2. Rosita Meñez recently sold an apartment house that she owned for $177,000. Because she had adequate savings and insurance, she decided to invest the money in a limited portfolio of stocks and bonds. Assuming that she purchased the following securities at the indicated prices, and that commissions averaged 1.75 percent of the cost of the securities, how much did Meñez invest?

Units	Security	Unit Price
500	Bank of America common stock	20 1/8
1000	General Motors common stock	62 1/4
2000	Xerox common stock	37 1/2
400	GAF $1.20 preferred stock	17 5/8
10	IBM 9 3/8%, 2004 bond	88 7/8
15	Sears 8%, 2006 bond	70 1/4

3. For many years midwesterner Jimmy Paxson had been dreaming of returning to the Sun Belt. He had recently sold his Chevrolet dealership for a tidy $525,000 which, after taxes and expenses were paid, netted him about $400,000. Now, he wants to bask in the southern sun and leisurely enjoy his twilight years. With retirement in mind, Paxson began the difficult task of developing an investment portfolio. Because he had always plowed his earnings back into his business, he was relatively unfamiliar with investments in securities. Thus, he called upon an investment counselor for assistance.

After becoming familiar with Paxson's situation, the counselor asked for an outline of his investment objectives. Paxson responded that on half of his funds he would be willing to accept certain risks in order to obtain some capital appreciation. In fact, he told the counselor that he would like to put about $20,000 into some type of speculative venture that would result in either a tremendous gain or a bearable loss. On the other half he wanted safety of principal. He added that he would like some funds invested in a bank or a savings and loan association so he could withdraw them rapidly in an emergency. From all of his funds he would like a reasonably assured annual return of $25,000.

Assume that you are the counselor. Indicate the types of investments that you would recommend for Paxson and the funds that you would place in each investment. In addition, indicate the income that each investment should generate for Paxson. If you include bonds, preferred stocks, and common stocks in your recommendations, name the exact company selected. Set up your answer in the following manner:

Type of Investment	Amount	Current Annual Yield (%)	Estimated Annual Income

Thrifts Strive for Equal Footing with Commercial Banks

Commercial banks and many thrift institutions have already become look-alikes. They could soon become something close to identical twins. Massachusetts may soon hasten this transformation by passing legislation, the first in the nation, that would provide the same legal status and banking powers to state-chartered commercial banks, mutual savings banks, and cooperative banks (the state equivalent of savings-and-loan associations).

The legislature's Committee on Banks and Banking unanimously approved this comprehensive banking legislation at the end of last month. It would by 1986:

1. Give thrifts completely the same banking powers as commercial banks. There would be no ceiling, for instance, on the proportion of their assets that could be invested in commercial loans.
2. Authorize statewide mergers by commercial banks, mutual savings banks, and cooperative banks in any combination.
3. Over three years, thrifts would convert to the same tax formula as commercial banks.

In other words, all state depository institutions would be playing on a "level playing field"—the same law would apply to all of them. Each depository institution could shape its future as it wished,

concentrating on mortgages, commercial loans, personal loans, or whatever on the asset side, and free to accept demand deposits, NOW accounts, various savings certificates, issue certificates of deposit, etc., on the liability side.

Should the legislation pass here, it will spread to other states, predicts Elliott G. Carr, president of the Savings Bank Association of Massachusetts. "Massachusetts has a reputation for being on the cutting edge of legislation," he says, recalling how NOW accounts got their start in the state in 1972.

In Massachusetts, the three major trade groups—the Massachusetts Banking Association (MBA), the Savings Banks Association of Massachusetts, and the Massachusetts Co-operative Bank League—favor the bill.

One reason is that the commercial bankers decided it was important to them that thrifts remain healthy institutions and that depository institutions as a group be able to compete with nonbanking entities, such as Merrill Lynch, American Express, Sears, Roebuck, and Fidelity (the expanding mutual fund group), companies that are increasingly invading the banking field.

If...state-chartered thrifts get more banking powers, Congress will soon come under pressure to give federal thrifts greater powers. Consumers could soon have a hard time trying to tell a thrift from a commercial bank.

SOURCE: Adapted from David R. Francis, "Commercial Banks, Thrifts May Soon Be on Equal Footing," *The Christian Science Monitor,* April 13, 1982, p. 11. Reprinted by permission from *The Christian Science Monitor.* © 1982 The Christian Science Publishing Society. All rights reserved.

20

Money and Banking

Objectives:

- Define money and identify some current forms of money.
- Distinguish between bank and nonbank depository institutions.
- Explain some major changes in the Monetary Control Act of 1980.
- Identify the major operations of the Federal Reserve System (Fed).
- Distinguish between the dynamic and defensive aspects of the Fed's operations.
- Explain the three basic parts of the Federal Reserve System.
- Discuss some key instruments of the Fed.
- Distinguish between special drawing rights (SDRs) and Eurodollars.
- Distinguish between the roles of the IMF and the World Bank.
- Define electronic funds transfer (EFT) and discuss three major forms of EFT.

Most people, when asked about money, will say that all they know about money is that they don't have enough! This lack of understanding is unfortunate, as the amount of money available to the economy is one of the most important factors influencing prices, incomes, business activity, and economic growth. Furthermore, we cannot have a modern, growing industrial economy without an efficient, up-to-date money and banking system.

In this chapter we will cover the basic aspects of money, the nature of our banking system, the functions and structure of the Federal Reserve system, some key institutions and money instruments in our international money and banking system, and the growing importance of electronic funds transfer systems.

BASIC ASPECTS OF MONEY

Over the span of history, money has existed in many forms and shapes. Different societies at different times have been willing to exchange goods or services for such items as the following:

seashells	bricks	beaver pelts
whale's teeth	coconuts	blankets
boar's tusks	cocoa beans	bronze axes
stones	iron rings	wheels
feathers	salt	

In colonial times, the earliest settlers used "wampum" more than anything else for money. Wampum consisted of clamshells strung like beads. It was surprising that the settlers, who previously had placed their faith in gold or silver, considered wampum valuable as money. When the settlers found that wampum was the most useful material they could have for trading with the native Indians, they began to use it for trading among themselves. Wampum had the same meaning to both Indians and settlers: it was money for both.

So, in 1637 the government of Massachusetts made wampum legal tender and fixed the exchange rate between the wampums of white and of black clamshells. Since a string of wampum represented a lot of money for fairly large purchases, small purchases often were made by counting out loose shells. This may be why people even today say they are "shelling out" money.

The Nature of Money

Any number of different materials—including paper IOUs—may serve as money. In primitive societies whatever material proves easiest to store, transport, and exchange may be used as money in "monetary" transactions. In any society, people may use anything they wish for money if the material being used has the same meaning to all of them. **Money** is anything that people will accept in exchange for their goods and services in the belief that they may in turn exchange it for other goods and services. The main point to remember is that the nature of money—how it functions and what it represents—is more important than the material money is made of.

Current Forms of Money

Today we use three forms of money in the United States: coins, paper money, and checking deposits (or demand deposits). How each of these forms of money is issued will be explained below.

Coins

The United States government mints our pennies, nickels, dimes, quarters, and half-dollars. Only the federal government may mint and issue American coins. This procedure is handled by the United States Treasury Department, and the coins are issued through the Federal Reserve Banks, which will be discussed later in this chapter.

Paper Money

The term *currency* is used collectively to denote both coins and paper money. Paper money (or "folding" money) consists of $1 bills, $5 bills, $10 bills, and bills in larger denominations. These bills are **legal tender,** which means that they are accepted in payment of taxes and of all private and public debts. Although there are other forms of currency used today, over 95 percent of all currency in circulation consists of Federal Reserve notes. While only the federal government may print paper money, it is the Federal Reserve Banks that issue the Federal Reserve notes.

Many Americans think that Federal Reserve notes can be exchanged for (or are "backed") by silver on deposit at the U.S. Treasury. This is not true. Federal Reserve notes are legal tender, but they can be exchanged only for other Federal Reserve notes. The only "backing" to Federal Reserve notes is the federal government's power to levy taxes.

Checking Deposits

A checking deposit (or checking account) at a commercial bank is a type of demand deposit. **Demand deposits** are generally bank debts that are payable on demand. This means that demand deposits are claims against a bank which can be transferred by means of checks from one person or business to another. Checking deposits are so close to coins and paper money in immediate purchasing power that they are considered to be a form of money. Savings accounts or time deposits at commercial banks that are not transferable by check are *not* included in measuring the supply of money. Figure 20-1 shows the breakdown in deposits at commercial banks in 1970 and 1981. In the past, banks paid interest only on savings accounts and time deposits. Today, they pay interest also on individuals' checking accounts.

The Federal Reserve System (Fed) controls the amount of demand deposits, or "checkbook money," that commercial banks may create. But how does a commercial bank create demand deposits which may be exchanged for currency when the depositor wishes? The mechanics of this process are a little involved, but Figure 20-2 shows what is meant when we say that banks create demand deposits. After looking at Figure 20-2 you may ask, "Where does the bank get the extra $50 to issue and lend to Kim?" The answer is that the bank didn't "get" the money. Rather, it created the money. But, as noted above, the Federal Reserve sets limits on this power of banks to create money by establishing legal reserves which banks must maintain.

Demand deposits in commercial banks, plus currency, make up our **money supply** — the total amount of money which could be spent for goods and services at any one time. Federal Reserve officials and economists often are concerned with the question of what size of money supply is right for a certain level of economic activity. Too little money may slow down economic growth. Yet, as we saw in Chapter 9, too much money relative to our needs and productive capacity may spur demand and jack up prices, thus causing inflation.

Figure 20-1   Changes in Commercial-Bank Deposits, 1970 and 1981

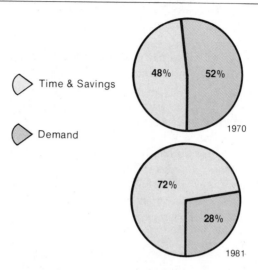

SOURCE: "Challenges for Retail Banking in the 1980s," *Economic Review of the FRB of Atlanta* (May, 1982), p. 16.

Figure 20-2   How a Commercial Bank "Creates" Money

Imagine that National Bank has only two individual depositors, Ann and Bill, who each has a $50 checking account. Total demand deposits at the bank are $100.

Suppose Kim asked the bank for a $50 loan and the loan was approved. By opening a checking account for Kim with $50 in it, the bank's total demand deposits are now $150.

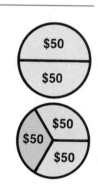

OUR BANKING SYSTEM

The decade of the 1980s will likely see more changes in our banking system than during the past 25 years. The face of U.S. finance is changing at breakneck speed, challenging time-worn ideas about what constitutes a bank and a thrift institution, which financial services each can offer, and where each can do business. These changes have been helped by the recent passage of one of the most sweeping financial laws in U.S. history.

In this section we will pinpoint the main types of depository institutions (bank and nonbank) in our banking system. Then we will take a look at the far-reaching provisions of two laws that have changed the functions of the depository institutions in our banking system: the Depository Institutions Deregulation and Monetary Control Act of 1980 and the Garn-St. Germain Depository Institutions Act of 1982.

Depository Institutions

We have seen that commercial banks, with their demand deposits, can create checkbook money. Yet commercial banks are not the only **depository institutions,** or institutions that can create demand deposits. One of the most interesting financial developments of the past 30 years has been the growth of nonbank financial institutions, some of which are also depository institutions. Among the more important types of nonbank financial institutions are:

1. Life insurance companies.
2. Mutual savings banks.
3. Finance companies.
4. Investment companies.
5. Real estate trusts.
6. Savings and loan associations.
7. Pension funds.
8. Credit unions.

Mutual savings banks, savings and loan associations, and credit unions are known as **thrift institutions or thrifts,** in which funds can be deposited, saved, and loaned. Like commercial banks, the thrifts are also called depository institutions. There are 40,000 depository institutions in our financial system which are either federally insured or eligible for federal insurance. The **commercial bank** is the main *bank* depository institution, and the savings and loan association is the main *nonbank* depository institution.

Role of Commercial Banks

In 1933 and 1935, Congress passed banking acts which still influence the structure of the banking industry in the United States. The 1930s was a time of great financial distress when over one-third (9,096) of the commercial banks failed. As a result, Congress faced pressure to restructure our financial system.

As a first priority, Congress aimed to ensure the survival of a large number of independent banks. A major step in this direction was the Glass-Steagall Act of 1933, which separated commercial banking from the investment companies and the securities business. The Act prohibited commercial banks from dealing in corporate securities and prohibited investment companies from offering deposit services. This action reflected congressional concern for the basic stability of the nation's payment system. Since that time, commercial banks were the only type of financial institution capable of offering *third-party transaction accounts* (or checking accounts) to individuals and businesses. This unique function distinguished commercial banks from all other types of financial institutions.

The Monetary Control Act of 1980, discussed on page 496, wiped out the unique position of commercial banks in the financial services industry. Thrift institutions today may offer third-party transaction accounts, as well as NOW accounts and other interest-bearing checking accounts to noncorporate customers. As we will see later, the Act also blurred the distinction between classes of financial institutions. Thus, the financial marketplace has seen an explosion of new financial services and instruments offered by both financial and nonfinancial firms, as Figure 20-3 indicates. There is some question now as to whether or not commercial banks may realistically be viewed as a distinct type of financial institution.

Figure 20-3   Growth of Financial Services, 1960-1982

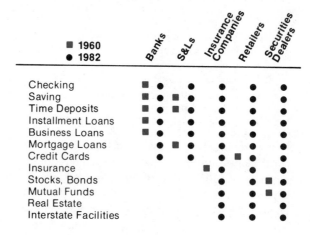

SOURCE: "Challenges for Retail Banking in the 1980s," *Economic Review of the FRB of Atlanta* (May, 1982), p. 14.

The deregulation of banking may be a difficult challenge for some commercial banks. Bankers will need new strategies to survive. Some banks, called "boutique banks," will choose to cater to higher-income customers and develop individual packages that meet their needs. Other banks will emphasize **specialty banking,** which is aimed at serving a defined market of business clients such as lending to high-technology companies. Still other banks will emphasize diversification, such as building up a data processing subsidiary. To summarize, commercial banks face real challenges in the 1980s. Creativity and innovation will be the keys to their survival in this industry.

Role of Savings and Loan Associations

On January 3, 1831, a group of citizens assembled at Thomas Sidebotham's Inn at Frankford, PA, now a part of Philadelphia. This assembly gave birth to the Oxford Provident Building Association of Philadelphia County — the first cooperative home-financing society in the United States. Soon other neighborhood associations formed to lend money for buying homes to their members. Each member of an association contributed some savings. When a member's name came up — sometimes drawn from a hat — this person could borrow money to buy a home.[1]

These cooperative home-financing associations have evolved into the institutions we now call **savings and loan associations (S&Ls).** While S&Ls have added non-borrowing savers as a principal source of funds, their business is still largely that of channeling savings into residential mortgage loans. This emphasis on residential mortgage loans has been a disaster recently for many S&Ls. The reason why S&Ls have become a troubled industry is that most of them are stuck with low-yielding mortgage loans made in past years, while savers can get higher interest rates through money-market instruments. Figure 20-4 shows the recent shift of interest-bearing deposits from commercial banks and thrifts to the money-market funds.

Figure 20-4   Shift in Interest-Bearing Balances, 1978-1981

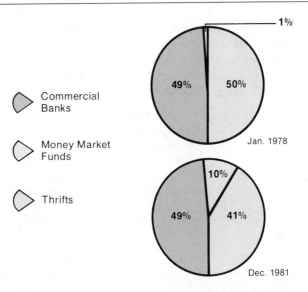

SOURCE: "Challenges for Retail Banking in the 1980s," *Economic Review of the FRB of Atlanta* (May, 1982), p. 16.

---

1. Doris E. Harless, *Nonbank Financial Institutions* (Federal Reserve Bank of Richmond, 1975), p. 54.

Monetary Control Act of 1980

Banks and thrifts have long operated under a hodgepodge of regulations under the uneven hand of state and federal governments. Furthermore, they were hobbled by the Federal Reserve's **Regulation Q,** which set interest-rate ceilings that have fallen well below market rates on savings deposits. As a result, some banks and thrifts have been unable to compete with money-market funds that pay higher interest rates and other nonbank institutions that offer innovative services. Thus, the strongest competitive battles for the consumer's savings deposits which began in 1980 were brought on by the Depository Institutions Deregulation and Monetary Control Act of 1980 (sometimes simply called the Deregulation Act or the Monetary Control Act).

Scope of the Act

Figure 20-5 summarizes the major points of the Monetary Control Act of 1980. By the mid-1980s, most of its provisions will be in effect. The Act sets a gradual elimination of controls on interest rates in the banking industry and gives new powers to traditional home-mortgage lenders. These include limited powers to expand beyond home-mortgage loans and to lend to business. In addition, the Act brings all financial institutions under a wider regulatory net of the Federal Reserve.

Effects of the Act

The Monetary Control Act parallels the deregulation of the transportation and energy industries. It guarantees a fiercely competitive environment in banking during the coming years by lifting controls on interest rates and other services provided by all financial institutions. Banks and thrifts will be slugging it out among themselves, as well as against nonbank giants. This face-off is expected to bring the following:

1. Less differentiation between commercial banks and thrifts and less segmentation in types of services offered. For example, S&Ls are expected to become known as full-service banks.
2. More conflict between depository institutions and nonbanking giants—such as Sears, Roebuck—to retain and expand market share of financial services.
3. Expansion of financial institutions, with states' rights challenged by some form of interstate banking system using electronic banking technology.
4. Fewer financial institutions, with many less competitive banks and thrifts selling out to stronger and larger institutions.

Clearly, the entire customer relationship of all financial institutions is at stake. In addition, expanded regulatory powers and responsibilities for the Federal Reserve have been created.

Garn-St. Germain Depository Institutions Act of 1982

On October 15, 1982, President Reagan signed into law an act which some people in financial circles have termed the most important legislation on depository institutions in the last 50 years. It is known as the Garn-St. Germain Depository Institutions

Figure 20-5   Summary of the Major Provisions of the Monetary Control Act of 1980

Change	Explanation
• Permits nationwide "NOW" accounts	• All depository institutions can offer interest-earning checking accounts, or negotiable order of withdrawal (NOW) accounts.
• Phases out interest-rate ceilings on deposits	• Interest ceilings, which discourage saving, are phased out over a six-year period. Also phased out is the Fed's Regulation Q.
• Eliminates usury laws	• State usury laws governing certain loans are wiped out unless a state adopts a new ceiling before April 1, 1983.
• Increases level of federally insured deposits	• Federal deposit insurance at commercial banks, mutual savings banks, S&Ls, and credit unions is increased from $40,000 to $100,000.
• Requires uniform reserve requirements for all depository institutions	• The previously lower reserve requirements for commercial banks, mutual savings banks, S&Ls, and credit unions—which are not members of the Fed—are phased *up* over a period of eight years. If the new reserve requirements represent a reduction in reserves, as is the case with member banks of the Fed, the phase-down period will be four years.
• Provides access to the Fed discount window	• Any depository institution will have the same discount and borrowing privileges at the Federal Reserve as member banks have.
• Expands lending and investing powers of thrifts	• Credit unions can make residential real estate loans. S&Ls and mutual savings banks can make consumer loans, offer credit cards, handle trust matters, and invest in commercial paper and public debt.

SOURCE: *Economic Review of the FRB of Atlanta* (March-April, 1980), pp. 4–5.

Act of 1982. This Act gives banks and savings and loans institutions the opportunity to offer a money-market deposit account (MMDA) that is "directly equivalent to and competitive with money-market mutual funds."

Other major provisions of the Garn-St. Germain Act allow federally chartered savings and loans institutions to:

1. Offer commercial lending in amounts up to 10 percent of their assets after 1983.
2. Expand nonresidential real estate lending up to 40 percent of their assets.
3. Authorize investments in consumer loans up to 30 percent of their assets.

The Act also states that interest-rate differentials between banks and savings and loans institutions must be eliminated.[2]

---

2. "Reagan Signs Landmark Banking Law," *Dallas Fed Roundup* (Federal Reserve Bank of Dallas, November, 1982).

THE FEDERAL RESERVE SYSTEM _____

In the early years of our nation, the economic system was reasonably simple and there were few demands on our monetary system. But as the economy produced more and more goods — of greater variety and in more places — it seemed that more frequent and severe mechanical failures occurred in the monetary system, which was supposed to provide the money to keep it in motion. The failures took the forms of currency shortages, lags or defaults in the collection of checks, and sharp regional shifts in currency and deposits. Thus, the Federal Reserve System was created in 1913 to provide relief from these various failures or abuses of the nation's monetary system. In this section we will take a look at the basic functions of the Fed, its structure, and some basic tools or instruments it uses to perform its many functions.

The Fed's Functions

The Federal Reserve System operates within the framework of national goals established by the legislative and executive branches of the federal government. Its main function is to help achieve the nation's economic goals through its *policy* operations (or monetary policy), which influence the availability of bank reserves, bank credit, and money. This function has been called the "dynamic" side of the Fed's duties. The Fed also performs important supervisory and service functions for the public, the U.S. Treasury, and commercial banks. These functions are performed through the Fed's *routine* operations and *regulatory* operations — the "defensive" side of the Fed's duties.[3] Figure 20-6 shows the key elements of the Fed's routine, regulatory, and policy operations.

In practice, the defensive and dynamic functions of the Fed are carried out side by side, and most of its operating areas are involved to some degree in each function.

The Fed's Structure

Figure 20-7 shows the organization of the Federal Reserve System which depicts the parts of the system and the processes that link these parts together. The three basic parts of the system are the Board of Governors, the 12 Federal Reserve Banks, and the approximately 5,500 private commercial member banks. Other parts are the Federal Open-Market Committee and the Federal Advisory Council.

Board of Governors

The Fed's Board of Governors is an agency of the federal government. It deals mainly with the formulation of monetary policy. It also has broad supervisory and regulatory responsibilities over the activities of commercial banks and the operations of the Federal Reserve Banks.

---

3. The terms "defensive" and "dynamic" were first set forth by Robert V. Roosa, *Federal Reserve Operations in the Money and Government Markets* (Federal Reserve Bank of New York, 1956), pp. 8-9.

Figure 20-6   **The Fed's Functions**

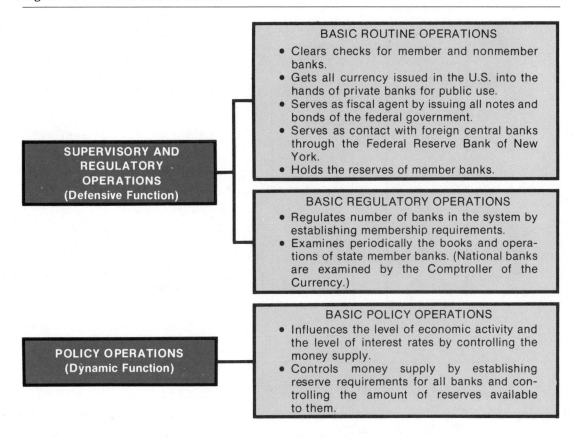

Federal Reserve Banks

The operations of the Federal Reserve System are conducted through a nation-wide network of 12 Federal Reserve Banks located in the cities of Boston, New York, Philadelphia, Cleveland, Richmond (VA), Atlanta, Chicago, St. Louis, Minneapolis, Kansas City (MO), Dallas, and San Francisco. Branches of Federal Reserve Banks have been established in 24 additional cities. The headquarters of the Board of Directors are in Washington, DC, but no operations are conducted from these offices. Figure 20-8 on page 501 shows the boundaries of the 12 Federal Reserve districts and the locations of the various Reserve Banks and branch offices.

Member Banks

About 5,500 commercial banks — out of a total of some 14,000 in the country — are members of the Federal Reserve System. Most of these banks are national banks chartered by the federal government. State-chartered banks may also join the system if they meet the rules laid down by the Fed's Board of Governors.

Figure 20-7   Organization of the Federal Reserve System

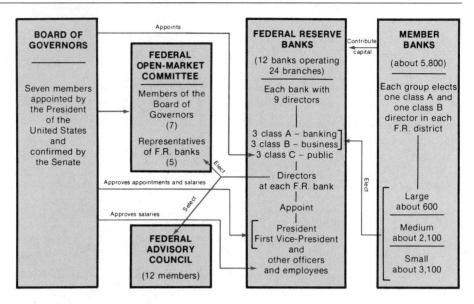

SOURCE: Board of Governors, *The Federal Reserve System: Purposes and Functions* (1974), p. 18.

Federal Open-Market Committee

The 12-member Federal Open-Market Committee decides what actions the Fed will take in the open market (see open-market operations on pages 501-502). It also has jurisdiction over the purchases and sales of foreign exchange by the Federal Reserve System. Therefore, it is the most powerful monetary policy arm in the system.

Federal Advisory Council

Also composed of 12 members, the Federal Advisory Council has the sole function of acting in an advisory capacity to the Board of Governors. Its members usually are prominent persons who have been selected by the board of directors of each Federal Reserve Bank.

The Fed's Key Instruments

We have noted that the Fed relies on monetary policy to regulate the nation's supply of money and credit. This monetary policy is put into action through three key instruments: open-market operations, administration of the Fed's discount window, and determination of reserve requirements of banks. The relationship of these three key instruments to the system's monetary policy is shown in Figure 20-9. These key instruments are a set of complementary instruments rather than alternatives for one another. Of these three, the open-market operations are the most flexible and widely used instrument.

Open-Market Operations

The Fed buys and sells government securities in the open market in order to adjust the level of bank reserves. These reserves are increased when the Fed buys securities,

---

Figure 20-8   Boundaries and Locations of the Federal Reserve System

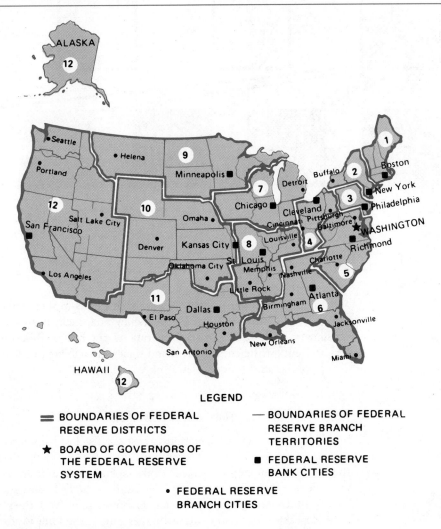

LEGEND

═══ BOUNDARIES OF FEDERAL
        RESERVE DISTRICTS

── BOUNDARIES OF FEDERAL
        RESERVE BRANCH
        TERRITORIES

★ BOARD OF GOVERNORS OF
        THE FEDERAL RESERVE
        SYSTEM

■ FEDERAL RESERVE
        BANK CITIES

• FEDERAL RESERVE
        BRANCH CITIES

SOURCE: *Federal Reserve Bulletin.*

Figure 20-9   Relationship of the Fed's Key Instruments to the System's Monetary Policy

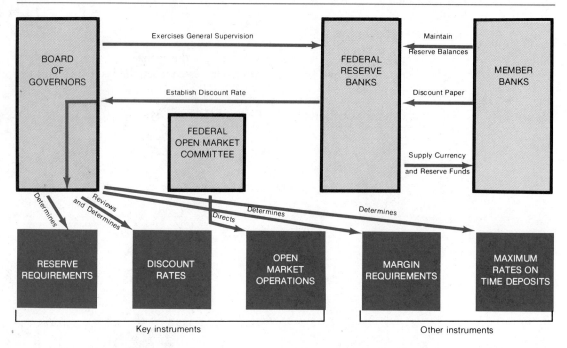

SOURCE: Board of Governors, *The Federal Reserve System: Purposes and Functions* (1974), p. 50.

and decreased when the Fed sells securities. By expanding or contracting bank reserves, the Fed can control the amount of money and credit available to businesses and consumers. In these **open-market operations,** the Federal Reserve Bank of New York acts as agent for the entire system and trades through approximately 31 large private dealers whose offices are in New York City.

Administration of the Fed's Discount Window

While open-market operations adjust the level of bank reserves, the Fed's loan function helps individual depository institutions by loaning funds. In its earlier years, the Fed loaned money to member banks by buying notes from them at a discounted rate. Hence, this loan function is referred to as the Fed's **discount window.**

With the passage of the Monetary Control Act of 1980, the Fed now makes loans to all depository institutions. Usually these are in the form of advances (or loans on promissory notes) which are secured by collateral. The interest rate charged by the Reserve Banks on their loans is the discount rate. When the Fed increases discount rates, the cost of acquiring reserves by borrowing goes up. When the Fed decreases the discount rates, the cost of acquiring reserves goes down. The Fed, however, often is called the *lender of last resort* because it expects depository institutions to try other sources of funds before turning to the Fed.

Determination of Reserve Requirements

The **reserve requirements** for banks consist of a percentage of their deposits (savings deposits, time deposits, and demand deposits) which must be held as legal reserves at a Federal Reserve Bank. The reserve requirements on third-party transaction accounts vary according to the size of the borrowing bank. However, the reserve requirements on savings deposits are the same at all banks.

Since the Banking Act of 1935, the Fed's Board of Governors has been empowered to make changes in reserve requirements. The Board can reduce the reserve requirements to increase the money and credit available to banks. Likewise, it can increase the reserve requirements to reduce the money and credit available to the banks.

Some banks have *nondeposit* liabilities, such as Eurodollar borrowings and loans from foreign banks. Reserve requirements are also set against these liabilities to control the expansion of bank credit.

INTERNATIONAL MONETARY OPERATIONS

In most economically developed nations, money is held mainly in the form of checking-account deposits in commercial banks while coins and paper money play smaller roles. People's faith in money depends on its purchasing power. We have noted that purchasing power depends upon how governments, through central banks, balance the amount of money in relation to the quantity of goods and services available.

International trade complicates money matters greatly. Different countries use different currencies. But when businesses sell goods abroad, they usually want to be paid in their own currency. Thus, importing and exporting means that currencies must be exchanged in what are called **foreign-exchange transactions.** The **exchange rate** is simply the price of one country's money in terms of another's.

Foreign exchange means different things to different people. Most Americans encounter foreign-exchange transactions only as tourists. But foreign-exchange transactions arising from the international trade and investments of importers, exporters, corporations, central banks, and financial institutions often are large and occur round the clock.

The topic of international monetary operations is wide in scope and often very technical. Since the U.S. economy is an important, interdependent part of the world economy and since the U.S. dollar has long played a key role in international monetary operations, we shall at least touch on some important concepts and processes that relate to international monetary operations. These include two major international money instruments and the various roles of the International Monetary Fund (IMF), the World Bank, commercial banks, and central banks.

International Money Instruments

Until the early 1970s, most countries had agreed upon the relative values of their currencies and attempted to preserve these relationships in the foreign markets. The International Monetary Fund had pegged (or anchored) the value of all currencies in relation to the U.S. dollar. In turn, the value of the U.S. dollar was pegged to gold and was convertible to gold by certain monetary institutions.

In August, 1971, President Nixon declared that official U.S. dollar holdings were no longer convertible to gold. After a period of turmoil, new currency rates were set at the Smithsonian Agreement in December, 1971. These new currency rates lasted about a year. Since 1973 the world's currencies basically have been **floating currencies,** which means that their values are determined by supply and demand instead of by administrative decisions. More accurately, this is a case of **managed floating** in which governments reserve the right to influence the money market actively.

But governments are not the only forces acting on the international money market. Two other important developments in this market are the emergence of the Special Drawing Rights and of the Eurodollar.

Special Drawing Rights

In a move away from pegging the currencies of IMF members to the U.S. dollar, which has fluctuated widely in recent years, the IMF created **Special Drawing Rights (SDRs).** These SDRs peg the currencies of IMF members to the market value of a basket of major world currencies. The SDR is called a *basket currency* because it is composed of more than one currency, with each currency in the basket assigned fixed weights. Actually, SDRs are not a form of currency. They are simply bookkeeping entries that are transferred between central banks in the settlement of balance-of-payment deficits.

In 1981 the IMF decided to simplify the SDR by reducing the currencies in the basket from 16 to 5. The five currencies were assigned weights to reflect their importance in international trade and finance. Table 20-1 shows the basket of currencies for 1978 and 1981. The five currencies in the basket for 1981 will be reviewed by the IMF every five years beginning January 1, 1986. We should note that the use of SDRs as international units of account has grown rapidly in recent years.

Eurodollars

Since 1971 the United States has had a generally deepening balance-of-trade deficit (see Chapter 16). Paying for these trade deficits has caused a huge *overhang* (or outflow) of U.S. dollars. These dollars have become **Eurodollars,** which are U.S. dollar deposits held and used by major American or foreign banks outside the United States. Eurodollars are borrowed or lent by major international banks when they need to acquire or invest additional U.S. dollar funds. The market in which this borrowing and lending is done is called the **Eurocurrency market** (or Eurodollar market or Euromarket).

Despite its name, the Eurocurrency market goes beyond Europe and involves currencies other than the dollar. This market is a global network of banks in centers

Table 20-1 Units of Currencies in the Special Drawing Rights Basket
(Percentage Weights Are Given in Parentheses)

Currency	Effective January 1, 1981		Effective July 1, 1978	
United States dollar	0.54	(42.0)	0.40	(33.0)
German mark	0.46	(19.0)	0.32	(12.5)
Japanese yen	34.00	(13.0)	21.00	(7.5)
French franc	0.74	(13.0)	0.42	(7.5)
British pound sterling	0.071	(13.0)	0.05	(7.5)
Italian lira	—		52.00	(5.0)
Dutch guilder	—		0.14	(5.0)
Canadian dollar	—		0.07	(5.0)
Belgian franc	—		1.60	(4.0)
Saudi Arabian riyal	—		0.13	(3.0)
Swedish krona	—		0.11	(2.0)
Iranian rial	—		1.70	(2.0)
Australian dollar	—		0.017	(1.5)
Spanish peseta	—		1.50	(1.5)
Norwegian krone	—		0.10	(1.5)
Austrian shilling	—		0.28	(1.5)

SOURCE: "The SDR in Private International Finance," *Quarterly Review of the FRB of New York* (Winter, 1981-1982), p. 32.

such as London, Paris, the Caribbean, Singapore, and Bahrain. The Eurocurrency market is huge, amounting to about $500 billion. Most importantly, governments have no effective control over this market. There are no legal reserve requirements, interest ceilings, or other rules to be observed while operating in this market. This is one reason that the Eurocurrency market attracts more money year after year. It now provides the world with a truly international financial market.

Roles of the IMF and the World Bank

In July, 1944, experts from 44 governments met for the Bretton Woods Conference sponsored by the United Nations. Their job was to make financial arrangements for the rehabilitation and reconstruction period after World War II. Two of the major actions of this conference were the establishment of the International Bank for Reconstruction and Development (usually called the World Bank) and the International Monetary Fund.

The World Bank, with headquarters in Washington, DC, is designed to make long-term capital available to the world's poorer nations. Its capital is provided by the industrial countries, about 25 percent of which is backed by the United States. The IMF covers short-term imbalances in payments between its 130 member nations. It also works to secure international cooperation, stabilize exchange rates, and expand international liquidity. It operates with funds provided by the member nations. The quota of funds for each member nation is set on the basis of its volume of international trade, national income, and international reserve holdings.

Role of Commercial Banks

The foreign-exchange market in the United States consists of a network of commercial banks located mainly in New York City and other major cities. While most banks offer foreign-exchange service to customers, there are only about 50 major money-center banks. These are called **market-maker banks** because they quote prices of various foreign currencies and actively trade in one or more currencies with other banks and for their own accounts. Market-maker banks, along with major U.S. branches of foreign banks, are the core of the *interbank* market. They seek to anticipate exchange-rate movements and even out fluctuations in supply and demand for foreign exchange.

Role of Central Banks

The foreign-exchange operations of a country's central bank are important to that country's currency. In fact, in many countries the central bank serves as its government's banker for domestic and international payments. In addition, central banks often work together to influence market conditions or exchange-rate movements. For example, the Federal Reserve Bank of New York handles foreign-exchange operations for the Fed and the U.S. Treasury. It uses various intervention techniques, depending on the market conditions and the Fed's objectives. The Fed also is an advisor and consultant within the federal government on international financial matters.

ELECTRONIC FUNDS TRANSFER SYSTEMS

The electronic transfer of funds includes a wide variety of new developments. To some, an electronic funds transfer system means a system to replace checks, cash, or credit cards with a network of computer terminals. To others, it simply means getting cash out of a machine. Generally **electronic funds transfer (EFT)** can be defined as the application of computer and telecommunications technology in making or processing payments.[4] EFT is tying thrift institutions to payment mechanisms, thus bringing them into direct competition with commercial banks. EFT also affects the broader areas of economic life, such as the documentation of transactions, security of funds from fraud and theft, and privacy of records. While these areas give rise to negative

---

4. This definition and the basic concepts discussed in this section are from E.J. Stevens, "Electronic Funds Transfer Systems," *Annual Report of the Federal Reserve Bank of Cleveland* (1977), pp. 3–4.

issues about EFT, we must recognize that these issues are products of a modern computerized society.

EFT initially was conceived as a nationwide replacement for paper documents in the banking system. It now exists in various forms, and the development and use of EFT technology is still changing. The three major forms of EFT in use today are: automated clearinghouses, automated teller machines, and point-of-sale terminals.

Automated Clearinghouses

The **automated clearinghouse** is a system for clearing interbank debits and credits. It is the cornerstone of the EFT system. Instead of paper checks, the information entered in the automated clearinghouse consists of magnetic tape. The automated clearinghouse is especially economical in handling large volumes of recurring transfers such as payroll deposits, mortgage payments, insurance payments, and various kinds of Social Security payments made by the federal government.

Automated Teller Machines

An **automated teller machine** is a device used by financial institutions, either on or off premises, to perform several basic teller functions electronically. These functions typically include receiving deposits, dispensing funds, transferring funds between accounts, making cash advances on credit cards, and receiving payments. A customer usually operates the automated teller machine by inserting a magnetic-stripe card, called an **access (or debit) card**, and punching in a personal identification number known only to that customer and the card issuer. Automated teller machines are usually found in banks. However, they are beginning to appear in supermarkets, airports, and other places with large numbers of potential customers.

Point-of-Sale Terminals

The **point-of-sale terminal** is a device that allows the paperless transfer of funds between customers and businesses at the time and place of sale. It also allows the customer to transfer funds from his or her checking or credit-card account to the merchant's account at the end of the month rather than immediately. The point-of-sale terminal permits the merchant to verify the funds in the customer's account. As with automated teller machines, point-of-sale terminals are activated by a customer's access card and personal identification number.

SUMMARY   Money and banking used to be regarded as the most stable of the financial components of business. Managers of financial institutions were seen as defenders of the status quo and caretakers of conveniently regulated and protected domains. While this image of stability and conservatism never did hold across the board, it certainly is not justified today. The process now going on in the domestic and international financial scenes is an aggressive and innovative integration of financial markets across institutions and geographical space. This current upheaval in the financial services industry is touching aspects of our monetary system, banking system, Federal Reserve System, international financial system, and electronic funds transfer systems.

In the money arena, checking accounts (demand deposits) have gone beyond the commercial banks. All depository institutions can offer interest-earning checking accounts, and interest-rate ceilings are being phased out. Thus, depositors are placing their funds in financial institutions that pay the highest interest on checking accounts.

In banking, the far-reaching provisions of the historic Monetary Control Act of 1980 are touching every depository institution in the system. Deregulation of the banking industry, along with the Garn-St. Germain Act of 1982, has blurred the usual distinctions between banks and thrifts, and depository and nonbanking institutions.

In the face of this competitive battle, the Federal Reserve System will take on greater powers and responsibilities in its routine, regulatory, and policy operations. The MCA sets reserve requirements for all banks, mutual savings banks, S&Ls, and credit unions. But any depository institution will have the same access to the Fed's discount window as member banks.

In international money and banking, governments and central banks face the challenge of managing their currencies despite widely fluctuating interest rates and market conditions. Furthermore, the huge Eurocurrency network provides the world with a $500 billion financial market, and governments have no effective control over this market.

The growing competition in domestic and worldwide financial services is a key factor in the development of electronic funds transfer systems which use computer and telecommunications technology to process payments. In the domestic financial services industry, the three major forms of EFT systems are automatic clearinghouses, automated teller machines, and point-of-sale terminals.

BACK TO THE CHAPTER OPENER

1. How does a commercial bank differ from a thrift institution?
2. What is the main type of thrift institution, and what is its major function?
3. What is a depository institution?
4. Which depository institution now makes commercial loans?
5. What does "NOW" stand for in NOW accounts?
6. Do you think greater banking powers will improve the financial shape of thrifts?

BUSINESS TERMS

money	490	foreign-exchange transactions	503
legal tender	491	exchange rate	503
demand deposits	491	floating currencies	504
money supply	491	managed floating	504
depository institutions	493	Special Drawing Rights (SDRs)	504
thrift institutions or thrifts	493	Eurodollars	504
commercial bank	493	Eurocurrency market	504
specialty banking	494	market-maker banks	506
savings and loan associations (S&Ls)	495	electronic funds transfer (EFT)	506
Regulation Q	496	automated clearinghouse	507
open-market operations	502	automated teller machine	507
discount window	502	access (or debit) card	507
reserve requirements	503	point-of-sale terminal	507

1. Take a look at a dollar bill. Can you exchange this bill for a dollar's worth of silver or gold?
2. What is the basic handicap that S&Ls face in competing with banks and mutual funds for new deposits?
3. Will the consumer win or lose as competition transforms financial services?
4. Will deregulation be good for smaller financial institutions such as credit unions?
5. We hear a lot about the policy operations of the Fed, especially in its dynamic function of altering the money supply. What are two other functions of the Fed?
6. Are all Eurodollars and other Eurocurrencies held or used in Europe?
7. Does the Euromarket help or hinder national governments?
8. What is the basic difference between the World Bank and the International Monetary Fund?
9. How do access (or debit) cards differ from credit cards?
10. How would consumers benefit from an extensive EFT network?

PROJECTS, PROBLEMS, AND SHORT CASES

1. The possibility of interstate banking—branch banking across state lines—looms on the horizon for the 1980s. What effect will it have on smaller community banks? Talk with a community-bank manager and see what steps he or she feels will be necessary in order to compete successfully with out-of-state banks. Give a five-minute talk in class summarizing the results of your interview.
2. One of the most popular means of transferring funds electronically is through the use of automated teller machines, either on or off premises. Prepare a two-page report on how the use of these machines may affect bank staffing patterns and the cost and training of human resources.
3. Sally Beauchamp, manager of EFT systems for Backwater National Bank, was concerned about the slowness in customer acceptance and use of the bank's EFT services. The bank had made large capital investments for installing the components of the EFT system—hardware, software, telephone lines, and support systems. In addition, it had made a large investment in traditional check-processing equipment. So, Beauchamp was especially dismayed when a male student in her night class in banking management attacked EFT systems as a tool to invade the privacy of a person's financial and personal life. The student argued that the Bank Secrecy Act of 1970 requires that banks collect, report, and store for at least five years all information on individual banking transactions for potential use in criminal and tax investigations. He further argued that EFT technology makes it easy for a bank to comply with the Bank Secrecy Act and that information for investigations of any type is easily transferred.

   Prepare a short report and discuss the following:

   a. Whether the student's fears were realistic.
   b. What steps, if any, may be needed to protect individual privacy.

Stressing Safety, a Tiny Insurer Cuts Risks
of Small Enterprises

Getting adequate insurance at reasonable cost is a major headache for many small businesses. Until recently, large insurance companies weren't anxious to sell them policies covering fire, robbery, or product liability. The insurers had all the business they wanted at big companies, which they considered better risks.

That's where Proprietors Corp. came in. Proprietors is a tiny Delaware, Ohio, concern that specializes in insuring "Ma and Pa" businesses. It was founded in 1969 by members of the Ohio Bowlers Proprietors Association who were having difficulty getting sufficient insurance. John Morgan, owner of Capri Bowling Lanes in Worthington, Ohio, says that he had 26 different policies on his business at one time in the 1960s. And at that, he says, "I don't think we were ever one-half insured."

Today, Proprietors sells insurance programs tailored for groups of neighborhood bicycle shops, small marine and aviation operations, automobile and tire dealers, and nursing homes. It works through trade organizations and picks up its customers carefully. Such high-risk businesses as scrap dealers have been turned down.

At the request of the Independent Bankers Association, Proprietors is developing a blanket-bond insurance program covering robberies and embezzlements for "cow-town, Corn Belt banks," says Paul Brislen, vice president of a subsidiary.

The program promises cheaper rates for small bankers, who are paying premiums that largely reflect the loss experience of big city banks. "In the beginning, our rates will be based on the overall industry loss record as well," Mr. Brislen says. "But eventually the premium will be based on the loss record for that group of banks." Similarly, an insurance package for tire dealers, initiated in July, is expected in time to reduce premiums 5% to 10%, the company says.

Proprietors has 15 safety experts on its staff, who, with others, analyze how customers' losses occur and how they can be prevented. Fewer claims don't only mean more profit for Proprietors but also lower rates for customers. Most of the prevention measures are "of a housekeeping nature," says Robert Pierce, chairman of Proprietors.

For example, tire dealers should strictly control access to customers' car keys to prevent theft, emergency exits shouldn't be locked, and waste material should be disposed of daily. Bowling alleys should install fireproof wastebaskets. Proprietors dispenses its safety advice mainly through trade groups and some 100 independent insurance agencies. (The company has only 10 agents of its own.)

But now big insurers are moving into the small-business market that previously had been the domain of Proprietors and a few other specialty insurance companies. They're attracted by the success stories, such as Proprietors', and eager to use what amounts to excess capacity in the insurance business. One big insurer, Aetna Life & Casualty Co., says small businesses don't require complex, individualized coverage that large concerns do and that takes considerable effort to administer.

SOURCE: Michael L. King, "Stressing Safety, a Tiny Insurer Cuts Risks of Small Enterprises," *The Wall Street Journal*, September 29, 1980, p. 25. Reprinted by permission of *The Wall Street Journal*, © Dow Jones & Company, Inc. (1980). All Rights Reserved.

Risk Management and Insurance

Objectives:

- Illustrate avoidable, uninsurable, and insurable types of business risks.
- State five characteristics of insurable business risks.
- Explain why governments underwrite certain types of risks.
- Identify two types of privately owned insurance companies according to ownership and specialization.
- Explain the types of health insurance coverages.
- Explain why fire insurance policies frequently contain coinsurance clauses.
- Decide whether no-fault automobile insurance should be required in all states.
- Identify at least five types of property and liability insurance other than fire and automobile.
- Explain the differences among ordinary life, group life, industrial life, and credit life insurance policies.
- Justify the type of ordinary life insurance you have or probably will purchase.

The bad news is that little Fred Finn Mazanek was less than a year old when he died. The good news is that he left an estate of $5,000 — which was sizable considering Fred was a guppy. The story of Fred's legacy began when Stan Mazanek, a student at the University of Arizona, filled out a life insurance application in the name of his fine-finned friend. The application had been addressed to "occupant" and sent to Stan's apartment. The protection offered was a deal that Stan could not refuse — for a premium of one dollar, $5,000 of life insurance protection could be obtained for six months.[1]

Because he was in good health and had a sound — but devious — mind, Stan completed the application in the name of his pet, Fred Finn. Every question was answered honestly. Stan indicated that Fred's age was 6 months; his weight, 30 centigrams; and his height, 3 centimeters. To Stan's surprise, the application was accepted by the Globe Life and Accident Insurance Company and Fred was issued policy 3261057.

When Fred died and a claim was filed by Stan, Globe suddenly became aware of its clerical error. Claiming that no jury would award $5,000 for a dead fish, Globe was reluctant to pay the claim. Stan stubbornly pointed out that the contract was legally entered into and accepted by the company. Finally, the two parties compromised and Stan was paid a $650 death benefit. With the money he purchased a couple of new guppies, a fish dinner for his family, and considered buying some life insurance for his own protection.

Is there a single industry in the United States that has an income of $152 billion a year, owns assets of over $733 billion, and employs 1.9 million men and women?[2] These figures not only stagger the imagination but happen to reflect the gigantic size of the insurance business. Some of the famous people who have worked in the insurance industry are identified in Figure 21-1.

With only three broad categories — life, health, and property and liability — and despite governmental competition in all areas, the thousands of companies that underwrite risks comprise a substantial segment of economic activity in the United States. The large size of the industry might seem to indicate that risk management always involves insurance. Actually, some types of risk are not insurable; for others an

---

Figure 21-1   Famous People Who Have Worked in the Insurance Industry

George Eastman — Inventor of the Kodak camera and industrialist
Col. Harland Sanders — Developer of Kentucky Fried Chicken
Warren E. Burger — Chief justice of the U. S. Supreme Court
Mildred "Babe" Didrikson Zaharias — Athlete
Spiro Agnew — U. S. vice-president
Medgar Evers — Civil rights leader
Jody Powell — Press secretary to President Jimmy Carter

SOURCE: 7 items (#1, 6, 8, 9-12) on page 288, "Renowned People Who Worked for Insurance Companies" in THE BOOK OF LISTS #2 by Irving Wallace, David Wallechinsky, Amy Wallace, and Sylvia Wallace. Copyright © 1980 by Irving Wallace, David Wallechinsky, Amy Wallace, and Sylvia Wallace. By permission of William Morrow & Co.

---

1. "Owner of Dead Fish Collects on Policy," *Muncie Star,* April 17, 1974, p. A7.
2. Insurance Information Institute, *Insurance Facts* (1982-1983), pp. 5, 17; and American Council of Life Insurance, *1982 Life Insurance Fact Book,* p. 55.

alternate solution is preferable. All businesses that operate in a capitalistic system constantly face **risks**, which may be defined as exposure to losses. When a potential loss is identified, management first hopes that steps can be taken to avoid it. If this solution is out of the question, it may still be possible to adopt a plan that reduces the loss exposure to an acceptable level that may or may not involve insurance.

Assume, for example, that one of our industrial giants has plants and offices in all 50 states. Management consists of five key executives. If this corporation has a rule that none of the five may fly, it has avoided the risk of a fatal airplane accident. Since such a rule would not be practicable, a policy that not more than one of the five may fly in any one airplane is more realistic. Furthermore, the company might carry a $1,000,000 life insurance policy on each of the five executives with the proceeds payable to the corporation, should one be killed in an accident. If one executive were to die in an accident, the $1,000,000 payment might well equalize the loss of profits for which this executive would have been responsible.

This chapter will first deal with some risks that must be absorbed in their entirety and with noninsurance methods of protection against risk losses. The balance of the chapter will be devoted to **insurance**, which is a social device by which many share the losses of a few. By a process known as underwriting, an insurance company contracts to reimburse an insured person for certain described losses. The company issues a printed document called an insurance policy for which the policyholder pays a fee known as an **insurance premium**.

BUSINESS RISKS

The large number of risks facing a business is indicated by the 7,000 claims that are filed annually against Esmark, a large consumer products company. This is equivalent to one claim every 18 minutes of a working day. If a risk is uninsurable, the company must either absorb it or resort to a noninsurance solution. If the risk appears to be insurable, management needs to know the characteristics it must have before an insurance company will write a policy. Figure 21-2 is a graphic illustration of the risk management process.

Categories of Uninsurable Risks

The major uninsurable, internal risk facing any business is the ever-present possibility that it cannot be operated at a profit. If the income from sales or services is inadequate to meet necessary expenses, losses result. If losses continue for any length of time, sooner or later the business will have to discontinue operations. Each year more than 10,000 industrial and commercial enterprises fail. Many of these are small businesses, but the bankruptcies of Braniff International Airlines and Wickes (a major home improvement company) indicate that large size is no guarantee of financial success.

In addition to management's inability to insure against operating losses, many other internal and external risks are not insurable. For example, a manufacturing

Figure 21-2   The Risk Management Process

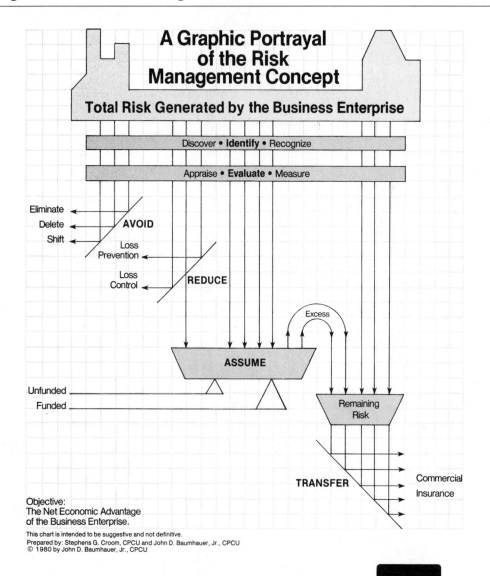

A Graphic Portrayal
of the Risk
Management Concept

Total Risk Generated by the Business Enterprise

Discover • **Identify** • Recognize

Appraise • **Evaluate** • Measure

Eliminate
Delete   **AVOID**
Shift
                Loss
        Prevention
                Loss
        Control   **REDUCE**

                                Excess

                        ASSUME

Unfunded
Funded
                                        Remaining
                                        Risk

                                TRANSFER   Commercial
                                                    Insurance

Objective:
The Net Economic Advantage
of the Business Enterprise.

This chart is intended to be suggestive and not definitive.
Prepared by: Stephens G. Croom, CPCU and John D. Baumhauer, Jr., CPCU
© 1980 by John D. Baumhauer, Jr., CPCU

Baumhauer-Croom
BCI *Insurance*

BAUMHAUER-CROOM-INSURANCE / 105 NORTH BELTLINE HIGHWAY / MOBILE, ALABAMA 36608 / TELEPHONE 205/344-6611

SOURCE: Reprinted with permission of Baumhauer Croom Insurance, Mobile, AL.

business may have been built on ownership of a patent that is about to expire. Employees may cause losses by striking and closing down operations. In most cases, businesses are able to keep losses of these types within acceptable limits. The most serious types of risks that are uninsurable are external rather than internal. A business frequently has little or no control over events that may bring disaster to it. On the other hand, disaster may strike because a company refused to anticipate the future or adjust to change.

Several uninsurable external risks are: continued consumer acceptance of established products which results in the failure of new products, changes in distribution methods and customer preferences, fluctuations in prices and price levels, and changes in laws. The development of microprocessors, laser technology, and satellite television has altered our life-style. Companies that fail to adjust to change are making obsolete products and will eventually be forced out of business.

The growth of chain stores, supermarkets, and shopping centers has caused many "mom and pop" retail stores to close. Fast-food franchisors, such as McDonald's and Kentucky Fried Chicken, have dealt a death blow to many restaurants. Sharp cost increases for fuel and materials may cause losses to firms unable to make offsetting increases in their selling prices. For example, when the price of imported oil greatly increased in 1974, many public utilities sustained losses until various state commissions allowed them price increases. Tariff changes that permit increased imports of competitive goods may ruin the sales of a domestic firm. Enforcement of certain environmental protection laws may force a polluting firm out of business.

Noninsurance Methods of Risk Protection

For a limited number of firms, there are two methods that provide protection against certain types of risks without using an insurance company. One method is hedging, which was explained in Chapter 19. However, futures transactions are not available to the many manufacturers whose production does not involve commodities. The other method is **self-insurance**, whereby a firm deliberately assumes a risk but provides a system for absorbing losses.

For example, a large corporation might own hundreds of factories, warehouses, and office buildings valued at millions of dollars and scattered among the 50 states. An insurance policy covering these properties against loss by fire would demand a substantial premium payment year by year. The corporation can reduce its expenses by setting aside an amount each year that will be adequate to pay for fire losses should they occur. For example, 50 hospitals in Alabama banded together to insure themselves. Instead of paying an annual premium of $1,500 a bed for malpractice and general liability insurance, now they set aside only $500 a bed for self-insurance.[3]

---

3. Christopher Evans, "To Cut High Premium Costs, More Firms and Institutions Are Insuring Themselves," *The Wall Street Journal,* April 14, 1978, p. 36.

Characteristics of Insurable Risks

Any insurable risk must have the characteristics identified in Figure 21-3 before an insurance company is willing to underwrite possible losses against it. On the basis of these requirements, the following question may well be asked: How would the $1 million injury insurance policy on football star Herschel Walker fit into the classification of insurable risks? The answer is that Walker's policy and other similar policies usually are written by Lloyd's of London. While not an insurance company, Lloyd's of London is an association through which members offer to underwrite hazards of all types. Marine insurance, which falls within the classification of insurable risks, forms the bulk, though not the spectacular portion, of the underwriting business of Lloyd's.

Figure 21-3   Characteristics of Insurable Risks

Characteristic	Explanation
• Predictability of annual loss	• Number of people who will die each year or the number of houses that will burn each year must be predictable, except in the case of nuclear war.
• Geographic dispersion	• A fire insurance company could not afford to insure all the houses in one city only. A disastrous fire such as the Chicago fire in 1871 would bankrupt a company.
• Selectiveness of the insured	• No company can afford to insure only people who are seriously ill, have heart trouble, or make their living testing new airplanes.
• Applicability of law of averages	• The risks must be numerous. Insuring one life for a small annual premium could not be done on a scientific basis, but insuring the lives of 100,000 can.
• Low cost relative to recovery	• Premium must be low in relation to the insured's recovery possibilities. If the annual cost of a policy insuring a $5,000 truck against loss by theft was $1,000 instead of about $10, a business would try some form of self-insurance.

THE INSURANCE BUSINESS

Although frequently taken for granted, the separation between public and private insurance underwriters is extremely important. Also, within the private sector the specialization of insurance companies helps to explain why most firms and individuals purchase numerous insurance policies. A medium-size business may have as many as two dozen different insurance policies costing over $500,000 annually. A large firm may spend $5 million to $50 million for 50 or more policies with several insurers.

Governments as Underwriters

The extent to which governments underwrite various risks, sometimes in competition with private industry, is startling for a capitalistic system. All states participate in a nationwide plan of unemployment insurance, which is required by federal law. Workers' compensation insurance, also required by all states, is frequently a monopoly of state government. Although not universal, many states operate retirement plans for state employees including public school teachers.

By far the most extensive entry of the federal government into the insurance business began in 1935 when the first Social Security Act was passed. This activity was expanded in 1966 with the introduction of the related Medicare program. The Old-Age, Survivors, and Disability Insurance System, commonly called Social Security, provides a program of monthly payments to retired or disabled workers or surviving dependents. **Medicare** covers hospital and medical insurance for those 65 years of age or older who are drawing retirement benefits. These programs require contributions on the part of the insured both before and after retirement, although the cost of the programs is shared by employers and the United States Treasury. Another public health activity, **Medicaid**, is operated by the states with the federal government providing matching funds. Medicaid covers persons, regardless of age, whose incomes are insufficient to pay for health care. Several of the other major federal insurance agencies and their programs are described in Figure 21-4.

Private Insurance Companies Classified by Ownership

The two major types of private insurance companies based on ownership are mutual companies and stockholder-owned companies, both of which were explained in Chapter 3. In 1982 over 90 percent of some 1,842 companies in the life insurance field were owned by stockholders. However, the 136 mutual companies owned nearly 60 percent of all the assets of United States insurance companies and accounted for 44 percent of the life insurance in force.[4]

Private Insurance Companies Classified by Specialization

Until a few years ago, partly because of state legal restrictions, insurance companies tended to specialize in a limited area such as life, fire or surety bonds. In recent years all states have liberalized their regulatory laws to permit a single insurance company to write many different coverages. This change has reduced specialization to two distinct types of insurance companies: property and liability, and life.

Classifying private insurance companies into the two specialized types mentioned above is in line with their sales outlets. Insurance salespersons customarily are either general insurance agents or life insurance agents. A general insurance agency repre-

---

4. American Council of Life Insurance, *1982 Life Insurance Fact Book,* pp. 18, 89.

Figure 21-4   The Major Federal Insurance Programs at a Glance

Federal Crop Insurance Corp.
Insures farmers against crop losses
Premium Income: $319.3 million ($366 million with Federal subsidy)
Claims or Losses: $390.5 million
Reserves: not available

National Credit Union Share Insurance Fund
Insures Federally-chartered credit union share accounts
Premium Income: $41.7 million
Claims or Losses: $27.6 million
Reserves: $174.8 million

Pension Benefit Guaranty Corp.
Insures the pension benefits of about 28 million Americans
Premium Income: $74.9 million
Claims or Losses: $57 million
Reserves: -$189 million

Federal Emergency Management Agency
Flood Insurance
Premium Income: $228.4 million

Claims or Losses: $118.4 million
Reserves: $371 million

Crime Insurance
(available only in high-risk areas)
Premium Income: $13.5 million
Claims or Losses: $39.2 million
Reserves: -$10 million (joint reserve with Riot Insurance)

Riot Insurance
Premium Income: $857,000
Claims or Losses: none
Reserves: See Crime Insurance

Federal Deposit Insurance Corp.
Insures accounts at most commercial banks and mutual savings banks
Premium income: $1 billion
Claims or Losses: $700 million
Reserves: $12.2 billion

Foreign Credit Insurance Association
A consortium of 50 companies that underwrites commercial credit risks for U.S. exports
Premium Income: $26.6 million
Claims or Losses: $19.6 million
Reserves: not available

Overseas Private Investment Corp.
Insures U.S. corporations' overseas investments against political risks
Premium Income: $30.1 million
Claims or Losses: $1.8 million
Reserves: $530.9 million

Federal Savings and Loan Insurance Corp.
Insures accounts at all Federally- and most state-chartered savings and loans
Premium Income: $425.1 million
Claims or Losses: 998.5 million
Reserves: $7 billion

Securities Investor Protection Corp.
Insures investors against the bankruptcy of their stockbroker
Premium Income: $259,000
Claims or Losses: $63.2 million
Reserves: $167 million

sents a number of different companies, including competing firms. Although it may represent a life insurance company, it does not stress this area of insurance. The life insurance agent, on the other hand, normally sells policies on a commission basis for only one company.

Further evidence of these two specialized types of private insurance companies is found in the professional designations that are granted to individuals who qualify for and pass certain examinations. The CLU (Chartered Life Underwriter) certificate is granted by the American College of Life Underwriters. In a similar manner the American Institute for Property and Liability Underwriters grants the designation CPCU (Chartered Property and Casualty Underwriter).

HEALTH INSURANCE

Health insurance, sometimes identified as accident and sickness insurance, covers one or any combination of the following: hospital, surgical, and other medical expenses; loss of income during the period of disability; and major medical expense. Health insurance is sold by both life insurance companies and property and liability insurance companies. It is also sold by nonprofit associations such as Blue Cross and Blue Shield.

Assume that Jerry Kahn, married, with three children, is involved in a serious automobile accident while driving home after work. He is hospitalized for three weeks and another four weeks elapse before he can return to his job. If he was properly insured, all or substantially all of his hospital expenses including surgeon's fees would be covered. He would also receive a stated weekly income for the entire seven weeks, such as two-thirds of his regular salary. If he owned a major medical policy and if his personal medical expenses exceeded an agreed-upon deductible amount such as $300, he would receive reimbursement for the excess. Health insurance policies also may provide that, if the insured loses an eye or a hand or a foot, he or she will receive either a flat sum or weekly amounts for several weeks.

A substantial percentage of all types of health insurance is written on a group basis with employers providing the entire cost as a fringe benefit. For example, General Motors pays more to Blue Cross and Blue Shield for employee health insurance than to U.S. Steel for its steel.[5] In some instances, employees bear all or a share of the cost under a payroll deduction plan. The extent of the use of health insurance is far greater than most people realize. More than 186 million Americans, or approximately 85 percent of our population, are covered by some type of health insurance. Figure 21-5 shows that nearly $126 billion was paid in health insurance benefits in 1980.

Figure 21-5   Health Insurance Benefit Payments, 1980

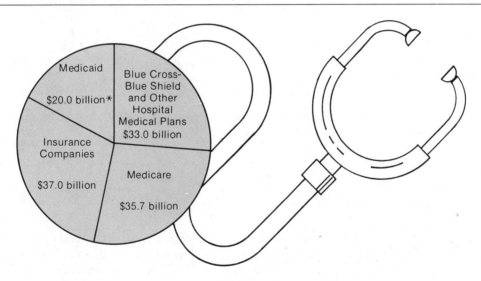

*Benefits for 1979.

SOURCE: *Source Book of Health Insurance Data, 1981-1982,* pp. 23, 32.

5. "GM Wants $3 Billion Savings: UAW Gave Ford $1 Billion," *The Muncie Evening Press,* March 17, 1982, p. 32.

PROPERTY AND LIABILITY INSURANCE

Approximately 3,000 insurance companies sell property and liability insurance and related lines. They own about $212 billion in assets and are responsible for employing nearly a million people. Table 21-1 shows the ten leading companies in the property and liability insurance fields. As indicated by Figure 21-6, a keen competition exists among the companies for insurance business. Figure 21-7 shows the major classifications of property and casualty insurance, as well as the various coverages available under each classification.

Table 21-1	The Ten Largest Property and Liability Insurance Companies, Based on Cost of Premiums Written, 1981

Rank		Total Premiums*
1	State Farm	$8,642,362,000
2	Allstate	5,348,263,000
3	Aetna Life & Casualty	4,428,893,000
4	Travelers	3,059,915,000
5	Liberty Mutual	2,826,480,000
6	Continental Insurance	2,818,200,000
7	Hartford Fire	2,689,859,000
8	INA	2,606,534,000
9	Farmers Insurance	2,598,010,000
10	Fireman's Fund	2,388,454,000

*Includes property, liability, and accident and health premiums.

SOURCE: *Best's Aggregates & Averages, Property and Casualty, 1982,* p. 8. Reproduced with permission.

Fire Insurance

Almost every type of building and its contents can be insured against loss resulting from fire. Policies are sold on a one- or three-year basis—with a strong preference for a three-year contract. The advantages of a three-year policy over a one-year policy are that the buyer is guaranteed against a rate increase in the second and third years and that a discounted rate may be granted.

Premium Rates

Figure 21-8 shows how fire insurance rates are set. Premium rates are relatively low but vary considerably in different geographical areas and among types of construction. For example, cities are graded on such items as water supply, fire alarms, building

Figure 21-6   Competition for Big Mac's Insurance

Kansas City Insurance Broker Wins Most McDonald's Franchises

Financial Guardian Inc. and Great American Insurance Co. finished first in the sizzling competition to provide insurance to McDonald Corp.'s franchises.

Overcoming McDonald's endorsement of a competing program, the Kansas City, Mo.-based broker captured about 1,500 of the approximately 4,000 McDonald's stores whose property and liability insurance programs were up for renewal.

Financial Guardian outsold the corporation-sponsored package brokered by Marsh & McLennan Inc. (M&M) and underwritten by Insurance Co. of North America (INA). The insurance marketing war was unleashed when McDonald's and Marsh & McLennan switched the company-owned policies to INA from American International Group (AIG) and AIG decided to fight for the business of McDonald's franchised stores.

Food franchise experience was the turning point in most Financial Guardian sales, according to President Donald Weber. "We've been in the fast-food franchise business since the 1970s. We do Pizza Hut and a variety of others," he explained.

Rates quoted by Great American also made a difference, Mr. Weber said, though he denied Financial Guardian slashed prices unreasonably as competitors charged.

"Because of the amount of franchise business we already do and our experience, we were able to create a rating program that may have been more effective than others in some areas . . . ," he noted.

Although competitors charged Financial Guardian had cut premiums to less than $1,500 per store in many cases, Mr. Weber said individual premiums averaged about $3,000.

Marsh & McLennan, selling the McDonald's-sponsored program, finished second in the sales battle, industry sources said. Although M&M did not have financial results compiled, competitors estimated the INA-underwritten plan finished with 1,000 to 1,200 stores.

SOURCE: "K. C. Insurance Broker Wins Most McDonald's Franchises," *Crain's Chicago Business,* November 2, 1981, p. 23. Reproduced with permission.

laws, and the efficiency of the fire department. The location of a building is important as it may stand between two old buildings or at some distance from other structures. If the construction is considered fireproof, the rate will be lower than on frame buildings. The lowest rates are around 10 cents for each $100 of coverage, and more hazardous risks may cost $2 for each $100 of coverage.

Standard Fire Policy

As indicated in Table 21-2, the fires and damage from the San Francisco earthquake of 1906—which was the most costly in the history of the United States—caused a loss of $350 million. However, fire damage to industrial property resulting in complete destruction is rare. If it were permissible to buy a fire insurance policy for only one-third or one-half of the total value of a property, the insured party would have an annual saving in insurance premiums which would probably offset a total fire loss. Insurance companies protect themselves against this reduced premium income by inserting a **coinsurance clause** in the policy. This clause requires that the insured buy coverage up to a stated percentage of the value of the property—usually

Figure 21-7   Major Classifications of Property and Liability Insurance and the Coverages Available

Classification	Coverages Available
Fire insurance	1. Standard fire policy 2. Special riders covering damage caused by factors other than fire such as lightning, explosion, aircraft, smoke, vehicles, vandalism, falling objects, weight of ice or snow, freezing of plumbing, collapse of buildings, business interruption, and depreciation.
Automobile insurance	1. Fire and theft insurance 2. Bodily injury liability insurance 3. Property damage liability insurance 4. Collision insurance 5. Comprehensive coverage 6. Medical payments endorsement 7. Protection against uninsured motorists 8. No-fault insurance
Burglary, robbery, and theft insurance	Comprehensive burglary and robbery policy
Workers' compensation insurance	Medical expenses, salary payments, death benefits
Marine insurance	1. Ocean marine insurance 2. Inland marine insurance
Fidelity and surety bonds	Losses due to dishonesty of individuals, groups, or persons holding key positions; losses arising from nonperformance of a contract
Specialized liability insurance	1. Personal excess liability policy 2. Malpractice insurance 3. Products liability insurance 4. Other multiperil policies

Figure 21-8   How Fire Insurance Rates Are Set

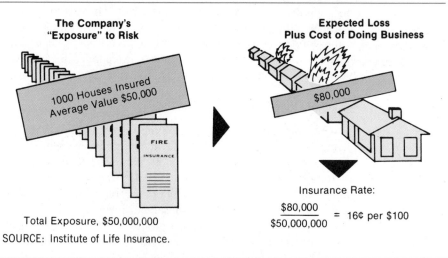

The Company's "Exposure" to Risk

1000 Houses Insured Average Value $50,000

FIRE INSURANCE

Total Exposure, $50,000,000

SOURCE: Institute of Life Insurance.

Expected Loss Plus Cost of Doing Business

$80,000

Insurance Rate:

$$\frac{\$80,000}{\$50,000,000} = 16¢ \text{ per } \$100$$

Table 21-2   The 12 Most Costly Fires in the United States

Date	Place	Property Destroyed	Estimated Loss
April 18, 1906	San Francisco, CA	28,000 buildings	$350,000,000
Oct. 8-10, 1871	Chicago, IL	17,340 buildings	175,000,000
Nov. 9, 1872	Boston, MA	776 buildings	75,000,000
Sept. 1, 1979	Deer Park, TX	Tank ship	70,000,000
Nov. 28, 1981	Lynn, MA	31 buildings	70,000,000
April 16, 1947	Texas City, TX	Waterfront industrial area	67,000,000
Feb. 27, 1975	New York, NY	Telephone central office	56,500,000
Feb. 7, 1904	Baltimore, MD	80 city blocks in business section	50,000,000
Aug. 12, 1953	Livonia, MI	Auto transmission plant	50,000,000
Dec. 5, 1970	Linden, NJ	Oil refinery, nearby buildings	50,000,000
Jan. 20, 1980	Borger, TX	Refinery	50,000,000
Nov. 21, 1980	Las Vegas, NV	Hotel	50,000,000

SOURCE: Insurance Information Institute, *Insurance Facts* (1982-1983), p. 52. Reproduced with permission.

80 percent—or assume a proportion of each fire loss. In most states residential property is not subject to coinsurance clauses.

For example, assume that a factory is properly valued at $100,000 but is insured against fire for only $50,000. The risk is only partially covered because the minimum insurance for full protection against partial losses under a coinsurance clause is 80 percent, or $80,000. If a fire occurs with a total damage of $20,000, the insurance company will pay only $12,500 ($50,000 ÷ $80,000, or ⅝ of the loss).

Multiple-Peril Policies

Since the mid-1950s, property owners have been able to obtain a multiple-peril homeowner's policy that, in addition to fire protection, provides coverage against such perils as windstorm, burglary, theft, and liability. In the past, homeowners would purchase fire and extended coverage insurance, but they would neglect to buy other forms of protection. A multiple-peril homeowner policy provides protection against numerous perils at a price that is lower than the combined costs of the separate coverages. Making the coverage even more reasonable is a deductible of $100 or $200 that is usually part of the policy.

Businesses can purchase multiple-peril policies, too. One type of coverage is the special multiperil policy which has minimum coverage requirements. This policy leaves most of the coverage choices to the insured. Another type of coverage is the businessowner's policy which applies the concept of a homeowner's policy to the small and medium-size business. This policy provides less flexibility than the special multi-peril policy, but it offers broad coverage. The businessowner's policy contains business-interruption coverage which protects an insured against loss of earnings due to a total or partial shutdown resulting from property damage. Business-interruption coverage is available with the special multiperil policy, too.

Automobile Insurance

Of the different coverages under automobile insurance listed in Figure 21-7 on page 522, those that are usually included in a policy are fire and theft, bodily injury liability, property damage liability, and collision. The need for theft coverage is indicated by the statistics that one car is stolen every 28 seconds, and only 15 percent of these thefts result in an arrest.

Insurance Settlements

Bodily injury liability insurance will pay the policyholder's legal liability for injury to one person or to a group. The insurance company will pay damages up to the amount of coverage carried. A common policy fixes a maximum of $10,000 for liability resulting from the death or disability of one person and $20,000 for similar reasons to a group. Higher maximum coverages can be obtained by paying a higher premium. A medical payments endorsement will pay hospital and doctor bills up to a specified maximum for each occupant of the insured's car who is injured in an accident, including the policyholder. Many states have enacted "guest laws" which relieve drivers from liability for injury to their passengers arising from an accident. These laws were passed to prevent friendly suits against car owners with the understanding that the insurance companies would finance the settlements.

Property damage liability insurance will pay for damage caused by the insured car to another car or other property not belonging to the insured. It is stated at a single amount such as $5,000. The insurance company will settle the claim up to the amount of the policy. It will not pay anything for damages to the policyholder's car unless collision or upset insurance is carried. Collision insurance protects car owners against any damage to their cars resulting from accidents and is relatively expensive unless it is bought with a deductible allowance such as $100 or $250. In this event the insurance company pays for damages that are in excess of the stated deductible amount. The savings that occur through the use of deductibles are shown in Table 21-3.

Comprehensive coverage is a contract that covers practically all damage to the insured's automobile — including fire and theft — except that resulting from collision

Table 21-3   Impact of Deductibles on Automobile Insurance

Amount of Deductible	Six-Month Premium for Insurance on a New Chevrolet	Savings with Deductible Larger Than $100
$100	$173	—
$200	$147	$26 or 15%
$250	$134	$39 or 23%
$500	$101	$72 or 42%
$1,000	$ 81	$92 or 53%

and upset. For example, claims have been paid for accidental damage to upholstery and for windshields broken by flying stones.

Financial Responsibility Laws

In an effort to get uninsured motorists off the roads, all the 50 states have financial responsibility laws. These laws usually provide that the driver of a car at fault in an accident must show evidence that he or she has taken care of the resulting costs to the innocent car driver. However, the preferred method of demonstrating the required financial responsibility is to own an insurance policy covering bodily injury and property damage liabilities.

No-Fault Insurance Laws

Under the **no-fault rule** the person injured in an automobile accident collects from his or her insurance company rather than from the insurance company of the person who caused the accident. In the 1970s there was considerable agitation in most states to enact a no-fault automobile insurance plan. Now, nearly half of the states have passed some type of no-fault insurance law. Advocates of no-fault insurance maintain that:

1. Most suits would be avoided.
2. Injured persons would receive prompt reimbursement for medical expenses, loss of income, and cost of repairs.
3. The cost of a policy would be less than the common type of policy.

Opponents of no-fault insurance, including some lawyers who would suffer a reduction in income, dispute these claims.

Burglary, Robbery, and Theft Insurance

An act of burglary is the unlawful taking of property within closed premises where evidence of forcible entry is visible. Robbery is the forcible taking of property from another person. Theft, or its legal synonym larceny, covers any act of stealing without regard for forceful entry or violence and hence includes both burglary and robbery.

Insurance companies underwrite more burglary insurance for residences than for businesses. For businesses a comprehensive burglary and robbery policy will cover the following:

1. Business safes.
2. Mercantile open stock.
3. Damage to or theft of money, securities, merchandise, or equipment.
4. Kidnapping of an employee to gain entrance.
5. Robbery inside or outside the business premises.

Insurance covering shoplifting losses is usually not carried because such losses are frequently difficult to prove and the cost is high.

Workers' Compensation Insurance

The purpose of workers' compensation insurance is to guarantee medical expenses and salary payments to workers who are injured on the job unless it can be shown that the employee's injury or death was willful or caused by intoxication. The usual practice is to specify weekly benefits. These are set at a fraction of the regular wage, such as one-half or two-thirds, to discourage those who might prefer to draw benefits rather than work. A waiting period of a few days to two weeks is also a common provision of many laws. This means that no benefits can be drawn until the expiration of the waiting period, thus eliminating claims for minor accidents. In case of death, weekly payments are made to the dependents of the deceased for a specified period, frequently eight years. Figure 21-9 shows the length of certain disability payments in the state of Illinois.

Workers' compensation insurance is compulsory in all 50 states although state laws are not uniform. Certain classes—notably farm and domestic employees, and employees in businesses with less than a stated number of personnel—frequently are exempt. In some states, workers' compensation insurance is a monopoly of the state; in others, private insurance companies compete with state plans. In a few states only private insurance companies write the policies unless a business is large enough to obtain approval for self-insurance programs. Rates vary with the hazard of the industry.

Figure 21-9   Length of Disability Payments in Illinois

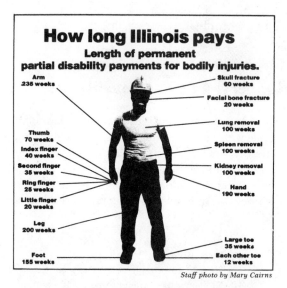

Staff photo by Mary Cairns

SOURCE: Marcia Stepanek, "Finely Balanced Work Comp Plan Seeks to Cut Costs, Keep Benefits," *Crain's Chicago Business,* April 7, 1980, p. 2. Reproduced with permission.

Marine Insurance

As Figure 21-7 on page 522 shows, marine insurance covers ocean marine and inland marine transportation. Inland marine insurance, however, need not involve shipment by water.

Ocean marine insurance is the oldest form of insurance. It covers practically all perils involving shipments on the high seas, including all degrees of loss from damage to the vessel and its contents up to a complete loss of both if the vessel sinks. Fire insurance is included as part of an ocean marine insurance policy.

A typical inland marine insurance policy covers loss caused by fire, theft, or damage of movable goods while being transported by rail, truck, airplane, inland and coastal steamers, and barges. An important type of inland marine insurance is the personal property floater. It protects personal property from all hazards, including fire and theft, wherever located — in the home, in transit, or abroad. Under a personal property floater the personal effects of students attending college away from home can be covered while in transit or at their college residences.

Fidelity and Surety Bonds

Fidelity bonds are usually written to cover employees occupying positions of trust in which they have jurisdiction over funds. The employer is guaranteed against loss caused by the dishonesty of such employees, and the insurance company will reimburse the policyholder for losses up to the amount specified in the policy. A policy may cover an individual, a group, or a named position. For example, a firm may secure a fidelity bond on certain employees for the amount of funds to which each has access. Or a firm may purchase a policy in which positions and the amounts of coverage are specified, such as treasurer — $50,000. Whoever is hired for a specified task is bonded for the stated amount.

Surety bonds are written to protect the insured against loss from the non-performance of a contract or of any agreed-upon act or business transaction. For example, a building contractor who agrees to erect a factory according to specifications within a certain time might be required to furnish a surety bond guaranteeing performance of the contract.

Specialized Liability Insurance

In recent years no other area of insurance has received as much attention as specialized liability insurance, which covers various risks shown in Figure 21-7 on page 522. Damage suits frequently are filed against car owners, homeowners, professionals, hospitals, and businesses. A study of verdicts in liability suits indicated that uninvited guests, mainly those who fell on the insured's sidewalk, won their cases 50 percent of the time. Those claimants who were invited to the insured's home and had an accident there won 36 percent of the time. Juries have been so generous in their awards to injured parties that people and business firms have had to supplement their regular insurance coverages with specialized liability policies (see Figure 21-10).

Figure 21-10   The $2,000,000 Verdict

The $2,000,000 personal injury verdict may become commonplace, says the editor of *Trial Lawyers Quarterly*. Since the first $1,000,000 verdict was returned in 1963, there have been 318 more seven-figure decisions in the appellate court. In 1970 a brain-damaged child could expect average compensation of $400,000. Today, amputee victims receive up to $800,000, while paraplegics and quadruplegics can expect as much as $1.9 million.

If this prediction sounds extreme, consider the case of nine-year-old Margaret Noble of Ronkonkoma, New York, who suffered brain damage and was rendered blind and partially paralyzed after remaining under anesthesia and left unattended for twenty minutes following an operation. The court approved a settlement of $6.7 million with her surgeon and anesthesiologist — $500,000 up front plus annual payments for the rest of her life.

SOURCE: Insurance Marketing Service, Inc., *Insurance and Risk Management Newsletter* (February/ March, 1981). Reproduced with permission.

A personal excess liability policy, for example, may be purchased to supplement other liability insurance carried by car owners, homeowners, and businesspersons. Among the malpractice insurance policyholders are physicians, hospitals, pharmacists, lawyers, public accountants, and architects. Due to the astronomical costs of malpractice insurance, some doctors are retiring early from practice; in some states legislation to relieve this situation has been enacted. Also soaring are the costs of product liability insurance. If, for example, a drug manufacturer of pills to relieve the common cold should unknowingly release a batch that caused dangerous side effects, several separate legal actions might be incorporated into a class-action suit against that manufacturer. This would mean that all users of such pills would be seeking damages that might well run into millions of dollars. Shortly after cyanide-laced Tylenol capsules caused several deaths in 1982, the first of several liability suits that were filed was for $15 million!

Other Insurance Coverages

In addition to the types of property and liability insurance that have been discussed above, the following specialized coverages are available for businesses:

1. Glass breakage.
2. Boiler and machinery insurance (which features preventive engineering service provided by the company writing the insurance).
3. Power interruption.
4. Title insurance.
5. Aircraft hull and liability coverage.
6. Electronic data processing liability coverage.
7. Environmental impairment liability coverage.
8. Kidnap and ransom coverage.
9. Political risk coverage (takeover of company by foreign nations).

LIFE INSURANCE

Life insurance policies are written by 2,000 different companies. These companies own assets of approximately $526 billion and employ about 900,000 people. The ten largest life insurance companies in the United States are identified in Table 21-4. In the United States there are 150 million policyholders whose lives are insured for $4.1 trillion. In 1981 these policyholders paid $76 billion in premiums. Benefit payments to policyholders and to the beneficiaries of policyholders who died were $43 billion.[6] Thus, the life insurance industry is truly gigantic in all dimensions.

As in the case of other forms of insurance, life insurance is based on the law of averages. No one can predict who will die during any given year, but the number of people living at the beginning of a year who will die within 12 months can be computed within narrow margins. The annual premium on a life insurance policy is related to statistics covering deaths as compiled by actuaries. An **actuary** is an expert at computing risks and the size of insurance premiums necessary for the profitable operation of an insurance company. Although insurance companies rely on more than one table, many states require the use of a mortality schedule compiled by the National Association of Insurance Commissioners, an organization of state insurance commissioners. In 1958 this body adopted the Commissioners Standard Ordinary Mortality Table, which is still in use. Table 21-5 shows the rates of male mortality according to the CSO Mortality Table. Figure 21-11 shows one way of classifying the various types of life insurance.

Table 21-4	**The Ten Largest Life Insurance Companies** **Based on Insurance in Force, 1981**	
	Insurance in Force	Assets
1. Prudential Ins. Co. of America	$456,174,631,000	$62,498,540,000
2. Metropolitan Life Ins. Co.	393,590,726,000	51,755,845,000
3. Equitable Life Assurance Soc., U. S.	223,874,676,000	36,768,160,000
4. Aetna Life Ins. Co.	163,873,853,000	25,158,904,000
5. John Hancock Mutual Life Ins. Co.	145,609,204,000	19,936,798,000
6. New York Life Ins. Co.	137,456,394,000	21,119,316,000
7. Transamerica Occidental Life Ins. Co.	123,624,304,000	2,601,874,000
8. Travelers Insurance Co.	116,498,216,000	14,803,168,000
9. Connecticut General Life Ins. Co.	90,809,773,000	15,103,332,000
10. Transamerica Assurance Company	89,665,951,000	1,322,678,000

SOURCE: *Best's Agents Guide to Life Insurance Companies, 1982,* pp. IX, XX. Reproduced with permission.

---

6. Insurance Information Institute, *Insurance Facts* (1982-1983), pp. 5, 11; and American Council of Life Insurance, *1982 Life Insurance Fact Book,* pp. 5, 14, 91.

Table 21-5   **Rates of Male Mortality**

Age	Number Living	Deaths Each Year	Death Rate per 1,000
20	9,664,994	17,300	1.79
30	9,480,358	20,193	2.13
40	9,241,359	32,622	3.53
50	8,762,306	72,902	8.32
60	7,698,698	156,592	20.34
70	5,592,012	278,426	49.79
80	2,626,372	288,848	109.98
90	468,174	106,809	228.14

SOURCE: 1958 Commissioners Standard Ordinary Mortality Table.

Figure 21-11   **Classification of Life Insurance Policies**

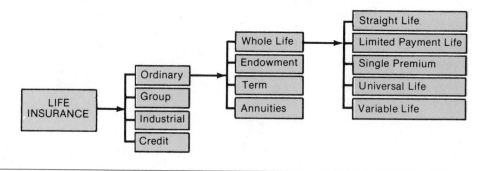

Ordinary Life Insurance

Ordinary life insurance is bought in individual policies of $1,000 or more, and the buyer is usually required to pass a physical examination before the policy becomes effective. Ordinary life policies account for over one-half of all types of life insurance in force. Figure 21-12 compares three of the most common types of ordinary life insurance: whole life, endowment life, and term life.

Premium payments on ordinary life insurance policies may be made quarterly, semiannually, or annually, except in the case of the single-premium life and the annuity, which are purchased with a lump sum. With the exception of term life insurance, all other forms of ordinary life insurance have a **cash surrender value** if the policy has been in effect at least two years and is cancelled before its expiration date.

The cash surrender value is also the amount that the insured can borrow at a stated interest rate from the insurance company.

Premium payments are used by the insurance companies for three items: operating expenses (including a profit), risk protection, and an investment element. The investment element earns funds that help to pay for the risk protection.

Whole Life Policies

A whole life policy is bought for its protective features. It pays its face value to a beneficiary when the insured dies, provided that premium payments are current and that a loan on the policy is not outstanding. There are five types of whole life policies: straight life, limited-payment life, single-premium life, universal life, and variable life. If premiums are payable every year as long as the insured lives, the insurance is known as straight life. If premiums are payable for only a stated number of years, the insurance is called limited-payment life. As the term implies, a single-premium life involves only one premium payment.

Universal Life Policies. In recent years over 100 companies have introduced universal life and variable life policies which are special types of whole life insurance.

Figure 21-12   Comparison of Whole Life, Endowment Life, and Term Life

	Whole Life		Endowment Life	Term Life
	Straight Life	Limited Payment Life		
• Relative cost of premium per $1,000	• Lowest of all whole life policies	• Lower than endowment for the same number of years	• Higher than whole life and term policies	• Lowest of all forms of ordinary life policies
• Length of premium payments	• Lifetime of the insured	• Stated number of years	• Stated number of years	• Stated number of years
• Cash surrender value	• Lowest of whole life policies	• Lower than endowment life	• Highest of ordinary life policies; equals face value when policy matures	• None
• Collectibility of face value of policy	• Upon the insured's death	• Upon the insured's death	• Upon the insured's death; by the insured if living at expiration of policy	• Upon the insured's death

---

A **universal life policy** is an attempt to make life insurance inflation-proof by offering the insured a high interest rate on the cash surrender value of the policy. The portion of the premium that is not used for insurance protection typically is invested in high-yielding short-term securities. By drawing on the investment portion of the insurance, policyholders are able to vary the amount or timing of their premium payments and to change their death benefit.

Variable Life Policies. A **variable life policy** has a fixed premium and a guaranteed minimum death benefit, but it does not have a minimum guaranteed cash surrender value. The amount of the death benefit varies, depending on the rate of return that is obtained from the investment portion of the insurance. The insured can choose how the investment element of the policy is to be invested. Investments range from short-term securities to common stock.

Evaluation of Straight Life Policies. Of the five types of whole life policies, straight life is the most widely purchased because it has the lowest cost per $1,000 and thus provides the most protection for the same amount of premium. Its disadvantage over the limited-payment life is that, unless the insured dies before retirement, the insured continues to pay premiums at a time when her or his income is most likely reduced. The single-premium life policy is relatively expensive and is therefore not commonly used. For example, a single-premium policy for a 40-year-old male would be $430 for each $1,000 coverage.

The face amount of a life insurance policy can be divided into two parts: an *amount at risk* and a *reserve* (or investment) *fund.* During the early years of a straight life policy, the amount at risk to an insurer is nearly the entire face value of the policy. If the insured should die, there is no reserve fund from which an insurer can draw to pay the death benefits. In later years, however, a reserve fund accumulates because the early premiums paid by the insured were not needed for death benefits. Figure 21-13 shows the division between the amount at risk and the reserve fund of the premium for straight life with a $1,000 face value for a 30-year-old person.

Endowment Life Policies

Endowment life insurance emphasizes savings over a stated period rather than protection. Since the annual premium for this policy is larger than for straight life or limited-payment life, its cash surrender value increases at a faster rate and eventually equals its face value when the policy matures. At this time the insured may collect the face value of the policy or elect to receive annual payments. Endowment life is the only type of life insurance that allows the insured rather than the beneficiary to collect the face value of the policy.

Term Life Policies

Term life insurance is the least costly of all types of life insurance available. For a given premium payment, term life gives the most protection over a stated time period. Table 21-6 compares annual premium costs per $1,000 insurance charged by one company for four different types of life insurance policies.

Figure 21-13   Proportions of Amount at Risk and Reserve Fund in a Straight Life Policy with a $1,000 Face Value

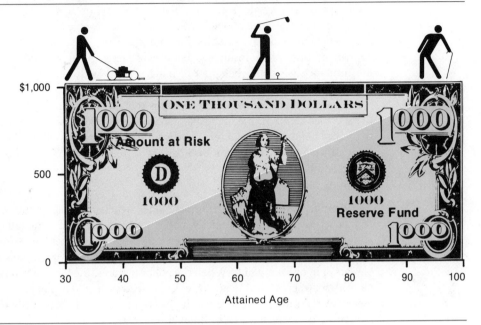

Table 21-6   Comparative Annual Premium Costs per $1,000 Insurance

Age	5-Year Renewable Term	Straight Life	20-Pay Life	20-Year Endowment
20	$ 4.88	$15.21	$26.71	$47.96
30	5.41	20.00	32.29	48.58
40	7.90	27.85	40.12	50.86
50	15.20	41.09	51.74	57.05

The CSO 1958 Mortality Table can be used to compute the basic cost of term life insurance policies written on an annual basis. Assume that all of the 9,664,994 twenty-year-old males (see Table 21-5 on page 530) were insured for $1,000 each for one year. The insurance company would have to pay out $17,300,000 to the beneficiaries of the 17,300 males who would die during the year. If a premium payment of $1.79 ($17,300,000 ÷ 9,664,994 = $1.79) were made for each $1,000 policy, the insurance company would have just enough money to meet the necessary outlay. The actual premium would obviously need to be higher than $1.79 for the insurance company to meet business expenses and make a profit. Note that the costs of term insurance computed on this basis would increase year by year, amounting to $3.53 per $1,000 at age 40 and to $20.34 at age 60. Rather than changing the rate every year, term insurance is usually sold on a 5-year, 10-year, or 20-year level premium plan.

Term life insurance policies are customarily renewable up to the age of 65 without the need to provide evidence of insurability. They are also convertible into more permanent forms of life insurance. Because of these advantages and the low cost, term life insurance is usually bought by young persons with family and home mortgage responsibilities.

The chief disadvantage of term life is that, if the insured is living at the end of the specified term, all premiums paid are the property of the insurance company and the policy automatically expires. The insurance company is obligated to pay the face value of the policy only if the insured dies within the time limit of the policy.

Annuities

Annuity insurance is a contract under which the insurer promises to make a regular series of payments, usually monthly, to the insured. Generally a person buys annuity insurance to be assured of an income other than a possible pension or a modest Social Security check after retirement. The insured may pay premiums over a number of years or in one lump sum. When the policy matures, the insured will begin to receive monthly payments until death or elect to receive a stated number of monthly payments. A monthly payment until the insured's death will necessarily be smaller than a monthly payment for a fixed number of years.

Annuities are of greatest interest to elderly people with no dependents who are in need of a maximum return after retirement. But businesses also take a vital interest in annuities because these offer one solution for employee pension plans, as discussed on pages 535-536 concerning business uses of life insurance.

Group Life Insurance

The purpose of group life insurance is to cover employees of business firms. An employer, for example, may take out a policy covering each employee for a sum such as $5,000; the amount may vary with different categories of employees. The employer usually pays all or a major portion of the premium, which is actually a bonus to the employee. Medical examinations are not required of the employees. This is possible because most employers do not hire employees who are not physically fit, and most employees are in a relatively healthy age bracket. Beneficiaries of the employee collect the face value of the policy if the employee dies at any time during the life of the policy.

Group life insurance usually is written on a one-year renewable term plan. Rates are lower than for any form of individual policy because the premiums are paid to the company in one check, which greatly reduces collection costs. The $1.9 billion in group life insurance outstanding at the end of 1981 gives some idea of the extensive use that businesses make of this form of life insurance.[7]

---

7. American Council of Life Insurance, *1982 Life Insurance Fact Book,* p. 5.

Industrial Life Insurance

Life insurance companies such as Metropolitan, John Hancock, and Prudential all owe their early growth to the sale of industrial life insurance. This type of insurance has substantially the same subtypes as ordinary life (i.e., whole life, endowment life, term life, and annuities). However, policies for industrial life insurance are usually for less than $1,000. In 1981 the average-size policy in force was $630. The insurance agent collects the premium weekly or monthly from the policyholders, frequently at their homes. Ordinarily no physical examination is required.

Rates for industrial life insurance are quoted at 10 cents or 25 cents a week rather than in dollars per year per thousand. Despite the small size of such policies, in 1981 the 55 million policies accounted for $34.5 billion of life insurance.

Credit Life Insurance

Credit life insurance guarantees repayment of amounts due on installment contracts or personal loans in case the debtor dies. Banks, finance companies, credit unions, retailers, and some mortgage lenders are the chief buyers of credit life insurance, and they add this cost to the price of the borrower's purchase or loan. It is written on a one-year basis, and the amount applicable to a borrower decreases as the debt is repaid. Practically all credit life insurance is written on a group basis, although individual policies are available.

Due to extensive consumer installment buying and short-term borrowing, credit life insurance is the fastest-growing form of life insurance. It has assumed one of the risks of consumer financing, both for the lender and the borrower. In 1981, outstanding policies on credit life insurance were in excess of $162 billion.[8]

Credit life insurance should not be confused with *credit insurance,* which a firm buys to protect itself against unusually high losses resulting from credit extended on open-book accounts. A requirement of credit insurance policies is that the insured firm must bear part of each loss, which keeps it from being too generous in extending credit.

Business Uses of Life Insurance

Proprietorships, partnerships, and corporations make extensive use of life insurance. The most common type used is group life insurance, which many firms provide as a fringe benefit for their employees. As previously mentioned, credit life insurance is widely used by businesses that sell to consumers on installment plans. The cash surrender values of life insurance policies owned by businesses are also potential sources of borrowing at interest rates lower than those available from a commercial bank.

Two other important adaptations of life insurance to the needs of business — insurance on owners or executives and employee pension plans — are described below.

---

8. *Ibid.,* p. 19.

Insurance on Owners or Executives

When a proprietor dies, his or her firm may have to be liquidated to pay funeral, administrative, and tax expenses. To avoid the need for heirs to sell the business, an adequate life insurance policy payable to the estate can be purchased. This policy could be on a straight life, limited payment life, or endowment life basis, which would provide the extra advantage of a cash surrender value.

When a partner dies, the partnership must be dissolved. The question then arises as to who will buy the deceased's interest in the firm. A term life insurance contract payable to the surviving partner or partners can provide a fund with which to buy this interest and thus avoid the need to take in a new partner. Likewise, if it is assumed that a partner will retire at a given age, an endowment policy maturing at the agreed retirement age guarantees that needed funds will be available.

Some corporations have found that their profitability greatly depends on the abilities and contacts of some of their key executives. To absorb the reduction in earning power that might result from the death of such executives, a corporation may carry an insurance policy on their lives payable to the corporation.

Employee Pension Plans

Firms interested in providing pensions beyond Social Security benefits to their retired employees can finance pension plans through insurance companies. Currently some 28 million employees are covered by insured pension plans, and the number is growing rapidly each year.

In 1974, Congress passed a pension reform act known as the Employee Retirement Income Security Act. This law, which provides for vesting rights, was discussed in Chapter 7. The provision for vesting rights means that pension plans must be funded. Although alternative methods can fulfill ERISA requirements, the use of a plan available from life insurance companies provides a safe haven for pension-fund assets.

SUMMARY   All businesses in a capitalistic system constantly face numerous types of risks. Because each hazard may result in losses, risks must be managed. Although some risks must be absorbed, others can be avoided or at least reduced to acceptable levels. Still others can best be handled by transfer to a third party, usually an insurance company.

To be insurable, risks must have certain characteristics. One of these is that they must be numerous enough so that premiums paid by many can be low and still provide adequate funds to pay the losses of a few. Institutions that underwrite losses include governments, nonprofit organizations, and stockholder-owned and mutual insurance companies.

The major divisions of the insurance business are health, property and liability, and life. Health insurance is written by all types of underwriters. It is a common practice for businesses to provide a group health insurance program for their employees and to pay all or at least a portion of the premium. This fringe benefit is the main reason that approximately 85 percent of the population of the United States is covered by some type of health insurance.

There are numerous types of property and liability insurance. A major division of interest to businesses of all sizes is fire and allied coverages. Coinsurance clauses require that business properties be insured for their approximate current values, unless the insured is willing to absorb a portion of each loss. Automobile insurance is also carried by almost all companies that own vehicles. Other types of property and liability insurance that concern businesses are theft, workers' compensation, marine, fidelity and surety bonds, and specialized liabilities. Product liability insurance has loomed large in recent years because of class-action suits and court attitudes that favor consumers.

The largest division of the insurance business is life insurance. Although most life policies are sold to individuals, many of them are also sold to businesses. A common employee fringe benefit is a group life insurance policy that is paid by the employer. Life insurance is also used by businesses to absorb credit losses, to finance employee pension plans, and to provide for funds when an owner or executive dies.

BACK TO THE CHAPTER OPENER

1. What are some of the uninsurable risks of a small business?
2. What are the characteristics of insurable risks?
3. What types of property and liability insurance should a small business have?
4. Would a small business have as great a need for fidelity bonds as a large business?
5. How can life insurance be used to assure the continuity of a small business where the owner-manager dies?

BUSINESS TERMS

risks	513	no-fault rule	525
insurance	513	fidelity bonds	527
insurance premium	513	surety bonds	527
self-insurance	515	actuary	529
Medicare	517	cash surrender value	530
Medicaid	517	universal life policy	532
coinsurance clause	521	variable life policy	532

QUESTIONS FOR DISCUSSION AND ANALYSIS

1. What is meant by the statement that the insurance industry is based on the "law of large numbers"?
2. How large should a company be in order to use self-insurance effectively?
3. Why should some members of the U.S. Congress want a national health insurance plan when 85 percent of the population is already covered by private health insurance plans?
4. How does a coinsurance clause differ from a deductible allowance?
5. Isn't careless driving encouraged by the no-fault insurance laws?
6. Why have all states enacted legislation requiring employers to carry workers' compensation insurance?
7. Why don't retailers who experience cash losses by their salespersons have fidelity bonds written to cover all salespersons?
8. What reasons can be given for the recent sharp increases in the premiums charged for specialized liability insurance?
9. What is meant by the statement "Buy term and invest the difference"?
10. Is credit insurance more important than credit life insurance to a producer of auto parts? to a finance company?

1. Consult the *Business Periodicals Index* or a similar index in your library and note the articles on insurance. A review of the subjects of these articles will indicate topics that are of current concern in the insurance industry. Choose a topic, read the appropriate articles, and prepare a well-written report that discusses all aspects of the topic.

2. Visit a large local retailer, such as a department store or supermarket, and prepare a list of ten insurable and ten uninsurable risks that are either present in the store or a result of business practices. For the insurable risks that you identified, indicate the type of insurance that can be used to reduce the risk.

3. The Clandell Corporation has just completed the best year in its history. It had a record after-tax income of $12,000,000. For many years it has paid a $2.00 annual dividend on the 3,000,000 shares of its common stock. The company wants to continue this same dividend policy into the future. Over the next two years the company will make a capital investment of $6,000,000 each year. These funds will be generated from retained earnings. For next year management is forecasting a 6 percent increase in its after-tax earnings. The company's state and federal income tax rate is 40 percent.

   Over the ten years of its existence, the Clandell Corporation has been relatively free of labor problems and has operated without a labor union. Corporate officers often have stated that they are willing to pay a good day's wage for a good day's work. Recently, however, the knowledge of record corporate earnings has given some rise to worker demands for higher wages, increased fringe benefits, and union representation. In fact, at this time union representatives are actively pushing efforts to organize the 5,000 workers.

   The union has declared that its first priority in bargaining with Clandell management is to obtain more company-paid insurance coverages for the employees. In order to blunt this union drive, Clandell's officers have hastily put together an insurance package of six coverages for their workers. However, they are now concerned that providing all six coverages to the workers would be too costly for the company. They have asked the workers to select a committee which will sit down with the management and carefully evaluate the importance of the coverages and their costs. The company officers believe that a well-conceived insurance plan containing any four of the six coverages will defeat the union. The employees are aware that the union charges a $100 initiation fee and membership dues of $10 monthly. The annual costs per employee for the six types of coverages are:

Group life ($20,000 per employee)	$ 50
Blue Cross (hospital expenses)	
Family coverage	280
Single coverage	120
Blue Shield (surgeon's fees)	
Family coverage	70
Single coverage	30
Major medical (all costs in excess of $300)	40
Health and accident insurance (supplement to	
workers' compensation)	50
Pension program	250

   Prepare a cost-and-need evaluation of these coverages and recommend an insurance plan that would contain four of the coverages.

VI. Information Management and Controls

Chapter 22. Business Information and the Computer
        23. Laws and Ethics for Business
        24. Regulation of Business

Grumman Corporation/Fred Annette, Photographer

The Texas Edison

Except for one little hitch, this scene would work nicely in one of those American Express card commercials: Here's the internationally acclaimed inventor—a man whose idea changed the daily life of the world—walking through the Dallas-Fort Worth Airport, and nobody knows who he is. No eyes light up with the spark of recognition. No kids come up to ask for autographs. Nobody pays any attention at all. Eventually, the tall, balding Texan pulls out his wallet to pay for something, and now at last we find out who he is: Jack St. Clair Kilby.

Okay, there's the hitch. Even after learning his name, most people have no idea who Jack Kilby is. A century ago, men of his ilk—men like Edison and Bell, whose inventions entered every home and spawned giant industries—were accorded enormous prominence almost overnight. Not so today. It has been not quite a quarter century since Jack Kilby, experimenting on his own in his lab at Texas Instruments, worked out the idea for the monolithic integrated circuit, the semiconductor chip in which the components of an electric circuit (originally a half dozen; today, a quarter million or more) can be put together on a sliver of silicon no bigger than an infant's thumbnail. It has been a decade since he filed his patent application for the chip's most famous offspring, the pocket calculator.

At first meeting, Kilby seems an unlikely miracle worker. A lanky 59-year-old with a big, leathery face, black horn-rimmed glasses, and a few wayward tufts of gray hair poking up from his temples, he looks precisely opposite of high-tech. Plain-spoken and plainly dressed, he is a quiet, introverted, grandfatherly type; he talks slowly in a deep, rumbling voice that still has some of the twang of Great Bend, Kansas, where he grew up. For all his pioneering work in the most modern of technologies, Kilby has an intriguing old-fashioned streak. He won't wear a digital watch. A computer would be useful in his work, but he doesn't use one because "I don't really know how." Although he is probably the single person most responsible for the demise of the slide rule, he still keeps his favorite Keuffel & Esser Log-Log Decitrig handy in the center drawer of his desk, and in some ways he prefers it to the calculators that rendered it obsolete. "It's an elegant tool," he says affectionately. "With the slide rule, there're no hidden parts. There's nothing going on that isn't right there on the table. It has sort of an honesty about it."

SOURCE: T. R. Reid, "The Texas Edison," *Texas Monthly* (July, 1982), p. 19. Reproduced with permission.

22 *Business Information and the Computer*

Objectives:

- Understand the meaning of electronic data processing and word processing.
- Explain the differences between an analog computer and a digital computer.
- Identify the basic components of a computer system.
- Discuss the meaning and use of computer hardware.
- Discuss the meaning and use of computer software.
- Understand the total systems concept.
- Discuss the advantages and disadvantages of time sharing, facilities management, and service bureaus.
- Explain some of the social concerns that are related to the computer.
- Describe the use of operations research techniques in solving management problems.
- Explain how statistics is used to handle business data.

Several years ago the Chatty Cathy doll was a hit in the toy stores. Now we have the chatty electric range that General Electric is developing. The talking range has a vocabulary of 150 words and phrases, including "please" but not "thank you." The conversation is controlled by a voice synthesizer that generates the human voice from a prerecorded set of words stored in a computer memory. The range makes such profound remarks as: "Please select automatic or manual cooking," "Select start or delayed start," and "Remove utensils from oven." In the future there probably will be clothes dryers that sing "How dry I am" and toasters that screech "My buns are burning."

In recent years the computer has become an essential part of our lives. Computers design cars, mix drinks, process student grades, knit sweaters, write letters, and do many other things (see Figure 22-1). The development of the microprocessor, a collar-button size silicon chip, has increased the speed and decreased the cost of computer power.

Today a single computer can do more calculations in a second than all the computers in the world could do 30 years ago. Some computers perform a calculation in 50 nanoseconds. (A nanosecond is a billionth of a second.) For comparison, a blink of an eye is usually about one-tenth of a second. Thus, a computer that performs a computation in 50 nanoseconds can handle 2 million computations during the blink of an eye!

As indicated in Table 22-1, from the early 1950s to 1985 the cost of performing one million calculations on a computer dropped from $250 to 1¢. If there had been similar technical progress in the auto industry, the luxurious Rolls Royce would be selling for $2.50 and would have a gas rating of 2,000,000 miles per gallon! The telephone industry has indicated that without the computer it would need to be employing nearly half the nation's work force to operate the telephone system.

Figure 22-1   "Anything you can do, I can do better"

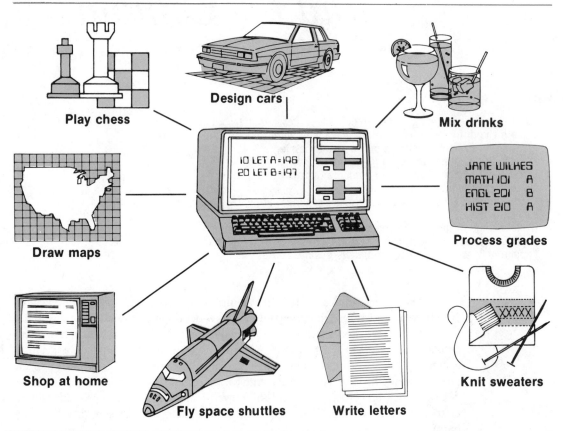

Play chess

Design cars

Mix drinks

Draw maps

Process grades

Shop at home

Fly space shuttles

Write letters

Knit sweaters

Table 22-1   Decreasing Cost of Computers and Calculations

Year	No. of Computers Installed	Average Sale Price	Percent of 1951 Sale Price	Average Cost per 1 Million Calculations
1951	10	$3,000,000	100.0	$250.00
1953	50	2,750,000	91.8	250.00
1955	244	2,250,000	75.0	165.00
1959	3,000	1,225,000	41.8	20.00
1965	23,000	700,000	23.3	2.75
1969	59,500	400,000	13.3	.25
1971	82,000	375,000	12.5	.10
1972	100,420	350,000	11.7	.09
1975	155,000	300,000	10.0	.08
1980	300,000	265,000	8.1	.04
1985 (est.)	500,000	210,000	7.0	.01

SOURCE: Elias M. Awad, *Business Data Processing,* 5th ed., © 1980. Reprinted by permission of Prentice-Hall, Inc., Englewood Cliffs, New Jersey.

SCOPE OF DATA PROCESSING

Data are the raw facts that must be converted into information. There are many classes of data, but the common ones used in business identify individuals, locations, objects, quantities, and monetary values. Information is the result of data processing and may be made available to company personnel as operating documents, reports, and analyses of problems. When data are processed through a computer, the procedure is called **electronic data processing (EDP).**

The first truly electronic computer was made at the University of Pennsylvania in 1946. It was called ENIAC (Electronic Numerical Integrator and Calculator) and was built to produce mathematical tables required for the accurate firing of projectiles. ENIAC weighed nearly 30 tons, contained almost 19,000 vacuum tubes, and required an operating area of 1,500 square feet. As Table 22-1 shows, within the past 30 years the growth of computer utilization has been phenomenal. The number of computers installed increased from a few hundred in the 1950s to an estimated 500,000 by 1985.

In recent years data processing equipment and techniques have been developed to simplify the tasks of writing repetitive letters, revising short documents, editing reports, and performing other office functions. A 10-page report that takes 90 minutes to type and correct manually can be prepared in 20 minutes on a word processor. The end result is a more efficient exchange of information and a reduced flow of paper in an office. Since these techniques involve a series of actions concerning words, the activity is called **word processing.** Although a word processing system runs from $5,000 for a single station to over $100,000 for a large center, an installation can result in substantial savings. One public utility installed a central word processing system and saved more than $200,000 in labor costs the first year. Figure 22-2 illustrates how word

Figure 22-2 MAILWAY Moves Messages Instantly Across the Seas

Mailway moves messages instantly across the seas

ILLUSTRATION SVEN SINDING

On a recent trip to Europe, Chairman Bill Butcher and members of the board of directors had a new assistant traveling with them: Electronic Mail.

Final drafts of speeches, itineraries, attendance lists, news summaries and the Chase "Flash!" publication followed the senior officers along their route, through the cooperative efforts of Corporate Communications and the International Sector's Global Electronic Mail System, or Mailway as it is commonly called.

Moving documents using Mailway from Headquarters to overseas offices is simple: operators key in memos or documents on Wang word processors, address the mail by entering an individual's name, and then use a series of function keys to place the items on a delivery list. System directories determine where the mail is to be delivered.

The mail is transmitted over the Chase Voice Network, an automated telephone system, to and from distribution centers. These centers, in turn, transmit the mail to other areas in the Network.

There are currently two distribution centers in operation. The New York distribution center, at the World Trade Center, serves three New York sites and Toronto, Canada, while the London center serves 10 European sites. A third distribution center, in Hong Kong, is scheduled to be added in September 1982, and after upgrading in the first quarter of 1983, will start distributing mail throughout Asia. By the end of 1983, 28 overseas locations will be connected to the Global Electronic Mail Network.

The drive to bring Mailway to the Bank has largely been led, to date, by the International Sector. The system was conceived and initiated by Frederick Siegle, Technical Services Division, International Operations and Systems. Siegle describes the sector's effort as "an attempt to utilize existing word processing and communications equipment to provide a timely and cost-effective alternative to pouch, facsimile and telex, for the exchange of administrative documents and messages."

SOURCE: Chase Manhattan Bank, *Chase News* (September, 1982), p. 3. Reproduced with permission.

processing has contributed to the development of a global electronic mail network at New York's Chase Manhattan Bank.

ANALOG AND DIGITAL COMPUTERS

The two general classes of computers are analog and digital. There are also hybrid computers that combine the features of both.

An **analog computer** carries out its calculations by making measurements. It translates such physical conditions as temperature, pressure, angular position, or voltage into related mechanical or electrical quantities. Analog computers are used in industry to make scientific computations, to solve equations, and to control manufacturing processes.

The operating principle of an analog computer may be compared to that of an ordinary weather thermometer. As the weather becomes cooler or warmer, the mercury in the glass tube rises or falls. The expansion and contraction of the mercury has a relationship to the conditions of the weather. The thermometer provides a continuous measurement that corresponds to the climatic temperature.

The **digital computer** deals with coded symbols and numbers. Whereas analog computers measure physical relationships, digital computers count numbers. A digital computer has the following characteristics:

1. It can perform arithmetic operations according to directions at speeds measured in billionths of a second.
2. It has the capability of making logical decisions, such as comparing one number with another and determining which is larger.
3. It has the capacity to store data and have them available for immediate recall.
4. It can follow a set of written instructions.

The remainder of this chapter will be devoted to digital computers because they are the type most commonly used in business.

COMPONENTS OF A COMPUTER SYSTEM

A computer system consists of one or more input devices, a central processing unit, and one or more output devices. The heart of the computer system is the **central processing unit (CPU),** which has three basic sections: memory, arithmetic, and control. The CPU processes the data which are received from an input device and then transmits the processed data to an output device. Figure 22-3 shows a diagram of the basic components of a computer system.

Input Devices

The purpose of an input device is to permit the computer operator to communicate with the computer. Input consists of data to be processed and the instructions required to process the data. The input device "reads in" data and instructions from various media. The data translated and stored may be numbers used in calculations, instructions that tell the computer what to do, or numbers or letters to be used as names and addresses. A recent development is the voice recognition system that converts the spoken word into data for the computer. Such a system has been installed at New York's Kennedy Airport to route outgoing luggage. Several forms of input media are illustrated in Figure 22-4.

Sections of the Central Processing Unit

As stated earlier, the CPU is composed of a memory unit, an arithmetic unit, and a control unit. The memory, or storage, unit is the center of operations of a CPU. All data being processed by the computer pass through the memory unit. This unit makes immense quantities of data available to the commands of the computer. The memory holds:

Figure 22-3   A Computer System

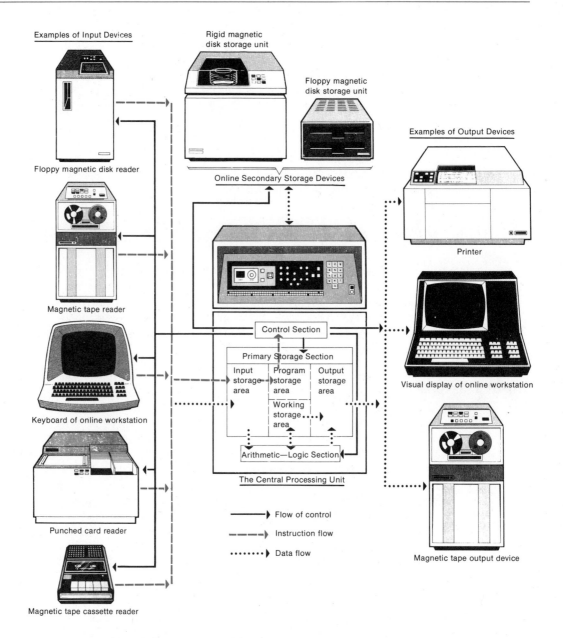

Examples of Input Devices

Rigid magnetic disk storage unit

Floppy magnetic disk storage unit

Floppy magnetic disk reader

Online Secondary Storage Devices

Examples of Output Devices

Magnetic tape reader

Printer

Keyboard of online workstation

Control Section

Primary Storage Section

| Input storage area | Program storage area | Output storage area |

Working storage area

Arithmetic—Logic Section

The Central Processing Unit

Visual display of online workstation

Punched card reader

⟶ Flow of control

- - - ➤ Instruction flow

........➤ Data flow

Magnetic tape output device

Magnetic tape cassette reader

SOURCE: From *Computers Today* by Donald H. Sanders. Copyright © 1983 by McGraw-Hill Book Company. Used with permission of McGraw-Hill Book Company.

Figure 22-4   Input Media Containing Data

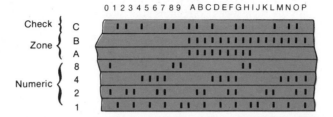

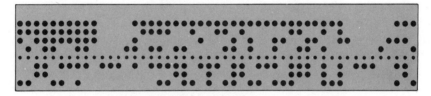

Magnetic tape is tape upon which data are recorded by the presence and absence of magnetized areas arranged according to code. Actual tape is one-half inch wide.

Punched paper tape is a special tape upon which data may be stored in the form of punched holes. Holes are located in columns across the width of the tape. Each column usually contains 5 to 8 positions, which are known as channels.

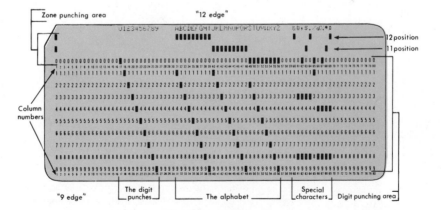

A **punched card** is made of heavy, stiff paper of constant size and shape. Data are stored in the form of punched holes arranged in 80 vertical columns. All holes in a single column are sensed simultaneously when a card is read by automated equipment. In each column there are 12 punching positions; (0-9) are identified as numeric punches and 11 and 12 are identified as zone punches.

1. The input data.
2. The intermediate results of calculations.
3. The final results to be "read out."
4. The program of instructions telling the computer what to do.

Memory units may be primary or secondary. Primary memory units used in most of the high-speed computers consist of silicon-chip semiconductors or magnetic cores. Secondary memory units that can be used to create a virtually unlimited memory include disks, drums, and magnetic tapes. Figure 22-5 shows the dramatic reduction in the size of the computer memory unit that has occurred since 1953.

Figure 22-5   Reduction in the Size of Memory Units

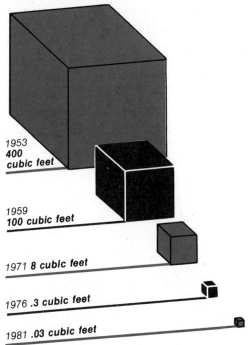

Age of Miniaturization

Computer space required to store 1 million characters of information—

1953
400 cubic feet

1959
100 cubic feet

1971 **8 cubic feet**

1976 **.3 cubic feet**

1981 **.03 cubic feet**

Thus, computer memory that would have required a room more than 7 feet in each dimension in 1953 can now be encased in the space taken by eight packs of cigarettes.

USN&WR chart—Basic data: International Business Machines

SOURCE: "A New—And Bigger—Computer Explosion," *U. S. News & World Report* (April 20, 1981), p. 62. Reprinted from "U. S. News & World Report." Copyright 1981, U. S. News & World Report, Inc.

The arithmetic unit of a CPU performs the operations of addition, subtraction, multiplication, and division, as well as comparison operations. The control unit interprets the program or instructions stored in the memory. It directs the various processing operations, issues proper commands to computer circuits to execute instructions, and checks to see that the instructions are properly carried out.

Output Devices

An output device "reads out" or translates into convenient form the results of processing or the contents of the memory unit. The output is the end product of the computer system. Printed pages are the most important form of output used solely by people. Some types of printed information produced are accounts, journals, financial statements, bills and invoices, and checks.

COMPUTER HARDWARE

The term **computer hardware** describes the central processing unit and its additional equipment. The CPU contains the circuits that control and execute the instructions. Additional equipment includes the input and output devices and secondary memory units that are linked to the CPU. For example, a system may consist of seven pieces of hardware: the computer, console, card reader, card punch, high-speed printer, magnetic tape units, and disk storage units. The last five of these are classified as peripheral equipment. One or more pieces of peripheral equipment may be located a few feet or many miles away from the CPU.

Terminals

A terminal is a form of peripheral equipment. It permits the input of data to the computer and/or the output of information to the user. A terminal satisfies the need for users in remote locations to communicate with the computer. Types of terminals include paper tape devices, visual display units, voice response units, touch-tone devices, and console typewriters.

A terminal has replaced the cash register in stores with computerized checkouts. On each item in these stores is a special rectangular label known as a **Universal Product Code (UPC)**, which is composed of thick and thin bars and spaces (see Figure 22-6). When the store checker slides each item's UPC over a laser-beam scanner, the terminal is instructed by a computer to print the item's code number, the department, the price, and the tax on the transaction slip. Figure 22-7 illustrates a system of computerized checkouts in a food store.

Generations of Computers

The computers introduced by manufacturers over the years are classified into computer generations. One of the characteristics that identifies a generation is com-

Figure 22-6   Decoding the Universal Product Code

The little striped patch now found on nearly every supermarket item is called a "universal product code" (UPC).

At the checkout, the cashier exposes the product's UPC to an "optical scanner" — either a pen-shaped "wand" or a window-like opening in the countertop. The scanner transmits the bar code to a computer, which pulls from its data bank the product's price and size or weight. The system relays the information back to the checkout and prints the product's name, price and size/weight on the register tape.

The scanner reads the bars, not the printed numbers, which are included only for the convenience of humans. The UPC bar code shown here is from a package of Jell-O Pudding Pops frozen pudding on a stick.

The first number in the 11-digit code, positioned to the left of the vertical bars, is the Number System Character which indicates one of five currently listed designations

"2" — Random-weight items such as meat and produce.
"3" — Health-related and drug items.
"4" — Retailer use only.
"5" — Coupons.
"0" — All items except the above.

The next five digits of the code are the Manufacturer Identification Number, assigned to manufacturers by the Uniform Product Code Council. The Manufacturer Identification Number for General Foods is "43000."

The last five digits of the code form the Item Code Number, which is controlled by the individual manufacturer and is unique to every product variation. The **item code in the** UPC indicates the Pudding Pops **flavor and package** size.

SOURCE: General Foods Corporation, *GF News* (August/September, 1982), p. 7. Reproduced with permission.

puter hardware. Figure 22-8 shows five generations of computers by name, period, hardware, organizational location, and effect on organization. In the first generation the circuitry was based on vacuum tubes. The second generation was identified by the use of transistors. The third generation employed large-scale integrated (LSI) circuits composed of tiny silicon chips. The fourth generation featured LSI circuits, low-cost disk storage, and satellite computers that communicate with a central computer. It is believed that the fifth generation will be marked by magnetic bubble storage, laser-holographic (three-dimensional image) technology, and Josephson junctions.

Figure 22-7   Computerized Checkouts in a Supermarket

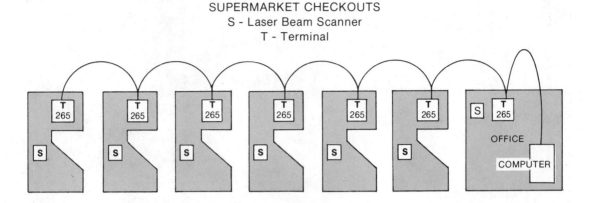

SUPERMARKET CHECKOUTS
S - Laser Beam Scanner
T - Terminal

Use of Minicomputers

Cabinet-sized minicomputers costing from $5,000 to $10,000 are challenging the larger and more costly mainframe computers for a greater share of the computer market. Figure 22-9 shows the expected change in the makeup of the computer market between 1980 and 1985. Using about as much electricity as a hair dryer (1,400 watts), a minicomputer is an economical data processing unit. Minicomputer systems can be designed to handle the processing needs of several users at the same time. They can be used for *distributed data processing*, too. This is where minicomputers are linked together so that they can process data at local sites while still having access to the information base of a mainframe computer.

Growth of Microcomputers

In recent years a variety of computers smaller in size than mainframe or cabinet-sized minicomputers have been developed. Although these smaller computers are identified by various names, such as personal computers and home computers, all of them have a common feature. The heart of their operations is a **microprocessor,** a tiny silicon chip (see Figure 22-10 on page 554). The chip contains the detailed circuitry that performs the arithmetic operations and controls the input and output functions. With the addition of various input and output devices and a memory unit to the microprocessor, a microcomputer is formed.

Personal computers are inexpensive forms of microcomputers that are intended for personal use rather than for large-business use. Because of their low cost and their multipurpose capability, personal computers are marketed to small-business users, to schools for student use, and to professionals. Physicians, writers, accountants, and farmers use this type of computer for their word processing, accounting, and inventory

Figure 22-8   Five Generations of Computers

Generation	Name	Period	New Hardware	Organizational Location	Effect on Organization
• First	• Gee whiz	• 1953–1958	• Vacuum tubes, magnetic records	• Controller's department	• First appearance of technicians (with salary, responsibility, and behavior problems); automation fears among employees
• Second	• Paper pushers	• 1958–1966	• Transistors, magnetic cores	• Movement to operating departments	• EDP group proliferation; some workers and supervisors alienated or displaced; introduction of new rigidity but also new opportunities
• Third	• Communicators	• 1966–1974	• Large-scale integrated circuits, remote terminals connected to central computer	• Consolidation into centrally controlled regional or corporate centers with remote terminals	• Centralization of EDP organization; division data visible to central management; some division managers alienated; response times shortened
• Fourth	• Information custodians	• 1974–1982	• Very large file storage, satellite computers, LSI circuits	• Versatile satellites instead of terminals, with control still centralized	• Redistribution of management functions, with logistic decisions moving to headquarters and tactical decisions moving out; resulting reorganization; field personnel pleased
• Fifth	• Action aids	• 1982– ?	• Magnetic bubble and/or laser-holographic technology, decentralized data processing	• Systems capabilities projected to all parts of organization; networks of different organizations interconnected	• Semiautomatic operating decisions; plans initiated by many individuals, leading toward flickering authority and management by consensus; greater involvement of people at all levels; central EDP group shrinkage

SOURCE: Frederic G. Withington, "Five Generations of Computers," *Harvard Business Review* (July/August, 1974), p. 101. Reprinted by permission.

Figure 22-9   Makeup of the Computer Market

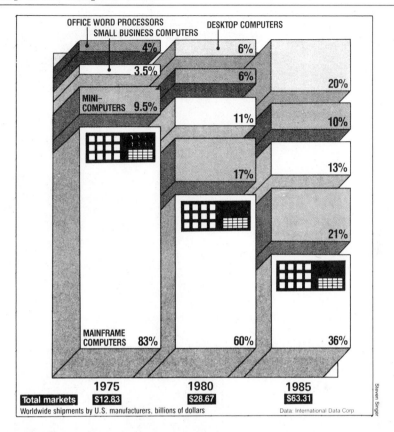

SOURCE: Illustration by Steven M. Singer, *Business Week* (February 15, 1982), p. 78. Reproduced with permission.

control requirements. Large firms also are providing certain employees, such as market researchers and engineers, with personal computers to replace or supplement the large mainframe computers. Personal computers generally sell for at least $2,000, including one or more disk storage devices to hold programs. Examples of personal computers are Radio Shack's TRS-80 models and Apple Computer's models Apple IIe and Apple III.

A simple home computer is an electronic keyboard that attaches to a television set for display purposes. It uses mainly floppy (flexible) disk drives or cassette tape recorders for external storage. Sometimes a home computer system includes a printer and/or a telephone modem which permits the computer to transmit data over the phone lines (see Figure 22-11). Although the primary use of many home computers is for playing video games, they can also be used for other tasks such as balancing checkbooks, word processing, and tax preparation. Some home computer keyboards, such as the Timex-Sinclair, sell for $100 or less.

Figure 22-10   Microprocessor on Top of a Dime

SOURCE: Courtesy of Motorola, Inc., Schaumburg, IL.

Figure 22-11   A Basic Home Computer System

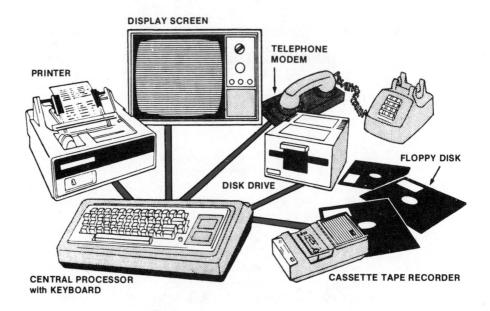

SOURCE: Peter J. Schuyten, "The Trials of Picking a System," *The New York Times,* June 24, 1980, p. D3. © 1980 by The New York Times Company. Reprinted by permission.

COMPUTER SOFTWARE

"Software before hardware" is a useful motto to follow if you are in the market for a computer. It means that you should first determine what you want the computer to do, then select the proper programs to do it, and finally choose the hardware that runs the software. Various programming aids that help make effective use of a computer are known as **computer software.** While computer hardware has become more economical and efficient over the years, computer software has become more elaborate. This has caused computer users to spend an increasing share of their money on software. The federal government, the largest computer user, spends $1.3 billion annually just maintaining old computer programs. This is equal to its annual expenditures on computer hardware. Figure 22-12 reveals that by 1985 software will be a $33.8 billion business, 60 percent as great as the hardware business.

Figure 22-12   Growth in Software Expenditures

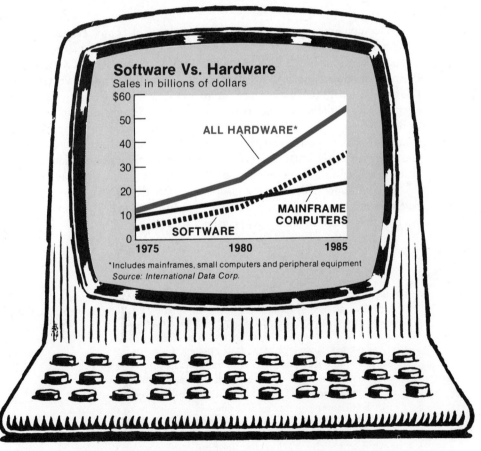

SOURCE: Andrew Pollack, "Computers: The Action's in Software," *The New York Times,* November 8, 1981, p. F1. © 1981 by The New York Times Company. Reprinted by permission.

Computer Programs

A **computer program,** which is a software item, is a series of operating instructions to be performed in processing the data supplied to the computer. The actual writing of a program is done by a person called a programmer. A program is prepared by listing in complete detail the logical steps which the computer must take to obtain the desired results. Some 500,000 steps are required for a computer to print a single insurance premium notice, for example. There are three basic considerations in the preparation of a program:

1. Defining the problem to be solved.
2. Outlining each logical step required to reach the solution.
3. Writing the program in a computer language.

Computer Language

A computer language is a basic combination of characters that is used in a computer program and that the computer understands. Four of the most popular computer languages are COBOL, FORTRAN, BASIC, and RPG. **COBOL** (Common Business Oriented Language) employs business terminology and is written in English-like words. **FORTRAN** (Formula Translation) is a widely accepted language for scientific and mathematical use. **BASIC** (Beginner's All-purpose Symbolic Instruction Code), also in English-like words, is an easy-to-learn language that allows the programmer to interact directly with a program. It often is used with personal computers and in time-sharing situations. **RPG** (Report Program Generator) language provides an easy method for programming a small computer to write a business report.

A continuing effort is being made to simplify the language used by computers. Scientists at Xerox Corporation have developed a language based on English words and symbols that even children can understand readily.

Flow Charts

A flow chart is a graphic representation of the logical steps to be used in solving a problem. It helps the programmer to do the following:

1. To break down a problem into workable segments.
2. To ensure that each step is accomplished in correct sequence.
3. To discover areas of the problem that need further clarification.
4. To prevent or to detect errors in a proposed solution.
5. To discover laborsaving and timesaving shortcuts to the solution.

There may be as many as 11 distinct steps in solving the problem of crossing an intersection where there is a traffic light but no oncoming vehicles. The problem may be stated: How does one go from corner A to corner B without diagonal crossing? The diagram of the problem and its flow chart are shown in Figure 22-13.

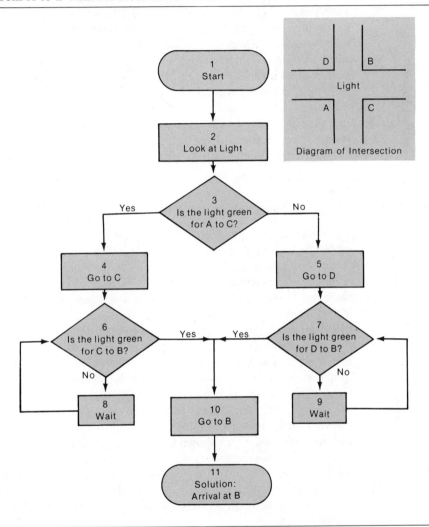

APPLICATIONS OF ELECTRONIC DATA PROCESSING

In the past many companies used a computer mainly to perform computations that formerly were done on mechanical calculators. Companies are now using computers in a broader total systems concept to satisfy their electronic data processing (EDP) requirements.

Total Systems Concept

The total systems concept relates departmental goals to the overall objectives of a company and gives its top management a broad, critical view of all its operations. Commonly, electronic data processing equipment has been used for processing routine subsystems such as sorting and calculating invoices. These subsystems usually feature a high volume of transactions and a large amount of routine processing which must be performed with each transaction. For these reasons it is typical to include accounts receivable, inventory control, the payroll, and similar subsystems in developing programs for a computer as the first steps toward a coordinated system.

A flow chart and its related program are developed for each data processing operation. Computer specialists, called systems analysts, develop ways of combining, expanding, and coordinating the separate data processing operations into a total system.

Use of Real-Time Systems

Real time is a type of data processing performed at the same time that the physical process or business transaction is occurring. The purpose of a real-time system is to produce results that are immediately useful in controlling an ongoing physical process or business transaction. The previously mentioned supermarket scanner with the Universal Product Code is an example of a real-time system.

A real-time system has three major features. First, data are maintained **on-line**, which means that all data and instructions used in the processing are transmitted to the computer at the time the transaction occurs. Second, the data are updated as events occur. Third, the computer can be "questioned" from remote terminals. That is, information stored in the computer can be obtained on request from a number of locations at some distance from the computer.

Many banks, department stores, and airline reservation offices use real-time systems to link numerous terminals together in a data-communication network. The real-time reservation system used by American Airlines is explained in Figure 22-14. Figure 22-15 shows the operation of a real-time system in a bank. The savings account balances of all customers are stored in the memory of a central computer. These terminals permit all deposits and withdrawals to be recorded as they are transacted. Thus, the current balance of any customer's account is available at any time in any branch terminal.

Use of Batch Processing

The batch processing of data is used when the data are not immediately needed for operations. In **batch processing**, the data are collected and sent periodically in groups or batches to the computer. The processing can be done during the slowest operating periods for a computer. This type of processing is appropriate for payroll operations or credit card billings where the output is needed only at certain periods of time.

Figure 22-14   American Airlines' SABRE (Reservations System)

One of the first commercial applications of real-time data processing was SABRE, a system built by IBM for American Airlines. Today, SABRE is the world's largest data processing system designed for business use. Updated with new equipment in 1972, 1975, 1978, 1980, and 1982, the real-time system receives from airline agents data pertaining to passenger reservations, ticketing, and airport passenger boarding functions from American's agents in the United States, Canada, Mexico, the Caribbean, South America, and Europe. American's baggage and freight tracing, crew scheduling, and flight progress information are processed by the SABRE system. SABRE also handles passenger reservations and ticketing for several other airlines and over 7,000 independent travel agents. It can immediately process the information and send a virtually instantaneous output message to the agent. SABRE is designed to handle tens of thousands of telephone inquiries every day together with requests for prices, passenger reservations on over 600 airlines, inquiries regarding seat availablility to and from other airlines, and specific flight seating location assignments. SABRE processes and prints tickets and boarding passes as well as invoice and itinerary documents. Over 8,000 hotels and 16 rental car companies can be automatically confirmed through the system. SABRE's data base stores over 3.5 million air fares and schedules. On most days SABRE processes upwards of 25,000,000 input transactions and has over 10,000,000 passenger records in its electronic files. The processing of a reservation or other transaction through SABRE takes approximately 1 to 3 seconds from agent input until the response is received.

SOURCE: Reproduced with permission of American Airlines.

Computer Service Firms

Part of the computer software industry has evolved into a computer services industry. Over the past few years many firms have been created to develop and sell computer programs and services to other firms. These firms own the computer hardware and employ skilled personnel in data processing, programming, and systems design. Some banks have entered this new industry by providing payroll, accounts receivable, billing, and other accounting and clerical services to their clients.

Time-Sharing

Time-sharing allows many customers to share the capabilities of a large central computer through the use of remote terminals hooked up to the computer. Although the computer actually services each user in sequence, the high speed of the computer makes it appear that the users are being serviced at the same time. It is estimated that there are over 20,000 users of time-sharing services. Both IBM and Control Data Corporation provide time-sharing services to businesses.

Facilities Management

If executives do not wish to use time-sharing nor desire to establish their own data processing system, they may turn to a computer service company specializing in

Figure 22-15   Operation of a Real-Time System for a Savings Account Transaction in a Commercial Bank

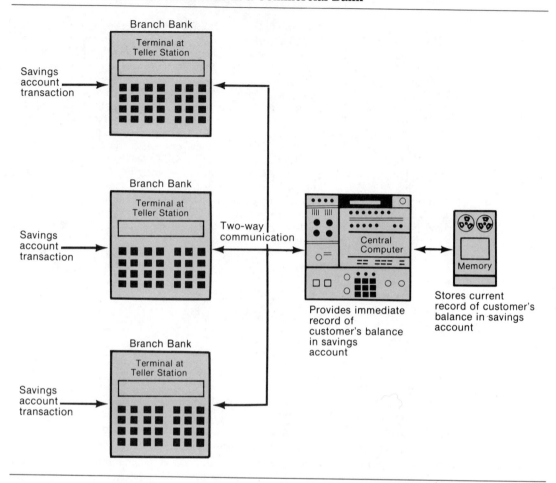

facilities management. This company sets up and operates all or a part of a firm's EDP requirements. The Chase Manhattan Bank of New York has placed its stock transfer activities into the hands of a facilities management company.

Service Bureaus

A **service bureau** has trained programmers and computer operators to handle computer operations for its clients. In the usual arrangement the data to be processed, such as sales slips, checks, and receipts, are delivered by the business to the service bureau. The bureau's computer then processes the input and prints the reports according to programs that were prepared earlier by the service bureau for its client. Figure 22-16 illustrates this procedure. The extent of this business is indicated by the nearly 40 service bureaus operating in the El Paso, TX market alone.

Figure 22-16   Operations of a Service Bureau

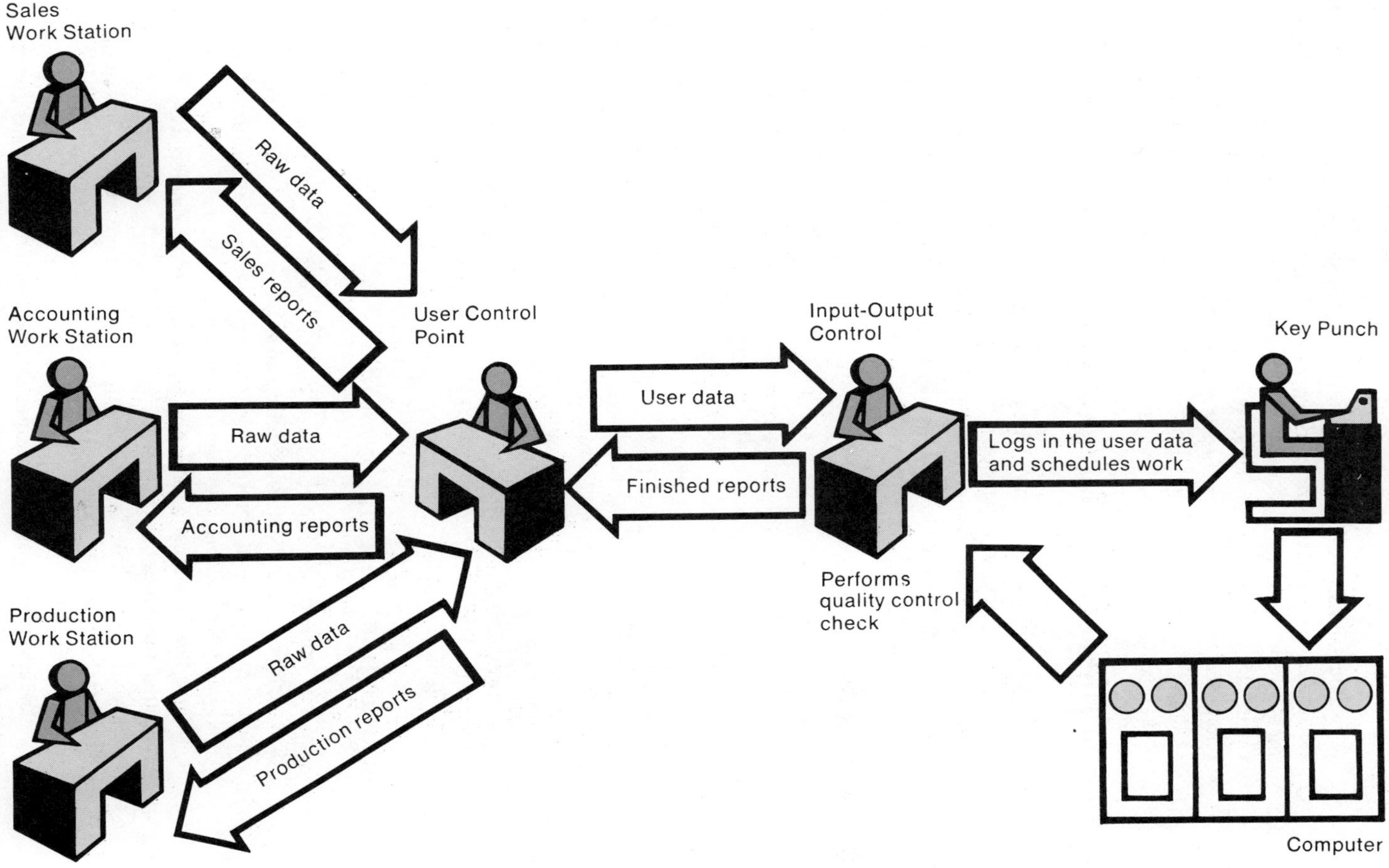

SOCIAL IMPACT OF THE COMPUTER _____

The explosive development of the computer has created change both inside and outside an organization. Inside the organization the computer has altered work assignments and provided management with new tools for decision making. Outside the organization the computer is greatly changing our way of life and will continue to exert a force for change. Some of the social concerns related to the computer are: generation of unnecessary information, organizational changes, fear of technological unemployment, invasion of privacy, depersonalization, and security of data.

Generation of Unnecessary Information

The ability of the computer to process a large amount of data at speeds exceeding 100 million operations per second should force management to select only the data which are necessary. Some managers are overwhelmed with computer printouts which are not needed and go unused. Someone has referred to this misuse of information as GIGO—garbage in, garbage out.

Organizational Changes

A central computer and a network of terminals make it possible to centralize decision making in a decentralized organization. Since the computer operates most efficiently with routine programs and procedures, it becomes a force in the standardization of some work assignments. The computer has also restructured various work assignments and has freed middle managers to supervise creatively rather than to become involved with the numerous routine details of a job. For example, the computer relieves credit managers from the repeated task of determining if their customers are approaching their credit limits.

The electronic data processing function has given rise to a group of specialists such as systems analysts, programmers, and computer operators. The U.S. Department of Labor estimates there will be 640,000 computer specialists employed by 1985. Figure 22-17 depicts a typical data processing department within a firm.

Fear of Technological Unemployment

For workers, one of the most fearful aspects of the computer is its capability of controlling machinery to perform tasks that formerly were done by human labor. The unemployment that results when machine labor is substituted for human labor is called *technological unemployment.* Even experts disagree on whether the economy can grow fast enough to absorb the workers who are displaced by robots, computers, and other machines.

Invasion of Privacy

By bringing many separate pieces of information together in one central data bank, there is the potential for an invasion of a person's privacy. Various types of data

Figure 22-17   Organization of a Data Processing Department

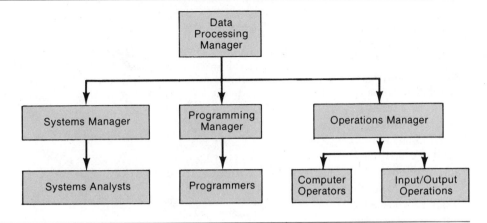

banks are already in existence. Table 22-2 reveals that the federal government has over 3.5 billion records on its citizens — the equivalent of 15 files on each American.

Depersonalization

When the computer replaces the human element in decision making, depersonalization occurs. Individuals feel they are viewed as numbers rather than separate personalities. Some organizations are taking actions to reverse this tendency toward depersonalization. The vice-president of service for Computervision, a high-tech company, says that after 20 years in the computer business he still does not use a computer. He states that even in the computer age managers must produce results by working through others.[1]

Security of Data

There are several reasons why computer security has become a topic of increasing concern to management. One reason is that usage of computer services facilities means trusting important business data to individuals outside the firm. Another factor is that the storage of substantial amounts of valuable data in a single location increases the risk of a large loss. Since the computer system can be programmed both to retrieve valuable data illegally and then to cover the theft, computer larceny is hard to detect.

Figure 22-18 cites several dramatic examples of computer crimes. In a report of 700 computer-aided crimes, the average loss was over $400,000. Some estimates indicate that the cost of both reported and unreported computer crimes is as high.

---

1.   Jack Falvey, "Real Managers Don't Use Computer Terminals," *Marketing News,* March 18, 1983, Sec. 1, p. 8.

Table 22-2   The Federal Government's Files on People

In thousands of computers and elsewhere, the federal government keeps track of Americans. Within these systems, at last count, were 3,529,743,665 files related to everything from payrolls to Social Security data to criminal charges to loans and grants — most available at the touch of a button.

Files on People

Departments of Education and Health and Human Services	1,033,999,891
Department of Treasury	780,196,929
Department of Commerce	431,427,589
Department of Defense	333,951,949
Department of Justice	201,474,342
Department of State	110,809,198
Department of Agriculture	33,727,730
Copyright Office	28,408,366
Department of Transportation	24,023,142
Federal Communications Commission	20,870,078
Department of Housing and Urban Development	20,340,642
Department of Labor	16,785,015
Department of Interior	16,708,016
Office of Personnel Management	16,016,779
Department of Energy	8,929,999
Executive Office of the President	30,655
All other federal agencies	452,043,345
Grand total	3,529,743,665

Or 15 files on average for each American

SOURCE: "Who Is Watching You," *U. S. News & World Report* (July 12, 1982), p. 35. Reprinted from "U. S. News & World Report." Copyright 1982, U. S. News & World Report, Inc.

The managements of many companies are now turning to computer security experts for assistance in safeguarding the computer. System commands, passwords, and secret codes are being utilized to protect computers against illegal entry. Surprise audits and checks are being conducted, too. One computer manufacturer — Honeywell, Incorporated — has devised a way to restrict the total amount of information available to any user of the computer. Other schemes seek to control access to the computer location through a system of electronically locked doors, electronic sensors, and closed-circuit television.

MANAGEMENT INFORMATION SYSTEMS

As organizations grow and become more complex, the need for adequate, accurate, and timely information becomes very important. The availability of the proper information reduces the possibility of a manager making a wrong decision. An important job for systems analysts is to design management information systems (MIS) that effectively meet the needs of business. These systems accumulate and organize the data that are necessary for planning, controlling, and decision making. Drawing from

Figure 22-18   Computer-Assisted Crimes

Dramatic crimes the computer helped commit

The case: Wells Fargo
The date: 1979-81
The take: $21.3 million

The modus operandi

L. Ben Lewis, an operations officer for the 11th largest U. S. bank, allegedly produced bogus deposits in an account at one branch belonging to a boxing promotion outfit. He did this by using the bank's computerized interbranch account settlement process to withdraw funds from a different branch. To keep the computer from flagging the imbalance, Lewis created new fraudulent credits to cover the withdrawal—and allegedly kept the rollover going for two years. Lewis denies the charges

The case: Morgan Guaranty
The date: 1980
The take: Zero

The New York bank reportedly accepted as legitimate a bogus telex from the Central Bank of Nigeria transferring $21 million. In response to subsequent instructions, the money was routed electronically to three banks. When an attempt was made to wire the funds to a new $50 account in a Santa Ana (Calif.) bank, the transfer was refused. This triggered inquiries by the other banks. The Nigerian bank branded the first message as fraudulent, and the funds were never collected

The case: Dalton School
The date: 1980
The take: Zero

Using a classroom terminal, teenage students at Manhattan's private Dalton School allegedly dialed into a Canadian network of corporate and institutional data systems. No funds were diverted —but damage was done to data files

The case: Security Pacific
The date: 1978
The take: $10.3 million

Stanley Mark Rifkin, who had been a computer consultant for the Los Angeles bank, visited the bank's wire transfer room, where he obtained the electronic funds transfer code. Later, posing as a branch manager, he called from a public telephone and used the code to send money to a Swiss account. By the time the bank's computers flagged the fraud, he had flown to Switzerland, converted the funds into diamonds, and returned to the U. S. Only when he boasted of the feat was he identified, convicted, and sentenced to prison

The case: Union Dime
The date: 1973
The take: $1.2 million

A teller at the New York City savings bank skimmed money from large new accounts by making a simple computerized correction entry. His embezzlement was discovered when police investigated a gambling parlor he frequented and questioned the source of his betting money

The case: Equity Funding
The date: 1973
The take: $27.25 million

The insurance holding company used computers to create phony insurance policies that were later sold to reinsurers. Of the company's assets, $143.4 million were found to be fictitious, of which an estimated 19% was the result of computer fraud

Data: BW

SOURCE: Reprinted from the April 20, 1981 issue of *Business Week* by special permission, © 1981 by McGraw-Hill, Inc. Illustration reproduced with permission of Joel F. Naprstek.

the computerized data base of an MIS, various operations research techniques and the use of statistics can help solve managerial problems.

Operations Research Techniques

Operations research (OR) is the application of mathematical techniques to a wide variety of management problems. It was originally used to enhance military efficiency during World War II. In a corporation, OR is usually conducted by a team of accountants, engineers, statisticians, economists, scientists, and mathematicians. The use of computers in OR is almost a necessity. In the OR process a problem is defined and analyzed, alternative solutions are tested, and a recommendation is made.

A study of manufacturing firms disclosed that 48 percent of them were using one or more OR techniques. One half of these firms use four or more OR techniques. The OR techniques used most often are shown in Table 22-3.

The **Program Evaluation and Review Technique (PERT)** establishes the estimated completion time for a project by arranging in a critical path the activities that must be accomplished. A critical path shows the sequence of activities that must be performed from the start of a project to its finish. Some of these activities can be done at the same time such as roofing a building and laying a concrete floor. Other activities, such as drilling a well and installing the well piping, must be done in succession. The **Critical Path Method (CPM)**, which is similar to PERT, establishes a path that considers cost, as well as the time involved, for the completion of a project.

Linear programming is a mathematical device for determining the best way to allocate a limited amount of resources. Using this technique, the H.J. Heinz Company developed a shipping schedule that economically matched the output of its 6 plants to the needs of its nearly 70 warehouses. *Exponential smoothing* is a moving average method that uses the values from past periods to forecast future business activity. Because it gives greater weight to the values in the more recent periods than in the older periods, this method has great appeal to managers.

A *computer simulation* provides a method for observing the interaction of a number of important elements in a business problem. By creating a model and using a computer, in just a few minutes United Airlines simulated the operations of a large airport over

---

Table 22-3 **The OR Techniques Most Often Used by Manufacturers**

Technique	Percent of Use
PERT	33.5
CPM	32.4
Linear programming	27.7
Exponential smoothing	26.9
Computer simulation	25.1
Queuing theory	14.2

SOURCE: Norman Gaither, "The Adoption of Operations Research Techniques by Manufacturing Organizations," *Decision Sciences* (October, 1975), p. 805. Reproduced with permission.

---

a period of several months. *Queuing theory* is a mathematical technique that attempts to minimize expenditures by determining the proper balance between the cost of service and the cost of a waiting line. Several uses of queuing theory are illustrated in Figure 22-19.

Figure 22-19   Examples of Uses for Queuing Theory

Uses	Input Unit	Service or Processing Needs
• Calls made at a coin-operated telephone	• Individual approaching telephone to place a call	• Telephone circuits and operator
• Automobile service station	• Vehicle driving into station for fuel and other service	• Attendant, gasoline pump, and other equipment
• Supermarket	• Customer seeking to have the amount of purchase tabulated and to pay for the purchase	• Clerk, cash register, and bagging operation at a check-out counter
• "Five-minute" car wash	• Automobiles arriving to be washed	• Attendants and automatic car-washing apparatus
• Medical clinic	• Patients entering to receive medical attention	• Physician, nurse, and clerical staff, and related equipment and drugs

SOURCE: Adapted from Charles T. Clark and Lawrence L. Schkade, *Statistical Analysis for Administrative Decisions* (2d ed.; Cincinnati: South-Western Publishing Co., 1974), p. 218. Reproduced with permission.

Use of Statistics

One of the most commonly used methods for handling the data in MIS is statistics. Statistics deals with numerical data related to the problems of business and involves four steps: collection; analysis, summarization, and measurement; presentation; and interpretation. The most important function of business statistics is to require the manager to explain situations or to state problems in a specific form. A study of manufacturers in Ohio disclosed that 23 percent used elementary statistical techniques, and an additional 22 percent utilized some advanced statistical methods in their operations.

Collection of Data

Numerical data must be collected before they can be summarized and used. If the figures are concerned with operations of a company, the data can be obtained from the company records. Financial statements, invoices, sales reports, and payroll records can supply vital information that is subject to statistical analysis. In many cases external data, such as census reports, are necessary in arriving at sound solutions to problems.

Analysis, Summary, and Measurement of Data

Once the data are available, the figures must be processed. Sometimes they need to be broken down into segments; at other times they are summarized in usable tables. Two types of statistical measurement—ratios and percentages—were illustrated in

Chapter 17 in connection with the interpretation of financial statements. Other common types of statistical measurements include averages, index numbers, correlations, and time series. An **average**, which is a measure of central tendency, is the typical value in a group of data such as weekly wages or daily stock prices. An **index number** is a device for measuring the change that has taken place in a group of related items over a period of time. The price indexes that were discussed in Chapter 15 are index numbers.

Presentation of Data

To present statistical material in a manner that will be useful for purposes of analysis, two devices are commonly used. These are summary tables and graphic presentations.

A summary table presents a considerable amount of statistical material in tabular form. Years, geographical areas, types of products, age groups, income groups, nationalities, and the like may be the bases for comparisons in summary tables.

The graphic presentation of statistical data has the great advantage of presenting a visual analysis of the facts. One of the most common graphic statistical presentations is the line or curve chart, which uses a line or a curve to indicate changes or trends over a period of time. Another graphic presentation is the bar chart, which is used for the comparison of figures. The pie chart divides a circle representing 100 percent or a dollar into many smaller portions. Finally, there are statistical maps, which are commonly used to present geographical information. Figure 22-20, which displays the division of expenditures for data processing over a five-year period, is an example of a pie chart.

Interpretation of Data

The final step in business statistics that aids management to make decisions and to control operations is the interpretation of data. Despite the best of intentions, several types of errors can creep into a manual computation. Arithmetic errors are likely to occur, particularly when the quantity of data to be processed is extensive. In surveys, the sample selected may not be representative of the whole. If a computer is used, the programmed instructions may be faulty. In some instances individuals use only selected information which supports their views. In other cases they may manipulate accurate figures to arrive at faulty conclusions. For example, the officers of one corporation announced that 2,000,000 shares of the corporation's stock were held by 3,003 persons who averaged 660 shares each. They did not state, however, that 3 persons held 75 percent of the stock and 3,000 persons held the other 25 percent.

SUMMARY   The processing of data through a computer is called electronic data processing. Data processing techniques, called word processing, have been developed to simplify the tasks of writing repetitive letters, editing reports, and performing other office functions.

There are two general classes of computers: analog and digital. The analog computer measures physical relationships. The digital computer, which is the type most commonly used in business, performs calculations by counting. A computer system consists of a central processing unit (CPU), input devices, and output devices. The term computer hardware describes the CPU and its additional equipment. A terminal, which is a special-purpose input/output device, satisfies the need for users in remote locations to com-

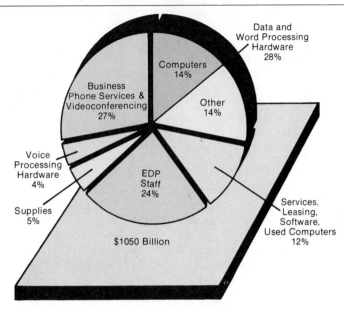

SOURCE: International Data Corporation. Reproduced with permission.

municate with the computer. Computers can be classified into five generations based upon technology.

The programming aids that help make effective use of a computer are known collectively as computer software. A computer program, which is a software item, consists of a series of operating instructions to be performed in processing the data supplied to the computer. Another software device is a flow chart, which is a graphic representation of the logical steps in programming. A total systems concept relates departmental goals to the overall objectives of the company. Part of the computer software industry has evolved into a computer service industry that sells computer services to other firms.

The explosive development of the computer has created the following social concerns: generation of unnecessary information, organizational changes, automation, invasion of privacy, depersonalization, and security of data.

Management information systems accumulate and organize the data that are necessary for planning, controlling, and decision making. Drawing from the computerized data base of an MIS, operations research procedures can be developed to solve managerial problems. The use of statistics permits the proper display of MIS data.

BACK TO THE CHAPTER OPENER

1. Is the invention of the microprocessor more important than the invention of the light bulb?
2. Is a microprocessor considered to be hardware or software?
3. What has the microprocessor done to the cost of computer calculations?
4. What computer functions are performed by silicon chips?
5. How is a microcomputer constructed from a microprocessor?

BUSINESS TERMS					
electronic data processing (EDP)	543		RPG	556
word processing	543		real time	558
analog computer	544		on-line	558
digital computer	545		batch processing	558
central processing unit (CPU)	545		time-sharing	559
computer hardware	549		facilities management	560
Universal Product Code (UPC)	549		service bureau	560
microprocessor	551		operations research (OR)	566
computer software	555		Program Evaluation and Review	
computer program	556		Technique (PERT)	566
COBOL	556		Critical Path Method (CPM)	566
FORTRAN	556		average	568
BASIC	556		index number	568

QUESTIONS FOR DISCUSSION AND ANALYSIS

1. Can word processing be more important than electronic data processing?
2. Will the use of the most advanced computer hardware compensate for the use of inadequate computer software?
3. How can a computer be used by hospital administrators? the legal profession? a railroad? the motion picture industry? a highway department?
4. Which of the five generations of computers represents the greatest advance in technology? Discuss.
5. What types of skills, education, and experience should a computer programmer possess?
6. Is a real-time system more useful to a commercial bank than to an airline reservation service? Explain.
7. How can computer service firms retain their customers when these customers are able to buy inexpensive personal computers?
8. Why do labor unions often resist the efforts of management to employ computer technology? Are the fears of unions justified? Discuss.
9. Does the need for large data banks outweigh the risk of invading a person's privacy? Discuss.
10. Cite several examples showing how statistics might be used in each of the following functional areas of business: marketing, production, finance, and personnel.

PROJECTS, PROBLEMS, AND SHORT CASES

1. Carefully study the data processing requirements in the following four areas of your school:

   a. Admissions.
   b. Registration.
   c. Course scheduling.
   d. Fee payments.

   If possible, visit the data processing center on your campus to gain a greater understanding of its relationship with these four areas. As a result of your study and visit, indicate how the computer is (or could be) used to process data in each of the four areas.

2. Select a topic of current interest in the computer field and prepare a well-organized report on it. The *Business Periodicals Index* in your library will help you to identify topics, such as computer crimes, computer insurance, and the computer and privacy, that are the subject of numerous articles. Stories on these and other computer topics are carried in periodicals such as *Datamation, Infosystems,* and *Mini-Micro Systems.*

3. "Complaints, complaints, complaints!" growled Harvey Ellsworth, president of a $10 million industrial distribution business. "I've been receiving from 10 to 50 letters of complaint a month from certain very unhappy customers."

Ellsworth was discussing a bothersome problem of the business with his administrative assistant, Kelli Conrad. Having a marketing background, Ellsworth recognized the need to keep in touch with his customers and to respond to their complaints. Before the monthly meetings with his management group, he often would telephone dissatisfied customers in order to learn first-hand of their complaints. He used these contacts as a basis for keeping his associates on their toes. They knew that he was not relying solely on their reports for market information.

Although his customer contacts kept him abreast of problems in the field, Ellsworth felt that he should develop a more systematic approach to collecting and analyzing the information he received. He approached the accounting department about using its minicomputer to process the customer-complaint data. (The accounting department had the only computer in the distributorship.) He was told that this computer was already being fully utilized. In fact, the lack of computer capacity throughout the company had caused several other departments to employ computer service firms. Therefore, Ellsworth decided to use a service firm for his data processing requirements, too. Because Conrad had some computer expertise, she was selected to handle the details of the new information system and to work with the service firm.

Ellsworth approached Conrad and remarked, "I would like you to develop a computer program that will permit us to classify our customers' letters by the state and city of the customer, type of product, and type of complaint. In order to provide us with the most useful information, the types of complaints probably should be divided into four or five distinct categories."

"The procedure we'll use to classify the information in each letter will be fairly simple," Ellsworth explained. "When a letter is received, my secretary will prescreen it and classify its contents according to the categories previously identified. Then, the letter will come to me for review and action. Next, I'll pass it on to you for processing and entry into the computer system.

"Another part of your job, Kelli, will be to develop the proper output from the information. Before my monthly management meetings, I would like a summary report that shows the types of complaints that were received during the month. I would also like to have annually a cumulative record of all of the complaints that were mentioned in the letters we received during the year. These data should be displayed in the form of summary tables and charts."

Ellsworth continued with an afterthought. "Kelli, I have another project for you, too. Analyze the pros and cons of purchasing additional minicomputers versus the use of a computer service firm!"

a. List five types of customer complaints that you believe will be identified by Conrad and entered into the computer.

b. Prepare an example of a summary table that you think would be useful to Ellsworth. Include in your table the proper top and side captions and title. You do not need to include any data within the table.

c. Prepare an example of a line or bar chart that you believe would be useful to Ellsworth. Make the necessary assumptions and construct a chart that can be clearly understood with the proper captions and title.

d. Discuss the advantages and disadvantages of buying minicomputers versus using a computer service firm.

Grounds for a Beef

Four ounces always make a quarter of a pound. But they don't always make a quarter pounder.

That's what McDonald's Corp. told Gary Johnson, who owns a meat company with four gourmet shops in Stickney, Ill. Earlier this year, Mr. Johnson started promoting his frozen meat patties as "quarter pounders." McDonald's decided it had grounds for a beef.

The 30-billion burger behemoth informed Mr. Johnson that "Quarter Pounder" is a registered trademark that describes a specific McDonald's sandwich, and he can't use it. Wrote McDonald's attorney William Horne: "It appears to be an effort on your part to trade off on the tremendous amount of advertising dollars McDonald's has spent to commercialize and popularize the 'Quarter Pounder.'"

Language Owners?

The company doesn't object to "the use of the generic term quarter-pound, or ¼-pound," Mr. Horne told Mr. Johnson. But using "Quarter Pounder" is out of bounds.

Mr. Johnson says he wouldn't dream of abusing McDonald's trademark. "I sell crab legs, sirloin, gourmet items," he says. "Ground beef is an after-thought. I'm not trying to capitalize on what they do. But they act like they own the language."

At first, Mr. Johnson says he considered dropping the name for his frozen patties, which represent only about 5% of his $3 million-a-year business. But now, he says, "I'm torn whether to fight it."

Lawyer's Views

His lawyer, Richard Angelotti, believes Mr. Johnson shouldn't fight, although he also believes McDonald's is wrong. "The trademark is for a Quarter Pounder sandwich. It doesn't say anything about a piece of meat being sold separately," Mr. Angelotti contends. "But the costs involved in litigating it would be high. I'm giving Gary practical advice."

Contends the McDonald's lawyer, Mr. Horne: "We have the trademark, and nobody can use it."

Mr. Horne acknowledges that "Quarter Pounder" is a weak trademark because it is "descriptive instead of nondescriptive." But he maintains that similarities between Mr. Johnson's product and the McDonald's sandwich are too great.

"If he took the quarter pounder name and used it on a car," suggests Mr. Horne, "he would have a case."

SOURCE: Lawrence Rout, "McDonald's Sizzles at Patty Label, Contending Trademark Is at Stake," *The Wall Street Journal*, October 31, 1980, p. 31. Reprinted by permission of *The Wall Street Journal*, © Dow Jones & Company, Inc. (1980). All Rights Reserved.

23

Laws and Ethics for Business

Objectives:

- Distinguish between civil law, common law, and statutory law.
- Explain the two basic court systems in the United States.
- Explain the four essential elements of a contract.
- Explain the principal-agent relationship.
- Distinguish between insolvency and bankruptcy.
- Identify the four basic steps in the bankruptcy process.
- Explain the importance of copyrights.
- Distinguish between ethics and morals.
- Discuss the "gray area" in ethical business behavior.
- Define ethical codes and audit committees.

Business is involved in just about every aspect of our lives. As a society we have put our trust in business firms to support, not weaken, our quality of life. Because business permeates our lives, we expect responsible behavior from a business, much as we would from a family member. At the minimum this expectation includes law-abiding behavior. In addition, however, the behavior should reflect the expectations and ethical norms of society—the greater "family" in which business firms exist.

Consider the following items that appeared in one day's edition of a Denver newspaper:

1. Representatives of two Japanese electronic firms allegedly attempted to purchase trade secrets from FBI agents posing as employees of a well-known firm.
2. A dispute between Lowry Air Force Base and a building firm in Colorado will go to a federal grand jury, with charges and counter-charges of fraud, shoddy work, and government harassment.
3. A real estate tycoon who fled Denver was arrested in Florida to face trial on charges of criminal conspiracy and securities fraud.
4. A party complained to "Action Line" about overbooking of reservations on a popular train.

These news items show that our laws cut across firms of various sizes, types, and geographical coverage. The framework of laws, often called "the Law," consists of constitutions, statutes, court decisions, rulings, and regulations that are administered by officials and enforced by various types of courts.

But what about the fourth news item on the overbooking of reservations? Is it a matter of law? If it were, then why did the concerned party resort to an "Action Line" newspaper column? Obviously it is a matter of business integrity and ethics that falls outside the formal scope of the law. The complaint deals with how well a business lives up to the expectations, moral principles, or values of those it touches. Eventually the railway company realized that its integrity was being challenged. So, it returned part of the fare paid by the party who was inconvenienced. Ordinarily the intent of laws is quite clear. But, as we shall see, there is far less agreement as to what is ethically right or wrong and what represents business integrity and sound professional ethics in specific situations.

DISTINCTIONS BETWEEN TORTS AND CRIMES

Before we move on, we should recognize that there is another way of looking at the news items previously mentioned. Do they involve torts or crimes? A **tort** is a private wrong concerned primarily with moral wrongs that one person may do to cause damage or loss to another. Examples of torts are deceit, libelous statements, and infringement on copyrights or trademarks. A **crime** is a public wrong in that it violates a law that has been passed. Forgery, extortion, and bribery are examples of crimes.

Another important distinction between crimes and torts is that, when a crime has been committed, the State will bring action to enforce the law that has been violated. Torts, on the other hand, require the injured party to bring legal action against the offender. Depending on the laws of a state, a crime can be a tort and some torts can be crimes. So, in some instances one action may follow the other if the wrong or injury is both a crime and a tort.

Without a doubt, today's managers must maintain an active and continuing concern for our system of laws that specify what behavior is right and what is wrong. Managers also must be aware of the ethical integrity being demanded increasingly by the public. Thus, the balance of this chapter will cover some basic aspects of our legal and court systems, the nature and scope of business law, the meaning of ethics, the challenge business faces in deciding what is ethical behavior, and the guidance managers receive from codes of ethics and audit committees.

OUR LEGAL AND COURT SYSTEMS

Most people have rather vague ideas about our legal and court systems. Much of what we pick up about legal matters probably comes from television programs, and the procedures these programs depict may be quite accurate. The programs also give us some insights into the bargaining that goes on behind the scenes. But we can better understand personal and business legal matters if we know some basics about the legal and court systems that operate in this country.

Bases of Laws

We have heard or read about such terms as civil law, common law, and statutory law. There are differences in the scopes of these types of laws. Common law and civil law are legal systems (bodies of laws that may be written or unwritten) that operate on a worldwide basis. Statutory law is written law that is effective only within the jurisdiction of the government under which it was enacted.

Civil Law and Common Law

Strictly speaking, **civil law** is concerned with the duties that exist between individuals. Torts, which were defined earlier, are violations of civil law. Civil law is based on formal codes comprised of laws, rules, and regulations. The Ten Commandments can be called civil law, as can ancient Roman law which was codified. The Code Napoleon, compiled in France in 1804, is also civil law. The legal systems of many European and Latin American countries are based largely on these earlier forms of civil law. In the United States the state of Louisiana, reflecting its French heritage, still uses some of these earlier civil laws.

Common law began in England centuries ago, and the United States inherited this legal system from England. A basic premise of **common law** is that each court decision becomes a precedent for future cases of a similar nature. This premise is known as the doctrine of *stare decisis,* a Latin phrase meaning "to stand by decided matters." Common law often is called unwritten law, judge-made law, or case law because it reflects legal opinions and decisions over the years. In fact, common law arises from traditions and customs and often becomes the basis for written law in the form of further legislative action.

Statutory Law

In contrast to common law, **statutory law** is written law in the form of acts passed by legislators at different levels of government. The U.S. Congress and various state legislatures enact statutory laws, while cities and counties pass ordinances. Any statutory law or ordinance which violates the Constitution of the United States—the supreme law of our land—will not be enforced by courts. In the United States, business law reflects civil, common, and statutory law.

Our Court Systems

As Figure 23-1 shows, two court systems exist in the United States: the federal court system and the state court system. If a case involves an alleged violation of a federal law or interstate commerce, it is heard in a federal court. Most legal disputes, however, are of such a nature that they are tried in state courts.

In both systems the court that first tries a case is known as a **court of original jurisdiction.** In the federal system the U.S. district courts and special courts, as well as the United States Supreme Court in a few instances, are courts of original jurisdiction. In the state systems the lower courts, and occasionally the state supreme court, are courts of original jurisdiction.

After a case has been decided by a lower court, the loser may appeal the decision to a higher court if it can be alleged that a principle of law has been violated. A court that has authority to review decisions reached in a lower court is known as an **appellate court.** If an appellate court believes that the case was improperly tried in the first place, it may dismiss the previous decision or refer it to the original court for a retrial. The United States Supreme Court is the highest appellate court for federal matters, and the supreme court of a state is the highest court for disputes with no federal implications.

Figure 23-1   Our Federal and State Court Systems

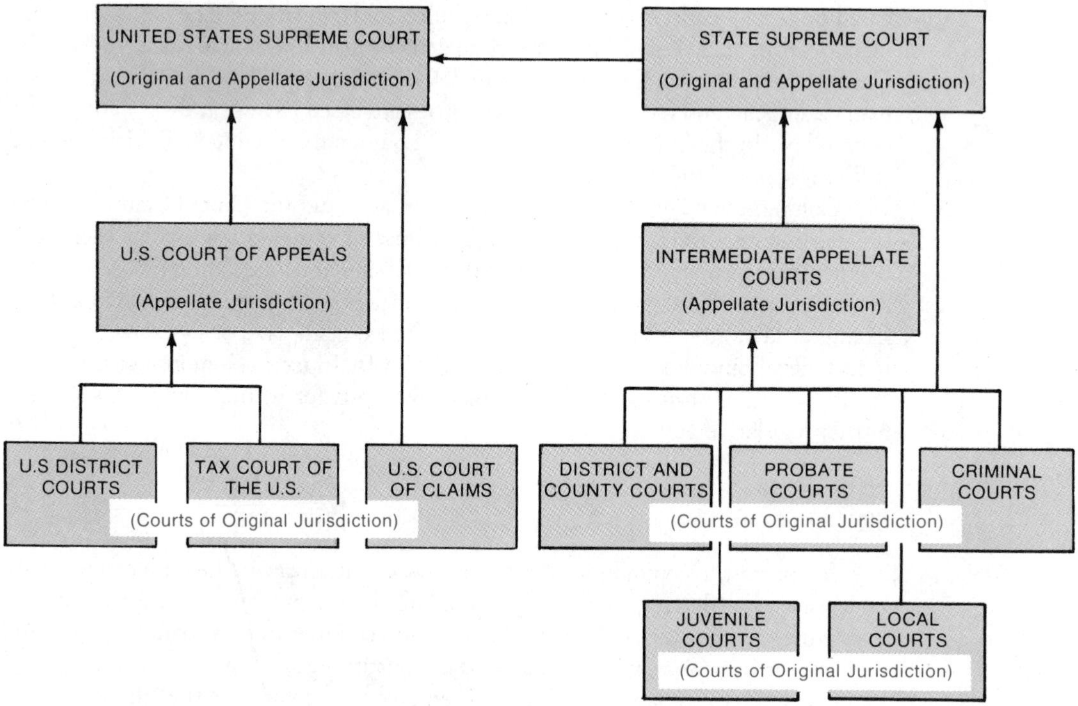

NATURE AND SCOPE OF BUSINESS LAW _____

Business law is concerned with any segment of the legal system that provides for a smooth and orderly flow of business transactions and the settlement of any disputes that may arise over these transactions. Any business, large or small, faces the possibility of being on the initiating or receiving end of a lawsuit or some other legal action. Most of these matters are handled through lawyers, and every business operator should have a professional working relationship with a competent lawyer. If the business operator has a general knowledge of some key concepts and issues in business law, she or he will be able to deal even more effectively with lawyers and legal processes. Some useful topics to be aware of, among many, include: the Uniform Commercial Code, the law of contracts, the law of agency, insolvency and bankruptcy, and copyrights.

Uniform Commercial Code

Most laws concerning business transactions in the United States are enacted by state legislatures. As these laws governing business were not always uniform in the past, businesses were forced to interpret the laws from state to state. This confusion led to the adoption of the Uniform Commercial Code (UCC) in 1957, a project of the National Conference of Commissioners on Uniform State Laws and the American Law Institute. The purpose of the UCC was to simplify, clarify, and reform the various laws concerning commercial transactions and to make them uniform among the various jurisdictions at the state level. The UCC has been adopted by all 50 states, the District of Columbia, and the Virgin Islands; however, the state of Louisiana adopted only certain articles of the UCC.[1]

Law of Contracts

Contracts are basic to business operations because practically every business transaction involves agreements between people. A **contract** is a voluntary agreement between two or more parties to do or not to do something. The four essential elements of a valid, enforceable contract are: mutual agreement on an offer and an acceptance, legally competent parties, consideration, and lawful acts enforceable in court. Generally a contract is unenforceable or becomes void when any of these essential elements is disregarded. Figure 23-2 summarizes the explanation for each of these essential elements.

While we cannot cover everything about the law of contracts in a few pages, we can at least note two important aspects of it: the statute of frauds, and express and implied contracts.

---

1. Kenneth W. Clarkson, Roger LeRoy Miller, and Bonnie Blaire, *West's Business Law: Text & Cases* (St. Paul, MN: West Publishing Co., 1980), p. 6.

Figure 23-2   Essential Elements of a Contract

ELEMENT	EXPLANATION
Mutual Agreement (offer and acceptance)	• The offer must be communicated in specific terms.
	• The offer and the acceptance must conform to specific terms, *not* counteroffers.
	• The offer and the acceptance can be oral or written except in certain cases that involve the Statute of Frauds.
	• The acceptance must be given within a reasonable time.
	• The agreement must be made in good faith and of one's own free will.
Legally Competent Parties	• The contracting parties must be of legal age, depending on state law.
	• Intoxicated persons, mentally retarded persons, and aliens are generally considered to be incompetent to enter into contracts.
Consideration	• One party promises to pay something of value (usually money) or to do something for the other party in return for something provided by the other party. Promises made, without consideration, are not legally enforceable as contracts.
Lawful Acts (enforceable in court)	• The subject of the contract must be lawful according to state law and public policy.

Statute of Frauds

The Uniform Commercial Code contains a provision known as the **Statute of Frauds**, which states that certain types of sales contracts must be in written form. These include sales of real estate, of personal property in excess of a certain value (usually $500), as well as agreements that cannot be performed within one year. The unusual name for this rule of law dates back to England when persons who wished to prove the validity of an oral contract would induce friends and relatives to give false testimony in court.

Express and Implied Contracts

Both oral and written contracts may be either express or implied. In an express contract the terms are agreed upon, such as a contract to buy 100 units at $2.00 each to be delivered within ten days and payment to be made at the end of the month. An implied contract is based on the conduct of the parties. For example, when a person telephones a broker to buy 100 shares of a named stock at the market price, there is an implied contract that is just as enforceable as an express contract.

Law of Agency

The word agency often is used for a type of franchise relationship such as an automobile agency or insurance agency. However, in its legal use, **agency** involves the delegation of authority to another person to act on one's behalf. The person who delegates the authority is the **principal.** An **agent** is the person who is authorized to represent the principal in dealings with third parties. An agent may be called such terms as a broker, attorney, or representative. Regardless of the term used, there are some basic obligations between the principal and the agent, and between the principal and third parties.

Obligations of Principal to Agent

The principal must pay the agent for services and expenses according to their contract. Also, if the agent is sued while legitimately representing the principal, then the principal must reimburse the agent for these expenses.

Obligations of Agent to Principal

Agents are obligated to follow instructions and to be loyal to the principal. Thus, agents should not use the agent relationship to enhance their own benefit. Agents are also expected to use a reasonable level of intelligence and care in the acts they perform for the principal. If agents exceed their authority, they may become personally liable to their principals.

Obligations of Principals to Third Parties

Principals are liable for all lawful acts and agreements that their agents make with third parties. For example, a bank officer (agent) might make a $50,000 loan to a businessperson (third party) even though this loan exceeded the agent's authority as a loan officer. If the businessperson was unaware of any loan restrictions, the bank (principal) would be expected to honor the commitment made by its loan officer.

Business Failures

Every year some businesses, including new and well-established ones, meet with financial reverses. The fault may lie with management or may be caused by outside factors it cannot control. Regardless of the reasons, continued losses will usually weaken the financial condition of a firm to a point where it cannot pay its debts and some action must be taken. If this condition does not improve, the firm may have to file for bankruptcy and thus be liquidated.

Financial face-offs are a serious matter to those caught in them. Although business failures are regarded as a continuing risk in our competitive enterprise system, in the past the condition of bankruptcy seemed to cast a stigma on a failed firm. By 1979, however, this condition was eased somewhat, especially for individual debtors. After 40 years without major change, our national bankruptcy laws have undergone a broad revision that makes it easier for debtors to "throw in the towel." The changes were brought about by the Bankruptcy Reform Act of 1978. By April 1, 1984, these changes were fully operational.

Insolvency

Under the Bankruptcy Reform Act of 1978, **insolvency** is defined as the insufficiency of fairly valued assets to pay debts. For example, a manufacturing firm may have assets valued at more than its liabilities. But if most of its capital is tied up in special machinery, it may not have the funds to pay its debts as they mature. If the firm is found to be legally insolvent, it can either be salvaged or liquidated (the firm's assets are sold and the proceeds distributed to its creditors according to law).

A business can be salvaged if the possibility of regaining its profitability can be assumed. It can be salvaged in two ways: through voluntary creditor agreements or through reorganization under Chapter XI of the Reform Act. In **voluntary creditor agreements** the creditors usually elect a representative who assumes active management of the business for a long enough period of time to guarantee that the agreement will be followed. As soon as the business is operating smoothly and successfully, the creditors' representative withdraws and allows the original managers to operate without supervision. If the creditors cannot agree on a voluntary solution or if there seems to be no hope of successful operation of the business, the only alternative is to turn to a court for help. The insolvent firm may take this step or the creditors may force the issue. **Reorganization** usually involves the scaling down of amounts owed, of interest rates on payments to be made, and of dividends paid to common stockholders.

Bankruptcy

An unsuccessful firm or individual may go from insolvency to **bankruptcy** by a written admission that liabilities owed exceed the value of assets. By filing for bankruptcy, a business or individual hopes to liquidate assets to help pay off creditors and to be released from remaining debts. In this way the bankrupt party can start a new business or a new job with a clear financial slate. Bankruptcy proceedings are handled by bankruptcy courts. However, the specific conditions to be satisfied vary between businesses and individuals. The basic steps in bankruptcy proceedings for businesses are shown in Figure 23-3.

Bankruptcy may be voluntary or involuntary. Voluntary bankruptcy is initiated by the debtor, while involuntary bankruptcy is petitioned by creditors.

Voluntary Bankruptcy Under the Reform Act. A voluntary petition for bankruptcy can be filed by any person or business, with the exception of the following:

Figure 23-3   Basic Steps in Bankruptcy Proceedings

COURT APPOINTS A RECEIVER
The receiver serves as temporary custodian of the firm's assets until they can be turned over to a trustee.

COURT APPOINTS A REFEREE IN BANKRUPTCY
The referee serves as the court's representative in the subsequent proceedings.

REFEREE CALLS A MEETING OF CREDITORS
TO ELECT A TRUSTEE IN BANKRUPTCY
The trustee liquidates the firm's assets, pays all secured claims, and distributes any remaining balance to general creditors according to a pecking order specified by the law.

BANKRUPT FIRM IS LEGALLY DISCHARGED
FROM ITS OBLIGATIONS
The firm is free to begin a fresh start without the weight of past failures.

1. Banking corporations.
2. Building and loan associations.
3. Insurance corporations.
4. Municipal corporations.
5. Railroad corporations.

These five types of businesses may seek relief under special provisions relating to liquidation and reorganization.

Many of the points that apply to a business filing a voluntary petition for bankruptcy apply also to individuals. But there are some other aspects of personal bankruptcy that we should note. The Reform Act provides two ways for filing personal bankruptcy. One way is to file under Chapter VII of the Act, which writes off all debt except for alimony, child support, taxes, and debts incurred by fraud or embezzlement. Federal student loans, except in hardship cases, cannot be excused until five years after they become first due. The other way is to file under Chapter XIII of the Act, which allows employed people with steady incomes to pay off at least a portion of their debts over a 36-month period while retaining their property. Under both methods the debtor is allowed to keep many of her or his assets, which include the following:

1. Up to $7,500 of equity in the debtor's house, or $15,000 if both spouses are filing.
2. Up to $1,200 of equity in an automobile.

3. Up to a limit of $200 per category of clothes and household goods.
4. Up to $500 worth of jewelry.

Many people feel that the big flaw in the Reform Act is its failure to require proof of financial distress on the debtor's part. In Chapter XIII of the Act, debtors must show only that they have regular income and can finance a reasonable payback plan. Chapter VII of the Act ignores a debtor's income. The upshot is that a debtor can file for bankruptcy, eliminate most outstanding debts, and keep much of what he or she owns. However, this varies by state. A state that thinks federal exemptions from property to satisfy claims of creditors are too generous can bar them under the state's own bankruptcy law. Florida and Virginia have passed such stringent laws. On the other hand, California's exemptions are more liberal than the federal exemptions.

Involuntary Bankruptcy Under the Reform Act. The conditions to be met in filing a petition of involuntary bankruptcy under the Reform Act are:

1. Debts must amount to at least $5,000.
2. If there are 12 or more creditors, at least 3 who have unsecured claims that total $5,000 or more can file the bankruptcy petition. If there are less than 12 creditors, only 1 need file if the unsecured claim is at least $5,000.
3. The petition need only allege that one of three possible situations exists: (a) that the debtor is generally not paying his or her debts as they become due, (b) that a custodian was appointed within 120 days preceding the date of the petition to take charge of less than substantially all of the debtor's property, or (c) that a custodian took possession of less than substantially all of the debtor's property within the 120 days.[2]

Farmers who expect to derive 80 percent of their income from farm work and certain nonbusiness corporations, however, are exempt from involuntary bankruptcy.[3]

Law on Copyrights

Copyrights are exclusive rights belonging to owners of "original works of authorship fixed in any tangible medium of expression."[4] The original works may consist of words, music, sound recordings, and so on. As in the area of bankruptcy, much has changed in copyright law that may be of great importance to business firms. The Copyright Act of 1976, which took effect on January 1, 1978, represents the first overhaul of our nation's basic copyright law since 1909. The new law gives longer protection to owners of copyrighted material against its unauthorized use. It also attempts to come to grips with the innovations in communications technology as they relate to the doctrine of fair use.

---

2. Raymond P. Neveu, *Fundamentals of Managerial Finance* (Cincinnati: South-Western Publishing Co., 1981), p. 521.
3. Clarkson, Miller, and Blaire, *op. cit.,* pp. 527-528.
4. *The New Copyright Law,* published by Scott, Foresman and Company, 1978.

Extended Copyright Protection

The period of copyright protection from works created and copyrighted after January 1, 1978, now runs for the author's lifetime plus 50 years. For works created and copyrighted before January 1, 1978, the copyright renewal term has been extended from 28 to 47 years. These changes bring United States law into conformity with international copyright provisions.

Public broadcasters, cable television systems, and juke boxes all have been heavy users of copyrighted material without paying royalties for it. Now they are required to pay into a pool administered by the Copyright Royalty Tribunal established by Congress.

The new law also deals with the use of photocopying. It permits "random" photocopying of copyrighted material, but bars "systematic" reproduction that might substitute for magazine subscriptions or book purchases.

Technological Developments and the Fair Use Doctrine

A key weakness of previous revisions of the copyright law was the failure to anticipate new technological developments such as computer systems, video cassette recorders, integrated circuits, and so on. As we saw in Chapter 22, the input devices in a computer system consist of information translated onto computer cards, tapes, or disks. Yet copyright owners are supposed to be protected against unauthorized translation of their works. Furthermore, with the translated material in storage, a collection of copyrighted works may well be held in the computer system.

The **doctrine of fair use**, as it has evolved in the courts, refers to the extent to which a copyrighted work may be used without the permission of the copyright owner. However, the new copyright law continues to use very general language so that the rules of fair use remain quite vague.[5] How, for example, should the fair use doctrine apply to the practice of **reverse engineering**, also called *second-sourcing* in the United States? In this process a producer of microprocessor chips can strip down a competitor's chip and analyze it to see how it works and what other functions it might be able to perform. Some producers build sales in new markets by copying, at least functionally, the best-selling integrated circuit in the market and then underselling the company that originally developed the chip.

In 1979, the American Electronics Association launched a project to extend federal copyright protection to semiconductor circuits. However, the project was scrubbed as so many member companies feel they have too much to lose from a restrictive chip-protection law. Reverse engineering is a universal practice that producers hesitate to give up. An unlikely solution is a copyright law that would ban flat out any copying without curtailing reverse engineering. But some large companies feel that copyright protection is essential to maintain profit margins, to fund R&D and capital investment, and to keep their creative employees.

In an effort to deal with all these issues, Congress in 1974 established a 13-member National Commission on New Technological Uses of Copyrighted Works. This com-

---

5. *Ibid.*, p. 4.

mission is supposed to make recommendations on changes in federal copyright law with respect to automatic systems capable of storing, processing, retrieving, and transferring information. The commission will be involved in a sticky area for a long time, and it has its work cut out for it.

BUSINESS ETHICS

To pinpoint what constitutes ethical business conduct is not an easy task. In doing this, some people equate ethical behavior with legal behavior—that is, if an action is legal, it must be acceptable. Most people, including managers, do recognize that legal limits on business must be obeyed. However, they see these legal limits as a bare-bones starting point for business behavior and managerial action.

Actually, ethical business behavior reflects the law plus our societal ethics, morals, and values as pictured in Figure 23-4. In turn, the formulation of law follows a society's ethical attitudes and results in a gradual merging of the two. Thus, a give-and-take relationship exists between what is "legal" and what is "ethical."

Figure 23-4   Elements of Ethical Business Behavior

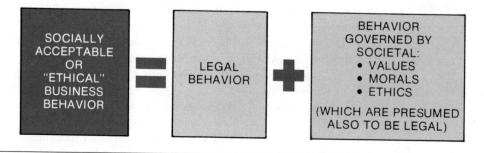

Ethics, Morals, and Values

Ethics is a branch of philosophy that deals with the "rightness" or morality of human conduct. The word ethics also relates to the object of human conduct in certain areas, such as medical ethics, business ethics, professional ethics, etc. Here we are interested mainly in ethics as the object of human conduct in business matters. In this sense we define **ethics** as the established rules of behavior that people accept as "good" or "bad."

Notice the quotation marks around the words *good* and *bad.* They are there to emphasize that the determination of good and bad is an ever-changing issue. One person puts it this way:

> Few words suffer semantic butchery as does the word "ethical." Some regard themselves ethical if their legal staff can keep them safely within the law. Others feel

ethical if they have a generally good "feeling" towards others—at least on the Sabbath. Still others construe themselves as ethical, even within the turmoil of hard, ambiguous "business" situations, if they execute exactly the boss's (or a client's) orders (although they might concede that the boss is unethical in some of those orders).[6]

Ultimately the decisions that managers make on questions involving ethics are individual decisions, as are the consequences. These decisions reflect many factors, including individual and societal morals and values.

Ethics *v.* Morals

Ethics and morals (or morality) often are used synonymously. This may be because the Greek word *ethos* from which "ethics" is derived and the Latin word *mores* from which"morals" is derived both mean habits or customs. However, **morals** differ from ethics in that morality contains an inevitable normative element. That is, morals refer to not merely what is done, but also what people ought to do and believe. This normative element, or "oughtness," conflicts with the changing aspects of business ethics.

Ethics and Values

As we noted in Chapter 2, values are cultural standards of behavior that act as guides to businesspersons in setting and pursuing goals. Thus, businesspersons use values in making ethical judgments whether they realize it or not. More and more, business managers are being challenged to increase their sensitivity to ethical problems. They are pressured to evaluate critically their value priorities to see how these fit with organizational and societal realities and expectations.

The Gray Area: Business Ethics

Bribing purchasing agents to buy your product is illegal, and cheating on a tax return can send a person to jail. But what about inadvertently leaking inside information about a company? Or putting pressure on a government official? When is a subordinate being ambitious and aggressive, and when is this person outright dishonest?

The term **ethical standards** is used to describe conformity to widely accepted modes of conduct. **Business ethics**, however, concerns both the ends and the means of business decision making. While the public wants stricter standards from government officials in this post-Watergate age, who can determine what is ethical and what is not? A major problem for business executives is that ethical standards often are situational. That is, what society considers good or right changes over time. For example, what looks ethical at first glance may not look that way in hindsight. Or what was acceptable yesterday may be out of bounds today. To illustrate, at one time child labor, 60-hour workweeks, polluted rivers, and dangerous conditions in factories were regarded as acceptable.

---

6. James Owens, "Business Ethics: Age-Old Ideal, Now Real," *Business Horizons* (February, 1978), p. 27.

Gray areas come up every day. Businesspersons may find themselves in situations where the law is not clear, the ground rules are not hard and fast, and the line between right and wrong is almost imperceptible. And this line is finer for the executive than for most other employees because of the pressures under which the executive works. Society rewards managers for their excellent performance but may penalize them harshly if they are found to be unethical in achieving that level of performance.

Basically there can be no ethical behavior — in or outside of business — without the individual's intent to do right. Besides relying on individual integrity, there are two other steps many companies are taking to throw some light on ethical gray areas and to encourage ethical decisions and actions on a uniform basis. These steps are: the development of codes of ethics and the use of audit committees.

Codes of Ethics

The search by corporate executives and boards of directors for some means of ensuring desirable business actions by employees has led to the development of corporate codes of ethics. Such codes are labeled as codes of conduct, ethical practices statement, guidelines for employee conduct, policy statement on corporate ethics, and the like. Regardless of the label used, the central instrument for making ethics operational and real in an organization is a *written* code of ethics. **Ethical codes** have been defined as "specific statements of what is regarded as right or wrong within a particular situation in the here and now."[7] In addition, an ethical code is specific, is both positive and negative in its ethical content, is based on general ethical standards, and is enforceable by appropriate sanctions.[8]

A code of ethics is not a luxury. Instead, it is a practical necessity. It provides clear-cut criteria for day-to-day actions and shows that an organization takes ethical behavior seriously.

Contents of Ethical Codes. Many corporations are clarifying their positions on employee conduct as part of their statements on ethics and behavior. The points covered in their positions vary from company to company. However, a recent analysis of corporate practice, prepared for the California Roundtable by Robert Chatov, shows that there is solid agreement on which areas of employee misconduct are of greatest concern to U.S. corporations. Chatov received usable material from 281 firms (a 26.3 percent response rate) and analyzed the subjects covered in their corporate ethics statements. Figure 23-5 and Figure 23-6 show the results of Chatov's analysis.[9]

Figure 23-5 shows 12 broad ethical dimensions under Part A. The first dimension concerns an employee's relation to the firm. The next group of 11 dimensions identify the firm's relation to its different constituencies. Under Part B of Figure 23-5 are listed 15 of the 16 behavioral variables contained in the first dimension (honesty and integrity are implied in all the variables). Figure 23-6 ties the ethical dimensions and behavioral variables together by showing the 14 most frequently prohibited employee

---

7. *Ibid.,* p. 30.
8. *Ibid.*
9. Robert Chatov, "What Corporate Ethics Statements Say," *California Management Review* (Summer, 1980), pp. 20–29.

Figure 23-5   Ethical Dimensions and Behavioral Variables of Corporate Concern

	PART A		PART B
	Ethical Dimensions	Variables Contained	Behavioral Variables
Employee's Relation to Firm		16 ⟶	Bribery
			Commercial espionage
Firm's Relation to:			Conflict of interest
	Employees	18	Executive piracy
	Shareholders	11	Expenses
	Dealers	9	Extortion, gifts, and kickbacks
	Suppliers	8	Insider information
	Unions	10	Moonlighting
	Local Community	8	Obligations of former employees
	Competitors	10	Payola
	Customers	16	Privacy
	Environment	7	Secrecy
	Government	20	Theft, company funds
	Miscellaneous Concerns	23	Loans and borrowing
			Honesty and integrity
Total Variables		156	

SOURCE: Robert Chatov, "What Corporate Ethics Statements Say," *California Management Review* (Summer, 1980), pp. 21-22. Reproduced with permission.

behaviors, the ethical dimension in which each variable occurs, and the typical treatment of these behaviors.

Ethical Codes and Managerial Behavior. In dealing with moral and ethical issues, a code of ethics helps a firm move from the abstract and general to the development of definitive answers for specific questions. Business must make an effort to redesign its own behavior or risk having heavy-handed standards imposed on it by government or other groups. But words can go only so far in developing a healthy ethical example within a corporation. Good conduct is best achieved through the force of example set from the top-down, rather than through the threat of punishment.

Use of Audit Committees

Corporate audit committees have been in existence prior to World War II. However, their growth in number and importance in the last 15 years makes them a key tool of corporate self-regulation. An **audit committee** is a group of outside directors—mostly in publicly held corporations—that monitors a management's recordkeeping practices and internal accounting control procedures. The audit committee discusses these matters with the firm's management, the internal auditors, the external accounting auditors, and the firm's legal counsel.

Figure 23-6 Fourteen Most Frequently Prohibited Employee Behaviors

Prohibited Behavior Variable	Ethical Dimension	Percent Firms Mentioning Variables Within Ethical Dimension	Typical Treatment in Ethics Statements
1. Extortion, gifts, kickbacks	Employee's relation to firm	67%	
	Firm's relation to suppliers	18	
a) Extortion			Explicitly prohibited
b) Gifts			Generally prohibited with minor exceptions
c) Kickbacks			Explicitly prohibited
2. Conflict of interest	Employee's relations to firm	65	Generally prohibited with minor exceptions
3. Illegal political payments	Firm's relation to government	59	Explicitly prohibited
4. Violation of laws in general	Firm's relation to government	57	Explicitly prohibited
5. Use of insider information	Employee's relation to firm	43	Explicitly prohibited
	Firm's relation to shareholders	8	
6. Bribery	Firm's relation to government	37	Explicitly prohibited
	Employee's relation to firm	34	
7. Falsification of corporate accounts	Firm's relation to shareholders (both variables)	28	Explicitly prohibited
Reporting full disclosure		34	
8. Violation of antitrust laws	Firm's relation to government	25	Explicitly prohibited
9. Moonlighting	Employee's relation to firm	25	Judgmental — usually tolerated if no conflict of interest
10. Legal payments abroad	Miscellaneous concerns	23	Some judgment
11. Violation of secrecy agreement	Employee's relation to firm	22	Explicitly prohibited
12. Ignorance of work-related laws	Firm's relation to government	22	Prohibited—employees to seek legal advice if in doubt
13. Fraud, deception	Firm's relation to customers	11	Explicitly prohibited
14. To justify means by goals	Miscellaneous concerns	10	Explicitly prohibited

SOURCE: Robert Chatov, "What Corporate Ethics Statements Say," *California Management Review* (Summer, 1980), p. 22. Reproduced with permission.

One of the main pressures for the use of audit committees came from the Foreign Corrupt Practices Act of 1977. The Act was an outcome of the investigations conducted during the Watergate era. In 1975 the Securities and Exchange Commission gathered proof of $300 million in illegal payments and bribes made by American corporations to high foreign officials to clinch business deals. While a few corporations made the headlines, they were not alone. About 450 corporations were involved!

The Foreign Corrupt Practices Act of 1977 provides a two-pronged attack on bribery. It contains antibribery provisions and establishes accounting rules that require corporations to keep more detailed records. The Act provides for prison sentences of up to five years for violators, and fines of up to $1 million for their companies. In addition, the Act places the SEC in an important position to monitor the conduct of corporate managements and to specify a corporation's disclosure responsibilities.

Clearly, the influence of the SEC brought about the growth of audit committees. Yet these committees have proved their usefulness far beyond that intended by the Foreign Corrupt Practices Act and the SEC. As one author comments about audit committees:

1. They are not required for auditor independence, but they help.
2. They are not essential for the performance of an audit, but they facilitate desirable communication with the board.
3. Members of the board do not need them to carry out their responsibilities, but they have found the committees to be quite useful in this respect.
4. Managements can function without audit committees, but many have found the committees to be a helpful source of guidance.
5. For the most confident managers, the audit committee idea seems to have forestalled more government intervention, at least for the time being.[10]

Thus, corporate audit committees exist for a number of reasons and can be an important link between the law and ethical practices in business.

SUMMARY   Business is involved in just about every aspect of our lives. Law and ethics are involved, to some degree, in just about every aspect of business. Even though most businesspersons deal with lawyers on legal matters, a basic knowledge of our legal and court systems and of some laws for business will make them better legal clients and managers.

Three main bases of laws are civil law, common law, and statutory law. Civil law, which is concerned with the duties that exist between individuals, is based on ancient codes of laws, rules, and regulations. Common law arises from legal opinions and decisions, as well as from customs and traditions. Statutory law is written law in the form of acts passed by federal, state, and local legislators.

We have two court systems in the United States: the federal court system and the state court system. Most business disputes will be tried in state courts unless they involve a violation of federal law or interstate commerce.

Five topics of business law that businesspersons should recognize are the: Uniform Commercial Code, law of contracts, law of agency, business failures involving insolvency and bankruptcy, and copyrights. Recent important legislation in these areas includes the Federal Bankruptcy Reform Act of 1978 and the Copyright Act of 1976.

To most people, ethical business conduct goes beyond legal conduct. Ethical behavior reflects law plus societal ethics, morals, and values. Legal behavior is a starting point for business behavior and managerial action. Ethical standards are not always clear as to what is right or wrong, good or bad. They are situational and tend to change over time. Two ways for businesses to clarify what they feel is ethical business behavior is to develop written codes of ethics and to use audit committees.

---

10. Frederick L. Neumann, "Corporate Audit Committees and the Foreign Corrupt Practices Act," *Business Horizons* (June, 1980), p. 63.

1. Does the issue in the article come under civil law, common law, or statutory law?
2. If McDonald's should litigate, which court system would it use?
3. If McDonald's should litigate, would the action be a crime or a tort?
4. Are the legal and ethical standards that govern business behavior clear in this matter?
5. How does the "intent" of both parties bear on their ethical business conduct?

BUSINESS TERMS

tort	574	insolvency	580
crime	574	voluntary creditor agreements	580
civil law	575	reorganization	580
common law	575	bankruptcy	580
statutory law	575	copyrights	582
court of original jurisdiction	576	doctrine of fair use	583
appellate court	576	reverse engineering	583
business law	577	ethics	584
contract	577	morals	585
Statute of Frauds	578	ethical standards	585
agency	579	business ethics	585
principal	579	ethical codes	586
agent	579	audit committee	587

QUESTIONS FOR DISCUSSION AND ANALYSIS

1. In the four news items cited on page 574, which are crimes and which are torts?
2. Would an owner or manager of a business be wiser to refer all legal matters to a lawyer than to rely on a personal knowledge of business law? Explain.
3. How is common law sometimes related to statutory law?
4. Would most business lawsuits be tried in state or federal courts?
5. Would a voluntary agreement by adults to deliver a stolen car to another party for an agreed price be a valid contract? Explain.
6. Is a voluntary creditor agreement, in effect, a vote of confidence in the abilities of the existing management of the firm?
7. In the first step of the bankruptcy process, the court appoints a receiver. Why, would you guess, is this such an important step?
8. Is there any difference between reverse engineering (or second-sourcing) and plain copying? Explain.
9. What is the difference, if any, between ethics and morals?
10. For most corporations, developing a code of ethics is an expensive, time-consuming, and unnecessary luxury. Do you agree? Explain.

PROJECTS, PROBLEMS, AND SHORT CASES

1. Interview the owner/managers of two businesses in your area—one in retail and one in service or manufacturing. Discuss the following and give a short class presentation of your findings:

   a. The legal issue that they deal with the most.
   b. For what purposes or problems do they consult a lawyer.

2. For the past three years, Trish Ochoa operated "Big Mama Shakeup," an ice cream and dessert shop. It has never been more than marginally profitable, but Trish felt she could survive the tough start-up years. But now she has run out of money, and filing

for bankruptcy seems the only solution to her financial problems. The trustee elected by her creditors found that Ochoa's accounting records showed the following:

Assets		Liabilities	
Cash	$ 140	Wages payable	$ 700
Inventories	1,890	Taxes payable	700
Equipment	6,400	Accounts payable	9,200
Land and building (net)	65,000	Mortgage payable	70,000
	$73,430		$80,600

The trustee sold the inventories for $1,000, the equipment for $4,900, and the land and building for $65,000. The costs of liquidation, lawyer's fees, and court costs amounted to $3,800.

Compute the amount available to general creditors. How much did they receive on a cents-on-the-dollar basis? (Note: Preferred creditors are paid before general creditors. Payments made to preferred creditors include the costs of liquidation, lawyer's fees, and court costs; the wages payable; and the taxes payable.)

3. Harry Trilby felt frustrated and discouraged. As chief sales engineer for a large construction company, he had worked for months to land a contract for a cement plant in the Middle East. "We thought we had it all wrapped up," he fumed. "We had a team of people over there for a month, the terms were agreed to, and we were told the contract was about to be signed. Then, at the last minute, a German firm got the contract." Trilby guessed that the German firm got the contract because it made a big payment to a high official. "Even worse," Trilby continued, "bribery by West German companies to obtain foreign contracts isn't illegal, and they can deduct the cost as a business expense for tax purposes! And we—we have the Federal Corrupt Practices Act and our company's audit committee to hold us back. I feel like I'm playing tournament tennis with a frying pan instead of a racket!"

Prepare a short report taking a position on whether or not American companies should be allowed to pay bribes (often called "sales commissions" or "fees for services rendered") to get foreign business.

A "Well-Regulated" Family

John Myrda lives in two worlds. He works in the crowded center of industrial Chicago, making machines to help keep the nation's commerce moving. He goes home to his wife and three young children in Mt. Prospect, where a well-manicured lawn, a clean home, and the sounds of family life surround him.

But both of Myrda's worlds are linked by the ever-present regulations set up and enforced by bureaucrats, mostly in Washington. For Myrda and his family, a typical day is filled with encounters with regulations.

The clock radio in the Myrdas' bedroom announces 5:15 a.m. with country music on WJEZ, a Chicago radio station licensed to operate at 104.3 FM by the Federal Communications Commission (FCC). Until earlier this year, WJEZ had to abide by FCC rules on the kind of programming mix it aired.

As Myrda, a 29-year-old Polish immigrant, dresses for work, his wife, Chris, packs his lunch. It includes some fruit, leftover soup, and a sandwich made with cold cuts. Like most processed meats, the cold cuts are made in plants heavily regulated by the Food Safety and Quality Service and the Food and Drug Administration (FDA) for cleanliness, the quality of the ingredients, and the processing.

Skipping breakfast at home, Myrda rushes to catch the 6:03 Chicago and North Western train to Chicago. Sometimes he walks eight blocks, but other times he takes his motorcycle, which must be registered with the Illinois secretary of state, just as the Myrdas' automobile is.

On the way to the train, he picks up a morning newspaper and a cup of coffee, which contains caffeine. The FDA warns that caffeine has caused birth defects in laboratory animals. (Mrs. Myrda drinks decaffeinated coffee.) Boarding the train, Myrda pays a fare set by the Regional Transportation Authority.

Twenty-five minutes later, the train deposits him in Chicago. After a five-minute walk, he arrives at Howe Corp., a small firm that makes refrigeration equipment for the food industry, one of the nation's more heavily regulated businesses. The parts for the machines Howe makes—and the finished products—are shipped to or from the North Elston Avenue plant in trucks regulated, though increasingly less so, by the Interstate Commerce Commission.

Back in Mt. Prospect, Chris Myrda, 25, is making the first of three meals she will prepare on this typical day. Feeding their three children—Jerry, 5, Monica, 2, and Annette, 2 months—is a big job and one she takes seriously. For Jerry and Monica, she fixes breakfast that includes eggs and milk. The price she pays for the milk is tied to the dairy price support the Agricultural Stabilization and Conservation Service gives to the dairy industry, which has a strong Washington lobby....

While she makes the beds and cleans the house, the two older children play with toys. But she is careful to make sure they have only safe toys—those without the little parts that come off and can be swallowed or without dangerous sharp edges or points or strings on which a child could choke. She can thank the Consumer Product Safety Commission (CPSC) for the fact that there are fewer hazardous toys these days because of regulations issued in recent years....

SOURCE: James Worsham, "A Day in 'Well-Regulated' Life of a Suburban Family," *Chicago Tribune*, July 12, 1981, p. 5. Copyrighted, 1981, *Chicago Tribune*. Used with permission.

Regulation of Business

Objectives:

- Explain the legality of governmental regulation of business.
- Distinguish between competitive businesses and approved monopolies.
- Identify and explain three federal laws, as amended, that were enacted for the purpose of promoting competition.
- Identify the federal regulations that are designed to protect consumer health and safety.
- Discuss the areas of business regulation common to most states.
- State three characteristics unique to public utility companies.
- State four principles of taxation.
- Itemize at least five tax sources, other than sales or income, used by states and local governments.
- Explain the differences between personal and corporate income taxes.
- Discuss the challenges facing the Social Security system.

Sometimes administering government regulations is like refereeing a feud between the Hatfields and the McCoys. You may not want to take sides, and whatever decision is rendered is going to make the other side grab their shotguns. The 1981 decision by the National Highway Traffic Safety Administration to rescind a regulation requiring automakers to install air bags or automatic seat belts brought out the smoking guns. Consumer advocates, such as Ralph Nader, complained loudly about the decision. The insurance industry, expecting passive restraints to reduce the cost of accident claims, joined in combat and brought a lawsuit to restore the regulation. On the other hand, the financially strapped automakers were all smiles. The decision saved them nearly $1 billion a year!

Most business executives feel that governmental regulations are strangling the free enterprise system. They point out that the regulatory agencies administering a law sometimes make rulings and interpretations which go far beyond the legislature's intent. The paperwork that is required by these agencies increases business costs and results in higher consumer prices. As shown in Figure 24-1, 1.338 billion hours (equal to 7,964,286 weeks) were spent in 1982 filling out federal forms. Advocates of additional regulation, however, feel that government has not done enough to curb the power of business corporations and to aid the consumer.

Figure 24-1   The Paperwork Burden

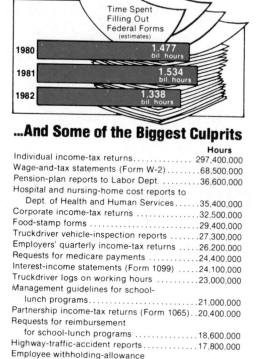

...And Some of the Biggest Culprits

	Hours
Individual income-tax returns	297,400,000
Wage-and-tax statements (Form W-2)	68,500,000
Pension-plan reports to Labor Dept.	36,600,000
Hospital and nursing-home cost reports to Dept. of Health and Human Services	35,400,000
Corporate income-tax returns	32,500,000
Food-stamp forms	29,400,000
Truckdriver vehicle-inspection reports	27,300,000
Employers' quarterly income-tax returns	26,200,000
Requests for medicare payments	24,400,000
Interest-income statements (Form 1099)	24,100,000
Truckdriver logs on working hours	23,000,000
Management guidelines for school-lunch programs	21,000,000
Partnership income-tax returns (Form 1065)	20,400,000
Requests for reimbursement for school-lunch programs	18,600,000
Highway-traffic-accident reports	17,800,000
Employee withholding-allowance certificates (Form W-4)	16,700,000
Corporate annual reports (Form 10-K)	16,200,000

Note: Figures are estimates for year ending September 30
USN&WR—Basic data: U.S. Office of Management and Budget

SOURCE: "Drive to Cut Red Tape Loses Some Steam," *U. S. News & World Report* (July 19, 1982), p. 49. Reprinted from "U.S. News & World Report." Copyright 1982, U.S. News & World Report, Inc.

Regardless of the viewpoint held, there is no doubt about the legality of governmental regulation of business. The Constitution of the United States gives the federal government the right to regulate interstate commerce and the right to tax. These two privileges are the bases for most business regulation at the federal level. Somewhat similar powers are granted the 50 states by each of their constitutions. As long as the laws passed by the Congress and by state legislatures are constitutional and are correctly enforced by administrative agencies, businesses must abide by their restrictions.

Fortunately for the economic development of this country, government showed little interest in the regulation of business for the first 100 years of this nation's existence. Although a few states exercised some regulation over canals, railroads, banks, and insurance companies, it was essentially a century of laissez-faire capitalism. Competition was an effective regulator because business was conducted by a large number of small units and there was little or no use of electricity, gas, and telephones.

Toward the close of the nineteenth century, conditions began to change. Railroads became important in the development of the country, and the need for regulating rates charged for rail transportation became apparent in the 1880s. Another development was the creation of monopolies. Competing firms turned their shares of stock over to trustees who then controlled and operated the formerly independent firms to minimize competition and maximize profits. These organizations, which became known as trusts, were extremely successful in the oil, sugar, tobacco, and whiskey industries.

COMPETITIVE BUSINESSES AND APPROVED MONOPOLIES

Two categories of business firms — competitive businesses and approved monopolies — were recognized by government when it finally decided that regulation of business was required. Competitive businesses included those that were expected to compete against one another, with prices being determined by supply and demand. Approved monopolies included businesses in which it was in the public interest to let monopolies exist. Gas, electricity, telephone, rail transportation, and similar areas were included in this category. It would be inefficient and costly to consumers, for example, if two gas and electric companies served one community.

Different methods of supervision and control were applied to each of these two categories. In the case of competitive businesses, efforts continue to be directed toward enacting and enforcing laws designed to create an economic climate in which business units can and must compete in a fair and equitable manner. For approved monopolies, specially created governmental commissions substitute for the marketplace in determining allowable prices and levels of service.

REGULATION OF COMPETITIVE BUSINESSES

The earliest federal laws regulating competitive businesses, passed between 1890 and 1914, were designed to enforce competition. Laws that affected such functional areas of business as marketing, labor, and finance were enacted much later and have been described in previous chapters. Additional regulatory laws applying to consumer goods have been enacted recently, and a section in this chapter will describe how this legislation protects public health and safety.

Federal Regulation to Promote Competition

Figure 24-2 briefly summarizes the provisions of the three federal laws in effect today that help promote competition. A relatively new direction in the federal regulation of business concerning environmental control laws was discussed in detail in Chapter 2.

Figure 24-2   Federal Laws to Promote Competition

Law	Provisions
1890 — Sherman Antitrust Act	• Declares illegal every contract, combination, or conspiracy in restraint of trade or commerce among the several states
1914 — Clayton Act, as amended by the Robinson-Patman Act of 1936 and the Celler-Kefauver Act of 1950	• Declares unlawful any act to discriminate in price between different purchasers of commodities or any exclusive agreement for the sale of goods where the effect may be to lessen competition substantially or tend to create a monopoly in any lines of commerce; eliminates favorable price treatment to quantity purchasers; declares unlawful any mergers that might lessen competition or tend to create a monopoly
1914 — Federal Trade Commission Act, as amended by the Wheeler-Lea Act of 1938	• Declares illegal every unfair method of competition and any unfair or deceptive practice that might prove harmful to the public

Impact of the Sherman Antitrust Act

A law against trusts was the first of a series of acts and amendments designed to protect the public by assuring a healthy competitive business climate. The extent of opinion favorable to the Sherman Antitrust Act of 1890 can be judged by the fact that it was passed by both houses of Congress with only one dissenting vote. Persons convicted of violating this law are now subject to a fine not to exceed $100,000 and/or imprisonment for up to three years. Triple damages can be awarded to those injured by the action of trusts.

The Sherman Antitrust Act was predicated on the fear, not without foundation in 1890, that large corporations were automatically harmful to the best interests of the public (see Figure 24-3). Bigness and badness were considered synonyms. This Act

Figure 24-3   Never Trust a Trust

By 1880, John D. Rockefeller was refining 95% of the nation's oil. At the time, American companies were prohibited from owning shares in other companies in other states. To get around this restriction, Rockefeller devised an oil trust, which owned shares in each of the component companies — pretending all the while that the companies were independent. He lavished bribes and "deals" on state legislators. He drove his competitors out of business by undercutting their prices until they gave up, and he expanded his power by buying oilfields across the country. At the same time he moved quickly into foreign markets. By 1885, 70% of Standard Oil's sales were overseas.

As the extent of Rockefeller's power gradually became known, public opinion forced the passage of antitrust laws in several states. But by 1888, Rockefeller was able to take advantage of a New Jersey law that allowed corporations to hold shares in companies outside the state. He reorganized the trust as a holding company, called Standard Oil (New Jersey),which owned shares of all the other companies. President Theodore Roosevelt's Justice Department brought suit in 1906, under the Sherman Anti-Trust Act of 1890. The case worked its way to the Supreme Court, which in a historic decision in 1911 declared Standard Oil an illegal monopoly that had sought to "drive others from the field and exclude them from their right to trade."

Out of the dissolution came 34 separate companies, including Standard Oil of New York (later Mobil) and Standard Oil of California. The companies were still owned by the same stockholders, and Rockefeller himself held a quarter of the shares. The money has held together well over the years: the Rockefeller family and Rockefeller Foundation now own about 1.75% of Exxon, 2% of Standard Oil of California, and 1.75% of Mobil.

SOURCE: Selected quote on pages 501-502 from EVERYBODY'S BUSINESS: AN ALMANAC by Milton Moskowitz, Michael Katz, and Robert Levering. Copyright © 1980 by Harper & Row, Publishers, Inc. Reprinted by permission of the publisher.

gave the Attorney General of the United States the authority to take action against the trusts. After extensive legal delays, most trusts were broken up. As time went on, the fear of giant companies subsided as more than one appeared in several industries such as steel, rubber, and oil. Today the Sherman Antitrust Act is more likely to be applied to specific corporate acts that may be construed as monopolistic if taken by two or more supposedly competing companies. For example, 22 manufacturers of boxes were indicted for conspiring to fix prices to the government. Recently, the medical and legal professions have been directed to refrain from price-fixing and other unlawful practices that restrict competition.

The business practices prohibited under the Sherman Antitrust Act are:

1. **Collusive bidding,** where supposedly competing firms either agree to submit identical prices or agree that one of them is to be the low bidder on a contract.
2. **Territorial pool,** where supposedly competing firms assign geographical areas for the exclusive benefit of each firm.
3. **Patent licensing,** where the owner of a patent allows others to use it upon payment of a royalty if this arrangement is used to restrain trade.
4. **Gentlemen's agreement,** where several competing firms agree that it would be desirable to raise prices in an effort to restrain competition.

Impact of the Clayton Act

By 1914 it was apparent that the Sherman Antitrust Act was not a complete answer to the trust problem. The Clayton Act recognized that the trust problem was no longer one of size but rather one of business practices. Among the practices that are unlawful under this Act are:

1. **Tying contracts,** where a buyer agrees to buy other goods from the same vendor to obtain the merchandise desired.
2. **Interlocking directorate,** where the majority of the members of two or more boards of directors are the same individuals, if either corporation has assets in excess of $1 million and if the corporations are competing businesses.
3. The purchase by one corporation of another corporation's stock if the effect is to lessen competition substantially or to tend to create a monopoly.
4. **Community of interests,** where a few stockholders dictate the composition of the boards of directors of two or more competing corporations.

There are several situations that permit sellers to charge different prices to similar buyers under the Clayton Act and its Robinson-Patman Act amendment. Such price discrimination takes into account differences in grade, quality, quantity, or cost, or where such discrimination was made in good faith to meet bona fide competition. The Celler-Kefauver amendment to the Clayton Act, which prohibited mergers, is one of the reasons in recent years for the rash of conglomerates that are created by the merger of firms in different lines of business. A company that desires to expand finds that it cannot legally acquire other firms engaged in the same line of business.

Impact of the Federal Trade Commission Act

The Federal Trade Commission Act of 1914 declared illegal any unfair method of competition in commerce. It created the Federal Trade Commission (FTC) to enforce this Act as well as many of the provisions of the Clayton Act. The FTC consists of five commissioners aided by a large staff of accountants, economists, and lawyers. It investigates alleged unfair methods of competition, issues complaints against offending firms, and conducts hearings. When necessary, the FTC issues cease-and-desist orders against those found guilty of engaging in forbidden practices. Penalties up to $10,000 per day can be assessed for violations. Under the Wheeler-Lea amendment to the Federal Trade Commission Act, it is no longer necessary to prove that competitors are injured if the unfair method is damaging to the general public. Prior to the Wheeler-Lea Act, consumers had no protection from misleading advertisements such as the classic one shown in Figure 24-4.

Over the years the powers of the FTC have been expanded. Its current activities include establishing "trade practice conferences" designed to secure voluntary agreement among firms in a particular industry as to what constitutes unfair competitive methods. Out of these may come a set of Trade Practice Rules that are mutually agreeable to the Commission and to the members of the trades affected. The mere fact that the FTC is in existence is a deterrent to the actions of firms that might be tempted to violate either laws or ethical principles. This is one of the reasons that the Commission is sometimes called "the police officer of the business world."

Figure 24-4   A Misleading Advertisement

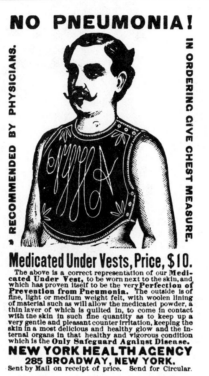

SOURCE: From *Advertising,* 4th edition, by John S. Wright, Daniel S. Warner, Willis L. Winter, Jr., and Sherilyn K. Ziegler. Copyright © 1977 by McGraw-Hill Book Company. Used with permission of McGraw-Hill Book Company.

Federal Regulation to Protect Consumer Health and Safety

Recent federal regulatory emphasis has shifted from laws designed to promote competition to laws that protect the health and safety of consumers such as those listed in Figure 24-5. Two federal agencies enforce the provisions of these laws: the Food and Drug Administration (FDA) and the Consumer Product Safety Commission (CPSC).

Food and Drug Administration

The FDA, which was established in 1906, is responsible for ensuring wholesome foods, safe and effective drugs and medical devices, harmless cosmetics, and truthful labeling of such products. The role of the FDA is vigorously to protect the consumer. It is responsible for setting and maintaining the standards required in the food, drug,

Figure 24-5   Federal Laws to Protect Consumers

Law	Provisions
1938 — Federal Food, Drug, and Cosmetic Act	• Requires package to show accurate weight, ingredients in proportion, and whether coloratives or preservatives have been used
1939 — Wool Products Labeling Act of 1939	• Requires the label of each product to show total fiber weight of the wool (and whether it is new, processed, or reused), percentage of nonwool filling, and name of manufacturer
1951 — Fur Products Labeling Act	• Requires correct name of the animal that produced the fur and other manufacturing details on the label
1956 — Refrigerator Safety Act	• Prohibits the interstate shipment of household refrigerators unless they contain a device that enables doors to be opened from inside
1958 — Textile Fiber Products Identification Act	• Requires label that shows the percentage of natural and synthetic fibers used
1960 — Federal Hazardous Substances Act	• Regulates the interstate distribution and sale of packages of hazardous substances intended or suitable for household use
1966 — Fair Packaging and Labeling Act	• Requires the use of understandable weights and measures and directs that efforts be made to reduce the number of sizes
1967 — Flammable Fabrics-Consumers Protection Act	• Amends the 1953 Flammable Fabrics Act to protect the public against undue risk of fire leading to death, injury, or property damage arising from ignition of wearing apparel and of interior household furnishings
1969 — Child Protection and Toy Safety Act	• Amends Hazardous Substances Act to protect children from toys and other children's articles which carry potential electrical, mechanical, or thermal hazards
1970 — Poison Prevention Packaging Act	• Provides for special packaging to protect children from serious personal injury or serious illness when handling, using, or ingesting household substances
1972 — Consumer Product Safety Act	• Establishes a Consumer Product Safety Commission to protect the public from injuries associated with consumer products and to develop uniform safety standards for consumer products
1975 — Magnuson-Moss Warranty and FTC Improvement Act	• Requires use of concise language in warranties and type of warranty, refunds, and corrective advertising

and cosmetic industries. The impact of the FDA and the Department of Agriculture regulations on food is shown in Figure 24-6. Note that the rules that govern what goes into a pizza include 310 separate regulations, covering more than 40 pages!

Since Congressional passage of the Delaney clause in 1958, the FDA has been required to ban any food additives that are shown to cause cancer in laboratory animals. When a Canadian study linked saccharin to cancer, a special act of Congress was necessary to keep this product — with a required warning label — on the market. After a two-year legal battle, the FDA ordered cosmetics manufacturers to list on their packages the ingredients of their products. The FDA initially required a warning label; then it prohibited the use of aerosol products propelled with chlorofluorocarbon gases. Many scientists had expressed concern that the release of these gases into the atmosphere was reducing the vital ozone layer.

A different concern of the FDA is prescription drugs. Although state laws govern whether pharmacists can substitute a less expensive drug for a more expensive one, the FDA encourages states to permit this substitution. The FDA declares there are no quality differences between drugs made by large and small firms or those sold under a brand name or *generic name* (chemical compound). For example, Squibb's Pentids (brand name) is Penicillin G (generic name).

Consumer Product Safety Commission

In 1972 the CPSC was created to identify the risks of household products and to establish safety rules for them. The CPSC reviews the effectiveness of industry self-

---

Figure 24-6   A Pizza with the Works

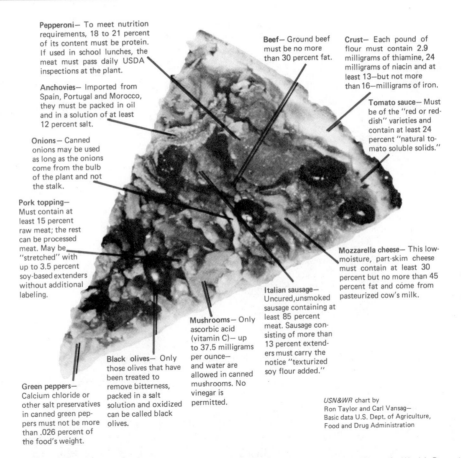

Pepperoni— To meet nutrition requirements, 18 to 21 percent of its content must be protein. If used in school lunches, the meat must pass daily USDA inspections at the plant.

Anchovies— Imported from Spain, Portugal and Morocco, they must be packed in oil and in a solution of at least 12 percent salt.

Onions— Canned onions may be used as long as the onions come from the bulb of the plant and not the stalk.

Pork topping— Must contain at least 15 percent raw meat; the rest can be processed meat. May be "stretched" with up to 3.5 percent soy-based extenders without additional labeling.

Green peppers— Calcium chloride or other salt preservatives in canned green peppers must not be more than .026 percent of the food's weight.

Black olives— Only those olives that have been treated to remove bitterness, packed in a salt solution and oxidized can be called black olives.

Mushrooms— Only ascorbic acid (vitamin C)—up to 37.5 milligrams per ounce—and water are allowed in canned mushrooms. No vinegar is permitted.

Italian sausage— Uncured, unsmoked sausage containing at least 85 percent meat. Sausage consisting of more than 13 percent extenders must carry the notice "texturized soy flour added."

Beef— Ground beef must be no more than 30 percent fat.

Crust— Each pound of flour must contain 2.9 milligrams of thiamine, 24 milligrams of niacin and at least 13—but not more than 16—milligrams of iron.

Tomato sauce— Must be of the "red or reddish" varieties and contain at least 24 percent "natural tomato soluble solids."

Mozzarella cheese— This low-moisture, part-skim cheese must contain at least 30 percent but no more than 45 percent fat and come from pasteurized cow's milk.

USN&WR chart by Ron Taylor and Carl Vansag— Basic data U.S. Dept. of Agriculture, Food and Drug Administration

SOURCE: "A Pizza with the Works—Including 310 Regulations," *U. S. News & World Report* (May 31, 1982), p. 55. Reprinted from "U. S. News & World Report." Copyright 1982, U. S. News & World Report, Inc.

---

regulation programs and of current federal, state, and local consumer protection laws. This agency has the responsibility for administering the following laws: the Flammable Fabrics Act, the Federal Hazardous Substances Act, the Poison Prevention Packaging Act, and the Refrigerator Safety Act. The CPSC compiles an annual list of the most dangerous consumer products, too (see Table 24-1). The need for this agency is demonstrated by the more than 100,000 product injury claims and lawsuits filed annually by businesses and consumers.

Table 24-1 — **Number of Injuries Requiring Emergency Room Treatment, July 1, 1980–June 30, 1981**

Product Group	National Estimate of Injuries
1. Stairs	763,000
2. Bicycles and bicycle accessories	518,000
3. Baseball	478,000
4. Football	470,000
5. Basketball	434,000
6. Nails, carpet tacks, screws, and thumbtacks	244,000
7. Chairs, sofas, and sofa beds	236,000
8. Roller and ice skating	225,000
9. Non-glass tables and unspecified tables	225,000
10. Glass doors, windows, and panels	208,000
11. Beds	199,000
12. Playground equipment	165,000
13. Lumber, boards, or panel pieces	151,000
14. Cutlery and knives (unpowered), including switchblades and pocketknives	140,000
15. Glass bottles and jars	140,000
16. Desks, cabinets, shelves, bookcases, magazine racks, and footlockers	126,000
17. Swimming pools and equipment	126,000
18. Drinking glasses	111,000
19. Ladders and stools	99,000
20. Fences (nonelectric or not specified)	99,000

SOURCE: U. S. Consumer Product Safety Commission, Washington, DC, 1982.

Initially, the CPSC was criticized for its inactivity. In its first five years it established safety standards for only three products: swimming pool slides, architectural glazing, and matchbooks. Recently the CPSC has been encouraging industries to develop information programs that help consumers to understand the choices and the risks among products. Firms are being urged to adopt "people" labeling, too. For example, a product that is perfectly safe for a six-year-old could be dangerous to a toddler.

State and Local Regulation of Competitive Businesses

Cities, villages, townships, counties, parishes, and other governing units within a state are created and exist under the constitution of that state. Consequently, state regulation of business encompasses all laws passed by the state legislature and any of its political subdivisions that have legislative authority. As long as these laws do not conflict with the state constitution, the federal constitution, or federal legislation, they are legal and enforceable.

Under what is known as the **police power,** it is not only the right but also the duty of a state to protect the health, safety, and morals of its citizens and to promote the general welfare. This power does not depend upon state constitutions or enabling legislation but is inherent in the power to govern. For example, a state can establish a weighing station and stop overloaded trucks—even those moving in interstate commerce. There may or may not be a law covering this activity, although in general most business regulation is covered by specific legislation.

Considering that there are 50 states and thousands of political subdivisions, it is obvious that the regulation of competitive business varies considerably among these governmental units. As shown in Figure 24-7, there are some areas that are quite commonly considered by governing bodies as proper restraints on business activities.

Figure 24-7   Areas of State and Local Regulation of Business

Area	Types of Regulations
• Labor conditions	• State regulations require that buildings be fireproof and hazard free. Mines should have the proper ventilating devices and emergency exits. Under the Taft-Hartley Act, states have the authority to pass right-to-work laws specifying that no one shall be required to join a union in order to obtain a job.
• Health and sanitation conditions	• Health and sanitation rules for factories, restaurants, and other establishments have been enacted at the state and local levels.
• Prices	• In nearly half the states unfair-trade laws have been passed. Most states have copied the federal laws against monopolies, trade practices, and pricing policies.
• Interest rates	• Usury laws that specify the maximum interest rates on different types of loans have been passed by most states.
• Zoning ordinances	• Most localities have enacted ordinances that establish specific locations for different types of property usage.
• Building codes	• Minimum building standards have been specified at the state and local levels.
• Licenses	• State and local regulations require licenses to engage legally in an activity. Certain licenses, such as for liquor stores and taverns, are used to control the number and types of these outlets. Some, such as for lawyers and other professionals, are used to certify their qualifications.

REGULATION OF APPROVED MONOPOLIES

In one sense the types of businesses currently considered to be approved monopolies can all be classified as public utilities, sometimes called public service companies. A public utility may be defined as a privately owned firm that renders a service so essential to its customers that it is allowed to operate legally as a monopoly under governmental regulation of rates and standards of service. Under this broad definition the following qualify as public utilities: electric, gas, water, telephone (local service only), and telegraph companies, as well as railroads, metropolitan buses, subways, oil and gas pipelines, and air, water, and motor transport companies.[1] The importance of investor-owned electric public utilities is shown by the fact that they supply 77 percent of the nation's electricity.

Characteristics of Public Utilities

Public utility companies have certain characteristics that are lacking in other forms of private business. One characteristic is the *public necessity* of the service rendered. Under present-day living conditions most people expect to have immediate access to water, electricity, gas, and a telephone. Another characteristic of public utilities is the economic efficiency that they achieve in providing their services. It would be undesirable, for example, to have two competitive firms build dams or lay pipes in one area. Finally, another characteristic of many public utilities is the right to secure special privileges from governmental units. These include the **right of eminent domain,** which is a government's power to take private property for a public purpose by the payment of a fair price. If necessary, the fair price will be determined by a court. The right of eminent domain is commonly extended to telephone, telegraph, gas, and electric services companies.

Regulatory Agencies for Approved Monopolies

The regulation of public utilities is largely centered on rates and service. Depending on the territory served by the utility, the determination and enforcement of what constitutes fair rates and satisfactory service falls under one or more of three levels of government: local, state, and federal.

Local Regulatory Bodies

If the public utility is a company operating buses within a municipality, it will be regulated by the city council or a comparable elected group. Regulatory conditions are

---

1. In 1982 the U.S. Department of Justice ordered AT&T to divest its 22 local telephone operations from its corporate structure. This left AT&T with three major units: its long-distance operations, its Western Electric manufacturing facility, and its Bell Laboratories research center. As a result of this divestiture, new competitors are providing long-distance services and telephone equipment.

imposed at the time a franchise, which is an exclusive right to serve the community for a specific number of years, is granted. These regulations would specify allowable fares and frequency of service.

State Public Utility Commissions

The bulk of all public utility regulation falls under the jurisdiction of a state public utility commission. This commission is a branch of the state government and usually consists of three to five commissioners aided by a clerical and legal staff. The competence of state public utility commissions varies among the 50 states. However, the general consensus is that they are effective in protecting consumers from excessive rates and in keeping the utilities in a healthy financial condition.

Providing Service. Because utilities are monopolies, a company cannot enter a new territory without first securing permission from the appropriate state commission. This usually involves securing a *certificate of convenience and necessity.* Also, a public utility cannot reduce or abandon the service it renders without first securing commission approval. The fact that one segment of its operations regularly operates at a loss is not sufficient reason for abandonment.

Determining Rates. At the state level, commissions have tried to develop rate structures that permit each public utility company to earn a fair return on a fair value of its property. A rate of return that is fair to the utility and to the public is extremely difficult to establish. In most instances the rates allowed have varied from 5 to 12 percent on the fair value of the utility's property — with 8 or 9 percent favored over these extremes. Even after a rate is established, there is no guarantee that earnings will equal the approved rate. If earnings are low, the utility can apply for an upward adjustment in rates.

During the late 1970s and early 1980s, the price of fuel increased so rapidly and sharply that most commissions allowed utilities to adjust their rates without following customary procedures. Also during this same time period, interest rates increased and utilities felt that they should be allowed to earn 12 percent or more. Otherwise they could not afford to borrow the capital needed for expansion purposes.

Determining the fair value of a public utility's property involves placing a price tag on every item of property. Two widely used measures are: original cost less depreciation, and reproduction cost new less depreciation. Original cost is also known as *historical cost,* and it corresponds to values shown on the balance sheet. The *reproduction cost new* method prices properties at current costs. Both methods have been approved by the United States Supreme Court.

Federal Regulatory Commissions

Although the operations of public utilities are primarily intrastate, electricity and natural gas move across state lines and are thus regulated as interstate commerce. Figure 24-8 lists the federal regulatory commissions that have jurisdiction over public utilities, as well as other regulated industries.

Figure 24-8   Federal Regulatory Commissions

Agency	Duties
● Federal Energy Regulatory Commission (FERC)	● Regulates interstate electric and natural gas rates; directs coordination and interconnection of transmission lines; controls sales and purchases of companies transmitting electricity in interstate commerce
● Nuclear Regulatory Commission (NRC)	● Issues licenses for nuclear power plants and has regulatory powers over their operations
● Interstate Commerce Commission (ICC)	● Regulates rates, service, valuation, security issues, consolidations, safety appliances, accounting, and many other phases of railroads, common carriers, water transportation, and oil pipelines involved in interstate commerce; prescribes safety regulations for all motor carriers; prescribes permits and minimum rates for contract carriers
● Civil Aeronautics Board (CAB)	● Promotes and regulates the civil air transportation industry within the U. S. and between the U. S. and foreign countries; establishes standards of service (to be abolished by 1985)
● Federal Aviation Administration (FAA)	● Supervises certification of aircraft, personnel, and development of airports
● Federal Communications Commission (FCC)	● Regulates rates and services for interstate communication by wire; supervises charges for cable and radio overseas messages, satellite communication, and cable TV; allocates television channels and radio frequencies

Deregulation of Certain Industries

In recent years several legislative acts have caused striking changes in the airline, trucking, and railroad industries. These acts are the Aviation Deregulation Act of 1978, the Motor Carrier Act of 1980, and the Rail Act of 1980. These laws greatly reduced the amount of government regulation and increased competition in these industries. Airline deregulation has led to bruising fare wars that reduced rates to as low as $99 between New York and Los Angeles (see Figure 24-9). Prior to deregulation, the President's Council of Economic Advisers estimated that regulating the trucking industry was costing the public $5 to $6 billion a year. Recent calls for less regulation reflect a major reversal in the long-run trend toward more government interference in our economic system.

PRINCIPLES OF TAXATION

Enacting a suitable program of taxation for any governmental unit is most difficult. The total revenue obtained should be adequate to meet necessary current expenditures. The burden should be distributed on an equitable basis. The tax law must be reasonably simple and the funds easy to collect. In some instances it may be desirable to use the tax as a means of regulation as well as revenue.

Taxation, particularly at the federal level, is also used to accomplish objectives beyond revenue and regulation. The income tax and estate and gift taxes tend to level wealth in this country. Some specific provisions, such as the investment tax credit that encourages firms to buy new equipment, are designed to encourage business expansion. When the economy appears to be headed for a recession, an income tax cut often is made to boost business. Whether or not such uses of taxation are desirable "principles" is questioned by those who believe that the only legitimate function of a tax is to raise revenue.

Bases for Taxation

A tax whose rate remains constant regardless of the size of the tax base is a **proportional tax.** For example, in a taxing district the tax rate is the same on the appraised value of property regardless of the amount of property that is owned by one person. A tax whose rate becomes lower as the tax base increases in size is a **regressive tax.** For example, the cost of securing a corporation charter, when based on the number of shares authorized, involves lower rates on the shares in excess of a stated minimum. The opposite of a regressive tax is a **progressive tax,** which applies higher and higher rates as the tax base grows in size. For example, income taxes usually are

---

Figure 24-9   Going Half Fare

SOURCE: Don Wright, *The Miami News.*

---

designed so that higher rates apply to the upper brackets of income. Likewise, the rates on inheritance, gift, and estate taxes become higher and higher for larger and larger transfers of wealth.

The reasons for selecting certain bases for purposes of taxation are not always apparent. Obviously such broad bases as sales, income, or property offer an opportunity to raise sizable sums without using excessively high rates. Taxes on gasoline have the advantage of raising funds from those who use the highways that are maintained and improved with these revenues. Taxes on liquor and tobacco are **sumptuary taxes,** which are designed to discourage consumption of the items taxed by increasing their retail prices.

Impact and Incidence of Taxes

From the businessperson's point of view, the impact and incidence of taxes are important. *Impact* refers to the person who is liable for the tax and who keeps the necessary records and mails out a check in payment of the amount due. In many instances it is possible to pass the tax on to others—usually the final consumer—through a process known as shifting. The place at which the ultimate burden falls is known as the *incidence* of the tax. For example, a gasoline tax may be paid by the owner of a service station but, if this tax is added to the purchase price paid by the customer, the owner is merely serving as a collection agency for a governmental unit. If the tax cannot be shifted, the businessperson must absorb it.

VARIATIONS IN STATE AND LOCAL TAXES

Rates and methods of collection of taxes may vary among states and local governments such as cities, counties, villages, school districts, and drainage districts. Figure 24-10 lists and defines the different types of taxes and license fees levied by almost all states. Among those listed are taxes which local governments may also impose such as general sales taxes, gross receipts taxes, income taxes, property taxes, and miscellaneous license fees. Figure 24-11 shows the collections from specific state and local taxes for the fiscal year 1981. Figure 24-12 shows per capita state and local taxes in 1982. Some of the more important state and local taxes are discussed below.

Sales Taxes

Sales taxes are levied on the retail price of goods or services at the time they are sold. These taxes may be given different names, as Figure 24-10 shows. General sales or gross receipts taxes provide the largest single source of revenue for 45 states. Only Alaska, Delaware, Montana, New Hampshire, and Oregon do not impose a sales tax. In some states food purchased but not consumed on the premises is exempted from the sales tax. In other states sales under a minimum amount are also exempted from the sales tax. City and county rates vary between 1 and 3 percent, except in New York

Figure 24-10   Taxes and License Fees Levied by State and Local Governments

SALES TAXES:
- General sales tax
- Selective sales tax, or excise tax

- Gross receipts tax

- Selective gross receipts tax

- Use tax

INCOME TAX

PROPERTY TAX

ORGANIZATION TAX/ANNUAL FEES:
- Incorporation fee
- Entrance tax
- Franchise tax
- Privilege tax

SEVERANCE TAX

PAYROLL TAX

MISCELLANEOUS LICENSE FEES

DEATH DUTIES:
- Estate tax
- Inheritance tax

GIFT TAX

- When tax rate applies to all or nearly all goods or services
- When tax rate applies to one or a few items such as tobacco, alcoholic beverages, gasoline, and motor oil consumed on public highways
- When tax rate on income from all sources, such as admission fees and interest, is the same as that applied to the sale of goods and services
- When tax rate is a percentage of gross receipts on specific items such as insurance premiums
- Tax on goods entering from another state

Tax on wages, salaries, commissions, dividends, interest, rents, and other similar sources of income to individuals; tax on net profits of businesses

Tax on value of real estate, of tangible personal property, and of intangibles owned by a taxpayer

- Organization tax on a domestic corporation
- Organization tax on a foreign corporation
- Annual fee on domestic corporations
- Annual fee on foreign corporations

Tax levied on owner of timberland or mineral deposits whenever the timber is cut or the minerals are removed from the ground

Tax on payrolls to be used for making payments to temporarily unemployed persons

Fees required to operate certain types of businesses, vehicles, and occupations

- Tax on entire net value of the deceased's holdings
- Tax on separate bequests made to individual heirs

Tax on substantial gifts made by a living person

City, which has a total city and state sales tax of 8½ percent. A sales tax is a regressive tax because individuals with smaller incomes pay a larger percentage of their money into the sales tax system than those with higher incomes.

Rates of selective sales taxes (or excise taxes) can be specific or ad valorem. For example, a specific rate would be 18.5 cents for a package of cigarettes. An example of an ad valorem rate is 10 percent of the item's selling price. Selective sales taxes on gasoline and motor fuels are paid to the state. However, it is common practice for a state to return a proportion of the amount collected to the county, township, city, or village on the basis of the collections made from these political subdivisions.

Selective gross receipts taxes on insurance companies are based on a percentage, such as 2 percent, of all premiums collected within the state. Taxes on the price of entertainment tickets range from 3 to 10 percent of the admission charge.

Figure 24-11   State and Local Taxes Collected in 1981

State Taxes
Tax Collections

Sales and Gross Receipts
General	$46,412 mil.
Motor fuels..................	$9,734 mil.
Public utilities	$4,296 mil.
Tobacco products	$3,893 mil.
Insurance	$3,321 mil.
Alcoholic beverages	$2,613 mil.
Other	$2,482 mil.

Licenses
Motor vehicles................	$5,266 mil.
Drivers	$429 mil.
Corporations	$1,612 mil.
Hunting and fishing............	$464 mil.
Alcoholic beverages	$212 mil.
Other	$1,510 mil.
Individual income..............	**$40,895 mil.**
Corporate income	**$14,143 mil.**
Severance......................	**$6,379 mil.**
Property	**$2,949 mil.**
Estate and gift..................	**$2,229 mil.**
Other taxes	**$899 mil.**

Total state taxes $149,739 mil.

Local Taxes
Tax Collections

Property	$65,607 mil.
General sales and gross receipts	$8,160 mil.
Individual income................	$4,990 mil.
Public utilities	$2,529 mil.
Motor-vehicle and operators' licenses..............	$388 mil.
Alcoholic-beverage sales	$164 mil.
Tobacco-product sales.............	$136 mil.
Motor-fuel sales	$100 mil.
Other taxes	$4,312 mil.

Total local taxes $92,191 mil.

SOURCE: "Tax Cut: Now You See It, Now You Don't," *U. S. News & World Report* (April 26, 1982), p. 89. Reprinted from "U. S. News & World Report." Copyright 1982, U. S. News & World Report, Inc.

Income Taxes

Forty-four states have enacted some type of personal income tax, and forty-five states tax the incomes of corporations.

Most states allow certain deductions and exemptions from gross incomes of individuals such as $1,000 for each member of a family. After this deduction, rates are graduated upward with a range from 0.5 percent on the first $1,000 of taxable income to 16 percent on taxable income over $35,915. A few states tax a percentage of the family's or person's federal income tax liability.

The tax rate for corporations is commonly a flat percentage of all net income. It ranges from 4 to 12 percent, although some states apply graduated rates. Foreign corporations are taxed in the same manner as domestic corporations to the extent that the taxable income of the foreign corporation can be allocated to its activities within the boundaries of the state levying the tax.

City income taxes customarily range from 1 to 4 percent of resident individuals' taxable incomes and the profits of resident firms (see Table 24-2). Nonresident individuals and firms pay the same rate on their incomes from employment or sales within the city limits.

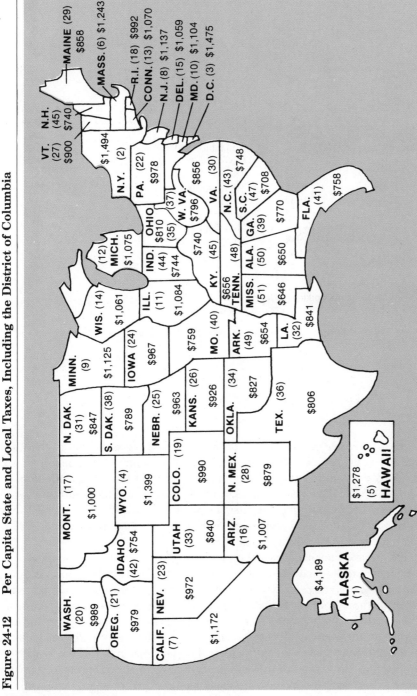

NOTE: Number in parentheses indicates standing of states according to burden of state and local tax. Dollars equal per capita tax in fiscal year 1980.

SOURCE: U. S. Bureau of the Census, *Statistical Abstract of the United States: 1982–1983* (103d ed.; Washington, DC: U. S. Government Printing Office, 1983), p. 284.

Table 24-2   City Income Tax in U.S. Cities with over 100,000 Population

	Present Rate	Date of Introduction		Present Rate	Date of Introduction
Alabama			New York		
Birmingham	1.0%	1970	New York	0.9% to 4.3%[3]	1966
Kentucky			Ohio		
Louisville	2.2	1948	Akron	2.0	1962
Maryland			Cincinnati	2.0	1954
Baltimore	50% of state income tax[1]	1966	Cleveland	2.0	1947
			Columbus	1.5	1947
Michigan			Dayton	1.75	1949
Detroit	3.0[2]	1962	Toledo	1.5	1955
Flint	1.0	1965	Youngstown	2.0	1948
Grand Rapids	1.0	1967	Pennsylvania		
Lansing	1.0	1968	Erie	1.0	1948
Missouri			Philadelphia	4⁵⁄₁₆	1939
Kansas City	1.0	1964	Pittsburgh	2⅛	1976
St. Louis	1.0	1948			

[1]Individual income tax only.
[2]1.5% for nonresidents working in Detroit.
[3]Plus surcharge of 2.5% to 5% effective June 15, 1982.

SOURCE: *1983 Hammond Almanac* (Maplewood, NJ: Hammond Almanac, Inc., 1983), p. 194. Reproduced with permission.

Property Taxes

Local governments rely on one or more forms of property taxes as their major source of revenue, whereas property taxes are a minor source of income for states. To tax real estate, local assessors value both land and buildings—frequently from one-third to one-half of true market value. A rate is then applied on an annual basis. For example, in a particular school district the rate might be $42.16 on each $1,000 of assessed value. This means that a factory building and land assessed at $2,000,000 would have an annual real estate tax of $84,320.

The value of tangible personal property owned by businesses includes the value of machinery; stocks of raw materials, goods in process, and finished goods; and office, store, and factory equipment. The usual valuation procedure is to use cost minus depreciation against which either a special rate or the real estate rate is assessed.

Intangibles subject to property taxes include stocks, bonds, mortgages, and notes. The value of these intangibles can usually be determined from market quotations or from the amounts stated on the instruments. Taxes on intangibles are the weakest form of property tax since assets of this type are easy to conceal. To encourage the listing of these assets, tax rates on them are sometimes less than those for real estate.

Miscellaneous License Fees

Ranking first in all states in total license fee revenue is the annual income from motor vehicle plates or renewal stickers. Fees are usually lowest for passenger automobiles and mopeds and highest for large trucks. For businesses that maintain their own fleets of passenger cars or trucks, or both, the annual cost for license plates is a substantial expense. In 1981, motor vehicle licenses contributed on a per capita basis an average of $23 to $31 to a state's revenue. Drivers' license fees are a related cost, but the charge for these fees is quite low.

License fees to sell alcoholic beverages and to operate gambling casinos produce substantial revenues for states. For example, in Indiana alcoholic beverage licenses run from $80 to $1,030. When New Jersey authorized casinos in Atlantic City, it specified an initial license fee of not less than $200,000—with a minimum $100,000 renewal fee plus $200 for each slot machine. In Nevada—the only state that has statewide legalized gambling—a license may run several thousand dollars annually, depending on the number of games operated.

States also license certain types of businesses such as the manufacture and wholesale distribution of beer and tobacco products. Several states license chain stores, with the annual rate based on the number of stores in the chain. Licenses for hunting and fishing are also mandatory in most states.

Cities license taxicabs, nightclubs, and sometimes even passenger automobiles. Other businesses frequently required by cities to obtain a license are bowling alleys, pool halls, movie theaters, and taverns. Each political subdivision within a state is free to select the types of businesses for which a license is required. There is little uniformity in this area.

FEDERAL TAXES

While tax collections by state and local governments are substantial, they can only be termed modest when compared with the tax dollars that flow into the federal treasury each year. For example, Table 24-3 shows that federal taxes collected in 1981 were estimated at $582 billion as contrasted with a $242 billion total estimate for all states. The sources from which billions of dollars are collected by the federal government each year are the taxes and customs duties listed in Figure 24-13.

Income Taxes

Income taxes levied on individuals and businesses comprise the largest source of revenue for the federal government. In recent years these taxes have produced receipts in excess of $340 billion annually. Of this huge sum individuals pay approximately 75 to 80 percent, and corporations the remainder. The rates and methods of computation vary considerably between taxes for individuals and for corporations.

Table 24-3   Federal Taxes Collected in 1981

	Tax Collections		Tax Collections
Individual income	$285,917 mil.	Miscellaneous excise taxes	
Corporate income	$61,137 mil.	Telephone, teletype service	$999 mil.
Social insurance		Foreign insurance policies	$75 mil.
Social Security	$160,515 mil.	Tax on foundations	$90 mil.
Railroad retirement	$2,457 mil.	Wagering	$13 mil.
State unemployment	$12,366 mil.	Employee pension plans	$5 mil.
Federal unemployment	$3,221 mil.	Other excise taxes	$1 mil.
Railroad unemployment	$176 mil.	Airports and airways	$1,201 mil.*
Alcohol		Highway trust fund taxes	
Distilled spirits	$3,819 mil.	Gasoline	$4,016 mil.
Beer	$1,604 mil.	Trucks, buses and trailers	$664 mil.
Wines	$244 mil.	Tires, inner tubes and tread rubber	$644 mil.
Special taxes	$21 mil.	Diesel fuel used on highways	$561 mil.
Tobacco		Use tax on certain vehicles	$237 mil.
Cigarettes	$2,539 mil.	Truck parts and accessories	$234 mil.
Cigars	$40 mil.	Lubricating oils	$101 mil.
Other tobacco products	$4 mil.	Other trust fund taxes	
Manufacturers' excise taxes		Black-lung disability insurance	$237 mil.
"Windfall profits" tax	$23,290 mil.	Inland waterway	$20 mil.
Gasoline	$32 mil.	Hazardous substances	$128 mil.
Firearms, shells, cartridges	$97 mil.	Estate and gift taxes	$6,787 mil.
Pistols, revolvers	$27 mil.	Customs duties	$8,083 mil.
Fishing rods, reels	$23 mil.	Other taxes	$291 mil.
Bows and arrows	$7 mil.	Total federal taxes $581,595 mil.	Up 16.1%

*After refunds.

SOURCE: "Tax Cut: Now You See It, Now You Don't," *U.S. News & World Report* (April 26, 1982), p. 88. Reprinted from "U.S. News & World Report." Copyright 1982, U.S. News & World Report, Inc.

Personal Income Taxes

For millions of Americans the old adage that there is nothing so certain as death and taxes is a truism. As Table 24-3 indicates, in 1981 personal income taxes added almost $286 billion to the U.S. treasury. Since 1982 the highest tax rate for a single person was changed from a hefty 70 percent to a lower 50 percent. Beginning in 1984, an individual does not pay this rate until he or she has a taxable income of $81,800. On the other hand, when a single person has a taxable income of $2,300 or less, there is no tax to pay. Many college students with summer or part-time jobs fall into this category.

Although Congress periodically passes new tax legislation, (see Figure 24-14), there are certain features of the personal income tax system that are constant. One is that it is progressive. Another is that the tax is collected on a pay-as-you-go basis. This means that as you receive the income, you pay the tax. This plan is achieved by requiring most employers to withhold the tax from your pay and send it to the government. Another feature is that allowances may be claimed for personal and dependency exemptions. An important aspect of the present tax system is the array of tax deductions for home and mortgage interest, state and local taxes, medical bills, consumer installment interest, union dues, charitable donations, alimony, and certain educational expenses.

Because of the numerous deductions allowed and the complexities of the tax system, a proposal periodically emerges for a flat rate of 10 to 20 percent that would replace the progressive income tax. The adoption of a flat-rate tax would levy taxes on billions of dollars of currently exempt income. Complaints that the rich are able to shelter much of their income would be stopped because all income, regardless of its source, would be taxed at the same rate. The flat-rate tax also would greatly simplify the tax code and eliminate the tendency of the tax system to misallocate financial resources. However, a drawback to a flat-rate tax is that the poor and lower-middle class would pay a much larger share of the taxes and the rich and upper-middle class would be paying much less.

Figure 24-13   Taxes Levied by the Federal Government

INCOME TAXES:
- Personal income tax
  - Tax on individual's annual income in excess of a stated amount
- Corporate income tax
  - Tax on earnings of corporations engaged in trade or industry

EXCISE TAXES:
- Manufacturers' excise tax
  - Tax on prices charged by manufacturers on selected items
- Retailers' excise tax
  - Tax on prices charged by retailers on selected items

SOCIAL SECURITY TAX

Tax on wages paid or received to finance old-age, survivors, and disability insurance benefits and for hospital insurance (Part A of Medicare)

ESTATE AND GIFT TAXES

Taxes on estates and gifts that exceed stated amounts

MISCELLANEOUS TAXES

Taxes on miscellaneous items for the purpose of obtaining additional revenue

REGULATORY TAX

Tax levied primarily for regulation rather than income

CUSTOMS DUTIES

Taxes on importation of foreign goods

Figure 24-14   Income Tax Time Line

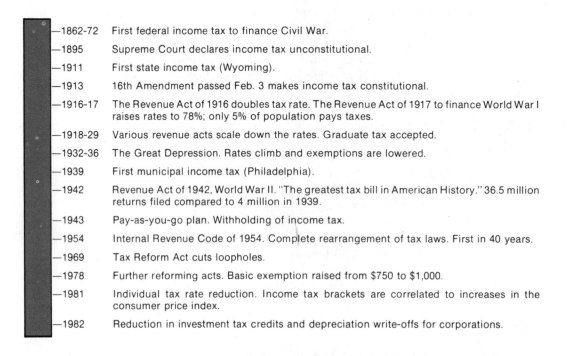

—1862-72	First federal income tax to finance Civil War.
—1895	Supreme Court declares income tax unconstitutional.
—1911	First state income tax (Wyoming).
—1913	16th Amendment passed Feb. 3 makes income tax constitutional.
—1916-17	The Revenue Act of 1916 doubles tax rate. The Revenue Act of 1917 to finance World War I raises rates to 78%; only 5% of population pays taxes.
—1918-29	Various revenue acts scale down the rates. Graduate tax accepted.
—1932-36	The Great Depression. Rates climb and exemptions are lowered.
—1939	First municipal income tax (Philadelphia).
—1942	Revenue Act of 1942, World War II. "The greatest tax bill in American History." 36.5 million returns filed compared to 4 million in 1939.
—1943	Pay-as-you-go plan. Withholding of income tax.
—1954	Internal Revenue Code of 1954. Complete rearrangement of tax laws. First in 40 years.
—1969	Tax Reform Act cuts loopholes.
—1978	Further reforming acts. Basic exemption raised from $750 to $1,000.
—1981	Individual tax rate reduction. Income tax brackets are correlated to increases in the consumer price index.
—1982	Reduction in investment tax credits and depreciation write-offs for corporations.

SOURCE: Adapted from *American Enterprise Teaching Notes,* Issue 10, p. 3.

Corporate Income Taxes

The federal corporate income tax is the most significant tax that most corporations pay. The Economic Recovery Tax Act of 1981 established the following corporate tax rates that became effective in 1983:

> 15 percent on the first $25,000 of net income
> 18 percent on the second $25,000 of net income
> 30 percent on the third $25,000 of net income
> 40 percent on the fourth $25,000 of net income
> 46 percent on net income over $100,000

Congress has structured the tax rates so that the lower rates on earnings under $100,000 are of more help to small corporations than to large ones. For example, compare the taxes paid by a corporation earning $150,000 with another earning $10,000,000, as follows:

Taxes on $150,000 Net Income		Taxes on $10,000,000 Net Income	
$ 25,000 × .15 =	$ 3,750	$ 25,000 × .15 = $	3,750
25,000 × .18 =	4,500	25,000 × .18 =	4,500
25,000 × .30 =	7,500	25,000 × .30 =	7,500
25,000 × .40 =	10,000	25,000 × .40 =	10,000
50,000 × .46 =	23,000	9,900,000 × .46 =	4,554,000
$150,000	$48,750	$10,000,000	$4,579,750

The small corporation pays about 32.5 percent of its net income in taxes while the larger one pays almost 46 percent. Through a variety of methods, corporations attempt to reduce their tax payments. These methods include depreciation and depletion allowances, investment tax credits, and an assortment of expenses. For example, in a recent year Philip Morris, Inc., shaved $58.6 million off its tax bill through the use of investment tax credits.[2] The Joint Committee on Taxation of the U.S. Congress revealed that the taxes paid on average by U.S. corporations were 35 percent of their earnings. The commercial banking industry paid the lowest tax rate — equal to 2 percent of earnings. Motor vehicle manufacturers had the highest actual tax rate at 48 percent.[3]

Tax-exempt organizations include the following:

1. Corporations operated exclusively for religious, charitable, scientific, literary, or educational purposes or for the prevention of cruelty to children or to animals.
2. Labor unions.
3. Fraternal societies.
4. Some mutual companies and cooperatives.
5. Civic organizations and clubs.

However, if any of the organizations mentioned above has income from the operation of a business enterprise which is not related to the purpose on which its exempt status is based, such income is taxable. Furthermore, tax-exempt organizations are required to file an annual information return which is examined to make sure that they are entitled to retain their favored tax status. Figure 24-15 calls attention to a strategy used by the residents of a small New York town in the mid-1970s in an effort to avoid unjustified taxes.

Social Security Taxes

The very first Social Security recipient in 1940, Ida M. Fuller of Ludlow, VT, paid only $22 into the Social Security system. She lived to be 100 and, by the time she died in 1974, had collected about $21,000 in benefits.[4] Mrs. Fuller's experience illustrates

---

2. "Why Taxes on Business Are Shrinking Fast," *U.S. News & World Report* (October 12, 1981), p. 86.
3. Leslie Wayne, "The Corporate Tax: Uneven, Unfair?" *The New York Times,* March 20, 1983, p. F1.
4. Conoco, Inc. "Putting the Security Back in Social Security," *Conoco 82,* Vol. 13, No. 2, p. 28.

Figure 24-15   A Religious Conviction About Taxes

The unhappy residents of Hardenburgh, New York, contend that they do not mind paying their fair share of taxes—but they do not want to pay the other guy's share, too. Half of the citizens of this small community nestled in the Catskill Mountains became tax-exempt clergy in order to escape a growing tax burden. They were ordained by a plumber in a nearby village who had become a bishop of the Universal Life Church through a series of correspondence courses.

Prior to their call to the ministry, the residents of Hardenburgh had seen their taxes increased by three or four times over a six-year period. Their turn to religion was a dramatic way in which they could demonstrate to the State Legislature the need for tax relief.

Some property owners were paying as much as two-thirds of their small incomes in school, town, and county taxes. The major reason for this heavy tax load was the great growth in the number of tax-exempt organizations locating in the area. These ranged from the Boy Scouts to the Zen Buddhists. The ordinary citizens of Hardenburgh were forced to pay more taxes in order to make up the revenue loss from the tax-exempt organizations.

SOURCE: Condensed from the *Fort Wayne Journal Gazette*, September 26, 1976.

one of the problems with the Social Security system. A person who makes the maximum contribution to the system and who retires at age 65 recovers his or her contribution within two years. Thus, a very small contribution may return very large benefits. Another major problem with the system is that retired people are becoming a large percentage of the total population. While in 1950 there was a ratio of 14 persons holding jobs for every Social Security recipient, by 1980 this ratio had declined to 3:1 (see Figure 24-16).

Congress passed the Social Security Act in 1935 to provide retirement benefits to the large middle- and low-income classes. The first payment which went to Mrs. Fuller was not made until 1940, when the Federal Old-Age and Survivors Insurance Trust Fund was established. In 1956, disability insurance was added to the system; and in 1965, medical insurance was included. The payroll taxes that employees pay for coverage are matched dollar for dollar by their employers. Social security is a pay-as-you-go system with a retiree's benefits being paid by those who are working. Table 24-4 indicates the changes over the years in the annual income base and the tax rate that generate funds for the Social Security program. Future benefits from the Social Security system are entirely dependent on taxes paid by the next generation. This is the reason why a low ratio of active workers to retirees is harmful to the system.

In 1983 a bipartisan National Commission on Social Security Reform recommended a program that would provide financial relief to the strapped system. The essential elements of the program, which was passed by Congress, include the following:

1. Acceleration of tax increases that were scheduled to go into effect in future years.
2. Reschedule of the cost-of-living increase in benefits to every January.

3. Taxation of half of Social Security benefits if the retiree's adjusted gross income plus half of the benefits exceed $25,000 (for couples, $32,000).
4. Requirement of *all* federal workers hired beginning January 1, 1984, and all employees of nonprofit organizations to join the Social Security system in January, 1984.
5. Prohibition of state and local government employees already in the system from dropping out.
6. Requirement of self-employed persons to pay 11.3 percent tax in 1984, rising to 13.02 percent in 1988–1989.

Time will tell how well the Social Security system weathers the challenges facing it.

Figure 24-16   Social Security Time Line

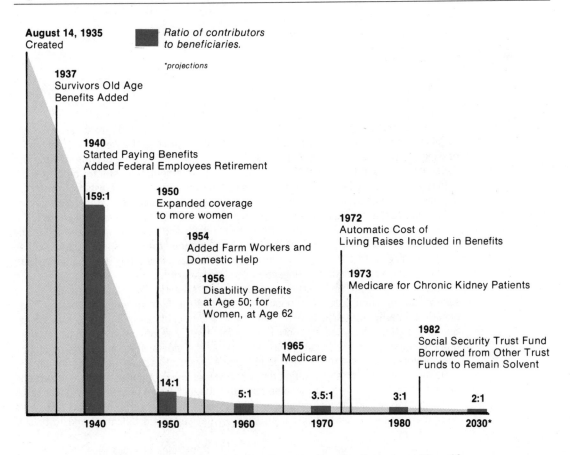

SOURCE: Adapted from *American Enterprise Teaching Notes,* Issue 10, p. 12.

Table 24-4   **Increases in Social Security Income Base, Tax Rates, and Taxes**

Year	Annual Income Base	Tax Rate[1]	Maximum Tax Payable
1937	$ 3,000	1.0 %	$ 30.00
1950	3,000	1.5	45.00
1970	7,800	4.8	374.40
1980	25,900	6.13	1,587.67
1981	29,700	6.65	1,722.35
1982	32,400	6.7	2,170.80
1983	35,700	6.7	2,391.90
1985	—[2]	7.05	—
1986	—[2]	7.15	—
1990	—[2]	7.65	—

[1]Tax rate is paid by both the employers and the employees.
[2]Wage base will increase automatically with any inflation-adjusted growth in average wages.

SOURCE: Social Security Administration.

SUMMARY

In the late 1800s certain competitive businesses found they could make larger profits by joining together in what became known as trusts. The federal government reacted by passing the Sherman Antitrust Act in 1890, followed in 1914 by the Clayton Act and the Federal Trade Commission Act. These laws, plus amendments, are still in force.

In recent years the federal government has shifted its regulatory interests from antitrust to consumer protection. Food, drugs, and cosmetics have been the subject of special legislation, and numerous labeling and consumer protection laws have been passed.

Laws in operation in most states affect labor, health and sanitation, prices, and maximum rates of interest on loans. At the local level, zoning ordinances and building codes restrict business. At both state and local levels, licenses frequently are required before individuals or corporations can engage in certain types of business.

Public utilities possess certain unique characteristics. They furnish a necessary service, are efficient only as monopolies, and have the right of eminent domain. They operate primarily intrastate and are regulated by city councils and state commissions. Such regulation, designed to allow them a fair rate of return on a fair value of their properties, concentrates on rates and services. At the federal level numerous regulatory commissions have jurisdiction over public utilities, as well as other regulated industries.

Some of the principles of taxation make business a prime target as a source of revenue for governments at all levels. For some taxes the impact falls on business, but these taxes can be shifted so that the incidence is felt elsewhere — usually by the consumer. Taxes can be and are used by government as a regulatory device, to aid business, and to bolster the economy.

States receive the largest amounts of revenue from sales or gross receipts taxes and income taxes. Cities also levy sales taxes and income taxes. Property taxes frequently account for almost all revenue at the local level unless the municipality also has a sales or income tax.

The federal government relies primarily on personal and corporate income taxes for the major source of its revenues. In recent years, the Social Security tax has become a greater burden to employers and employees.

BACK TO THE CHAPTER OPENER

1. Do government regulations affect individuals more than they affect businesses?
2. What government requirements cause the largest paperwork burden for individuals?
3. What are the federal regulations that promote competition?
4. What are the differences between the FTC and the FDA?
5. What is the significance of the Delaney clause to consumers?

BUSINESS TERMS

collusive bidding	597	police power	603
territorial pool	597	right of eminent domain	604
patent licensing	597	proportional tax	607
gentlemen's agreement	597	regressive tax	607
tying contracts	598	progressive tax	607
interlocking directorate	598	sumptuary taxes	608
community of interests	598		

QUESTIONS FOR DISCUSSION AND ANALYSIS

1. Why is competition more likely to be effective as a regulator of prices and services if the companies in an industry are both numerous and small?
2. Are territorial pools more harmful to competition than tying contracts?
3. Considering the existence of a well-seasoned FTC, why did Congress authorize a Consumer Product Safety Commission?
4. Is the federal regulation of competitive businesses more (or less) burdensome than state and local regulations? Cite specific examples to support your conclusion.
5. Is the use of a license as a method to regulate the number of liquor stores and other businesses more important than its use to certify the qualifications of lawyers and other professionals?
6. The railroads have always been regulated by the ICC, a federal agency. Why do states dominate the regulation of telephone, electric, and natural gas rates?
7. Is the recent federal deregulation of the transportation industry a sign that this country is moving in the direction of laissez-faire capitalism? Support your answer with specific examples.
8. Income taxes are levied by cities, states, and the federal government. Sales taxes are levied by states and municipalities. Is this duplication necessary? Discuss.
9. Property taxes provide most of the revenue collected by cities, townships, and other local governmental entities. What reasons can be given for this choice of a tax base?
10. Should employers and employees have a choice between joining or staying out of the Social Security system?

PROJECTS, PROBLEMS, AND SHORT CASES

1. Choose a particular industry, such as transportation, communications, or food, and prepare a paper that indicates the trend of regulation in the industry. Sources of articles for your paper are available from the *Business Periodicals Index* under "Regulations" and from the *Readers Guide to Periodical Literature* under "Industry and the Environment" and "Public Utilities."
2. From a nearby U.S. Internal Revenue Office, obtain a copy of the 1040 Personal Income Tax form and its instructions and a copy of the 1120 U.S. Corporation Income

Tax form and its instructions. Analyze each form and compare and contrast the type of information that is required by each. Identify the basic differences between the two forms. Organize your findings into a short report.

3. Juan Gomez was the driving force behind Taco Delight, a franchised chain of Mexican fast-food restaurants. Gomez had worked very long and hard to establish the operation. Using personal savings and loans from relatives and friends, he built his original restaurant in Phoenix, AZ. His tacos and burritos were immediately hailed as culinary delights. Gomez credited the acceptance of his tasty foods to the use of his Mexican grandmother's recipes that had been handed down through several generations of his family.

Believing there was a market in other communities for this type of food, Gomez decided to form a franchise organization. He strongly believed that Taco Delight could become the McDonald's of the Mexican fast-food business. Over a four-year period Gomez franchised 128 restaurants that extended from southern California to northern Missouri. His corporation owned another 15 units in Arizona and New Mexico. Wherever they were located, Taco Delight restaurants were acclaimed for their excellent Mexican food. Gomez continued to adhere to the formula that brought him success: his grandmother's recipes, quality ingredients, and high standards. To maintain this quality edge, he insisted on a rigid standard operating procedure for all of the restaurants. All items from napkins to buildings were standardized, and both food and nonfood items were supplied from a central warehouse.

Recently, Gomez had a franchisee in Missouri who expressed strong dissatisfaction with the chain's centralized buying procedures. This franchisee complained that his delivery of food supplies often was late. As a result, he began buying from a local supplier who offered him fast service and prices lower than those quoted by Gomez. Although Gomez attempted to improve his service to the franchisee, the individual continued to purchase from the local supplier. In fact, he began buying nonfood items from this supplier, too. Because the franchise agreement specified that franchisees would purchase all of their food and nonfood supplies from Gomez, he ordered the franchisee to discontinue the local purchases. Despite numerous warnings, the franchisee refused to comply. This caused Gomez to sue him for breach of contract.

To Gomez's surprise the court ruled in favor of the franchisee on the grounds that the provisions of the franchise agreement violated both the Sherman Antitrust and the Clayton Acts. Currently Gomez is pondering his next step. He could appeal the case and hope for the overthrow of the decision by a higher court. Another alternative would be to make changes in the provisions of the franchise agreement so he definitely would not be in violation of the antitrust acts. Finally, he could sit tight and hope that the other franchisees would not follow the lead of the Missouri franchise. Realizing that the future of his franchise system was at stake, Gomez was plagued by uncertainty.

a. Indicate specifically how the provisions of the franchise agreement violated the provisions of the antitrust acts.

b. What action should Gomez take next?

c. Itemize the different taxes that Gomez's company probably is paying to the Arizona and New Mexico cities in which it has stores, the states of Arizona and New Mexico, and the federal government.

VII. Business and You

Chapter 25. *Business Career Opportunities*
26. *Small Business and Franchising*

Computerized Job Matching

A California entrepreneur, Tom A. Papke, is convinced that computers will soon play a much bigger role in show business. In early July, working with a staff of five salesmen from an office in his Hollywood condominium, he formed a new company called International Computer Casting.

"There's a great need to organize talent," Mr. Papke says. "We intend to build an international computer network, or a kind of data base for the industry."

For a fee, Mr. Papke says, his new company will use a computer to catalogue the photographs and résumés of actors, models, singers, movie technicians, and others with specialized skills in the entertainment industry. Meanwhile, he adds, the company hopes to lease more than 1,000 computer terminals, as well as devices for receiving high-resolution photographs over telephone lines. This equipment, designed to "call up" candidates for a role or job, would be leased to movie studios, advertising agencies, modeling agencies and other concerns that hire entertainers.

Mr. Papke's company offers a new wrinkle in a broad trend toward what is called computerized job matching, a concept that's been in the experimental stage for more than a decade. In theory, job seekers in management, engineering, education, and many other fields could have their résumés, salary requirements, and other information assembled in large computer banks where employers would have instant access to lists of qualified job applicants.

Many corporations have already automated their personnel records and in some cases are keeping computerized records on job candidates. One example is the Hewlett-Packard Company, the electronics concern, which uses a computer for what it calls its Potential Employee Processing System. Margo Scott, the company's manager of staffing systems, said the two-year-old system was being used to keep track of the job movements, professional accomplishments, and other information supplied by the more than 100,000 applicants that Hewlett-Packard had on file.

In the future, Mrs. Scott added, the company hopes to use the system to track a far larger number of potential employees, sometimes beginning when they are in their teens and recommended by their high school teachers. "We feel that most of the people in the world are potential Hewlett-Packard employees," she said, "and this system could become a kind of headhunter."

Such extensive use of computers, however, is viewed with skepticism in some quarters. "You can't treat job applicants like pieces of inventory," declared Marc Silbert, president of the New York operations of Robert Half International, a major employment agency. He added that computers could "never provide the subtle nuance of experience and personality."

The largest use of computers in employment has been by government. In many states, job seekers receiving unemployment compensation are offered computerized job listings. Federal agencies, meanwhile, have increasingly used computers to screen job applicants.

SOURCE: Thomas J. Lueck, "Computerized Job Matching," *The New York Times,* August 5, 1982, p. D2. © 1982 by The New York Times Company. Reprinted by permission.

Business Career Opportunities

Objectives

- Identify the major factors that should be taken into consideration in making career planning decisions.
- Identify several important aids to occupational selection.
- Describe the various types of tests that are used to measure the vocational abilities of individuals.
- Understand the conditions necessary for establishing your own business.
- Describe the career paths in marketing, human resources, production, finance, accounting, computer operation, statistics, and government service.
- Identify the major elements of a job campaign.
- List several important sources of information about prospective employers.
- Comment on the construction of an effective letter of application.
- Write an appropriate résumé.
- Prepare for a favorable job interview.

Knowing he was betting against the odds, a young man wrote and asked to be interviewed for a copywriting job with a well-known advertising agency. Scores of candidates annually descend on advertising agencies for this type of assignment. In order to impress their prospective employers, most serious candidates bring a large portfolio of their work samples. This young man had none, so he knew that an extra creative effort would be necessary to demonstrate his ability to the agency management.[1]

The nervous candidate was ushered into the office of the agency's president, who was carefully reviewing the candidate's letter. The president looked up and declared, "You state that you are a skilled writer, but what have you written to prove this?"

"Well," replied the candidate confidently, "I produced a direct-mail piece that obtained a 100 percent response."

This amazing disclosure stunned the agency president for a moment. After all, a 5 percent return from direct mail is outstanding and a 100 percent response would rank with the seven wonders of the world. The president uttered in disbelief, "May I see it?"

The perspiring candidate rapidly responded, "You have it in your hand."

The president grinned and said, "And you have a job!"

Although this dramatic encounter led to a job, not all job candidates would be so lucky without some carefully planned and executed efforts. This chapter reviews the factors that you should consider in career planning. The various aids to occupational selection are identified and the areas of employment opportunities are discussed. A concluding section outlines the elements in a carefully prepared job campaign.

FACTORS TO CONSIDER IN CAREER PLANNING

An opportune time to establish career plans is at the beginning of a college program. The importance of including a college education in career plans is illustrated by the earnings difference between a college graduate and a high school graduate. The average college graduate can expect a lifetime income of more than $1,100,000, which is over 40 percent higher than the average for a high school graduate.

Selecting a career involves some complex decisions on your part. Several important factors should be taken into consideration when making these decisions. These factors include: type of occupation, kind of industry or organizational setting, size of company, line or staff position, and job location.

Type of Occupation

You may want to choose the type of occupation which is compatible with your interests and aptitudes, self-identity, personality, and social background. For example, one who is people-oriented may be strongly motivated toward a career in social work. Or, one who desires to attain power and status might be inclined to choose a managerial job.

---

1. William D. Ellis, "In Job Hunt, Mix Business, Humor," *Fort Wayne News-Sentinel,* August 23, 1982.

Kind of Industry or Organizational Setting

The kind of industry or organization in which you desire to work must also be considered. For example, in the accounting field you have a choice for a position among industrial firms, public accounting firms, and governmental agencies. Each of these types of settings provides a different work climate for an accountant.

In addition, the specific requirements of a position generally vary from industry to industry. For example, the responsibilities of a marketing researcher for U.S. Steel are different from those of one working for General Foods. Even within the same industry the duties of a particular job may differ from company to company because of the way the job is structured.

Size of Company

In a small company you often obtain a position that carries broader responsibilities than a similar position in a larger company with its more specialized assignments. On the other hand, the larger firm generally offers attractive promotions into many more types of managerial positions. Some individuals initially desire the training program, growth prospects, and high salaries offered by a large company. At a later period in their career, these same individuals may seek employment in smaller firms where they can assume a more important leadership role. Figure 25-1 shows the advantages of working for large and small employers.

Line or Staff Position

Do you seek a line position or a staff position? You may begin as a trainee or as an assistant in a staff position, such as marketing research or quality control, and eventually be promoted to head the staff. In many cases, however, this is as far as you will rise in a staff job. As indicated in Chapter 4, staff positions support the line activities. By working in staff positions, you are exposed to a variety of experiences that assist in your development as a future line executive. However, most top management positions are held by individuals who have spent the majority of their time in line jobs in either marketing, production, or finance. For example, the two top executives at General Motors are typically from production and finance.

Job Location

Choosing a community in which to work depends upon your personal preferences, life-style, and economic ambitions. For example, some individuals tend to feel more comfortable in the area of the country in which they have spent the longest period of their lives. This, however, is not a good reason for resisting a move to another geographic location. When job applicants restrict themselves to a particular location, they limit their number of job offers.

Figure 25-1   Advantages of a Large and a Small Employer

Large Employer	Small Employer
• More job levels, therefore greater promotional opportunities.	• Person of ability may stand out sooner and more prominently.
• Greater potential earnings.	• May offer eventual ownership possibilities.
• Starting salary often higher.	• Advancement often faster; competition may be less.
• More extensive training programs.	• Quicker assumption of responsibility and more immediate assignment to a specific job.
• Greater security and fringe benefits.	• More opportunity to benefit from growth of the organization.
• Greater financial strength to weather depressions and technological changes.	• Individual may be able to give more direction to work of organization and more readily see results of his own efforts.
• Promotion-from-within policies enable graduate to make career with one employer on a lifetime basis.	• More willing to hire older, experienced graduates.
• More staff resources available to help solve problems as they arise.	
• Greater expenditures on research to ensure progress.	• Often greater opportunity for the independent person who works best alone.
• Diverse operations permit functional and geographic transfers.	• Work is often more varied and not as routine.
• Often more scientific approach to management.	
• Less danger of being merged with large employer because of financial difficulties, competition of new products, or uneconomical size.	• Little need for geographical relocation, upsetting family life and friendships.
• More scientific promotion policies; little danger of relatives being favored as in a family-owned business.	• Policies and procedures more flexible; individual initiative may be more encouraged.
	• Often get better experience if you are interested in going into business for yourself.
	• Easier identification with goals of employer; more apt to be known by top management.

SOURCE: From *Planning Your Career* by Robert Calvert, Jr., and John E. Steele. Copyright ©1963 by McGraw-Hill Book Company, Inc. Used with permission of McGraw-Hill Book Company.

Individuals who desire employment in a large company should be willing to accept assignments wherever the company's plants and offices are located. An individual with a strong desire to reside in the Southeast, for example, may seek and accept a job with a large company in Atlanta only to be transferred several years later to Minneapolis. Some companies transfer their employees frequently.

For some job applicants the location of the job is more important than the nature of the job. Such individuals generally desire to locate in communities that reflect their life-styles. Job seekers often prefer communities that have a high job-growth potential and that offer good employment opportunities. Figure 25-2 shows the ten fastest growing U.S. cities during the 1980s. Seven of the cities are situated in the popular Sun Belt states.

AIDS TO OCCUPATIONAL SELECTION

Your college years should be the time to learn the relative merits of various careers. During this period, you can determine whether your own qualifications match the characteristics of a wide variety of occupations. Aids in selecting an occupation include tests, hobbies, college courses, work experience, vocational literature, industry contacts, and placement offices.

Tests

Various types of tests are used to measure your vocational abilities. Many colleges and universities have career centers or testing and psychological services centers where these tests are administered. The tests discussed on page 630 are measures of an individual's mental ability, aptitude, and interest and personality.

Figure 25-2   The 10 Fastest-Growing U.S. Cities for the Next 10 Years

Average annual job growth in per cent and growth industries, 1979-90*

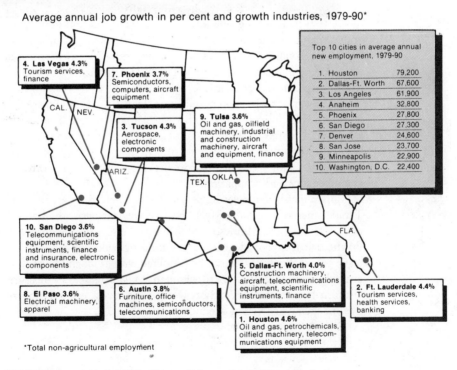

4. Las Vegas 4.3%
Tourism services, finance

7. Phoenix 3.7%
Semiconductors, computers, aircraft equipment

3. Tucson 4.3%
Aerospace, electronic components

9. Tulsa 3.6%
Oil and gas, oilfield machinery, industrial and construction machinery, aircraft and equipment, finance

10. San Diego 3.6%
Telecommunications equipment, scientific instruments, finance and insurance, electronic components

8. El Paso 3.6%
Electrical machinery, apparel

6. Austin 3.8%
Furniture, office machines, semiconductors, telecommunications

5. Dallas-Ft. Worth 4.0%
Construction machinery, aircraft, telecommunications equipment, scientific instruments, finance

2. Ft. Lauderdale 4.4%
Tourism services, health services, banking

1. Houston 4.6%
Oil and gas, petrochemicals, oilfield machinery, telecommunications equipment

Top 10 cities in average annual new employment, 1979-90	
1. Houston	79,200
2. Dallas-Ft. Worth	67,600
3. Los Angeles	61,900
4. Anaheim	32,800
5. Phoenix	27,800
6. San Diego	27,300
7. Denver	24,600
8. San Jose	23,700
9. Minneapolis	22,900
10. Washington, D.C.	22,400

*Total non-agricultural employment

SOURCE: Copyrighted, 1981, *Chicago Tribune.* Used with permission.

Intelligence Tests

Your ability to think, reason logically, and understand is measured by **intelligence tests**. Since these tests generally are prepared and validated on white middle-class Americans, they may contain a bias against other cultural and ethnic groups. The Wechsler Adult Intelligence Scale and the Stanford-Binet Test are individually administered tests that are quite accurate. The Wonderlic Personnel Test and the Otis Self-Administering Test of Mental Ability are short, group-administered tests that provide a reasonable estimate of mental ability.

Aptitude Tests

Your ability to learn how to perform certain jobs can be measured by **aptitude tests.** A purpose of these tests is to predict your future success in a particular occupation. Two aptitude tests are the Differential Aptitude Tests of the Psychological Corporation and the General Aptitude Test Battery (GATB) of the United States Employment Service. The GATB is available to job applicants who register with a State Employment Service.

Interest and Personality Tests

Patterns of likes and dislikes in various activities are shown in **interest tests.** These tests measure the similarity between your interests and those of successful men and women in a wide range of occupations. The Strong-Campbell Vocational Interest Blank is a popular interest test that in recent years has been carefully checked and refined to eliminate any sexism. The Kuder Interest Series is a group of interest inventories that has been in use since 1940.

A new test in the career guidance field is the Self-Directed Search, which was constructed by John Holland. This is a self-administered, self-scored guide to career selection. The user of Holland's test classifies herself or himself into one of six personality types. Each personality type is matched to a range of suggested occupations. Figure 25-3 shows the six personality types with their corresponding behavioral characteristics and occupations.

Instruments that measure personality characteristics are the Guilford-Zimmerman Temperament Survey, the Myers-Briggs Type Indicator, the Edwards Personal Preference Schedule, the Minnesota Multiphasic Personality Inventory, and the California Psychological Inventory. Although self-rating scales are available for most personality tests, personality traits cannot be measured with as much accuracy as can intelligence, aptitudes, and interests. Each **personality test** attempts to measure different personality attributes such as objectivity versus subjectivity, extroversion versus introversion, and independence versus dependence.

Hobbies

It is not at all unusual for students to gain a useful clue to their future choice of vocations through their hobbies or avocations. You may have certain likes and dislikes

Figure 25-3   Personality Types Matched with Behavioral Characteristics and Occupations

Personality Type	Behavioral Characteristics	Matching Occupations
● Realistic	● Involves aggressive behavior and physical activities requiring skill, strength, and coordination	● Forestry, farming, architecture
● Investigative	● Involves cognitive (thinking, organizing, and understanding) rather than affective (feeling, acting, or interpersonal and emotional) activities	● Biology, mathematics, oceanography
● Social	● Involves interpersonal rather than intellectual or physical activities	● Clinical psychology, foreign service, social work
● Conventional	● Involves structural, rule-regulated activities and subordination of personal needs to an organization or person of power and status	● Accounting, finance
● Enterprising	● Involves verbal activities to influence others and to attain power and status	● Management, law, public relations
● Artistic	● Involves self-expression, artistic creation, expression of emotions, and individualistic activities	● Art, music, education

SOURCE: Douglas T. Hall, *Careers in Organizations* (Pacific Palisades, CA: Goodyear Publishing Company, Inc., 1976), p. 13. Reproduced with permission.

that are shown by the activities in which you engage. If you enjoy sports, photography, or working with tools, you may discover that these interests are helpful in guiding you to a college major and a vocational selection.

College Courses

When you complete this course and others in business subjects, you will be more familiar with the various areas and activities of business. In most instances these activities can be translated into job opportunities. There may be some particular kind of work that has excited you during your course of instruction. It may prove to be the right answer to your problem of selecting a self-fulfilling and challenging vocation.

Work Experience

Some work experience during the school year and vacations is desirable. If it is financially possible, a variety of jobs should be sought. Each job will provide you with a basis for evaluating the various kinds of employment. If you have in mind a definite career choice, you should make a special effort to obtain some work experience in the chosen field.

The curricula of some schools offer internships and cooperative education programs which blend work experience with formal education. Through structured work assignments in a company, students are provided a realistic test of their career interests and aptitudes.

Vocational Literature

A wealth of vocational literature is available in your college library, as well as in the public libraries of your home community. The *Occupational Outlook Handbook* and the *Occupational Outlook Quarterly,* which are published by the Bureau of Labor Statistics, are particularly helpful in identifying trends and growth patterns for many different occupations. A useful reference in investigating specific jobs is the *Dictionary of Occupational Titles* (DOT) and *Supplements* prepared by the U.S. Employment Service. The DOT lists about 20,000 different occupations.

A great many books have been written about businesspersons and outstanding business firms. Many of these not only make fascinating reading, but also provide a description of an industry or an individual who achieved success. Articles appearing in *Fortune, Business Week, Time, Forbes, Nation's Business, The Wall Street Journal,* and other publications furnish information about companies and jobs, too.

Industry Contacts

Whenever the opportunity presents itself, visit a factory, a corporate office, a retailer, or a bank and note the activities being performed. Try to imagine yourself in some of the jobs you see others doing. Talk with employees at all levels of management about their jobs. Try to find out what they believe is important for success in their work. Industry contacts often are made through student organizations that invite businesspersons to their meetings.

Placement Offices

Many colleges and universities maintain placement offices. The primary purpose of a placement office is to provide a place where prospective graduates and employers may meet and discuss job offerings. Many of the firms that recruit college graduates describe their opportunities and positions in brochures that are usually available in the placement office.

AREAS OF EMPLOYMENT OPPORTUNITIES

Theodore Barry & Associates, a management consulting firm, has identified a "Big Ten" of job areas that will employ nearly 43 percent of all workers by 1990! These job areas are:

1. Medical/health services.
2. Educational services.
3. Eating/drinking establishments.
4. Retail/general merchandise.
5. Miscellaneous business services.
6. Wholesale.
7. Special trade contractors.
8. Finance.
9. Machinery (except electrical).
10. Food/dairy stores.[2]

Table 25-1 presents the employment trends and prospects for some of the occupations that are discussed below. As that table indicates, there will be wide variations in growth for the different occupations. Figure 25-4 indicates the career paths, or promotional opportunities, in selected occupations.

Establishing Your Own Business

Young persons who go into business for themselves find that the best opportunities are in their local communities and in a business that sells goods or services. The operation of a fast-food service, a home computer store, and a women's apparel shop are a few examples of such enterprises. Occasionally new manufacturing operations are established, but such firms are less common than new retailing organizations. The growth of franchising has provided new self-employment opportunities for persons who have the required capital and abilities.

Most individuals who hope to go into business for themselves realize that they must have adequate personal and financial resources. Many, however, fail to consider that they should have some experience in the proposed line of business. Without this experience it is wiser to work for someone else who is in the same or a related field.

Marketing

The field of marketing offers numerous and widely varied vocational opportunities for college graduates. In the areas of manufacturing and wholesaling alone there were nearly 1.5 million salespersons employed in 1980. Most firms believe that college-trained persons make the best salespersons. This belief is well-founded since the person who has completed college has demonstrated self-motivation, discipline, and persistence.

For those who achieve outstanding sales records and possess supervisory abilities, promotions to managerial positions are available. Figure 25-4 shows these promotional opportunities. Department stores usually promote salespersons first to the rank of

---

2. Elizabeth M. Fowler, "'82 Job Outlook," New York Times News Service, as printed in the *Muncie Star*, January 10, 1982, p. B2.

Table 25-1   Prospects to 1990 for Selected Business Occupations

Occupation	Estimated Employment, 1980	Expected % of Change by 1990	Job Growth
MARKETING OCCUPATIONS			
Manufacturers' salesworkers	440,000	*	As fast as average
Wholesale trade salesworkers	1,100,000	*	As fast as average
Retail trade salesworkers	3,300,000	*	As fast as average
Retail buyers	150,000	+20–27	As fast as average
Advertising workers	100,000	*	As fast as average
Public relations workers	87,000	+18–26	As fast as average
Marketing research analysts	29,300	*	Faster than average
PERSONNEL OCCUPATIONS			
Personnel and labor relations specialists	178,000	+15–22	As fast as average
Lawyers	425,000	+25–39	Faster than average
PRODUCTION OCCUPATIONS			
Blue-collar worker supervisors	1,300,000	+16–25	As fast as average
Industrial engineers	115,000	+26–38	Faster than average
Purchasing agents	172,000	+16–24	As fast as average
FINANCE OCCUPATIONS			
Bank officers and managers	400,000	+26–33	Faster than average
Credit managers	55,000	0	Slower than average
Insurance underwriters	76,000	+18–23	As fast as average
Claims representatives	210,000	+39–43	Faster than average
Actuaries	8,000	+40–48	Faster than average
Securities salesworkers	63,000	*	Faster than average
Real estate agents and brokers	580,000	*	Faster than average
Economists	44,000	+26–32	Faster than average
ACCOUNTING, COMPUTER OPERATIONS, AND STATISTICS			
Accountants and auditors	900,000	+25–34	Faster than average
Programmers	228,000	+22–27	As fast as average
Systems analysts	205,000	+68–80	Faster than average
Statisticians	26,500	+17–25	As fast as average
GOVERNMENT SERVICES			
City managers	3,300	+21	As fast as average
Occupational safety and health workers	80,000	*	As fast as average
Health and regulatory inspectors	112,000	+12–14	Slower than average

*Estimate not available.

SOURCE: "The Job Outlook in Brief," *Occupational Outlook Quarterly* (Spring, 1982), pp. 2–33; and *Occupational Outlook Handbook* (April, 1982).

assistant buyer and then to buyer for a particular department of a store. Many department stores have an executive training program for college graduates.

In 1980 there were 100,000 persons employed in advertising. Openings are available in the advertising departments of large firms and also in advertising agencies. Duties may involve copywriting and layout, or they may deal with such problems as buying or selling advertising space. In the advertising department of a firm, one can

Figure 25-4   Career Paths in Selected Occupations and Industries

Approx. Years of Service[1]	Marketing	Retailing	Personnel	Production Management	Banking	Public Accounting	Industrial Accounting
15	Vice-President Marketing	Corporate Vice-President	Vice-President Personnel	Vice-President Production	President	Partner or Principal	Vice-President Finance
14	National Sales or Advertising Manager	Nat'l Operations Manager					Division Controller
13		Nat'l Merchandise Manager	Corporate Personnel Staff	Division Manufacturing Manager	Senior Vice-President		
12	Product Group Manager	Zone Manager					
11		Divisional Buyer		Product Group Manufacturing Staff	Vice-President		Assistant Division Controller
10	Marketing Staff Analyst	Store Manager	Plant Personnel Manager	Plant Manager		Manager	Plant Controller
9					Asst. Vice-President Junior Officer		
8							Assistant Controller
7	Regional Sales Manager	Buyer	Employment Manager	Department Manager	Branch Manager Operations Dept. Manager Analyst Trust Commercial		
6	Branch Sales Manager					Senior Accountant	Department Manager
5		Asst. Store Manager					
4		Asst. Buyer or Dept. Manager		Production Supervision			
3	Sales Supervisor		Personnel Assistant			Staff Accountant	Staff Financial Analyst
2		Sales		Departmental Assistant	Banker in Training		
1	Sales	Trainee					General Accountant

[1]Of course, these estimates only approximate yearly progress in a purely hypothetical organization. More specific information is nearly impossible to obtain due to the wide variances between employers.

SOURCE: C. Randall Powell, *Career Planning Today* (Dubuque, IA: Kendall/Hunt Publishing Company, 1981). Reproduced with permission.

advance to the position of an assistant advertising manager and then to advertising manager. In agencies, the first step up might be to the position of account executive or assistant department manager.

There is an increasing demand for qualified personnel in marketing research. In 1980 there were about 29,300 market researchers employed in the United States. College graduates with a background in marketing and statistics are sought after by both marketing research firms and marketing research departments of many companies. The initial positions might be in sample construction, questionnaire design, or interviewing. Promotions lead to positions as supervisors or editors.

Human Resources

In 1980 employment in the field of human resources totaled 178,000. Employment possibilities in this field are greater in manufacturing firms than they are in distributive, financial, and other nonmanufacturing enterprises. Most of the larger factories maintain extensive human resources staffs. For those who become involved in labor negotiations, a law degree often is needed.

Within the human resources division, advancement possibilities include heading a department such as employment, training, personnel services, safety and health, personnel research, wages and salaries, and labor relations. From one of these posts an outstanding individual should be able to secure a position as a human resources manager. Many firms with complex labor-management problems now have a vice-president in charge of labor relations.

Production

Industries engaged in manufacturing employ about 22 percent of all workers in the United States. Within these organizations are many opportunities for college-trained students of business. Some graduates begin as trainees and advance to such supervisory positions as line supervisor, production manager, and plant manager. Others work in industrial engineering, quality control, production control, shipping and traffic, warehousing, and plant maintenance. The opportunities for advancement in this field are also shown in Figure 25-4 on page 635.

Purchasing for a manufacturing concern utilizes many of the skills and much of the knowledge acquired by a business student. Following an initial training program, a capable individual will progress from junior buyer, to buyer, to assistant purchasing agent, to purchasing agent. In large organizations, purchasing agents or managers of purchasing departments may become vice-presidents who are responsible for all aspects of materials management.

Finance

The field of finance offers a variety of vocational opportunities for persons with collegiate training in business. Many financial positions require an individual who has an aptitude for and an interest in working with numbers.

Commercial banking offers many exciting opportunities for those with a broad knowledge of business activities. Advancement possibilities include cashier or controller, branch manager, and trust officer. Figure 25-4 on page 635 shows the career paths in a typical banking organization. In 1980 there were 400,000 bank officers and financial managers employed. Positions are also available in governmental banking agencies.

Positions in the credit field include credit managers, who authorize credit transactions, and loan officers, who approve cash loans. Credit officials examine financial reports, interview credit references, and work with credit bureaus in gathering the information necessary for making decisions on credit granting.

One of the largest career fields for college-trained people is insurance. Life and property and casualty insurance companies are continually seeking qualified individuals who desire to become agents and brokers. Other occupations, such as underwriters, actuaries, claims adjusters, and claim examiners, are also available.

The broad area of finance also includes many other types of job openings. Investment banking companies and brokerage firms employ college graduates to sell stocks and bonds, to handle accounts, and to perform security analyses. The field of real estate offers both selling and property management opportunities.

Accounting, Computer Operation, and Statistics

Accounting is a large field with three major subdivisions—public, industrial, and governmental. In 1980 there were 900,000 persons employed in accounting and over a third of the accountants were women. Public accounting is a profession, and the usual goal is to qualify as a Certified Public Accountant. Experience is acquired by working as a junior accountant with a public accounting firm. Career progress will lead to either a partnership in the organization or the establishment of one's own office.

Industrial accounting embraces the accounting activities of all types of firms. A major activity of the industrial accountant in a manufacturing firm is cost accounting. Numerous companies also employ internal auditors whose duties are somewhat similar to those performed by public accountants. Although many starting positions are clerical, such as handling receivables or payrolls, opportunities for advancement are excellent.

Governmental accounting positions are open in many branches of the federal and state governments. The Federal Bureau of Investigation and the Internal Revenue Service have numerous positions available for college accounting majors. Other agencies, such as the Armed Services, General Accounting Office, and Department of Agriculture, employ accountants in civil-service positions.

The widespread introduction of electronic data processing equipment has provided a growing field for college graduates with a background in business. There are employment opportunities for data processing directors, systems analysts, computer programmers, business-systems coordinators, program managers, and other similar managerial positions. Some of these jobs require mathematical abilities and aptitudes in addition to a basic knowledge of business operations.

Persons qualified as statisticians are needed by industry, research organizations, and the government. Many large firms recruit college graduates for their own statistical departments. All types of research organizations have trained statisticians on their staffs. Advancement to more responsible positions may lead to such managerial posts as chief statistician or director of research.

Government Service

Government employment has surged to the point where nearly one out of every five employed persons works for the government. Many types of employment opportunities exist in government at city, state, and national levels. Federal jobs often carry some form of civil service classification. College men and women who expect to make their careers with the federal government should take the competitive Civil Service examinations that are given periodically. Individuals who pass are placed into one of the **General Schedule (GS) grades.** They often are employed as management trainees in a manner similar to the training programs available in private companies. There are 550 different white-collar occupations within the 18 GS grades in the federal government. Table 25-2 shows the GS grades, number of employees in each grade, pay range, and examples of the type of work done.

Table 25-2   **Distribution and Pay Ranges of Federal Workers by General Schedule (GS) Grades, 1982**

General Schedule Grades	Number of Employees in Grade	Pay Range (Year)	Type of Work
GS-1	2,375	$ 8,676–$10,857	Messenger
GS-2	17,734	9,756– 12,278	File clerk
GS-3	81,406	10,645– 13,840	Typist
GS-4	163,802	11,949– 15,531	Senior stenographer
GS-5	191,130	13,369– 17,383	Engineering technician
GS-6	90,739	14,901– 19,374	Secretary
GS-7	132,131	16,559– 21,527	Computer operator
GS-8	28,160	18,339– 23,838	Computer operator
GS-9	142,290	20,256– 26,331	Buyer
GS-10	28,037	22,307– 29,003	Electronics technician
GS-11	159,550	24,508– 31,861	Job analyst
GS-12	164,954	29,374– 38,185	Attorney
GS-13	111,485	34,930– 45,406	Chief accountant
GS-14	56,772	41,277– 53,661	Personnel director
GS-15	28,491	48,553– 63,115	Personnel director
GS-16 ⎫	739	56,945– 72,129 ⎫	Super grades — supervisors, directors of bureaus
GS-17 ⎬	163	66,708– 75,604 ⎬	
GS-18 ⎭	75	78,184– — ⎭	

SOURCE: *Federal Register,* Vol. 47, No. 198 (October 13, 1982), p. 4483.

PLANNING A JOB CAMPAIGN

When approaching graduation, the prospective graduate needs to prepare a carefully planned job campaign. The elements of this campaign should include: information on job opportunities, information on prospective employers, a letter of application, a résumé, adequate preparation for an interview, and some luck (see Figure 25-5). Similar to a military campaign, all elements of a job campaign are equally important and interrelated.

Figure 25-5	A Little Bit of Luck

Carter Burgess

Burgess has been president of TWA, president and then chairman of American Machine & Foundry, and is currently a director of Ford, J. P. Morgan, and Smith-Kline. He might have done a lot less but for a piece of luck in December 1941.

He was then a second lieutenant in the Army at Fort Myer near Washington, D.C. One day the post adjutant stuck his head out of a window as Burgess was passing and asked if he had a pressed uniform. Burgess did, and was told to report immediately to the Federal Reserve Building. It turned out that Roosevelt, Churchill, and their senior military aides were meeting there and urgently needed well-turned-out young officers who knew how to run a mimeograph and serve tea.

Burgess impressed the high-level military people at the meeting, and his military career took off like a rocket. When the war ended, the military contacts led to several middle-level executive jobs, then to a stint as Assistant Secretary of Defense for Manpower, then to TWA and AMF. Burgess says he often wonders how it would have all turned out if that uniform hadn't been pressed.

SOURCE: Daniel Seligman, "Luck and Careers," FORTUNE (November 16, 1981), p. 61. © 1981 Time Inc. All rights reserved.

Sources of Information on Job Opportunities

The first step in a job campaign is to locate job opportunities. For many college students the college placement office is the most important source of job leads. Many employers of college graduates list their specific job needs with the placement office. State employment offices and private employment agencies supply additional leads for job opportunities. A state employment office brings together prospective employers and employees, and its services are free. A private employment agency operates like a state employment office but charges a fee.

Some persons are hesitant to contact faculty members and friends about jobs. These acquaintances, however, often can supply valuable information about the availability of jobs. Research by the U.S. Department of Labor indicates that 48 percent of job seekers find employment through people they know. Professional groups, such as the American Marketing Association and the National Association of Accountants, frequently provide information on job openings in their fields. Some of these associations have collegiate chapters that can use the job placement services of the national association. Job fairs, where a number of employers have recruiting booths, often provide an opportunity for initial contacts with prospective employers.

Want ads in local newspapers and trade publications are another source of job openings. The ads in local newspapers usually are for lower-level positions than those in trade publications. The ads in trade publications, such as *Women's Wear Daily* and *Advertising Age,* are generally more appealing to career-oriented college graduates.

Sources of Information on Prospective Employers

With very little effort you can gather numerous facts about prospective employers. The type of information to be gathered about an employer is shown in Figure 25-6. Such information generally can be found in the college placement office or the school library.

Books, Periodicals, and Indexes

An important book that is found in most placement offices is the *College Placement Annual.* This book contains an alphabetical listing of large companies that intend to recruit college graduates.

School libraries contain a variety of materials on companies. These range from business histories about Sears, General Motors, and other firms to short periodical articles about a company. The *Business Periodicals Index* serves as a guide to numerous articles about companies and industries. The *Funk and Scott Index* is particularly suitable for use by job applicants since it identifies an article in a periodical by the name of the company featured.

Directories and Manuals

In most libraries there are several directories that supply useful company information to job applicants. Two of the best ones are Dun & Bradstreet's *Middle Market Directory* and *Million Dollar Directory.* The *Middle Market Directory* lists businesses that have a net worth ranging from $500,000 to $999,000. The *Million Dollar Directory* includes all businesses that have a net worth of $1 million or more.

Listings in the Standard and Poor's *Register of Corporations, Directors, and Executives* contain the company name, address, volume of sales, number of employees, principal products, and names of company executives. The Moody's *Manuals of Investment* provide very adequate financial information on companies. Five specialized Moody's manuals are published each year: *The Industrial Manual, Bank and Finance Manual, Transportation Manual, Municipal and Government Manual,* and *Public Utilities Manual*. For each firm listed in a manual there is information on its history, sales, profits, officers, and finances. The *Federal Career Directory: A Guide for College Graduates* is a complete guide to federal jobs that is published annually by the U.S. Civil Service Commission.

Figure 25-6   Information to Gather About an Employer Prior to an Interview

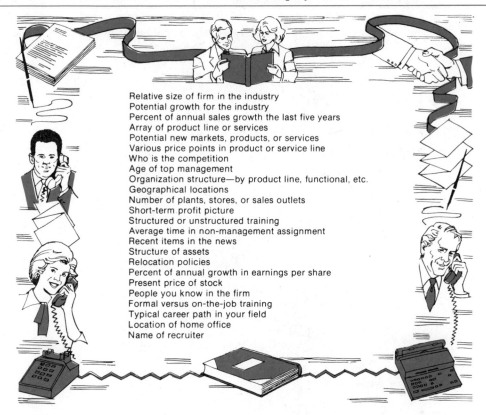

Relative size of firm in the industry
Potential growth for the industry
Percent of annual sales growth the last five years
Array of product line or services
Potential new markets, products, or services
Various price points in product or service line
Who is the competition
Age of top management
Organization structure—by product line, functional, etc.
Geographical locations
Number of plants, stores, or sales outlets
Short-term profit picture
Structured or unstructured training
Average time in non-management assignment
Recent items in the news
Structure of assets
Relocation policies
Percent of annual growth in earnings per share
Present price of stock
People you know in the firm
Formal versus on-the-job training
Typical career path in your field
Location of home office
Name of recruiter

SOURCE: C. Randall Powell, *Career Planning Today* (Dubuque, IA: Kendall/Hunt Publishing Company, 1981). Reproduced with permission.

Company Materials

Large companies, such as General Motors, Federated Department Stores, and Mead, furnish extensive materials on their company training programs and job opportunities. All large employers prepare annual reports that, in addition to financial information, often contain data on new ventures, product developments, and management changes.

Writing the Letter of Application

A **letter of application** such as that illustrated in Figure 25-7 reveals both the organizational and writing skills of its writer. It should be effective, personalized, and directed to the person who hires for the desired position.

Figure 25-7   A Letter of Application

> 3428 N. Tildale Avenue
> Apt. 278
> Muncie, IN 47304-4925
> March 6, 1984
>
> Ms. Jane Phillips
> Director of Human Resources
> Illinois Chemical Products Company
> Hofbrau, IL 58971-2218
>
> Dear Ms. Phillips:
>
> Do you desire to employ a self-motivated, conscientious person for your sales position? I have had three years of successful selling in a large furniture store. During these three years, I built a growing clientele and learned effective selling techniques. Because of my work experience, academic background, and personality, I believe that I qualify as a candidate for your sales position.
>
> My selling experience has convinced me that a sales position is most consistent with my values and objectives. My eventual career goal is to attain a responsible position in marketing management. As indicated in one of your booklets in our College Placement Office, you provide the opportunity for a capable person to move through sales into marketing management. A remark was made in the booklet that over 70 percent of the managers in your marketing area have been promoted from other marketing assignments within your company.
>
> My work at McIntyre Furniture provided me with a background for your type of sales activity. I have had experience in planning a sales campaign, preparing ads and promotions, developing an inventory control system, and handling customer complaints. The attached résumé provides other examples of the kinds of experiences that have prepared me for your sales position.
>
> May I have the privilege of an interview during the week of March 19? I will call you within the next few days to see if we can arrange a convenient time.
>
> Sincerely yours,
>
> Craig Bolton
>
> Enclosure

The initial paragraph should attract the attention and arouse the interest of the prospective employer in the applicant. An attention-grabbing statement, such as "Do you desire a self-motivated, conscientious, and proven salesperson?", is proper. An additional statement should indicate why the employer should be interested in the candidate.

The middle paragraphs should state the specific reasons for desiring to work for the firm. Your immediate job goals and long-term ambitions should be mentioned. If you declare that you will be successful in the job, this comment should be supported with adequate reasons. There should be some concrete evidence, too, that you are familiar with the employer's activities. This evidence may be shown by referring to company policies or product offerings. Another statement in this part of the letter should indicate that your résumé is enclosed.

In the final paragraph you usually request either a personal interview or additional information. At this point an effective letter will have created a desire on the part of the employer for an interview with you.

Preparing a Résumé

Your **résumé**, or personal data sheet, is a written summary of personal, educational, and experience factors that indicate your ability to perform a job. Since the major corporations receive more than 200 résumés every day, there is a need to distinguish your résumé from all the others. Your résumé should establish a link between your strengths and the demands of the position you desire (see Figure 25-8).

Figure 25-8	White Lies and Red Lights

White lies in a résumé can activate a red light in your job search. Since the Janet Cooke incident, employers are investigating the background of job candidates more carefully. Miss Cooke was a budding journalist who falsified her college experience on her résumé to *The Washington Post*. After being hired by the *Post*, she wrote a fabricated story that won high acclaim and subsequently a Pulitzer Prize. When it became known that the fascinating story was false, the award was taken away, leaving all parties thoroughly embarrassed.

According to one study, 80 percent of all résumés contain some white lies, of which almost a third relate to a person's education. At AT&T's corporate headquarters all job applicants must sign a form indicating that the applicant understands that the company will conduct an investigation to verify his or her employment history and education. Any false statement that is uncovered is reason for disqualification or dismissal.

Cheating on a résumé is not bad news for everyone, however. Many employers are using the services of a small Minneapolis firm, National Credential Verification Services, to detect faulty résumés. Within 24 hours after receiving an employer request, the firm can verify whether a particular applicant has the degree and years of attendance stated on a résumé. White lies on résumés became a green light for a new business!

In recent years the information in a résumé has become more important to employers. This is because some states have passed strict laws limiting the questions that employers can ask on application forms. Questions that often cannot appear on these forms generally involve race, religion, nationality, criminal record, marital status, sex, and age.

An effective résumé is short, concise, and well-organized. Figure 25-9 shows that a one-page résumé is usually adequate. Most résumés include the following parts:

Figure 25-9 **A Résumé**

CRAIG BOLTON

ADDRESS	3428 N. Tildale Avenue Apt. 278 Muncie, IN 47304-4925 Phone: (317) 286-8200
PERSONAL DATA	Date of birth: April 2, 1963 Height: 5'10" Weight: 145 lbs. Marital status: married Children: none Health: excellent
PROFESSIONAL OBJECTIVE	To be a sales representative for a marketing-oriented firm, eventually qualifying for management responsibilities.
EDUCATION	Ball State University, Muncie, IN, B.S. Marketing, May, 1984. Earned a 3.93 grade point average (based on a 4.0 scale). Relevant courses outside major field: chemistry and biology.
COLLEGE ACTIVITIES	While attending Ball State University, activities were: Blue Key National Honor Society; Junior Marshal for 1983 graduation ceremonies; Vice-President of Student Marketing Association, 1983–84; elected to Beta Gamma Sigma Honorary and Phi Eta Sigma Honorary; recipient of Ermal Marsh Business Scholarship, 1982–84.
WORK EXPERIENCE School year 1982–84:	Central Mailing Department, Ball State University: Mail carrier, delivering University-related mail.
1980–82:	McIntyre Furniture, Inc., Farmland, IN: Assisted in many aspects of the business, but concentrated in the sales area. Delivered papers for three years while in high school. Was 100 percent self-supporting during college.
Marketing internship:	McIntyre Furniture, Inc., Farmland, IN: Salesperson with various management responsibilities—planned, promoted, and implemented annual sale; developed inventory control system; and assisted with interior decorating.
INTERESTS	Tennis, golf, basketball, spectator sports, and photography.

CREDENTIALS AND REFERENCES ON FILE AT BALL STATE UNIVERSITY PLACEMENT OFFICE

1. *Identification.* This includes name, address, and telephone number.
2. *Personal data.* This includes marital status, birth date, height, and weight.
3. *Professional objective.* This should be general enough to cover any suitable job, yet specific enough to identify the applicant's major interest.
4. *Education.* The highest degree received should be identified first. High schools attended do not need to be listed, but all colleges attended should be shown. If the

applicant has a high grade point average (GPA), it should be identified. If the GPA is low, grades in major subjects and grade improvements should be emphasized and reasons for low grades should be stated.

5. *College activities.* A listing of college activities and the offices held in these activities provides an employer with an insight into the social skills and leadership ability of the applicant.

6. *Work experience.* For a new college graduate the type of work experience often is less important than the evidence that the applicant is a hard worker. Any work experience that indicates the graduate's time was spent in a productive manner is appreciated by the employer.

7. *Special skills, hobbies, or interests.* Any of these that relate to the desired job should be identified.

8. *References.* Some job counselors advise applicants to omit a list of references from their résumés. Instead, they recommend a statement be made that references will be furnished on request.

Preparing for an Interview

Table 25-3 reveals that your communication skills, personality, poise, and appearance are very important factors that a recruiter will evaluate in the initial job interview. These same factors are also very important in succeeding on the job and obtaining promotions, as Table 25-4 shows.

Because of the importance of the initial interview, a great deal of preparation should precede it. Pre-interview research serves the dual purposes of finding out about the company and building an applicant's confidence (see Figure 25-10). Armed with information about the company, you can ask intelligent questions and project an image

Table 25-3   Factors in Obtaining a Job

| | PERCENTAGE | | |
	Very Important	Important	Not Important
Grade point average	23.7	64.5	11.8
Oral communication skills	69.0	30.0	1.0
Written communication skills	38.3	52.2	9.5
Poise	42.9	57.1	0
Appearance	37.9	56.9	5.2
Social graces	6.8	64.0	29.2
Personality	44.1	51.6	4.3
School attended	1.1	51.6	47.3
Recommendations	16.9	52.8	30.3

SOURCE: Reprinted with the permission of Allen Blitstein, Southwest State University, from *The Collegiate Forum,* published by Dow Jones and Company, Inc., Princeton, NJ 08540. Copyright 1981, all rights reserved.

Table 25-4   Factors in Succeeding on the Job and Obtaining Promotions

	PERCENTAGE		
	Very Important	Important	Not Important
Grade point average	2.2	32.3	65.5
Oral communication skills	75.3	23.7	1.0
Written communication skills	61.7	35.1	3.2
Poise	43.0	51.6	5.4
Appearance	29.0	68.8	2.2
Social graces	8.8	61.2	30.0
Personality	52.7	44.1	3.2
School attended	0	12.9	87.1
Recommendations	11.3	33.7	55.0

Figure 25-10   A Rough Interview

of self-assurance. Figure 25-11 identifies some points you should remember in regard to the interview.

You should be prepared to answer any questions concerning your qualifications, goals, and personal interests. Figure 25-12 lists 20 questions that often are asked by interviewers. Since your résumé may serve as a guide for the interviewer, you should review it prior to the interview.

Applicants often are uncertain of how to respond to an interviewer's question about salary requirements. If the salary question arises in an interview, you should inform the interviewer that you are looking for future opportunities, not an enormous initial salary. Of course, the interviewer should understand that you expect a competitive salary. You should obtain from your college placement office the salary range for a position prior to interviewing for the position.

Figure 25-11 The Interview: Some Points to Remember

Analyze Strengths and Weaknesses. In preparing for interviews, start by doing some solid, honest self-assessment. Analyze your strengths and weaknesses, your background, your academic performance, your vocational interests, and your personal aspirations and values. In other words, begin to formulate, in your own mind, not only what you would like to do but also what you feel you are best prepared to do.

Read Employer Literature. Next, study your prospective employers. It is imperative that you have some knowledge about their policies, philosophies, products, and services. Failure to do your homework before an interview can be the kiss of death. Nothing turns recruiters off faster.

Dress in Good Taste. Although most employers are becoming more liberal in their standard of dress and appearance, let basic good taste be your guide. If a beard or "Alice-in-Wonderland" look is going to jeopardize your chances for a job, that's your decision. With some employers, appearance could be the deciding factor. The question you have to ask yourself is, "How important is it?"

Be Yourself. Your attitude is going to influence the interviewer's evaluation. Don't try to be something you aren't . . . just be yourself. Emphasize your strong points and remember that the recruiter is looking for inherent personal energy and enthusiasm. The interview is your opportunity to sell a product and that product is *you!*

Dwell on the Positive. Try always to dwell on the positive. While past failures and shortcomings need not be volunteered, don't try to cover them up or side-step them. Should recruiters ask about them, try to explain the circumstances rather than give excuses or blame others. Remember, they're human, too . . . and probably have made a few mistakes. You'll create a better impression by being honest and candid.

Ask Questions—When Indicated. If appropriate, ask meaningful questions, particularly if you're not clear about the details of the job, the training program, or other job-related concerns. But, don't ask questions just because you think that's what is expected.

Follow Up. Finally, follow up on the interview. Provide whatever credentials, references, or transcripts are requested by the prospective employer as soon as possible. Be sure to write down the name, title, and address of the recruiter. You may want to consider a brief typed letter of appreciation for the interviewing opportunity.

Use Your Career Planning and Placement Office. These are, of course, only general suggestions and observations. For more detailed and personalized advice, take advantage of the services of your college's career planning and placement office.

SOURCE: The College Placement Council, *The Campus Interview.*

Figure 25-12   Twenty Questions Often Asked by Job Interviewers

1. Tell me about yourself. Expand on your résumé.
2. For what position are you applying?
3. What are your long-term career goals? Where in ten years?
4. Why do you feel that you will be successful in . . . ?
5. What supervisory or leadership roles have you held?
6. How do you spend your spare time?
7. What have been your most satisfying and most disappointing experiences?
8. What are your strongest (weakest) personal qualities?
9. Give me some examples that support your stated interest in . . . .
10. Why did you select us to interview with?
11. What courses did you like best? least? Why?
12. What did you learn or gain from your part-time and summer job experiences?
13. Which geographic location do you prefer? Why?
14. Would you prefer on-the-job training or a formal program?
15. What can you do for us now? What can I do for you?
16. What are your plans for graduate study?
17. Why did you choose your major?
18. Why are your grades low?
19. Tell me about your extracurricular activities and interests.
20. Why did you quit your various jobs?

SOURCE: C. Randall Powell, *Career Planning Today* (Dubuque, IA: Kendall/Hunt Publishing Company, 1981). Reproduced with permission.

SUMMARY

Selecting a career involves several complex decisions on your part. These decisions relate to: type of occupation, kind of industry or organizational setting, size of company, line or staff position, and job location. In the small company a position usually carries broader responsibilities than a similar position in a larger company. The larger firm, however, offers attractive promotions into many more types of managerial positions.

Aids to occupational selection include: tests, hobbies, college courses, work experience, vocational literature, industry contacts, and college placement offices. Intelligence tests measure the capacity of a person to think, reason logically, and understand. Aptitude tests measure the ability of a person to learn how to perform certain jobs. Interest tests measure the similarity between one's interests and those of successful people in a wide range of occupations. Personality tests measure personality traits. The college placement office serves as a place where prospective graduates and employers can meet and discuss job offerings.

As the supply of college graduates approaches the demand, a knowledge of specific employment opportunities becomes vitally important. Some individuals with adequate personal and financial resources and experience in a particular line of business go into business for themselves. In the field of marketing there are numerous career opportunities in sales, retailing, advertising, and marketing research. Within the human resources division, individuals may seek positions in the following areas: employment, training, personnel services, safety and health, personnel research, wages and salaries, and labor relations. In the production area there are employment opportunities in factory supervision, industrial engineering, quality control, production control, shipping and traffic, warehousing, plant maintenance, and purchasing. In the field of finance, jobs are available in commercial banking, credit operations, investment banking, stock brokerage firms, and real estate organizations. Other career fields include accounting, computer operations, and statistics. In recent years, the government has offered many opportunities for qualified individuals.

The major elements of a job campaign include: information on job opportunities, information on prospective employers, a letter of application, a résumé, and preparation for an interview. Each of these elements is equally important and interrelated.

BACK TO THE CHAPTER OPENER

1. What type of information should a job candidate place in a computerized job matching system?
2. In what type of industries will computerized job matching be most successful?
3. Will computerized job matching for college graduates eventually replace college placement offices?
4. How will computerized job matching reveal the personality and attitudes of job candidates?
5. If computerized job matching becomes accepted, how will planning a job campaign change for college graduates?

BUSINESS TERMS

intelligence tests	630	General Schedule (GS) grades	638
aptitude tests	630	letter of application	641
interest tests	630	résumé	643
personality test	630		

QUESTIONS FOR DISCUSSION AND ANALYSIS

1. When is the best time for a student to establish a career plan? Discuss.
2. Why do the specific requirements of a position generally vary from industry to industry and from company to company?
3. Should a person's first job be with a small or a large company? Discuss.
4. Why do persons who remain in staff positions throughout their careers have difficulty in advancing to chief executive in their companies?
5. Are aptitude tests more important than intelligence tests to employers who are recruiting college graduates?
6. Is a college placement office doing its job if less than 90 percent of those registered with the office obtain employment?
7. Should one choose a career field in which the availability of jobs is limited? Discuss.
8. Why would a graduate choose employment in the government over private industry?
9. Is a letter of application more important than a résumé? Discuss.
10. If a recruiter offers you a cigarette, should you accept it—assuming you are a smoker?

1. Choose a large company in which you have an interest. Assume that you are going to interview for a job with this company. Go to the library or your college placement office and gather all the pre-interview information that is necessary for a successful interview. Then do the following:

a. Indicate how each piece of information that you gathered will be useful in a job interview.

b. List the sources of your information.

2. The purpose of this project is to acquaint you with the requirements of a specific vocation. The project is divided into three assignments. Prepare a concise, well-organized paper on these assignments.

a. Identify a vocational objective which you would like to attain in 10 to 15 years. Indicate the major job duties, places of employment, training, qualifications, working conditions, and employment outlook for this selected vocational objective. Library references, such as the *Dictionary of Occupational Titles,* the *Occupational Outlook Handbook,* and the *Encyclopedia of Careers and Vocational Guidance,* should be especially helpful.

b. Relate your personal qualifications, such as education, aptitudes, skills, and personality, to the requirements of the selected vocation.

c. Interview a person who is working in the selected career. From this interview you should learn firsthand about the requirements and responsibilities of the selected career field. Friends, professors, and members of your family may provide you with suggestions concerning whom to interview.

3. After reading a description of the following jobs, answer the questions that follow Job 3.[3]

Job 1

Company 1 is an international electronics firm with sales of $1 billion a year. It has offered you a job as assistant to the general manager of the Aerospace Division at a starting salary of $19,000 a year. The division headquarters is in a pleasant suburb of San Diego, California. The expectation is that if you perform satisfactorily, within two years you would be assigned to a line management position in one of the corporation's international subsidiaries, after which you would return to the United States. Your duties in the entry-level job would include studies of problems in a variety of functional areas. During the interviews, the division's general manager appeared to be competent, personable, and interested in your career aspirations. She mentioned that she thought a person should enjoy working, as she did, and should be able to strike a healthy balance between on-the-job development and commitments to family, community, and personal growth.

Job 2

Company 2 is a small solar energy equipment manufacturer in your hometown. The president, a somewhat absent-minded engineer who developed the solar heat-

---

3. James W. Schreier, "What Students Look for in Jobs." Reprinted from the Fall 1981 *Journal of College Placement* with the permission of the College Placement Council, Inc., copyright holder.

ing process that is the firm's main product, wants a person to handle "the business end of the business." This would include management of the firm's 82 employees, development of an internal accounting and control system, and negotiations with potential clients. With this arrangement, the president could concentrate on research and design of new products. The company can only afford to pay a $16,000 salary, but there is a provision for profit sharing once sales and new income begin to grow. In the future, the responsibilities of the position could be expected to expand rapidly, along with the company.

Job 3

Company 3 is one of the largest and most prestigious consulting firms in the world, with offices in New York, London, Paris, and San Francisco. You have undergone a rigorous series of correspondence, tests, and interviews before being offered a job in the London office. You would start as a consultant, working with a small team of professionals under the supervision of a seasoned project manager. The work would be highly challenging. You would stretch your analytical abilities and sharpen your interpersonal skills by associating with high-powered, interesting clients and colleagues. The starting salary is $22,000 a year, considerably above what is paid by other companies in Great Britain. However, the consultants you have spoken with have stressed that the firm "gets its money's worth." The typical workweek is 60 hours, with an average of 60 percent out-of-town travel. One of the partners mentioned that the company adheres to an "up or out" policy. Consultants at all levels are evaluated thoroughly and, if they do not consistently attain the high standards of professional performance for which Company 3 is known, they are placed in other careers outside the firm.

a. Indicate your order of preference for the three jobs and explain the reasons for your ranking.

b. Indicate how the two jobs that you did not choose could be changed to make them more attractive to you.

c. Relate the following job choice factors in a ranking order to Jobs 1, 2, and 3:

(1) Attractive job duties
(2) Attractive benefits
(3) Attractive job location
(4) Variety of assignments
(5) Job security
(6) Stimulating contact with colleagues

(7) Chance to learn new skills
(8) Attractive work climate
(9) Attractive salary
(10) Chance to exercise leadership
(11) Opportunity for advancement
(12) Proper pace/stress

d. From the twelve job choice factors mentioned above, select and rank the four that you believe are most important to job candidates.

Increasing Profits by Decreasing Weight

It's the sort of story that would-be business owners dream about. For nearly the first 20 years of her marriage, Sybil Ferguson was 50 pounds or more overweight. In the late 1960s, desperation drove her to devise her own diet based on vitamins, basic foods, and exercise. It worked for her and her friends and became a tiny business.

From that grew Diet Center Inc., a national network of 1,322 centers that sold about $140 million in weight-reducing services and products in the fiscal year ended September 30. Diet Center itself earned $3.4 million on about $19 million in revenue. Now Mrs. Ferguson's Cadillac and her husband's sit in reserved spaces at the company's headquarters in Rexburg, Idaho; a nearby hangar houses a company airplane and a small helicopter Mr. Ferguson is learning to fly.

Diet Center's success is largely the result of good timing and its owner's good business sense. Mrs. Ferguson's diet program came along when fitness was becoming an American fetish and any new way to lose weight was almost sure to attract interest. And Mrs. Ferguson's husband, Roger, president of the company, was an experienced franchise manager with financial acumen. "I come up with the ideas, and he tells me whether we can afford them," says Mrs. Ferguson, who shares control of the company with her husband but holds the titles of secretary and treasurer.

The Fergusons decided on a franchise system after ruling out direct management of diet centers as being too costly and complicated for them to handle at first. As a regional manager for a company which sold an agricultural soil conditioner, and a former owner of one of the company's franchises, Mr. Ferguson had learned how it made money from continuing license fees based on the amount of product sold.

Soon after incorporating in January, 1972, the Fergusons sold their first franchise for $2,500. Half the sum provided "go money" for their company, says Mr. Ferguson. The following June he quit his $30,000-a-year job. The Fergusons planned to devote a year to Diet Center, calculating that they and their five children (who now range in age from 17 to 28) could live off savings and income from the college students they boarded in their spacious basement. "We've always been willing to gamble on things, but with each other's permission," Mr. Ferguson says. By 1974, they were earning $800 a month from each of the 25 centers!

In early 1976, Diet Center began offering a $900 bonus to existing franchise holders for any additional buyers they found. A flood that wiped out the company's headquarters the same year may also have helped further Diet Center's growth. The Fergusons chose to rebuild in Rexburg, where many townspeople had cash to invest from federal reimbursement for flood damages. Prompted by stories about successful Diet Center franchises, many put their money into the company.

"The fever started," says James Myers, a Rexburg tax accountant who figures he and his wife will earn more than $100,000 this year from their one-third interest in a company holding 30 franchises in New York State — and that is only a portion of his total interest in Diet Center.

SOURCE: Erik Larson, "Couple's Venture in Diet Field Turns into a Big Success Story," *The Wall Street Journal,* November 23, 1981, p. 25. Reprinted by permission of *The Wall Street Journal,* ©Dow Jones & Company, Inc. (1981). All Rights Reserved.

Small Business and Franchising

26

Objectives:

- Understand the importance of small business in our society.
- Identify the factors necessary for new-business success.
- Discuss the differences between small businesses and large businesses in the areas of marketing, personnel, production, and finance.
- Recognize the behavioral qualities that should be possessed by an entrepreneur.
- Understand the major differences among proprietorships, partnerships, and corporations.
- Specify the different types of loans and services available through the SBA.
- State the benefits of a franchised operation to a small-business person.
- Identify several sources of information about franchise opportunities.
- Recognize the concerns that prospective franchisees have about the operations and intentions of franchisors.
- Identify the major provisions in a franchise contract.

After high school, Robert Tezak obtained a degree in mortuary science and joined his family's funeral operations in Joliet, IL.[1] Feeling that the business was somewhat of a dead end, he began to think about getting into something livelier. Mr. Tezak had always enjoyed bargaining with people and buying and selling things. Although the

---

1. Frederick C. Klein, "Uno Owners Have Made It Big by Playing Their Cards Right," *The Wall Street Journal,* November 1, 1982, p. 27.

funeral business provided the opportunity to see new faces, there was not much occasion to make deals.

On a visit to relatives in Louisville, KY in 1971, he played an exciting card game called Uno. Realizing the marketing potential for the game, he tracked down its inventor, a barber in Cincinnati, OH. With his savings and borrowed money, Mr. Tezak purchased the barber's copyright and inventory for $87,000. He proceeded to establish operations with one employee—his brother-in-law—in a spare room of the family florist shop, which was located next door to the funeral home. Mr. Tezak organized International Game, Inc.—a name to grow into—and began marketing a slightly altered version of Uno.

For the first few years, sales consisted mainly of reorders from existing retail outlets and direct orders from individuals who had played the game and wanted their own set. The young company hired its first salesperson in 1975 and saw sales grow to nearly 100,000 units. Sales continued to grow through the late 1970s and, by the end of 1982, the company had sold almost 38 million Uno sets. Mr. Tezak is confidently predicting that within a decade the total sales of Uno will move past all-time industry leader Monopoly, which has sold 85 million units since its introduction in 1935.

Mr. Tezak's company remains small, employing only 19 persons. All 9 stockholders and 3 key officers are family members. The company's manufacturing and warehousing are contracted to other firms. By remaining small, Mr. Tezak is able to engage in several other ventures, including a Burger King franchise, real estate investments, and a county coroner's job.

IMPORTANCE OF SMALL BUSINESS

Small businesses comprise 97 percent of all incorporated and unincorporated businesses, and they generate more than half of all business receipts. As indicated in Figure 26-1, the majority of small businesses are in the retail and service industries.

A Massachusetts Institute of Technology study revealed that 66 percent of all new jobs in the private sector are created by businesses with 20 or fewer employees. In contrast, the National Federation of Independent Business, Research and Education Foundation has indicated that over the past 10 years the 1,000 firms with the largest sales produced only 11 percent of all new jobs. Small firms also provide more than 80 percent of the jobs for the disadvantaged minorities. Table 26-1 shows the leading black-owned businesses in the country. Several of these fall into the small-business classification.

There are certain regions of the country where small businesses are particularly successful. As shown in Figure 26-2, small-business earnings are highest in the Southwest, Mountain States, and New England. These states contain numerous sparsely populated areas where small businesses dominate the local economy.

FACTORS NECESSARY FOR NEW-BUSINESS SUCCESS

The lure of operating freedom, fame, and fortune frequently draws individuals into a new-business venture. These individuals often start out on just a shoestring and

Figure 26-1   Small Business by Industry

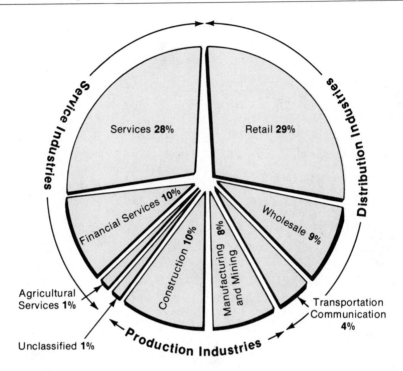

SOURCE: National Federation of Independent Business, Research and Education Foundation, "Small Business in America" (1981). Reproduced with permission.

a prayer. They are unprepared for the numerous pitfalls and challenges that await them. If they were aware of the number of new-business failures, many individuals would hesitate to take the giant leap from being a comfortable corporate employee to an overworked independent businessperson. Statistics indicate that one-third of all new businesses fail by the end of their first year, and only one-third are still operating after five years.

According to Table 26-2, managerial inexperience is the leading cause of business failure in nine out of ten cases. Of all new businesspersons, 24 percent either had no previous experience in the line or lacked managerial experience in the field in which they placed their lifetime savings! This inexperience was evident in all fields, but more so in retailing, where over 15 percent of the new businesspersons had no prior experience in the line and about 13 percent had no managerial exposure. Table 26-2 identifies the major causes of business failures.

Before engaging in a new-business venture, a person should identify the factors necessary for success. An evaluation of these factors will help in determining whether

Table 26-1   The Leading Black-Owned Businesses

Rank	Company & Location	Chief Executive	Year Started	Number of Employees	Type of Business	1982 Sales (000)
1	Motown Industries Los Angeles, California	Berry Gordy	1958	231	Entertainment	$104,300
2	H. J. Russell Construction, Inc. Atlanta, Georgia	H. J. Russell	1958	500	Construction/development/ communications	103,850
3	Johnson Publishing Company, Inc. Chicago, Illinois	John H. Johnson	1942	1,586	Publishing, cosmetics & broadcasting	102,650
4	Fedco Foods Corporation Bronx, New York	J. Bruce Llewellyn	1969	725	Supermarkets	85,000
5	Wardco Incorporated New Haven, Connecticut	Larry B. Wardlaw	1978	17	Commercial fuel oils	84,393
6	Thacker Construction Company Decatur, Georgia	Floyd O. Thacker	1970	475	Construction/engineering	77,300
7	G & M Oil Company, Inc. Baltimore, Maryland	Rudolph Gustus	1963	57	Petroleum sales	62,096
8	Soft Sheen Products, Inc. Chicago, Illinois	Edward G. Gardner	1964	570	Manufacturer & distributor of hair care products	55,000
9	Vanguard Oil & Service Company Brooklyn, New York	Kenneth Butler	1970	51	Petroleum sales	53,000
10	The Jackson Oil Company Baltimore, Maryland	Will D. Jackson	1965	53	Petroleum sales	50,801
11	M & M Products Company, Inc. Atlanta, Georgia	Cornell McBride	1973	380	Manufacturer & distributor of hair care products	43,000
12	Johnson Products Company, Inc. Chicago, Illinois	George E. Johnson	1954	541	Manufacturer of hair care products & cosmetics	42,400
13	Dick Griffey Productions Los Angeles, California	Dick Griffey	1975	95	Entertainment	41,200
14	The Smith Pipe Companies, Inc. Houston, Texas	George Smith	1976	85	Oilfield pipe & supply sales	35,000
15	Systems & Applied Sciences Corp. Riverdale, Maryland	Porter L. Bankhead	1973	800	Computer & electronic data systems	34,000

SOURCE: "The Top 100 Black Businesses," *Black Enterprise* (June, 1983). Copyright 1983. The Earl G. Graves Publishing Co., Inc., 295 Madison Avenue, New York, NY 10017. All rights reserved.

a proposed business will succeed. Answers to the following questions will help a prospective businessperson make the proper evaluation:

1. What kind of business, in an economic sense, will be created?
2. What will be the size of the business's market?
3. How marketable is the product that will be sold?
4. Are the start-up costs commensurate with the long-term prospects of the business?
5. What will be the relationship between profitability and investment in the new business?

6. Can the business be easily explained to potential investors?
7. What mechanism exists for investors to cash in their chips and get out of the business?[2]

DISTINCTIONS BETWEEN SMALL AND LARGE BUSINESSES

It is a mistake to think that a small business is just a firm with fewer employees, less capital, and a smaller scale of operations than a large one. The problems and opportunities of a small business differ greatly from those of a large business. Because of its size, a small business faces numerous challenges that are not found in large firms.

Figure 26-2   **Small-Business Earnings by Region**

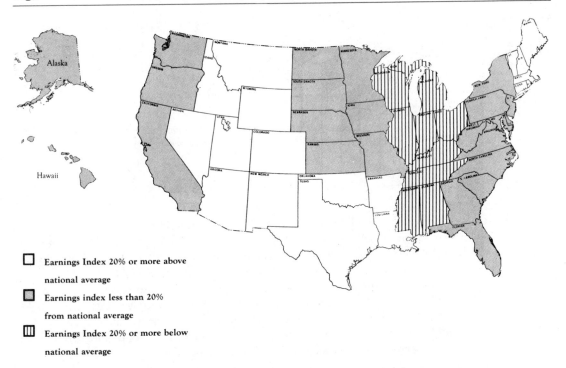

☐ Earnings Index 20% or more above national average

▦ Earnings index less than 20% from national average

▥ Earnings Index 20% or more below national average

SOURCE: National Federation of Independent Business, Research and Education Foundation, "The Small Business Economy—1981" (1981), p. 7. Reproduced with permission.

2. James McNeill Stancil, "Realistic Criteria for Judging New Ventures," *Harvard Business Review* (November/December, 1981), p. 60.

Table 26-2   Causes of 16,794 Business Failures in 1981

Underlying Causes	PERCENTAGE OF FAILURES IN BUSINESS AREA					
	Manufacturers	Wholesalers	Retailers	Construction	Commercial Services	All
Neglect	0.4%	0.9%	0.7%	0.6%	0.4%	0.7%
Fraud	0.4	0.8	0.3	0.1	0.4	0.3
Managerial inexperience:						
Lack of experience in the line	11.3	8.9	15.6	5.8	7.8	11.1
Lack of managerial experience	10.7	11.2	12.7	14.0	12.6	12.5
Unbalanced experience*	18.3	20.1	19.2	18.0	21.1	19.2
Incompetence	50.1	50.0	41.7	51.4	40.9	45.6
Disaster	0.7	0.6	0.5	0.2	0.3	0.5
Reason unknown	8.1	7.5	9.3	9.9	16.5	10.1
Total	100.0%	100.0%	100.0%	100.0%	100.0%	100.0%
Number of failures	2,224	1,708	6,882	3,614	2,366	16,794
Average liabilities per failure	$1,065,834	$660,792	$226,464	$235,689	$442,022	$414,147

*Experience not well rounded in sales, finance, purchasing, and production on the part of the individual in case of a proprietorship, or of two or more partners or officers constituting a management unit.

SOURCE: Dun & Bradstreet Corporation, *The Dun & Bradstreet Business Failure Record* (1983), p. 12. By permission of Dun & Bradstreet Credit Services, a company of The Dun & Bradstreet Corporation.

In many cases a small firm has neither the product lines nor the customers to compete with a larger firm. The major distinctions between small businesses and large ones will become clearer by examining the functional areas of marketing, personnel, production, and finance. Many of these differences are summarized in Figure 26-3.

Because a small-business owner cannot afford a large, specialized staff to resolve problems, she or he often seeks counsel from a variety of outside sources. The problem to be resolved determines the type of source to use. For example, a complex tax problem usually is handled by an accountant, and a trademark dispute is resolved by an attorney. Table 26-3 identifies the most useful sources of information for small-business owners.

Differences in Marketing

The outstanding marketing advantage of a small business over a large one is its closeness to its customers. Many small-business owners cater to a devoted group of customers by stocking special goods and personalizing services for them. By furnishing more and better services, the small business often can compete effectively with a large one. These services include deliveries, phone orders, gift wrapping, check cashing, credit, and a merchandise-on-approval program.

Among the marketing weaknesses of small firms are inadequate sales programs, lack of effective advertising programs, inadequate inventory control, and purchasing and pricing disadvantages. For example, many small businesses employ only part-time salespersons. Their sales presentations often are incomplete and ineffective because the only sales training these salespersons receive is from representatives of wholesalers and other suppliers. As a result, they lack the ability to turn interesting product features into needed customer benefits.

Figure 26-3   Differences Between Small Business and Large Business

Characteristics of a Small Business	Characteristics of a Large Business
• Serves a narrow market	• Serves a broad market
• Inadequate funding of promotional programs	• Adequate funding of promotional programs
• Close top-management contact with employees	• Top management isolated from employees
• Managers fill several roles	• Specialized management and large staffs
• Organization permits rapid decision making	• Complex organization slows decision making
• Minimum physical resources — plant and equipment	• Extensive physical resources — plant and equipment
• Additional physical resources represent a large portion of total investment	• Additional physical resources represent a small portion of total investment
• Proprietorship, partnership, or close corporation	• Publicly owned corporation
• Limited financial resources — own savings and bank loans	• Varied financial resources — stock offerings and bonds
• Cost of loans from 2 to 10% higher than prime rate	• Cost of loans is at the prime rate

Table 26-3   Ten Most Useful Sources of Information for a Small-Business Owner

Most Useful Source	Percent Responding
Accountant	89%
Attorney	86
Banker	77
Owners of other business	77
Suppliers	74
Trade association	68
Friends or relatives	65
Insurance companies	52
Political representatives	48
Public libraries	44

SOURCE: Jane S. Cromartie, Daniel S. Juhn, and Kenneth J. Lacho, "Help and Where to Find It: Dealing with Small Business Problems," *Louisiana Business Survey* (Spring, 1982), p. 15.

Many small firms lack both the creative talent and the money for an effective advertising program. In most cases they cannot afford to use an advertising agency. They rely mainly on satisfied customers to spread the message about their goods and services. When they advertise, they do so only in the classified section of the newspapers and in the Yellow Pages of the telephone directory. As a result, they are unable to evaluate the effectiveness of their advertising.

In a small firm, effective buying plans and tight inventory control procedures often are nonexistent. It is not too unusual to find obsolete merchandise and soiled goods on the shelves of some small businesses. In some instances they stock the wrong goods or offer the wrong services because they select what they like rather than what is wanted by their customers. Figure 26-4 shows the final advertising message from a car wash operator who went out of business.

When forced to compete with a large business, the small firm is at a price disadvantage because it usually has higher unit costs than the large one. Large businesses receive quantity discounts by buying in huge amounts directly from producers. On the other hand, small businesses with limited markets and lower inventory needs usually purchase in small quantities from wholesalers or other middlemen. Thus, they are unable to obtain quantity discounts on their modest purchases. This perplexing problem for small businesses is discussed in the "open letter" presented in Figure 26-5.

Differences in Personnel

In a small business there is the advantage of direct contact between the owner/manager and the employees. Since the employees often report directly to the owner/manager, directions can be communicated clearly and coordination can be achieved rapidly. Thus, close personal ties often are developed between the owner/manager and the employees. An unusual one-person small business is described in Figure 26-6.

Another advantage is the opportunity for some employees of the small business to gain experience in many different activities. By being generalists rather than specialists, such employees develop skills in a variety of fields and thus achieve more balanced experiences. Furthermore, some employees in a small business are given more responsibilities than their counterparts in a large business. As a result, they often make decisions that are made by department managers in large firms.

Personnel difficulties encountered by the small business lie in its inability to hire and maintain adequate work staffs for one or more reasons. First, most small businesses pay their employees less and provide fewer fringe benefits. As a result, they are handicapped in recruiting and maintaining qualified employees such as auto mechanics, television repairers, and pharmacists. In some instances the practice of industrywide contracts with labor unions imposes big-business wages and work rules on small businesses. This action increases the costs and reduces the flexibility of the small-business owner.

Second, since most small-business managers are not personnel specialists, they often lack the ability to screen, recruit, and train new employees properly. Third, the size of the small business does not permit its employees to specialize and to master a

Figure 26-4   The Final Advertisement from a Small-Business Owner

DON ROGERS

"I FER ONE...

would like to thank the people who turned out for 'SAVE YOUR CAR WASH' month, during September." The initial response was very gratitying, as we washed 508 cars the first 3 days. However, as the month wore on, we resumed our normal dismal pattern.

It is with regret that we now announce

THE CLOSING OF THE CLEAN CAR CORRAL EFFECTIVE SATURDAY, OCTOBER 2.

We thank our regular customers who have supported us. I hate to close, primarily because of you and our employees, but when it becomes more economical to close a business than to keep it open, the decision is obvious.

I would also like to thank Mayor Roman Beer and other city officials who were so much help in getting this business off the ground originally and for their other considerations shown during its operation.

A special thanks to Dick Andrew who has been a good, friendly competitor. We invite you to use his facilities at the Suds 'un Duds for your car washing needs.

We have four good employees who would like to find work. If you have anything for them please let them or me know.

The building and property are for sale, or I would consider developing and leasing to responsible parties. The car wash equipment is not for sale locally.

If anyone has unused car wash coupons please return to me at P.O. Box 291, Angola, and they will be refunded in full after October 18th.

So...we bid a fond farewell to the car wash business in Angola and return you now to the golden days of yesteryear.

You win some...you lose some.

Respectfully submitted,
DON ROGERS

Don Rogers

C.W.B. (Retired)

SOURCE: *Angola Herald-Republican* (Angola, IN), September 29, 1982. Reproduced with permission.

Figure 26-5   A Letter to the Community from a Small-Business Owner

A LETTER TO THE FAIR-MINDED CITIZENS OF OUR COMMUNITY

During the last winter, many of you drove your automobile into a service station or garage to have your radiator checked. In hotels and cafes it is customary to tip the employees even though at times they do not render extra service. How many car owners would think of tipping their favorite automotive serviceman who, in the severest of weather, performs services, such as checking radiators, oil, tires, etc., without cost to the owner?

Actually these people don't expect a tip for all this free service. But you should stop and think a minute how the operator must feel when he knows you bought your anti-freeze at a discount house, or grocery, or drug store at the same price he has to pay or even less than his cost. This season we see more and more stores using anti-freeze, oils, and other automotive items as loss leaders. So, Mr. Car Owner, the next time a severe cold spell moves in, stop back at the store where you purchased your anti-freeze and ask them to come out in the freezing, disagreeable weather and use an expensive, easily broken hydrometer to check your radiator. We think the results would be most interesting.

Here is a problem all motorists should consider — anti-freeze should be installed by the seller who, at the same time, will check connecting hoses and radiator for leaks and will install the correct amount of anti-freeze to assure proper protection for the cold season. Furthermore, he will be most happy to check your radiator several times during the winter months and advise you whether you have adequate protection. Usually the motorist will ask for his "free service" during the severest weather, thus imposing a hardship on the serviceman, but rarely does he complain.

Now, Mr. Car Owner, let us all bear in mind that, if you take this business away from the people who are willing to give free services with your purchases, then the time is near and justified that the serviceman will make a charge for these services.

SOURCE: Unknown.

skill. Finally, many small firms are unable to offer promotions to worthy employees. Without this incentive, employees will seek other employment opportunities. This situation often occurs in a family business where all the promotions go to family members.

Differences in Production

There are several advantages that a small business has over a large one in the area of production. First, a small business often has the freedom to innovate and develop new products. For example, the Polaroid camera and the Apple® personal computer were developed by relatively small organizations. Second, the small business can move rapidly in making decisions whenever necessary. This is because the decision making is concentrated in the hands of only one or a few key persons. Another reason for this decision-making flexibility is that the small firm is not restrained by large investments in specialized equipment, materials, and personnel. Third, the small manufacturer has

Figure 26-6   Something to Chirp About

Something to chirp about . . .

It seems as though things hatched at the right time for Ted Giannoulas. He came to the OSU area for the first time to appear in the Sports Imports Invitational April 3 at St. John Arena — as none other than the San Diego Chicken.

The invitational brought nationally-rated volleyball teams from OSU, UCLA, USC and Stanford to compete. Added attractions included the Ohio State and UCLA cheerleaders, the UCLA song girls and groups from the OSU and USC marching bands.

The 5-foot-4-inch Giannoulas has been playing the chicken for about seven years now. He began his career as a mascot for a San Diego radio station, but sued for his rights to work for himself in 1979, becoming, what he terms as "a free-agent chicken."

A high point of his chickening occurred after that court battle, when he had his "grand hatching" before a San Diego Padres game. The crowd of 47,000 gave him a 10-minute standing ovation following his emergence from a huge styrofoam egg, he recalled. "I'm a kind of folk hero in San Diego."

He has been making some tracks in Columbus as well. He travels about 250 days a year and has performed at two Columbus Clippers baseball games and recently at the Van-O-Rama show held at the State Fairgrounds.

As for the Invitational, he felt right at home. After all, he spent much of his early career with the San Diego Breakers, a member of the professional International Volleyball Association: "I like volleyball. The more intimate atmosphere of an arena helps the audience pick up subtleties. In large stadiums, you have to rely on exaggerated movements."

The chicken specializes in visual comedy: "I'm the feathered Harpo Marx. I always knew being a performer was in me and, as the years progress of doing the chicken, it's been easier for me to pioneer this new form of comedy.

"No one is inhibited by the chicken. It really helps break down defense barriers, so all I have to worry about is getting the laughs."

And he wants to keep on getting laughs for at least a few more years. The 26-year-old has no plans to hang up his feathers . . . and understandably so — his business nets in six figures and Giannoulas collects up to $5,000 for a given show.

But there seems to be more to it than that. "I think the chicken will always be a part of my life — I don't think I'll ever stop being the chicken," said Giannoulas, who is toying with the idea of transforming the foul into cartoon form. Look out, Roadrunner. — G.P.H.

SOURCE: *OSU/Alumni Magazine*, published by The Ohio State University Alumni Association (April, 1981). p. 20.

the ability to produce personalized products for its customers. Instead of a mass assembly operation, the output of a small firm, such as a job printing shop, can be specialized for each customer. Finally, the small business can exercise close control over its production activities.

The production weaknesses of many small manufacturing firms are numerous. First, due to capital limitations the small firm cannot mass-produce its goods in the same manner as General Electric or Ford Motor Co. Numerous small manufacturers limit their production to short-run, job shop operations.

Second, many small firms cannot afford the services of specialists in areas such as production scheduling, quality control, and technical research. For example, the production scheduling activity often is performed in a loosely organized and haphazard manner. Sometimes it is determined by the customer who cries the loudest and longest for his or her order. When it comes to a separate quality control activity, many small manufacturers do not recognize the need for it. Since they often produce small quantities in a job shop, they contend that quality is built into their products. Although this statement has some merit, there is still a need to ensure that a product meets certain predetermined quality standards.

Finally, small firms do not conduct any research and development activities because they have neither the funds nor the specialized talent for a research program. They usually are forced to copy the products and processes of larger firms in the industry. Small manufacturers are also often unaware of the usage of new materials and new equipment. In many cases they must rely upon information from suppliers and trade journals to learn about new technology.

Differences in Finance

One financial advantage of a small business is its lower overhead. It is not burdened by several levels of management and a large supporting staff. This permits most of its funds to be directed to revenue-producing activities. Another financial advantage lies in the fact that a small business may qualify as a Subchapter S corporation under the Internal Revenue Code. A Subchapter S corporation is one with 35 or fewer stockholders which can elect to be taxed as a proprietorship or a partnership. Finally, as will be discussed in a later section, a small business may seek financial help from the Small Business Administration.

Many of the major problems encountered by small businesses are financial ones, as indicated in Table 26-4. The lack of adequate short-term and long-term capital often limits the operations of a small business. Short-term funds are needed to cover cash requirements, accounts receivable, and inventories. Long-term capital is required to purchase the equipment, building, and land for the business.

Long-term capital usually is raised through owners' funds, sales of common stock, and borrowed funds. Many small-business owners, however, do not choose to raise funds through the sale of common stock. This is because a stock offering could reduce their control over their businesses. In addition, there may not be any market for their stocks if they are small, unknown companies. Borrowed funds consist of bank loans or bond issues. But banks often hesitate to make loans that are paid back over a period

Table 26-4   Major Problems Encountered by Small Businesses

Problems	Percent Responding[1]
Working capital	41%
Accounting/bookkeeping records	35
Forecasting demand for your product and/or service	33
Financial planning and use of financial information and ratios	33
Banking/financing	33
Legal problems/information	31
Sales/marketing	29
Credit and collections	29
Advertising of your product/services	28
Overall business organization	21

[1] Because the respondents could choose more than one problem, the total exceeds 100 percent.

SOURCE: Satish Mehra, "Operational Problems of Small Businesses in the Mid-South," *Mid-South Business Journal* (3d Quarter, 1982), p. 6. Reproduced with permission.

of several years. And bond issues are expensive to prepare and to sell for a small business. Thus, the owner's funds are the most important and often the sole source of long-term capital for a small firm. Figure 26-7 shows the primary sources of capital for both establishing a new business and purchasing an existing one.

Another financial concern for the small business is the accessibility of credit. The credit available to a small firm often is related to the credit standing of its owner or owners. Because the probability of success for a small business is unknown, many creditors insist that its owner guarantee the credit obligations of the firm. Since the owner uses credit for personal and family use also, this restricts the amount available for the business.

THE FIVE P'S OF ENTREPRENEURSHIP

In spite of the difficulties associated with a small business, many individuals dream about starting their own business. Yet few ever bring these dreams to reality. Young persons often declare that they eventually would like to have their own business but seldom do anything about it. When these persons become older, they often no longer have the desire to begin a new venture. The security, status, and salary provided by employment in an established organization have become more attractive than the risk of insecurity of entrepreneurship, or starting a new business.

Entrepreneurs such as Ray Kroc of McDonald's and Rich DeVos of Amway are adventurers, risk-takers, and profit-seekers. As noted in Chapter 1 on page 11, an

Figure 26-7   Sources of Capital for Starting a New Business and for Purchasing an Existing Business

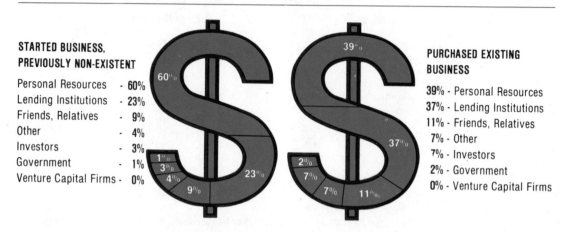

STARTED BUSINESS, PREVIOUSLY NON-EXISTENT

Personal Resources   - **60%**
Lending Institutions   - **23%**
Friends, Relatives   - **9%**
Other   - **4%**
Investors   - **3%**
Government   - **1%**
Venture Capital Firms -   **0%**

PURCHASED EXISTING BUSINESS

39% - Personal Resources
37% - Lending Institutions
11% - Friends, Relatives
7% - Other
7% - Investors
2% - Government
0% - Venture Capital Firms

SOURCE: National Federation of Independent Business, Research and Education Foundation, "Small Business in America" (1981). Reproduced with permission.

entrepreneur is an individual or group who engages in business under a capitalistic system. The entrepreneur gathers the capital, organizes the business, and manages it. The behavioral qualities of an entrepreneur can be identified as the five P's of entrepreneurship, which are:

1. *Purposeful.* Sets goals and strives diligently to accomplish them.
2. *Persuasive.* Influences others, such as bankers, suppliers, and customers, to assist in reaching desired goals.
3. *Persistent.* Pursues goals continually and often against great odds. Setbacks and disappointments do not halt the efforts toward goal attainment.
4. *Presumptuous.* Strikes out boldly and acts when others hesitate to do so. Is willing to take calculated risks and to accept innovative approaches.
5. *Perceptive.* Should be able to understand how each separate decision relates to accomplishing established goals.

CHOICE OF BUSINESS OWNERSHIP FORM

An initial decision in starting a new business is to determine the legal form of business ownership. As noted in Chapter 3, the major forms of business ownership are proprietorships, partnerships, and corporations. Although over 70 percent of all businesses are organized as proprietorships, sales of the typical proprietorship average only about $43,000 a year. Nevertheless, the ease and low cost of both forming and dissolving a proprietorship are important reasons for choosing this form of ownership.

Most partnerships are classified as small businesses even though they may be larger than proprietorships. Partnerships account for only 10 percent of all forms of business ownership, and the average partnership has revenues of $178,000 and profits of about $11,000 a year. Since partnerships are unincorporated forms of ownership, they can be organized with the same ease and low cost as proprietorships. In addition, they have the ability to raise additional funds and to obtain some degree of managerial specialization.

While corporations account for only 20 percent of all forms of business ownership, they produce 89 percent of business revenues. Many small businesses are organized as corporations because the corporate form is accorded definite legal status and offers limited liability for its owners. On the other hand, the cost and reporting requirements of corporations often are too restrictive for small firms.

In determining the most suitable form of ownership for a small business, an entrepreneur's decision can be guided by answers to the following questions:

1. What form of organization provides the best tax advantage?
2. What is the extent of the owner's personal liability for debts and other obligations?
3. What are the sources of funds and how much financing is needed?
4. What type of managerial expertise is needed in the organization?
5. What will happen to the business if the key person in the organization dies or is disabled?
6. How much control does the owner want over the business?
7. How important are ease and low cost of organizing the business?

As a business matures, its form of ownership undergoes changes. When it is new, it usually has little need for great amounts of capital or managerial specialization. Thus, it often is organized as a proprietorship. If the business grows, partners may be added to provide more funds and managerial help. At a later period, the expanding business may seek even larger amounts of capital, greater managerial expertise, and limited liability for its owners. At this time it forms a corporation.

SMALL BUSINESS ADMINISTRATION SERVICES

Over a seven-year period Charles Wallace, a former sharecropper from Georgia, expanded his fuel oil delivery business in New York from 1 truck to 19. During this time, his annual sales increased to $35 million. Mr. Wallace credits his success to the help he received from the Small Business Administration (SBA).

The SBA is a government agency created by Congress in 1953 to help small businesses grow and prosper. It offers small businesses financial aid, management assistance, help in obtaining government contracts, counseling services, and publications covering the numerous activities of small businesses. The limits for a business to be considered small and to qualify for government assistance are listed in Figure 26-8.

Types of SBA Loans

A major purpose of the SBA is to make available low-cost capital to small-business owners. The different types of loans it extends are:

Figure 26-8   Size Standards for a Small Business

A. For Loans   Annual Receipts Maximum

  Services   *$2–$8   million
  Retail   *$2–$7.5   million
  Wholesale   *$9.5–$22   million
  General construction   *$9.5   million
  Farming and related activities   *$1   million

                                                      Average Employment Maximum

  Manufacturing   *250 to 1,500

B. For Procurement   Annual Receipts Maximum

  Services   *$2–$9   million
  General construction   *$12   million

                                                      Average Employment Maximum

  Manufacturing   *500 to 1,500

C. For SBIC Assistance

  All industries   Net Worth Maximum
                                                      $6 million

                                                      Average Net Income
                                                      (after taxes) maximum
                                                      $2 million for the
                                                      preceding two years

D. For Surety Bonds   Annual Receipts Maximum

  All industries $3.5 million

*Varies by industry.

NOTE: A. and C. standards increase 25% if a firm operates in an area of high unemployment, as defined by the Labor Department.

SOURCE: U.S. Small Business Administration, *Facts About Small Business and the U.S. Small Business Administration* (February, 1981), p. 8.

1. **Direct loans.** If a small-business owner has been turned down by two banks, he or she becomes eligible for a direct loan of up to $150,000. However, the SBA's loan officers must be convinced that the applicant is willing and able to repay the loan. The funds which the SBA has for direct loans are very limited.

2. **Guaranteed loans.** To provide financial aid to as many small businesses as possible, the SBA has shifted its attention from direct loans to guaranteed loans. Under this

plan the SBA guarantees the lesser of 90 percent or $500,000 of a bank loan. Bankers are willing to participate in this program because they are given the opportunity to judge the credit risks of the applicants. Guaranteed loans account for nearly 90 percent of the SBA's overall business lending, and over 10,000 banks are active in this program. In 1982 the SBA guaranteed $2.8 billion in loans.

3. **Participation loans.** The SBA and a private financial institution share in the amount of a participation loan. The SBA's share is limited to 75 percent of the loan and no more than $350,000. A portion of these loans is directed to minority and low-income businesspersons.

Long-Term Financing Through SBICs

Small Business Investment Companies (SBICs) are privately owned, SBA-licensed companies that provide long-term financing to small firms for expansion, modernization, and everyday operations. Funds for an SBIC are generated through private capital and loans from the federal government. Although the SBICs are licensed and regulated by the SBA, their transactions with the small firms are strictly private.

The SBICs make long-term loans, purchase either stock or debt securities, or invest in a combination of equity and debt. The amount of funds available to small businesses through the SBICs is a small part of their overall capital needs. The SBICs are channeling only $200 million to $300 million annually into small businesses.

Financial and Management Aid Through Section 301(d) SBICs

To provide financial and management aid to minority businesspersons, the SBA has established a specialized type of SBIC known as a **Section 301(d) SBIC**, formerly called a MESBIC (Minority Enterprise SBIC). There are over 100 of these types of SBICs, which are operated by established industrial or financial firms, by community- or business-oriented economic development organizations, or by private or public investors. For example, Motor Enterprises is a Section 301(d) SBIC that was organized by General Motors Corporation. Its original investment of $3.5 million produced an additional $17.8 million in bank loans for 119 minority-operated firms.

Advice Through SBA Publications

The SBA prepares various types of publications for small-business owners. Three of the most important *free* series includes *The Management Aids* (MAs), *Small Business Bibliographies* (SBBs), and the *Starting Out Series* (SOSs). The MAs recommend methods and techniques for handling management problems and business operations. In the SBBs the key reference sources for many areas of business management are identified. The SOSs are one-page fact sheets that indicate the financial and operating requirements for selected manufacturing, retail, and service businesses. Included in the SBA list of publications for sale are books that discuss specific management techniques and problems and others that assist in the initial start-up of a business.

Miscellaneous SBA Services

Among the other services for small businesses that the SBA provides are:

1. Low-interest loans to victims of disasters.
2. Lease guarantee programs which often are necessary because small businesses with only fair or low credit ratings often are excluded from leasing good locations.
3. Help in obtaining contracts and orders from the federal government.
4. Service Corps of Retired Executives (SCORE), a group which gives free counseling and guidance to small-business owners.
5. Active Corps of Executives (ACE), a group of volunteers from industry, education, and the professions who act as management consultants to small businesses.
6. Small Business Institutes, groups of college students and faculty advisors on nearly 500 college campuses that provide on-site management counseling to small-business owners.
7. Small Business Development Centers, units that draw from the resources of local, state, and federal government programs, the private sector, and universities to provide technical and managerial assistance to small businesses.

FRANCHISING

Ronald McDentist is not a franchised dentist office next to a McDonald's restaurant, but it could be someday. The $436 billion franchise industry is growing in fields such as health care, computers, and home security in addition to the traditional areas of fast-food and lodging.

Since the 1960s, the franchising of complete businesses has provided many independent businesspersons with the operating expertise of a corporate chain. Today, nearly one-third of all retail sales is made through some type of a franchised business. A **franchise** is a continuing business relationship that requires a person to operate a business according to the methods advocated by the franchising organization. The party that develops the franchise and initiates the franchise agreement is the **franchisor**. A **franchisee** usually is a retailer who obtains the right to use a franchisor's name and trademark in his or her business. A franchisee often agrees to adopt standardized operating procedures imposed by a franchisor and to purchase equipment and supplies from approved sources. Table 26-5 shows the various kinds of franchised businesses, the number of establishments in each business, and their sales.

The total investment in a franchised operation can be quite high. The management of Burger King states that each unit costs more than $300,000 for the building, equipment, and initial franchise fee (see Figure 26-9). Franchise systems have been particularly successful in retail services such as fast-food restaurants (e.g., McDonald's), motels (e.g., Holiday Inn), auto rentals (e.g., Hertz), and employment agencies (e.g., Kelly Girls). Table 26-6 shows the top ten fast-food franchisors in the United States. As shown in the right-hand column of Table 26-6, the average sales of $1,200,000 for a McDonald outlet are nearly $400,000 greater than for a Burger King unit.

Table 26-5   Franchising in the Economy, 1983*

Kinds of Franchised Business	Establishments (Number)			Sales ($000)		
	Total	Company-Owned	Franchisee-Owned	Total	Company-Owned	Franchisee-Owned
TOTAL—ALL FRANCHISING	465,093	88,766	376,327	435,752,885	60,802,438	374,950,447
Automobile and truck dealers	27,390	50	27,340	192,475,000	354,000	192,121,000
Automotive products and services	41,496	4,178	37,318	9,269,724	2,779,796	6,489,928
Business aids and services	55,608	7,108	48,500	9,499,304	1,649,159	7,850,145
Accounting, credit, collection agencies, and general business services	2,789	44	2,745	153,027	10,480	142,547
Employment services	5,299	1,660	3,639	2,212,746	959,615	1,253,131
Printing and copying services	4,352	137	4,215	593,600	22,780	570,820
Tax preparation services	10,031	4,603	5,428	381,987	199,377	182,610
Real estate	17,698	258	17,440	3,891,686	142,850	3,748,836
Miscellaneous business services	15,439	406	15,033	2,266,258	314,057	1,952,201
Construction, home improvements, maintenance, and cleaning services	17,400	732	16,668	2,608,806	292,150	2,316,656
Convenience stores	17,276	10,205	7,071	10,167,670	5,847,256	4,320,414
Educational products and services	5,022	754	4,268	577,334	117,341	459,993
Restaurants (all types)	70,262	21,883	48,379	38,383,176	14,267,152	24,116,024
Gasoline service stations	139,250	25,065	114,185	114,534,000	20,616,000	93,918,000
Hotels, motels, and campgrounds	6,850	1,115	5,735	12,003,472	3,393,266	8,610,206
Laundry and drycleaning services	3,283	52	3,231	277,886	16,500	261,386
Recreation, entertainment, and travel	7,396	91	7,305	1,071,154	24,981	1,046,173
Rental services (auto-truck)	8,284	2,032	6,252	3,988,765	2,342,540	1,646,225
Rental services (equipment)	1,776	207	1,569	460,174	139,534	320,640
Retailing (non-food)	39,981	13,029	26,952	12,912,187	5,275,288	7,636,899
Retailing (food other than convenience stores)	18,429	1,978	16,451	9,520,531	2,412,805	7,107,726
Soft-drink bottlers	1,600	85	1,515	17,417,000	1,219,000	16,198,000
Miscellaneous	3,790	202	3,588	586,702	55,670	531,032

*1983 data estimated by respondents.

SOURCE: U.S. Department of Commerce, *Franchising in the Economy, 1981–1983* (January, 1983), p. 23.

Advantages to Franchisees

The franchising method permits a franchisee to start an enterprise that already has a strong consumer identification. A franchisee obtains managerial assistance from a franchisor in the areas of site selection, accounting systems, marketing, production, finance, purchasing, and personnel. Another advantage to the franchisee is the

Figure 26-9   Profile of a King—Burger King

The Burger King franchise community, as of October 1, 1981, was composed of 850 groups who own 2,668 restaurants. While the largest franchisee (Chart House of New Orleans) owns 365 stores, the average franchisee group owns three. The franchisee signs a 20-year agreement for $40,000 which gives him the rights to the Burger King name, system, expertise, training, and research and development. He pays a three and a half percent monthly royalty fee, a four percent monthly advertising fee, and a two percent additional contribution to local advertising in many markets. One percent of all those who express interest ultimately do become Burger King franchisees.

The average span of time between approval and opening of the restaurant is 14 months. The typical Burger King franchisee is a single investor. (Although there are investor groups, the operating partner has to have 50 percent equity.) He or she is 30 to 45 years old, possesses 10 to 15 years of previous business experience (not necessarily in food), and has a minimum of $120,000 in liquid assets and a $150,000 net worth excluding home ownership. The person will be expected to be a 100 percent Burger King franchisee who will manage the restaurant on a day-to-day basis. In addition, the franchisee must be willing to become active in the support of his community. "Community involvement is basic to our operating philosophy," says C. Ronald Petty, senior vice-president for development. "To be successful, the franchisee must be willing to make a commitment to make that community better. Over the years, the chains have realized that they can't just take money out of an area. Something has to be constantly put back in to improve it, no matter what type of neighborhood it is. The franchisee *is* Mr. Burger King in his community."

SOURCE: Kevin Farrell, "Burger King: 'Making It Special,'" *Restaurant Business* (October 1, 1981), p. 102. Reprinted with permission from RESTAURANT BUSINESS. Copyright 1981, Bill Communications, Inc.

managerial training provided by the franchisor. For example, McDonald's operates Hamburger University for its management trainees, and Long John Silver trains its future managers at Cod College. Figure 26-10 shows the benefits of a well-run franchise system to a franchisee.

Studies have indicated that the two primary causes of business failure are managerial incompetence and the lack of well-rounded business experience. By becoming

Table 26-6   The Top Ten Fast-Food Chains, 1982

Sales Rank	Company (Hqtrs. State)	Estimated Total Food Service Sales of All Units (000,000)	Number of Units (end of fiscal yr.)	Estimated Average Per-Unit Sales (000)
1	McDonald's (IL)	$7,800	6,739	$1,200
2	Burger King (FL)	2,600	3,255	800
3	Kentucky Fried Chicken (KY)	2,600	6,304	425
4	Wendy's (OH)	1,700	2,229	720
5	Hardee's (NC)	1,400	1,465	733
6	Pizza Hut (KS)	1,300	4,300	315
7	Int'l Dairy Queen (MN)	1,238	4,805	275
8	Shoney's (TN) (includes Famous Recipe)	700	728	1,100
9	Arby's (GA)	591	1,144	472
10	Taco Bell (CA)	590	1,350	440

SOURCE: "Top 100 Chains by Sales Volume," *Nation's Restaurant News* (August 2, 1982), p. 130. ©1982 *Nation's Restaurant News*.

Figure 26-10   Benefits of a Franchise System to the Franchisee

1. Location assistance.
2. Use of a regionally or nationally known name.
3. Initial employee and management training.
4. Continuing management and merchandising assistance.
5. Promotional and publicity aid.
6. Store development help, including lease negotiation.
7. Assistance with store layout and design.
8. Help with equipment purchasing.
9. Time-tested operating procedures.
10. Assistance in obtaining funds.
11. Identification of qualified suppliers.
12. Standardized accounting system.
13. Ability to market a well-known product or service.
14. Reduced risk of failure.

a part of a franchise system, the small-business operator reduces the risk of failure from these causes. Statistics compiled by the government indicate that less than 5 percent of franchised units fail each year. On the other hand, the Small Business Administration reports that 65 percent of all new independent businesses fail within five years.

Advantages to Franchisors

Franchising is a rapid way for a franchisor to obtain wide distribution. This distribution is achieved with a minimum financial outlay by the franchisor. In the late 1950s, McDonald's grew rapidly by offering its franchise to prospective restaurant operators. By 1982 the chain had 4,580 or 68 percent of its total units which were owned and operated by independent businesspersons. Some evidence of McDonald's size is illustrated in Figure 26-11.

Figure 26-11   McDonald's McFacts

An unusual McDonald's restaurant on the Mississippi River in St. Louis.

- Each year a half-million steers are converted into McDonald's hamburgers.
- McDonald's sells about one billion hamburgers every three months.
- It takes the equivalent of 300 square miles of forest to keep McDonald's restaurants stocked annually with paper products.
- McDonald's is the nation's biggest buyer of processed potatoes and fish.

SOURCE: "The Mammoth, Marvelous Money Machine," *Marketing & Media Decisions* (Spring 1982 Special), p. 112. Reproduced with permission.

Another advantage to a franchisor is that a self-motivated franchisee usually is more concerned about operating results than is a salaried manager. For some franchisors, a franchise system provides a continuous market for their goods. These franchisors, such as Pizza Hut and Midas Muffler, receive earnings from both the franchise fees and the sale of goods.

Sources of Information About Franchises

Among the different sources of information about franchising are various publications, franchise shows, franchise consultants, and the International Franchise Association (IFA). Most publications about franchises are available in business libraries. These include:

1. *The Franchise Opportunities Handbook,* published by the U.S. Department of Commerce, lists numerous franchise opportunities. Since the information in these publications is furnished by the franchisors, their claims should be carefully investigated. Figure 26-12 depicts the type of information shown.
2. *The Directory of Franchising Organizations*, published annually by Pilot Books, lists the types of franchises available and the requirements to obtain a franchise.
3. *Franchising World*, a monthly publication of the International Franchise Association, furnishes operating information, legislative coverage, and interviews with franchisees and franchisors.
4. *Franchising Today* and *The Info Franchise Newsletter* are periodicals that supply additional insights into franchising operations.
5. *Franchising in the Economy, 1981-1983,* a government publication, provides an overview of franchising and industry statistics.

Franchise shows are held annually in major cities throughout the country. At these shows franchisors provide information and materials to prospective franchisees. Franchise consultants usually are paid by franchisors. Thus, their advice should be considered with caution. The recognized spokesperson for responsible franchising is the International Franchise Association, a nonprofit trade organization of more than 350 franchisors in the United States and other countries. It annually distributes thousands of copies of its booklet "Investigate Before Investing" to potential franchisees.

Cautions for Franchisees

Investing in a franchise outlet may involve thousands of dollars. Therefore, the prospective franchisee should protect this investment by obtaining as much information as possible about the franchising organization. In 1979 the Federal Trade Commission issued a major rule that requires a franchisor to disclose material facts about its business and its franchise relationships. The rule, entitled "Disclosure Requirements and Prohibitions Concerning Franchising and Business Opportunity Ventures," also prohibits franchisors from making false statements concerning actual or potential sales, income, or profits. Figure 26-13 identifies the specific types of information that franchisors must disclose.

Figure 26-12   A Franchise Opportunity

INTERNATIONAL DAIRY QUEEN, INC.
P. O. Box 35286
Minneapolis, Minnesota 55435
B. V. Bloom, Director—New Store Development

Description of Operation: International Dairy Queen, Inc., is engaged in developing, licensing and servicing a system of franchised retail stores which offer a selected menu of soft dairy products, hamburgers and beverages marketed under "Dairy Queen," "Brazier" and "Mr. Misty" trademark.

Number of Franchisees: There are currently 4,780 "Dairy Queen" and "Dairy Queen/Brazier" stores located in all 50 states and 12 foreign countries.

In Business Since: The soft serve dairy product was first offered to the public in 1938 with the first "Dairy Queen" store being opened in 1940. In 1962 certain territorial operators formed International Dairy Queen, Inc., by contributing their respective "Dairy Queen" territorial franchise rights.

Equity Capital Needed: The franchise fees are $25,000 for plan "A." All prospective franchisees must meet certain financial requirements.

Financial Assistance Available: Qualified franchisees may purchase equipment on a conditional sales contract over a 5 year payment period with the required down payment.

Training Provided: International Dairy Queen, Inc.'s National Training Center in Minneapolis, Minnesota offers an intensive 2 week training course to all new and existing franchisees. The course covers sanitation, sales promotion, inventory control and basic functions of management. The company also offers new franchisees the services of a special opening team that assists operators in opening their new "Dairy Queen" or "Dairy Queen/Brazier" store.

Managerial Assistance Available: International Dairy Queen, Inc., maintains an operations specialty division in addition to regional and district managers, who provide continuing assistance involving store operation, product quality, customer convenience, product development, advertising, financial control, training, communication and incentives. A research and development department is engaged in developing new products, cooking methods and procedures. Sales promotion programs are conducted through newspapers, radio, television and billboards.

Information Submitted: March 1982

SOURCE: U.S. Department of Commerce, *Franchise Opportunities Handbook* (September, 1982), pp. 203–204.

At the state level, 15 states have enacted laws that require franchisors to register a franchise offer with a state agency and to furnish a prospective franchisee a separate disclosure form. This form contains useful information about the franchisor, the franchise system, and the franchise contract. Some 20 states have legislation that covers the procedures on the termination and renewal of the franchises. The purpose of this legislation is to restrict a franchisor's ability to end a franchise contract without just cause.

After having determined that the franchising organization has a strong financial base, an acceptable credit rating, and a history of successful competitive performance, the prospective franchisee should find out about all the costs associated with the franchise. Among these are:

1. Initial franchise fee, which may be as little as several hundred dollars for a franchise from a small regional franchisor to as much as $20,000 for one from a large national franchisor such as Dairy Queen.
2. Annual royalty fee, which most franchisors require in return for their managerial services. In the fast-food industry this fee is typically 4 percent of a franchisee's sales.
3. Contribution to an advertising fund that is administered jointly by the franchisor and franchisees. This may be 1 or 2 percent of each franchisee's annual sales.
4. Site evaluation fee, which is collected by some franchisors.

For some franchisees the total investment in building, equipment, and fees can run over $1 million. Table 26-7 shows the amount of owners' funds that are needed to start certain selected franchises.

Provisions in a Franchise Contract

The franchise contract plays an important role in the franchisor-franchisee relationship. As a legal safeguard, the prospective franchisee should have an attorney

---

Figure 26-13   **Information That Is Part of the "Disclosure Requirements and Prohibitions Concerning Franchising and Business Opportunity Ventures" Rule**

1. Business experience of the franchisor and its key management personnel.
2. Litigation and bankruptcy history of the franchisor and its key management personnel.
3. Financial information on the franchisor.
4. Costs, both initial and recurring, which will be required to be paid by the franchisee.
5. Statistical information on the number of franchises and company-owned outlets.
6. Termination, cancellation, and renewal provisions of the franchise agreement.
7. Number of franchisees terminated during the past year and the reasons for their termination.
8. Training offered by the franchisor.
9. Restrictions imposed by the franchisor on the manner in which the franchisee may operate his business. This includes restrictions on such things as the types of goods which can be sold, suppliers that can be used, and the geographic area in which the franchise may operate.

SOURCE: "New FTC Rule Requires Disclosures by Franchisors," *FTC News Summary* (December 22, 1978), p. 1.

Table 26-7   Equity Capital Needed to Start a Franchise

Franchise	Equity Capital Needed[1]
Command Performance (hair styling)	$75,000 to $100,000
Computerland Corporation	$60,000
Docktor Pet Centers, Inc.	$60,000 to $75,000
Hickory Farms of Ohio, Inc.	$85,000
Jellystone Campgrounds	$75,000 to $150,000
Manpower, Inc.	$50,000 minimum
McDonald's Corporation	$125,000 minimum
Travelodge International, Inc.	$350,000 to $1,000,000
Wendy's Old Fashioned Hamburgers	$500,000
Ziebart Rustproofing Company	$50,000 to $60,000

[1]Equity represents owner's funds. Total investment would be much more.

SOURCE: U.S. Department of Commerce, *Franchise Opportunities Handbook* (September, 1982).

review the franchise contract. In addition to the fees, the major contract provisions that should be closely checked for clarity and suitability relate to the following:

1. *Equipment and supplies.* Many contracts specify that the franchisees must purchase their equipment and inventories from specified suppliers. For example, 150 bakeries worldwide make buns for McDonald's.
2. *Product mix.* Some contracts indicate the exact product mix that a franchisee should carry. The franchisee should be certain that this product mix meets the needs of its particular market. For example, tacos or health foods might be a successful seller in one location but a failure in another.
3. *Territory restrictions.* The territory provided by the franchisor should be adequate to support the franchisee. For example, early in its operation McDonald's believed that a population of 50,000 was needed to support a fast-food restaurant. This figure now has been reduced to 25,000. In addition, a franchisee should be given territory protection. For example, another franchisee of the same franchising organization should not be permitted to operate within the territory of an established franchisee.
4. *Buy-back options.* For some franchisors a franchise system is an inexpensive and rapid way to establish a chain operation. When these franchisors obtain adequate funds and managerial expertise, however, they often buy out their franchisees.

Other contract provisions that must be examined carefully relate to such topics as termination, transfers, advertising, and quality control. In the long run, however, the success of a franchised operation depends not upon a contract but upon the mutual respect between the franchisor and the franchisee.

Future of Franchising

In the past some franchising ventures, such as Minnie Pearl's Chicken and Jerry Lewis Cinemas, have been disappointments. Numerous franchising failures have occurred because franchisors lacked the capital and managerial expertise necessary for success. Inexperienced and untrained franchisees have contributed to franchising failures, too. Since many of these problems have been resolved, the franchise industry should experience vigorous growth through the 1980s. A U.S. Commerce Department official predicts that in the future your chances of going into business and surviving will be very small unless you have a franchise. There are already 465,000 franchise businesses — including car dealers and gasoline service stations — that generate $436 million in sales annually.

In the future the most successful franchises will be in areas that stress convenience, service, and new technology. The fast-food industry will continue to be a stronghold for franchising, with an increasing interest in ethnic offerings such as Chi-Chi's Mexican food and the Spaghetti Pot Italian dishes. Franchising should become more important in dental, optical, physical fitness, legal, tax, and real estate services. An increasing interest in video equipment and home computers should cause the expansion of franchised operations such as the Video Connection and Computerland.

The lure of growing and profitable markets has caused franchisors to expand overseas. A Department of Commerce survey indicated that 288 U.S. franchisors operated 21,416 units in other countries in 1981. McDonald's international sales of $1.4 billion represented 19 percent of its total system-wide sales. The chain has 1,185 units scattered in 29 foreign countries and territories. Figure 26-14 shows the German translation of a famous McDonald's advertising slogan.

Figure 26-14   A Big Mac in Any Language

100% saftig reines Rindfleisch auf einem getoasteten Sesambrötchen, feine Zwiebeln, milder Chesterkäse...

...Spezialsauce, knackiger Eissalat und zart-würzige Essiggurken...

NOTE: The translation is "Twoallbeefpattiesspecialsaucelettucecheesepicklesonionsonasesame-seedbun." This tongue-twisting phrase, which has been translated into 12 languages and has delighted consumers from Japan to Jacksonville, means the Big Mac sandwich to people in 27 countries and territories around the world. And this phrase, or variations of it, first used in the late 1960s, ranks among the top advertising slogans in the history of modern marketing.

SOURCE: McDonald's Corporation, 1980 Annual Report, p. 14. Reproduced with permission.

SUMMARY

Small businesses comprise 97 percent of all businesses, and they generate more than half of all business receipts. A university study revealed that 66 percent of all new jobs in the private sector are created by businesses with 20 or fewer employees. Small firms provide more than 80 percent of the jobs for the disadvantaged minorities.

To be a successful businessperson, an individual should have some previous managerial experience. In addition, the individual should know the following about his or her proposed business: the type of economic values that will be created, size of the business's market, marketability of the product, correlation between the start-up costs and the long-term business prospects, relationship between profitability and investment in the new business, ease of explaining the business to potential investors, and the mechanism for investors to get out of the business.

A major marketing advantage of a small business over a large one is closeness to its customers. In the personnel field, the advantages include the direct contact between the owner/manager and the employees and the opportunity for employees to gain experience in many different activities. In the production area, the advantages include the freedom to innovate and develop new products and the flexibility to make rapid decisions and to develop personalized products for customers. A major financial advantage of a small business is its low overhead, which permits most of its funds to be directed to revenue-producing activities.

In order to be their own boss, many individuals start their own business. These individuals should possess the entrepreneurial qualities of being purposeful, persuasive, persistent, presumptuous, and perceptive. A new business often is established as a proprietorship. When it grows, partners are added to provide more funds and managerial help. At a later period, the expanding business may want greater access to capital and limited liability for its owners; so, a corporation is formed.

The major types of loans that the SBA extends to small businesses are direct loans, guaranteed loans, and participation loans. The SBA licenses privately owned SBICs that provide long-term financing to small firms. Other services and organizations provided by the SBA for small businesses include: business publications, low-interest loans to disaster victims, lease guarantee programs, help in obtaining government contracts, SCORE, ACE, Small Business Institutes, and Small Business Development Centers.

The franchising method permits a small-business operator to start an enterprise that already has a strong consumer identification. A franchisee obtains managerial assistance from a franchisor in the areas of site selection, accounting systems, marketing, production, finance, purchasing, personnel, and management training. Sources of information about franchising are available from various franchise publications, franchise shows, franchise consultants, and the International Franchise Association.

After having determined that the franchisor has a strong financial base, an acceptable credit rating, and a history of successful competitive performance, the prospective franchisee should find out about all the costs associated with the franchise. These often include an initial franchise fee, annual royalty fee, advertising fee, and site evaluation fee. Prior to signing a franchise agreement, a prospective franchisee should check for clarity and suitability the contract provisions that cover equipment and supplies, product mix, territory restrictions, and buy-back options.

BACK TO THE CHAPTER OPENER

1. Do the Fergusons exhibit any of the behavioral qualities of entrepreneurs?
2. Why did the Fergusons form a corporation?
3. How could the Small Business Administration have helped the Fergusons?
4. Why did the Fergusons decide on a franchise system?
5. What type of information concerning their franchise must be disclosed by the Fergusons to prospective franchisees?

BUSINESS	direct loans (SBA)	668	franchise	670
TERMS	guaranteed loans (SBA)	668	franchisor	670
	participation loans (SBA)	669	franchisee	670
	Section 301 (d) SBIC	669		

QUESTIONS FOR DISCUSSION AND ANALYSIS

1. Why should the United States have a policy of attempting to preserve and strengthen small business?

2. How can small-business owners overcome the problem of a lack of managerial experience?

3. How can small businesses overcome their marketing weaknesses and compete effectively with large businesses?

4. What are the differences in the personnel function between large businesses and small businesses?

5. Is the granting of an SBA loan to a business unfair to the competing small businesses that do not have one?

6. What are the differences between General Motors' franchising a car dealer and McDonald's franchising a restaurant?

7. Why would a mature franchise with adequate funds and management want to retain a franchise system of operation rather than a corporate chain?

8. Does a franchisor usually want a prospective franchisee to have prior business experience in the franchisor's field?

9. What are some of the attributes of a successful businessperson that a franchise cannot provide to a franchisee?

10. How can a prospective franchisee check out the business performance and earnings claims of a franchisor?

PROJECTS, PROBLEMS, AND SHORT CASES

1. From articles listed in the *Business Periodicals Index* (BPI) and other indexes, prepare a report that discusses a topic of current interest in the field of small business. A review of the BPI will indicate that the following classifications under "Small Business" list numerous articles from which you can choose for your report: *accounting, data processing, employee relations, export-import trade, finance, laws and regulations, management, marketing,* and *taxation.*

2. The purpose of this project is to acquaint you with some of the problems in establishing a small business. In answering these questions, assume that you are starting a new fast-food franchise. This franchise will require an initial investment of $500,000 for land, building, equipment, and fees. You have savings of only $50,000 to invest in the franchise. Provide complete and concise answers to the following questions:

a. What are the basic differences between the operations of a single fast-food franchise and a large corporate chain of restaurants? Answer this by examining the areas of marketing, personnel, and finance.

b. Do you feel that you possess the behavioral qualities of an entrepreneur? Explain.

c. Which three of the five behavioral qualities of an entrepreneur are the most important ones for an operator of a fast-food franchise?

d. What are the major advantages and disadvantages of the proprietorship and the corporation?

e. What type of business ownership should you use for your fast-food franchise? Provide specific reasons for your choice.

f. If you desire financial aid from the Small Business Administration, what type of loan will you seek and why will you seek it?

g. How could an SBIC help in financing your fast-food franchise?

h. How does a small-business owner benefit from being a member of a franchise system?

i. What qualities should you as a potential franchisee look for in a fast-food franchisor?

j. What are some of the important provisions of a franchise contract that you should examine carefully?

3. Peter and Tony Brown, two brothers, bought a Danny Donut Shop franchise early in the year. They paid the franchisor $12,000. But now, to their dismay, their total commitment is almost $100,000 which they have had to cover with loans, guarantees, and a personal mortgage. Peter and Tony are not happy with their situation.

"We're making money, but...," said Tony, one evening after they had closed.

"I know," replied Peter. "But not as much as we expected. We should have checked those market estimates that the franchisor gave us."

"We could have spoken to that other Danny Donut Shop franchisee out in the suburbs. He'd have given us a good idea of what to expect," Tony added.

"Well, there's a new Danny Donut Shop coming into town. Do you want to do him a good deed and talk to him?" suggested Peter.

"What do you mean, another franchisee?" asked Tony indignantly. "This city is our territory!"

Replied Peter, "The contract we signed says the city is our territory in the sense that we have the right of first refusal on any new franchises. Do you think we can afford to buy another Danny Donut Shop franchise?"

"No way," said Tony, shaking his head. "Not after all the money we had to lay out for equipment and fixtures. Sure the franchise purchase price was a good deal, but I thought we could have bought just any equipment and preferably secondhand."

"Our contract specified new equipment. And, as you know, it specified the type of cookers; counters; everything, in fact, that we needed, along with the supply source," remarked Peter.

"OK," interrupted Tony, "the shop looks nice but they wouldn't let us even modify the layout. If we had smaller tables, we could get more people in. But our franchisor said no."

"It's all in the contract," answered Peter flatly. "Just like I had to say no to that fellow who said he could sell us donut batter cheaper than what we buy from the franchisor."

"Why say no?" asked Tony. "That's the only way we can increase our margin, seeing that the franchisor doesn't want us to adjust the suggested retail prices."

"Sorry, Tony. The contract says we buy our batter and all other supplies from the franchisor," reminded Peter.

Driving home with Tony, Peter remembered something else concerning their Danny Donut Shop franchise. "I got a call from the franchisor's agent today. We're late on our six-month royalty payment."

"What do you mean by a 'royalty payment'? We paid the purchase price and we pay a service fee. What is this royalty business?" queried Tony.

"That is in the contract also," explained Peter patiently. "Over a certain volume of sales, we must pay the franchisor a royalty."

"And, of course," added Tony, "the franchisor is always sending his agent down to check our operations and to see our books. So he'll always know what our sales are."

"They have to send someone down to make sure that Danny Donut Shop standards are the same everywhere. We've agreed to operate by their rules. It's in the contract," said Peter.

"It's a pity that you know the contract only now," commented Tony bitterly.

"It's both our faults," retorted Peter. "We should have examined the contract more carefully and should have checked out everything about the franchise first."[3]

a. What specific factors of the contract did the Browns overlook when they bought a Danny Donut Shop franchise?

b. Should the Federal Trade Commission's disclosure rule on franchising and the state franchising laws have prevented the difficulties that the Browns encountered?

c. What are the major points that a prospective franchisee should investigate when considering the purchase of a franchise?

3. From *Buying a Franchise,* Chapter 1, Volume 3 of the series, "Minding Your Own Business," Federal Business Development Bank, Montreal, Quebec, Canada, pp. 12 to 13.

Comprehensive Case
PAWS, Inc. — The Tale of GARFIELD[1]

The "Paws that refreshes" refers to a remarkable organization — PAWS, Inc., headed by cartoonist Jim Davis. It produces one of the most widely read comic strips — GARFIELD® — in the United States. This lovable, smart-aleck cat is the creation of Jim Davis, a skillful artist who is tickling the funny bone of newspaper readers (see Figure A-1).

Jim Davis was born in Fairmount, IN, where he grew up with about 25 cats rambling in and out of his rural home. (Because of his wife's allergy to cats, he no longer has one.) From 1963 through 1967, Jim studied art at Ball State University in Muncie, IN. After leaving college, he worked for an advertising agency where he did paste-ups and a variety of other assignments. In 1969, he became an assistant to cartoonist Tom Ryan, who draws the syndicated comic strip Tumbleweeds. Although the pay was meager, Jim perfected his drawing skills and obtained an introduction into the syndicated cartoon industry.[2] To supplement his income, Jim moonlighted as a freelance commercial artist, copywriter, radio personality, and political campaigner.

---

1. The authors are indebted to Jim Davis for his cooperation in providing the information for this case.
2. A syndicate is a business concern that buys comic strips, articles, and other materials and then sells them for simultaneous publication in many newspapers. A syndicate varies the selling price of its materials according to the circulation of a newspaper.

SOURCE: GARFIELD: ©1978 United Feature Syndicate, Inc.

Starting a New Comic Strip

After several restless but creative years with Ryan, Jim decided to initiate his own comic strip. Believing he had the perfect idea for a strip, Jim created one that featured a bug called Gnorm Gnat. His experience with comic strips had convinced him that nonhuman cartoon characters could be placed in many more interesting situations with more flexibility than humans could. An animal or bug is not perceived by readers as being white, black, male, female, young, or old. For the next six years, Jim repeatedly tried to sell his strip to the cartoon syndicates. The overwhelming negative responses that were received finally caused Jim to bug off. As one syndicate editor consoled him, "Your art is good, your gags are great, but bugs—nobody can identify with bugs!"

Although the bug comic strip did not fly, Jim still had the entrepreneurial urge to develop his own strip. A thorough review of the successful strips revealed to him that dogs were very popular. SNOOPY, MARMADUKE, Belvedere, and Fred Bassett were carried by numerous newspapers and enjoyed an immense audience. Conversely, there were very few cats in the comics at this time. He believed that there was a large group of cat lovers who, as readers, would sustain a comic strip about a cat. This caused Jim to make a carefully calculated business decision to develop and market a strip featuring a cat. Jim reasoned that cat lovers would support a cat-centered strip even more than dog lovers would support a dog-centered strip. Dog owners are attracted to a certain breed of dog such as German shepherd, boxer, or golden retriever; but cat lovers love all kinds of cats. In effect, cat fanciers own generic cats.

Creating GARFIELD

In 1975, Jim's talented pen gave birth to an obstinate, overweight, and cynical cat called GARFIELD. As one writer commented, "The cat has all the Boy Scout virtues turned inside out." GARFIELD is named after Jim's paternal grandfather, James A. Garfield Davis, who was a large, cantankerous character. Other central personalities in the strip included Pooky, a teddy bear named after his wife's childhood toy bear; Jon, GARFIELD's master, whose name is drawn from a vaguely recalled coffee commercial; Nermal, a cute little kitten whom GARFIELD jealously tries to upstage; and Odie, a not-too-smart slobbering dog who is usually overwhelmed by the shrewd GARFIELD (see Figure A-2).

In 1978, after spending nearly one and a half years painstakingly developing and perfecting the concept of the GARFIELD® comic strip, Jim felt confident enough to attempt to peddle the strip to a syndicate. Much to Jim's disappointment the first two syndicates that he contacted, King Features and the *Chicago Tribune-New York News*, refused to buy the strip. Happily, the third one—United Feature Syndicate, Inc.—signed him to a contract.

As Jim readily discovered, the life of any new entrepreneur—whether illustrator or retailer—is not easy. After four months of test runs, GARFIELD® was cancelled

Figure A-2   GARFIELD, Pooky, and Odie

by the *Chicago Sun-Times* and major papers in Salt Lake City and Little Rock. Knowing that it takes from one to three years for a strip to attract and retain a loyal group of readers, Jim gloomily thought that the cancellations meant the end to his fledgling venture.

To the surprise of the newspapers, a legion of GARFIELD fans had already developed; and they strongly protested the removal of their favorite comic strip. Within a few days of the cancellation, the *Sun-Times* had heard from 1,300 angry readers who strongly insisted that the strip be continued. As a result of this outpouring of sentiment for the roguish cat, the papers promptly reinstated GARFIELD.® Turning what appeared to be certain failure into good fortune, Jim used the publicity and support to sell the strip to other newspapers. This breakthrough established the feisty GARFIELD® as a dominant comic strip personality.

The Advantages of a Licensing Program

While developing the GARFIELD® strip, Jim kept in mind the licensing opportunities that would become available to a successful strip. Without a licensing program, a cartoonist's income is only a percentage of the fees that newspapers pay to the syndicate. For example, a paper carrying a daily comic strip ordinarily pays a syndicate from $5 to over $100 weekly for the right to run the strip. Under a licensing program, however, the cartoonist can obtain considerable revenue. Most licensing agreements call for a 5 to 7 percent royalty fee to be paid to the licensor (the syndicate). Fortunately United Feature Syndicate has an outstanding track record in developing licensing programs for its comic strip characters. (This syndicate handles PEANUTS, which has enjoyed an active licensing program for the last 20 years.) In GARFIELD's case, the royalty fee is split fifty-fifty between PAWS, Inc., and the syndicate. In 1981, GARFIELD retail sales grossed over $15 million.

The sales of licensed products that are based on popular comic strips are fairly steady and not particularly affected by general economic conditions. In fact, there appears to be an inverse relationship between the sales of these products and economic conditions. For example, during the Great Depression of the 1930s, comic strips attained a high degree of popularity as people were seeking a psychological lift from their problems. This was an excellent period for the sales of licensed products that were based on Popeye, Mickey Mouse, and other comic strip characters.

In retrospect, Jim's decision early in the GARFIELD era to develop a strong licensing program was masterful. The retail sales of all licensed products climbed spectacularly during the early 1980s. By 1982, the retail sales of all licensed products were generating $20.6 billion. This was a 50 percent increase over 1981, more than twice 1980, and over three times the 1978 sales.[3]

A licensing arrangement based on the proper character benefits both the licensee and the licensor. When licensed popular characters appear on products, these products sell much more rapidly than similar products without a licensed character. There are large variations in the life span of a licensed character. One based on a movie may enjoy popularity for six months or a year. If the character is based on a Saturday morning television cartoon, it may last for the duration of the cartoon series. Some licensed characters have a very short life and others, such as Mickey Mouse (who is over 50) and SNOOPY, endure for generations.

Building the Foundation of a Licensing Program

In order to build the foundation for an active licensing program, Jim wanted to establish GARFIELD® in as many newpapers as possible. There are two reasons why it is often difficult for a new comic strip to obtain space in a newspaper. One reason is that, every time a paper shortage occurs, a newspaper eliminates some of its comic strips. When the shortage ends, however, the comic strip section never returns to its original size. Another reason is that a large portion of a comic page is locked up by what the industry calls the "undroppables." These are enduring features, such as PEANUTS®, Blondie, and Beetle Bailey, that are assured of space as long as they exist. Thus, for a newspaper editor to add a new comic strip, a current one must be dropped. But a strip that has run in a paper for a period of time is viewed as an old friend by its readers; so, dropping it is a difficult decision to make.

Jim carefully estimated the time frame that would be necessary to gain reader acceptance and recognition of GARFIELD. He concluded that it would take from three to five years to establish a solid foundation on which to base a licensing program for his furry friend. In order to accelerate this timetable, Jim met with his staff and planned a strategic marketing move that significantly affected the GARFIELD pro-

---

3. Marcie Lynn Avram, "Winning Characters," *Stores* (May, 1983), p. 63.

gram. As an avid comic book reader, Jim could never understand why all of the comic strip panels were stacked one on top of another and placed between the covers of a conventional vertical book. It seemed logical and more readable to print the strips on a horizontal format as they appear in the newspapers. Another benefit from publishing a horizontal book is that it could not be displayed in the same area as the other books. Because of its odd shape, it would have to be displayed in its own area and therefore attract more attention.

Thus, the staff swiftly developed a mockup of a horizontal book. Then they designed and built a display dump that would hold the books. All of this activity was accomplished without contacting the printers, cutters, packagers, shippers, and rack jobbers who generally provide advice on the feasibility of such a project. Looking back, Jim feels that if these individuals had been consulted, the entire concept would have been dropped.

In order to market the GARFIELD® strips most effectively, Jim made the decision to publish the strips in chronological order — both daily and Sunday. They would be placed in a series of matching books with a bright new cover color for each edition. Jim's objective was to establish a subscription mentality for GARFIELD® readers so that they instinctively would buy the next book as it was published. The cover of a book would spell out in large letters its number in the series. If a reader had the first book, the second book, and the fourth book, he or she would readily know to buy the third book.

With the production and marketing concepts for the books worked out, Jim presented it to officials at United Feature Syndicate, Inc., in New York. Their reaction was that it was unrealistic and unworkable. A disillusioned Jim Davis returned to his studio in Muncie, IN, on a Saturday. In the mail on the next Monday was a letter from Ballantine Books asking how they could obtain the publishing rights to GARFIELD. Jim immediately contacted United Feature Syndicate's licensing representative and took the mockup to Ballantine, which accepted the entire concept.

In the publishing industry a book which is the shape of the GARFIELD books is known as the GARFIELD format. The success of this venture is evidenced by the fact that Jim had eight GARFIELD® books on the prestigious *New York Times* Best Seller List at one time — the only author ever to have accomplished this!

As a result of the book sales, reader acceptance of GARFIELD® increased greatly. To accelerate this momentum, Jim initiated a book tour in 20 major U.S. cities in April, 1980. At the start of Jim's travels GARFIELD® was being added to newspapers at the rate of about seven papers a month. Within two months after the tour began, the strip was being added to newspapers at the rate of one a day. During the book tour, Jim learned that best sellers are self-perpetuating. When booksellers learn that a book is on the best seller list, they immediately order it. This places the book in more stores and in more advantageous displays where additional sales keep it on the best seller list.

Developing Licensing Programs for GARFIELD Products

With GARFIELD's popularity rapidly increasing, Jim decided to pursue licensing arrangements actively. In order to gain insight into the marketing of licensed products,

Jim reviewed the marketing of the Kliban Cat products. Although this character was still very popular on licensed items, its appeal was beginning to decline. Jim attributed this loss of appeal to the fact that the same cat was being placed on every item without regard to the item's size, shape, printing process, or market. The artist's input on the character had ceased years before, and repetition was beginning to take its toll.

Learning from the Kliban experience, Jim decided to take full creative and artistic control of the GARFIELD licensing program. This would enable him to design the appropriate art for each licensed item, taking into consideration the type of reproduction process and the target market for the item. He could readily check and maintain the quality of the licensed products, too. Jim discovered that this personalized approach was very demanding and difficult to achieve. The GARFIELD licensing program involved working in the publishing, ceramics, textile, game, and electronics industries, among others. Each industry had its own requirements. The four-color process in one industry might be full color in another, reflective art in another, and five color in yet another.

The success of the Gibson line of GARFIELD® greeting cards provided an early gauge of consumer response to the GARFIELD products. Gibson test marketed the GARFIELD® cards in several stores by placing them in the regular display racks next to the other cards. Gibson ordinarily test markets a new line of cards for three to six months. After a few weeks, it was evident that the GARFIELD® cards were hot items.

As the product line began to grow, it became painfully obvious to Jim that he did not personally have the time to design each product. His 5:30 A.M. to late-night working schedule was already woefully overcrowded. As a result PAWS, Inc., was established. This is a close corporation of 17 artists and administrators who are responsible for the design and maintenance of the GARFIELD image throughout the world. There are two groups of artists. One group consists of Jim and two others who work on the comic strip. Jim continues to dream up the GARFIELD capers and does the first pencil drawing of each strip himself. The other group is composed of a production manager and seven artists, who create the illustrations for GARFIELD's licensing ventures. The administrative area includes a business manager, an office manager and her assistant, a fan mail correspondent, a corporate pilot, and an account executive who markets GARFIELD to commercial enterprises.

With the organization of PAWS, Inc., Jim has the personnel to create original art for almost every item that is being licensed. Some licensees resisted this individualized approach because they did not want to pay for new artwork. These licensees were accustomed to utilizing the art from either the strips or the licensor's file. This resistance faded rapidly when the licensed products began selling briskly in the marketplace.

In developing the licensing program in the United States, a decision was made to confine the GARFIELD visage only to products such as coffee mugs, T-shirts, and sleepwear (see Figure A-3), but not to endorse a particular branded product such as cereal or peanut butter. GARFIELD lines include toys by Mattel Co., glassware by Anchor Hocking, and outdoor footwear by Brookfield Athletic Shoe Co. These are a notable few of the over 50 companies marketing GARFIELD's visage. Jim believed that, if GARFIELD were a commercial spokesperson or spokescat for a line of goods, he would receive too much exposure or possibly the wrong kind of exposure for his

SOURCE: GARFIELD Characters: ©1978, 1979 United Feature Syndicate, Inc.

personality. In certain foreign markets, product endorsements may be the most effective way to establish GARFIELD's name. However, in other countries GARFIELD does not have the strong media acceptance that he does in this country and in Canada.

An outstanding marketing advantage for GARFIELD is that he is seen daily by over 80 million readers in 1,400 newpapers. For the GARFIELD licensees, this means there are 1,400 advertisements a day in all of the major United States markets. Additional promotional exposure is obtained for the GARFIELD licensees through the GARFIELD television specials and a record album. The strong impact of television on consumers ensures GARFIELD's credibility in the marketplace.

The Dakin Company, the world's largest manufacturer of plush dolls, was a licensee that discovered the unexpected strength of GARFIELD's power. In order to obtain the appropriate GARFIELD® doll, eight versions of it were shipped back and forth in one year to the Dakin plant in Korea. When the doll was finally perfected, Dakin test-marketed 10,000 of them in stores in the San Francisco Bay area. To determine the vigor of the doll's sales, Dakin representatives returned to the stores after 48 hours to check on the number of dolls on hand. To their surprise all of the dolls had been sold. The brisk demand for these dolls was soon duplicated throughout the United States. Although Dakin began producing the dolls in four additional plants, it took over a year before supply caught up with demand! Today, there are nearly 200 Korean workers whose full-time pursuit is spray-painting stripes on GARFIELD® dolls.

Keeping GARFIELD Purring

A major concern of Jim's was to maintain a fresh and vibrant image for GARFIELD. Through 1980 and 1981, GARFIELD was depicted on licensed products in a sitting position against a bright red, blue, or yellow background. Because the GARFIELD items were selling well, some of the licensees were reluctant to alter the successful marketing formula. The PAWS staff, however, believed that these licensees did not understand the depth of reader loyalty that had been generated for GARFIELD through the newspapers and other media. GARFIELD fans would want the newest creations.

By 1981 the PAWS staff was doing conceptual work on GARFIELD products that would be marketed in 1983. The decision was made to modify GARFIELD by using an airbrush treatment that would round him out and make him look a little more human. Fresh color combinations, such as powder blue, purple, rose, and lavender, were to be worked into GARFIELD creations. When informed of these changes, some of the licensees were aghast. They insisted that the original GARFIELD be continued; otherwise the delicate combination of elements that created his success would be destroyed. To counter this opposition, Jim pointed out to the licensees that GARFIELD's long-term success depended on innovative approaches and new presentations. Although Jim felt that GARFIELD could have been successfully continued as a fat orange cat on a red background for another two years, he knew that the public eventually would have become bored with GARFIELD. It was difficult, however, to convince the licensees' product managers, whose jobs depend on GARFIELD's success, that this was the correct approach. Nevertheless, the more than 1,600 products bearing GARFIELD's visage provide evidence of the success of the PAWS program. As GARFIELD said, "The meek may inherit the earth, but in the meantime the powerful will make a pretty comfortable living."

QUESTIONS

1. What entrepreneurial qualities does Jim possess? Discuss.
2. Why did Jim choose the corporate form of ownership for PAWS rather than a proprietorship or a partnership?
3. Draw what you believe should be the organization chart for PAWS, Inc., and indicate the appropriate line and staff positions.
4. What types of compensation systems might be used for the employees of PAWS, Inc.? How could these employees be encouraged to be innovative, careful, and productive in their work?
5. What type of production process is used for the manufacture of the GARFIELD® doll? How do production control and quality control enter into the GARFIELD program?
6. Explain how Jim practices the marketing concept with GARFIELD.
7. How has Jim blended the four P's of the marketing mix in promoting GARFIELD?
8. In what stage of the product life cycle is the GARFIELD® comic strip? How can Jim keep GARFIELD from reaching the decline stage?
9. How does the licensing of GARFIELD differ from General Electric's licensing of a Japanese company to produce washing machines for the Japanese market?
10. Identify areas in Jim's operations where the services of an accountant would be useful.
11. Indicate the types of risks that the PAWS organization faces and the insurance or methods that can be used to reduce these risks.

Glossary

absolute advantage   a nation's economic advantage over other nations by being the sole producer of a good or by producing a good more cheaply than others can

access (or debit) card   a magnetic-stripe bank card, encoded with a personal identification number known only to the customer and the card issuer, used to operate automated teller machines

accounting   the recording, classifying, and summarizing of business transactions, and the interpretation of them

acid-test ratio   the ratio of the total of cash, net receivables, and marketable securities held on a temporary basis, to current liabilities

actuary   an expert at computing risks and the size of insurance premiums necessary for the profitable operation of an insurance company

administrative management or middle management   managerial level comprised of managers of divisions or services with a coordinating and unifying orientation

administrative skill   conceptual skill that involves the ability to see the company as a whole

advertising   any paid form of nonpersonal presentation and promotion of ideas, goods, or services by an identified sponsor

advertising agency   an organization equipped to handle all phases of advertising for its clients

advertising media   the different devices through which advertising reaches its audience

affirmative-action program   an employer's analysis of its deficiencies in hiring minorities and women, including steps to take in removing the deficiencies

agency   the delegation of authority to another person to act on one's behalf

agent   the person who is authorized to represent the principal in dealings with third parties

AIDA   abbreviation derived from the first letter in each of the major tasks of advertising: to attract Attention, to draw Interest, to create Desire, and to get Action

alien corporation   state classification of a corporation doing business in that state but chartered by a foreign government

American capitalism   economic system in which individuals competitively produce goods and services for society with comparative freedom from outside controls

analog computer   a computer that carries out its calculations by making measurements

appellate court   a court that has authority to review decisions reached in a lower court

aptitude tests   tests that measure the ability of a person to learn how to perform certain jobs

arbitration   the method by which both parties to a labor dispute agree to submit the dispute to a third party for a binding decision

assets   items owned by a firm such as cash, receivables, inventories, equipment, land, and buildings

audit committee   a group of outside directors that monitors a management's recordkeeping practices and internal accounting control procedures

automated clearinghouse   a system for clearing interbank debits and credits

automated teller machine   a device used by financial institutions, either on or off premises, to perform several basic teller functions electronically

automation   the control of machine tools by computers

average   a measure of central tendency that is the typical value in a group of data

average inventory   the minimum inventory plus one-half of the order quantity over a period of the inventory cycle

bait pricing   advertising a low-priced shopping good to lure customers into the store and then attempting to persuade them to buy higher-priced models

balance of payments   the difference between a nation's total payments to and total receipts from foreign nations during a given time

balance of trade   the difference between the monetary values of a nation's imports and exports of goods and services

balance sheet   a financial statement that lists a firm's assets, liabilities, and capital as of a specific date

balance-sheet equation   assets equal liabilities plus capital

bank acceptances   instruments that indicate a bank will accept sight drafts covering merchandise shipped to one of its customers

bank discount   interest deducted in advance from a loan by a bank

bankruptcy   the state in which liabilities owed by a firm exceed the value of assets owned

BASIC (Beginner's All-purpose Symbolic Instruction Code)   an easy-to-learn computer language in English-like words that allows the programmer to interact directly with a computer program

batch processing   method by which data are collected and sent periodically in groups or batches to the computer

bears   speculators who sell stock, expecting the market to go down

behavioristic market segmentation   the classification of consumers according to their response, knowledge, or attitude about a good or service

behavior modification or positive reinforcement   the theory of B. F. Skinner that holds that human behavior is controlled by its immediate consequences

billings   dollar amounts of all advertising space, time, and services billed by advertising agencies to their clients

blacklist   a secret list of names, compiled by employers' associations, of persons thought to be union agitators or sympathizers

blue-sky laws   state laws regulating security sales

board of directors   group elected by corporate stockholders to represent them, to elect corporate officers, and to take final action on important policies

bond   a debt of the issuing corporation that matures at a stated future date and on which interest is paid annually or semiannually

bottom line   another term for net income (or net earnings) or net loss, the final figure on an income statement

boycott   a refusal to purchase products from companies whose employees are on strike or from firms who sell the goods of a struck or nonunion plant

brand names   names used by firms to identify their products and to distinguish them from competing goods

break-even point   the volume of sales for a product needed to cover its total variable and fixed costs

budget   a written plan of action in numerical form against which actual performance may be compared

bulls   speculators who buy stocks in anticipation of a rise in price

business   all the commercial and industrial activities that provide goods and services to maintain and improve our quality of life

business ethics   ethical standards that concern both the ends and the means of business decision making

business law   principles and regulations that provide for a smooth and orderly flow of business transactions and the settlement of disputes that may arise over these transactions

business legitimacy   the recognition by society that businesses are fulfilling the role for which they were created

business trust   unincorporated business managed by a small group of trustees who issue shares to its owner-investors but are not elected or controlled by them

buying motive   an influence that occurs when bodily energy is activated and selectively directed toward satisfying a need

CAD (Computer-Aided Design)   the use of computer graphics displayed on a screen to design, draft, and analyze

call   an option to buy a named stock at a specified price within a stated time period

callable or redeemable bonds   bonds that have an indenture clause providing they can be called or redeemed at the option of the issuer

call price   the exact amount at which a bond can be redeemed at the option of the issuer

CAM (Computer-Aided Manufacturing)   the computerized control of production machines

capital   ownership interest in assets consisting of the original and subsequent invested funds plus retained profits

capital-labor ratio   the proportion of capital investment that each worker has to work with

capital statement   a financial statement that shows the changes in a firm's capital since the previous balance sheet

cartel   a group of companies or countries handling similar goods joined together in an effort to control the market for these goods

cash discount   an inducement offered by the seller to

encourage buyers to pay their bills within a short time after the goods are delivered

cash surrender value   the amount a policyholder receives when a life insurance policy is cancelled or, more commonly, the amount that can be borrowed from the insurance company

centralized management   managerial authority that occurs when a central manager is heavily involved in decisions made by other managers down the line

central processing unit (CPU)   the heart of a computer system that processes the data from an input device and transmits the processed data to an output device

Certified Public Accountants (CPAs)   independent individuals or firms who provide accounting-related services to the public and have complied with state certification rules

chain of command or hierarchy of authority   formal authority relationships that run in a direct line from the top to the bottom of the organization

chain stores   two or more stores in the same general line of business which are centrally owned and managed by a corporate chain

channels of distribution   the routes that goods take in their progress from producers to consumers

charter   document issued by a state authorizing and recording the formation of a corporation

checkoff   the union goal of collection of union dues by the employer through payroll deductions

CIM (Computer-Integrated Manufacturing)   a feature of the automated factory in which computer-assisted designs can be translated directly into machine-tool or robotics language which can run machines at any location

circulating capital   the current assets of a business

civil law   legal system based on formal codes comprised of laws, rules, and regulations and concerned with the duties that exist between individuals

coalition bargaining, coordinated bargaining, or conglomerate bargaining   in companies where several unions have contracts, the unions join together in the bargaining process with the company

COBOL (Common Business Oriented Language)   a computer language that uses business terminology and is written in English-like words

coinsurance clause   a provision in a fire insurance policy that limits the amount of a loss that will be paid by the insurer unless a stated percentage of the value of the property is insured

collective bargaining   the process by which a union becomes the bargaining agent for its members in place of individual company-employee bargaining

collusive bidding   an illegal business practice whereby supposedly competing firms either agree to submit identical prices or agree that one of them is to be the low bidder on a contract

commercial bank   the main bank depository institution

commercial draft   a credit instrument similar to a promissory note except that it originates with the party who is to receive the money

commercial paper   unsecured promissory notes that well-known corporations sell on the open market

commission broker   a member of a security exchange who buys and sells stock on the trading floor of the exchange

commodity exchange   an organized market for a selected list of commodities

common law   legal system that reflects legal opinions and decisions over the years, in which each court decision becomes a precedent for future cases of a similar nature

common stocks   certificates that represent corporate ownership on which no dividend rate is stated

communism   a socialist economy ruled by a single political party and based on the economic and political doctrines of Karl Marx

community of interests   an illegal practice by which a few stockholders can dictate the composition of the boards of directors of two or more competing corporations

comparable worth   the theory of equal pay among men and women doing similar work

comparative advantage   a nation's economic advantage over other nations by specializing in those goods and services in which it has the greatest cost advantages

compensation equity   pay seen as fair and consistent by employees when compared to pay for jobs of a similar level within the organization and for similar jobs with other employers

computer hardware   the central processing unit and its additional equipment

computer program   a series of operating instructions to be performed in processing the data supplied to a computer

computer software   various programming aids that help make effective use of a computer

concessionary bargaining   method by which managers aggressively try to get unions to make cuts in wages and benefits in existing contracts because of the employer's competitive needs

conciliation   a method used in a labor dispute by which a mediator tries to get the parties to agree to offers freely made by either party

consensus management   a top management style keyed to group decision making and implementation

consumer co-ops   user-owned retail outlets of goods and services

consumer goods   goods used by ultimate consumers or households without further commercial processing

Consumer Price Index (CPI)   a widely used measure, prepared monthly by the U. S. Department of Labor, of the changes in the purchasing power of the dollar

consumption ethic   principle or value practiced by those who view consumption and material comfort as the most important goals in life

containerization   the shipping of cargo in large aluminum or steel boxes

contingency management   a managerial technique that recognizes the factors, forces, and variables in the relationship between the organization and its environment

contract a voluntary agreement between two or more parties to do or not to do something

contract purchasing a policy involving an agreement with vendors to have purchased materials delivered over a period of time

controlling the managerial function that measures current performance against expected results and takes necessary action to reach the goals

convenience goods goods that are bought by the consumer after little shopping effort, purchased frequently, bought by habit, and sold in numerous outlets

convertible bonds bonds that the holder can convert at any time into common stock of the issuing corporation

cooperative advertising· a form of product advertising where the costs are shared by manufacturers and their middlemen

cooperative or co-op incorporated, nonprofit business in which members each have a single vote, interest is paid on the amount each owner invests, and patronage dividends are paid in proportion to the volume of purchases by each user-member

copyrights exclusive rights belonging to the owners of original works of authorship

corporate accountability the concept that corporate managers are responsible for how well they handle the resources under their control

corporate social audit systematic attempt to measure and evaluate a corporation's impact on society

corporation a business that is an artificial being as a legal entity created by law

cost of merchandise sold the purchase price of the merchandise that was sold by the firm during the year or accounting period

court of original jurisdiction the court that first tries a case

credit union a cooperative chartered by either the state or the federal government to allow members of a specific group to save money and loan it to one another

crime a public wrong that violates a law that has been passed

Critical Path Method (CPM) operations research technique which establishes a critical path that considers both cost and time involved for a project's completion

cumulative voting system by which a stockholder can cast as many votes for one person as the number of board directors to be elected times the number of shares owned

current assets assets that will be converted into cash or used within one year

current liabilities debts that are owed and payable within one year

current ratio the ratio of total current assets to total current liabilities

custom contract a contract arrangement where unions soften the usual contractual demands in the face of wage competition from open shops

customs union a form of economic integration where nations agree not only to abolish trade restrictions among themselves, but also to adopt common policies regarding trade outside the union

debenture bonds bonds with no security backing except the good name of the issuer

decentralization delegation of authority for making managerial decisions to subordinates at lower levels in the organization

defined-benefit plan a pension plan that provides a fixed benefit although contributions to the plan may vary over the years

defined-contribution plan a pension plan in which contributions are fixed but the actual amount of the benefits is not known before retirement

dehiring the process of getting an employee to quit voluntarily so that it is unnecessary to fire that person

delegation managerial technique by which a manager assigns tasks or goals to subordinates, grants them necessary authority, and creates an obligation to do the task

demand deposits claims or debts against a bank that are payable on demand

demand elasticity the effect that a change in price for an item has on the quantity demanded

demand management current name for Keynesian economics that attempts to increase output by increasing demand for it

demography the study of vital and social statistics such as births, deaths, marriages, and population fluctuations

departmentation the element in the organizing process that rationally groups the work necessary to achieve the goals of the organization in ways that encourage cooperation and communication

depository institutions financial institutions that can create demand deposits

digital computer a computer that deals with coded symbols and numbers

directing the managerial function that includes the three basic elements of leadership, motivation, and communication in achieving the goals of the organization

direct loans (SBA) loans of up to $150,000 made by the SBA to small-business owners turned down by two banks

discharge the permanent separation of an employee from a company, and usually of a negative nature

discount a reduction in price made by a seller to a buyer

discount window the Federal Reserve's loan function in which it loans money to member depository institutions

discretionary income the income available after necessities have been purchased and a certain standard of living has been met

disposable personal income the aggregate amount available for spending and saving in a country during a particular period of time

distribution management the control of total costs of transportation, warehousing, inventory control, protective packaging, and materials handling

doctrine of fair use the principle referring to the extent to which a copyrighted work may be used without permission of the copyright owner

domestic corporation state classification of a corporation doing business in the state in which it is chartered

dormant or sleeping partner a partner neither known to the general public as a partner nor active in managing the partnership

dumping selling a good abroad at less than home prices for that good

earnings per share (EPS) earnings per share of common stock computed by dividing the amount available to common stockholders by the number of shares of common stock outstanding

Economic Man one concerned mainly with producing goods and services and who considers advantages and disadvantages in terms of one's own self-interest

effective rate of interest the true interest cost rather than the nominal rate stated on the loan instrument

electronic data processing (EDP) the processing of data through a computer

electronic funds transfer (EFT) the application of computer and telecommunications technology in making or processing payments

Employee Stock Ownership Plans (ESOPs) a concept originated by Louis Kelso that allows workers to use corporate credit to buy a piece of the business in which they work

employment or job counselor firms companies that help job seekers to prepare résumés, use job-search techniques, and pinpoint possible employers

employment security a union goal of a steady lifetime job or income for workers

enlightened self-interest (ESI) model of business responsibility based on a mixture of self-interest and public interest

entrepreneur one who initiates economic activity and is a prime risk taker in a capitalistic system

environmental scanning management process of seeking useful information about events and relationships in a company's external environment

equilibrium theory of prices a theory based on the assumptions of pure competition with the two forces of supply and demand determining the price

ethical codes specific statements of what is regarded as right or wrong within a particular situation in the present

ethical standards widely accepted modes of conduct

ethics the established rules of behavior that people accept as "good" or "bad"

Eurocurrency market the international financial market in which Eurodollars are borrowed or lent by major international banks

Eurodollars U.S. dollar deposits held and used by major American or foreign banks outside the United States

exchange rate the price of one country's money in terms of another country's money

executive search firm or "headhunter" a firm hired and paid by an employer to seek out a person for a specific position

exporting selling goods produced in one country to another country

facilities management the service provided by a computer service company that sets up and operates all or part of a firm's EDP requirements

factor a financial institution that makes outright purchases of a business's accounts receivable

fair-trade laws the practice (now illegal) in which manufacturers of branded goods could require retailers to charge a minimum specified price for the goods

feedback knowledge of results, often of an informational, corrective, or reinforcing nature

fidelity bonds insurance policies that protect employers against losses due to the dishonesty of covered employees

FIFO "first in, first out" valuation policy which assumes that items first acquired or produced are priced out ahead of similar items acquired later

financial audit a periodic examination and evaluation of the accounting records of a firm

fiscal policy major economic policy tool based on the taxing and spending efforts of the federal government

fixed assets assets that are intended for use rather than sale and are expected to last beyond a year

fixed capital all types of assets other than current assets

fixed costs the inescapable costs, such as plant, equipment, and overhead expenses, that are present regardless of production levels

flexible or "cafeteria" benefits plan a fringe benefits program in which employees are given certain basic benefit items and are allowed to select other benefits from a package of optional items

floating currencies currencies whose values are determined by supply and demand in the open market

floating lien a lien held by the lending agency on all the inventories of the borrower

f. o. b. (free on board) destination the price of a product quoted to buyers that includes transportation costs to their city or place of business

f. o. b. shipping point (or factory) the price of a product quoted to buyers that does not include transportation costs

focus group a form of personal interviewing which involves interviewing 8 to 12 persons at the same time in order to probe attitudes and obtain group interaction

foreign corporation state classification of a corporation doing business in that state but chartered by another state

foreign-exchange transactions the exchange of currencies by the central banks of various countries to be used in international trade

form utility intangible satisfaction derived from a physical change in a product

FORTRAN (Formula Translation) a computer language widely used in scientific and mathematical operations

forward buying the purchasing policy involving orders

for larger amounts of an item placed less frequently

fourth market   large blocks of listed securities traded off the floor of the exchange directly between two institutional investors

franchise   a continuing business relationship that requires a person to operate a business according to the methods prescribed by the franchising organization

franchisee   the person, usually a retailer, who obtains the right to use a franchisor's name in his or her business

franchisor   the party that develops the franchise and initiates the franchise agreement

free-trade associations   a form of economic integration where goods flow freely among member nations without being subject to tariffs

free-trade zone   an area in a country where foreign goods can be stored, processed, or assembled without being subject to tariffs until they are moved to another part of the country

freight forwarder   a broker for companies that ship in less-than-carload, truckload, or airplane-load lots

fringe benefits   benefits of all kinds given to employees apart from their regular pay

functional authority   right to issue policies and procedures for specific functions throughout the organization and to expect compliance

functional middlemen   a group of wholesalers who do not take title to the goods which they sell

futures market   the market in a commodity exchange in which contracts for purchase or sale call for delivery some months in the future

generally accepted accounting principles (GAAP) broadly defined standards that accountants follow in preparing financial statements in order to achieve uniformity

general-merchandise stores   retailers that offer a wide variety of goods, among which are general stores and department stores

general partner   a partner who has unlimited liability and is usually active in managing the partnership

general partnership   legal business ownership in which all partners have unlimited liability

General Schedule (GS) grades   the classification of Civil Service jobs into 18 grades

gentlemen's agreement   an illegal business agreement in which competing firms decide to raise or fix prices

give-backs   the giving up by unionized employees of hard-won pay hikes, fringe benefits, or work rules that hamper productivity

goodwill   the price paid for a firm's intangible assets, such as its good name, trade connections, or earning capacity

gross profit   the difference found by subtracting the cost of merchandise sold from the net sales

guaranteed loans (SBA)   plan under which the SBA guarantees the lesser of 90 percent or $500,000 of a bank loan to a small business

hand-to-mouth buying   the purchasing policy of ordering small amounts of an item at frequent intervals

hedging   the act of using the futures market to protect a legitimate manufacturing profit on a product

hierarchy of needs   a theory by A. H. Maslow that arranges five basic human needs in an ascending order

horizontal differentiation   dividing operating tasks in an organization

human relations skill   the ability to work effectively with people individually and in groups

human resources approach   a concept that formally recognizes that all persons in an organization are potential sources of innovation and talent

IMPROSHARE Plan   an incentive pay plan based on the number of employee-hours required in production

Incentive Stock Option (ISO)   a qualified stock option that gives an executive the right to pay today's price for a block of shares in the company at a future time

income statement   a financial statement that summarizes the income and expenses of a business for a stated period of time, usually a year

indenture   the legal agreement under which bonds are issued

independents   stores that are individually and usually locally owned

index number   a device for measuring the change that has taken place in a group of related items over a period of time

industrial goods   goods sold primarily for use in producing other goods or in providing services

inflation   an economic condition that reduces the purchasing power of money because of an excess of economic demand relative to the supply of goods and services

informal organization   activities and human interactions that are not a formal part of the organization

information utility   intangible satisfaction created by the promotion function, which informs the consumer about a product

injunction   a court order that restrains a union from interfering with a plant's production, usually during a strike

insolvency   insufficiency of fairly valued assets owned to pay off debts

institutional advertising   a form of advertising created for the purpose of getting a message from a firm or group of firms across to the public

institutional management or top management   the managerial level comprised of the board of directors, president, and group executives whose orientation is to establish the relationship of the firm to other institutions in its environment

insurance   a social device by which many share the losses of a few

insurance premium   the fee charged for an insurance policy

intangible assets   assets that have no physical substance but have some other value, such as goodwill

intelligence tests   tests that measure the ability of a person to think, reason logically, and understand

interest tests   tests that show a pattern of a person's likes and dislikes in various activities

interlocking directorate   the illegal business practice of having the same persons comprise the majority of two or more boards of directors

internalization of social costs process by which industrial firms and their customers pay for their share of the social costs of pollution created by the production of a needed product

inventory control a system designed to find the optimum level of stock to keep on hand under conditions of changing market demand, production requirements, and financial resources

inventory turnover the frequency with which a firm sells its present stock of salable goods, usually found by dividing cost of merchandise sold by an average monthly inventory

investment banking company a financial institution that acts as a middleman between the new securities market and firms with long-term capital needs

investment companies financial organizations that sell shares of stock to individuals and other investors and then use the cash received to purchase securities of other firms as their only assets

job analysis the process of collecting and organizing information about jobs to be filled

job burnout a job-related syndrome that may affect employees who deal extensively with other people on the job

job description the formalized, written statement about the various requirements of a specific job

job induction introducing a new employee to the job and to fellow employees

job orientation instructing employees about policies, rules, and other matters concerning the company and their jobs

job specification a listing of the personal qualifications, skills, aptitudes, or background needed of the person filling a certain job

joint venture a single undertaking by two or more persons, usually of short duration

Kanban a "just-in-time" Japanese inventory and quality control system, involving a close relationship among managers, assembly workers, and suppliers, that allows factories to keep on hand only the parts needed for immediate production

labor the human factor in the production and distribution of goods and services

labor productivity a measure of output per employee-hour

layoff either a permanent or a temporary separation of an employee from a company, which usually does not reflect negatively on the employee

leader pricing a policy of setting a low price on a high-demand good and promoting it highly to attract customers to the store

leadership the ability to persuade or influence others in a dynamic two-way process between the leader and followers

legal entity an artificial being legally given the rights, duties, and powers of a person

legal tender bills or "paper money" that are accepted in payment of taxes and of all private and public debts

letter of application a letter written to a prospective employer by a job seeker

liabilities the amounts owed, or the claims of creditors against a firm's assets

licensing shifting the technology and property rights from one company to another

LIFO "last in, first out" valuation policy which assumes that the most recent items acquired or produced are priced out ahead of similar items acquired earlier

limited or special partner a partner with limited liability who is inactive in managing the partnership

limited partnership one or more partners can have limited liability as long as at least one partner has unlimited liability

line-and-staff organization an organization structure where line managers get help from specialized or general staff outside the direct chain of command

line authority authority possessed by managers who directly supervise subordinates in the chain of command or hierarchy of authority

line organization an organization structure based on clear and simple relationships in a direct chain of command

listed securities stocks and bonds that have been approved for trading on a security exchange

lockout an employer's refusal to allow workers to enter the plant to work

long-term liabilities debts that will not be due for several years

loss leader a leader item sold at cost or below cost

maintenance the activities involved in keeping machinery and equipment working at a desired level of reliability

make-or-buy decision the decision to make or to purchase a certain part required in manufacturing a product

managed floating process by which governments reserve the right to influence the money market actively

management by objectives a concept and process in which superiors and subordinates jointly set goals and focus on goal attainment rather than on the work process itself

manufacturing a form of production by which raw and semifinished materials are processed and converted into finished products

margin trading process in which a stock buyer pays only a portion of the purchase price and borrows the balance from a broker or bank

marketing the human activity directed at satisfying needs and wants through exchange processes

marketing concept a concept that involves satisfying consumer needs, coordinating all activities in support of marketing, and achieving organizational objectives through customer satisfaction

marketing functions the inescapable economic activities of buying, selling, transportation, storage, financing, research, risk taking, and product standardization that are found throughout the marketing system

marketing mix the combination of decisions in a company's marketing program that commonly includes the four P's of product, place, promotion, and price

marketing research the systematic gathering, recording, and analyzing of data about problems relating to the marketing of goods and services

market-maker banks major money-center banks that actively trade in one or more currencies with other banks and for their own accounts

market segmentation a product development strategy in which the market for a product is divided into two or more homogeneous groups of customers and variations of the product are developed to satisfy each group

markup a percent of a product's cost or selling price that should cover the cost of handling the article to be priced, a portion of the firm's expenses, and a certain amount of profit

mass production the effective combination of specialized labor, machine power, and interchangeable parts

material requirements planning (MRP) an inventory control system based on end-product sales forecasts adjusted to reflect manufacturing plans and lead time, plus vendor capabilities

materials control a system of records and procedures designed to inform management of the quantity and location of materials in the plant

materials management all the activities relating to the acquisition, control, and movement of materials and supplies used in the production of a firm's finished products

materials managers specialists who control a company's material requirements by deciding what to buy, how much to buy, how to schedule shipments, and how to keep inventories at proper levels

materials movement internal handling of materials and external transport of goods to and from the company

matrix or project organization a hybrid form of organization that involves temporary, fluid work teams within the framework of the formal organization

mechatronics the linking of mechanical devices with the electronics of computerized robots to produce hybrid machines and processes that contain the best features of mechanical and electronic machinery

mediation a method used in a labor dispute in which the mediator makes suggestions to both sides in an attempt to reach an agreement

Medicaid insurance program operated by the federal and state governments to cover persons, regardless of age, whose incomes are insufficient to pay for health care

Medicare federal government insurance program that covers hospital and medical insurance for persons 65 years of age or older who are drawing retirement benefits

merchant wholesalers wholesale establishments that buy and sell merchandise on their own account

microprocessor a tiny silicon chip that contains detailed circuitry that performs arithmetic operations and controls input and output functions

mikoshi a Japanese management model that encourages and stimulates the performance of subordinates

minimum wage the lowest hourly rate that can be paid to workers covered by the Fair Labor Standards Act (FLSA)

monetary policy major economic policy tool based on our nation's supply of money and credit

money anything that people will accept in exchange for their goods and services in the belief that they may in turn exchange it for other goods and services

money-market fund a type of mutual fund that consists of short-term money-market securities

money supply the total amount of money which could be spent for goods and services at any one time

morals principles that involve both what is done and the normative question of what people ought to do and believe

most-favored-nation (MFN) treatment trading nations sign treaties providing equal treatment to each other in regard to tariffs, customs regulations, and taxes

motivation the willingness to behave in a certain way

multinational corporation (MNC) a corporation that has direct investments in several countries and whose managers operate under a worldwide strategy

mutual aid pacts (MAPs) and strike insurance management bargaining tactics in which struck firms are aided by other firms so that the struck firms can hold out over long strikes

mutual company a life insurance company or savings bank that does not issue stock but is owned by the users of its services

mutual funds a popular name for open-end investment companies

national market system (NMS) a computerized trading system that links the organized stock exchanges and the over-the-counter market

national or manufacturer's brand a brand promoted and distributed by a manufacturer

negotiable instrument a written debt instrument that can be passed to a third party by endorsement

nemawashi the Japanese use of careful persuasion to get others to align with a particular position, thus achieving consensus

no-fault rule an insurance law in which the person injured in an automobile accident collects from his or her own insurance company rather than from the insurance company of the person who caused the accident

nominal rate of interest interest stated on a loan instrument

nontariff trade barriers (NTBs) measures other than tariffs or quotas, public or private, that distort trade flows

nonvoluntary rotation a partial layoff in which employees work shorter weeks

odd-lot dealers security dealers who buy and sell less than round lots (100 shares) of stock

one-price policy policy in which the established price applies to all comers and is not subject to haggling by individual customers

on-line a feature of a real-time system in which all data and instructions used in the processing are transmitted to the computer as the transaction occurs

open-book account an account receivable or payable of manufacturers, wholesalers, and retailers

open-market operations a key instrument of the Federal Reserve in which the Fed buys and sells government securities in the open market in order to adjust the level of bank reserves—the amount of money and credit—available to businesses and consumers

operating management or technical management managerial level comprised of department managers and persons of professional technical competence oriented to basic operations such as producing goods

operations management the production of services, such as health care

operations research (OR) the application of mathematical techniques to a wide variety of management problems

option exchange security exchange devoted to the trading of stock options provided by brokers, speculators, and investors

orderly marketing arrangements market-sharing arrangements negotiated between importing and exporting countries

organization a group of people occupying a formal structure of positions to achieve a particular purpose

organizational behavior modification the use of B. F. Skinner's behavior modification in business organizations as a contingency management technique

organization chart company diagram that shows graphically how the work load of an organization is divided and assigned to specific individuals or departments

organization structure the formal pattern of relationships among the parts of an organization

organizing process the managerial process of dividing the organization's work and assigning the authority and responsibility necessary to achieve the organization's goals

Ouchi's Theory Z a management style set forth by William Ouchi that focuses on a strong company philosophy, a distinct corporate culture, long-range staff development, and consensual decision making

over-the-counter markets the markets in which unlisted securities are bought and sold

partial productivity a measure of productivity in terms of only one element of input, such as labor

participation loans (SBA) loans in which the SBA and a private financial institution share in the amount lent

partnership association of two or more co-owners to carry on a business for profit

parts redundancy a feature of computers based on self-diagnostic programs that allow computers to diagnose their own problems and keep on running even if major parts fail

patent licensing a business practice whereby a patent holder allows others to use the patent for a fee, which is illegal if this arrangement is used to restrain trade

penetration pricing a low pricing policy used to secure a dominant position for a new product in the market

pension portability the right to transfer a pension program when a person changes jobs

personality test a test that measures different personality attributes

personal selling a salesperson's oral presentation to a prospective buyer for the purpose of making sales

picketing the act of posting one or more persons at the gates of a struck plant to block or harass persons trying to enter the plant

place utility intangible satisfaction created by transporting a product to a desired location

planned obsolescence a purposeful plan to phase out old products

planned shopping centers areas carefully designed, constructed, and managed by developers who lease space to a variety of retailers

planning the process of establishing and clarifying objectives, determining the policies and procedures necessary to reach the objectives, and preparing a plan of action

point-of-sale terminal a device that allows the paperless transfer of funds between customers and businesses at the time and place of sale

police power principle that the states have not only the right but the duty to protect the health, safety, and morals of their citizens and to promote the general welfare

possession utility intangible satisfaction created by the successful selling of a product

preferred stocks stocks on which dividend payments are stated and which rank above common stocks

Prevention of Significant Deterioration (PSD) rules regulations that provide three classes of areas for which pollution control plans of various degrees must be developed

price lining a policy that limits prices of goods to a few specific pricing points

primary data internal and external data gathered by or for a firm for its use

primary job a steady, modern job that offers a chance to advance in one's work

prime rate the interest rate charged by large banks on loans made to their most creditworthy customers

principal the person who delegates authority to an agent to act on her or his behalf

private employment agency a firm that interviews and classifies job candidates and sends the appropriate ones to employers who have job openings

private or dealer's brand a brand sponsored by a wholesaler or a retailer

process innovation skill and care in the way managers organize the processes of production

procurement the combined functions of purchasing, inventory control, and traffic control

Producer Price Indexes measures of the average price changes received in primary markets by producers of commodities that are in various stages of processing

product a combination of physical components which provides a bundle of satisfactions or utilities to consumers

product advertising a type of advertising designed to sell one or more definite, identified products

product differentiation the effort by marketing managers to secure some control over demand by promoting distinctions between their products and the competition

production the transformation of inputs from human and physical resources into outputs desired by consumers

production control coordination of all the elements in the production process into a smoothly operating whole

productivity a measure of the efficiency with which a person, business, or entire economy produces goods and services

product life cycle the stages of introduction, growth, maturity, saturation, and decline of a product

product line a group of products that are closely related as to the needs they satisfy, their use, their markets, or their price ranges

product mix a company's combination of product lines

profit earnings that remain in a business firm after the costs of its operations are covered

Program Evaluation and Review Technique (PERT) operations research technique which establishes a project's estimated completion time by arranging in a critical path the activities to be accomplished

programmable or instructible machine a machine that can do a series of tasks when a set of instructions is fed into it by the human who controls it

progressive tax a tax whose rate becomes higher as the tax base grows in size

promissory note a written instrument in which the maker promises to pay a named party a definite sum of money at a specific future date

proportional tax a tax whose rate remains constant regardless of the size of the tax base

proprietorship a business owned by one person and operated for one's own profit

protectionism a policy which advocates government economic protection for domestic producers through restrictions on foreign competitors

proxy a stockholder's signed authorization giving someone else the right to cast that person's vote at an annual corporate meeting

psychographic market segmentation the process of segmenting markets by identifying individuals who share the same type of lifestyle or personality traits

publicity favorable information about a product or institution that is supplied to the advertising media

purchasing the buying of materials and supplies

purchasing agent the head of a firm's purchasing department (also called the purchasing manager)

Puritan ethic (Protestant ethic or work ethic) a principle of moral conduct that emphasizes individual effort, hard work, self-discipline, reinvestment rather than consumption of earnings, and obedience to God's will

put an option to sell a named stock at a specified price within a stated time period

Quality Circle a group of workers and supervisors that meets regularly to identify, analyze, and solve product-quality and production problems, as well as to improve general operations

quality control the maintenance of established manufacturing standards

quality of work life (QWL) management programs to share responsibility with employees in devising ways to increase job satisfaction and improve product quality and productivity

quantity discount a discount from selling price granted to buyers who order in large quantities

quota a form of protectionism that sets a ceiling on the volume of imports no matter how noncompetitive the domestic prices become

R&D limited partnership approach in which investor-partners supply tax-sheltered financial backing to an inventor of an innovative product, who buys out the partners if the project is successful

rate of return on capital ratio calculated by dividing the net income by the average investment

rate of return on total assets a measure of a firm's efficiency found by dividing net income by total assets

ratio of ownership to debt ratio showing the relative proportion of capital secured from owners and from creditors

real time a computerized data processing system that produces results that are immediately useful in controlling an ongoing physical process or business transaction

rebate a temporary pricing practice that permits a seller to maintain a product's original selling price while still providing a price concession to stimulate sales

reciprocal buying an arrangement in which a company buys from customers who, in turn, buy from that company

redundancy the use of a backup system so that breakdowns will not stop production operations

regressive tax a tax whose rate becomes lower as the tax base increases in size

Regulation Q a regulation of the Federal Reserve that set bank and S&L interest-rate ceilings that now have fallen well below market rates on savings deposits

reliability the probability that a production system or piece of equipment will function properly for a specified time

reorganization the scaling down of amounts owed, of interest rates on payments to be made, and of dividends paid by an insolvent firm

reprogrammable industrial robot a robot that can be reprogrammed to do a sequence of tasks in a job and to do different jobs

reserve requirements the percentage of bank's deposits that must be held as legal reserves at a Federal Reserve Bank

résumé a written summary of personal, educational, and experience factors that indicate the ability of the applicant to perform a job

retailing the activity that involves selling consumer goods to ultimate consumers for their own use

retained earnings statement a financial statement that shows the detailed changes that have taken place in a firm's capital account during the year

reverse engineering the process of stripping down a competitor's product, analyzing its functions and how it works, and — sometimes — copying the product

right of eminent domain a government's power to take private property for a public purpose by the payment of a fair price

right-to-work laws state laws stipulating that no one shall be required to join a union in order to get or keep a job

ringi the Japanese practice of involving people at various levels of the organization in decision-making processes

risks exposures to losses

robotics the use of robots in production and manufacturing

RPG (Report Program Generator) a computer language that provides a simple method for programming a small computer to write a business report

Rucker Plan an incentive pay plan based on value added in manufacturing

salary compensation of a fixed amount regularly paid to an employee

salary reduction plan a pension plan that allows employees to put a certain percentage of their salaries into a company's profit-sharing or savings plan

sales finance company a financial institution that buys installment sales contracts from dealers who have sold merchandise to consumers

sales presentation a demonstration by a salesperson to a prospect showing how the product's features produce consumer benefits

sales promotion all marketing activities, other than personal selling, advertising, and publicity, that stimulate consumer buying and dealer effectiveness

savings and loan associations (S&Ls) financial institutions that accept deposits from savers and lend these funds to borrowers mainly for home construction

Scanlon Plan an incentive pay plan and style of management in which bonus payments are based on a ratio of the total labor cost to the company's sales

secondary data facts previously published or released to other users

secondary job a temporary, dead-end job where a person does grubby work with inefficient processes and bosses

secret partner an active managing partner who is not publicly known as a partner

Section 301(d) SBIC special type of Small Business Investment Company which provides financial and management aid to minority businesspersons

security exchange an organization, commonly called a stock exchange, which provides facilities for its members to buy and sell listed securities

self-insurance method by which a firm deliberately assumes a risk but provides a system for absorbing losses

seniority rights a union goal in which decisions about job issues, such as layoffs and promotions, are based on the worker's length of service on the job

sensory or "smart" robots robots with one or more artificial senses that are integrated with sophisticated computer software

service bureau a computer service that has trained programmers and computer operators to handle computer operations for its clients

7-S model a management model in which organizational performance reflects careful consideration of strategy, structure, systems, staff, style, skills, and superordinate goals

sexual harassment deliberate or repeated unsolicited verbal comments, gestures, or physical contact of a sexual nature which are unwelcome

shopping goods goods that are bought after comparison shopping, purchased infrequently, and sold in a limited number of selected outlets

short selling procedure in which the bear sells borrowed stock today, expecting to buy the same stock soon at a lower price, cover the borrowed stock, and make some profit

silent partner a partner known to the general public as a partner but not active in managing the partnership

Simplified Employee Pensions (SEPs) company-established retirement plans, such as Individual Retirement Accounts (IRAs), that are funded from payroll deductions

single-line store a retail store that usually is recognized by its most important product line but which may carry a variety of other related merchandise

skimming the cream pricing a high pricing policy generally associated with a product in the initial stages of its life cycle

social costs of pollution the harmful effects of productive processes that fall outside the market's pricing mechanisms

socialism an economy in which the government is heavily involved in economic decisions

Social Man one who stresses people instead of things and human rather than monetary values as routes to the good life

social performance index a voluntary measure developed by the U. S. Chamber of Commerce to help firms determine where they can be more socially active

span of management the number of subordinates that a manager can effectively supervise

Special Drawing Rights (SDRs) a composite currency created by the International Monetary Fund in the form of bookkeeping entries that are transferred between central banks in the settlement of balance-of-payment deficits

specialist a stock trader who spends most of the time at one post on the trading floor of an exchange and concentrates on a limited number of securities

specialty banking banking aimed at serving a defined market of business clients

specialty goods goods bought very infrequently by the consumer after special shopping effort in exclusive outlets in which price is not a major factor

specialty store a retail store (such as a meat market or a dairy store) that offers a depth of assortment in one portion of a line of goods

speculative purchasing a policy that goes beyond purchasing the normal needs in the amounts ordered and prices paid because of anticipation of higher prices for the items needed, fear of strikes against major suppliers, or the chance to make a quick profit on excess inventories when prices go up

spot market the cash market of a commodity exchange in which the buyer usually expects delivery of the purchased product and the seller usually owns the product sold

spot television the purchase of time on a local station

spread the difference between a put and call for the same stock, usually with different expiration dates

staff authority authority based on expertise in specialized activities including the authority to advise, plan, gather information, and provide guidance to line managers

staffing the managerial function of recruiting, hiring, training, and developing the right person for each job

statement of changes in financial position a financial statement that shows a firm's sources, uses, and results of working capital obtained during a specific period

Statute of Frauds a provision of the Uniform Commercial Code that specifies that certain kinds of sales contracts must be in written form

statutory law written law in the form of acts passed by legislators at different levels of government

Stock Appreciation Right (SAR) an executive incentive in which an executive can take a cash bonus equal to the value of a stock's appreciation over a span of time

stock certificates the evidence of ownership in corporations

strategic planning developing goals that build on a company's strengths and avoid its weaknesses

strike or walkout a temporary refusal by employees to continue their work until their demands are met by management

striking price the price at which a stock option can be exercised

Subchapter S corporation a firm that is limited to 35 stockholders and elects to have its income taxed by the federal government as if it were a proprietorship or a partnership

sumptuary taxes taxes that are designed to discourage consumption of the items taxed, such as liquor and tobacco, by increasing their retail prices

supply-side economics current version of classical economics, based on Say's Law, that holds that supply creates its own demand because people produce in order to consume

surety bonds insurance policies that protect the insured against loss from the nonperformance of a contract or any agreed-upon act

tariffs the taxes imposed by a nation on imported goods

technical skill the managerial skill that involves functions dealing with the production and distribution of the company's products or services

telemarketing the use of the telephone as a communication medium for industrial selling

territorial pool an illegal business trade practice where supposedly competing firms assign geographical areas for the exclusive benefit of each firm

Theory Z Organization an organization that exhibits definite "Z" tendencies such as long-term employment and training, careful promotions, and career development across functional lines

third market large blocks of listed securities traded off the floor of the exchange with a brokerage firm acting as an intermediary between two institutional investors

thrift institutions or thrifts mutual savings banks, savings and loan associations, and credit unions in which funds can be deposited, saved, and loaned

time-sharing a computer service that allows many customers to share the use of a central computer from remote terminals

time utility intangible satisfaction created by the storage function which makes a product available when it is needed

tort a private wrong concerned primarily with moral wrongs that one person may do to cause damage or loss to another

total productivity the measure that relates output to an entire set of resources used in the production process, the resources being weighted on the basis of their relative importance to the process

total quality control or process control reliance on statistical techniques to control a product's quality, uniformity, and cost at every stage of the manufacturing process

trade acceptance a time commercial draft prepared for a shipment of merchandise

trade discount a discount from the list price of a product that recognizes the different functions performed by wholesalers and retailers

trademark a word, name, symbol, or any combination of the three that provides a unique company identification

trading companies firms that buy and sell goods from many foreign companies and assist in financing and forming business combinations that compete for international contracts

Traditional Man one whose values are rooted in John Locke's "Natural Laws," in John Calvin's Puritan ethic, and in Adam Smith's principle of self-interest

tying contracts an illegal business practice where a buyer agrees to buy other goods from the same vendor in order to obtain the merchandise desired

unfair-trade laws state laws that restrain sellers from selling goods at less than their cost plus a specified markup

union security the goal of organized labor to have management recognize a union as the sole bargaining agent of its employees

unit pricing the identification of a product's price in terms of established units such as ounces, pounds, or quarts

universal life policy a special type of whole life insurance in which the portion of the premium that is not used for insurance protection typically is invested in high-yielding short-term securities

Universal Product Code (UPC)   a label consisting of thick and thin bars and spaces which is printed on consumer goods to permit computerized checkouts

unlisted securities   bonds and stocks traded over the counter and not listed on a security exchange

uzekara   the Japanese practice of carefully seeking consensus on management changes rather than imposing them on a one-way basis

value analysis   a systematic appraisal and examination of products and parts to see if any cost-saving changes in design, materials, or processes can be made and to make sure the products or parts fulfill their functions at the lowest possible cost

variable costs   the escapable, or out-of-pocket, costs (such as labor and materials) which are incurred when units are produced

variable life policy   an insurance policy with a fixed premium and a guaranteed minimum death benefit, but the amount of the death benefit varies depending on the rate of return from the investment part of the insurance

varying-price policy   a policy in which large buyers may secure lower prices than their smaller competitors

vertical differentiation   dividing levels of managerial decision making in an organization

vesting rights   the right to pension benefits that legally belong to employees after a stated time

voluntary chains   a group of independent stores sponsored by independent wholesalers, or a group of cooperating retailers who own the wholesale operation that serves them

voluntary creditor agreements   arrangements in which creditors elect a representative who assumes active management of an insolvent firm until the business can operate successfully

warehouse receipt   an inventory receipt which specifies that the stored goods will be released to the person who rented the space — or to order of bearer — upon payment of the storage charges

wholesaling   all the marketing activities of firms that sell to retailers, industrial firms, and other commercial users

word processing   a system of data processing techniques and software involving a series of actions with words to simplify writing letters, revising documents, and other office functions

working capital   the dollar difference between total current assets and total current liabilities

yellow-dog contract   an agreement signed by workers, usually as a condition of securing jobs, promising not to join a union while working for the employer

zero-base budgeting (ZBB)   the practice of requiring that all budgets be justified in detail and evaluated from scratch each year

Index

A

absolute advantage, 370-371
access (or debit card), 507
accountants:
  certified public (CPAs), 403
  types of, 403-404
accounting:
  as area of employment opportunity, 637
  defined, 402
  standardization and regulation of, 425-426
accounting procedures:
  basic steps in, 404-406
  standardization and regulation of, 425-426
accounts receivable, 455
acid-test ratio, 418, 420
Action for Children's Television, 339
Active Corps of Executives (ACE), 670
actuary, 529
administrative management, 90
administrative skill, 91

ad valorem tariff, 387
advertising:
  class, 321
  consumer actions in, 339
  cooperative, 321
  criticisms of, 335-337
  defined, 314
  ensuring truth in, 337-339
  government regulation in, 338-339
  institutional, 321, 322
  mass, 321
  objectives of, 320-321
  primary, 321
  product, 321-322
  selective, 321
  self-regulation in, 338
  tasks of, 321
  types of, 321-322
advertising agency, 335
advertising media, 322, 331-335
affirmative-action program, 128-129
affirmative defenses, 145-146
AFL-CIO, 165, 173, 180
Age Discrimination in Employment
  Act (ADEA) of 1967, 133-134

agency, 579
agency shop, 168
agent, 579
AIDA, 321
airfreight, 254-255
air pollution:
  control of, 31-32
  nature and sources of, 31
air transportation, 254-255
alien corporation, 54
American Federation of Labor (AFL), 163-165
American Institute of Certified Public Accountants (AICPA), 425
American Stock Exchange (Amex), 465, 479
amount at risk, 532
analog computer, 544-545
analytic production processes, 215-216
annuity insurance, 534
anticipative management, 99
anti-union management consultant, 172
appellate court, 576
application, letter of, 641-643

approach, 318
approved monopolies:
    and competitive businesses, 595
    regulation of, 604-606
aptitude tests, 630
arbitration, 173
assembly line, 216
assets:
    current, 412
    defined, 412
    fixed, 412, 414
    intangible, 414
Associated Credit Bureaus of
    America, 450, 452
Association of Southeast Asian Na-
    tions (ASEAN), 388, 390
assumptive close, 319
Athos, Anthony G., 202, 204-205
audit, 422-423
audit committee, 587-589
authority:
    functional, 75-76
    hierarchy of, 74
    line, 74-75
    managerial, decentralization of,
        78-79
    staff, 75
authority relationships, establish-
    ment of, 74-76
automated clearinghouse, 507
automated teller machine, 507
automated factory, 221-227
automation, 221
automobile insurance, 524-525
average, 568
average cost pricing, 350-351
average inventory, 243
averages, stock, 471
Aviation Deregulation Act of 1978,
    606

B

baby bonds, 437
bait pricing, 357
balance of payments, 390-391
balance of trade, 390-391
balance sheet, 411-415
balance-sheet equation, 412
bank acceptances, 454
bank discount, 452

banking, specialty, 494
Banking Act of 1935, 503
banking system, U.S., 492-497
bankruptcy:
    defined, 580
    involuntary, 582
    voluntary, 580-582
Bankruptcy Reform Act of 1978,
    580-582
banks:
    central, 506
    commercial, 493-494, 506
    market-maker, 506
bar-code scanners, 241
bargaining:
    coalition, 169
    collective, 168-169
    concessionary, 178-179
    tactics and tools of, 169-173
barge transport, 252-253
base pay, considerations in deter-
    mining:
    compensation equity, 142-143
    external competitiveness of the
        firm, 142
    federal legislation, 143-146
BASIC (Beginner's All-purpose
    Symbolic Instruction Code),
    556
basket currency, 504
batch processing, 558
bears, 472
behavioristic market segmentation,
    271
behavior modification:
    defined, 105
    organizational, 105-106
    v. needs satisfaction, 106
benevolent societies, 162
Better Business Bureau, 338
Big Board, 465
billings, 335
bill of materials, 218
bird dogs, 317
blacklist, 172
black unionists, 179-180
blue-sky laws, 475
board of directors:
    changing responsibilities of, 51
    defined, 50
    women as members of, 52
Board of Governors of the Federal
    Reserve System, 498, 499,
    500, 503

bond:
    baby, 437
    callability, terms of, 440
    callable, 440
    chattel mortgage, 438
    collateral trust, 438
    convertibility, terms of, 440
    convertible, 440
    coupon, 438
    debenture, 438
    defined, 435
    denominations of, 437
    equipment trust certificate, 438
    evidence or lack of evidence of
        ownership of, 438
    fidelity, 527
    general features of, 435-438
    maturity dates of, 438
    provision for trustee, 436
    real estate mortgage, 438
    redeemable, 440
    registered, 438
    repayment, method of, 438-440
    special features of, 438, 440
    surety, 527
    type of security offered, 438
bonus plan, 148
bottom line, 411
boycott, 171
brand names, 294
break-even analysis pricing, 348-
    350
break-even point, 348
broker, commission, 466
brokerage firms, 445
budgets, 423-424
bulls, 472
burglary, robbery, and theft insur-
    ance, 525
business:
    as a key social institution, 4, 6
    competitive, regulation of,
        595-603
    constitutional support for, 8
    defined, 3-4
    establishing your own, 633
    institutional framework of, 6
    large, 657-665
    new, factors for success of,
        654-657
    physical environment of, 30-35
    relationship of, with govern-
        ment, 8
    small, 654, 657-665

social environment of, 24-26
structure of, 4
business enterprise system, American, 4-13
business ethics, 584-589
business failures, 579-582
business firms, sizes and types of, 4, 6
business law, 577-584
business legitimacy, 35
business loans from commercial banks, 452-453
business ownership, legal forms of:
  business trusts, 56-57
  choosing, 666-667
  cooperatives, 58-60
  corporations, 48-56
  credit unions, 60
  joint ventures, 56
  mutual companies, 60
  partnerships, 44-48
  proprietorships, 42-44
  syndicates, 56
  unincorporated associations, 58
business responsibility, social values and models of, 26-30
business risks, 513-516
Business Roundtable, 33
business trust, 56-57
buying:
  forward, 236
  hand-to-mouth, 236
  manufacturing v., 235
  reciprocal, 237
buying cooperative, 59
buying intentions, 276
buying motives, 277-279
buying process, 279-280

C

CAD-CAM systems, 224-226
call, 480
callable bonds, 440
callable preferred stock, 441
call price, 440
Calvin, John, 25
capital:
  as key factor of capitalism, 10
  circulating, 434

debt, 434
defined, 412
equity, 434-435
fixed, 434
working, 415, 417
capitalism:
  American, 9
  basic freedoms of, 9
  economic theories of, 14-16
  key factors of, 10-11
  roles and gainful relationships in, 11
capital-labor ratio, 193
capital statement, 414
career planning, factors to consider in, 626-628
cartels, 381
cash discount, 358
cash surrender value, 530
Celler-Kefauver Act of 1950, 596, 598
Central American Common Market (CACM), 388
central banks, 506
centralized management, 79
central processing unit (CPU), 545, 548-549
certificate of convenience and necessity, 605
certified public accountants (CPAs), 403
chain of command, 74
chain stores, 305
channels of distribution, 295-298
charge accounts, 450
charter, 50
chattel mortgage bonds, 438
checking deposits, 491
checkoff, 167
Chicago Board of Trade, 480
Chicago Board Options Exchange (CBOE), 479, 480
Child Protection and Toy Safety Act of 1969, 600
choice, freedom of, 9
choice close, 319
circulating capital, 434
Civil Aeronautics Board (CAB), 606
civil law, 575
Civil Rights Act of 1964:
  and the EEOC, 128
  Title VII of, 128, 131, 133, 134
class advertising, 321

classical theory of capitalism, 14-15
Clayton Act, 596, 598
Clean Air Act Amendments of 1970, 31-32
Clean Air Act Amendments of 1977, 32
Clean Air Act of 1963, 31
close, 319
close corporation, 54
closed-end investment companies, 447
closed shop, 168
coalition bargaining, 169
Coalition for Better Television, 339
Coalition of Black Trade Unionists, (CBTU), 180
Coalition of Labor Union Women (CLUW), 180
COBOL (Common Business Oriented Language), 556
codes of ethics, 586-587
coins, 490-491
coinsurance clause, 521
collateral trust bonds, 438
collective bargaining, 168-169
collusive bidding, 597
command economy, 17
commercial bank:
  defined, 493
  role of, 493-494, 506
commercial drafts, 453-454
commercial paper, 454-455
commission broker, 466
Commissioners Standard Ordinary Mortality Table, 529, 533
commission plan, 147-148
Committee on Political Education (COPE), 173
Commodity Credit Corporation, 453
Commodity Exchange Authority, 484
commodity exchanges, 480-484
Commodity Futures Trading Commission (CFTC), 484
common law, 575
common situs picketing, 171
common stocks, 443
communication:
  as part of the manager's jobs, 106-108
  differences between information and, 108
communism, 17

community of interests, 598
community shopping center, 306-307
company size, as factor in career planning, 627
comparable worth, 146
comparative advantage, 371-373
compensation equity:
  defined, 142
  external equity, 142-143
  internal equity, 142
competition:
  as uncontrollable marketing factor, 272-273
  federal regulation for promotion of, 596-598
competitive approach in pricing, 351-352
competitive businesses:
  and approved monopolies, 595
  federal regulation of, 595-602
  state and local regulation of, 603
composite quotation system, 469-470
compound tariff, 387
compulsory arbitration, 173
Computer-Aided Design (CAD), 225
Computer-Aided Manufacturing (CAM), 225
computer hardware, 549-553
Computer-Integrated Manufacturing (CIM), 225
computer language, 556
computer operation, as area of employment opportunity, 637
computer program, 556
computers:
  analog, 544-545
  digital, 545
  generations of, 549-550
  social impact of, 562-564
computer service firms, 559-560
computer simulation, 566
computer software, 555-556
computer system, components of a, 545-549
concessionary bargaining, 178-179
conciliation, 173
conglomerate bargaining, 169
Congress of Industrial Organizations (CIO), 165
conscious buying motives, 278
consensus management, 94

consolidated tape, 469-470
constitutional democracy, 6, 8
consumer behavior, 277-280
consumer co-ops, defined, 59
consumer goods, 288
consumer health and safety, federal regulation for protection of, 599-602
Consumer Price Index (CPI), 363
Consumer Product Safety Act of 1972, 600
Consumer Product Safety Commission (CPSC), 601-602
consumers:
  actions of, in advertising, 339
  role of, 13
consumption ethic, 26
containerization, 254
contingency management, 109-111; defined, 109
continuous production processes, 215
contract:
  custom, 167
  defined, 577
  express, 578
  implied, 578-579
  industrywide national union, 179
  law of, 577-579
  management, 380
  open shop, 168
  tying, 598
  yellow-dog, 172
contract purchasing, 236
control:
  inventory, 241-242
  materials, 241
  production, 218
  quality, 220
  total quality (or process), 220
controlling:
  and the economic climate, 98
  at different managerial levels, 98
  defined, 97-98
convenience goods, 289
convertible bonds, 440
convertible preferred stock, 442
cooperative advertising, 321
cooperative (or co-op):
  advantages and disadvantages of, 59-60
  buying or supply, 59
  consumer, 59
  defined, 58

  kinds of, 58-59
  producer, 59
coordinated bargaining, 169
Copyright Act of 1976, 582
Copyright Royalty Tribunal, 583
copyrights:
  defined, 582
  law on, 582-584
corporate accountability, 35-36
corporate income taxes, 615, 616-617
corporate social audit, 35-36
corporation:
  advantages of, 55
  alien, 54
  annual meetings of, 52
  classifications of, 53-54
  close, 54
  defined, 49
  disadvantages of, 55-56
  domestic, 54
  foreign, 54
  formation of, 50
  governmental, 53
  monitoring social performance of, 35-36
  multinational, 391-396
  nature of, 49-50
  nonprofit, 53-54
  nonstock, 54
  open, 54
  private, 53
  professional, 54
  profit, 53
  separation of ownership and management in, 53
  stock, 53
  structure of, 50-53
  subchapter S, 54
  voting practices of, 52-53
cost approach in pricing, 345-351
cost-benefit relationships, 33
cost of merchandise sold, 407, 409
costs:
  fixed, 348
  historical, 605
  of trading, 471-472
  variable, 348
countertrade, 384
coupon bond, 438
court of original jurisdiction, 576
court systems, 576
credit information, 450, 452
credit insurance, 535

credit life insurance, 535
credit terms, 450
credit union, 60
crime, 574
crisis management, 99
Critical Path Method (CPM), 566
culture, role of, in international trade, 376, 378-379
cumulative preferred stock, 441
cumulative voting, 52-53
Curb Exchange, 465
currency:
    basket, 504
    defined, 491
    floating, 504
current assets, 412
current liabilities, 414
current ratio, 417-418
customary prices, 351
custom contract, 167
customer sales organization, 317
custom products, 213
customs duties, 615
customs union, 388

D

data:
    analysis, summary, and measurement of, 567-568
    collection of, 567
    interpretation of, 568
    presentation of, 568
    primary, 280
    secondary, 280
    security of, 563-564
    sources of, 280
data-gathering methods, 281-282
data processing. See electronic data processing.
Davis-Bacon Act, 174, 176
dealer's brand, 294
death duties, 609
debenture bonds, 438
debt capital, 434
decentralization of managerial authority:
    and physical dispersion, 79
    defined, 78
    factors in, 79

decision making:
    consensus management, 94
    intuitive, 94
    process of, 93-94
    steps in, 93-94
defined-benefit plan, 154
defined-contribution plan, 154
dehiring, 126-127
delegation:
    defined, 79
    process of, 79-80
delivered prices, 354-355
demand:
    as an aspect of inflation, 191
    as an uncontrollable marketing factor, 274-276
demand deposits, 491
demand elasticity, 361
demand management:
    defined, 15
    economics of, 15-16
    policy tools of, 16
Deming, W. Edwards, 220
democracy, constitutional, 6, 8
demography, 271
departmentation of operating tasks:
    by customer, 73-74
    by function, 72
    by geographic territory, 73
    by process or equipment, 72-73
    by product, 73
    defined, 72
depersonalization, 563
depository institutions, 493
deposits, checking, 491
deregulation, 606
development and training, 122-126
differentiation:
    horizontal, 69
    product, 271-272
    vertical, 69
digital computer, 545
directing, 97
direct mail, 333
disabled, discrimination against the, 134
Disaster Loan Corporation, 453
discharge, 127
discount:
    bank, 452
    cash, 358
    defined, 357
    quantity, 358
    trade, 357

discount pricing, 357-358
discount window, 502-503
discretionary income, 275-276
discrimination:
    against minorities, 132-133
    against older employees, 133-134
    against the disabled, 134
    against women, 129-132
    in employment, 128-134
DISCs, 384
disposable personal income, 274
distributed data processing, 551
distribution:
    channels of, 295-298
    policies of, 295-298
    structure of, 273-274
distribution management, 241-256
dividend:
    pass the, 441
    patronage, 58
doctrine of fair use, 583
domestic-content law, 177
domestic corporation, 54
Domestic International Sales Corporations (DISCs), 384
dormant buying motives, 277-278
dormant or sleeping partner, 46
Dow Jones Industrial Average (DJIA), 471, 473
drawee, 453
drawer, 453
dumping, 385
Dun & Bradstreet, Inc., 450
duties:
    customs, 615
    death, 609

E

earnings per share (EPS), 422
economic integration, 385-390
Economic Man, 25-26
Economic Recovery Tax Act of 1981, 154, 199
economic systems:
    capitalism, 14-16
    communism, 17-18
    socialism, 17
effective rate of interest, 456

elasticity, demand, 361
electronic data processing (EDP):
  applications of, 557-560
  defined, 543
  scope of, 543-544
electronic funds transfer systems, 506-507
eminent domain, right of, 604
emotional buying motives, 277
Employee Assistance Programs (EAPs), 153
employee attitudes, and declining productivity, 197-198
employee benefits:
  fringe benefits, 151-156
  pension plans, 153-155
  profit sharing, 149
Employee Retirement Income Security Act (ERISA), 153
employees:
  prospective, 640-641
  recruiting, 120
  relations of, with management, 201-207
  wage incentives for, 147-148
Employee Stock Ownership Plans (ESOPs), 149-150
employment, discrimination in, 128-134
Employment Act of 1946, 16
employment opportunities:
  areas of, 632-638
  in accounting, 637
  in computer operation, 637
  in finance, 636-637
  in government service, 638
  in human resources, 636
  in marketing, 633-634, 636
  in production, 636
  in statistics, 637-638
  self-employment, 633
  sources of information on, 639-640
employment or job counselor firms, 120
employment process, 120-122
employment security, 166-167
endowment life insurance, 532
energy problems, and declining productivity, 197
enlightened self-interest (ESI), 28-30
enterprise, private, 9
entrance tax, 609

entrepreneur, 11
entrepreneurship, 633; five P's of, 665-666
environmental costs, and declining productivity, 197
environmental issues, managerial response to, 34
Environmental Protection Agency (EPA), 31
environmental scanning, 36
Equal Employment Opportunity Act of 1972, 128
Equal Employment Opportunity Commission (EEOC), 128, 131, 133, 134
Equal Pay Act of 1963, 133, 145-146
equilibrium theory of prices, 360-361
equipment:
  installment purchase of, 453
  maintenance of, 219
equipment trust certificates, 438
equity, compensation, 142-143
equity capital, 434-435
estate taxes:
  federal, 615
  state and local, 609
ethic:
  consumption, 26
  Protestant, 25
ethical codes, 586-587
ethical standards, 585
ethics:
  business, 584-589
  codes of, 586-587
  defined, 584
Eurocurrency market, 504
Eurodollars, 504-505
European Coal and Steel Community, 389
European Common Market, 388, 389
European Free Trade Association, 388
exchange:
  commodity, 480-484
  option, 479
  security, 464-477
exchange rate, 503
excise taxes:
  federal, 615
  state and local, 609
Executive Order No. 11246, 128
Executive Order No. 11375, 128

executives, wage incentives for, 150-151
executive search firm (or "head-hunter"), 120
Eximbank (U.S. Export-Import Bank), 383-384
experiment method, 282
exponential smoothing, 566
exporting, 379
express contract, 578
external audit, 422

F

facilities management, 559-560
factor, 455
factoring, 455
factory, automated, 221-227
failures, business, 579-582
Fair Labor Standards Act (FLSA) of 1983, 144, 145, 146
Fair Packaging and Labelling Act of 1966, 600
fair-trade laws, 359-360
fair use, doctrine of, 583
fast-track, 124
Federal Advisory Council, 500
Federal Aviation Administration (FAA), 606
Federal Communications Commission (FCC), 339, 606
Federal Deposit Insurance Corporation (FDIC), 458
Federal Energy Regulatory Commission (FERC), 606
Federal Food, Drug, and Cosmetic Act of 1938, 338, 600
Federal Hazardous Substances Act of 1960, 600, 602
Federal Mediation and Conciliation Service (FMCS), 173
Federal Old-Age and Survivors Insurance Trust Fund, 618
Federal Open-Market Committee, 500
Federal Reserve Banks, 491, 499, 502, 503
Federal Reserve Board, 191

Federal Reserve System (FED), 491,
    496, 506:
  functions of, 498
  key instruments of, 500-503
  structure of, 498-500
federal taxes:
  corporate income, 615, 616-617
  customs duties, 615
  estate, 615
  excise, 615
  gift, 615
  income, 613-617
  miscellaneous, 615
  personal income, 614-615
  regulatory, 615
  Social Security, 617-619
Federal Trade Commission (FTC),
    320, 338, 339, 598, 675
Federal Trade Commission Act of
    1914, 596, 598
feedback, 107
feedback loop, 107
feedstocks, 197
fidelity bonds, 527
FIFO ("first in, first out"), 407
finance:
  as area of employment oppor-
    tunity, 636-637
  differences in, between small and
    large businesses, 664-665
Financial Accounting Standards
    Board (FASB), 425-426
financial audit, 422
financial responsibility laws, 525
financial statements:
  balance sheet, 411-415
  income statement, 407-411
  interpretation of, 417-422
  statement of changes in financial
    position, 415-417
financing:
  long-term, 434-449
  short-term, 449-458
fire insurance, 520-523
fiscal policy, 15
fishyback freight, 254
fixed assets, 412, 414
fixed capital, 434
fixed costs, 348
Flammable Fabrics-Consumers Pro-
    tection Act of 1967, 600, 602
flexible or "cafeteria" benefits plan,
    153
flexible price agreement (FPA), 236

floating currencies, 504
floating lien, 455
flow charts, 556
f.o.b. (free on board) destination,
    354
f.o.b. shipping point (or factory),
    355
focus group, 281-282
Food and Drug Administration
    (FDA), 338, 599-601
Ford, Henry, 245
foreign corporation, 54
Foreign Corrupt Practices Act of
    1977, 384, 396, 588-589
foreign-exchange transactions, 503
form utility, 264
FORTRAN (Formula Translation),
    556
forward buying, 236
fourth market, 478
franchise:
  defined, 670
  sources of information about, 675
franchise contract, provisions in a,
    677-678
franchisee:
  advantages to, 671, 673-674
  cautions for, 675-677
  defined, 670
franchise tax, 609
franchising, 670-679
franchisor:
  advantages to, 674
  defined, 670
Fraser, Douglas A., 165
freedom of choice, 9
free-trade associations, 388
free-trade zones, 382-383
freight forwarders, 255-256
fringe benefits:
  as goal of organized labor, 168
  cost of, 151
  defined, 151
  flexible or "cafeteria" plan, 153
  Employee Assistance Programs
    (EAPs), 153
  pension plans and ERISA,
    153-155
  reduction in, 152-153
  scope and trends of, 152-153
  unemployment benefits, 156-157
Full Employment and Balanced
    Growth Act of 1978 (Humph-
    rey-Hawkins bill), 16

functional authority, 75-76
functional middlemen, 301
Fur Products Labeling Act of 1951,
    600
futures market, 482

G

gains-sharing plans, 148-149
Garn-St. Germain Institutions Act
    of 1982, 496-497
General Agreement on Tariffs and
    Trade (GATT), 381-382
generally accepted accounting prin-
    ciples (GAAP), 402
general-merchandise stores, 304
general partner, 46
general partnership, 44
general sales tax, 609
General Schedule (GS) grades, 638
general staff, 81
generic name, 601
Geneva Meeting, 382
gentlemen's agreement, 597
geographic sales organization, 316
gift taxes:
  federal, 615
  state and local, 609
give-backs, 178
Glass-Steagall Act of 1933, 493
Gompers, Samuel, 163-164
goods:
  consumer, 288-290
  convenience, 289
  industrial, 288
  receiving, 240
  shopping, 289
  specialty, 289
  types of, 288-290
goodwill, 414
goofing-off, 170
government, relationship of, with
    business, 8
governmental corporation, 53
government service, as area of em-
    ployment opportunity, 638
gross profit on sales, 409
gross receipts tax, 609
group executives, 77-78
group life insurance, 534

H

hand-to-mouth buying, 236
hardware, computer, 549-553
health insurance, 518-519
hedging, 483
hierarchy of authority, 74
hierarchy of needs:
　defined, 104
　v. behavior modification, 106
hiring halls, union, 168
historical cost, 605
horizontal differentiation, 69
house-to-house selling, 307
human relations skill, 92
human resources:
　as area of employment oppor-
　　tunity, 636
　compensation for, 140-147
　fringe benefits for, 151-156
　wage incentives for, 147-151
human resources approach, 117
human resources management,
　116-117

I

impact, 608
implied contract, 578-579
IMPROSHARE Plan, 149
incentives, wage, 147-151
incentive stock option (ISO),
　150-151
incidence, 608
income:
　discretionary, 275-276
　disposable personal, 274
income from operations, 410
income patterns, 274-276
income statement, 407-411
income taxes:
　corporate, 616-617
　federal, 613-617
　personal, 614-615
　state and local, 610
incorporation fee, 609
indenture, 436
independents, 305
indexing of wages, 144

index numbers, 568
Individual Retirement Accounts
　(IRAs), 154
industrial goods, 288
industrial life insurance, 535
industry, kind of, as factor in career
　planning, 627
industry-specific research and devel-
　opment, 195
inflation, 191
informal organization, 84-85
information utility, 264
inheritance tax, 609
injunction, 172
innovating, as a managerial func-
　tion, 99-100
input devices, 545
inside board member, 51
insolvency, 580
Instinet (Intermarket Trading Sys-
　tem Network), 465
institutional advertising, 321, 322
institutional management, 90
instructible machine, 222
insurance:
　annuity, 534
　automobile, 524-525
　burglary, robbery, and theft, 525
　business of, 516-518
　credit, 535
　defined, 513
　fidelity bonds, 527
　fire, 520-523
　health, 518-519
　life, 529-536
　marine, 527
　no-fault, 525
　property and liability, 520-528
　specialized liability, 527-528
　strike, 172
　surety bonds, 527
　workers' compensation, 526
insurance companies, private,
　517-518
insurance premium, 513
insurance settlements, 524-525
intangible assets, 414
integrated wholesaling, 302
intelligence tests, 630
interbank, 506
interest rates, 456
interest tests, 630
interlocking directorate, 598
interlocking directorate boycott, 171

Intermarket Trading System (ITS),
　478-479
Intermarket Trading System Net-
　work (Instinet), 465
intermittent production processes,
　215
intermodal shipments, 247
internal audit, 422
internalization of social costs, 30
International Bank for Reconstruc-
　tion and Development, 505
International Franchise Association
　(IFA), 675
International Monetary Fund (IMF),
　383, 504, 505-506
international monetary operations,
　503-506
international payments, and trade
　balances, 390-391
international trade:
　defined, 391
　economic reasons for, 370-373
　methods of conducting, 379-381
　other reasons for, 373-374
　political reasons for, 373
Interstate Commerce Commission,
　(ICC), 250, 606
interview, preparing for an, 645-647
inventories, used as collateral,
　455-456
inventory control, 241-242
inventory turnover, 420
investment:
　increasing, in capital goods, 200
　increasing, in R&D, 200-201
investment banking company, 443
investment companies, 447, 449
investments, 414
involuntary bankruptcy, 582
involuntary termination, 127

J

job analysis, 118
job burnout, 127
job campaign, planning a, 639-647
job description, 119
job induction, 122
job location, 627-628

job orientation, 122
job specification, 119
job termination, 126-127
joint venture, 56, 380
jurisdictional strike, 170

K

Kanban, 245-246
Kelso, Louis, 149
Kennedy Round, 382
Keogh Plans, 154
Keynes, John Maynard, 15, 242
Keynesian Theory, 15-16
Kirkland, Lane, 165, 180
Knights of Labor, Noble Order of, 163

L

labels, 294-295
labor:
    bargaining tools of, 169-171
    defined, 162
    organized, emergence and growth
        of, 162-165
    organized, goals of, 166-168
labor disputes, methods of settling, 173
labor issues and trends, current, 178-183
labor legislation, 173-178
Labor-Management Relations Act
    (Taft-Hartley Act), 171, 173, 175, 176, 177
Labor-Management Reporting and
    Disclosure Act of 1959
    (Landrum-Griffin Act), 175, 176
labor productivity, 192
laissez-faire, 9
Landrum-Griffin Act, 175, 176
Latin American Free Trade Associa-
    tion (LAFTA), 388
law:
    business, 577-584
    civil, 575

common, 575
statutory, 575
layoff, 127
leader pricing, 357
leadership:
    defined, 101
    managerial, 101-104
legal entity, 50
legal tender, 491
lender of last resort, 503
letter of application, 641-643
Lewis, John L., 165
liabilities:
    current, 414
    defined, 412
    long-term, 414
license fees, 609, 613
licensing:
    defined, 380
    patent, 597
life insurance:
    annuity, 534
    business uses of, 535-536
    credit, 535
    endowment, 532
    group, 534
    industrial, 535
    ordinary, 530-534
    on owners or executives, 536
    straight, 532
    term, 532-534
    universal, 531-532
    variable, 532
    whole, 531-532
LIFO ("last in, first out"), 407
limited-function wholesalers, 301
limited or special partner, 46
limited partnership, 44-45, 46-47
line-and-staff organization, 81-82
linear programming, 566
line authority, 74-75
line organization, 80-81
line position, as factor in career
    planning, 627
listed securities, 464
load ahead schedules, 218
loans, business:
    from commercial banks, 452-453
    from governmental agencies, 453
    short-term, 455-456
Locke, John, 25
lockout, 171-172
Long, Russell B., 149
long position, 483

long-term financial institutions, 443-449
long-term financing, 434-449
long-term liabilities, 414
loss leader, 357
Lynch, Leon, 180

M

McGregor, Douglas, 102
machines:
    programmable or instructible, 222
    simple, 221-222
magazines, 334-335
Magnuson-Moss Warranty and FTC
    Improvement Act of 1975, 600
mail, direct, 333
mail-order houses, 307
maintenance, 219
make-or-buy decision, 235
maker, 452
Maloney Amendment to the Securi-
    ties Exchange Act, 478
managed floating, 504
management:
    administrative, 90
    anticipative, 99
    bargaining tools of, 171-172
    centralized, 79
    consensus, 94
    contingency, 109
    crisis, 99
    decentralized, 78
    distribution, 241-256
    facilities, 559-560
    human resources, 116-117
    institutional, 90
    levels of, 76-77, 90-91
    materials, 232
    of automated factories, 226-227
    operating, 90
    operations, 212
    project, 82, 84
    relations of, with employees, 201-207
    span of, 76-78
management by objectives (MBO):
    concept of, 109
    defined, 108
    process of, 109

management contracts, 380
management information systems, 564, 566-568
management perspective, long-term, 201
manager:
  and enlightened self-interest, 28-30
  as trustee of power, 28
  as trustee of profit, 26-28
  forces in the, 102
  materials, 232-234
  purchasing, 234
  role of, 11-12
  responses of, to environmental issues, 34
  sourcing, 234
  training and development of, 122-126
managerial authority, decentralization of, 78-79
managerial behavior, and ethical codes, 587
managerial development, 122-126
managerial functions:
  controlling, 97-98
  directing, 97
  innovating, 99-100
  organizing, 97
  planning, 95-96
  representing, 98-99
  significance of, at different managerial levels, 100-101
  staffing, 97
managerial leadership, 101-104
managerial levels, 90-91
managerial skills, 91-92
managerial tools, 92-93
managerial training, 122-126
managerial work, division of, 76-79
manufacturer's brand, 294
manufacturing:
  defined, 211
  organization and orientation of, 214-215
  v. buying, 235
manufacturing systems, 212-216
margin trading, 473
marine insurance, 527
market:
  Eurocurrency, 504
  fourth, 478
  futures, 482
  option, 479-480

over-the-counter (OTC), 477-478
primary, 473
secondary, 473
spot, 482
third, 478
market approach in pricing, 351-352
marketing:
  as a productive system, 264
  as area of employment opportunity, 633-634, 636
  defined, 262
  differences in, between small and large businesses, 658-660
  employment in, 263
  importance of, 262-263
marketing concept, 262
marketing costs, 263
marketing environment, uncontrollable factors in, 272-276
marketing establishments, number of, 263
marketing functions, 267
marketing legislation, as uncontrollable marketing factor, 273
marketing mix, 267-272
marketing operations, 265-266
marketing organization, structure of, 264-266
marketing research, 280-282
marketing staff services, 266
marketing strategy, 268
market-maker banks, 506
market segmentation, 268-272
markup on total costs, 346, 348
Marshall, John, 49
Marx, Karl, 17
Maslow, A. H., 104-105
mass advertising, 321
mass picketing, 171
mass production, 216
master schedules, 218
material requirements planning (MRP), 243-245
materials control, 241
materials handling, internal, 247
materials management:
  defined, 232
  evolution of, 232-234
materials management organizations, 232
materials managers, 232-234
materials movement, 247

materials transport, external, 247-256
matrix organization, 82, 84
Meany, George, 165
mechatronics, 223-224
mediation, 173
media, advertising, 322, 331-335
Medicaid, 517
Medicare, 517
mentor, 124
merchant wholesalers, 300-301
merit shop, 168
microcomputers, 551, 553
microprocessor, 551
middle management, 90
Midwest Stock Exchange, 465, 479
mikoshi, 204
military organization, 80
milline rate, 332
minicomputers, 551
minimum wage, 144-145
minorities, discrimination against, 132-133
Monetary Control Act of 1980, 494, 496, 502
monetary policy, 15
money:
  basic aspects of, 490-491
  checking deposits, 491
  coins, 490-491
  current forms of, 490-491
  defined, 490
  nature of, 490
  paper, 491
money-market fund, 458
money supply, 491
monopolistic competition, 362
monopoly:
  approved, 595, 604-606
  as a pricing theory, 362
morals, 585
most-favored-nation (MFN) treatment, 382
motivation, 104
Motor Carrier Act of 1980, 250, 606
motor truck transport, 250-251
multinational corporations (MNCs):
  benefits from, 394-395
  criticisms of, 395-396
  defined, 393-394
  motives of, 394
  role of, 394
multinational trade, 391
mutual aid pacts (MAPs), 172

mutual aid societies, 162-163
mutual company, 60
mutual funds, 447, 449

N

National Advertising Division
    (NAD), 338
National Advertising Review Board
    (NARB), 338
National Association of Insurance
    Commissioners, 529
National Association of Purchasing
    Management, 237
National Association of Securities
    Dealers, Inc. (NASD), 465,
    478
National Association of Securities
    Dealers Automated Quotations
    (NASDAQ), 478
National Board of Mediation, 173
national brand, 294
National Coalition on Television
    Violence, 339
National Commission on New
    Technological Uses of Copy-
    right Works, 583-584
National Commission on Social
    Security Reform, 618
National Consumer Cooperative
    Bank Act of 1978, 59-60
National Credit Interchange Sys-
    tem, 450, 452
National Environmental Develop-
    ment Association (NEDA), 33
National Labor Relations Act
    (Wagner Act), 174-175
National Labor Relations Board
    (NLRB), 172, 174, 176
national market system (NMS),
    478-479
negotiable instrument, 452
neighborhood shopping center, 306
nemawashi, 204
net income, 411
newspapers, 331-332
New York Stock Exchange (NYSE),
    464-465, 468, 469, 471, 474,
    479
"Nine-to-Five," 181

Noble Order of the Knights of
    Labor, 163
no-fault rule, 525
nominal rate of interest, 456
noncallable preferred stock, 441
nonconvertible preferred stock, 442
noncumulative preferred stock, 441
nonmarketing costs, as uncontrol-
    lable marketing factor, 273
nonparticipating preferred stock,
    441
nonprofit corporation, 53-54
nonstock corporation, 54
nonstore operations, 307
nontariff trade barriers (NTBs),
    387-388
nonvoluntary rotation, 127
no-par stock, 442
Norris-LaGuardia Act, 172
notes payable, 452-453
Nuclear Regulatory Commission
    (NRC), 606

O

objections, answering, 319
observation, technique of, 281
obsolescence, planned, 294
occupational selection aids, 629-632
occupational type, as factor in career
    planning, 626
odd-lot dealers, 468
odd prices, 354
Odiorne, George, 108, 109
Office of Federal Contract Compli-
    ance (OFCC), 128, 134
oligopoly, 362
one-price policy, 356
on-line, 558
open-book accounts, 450, 452
open corporation, 54
open-end investment companies,
    447
open-market operations, 501-502
open shop, 168
open shop contract, 168
operating expenses, 409
operating management, 90
operations management, 212
operations research (OR), 566

option exchange, 479
option markets, 479-480
order, placing and following up of,
    239-240
orderly marketing arrangements,
    387
order-point analysis, 242-243
ordinary life insurance, 530-534
organization:
    complexity of, and contingency
        management, 109-111
    coordinating the, 69-70
    defined, 68
    developing effective, 85
    dividing the, 68-69
organizational behavior modifica-
    tion (OB Mod.), 105-106
organizational effectiveness, 85
organizational picketing, 176
organization charts, 70
organization structure:
    defined, 80
    forms of, 80-84
    informal, 84-85
    line, 80-81
    line-and-staff, 81-82
    matrix, 82-84
    premises of, 80
organization tax, 609
organized labor:
    emergence and growth of, 162-165
    goals of, 166-168
organizing, 97
organizing process, 68
other income and other expense,
    410-411
Ouchi, William G., 202-204
Ouchi's Theory Z, 202-204
outlaw strike, 170
outplacing, 126
output devices, 549
outside board member, 51
overhang, 504
over-the-counter (OTC) markets,
    477-478

P

paper money, 491
par stock, 442
partial productivity, 192
participating preferred stock, 441

partners, kinds of, 46
partnership:
    advantages of, 47-48
    characteristics of, 45
    contract of, 46
    defined, 44
    disadvantages of, 48
    general, 44
    limited, 44-45, 46-47
parts redundancy, 219
Pascale, Richard T., 202, 204-205
pass the dividend, 441
patent licensing, 597
patronage buying motives, 279
patronage dividends, 58
payee, 452
payment, wage, 146-147
payments, balance of, 390-391
payroll tax, 609
penetration pricing, 353
Pension Benefit Guarantee Corporation (PBGC), 153
pension plans:
    and ERISA, 153-155
    and Social Security, 155-156
    defined-benefit and defined-contribution, 154
    IRAs and Keogh Plans, 154
    portability of, 155
    salary reduction plans, 154-155
    vesting rights in, 155
pension portability, 155
performance shares, 151
personal income taxes, 614-615
personality test, 630
personal selling, 314-319
personnel, in small and large businesses, 660, 662
phantom security, 167
pick-and-place robots, 223
picketing, 171
piece-rate plan, 147
piggy-back service, 250
pipelines, 254
placement offices, 632
place utility, 264
planned obsolescence, 294
planned shopping centers, 306
planning:
    defined, 95
    information needed for, 96
    strategic, 96
pledging, 455
point-of-sale terminal, 507

Poison Prevention Packaging Act of 1970, 600, 602
police power, 603
pollution:
    air, 31-32
    control of, 31-35
    social costs of, 30
population trends, 274
portfolio, 447
positive reinforcement. *See* behavior modification theory.
possession utility, 264
power, trustee of, 28
preapproach, 317
preferential tariffs, 388
preferred stocks, 441-442
prevailing prices, 351
Prevention of Significant Deterioration (PSD) rules, 32
price:
    approaches in determining, 344-352
    call, 440
    stock, variations in, 471
    striking, 480
price indexes:
    Consumer Price Index (CPI), 363
    Producer Price Indexes, 364
price leadership, 352
price legislation, 359-360
price lining, 355
price of substitute products, 351
pricing objectives, 344
pricing policies:
    bait pricing, 357
    delivered prices, 354-355
    discount pricing, 357-358
    higher, competitive, and low prices, 352
    leader pricing, 357
    odd prices, 354
    one-price policy, 356
    penetration pricing, 353
    price lining, 355
    skimming the cream pricing, 352-353
    unit pricing, 356
    varying-price policy, 357
pricing theories:
    demand elasticity, 361
    equilibrium theory, 360-361
    monopolistic competition, 362
    monopoly, 362
    oligopoly, 362

primary advertising, 321
primary boycott, 171
primary data, 280
primary job, 190
primary market, 473
prime rate, 456
principal, 579
"Printers' Ink" statute, 339
private brand, 294
private corporation, 53
private employment agency, 120
private enterprise, 9
private placement, 449
private property, 9
privilege tax, 609
process control, 220
process innovation, 212
procurement, 232
producer cooperative, 59
Producer Price Indexes, 364
product advertising, 321-322
product boycott, 171
product differentiation, 271-272
production:
    as area of employment opportunity, 636
    defined, 211
    differences in, between small and large businesses, 662, 664
    mass, 216
production control, 218
production function, ongoing, 216, 218-220
production processes, 215-216
productivity:
    and inflation, 191
    and opportunity, 190
    and social justice, 190
    decline in, 193-198
    defined, 190
    labor, 192
    measures of, 191-193
    partial, 192
    steps to improve, 198-207
    total, 193
product life cycle, 291-293
product line, 293-294
product line organization, 316-317
product mix, 294
product policies, 290-295
products:
    custom, 213
    defined, 288
    new, development of, 290-293

standard, 213-214
type or character of, 213-214
professional corporation, 54
profit:
    as key factor of capitalism, 11
    defined, 11
    trustee of, 26-28
profit corporation, 52
profit-sharing plans, 149
Program Evaluation and Review
    Technique (PERT), 566
programmable machine, 222
progressive tax, 607
project management, 82, 84
project organization, 82, 84
promissory note, 452
promotion, sales, 314
property:
    movable, 456
    private, 9
property and liability insurance,
    520-528
property tax, 609, 612
proportional tax, 607
proprietorship:
    advantages of, 43-44
    characteristics of, 42-43
    defined, 42
    disadvantages of, 44
prospecting, 317
protectionism, 385-390
Protestant ethic, 25
proxy, 52
psychographic market segmenta-
    tion, 271
publicity, 322
public necessity, 604
public utilities, 604, 605
public utility commissions, state,
    605
purchasing:
    contract, 236
    defined, 232
    nature and functions of, 235-241
    speculative, 237
purchasing agent, 234
purchasing department, organiza-
    tion of, 234-235
purchasing functions, 238-241
purchasing policies:
    contract purchasing, 236
    hand-to-mouth v. forward buy-
        ing, 236
    manufacturing v. buying, 235

reciprocal buying, 237
sealed bids, use of, 237
speculative purchasing, 237
Puritan ethic, 25
put, 480

Q

qualified stock option, 151
Quality Circles (QCs):
    defined, 205-206
    nature of, 205-206
    use of, 206-207
quality control, 220
quality of work life (QWL), 202
quantity discount, 358
queuing theory, 567
quotas, 387
quotation system, composite,
    469-470

R

radio, 333-334
Rail Act of 1980, 606
rail transport, 248-250
Railway Labor Act, 173
R&D limited partnership, 47
Randolph, A. Philip, 179
rate of return on capital, 421
rate of return on total assets, 421
rate-of-return pricing, 348
rational buying motives, 277
ratio of ownership to debt, 420-421
ratios:
    acid-test, 418, 420
    capital-labor, 193
    current, 417-418
real estate mortgage bonds, 438
real time, 558
real-time systems, 558
rebate, 357
reciprocal buying, 237
recruitment of employees, 120
redeemable bonds, 440

redundancy, 219
referral unions, 168
Refrigerator Safety Act of 1956,
    600, 602
regional shopping center, 307
registered bond, 438
registered representative, 445
regressive tax, 607
regulation of business:
    federal, 595-602
    state and local, 603
Regulation Q, 496
regulatory agencies:
    federal, 605
    local, 604-605
    state public utility commissions,
        605
regulatory tax, 615
reliability, 219
reorganization, 580
representing, 98-99
reproduction cost new, 605
reprogrammable industrial robot,
    223
research and development (R&D):
    decline in, 195
    increased investment in, 200-201
reserve fund, 532
reserve requirements, 503
résumé, 643-645
retailing:
    by geographic location, 306-307
    by lines of goods handled, 304
    by ownership, 305
    by type of operation, 307, 309
    defined, 302
retained earnings statement, 415
retirement, 127
Reuther, Walter, 165
revenue from sales, 407
reverse engineering, 583
Revised Order No. 4, 128
right of eminent domain, 604
right-to-work laws, 177-178
ringi, 205
risk, as key factor of capitalism,
    10-11
risk protection, noninsurance meth-
    ods of, 515
risks:
    business, 513-516
    defined, 513
    insurable, 516
    uninsurable, 513, 515

Robinson-Patman Act, 360, 596, 598
robot:
  pick-and-place, 223
  reprogrammable industrial, 223
  sensory or "smart," 223
  servo, 223
robotics, 221
Ro/Ro shipping, 254
RPG (Report Program Generator), 556
Rucker Plan, 149

S

salary:
  defined, 140
  straight, 146
salary reduction plans, 154-155
sales:
  gross profit on, 409
  revenue from, 407
sales organizations, 316-317
salespersons, types of, 315
sales presentation, 318
sales process, steps in, 317
sales promotion, 314
sales taxes, 608-609
savings, increasing, to improve productivity, 199
savings and loan associations (S&Ls), 495
Say's Law, 14-15
scalar organization, 80
Scanlon Plan, 148-149
schedule of cost of goods manufactured, 409, 410
sealed bids, use of, 237
secondary boycott, 171
secondary data, 280
secondary job, 190
secondary market, 473
second-sourcing, 583
secret partner, 46
Section 301(d) SBICs, 669
sector executives, 77-78
securities:
  listed, 464
  unlisted, 477
Securities Act of 1933, 475

Securities and Exchange Commission (SEC), 426, 465, 472, 475-479, 588-589
Securities Exchange Act of 1934, 475-477
Securities Investor Protection Act of 1970, 474
security:
  employment, 166-167
  of data, 563-564
  phantom, 167
  union, 167
security exchanges:
  defined, 464
  national and regional, 464-473
  regulation of, 475-477
  role of, 473-474
security sales, regulation of, 475-477
selecting-out, 126
selective advertising, 321
selective gross receipts tax, 609
selective sales tax, 609
selection and hiring, steps in, 118-122
self-insurance, 515
self-interest, enlightened, 28-30
selling:
  house-to-house, 307
  personal, 314-319
  short, 472-473
seniority rights, 167
sensory or "smart" robots, 223
service bureaus, 560
Service Corps of Retired Executives (SCORE), 670
service wholesalers, 301
servo robot, 223
7-S model, 204-205
severance tax, 609
sexual harassment, 131-132
Sherman Antitrust Act of 1890, 596-597
shift premium plan, 147
ship transport, 253-254
shopping centers, 306-307
shopping goods, 289
short position, 483
short selling, 472-473
short-term debt, types of:
  bank acceptances, 454
  commercial drafts, 453-454
  commercial paper, 454-455
  notes payable, 452-453
  open-book accounts, 450, 452

short-term financing:
  cost of, 456-458
  security for short-term loans, 455-456
  types of short-term debt, 449-455
short-term financing institutions, 458
sight drafts, 453
silent partner, 46
silver platter unionists, 182
similar work, 145
simple machines, 221-222
Simplified Employee Pensions (SEPs), 154
single-line stores, 304
sitdown strike, 170
situation, forces in the, 104
skimming the cream pricing, 352-353
Skinner, B. F., 105-106
slot-machine unionists, 182
slowdown strike, 170
small business, importance of, 654
Small Business Administration (SBA):
  loans from, 667-669
  publications of, 669
  Section 301(d) SBICs, 669
  services of, 667-670
  Small Business Investment Companies (SBICs), 669
Small Business Development Centers, 670
Small Business Institutes, 670
Small Business Investment Companies (SBICs), 669
Smith, Adam, 25, 29
Smithsonian Agreement, 504
Smoot-Hawley Tariff Act, 381
social costs of pollution, 30
socialism, 17
Social Man, 26
social performance index, 36
Social Security, pensions and, 155-156
Social Security Act of 1935, 517, 618
Social Security taxes, 617-619
software, computer, 555-556
soldiering on the job, 170
sourcing manager, 234
Southern Strategy, 182
span of executive control, 76
span of management, 76-78

Special Drawing Rights (SDRs), 504
specialist, 468
specialized liability insurance, 527-528
specialized staff, 81
specialty banking, 494
specialty goods, 289
specialty stores, 304
specifications, establishing, 239
specific tariff, 386-387
speculative purchasing, 237
speculative transactions, 472-473
spot market, 482
spot television, 332
spread, 443, 480
staff authority, 75
staffing:
    basic steps in, 117-127
    defined, 97
    function of, changes in, 116-117
staff position, as factor in career planning, 627
Staggers Act of 1980, 249
standard products, 213-214
standards, ethical, 585
stare decisis, 575
state and local taxes:
    annual fees, 609
    death duties, 609
    gift, 609
    income, 610
    license fees, 609, 613
    organization, 609
    payroll, 609
    property, 609, 612
    sales, 608-609
    severance, 609
    variations in, 608-613
state capitalism, 17
statement of changes in financial position, 415-417
statistics:
    as area of employment opportunity, 637-638
    use of, 567-568
Statute of Frauds, 578
statutory law, 575
Stephens, Uriah S., 163
Stock Appreciation Right (SAR), 151
stock corporation, 53
stock exchanges. See security exchanges.

stock certificates, 435
stocks:
    common, 443
    costs of trading, 471-472
    preferred, 441-442
    price valuations and averages, 471
    speculative transactions, 472-473
    trading procedures, 466-470
stores:
    chain, 305
    general-merchandise, 304
    independent, 305
    single-line, 304
    specialty, 304
    voluntary chain, 305
straight life policies, 532
straight salary, 146
strategic planning, 96
Strategy, Southern, 182
strike:
    defined, 169
    jurisdictional, 170
    sitdown, 170
    slowdown, 170
    sympathy, 170
    wildcat (or outlaw), 170
strike insurance, 172
striking price, 480
structure of distribution, 273-274
Subchapter S corporation, 54, 664
subordinates, forces in the, 102
sumptuary taxes, 608
supply, as an aspect of inflation, 191
supply cooperative, 59
supply-side economics:
    defined, 14
    policy tools of, 15
surety bonds, 527
surface transport, 248-251
survey technique, 281-282
sympathy strike, 170
syndicate, 56
synthetic production processes, 215-216
systems concept, total, 558

T

Taft-Hartley Act, 171, 173, 175-177, 603
tape, consolidated, 469-470

tariffs:
    ad valorem, 387
    compound, 387
    defined, 386
    preferential, 388
    specific, 386-387
taxation:
    bases for, 607-608
    principles of, 606-608
taxes:
    corporate income, 615, 616-617
    customs duties, 615
    death duties, 609
    entrance, 609
    estate, 609, 615
    excise, 609, 615
    federal, 613-619
    franchise, 609
    general sales, 609
    gift, 609, 615
    gross receipts, 609
    impact and incidence of, 608
    income, 610, 613-617
    inheritance, 609
    miscellaneous, 609, 613
    organization, 609
    payroll, 609
    personal income, 614-615
    privilege, 609
    progressive, 607
    property, 609, 612
    proportional, 607
    regressive, 607
    regulatory, 615
    sales, 608-609
    selective gross receipts, 609
    selective sales, 609
    severance, 609
    Social Security, 617-619
    state and local, 608-613
    sumptuary, 608
    use, 609
tax-free rollover, 155
technical management, 90
technical skill, 92
technological unemployment, 562
teenwage, 145
telemarketing, 319
television, 332-333
terminals, 549
termination, involuntary, 127
term life insurance, 532-534
territorial pool, 597
tests, 629-630

Textile Fiber Products Identification Act of 1958, 600
Theory X, 102, 103
Theory Y, 102, 103
Theory Z, Ouchi's, 203
Theory Z organization, 204
third market, 478
third-party transaction accounts, 494
thrift institutions (or thrifts), 493
time drafts, 453
time-of-day pricing, 351
time-sharing, 559
time utility, 264
time wages, 146
Title VII of the Civil Rights Act of 1964, 128, 131, 133, 134
Toffler, Alvin, 108
Tokyo Round, 382
top management, 90
tort, 574
total productivity, 193
total quality control, 220
total systems concept, 558
trade:
    balance of, 390-391
    international, 370-374, 379-381
    multinational, 391
    world, conducting, 375-381
    world, promoting, 381-384
trade acceptance, 453
trade discount, 357
Trade Expansion Act of 1962, 382
trademark, 294
Trade Practice Rules, 338, 598
trade unions, 163
trading, of stocks:
    costs of, 471-472
    margin, 473
    procedures of, 466-470
trading companies, 384
Traditional Man, 25
training and development, 122-126
transfer agent, 447
transport, of external materials:
    air, 254-255
    barges, 252-253
    freight, 255-256
    motor trucks, 250-251
    pipelines, 254
    rails, 248-250
    ships, 253-254
transportation:
    air, 254-255
    water, 252-254

trial close, 319
trust, business, 56-57
trust certificates (or trust shares), 56
trust companies, 445, 447
trustee, 436
trustee of power, 28
trustee of profit, 26-28
tying contracts, 598

U

underwriters, governments as, 517
underwriting syndicate, 56
unemployment, technological, 562
unemployment benefits, 156-157
unfair-trade laws, 359-360
Uniform Commercial Code (UCC), 577
unincorporated associations, 58
union contracts, industrywide national, 179
unionists:
    black, 179-180
    silver platter, 182
    slot-machine, 182
    women, 180-181
unions:
    modern, growth of, 163-165
    referral, 168
    trade, 163
union security, 167
union shop, 168
union solidarity, challenges to, 181-183
unit pricing, 356
universal life policy, 531-532
Universal Product Code (UPC), 549
unlisted securities, 477
unqualified stock option, 151
use tax, 609
utilities, public, 604, 605
uzekara, 205

V

value analysis, 240-241
values, ethics and, 585
variable life policy, 532
variable cost pricing, 348

variable costs, 348
varying-price policy, 357
vending machines, 309
vendors:
    evaluating performance of, 240
    selecting, 239
vertical differentiation, 69
vesting rights, 155
Vietnam Era Veterans Readjustment Assistance Act, 134
Vocational Rehabilitation Act of 1973, 134
voluntary arbitration, 173
voluntary bankruptcy, 580-582
voluntary chains, 305
voluntary creditor agreements, 580

W

Wage and Hour Act of 1938, 144
wage incentives:
    bonus plan, 148
    commission plan, 147-148
    employee stock ownership plans (ESOPs), 149-150
    gains-sharing plans, 148-149
    incentive stock options (ISO), 150-151
    performance shares, 151
    piece-rate plane, 147
    profit-sharing plans, 149
    stock appreciation rights (SARs), 151
wage payment, forms of:
    shift premium, 147
    straight salary, 146
    time wages, 146-147
wages:
    defined, 140
    higher, as goal of organized labor, 167
    minimum, 144-145
Wagner Act, 174-175
walkout, 169
warehouse receipt, 455
water transport, 252-254
weekly department schedules, 218
what the traffic will bear, 351-352
Wheeler-Lea Act of 1938, 338, 596, 598
Whitney, Eli, 216
whole life insurance, 531-532

wholesalers, merchant, 300-301
wholesaling:
  defined, 299
  integrated, 302
  reasons for, 299-300
wholly owned manufacturing operations, 381
wildcat strike, 170
women:
  occupational discrimination against, 130-131
  sexual harassment of, 131-132
  wage discrimination against, 131
Women Employed's (WE), 181

"Women Organized for Employment," 181
Women's Trade Union League, 180
women unionists, 180-181
"Women Working," 181
Wool Products Labeling Act of 1939, 600
word processing, 543
workers, role of, 12-13
workers' compensation insurance, 526
work ethic, 25
work force, changing composition of, 195, 197

work groups, wage incentives for, 148-150
work improvement, 218
working capital, 415, 417
work life, quality of, 202
World Bank, 383, 505
world trade:
  conducting, 375-381
  promoting, 381-384

Y, Z

yellow-dog contract, 172
zero-base budgeting (ZBB), 423-424